Secondary and Middle School Teaching Methods

Allan C. Ornstein

Loyola University of Chicago

 HarperCollins*Publishers*

Executive Editor: Christopher Jennison
Project Coordination, Cover Design: Publishing Synthesis, Ltd.
Photo Researcher: Rosemary Hunter
Production Manager: Michael Weinstein
Compositor: Publishing Synthesis, Ltd.
Printer and Binder: R.R. Donnelley & Sons Company
Cover Printer: New England Book Components, Inc.

Secondary and Middle School Teaching Methods

Library of Congress Cataloging-in-Publication Data
Ornstein, Allan C.
    Secondary and middle school teaching methods / Allan C. Ornstein.
        p. cm.
    Includes bibliographical references and index.
    ISBN 0-06-044928-4
    1. High school teaching.   2. Teaching   I. Title
    LB1737.A3076 1991
    373.13—dc20
                                                                                            91–31365
                                                                                            CIP

91 92 93 94 9 8 7 6 5 4 3 2 1

To:

The Baltic people:
May they rejoice in their new independence

The Israeli people:
May they find peace in their homeland

The American Indians:
May they regain their spirit and soul

Contents

Chapter 2 Learning: A Developmental Approach 47

Chapter 3 Classroom Management and Discipline 101

Chapter 4 Testing Students 155

Chapter 5 Evaluating Students 221

PART TWO   Instruction

Chapter 6   Instructional Objectives   273

Chapter 7   Instructional Methods   319

Chapter 8   Instructional Materials   379

Chapter 9 Instructional Technology 435

Chapter 10   Instructional Grouping   473

Tips for Teachers

Preface

Secondary and Middle School Teaching Methods aims to prepare secondary school teachers—particularly middle school, junior high school, and senior high school teachers—and help experienced teachers improve their teaching and instruction. The emphasis is on methods, principles, and strategies of teaching—what some educators call the "how to" approach.

Like the master engineer or artist, the effective teacher must have a thorough knowledge of the methods and principles essential for professional competence. One purpose of this text is to help the prospective teacher understand these methods and principles.

In this text, a broad approach to methodology is offered, which combines research, theory, and practice. To enhance the practical aspects of the text, each chapter has several "Tips for Teachers" and "Guidelines for Implementing . . ." features that link research and theory. These sections are designed to help the reader apply research and theory to practical teaching situations.

The book combines traditional teaching methods with the latest advances in educational psychology, particularly cognitive science and humanism. The attempt is to blend current concepts and practices of critical thinking and learning strategies with what we know about student motivation and self-esteem. Thus both cognitive and affective domains of learning are considered.

The text contains 13 chapters. The first two chapters discuss the general methods of teaching and learning. Chapters 3 through 5 examine the basic dynamics of managing, testing, and grading students. The next six chapters focus on instructional techniques, based on effective educational practices, and include topics such as instructional objectives; instructional methods (i.e., practice and drill, explaining, questioning, and problem-solving); instructional materials (i.e., textbooks, workbooks, duplicated materials, magazines and newspapers, and simulations and games); instructional technology (i.e., instructional television, computers, and videos); grouping for instruction (i.e., whole, small, and individual groups, as well as mastery learning and cooperative learning); and instructional planning (i.e., strategic planning, unit planning, and lesson planning). The last two chapters deal with teacher professionalism, namely the effective teacher and professional growth.

Each chapter begins with a set of focusing questions. Within the chapters short headings and key terms (terms in bold print) help the reader conceptualize main ideas. The end of each chapter includes a detailed summary of chapter content, a case study, questions to consider, activities, recommended readings, and key terms. All elements are designed to assist the reader in reviewing and integrating the material.

The text's focus is on how teachers teach and students learn—that is, the teaching and learning process. The content discussed is most often covered in general methods of teaching courses, secondary methods of teaching courses, and student teaching. The methods apply to secondary school settings, grades 6 to 12, urban and rural schools, large and small schools, and multicultural settings.

I wish to thank the following reviewers for their insights and comments: Burton Boxerman, University of Missouri at St. Louis, Joseph Eulie, State University of New York at New Paltz, Frank Olson, Pacific Lutheran University, and Fred Rodriguez, University of Kansas. Special thanks goes to Paula Cousin, project editorial supervisor, who did a fine, professional job. Both Alan McClare and Chris Jennison, sponsoring editors, must be recognized for their experience and wisdom. Finally, I am always grateful to my children—Joel, Stacey, and Jason, and my wife Valerie, for their patience and understanding. Writing is a lonely venture that takes time away from family and other human endeavors. My family members have come to accept my role as author.

Allan C. Ornstein

ONE

Teaching and Learning

Chapter 1

Teachers and Teaching

FOCUSING QUESTIONS

1. How can teacher education be improved?

2. What is the proper mix of arts and science and education courses?

3. Is teaching a science or art? Explain.

4. Do teachers make a difference in student achievement? Explain.

5. Based on research findings, how would you define an effective teacher?

6. How would you describe the dominant characteristics of most classrooms?

7. What classroom variables can be modified to improve academic achievement?

8. What are the major distractors of academic time? How can academic time be improved in the classroom?

*T*his chapter discusses a number of important issues related to teaching, such as the proper mix of teacher education courses, whether teaching is a science or an art, whether teachers make a difference, and whether we can identify effective teachers. Next we look at classrooms—what goes on and what works. We examine historical classroom changes and classroom organization, interactions, and tasks. Finally, we look at various ways to improve academic time and productivity.

TEACHER PREPARATION

The preparation of teachers consists of three components: (1) *general* or liberal education, with the bulk of the student's program combining courses from the arts and sciences in order to give students a broad cultural background; (2) *specialization*, a cluster of courses in a specific area, described in most colleges as the student's major; and (3) *professional education*, those education courses designed to prepare teachers in the foundations of education (history, philosophy, and/or psychology) and methods and basic principles of teaching. For example, the book you are reading is designed to meet the needs of a methods or teaching course.

Almost all educators agree that the preparation of good teachers rests upon these three components. The relative emphasis that each area should receive, however, provokes strong arguments among educators and especially between professors of education and professors of arts and sciences. How much time should the education student devote to a general or liberal education, to specialization, and to professional education? James Conant, one of the most influential educators of the twentieth century, once defined this quarrel "as a powerful struggle among professors, which has come to involve parents, alumni, legislators, and teachers."[1]

More recently, Andrew Porter points out that beliefs about good teacher preparation tend to focus on "two sharply contradictory" views. At one extreme are "those who maintain that mastery of the subject matter to be taught is all that is required for good teaching." At the other extreme are "those who view good teaching as primarily a matter of pedagogical expertise."[2] The **Holmes Group** (a number of reform educators who are based at research institutions) represents the first position and prefers that teachers invest their preparation time in earning a baccalaureate degree in academic disciplines and a master's in education. The second position, that pedagogical knowledge and

---

1 James B. Conant, *The Education of American Teachers* (New York: McGraw-Hill, 1963), p. 11.

2 Andrew C. Porter, "Understanding Teaching: Model for Assessment," *Journal of Teacher Education* (July-August 1988), p. 3.

skills are more important than subject matter knowledge, is best illustrated by the recent emphasis on **cognitive psychology**, with its focus on teaching methods, thinking skills, and student learning strategies.

A middle position interfaces what is to be taught (subject matter) and how it is best taught (pedagogy). According to Lee Shulman, generic teaching strategies—once considered applicable to teaching in any subject—must be modified to fit the subject.[3] (And if I may add, they must also fit the grade level or developmental stage of the student.) This position supports the idea that students cannot critically think in their subject without a knowledge base; content provides the tool for understanding the world around us as well as for controlling and applying our mental processes. But this idea seems to operate more at the secondary grade levels, where a knowledge base is important for proceeding to higher levels of thinking, than at the elementary grades.

Carolyn Evertson also represents a middle position. She and her colleagues contend there is no evidence that greater emphasis on the arts or sciences for prospective teachers results in greater teacher effectiveness (in terms of methods or techniques), but that does not prove that such changes are undesirable. They see no reason why courses defined as "professional" cannot be as intellectual or rigorous as courses described as "liberal arts."[4]

Education Courses: How Many?

In the last 40 years, especially since the Sputnik era, there has been a substantial reduction in the number of education courses required, as well as a decrease in education electives taken in place of general and specialized courses in the arts and sciences. For example, in a tabulation of 1600 transcripts of students from 32 colleges of education in the late 1950s, it was found that 22 percent of the total program of secondary teachers and more than 41 percent of the program of elementary teachers were devoted to education courses. The percentages were even higher among those attending teachers' colleges. In these schools, more than 25 percent of the secondary teacher education and 45 percent of the elementary program were allocated to education courses.[5]

As of 1990 most colleges and universities require about 18 educational semester credits (or about 12 percent of the total program) for secondary teachers and about 24 credits (or about 20 percent) for elementary teachers.[6] There is variation among states and within each state among colleges and

3 Lee S. Schulman, "Those Who Understand: Knowledge Growth in Teaching," *Educational Researcher* (February 1986), pp. 4-14.

4 Carolyn M. Evertson, Willis D. Hawley, and Marilyn Zlotnik, "Making a Difference in Educational Quality Through Teacher Education," *Journal of Teacher Education* (May-June 1985), p. 6.

5 James D. Koerner, *The Miseducation of American Teachers* (Boston: Houghton Mifflin, 1963).

6 Telephone conversation with Cherly Stein, Department of Government Relations, American Association of Colleges for Teacher Education, March 15, 1990.

universities preparing teachers. Although some institutions still encourage courses beyond state certification requirements, the general trend is to reduce the number of education courses.

The content of these education courses also varies considerably from institution to institution, and even courses with similar titles usually vary in content, since the professors who teach them cannot agree on a common body of knowledge that they all feel should be held by teacher candidates. (Whereas your professor has chosen to use this text, a high cognitive approach to teaching, another professor teaching the same course may decide on a totally different text and approach.) Furthermore, standards in these courses vary, depending on the institution and professor, so that it is difficult to determine what has been taught and learned in these courses.

The point is, that with a continuous reduction in education courses, coupled with lack of agreement on important pedagogical knowledge, we leave it to chance or accident whether beginning teachers acquire professional knowledge suitable for good teaching.

In recent years (1985 to 1990) more than one-third of the teacher education institutions that have applied for NCATE (National Council for Accreditation of Teacher Education) accreditation have been denied it, largely due to the fact that their knowledge base has been vague: it is unclear by the colleges and universities exactly *what* is distinctive about their teacher education program and *why* their specific program (the courses required and competencies or outcomes being attempted) is important to prospective teachers. A **professional knowledge base** is supposed to provide a framework for preservice teachers of what content and skills are important in the program, as well as direction for professors and administrators of the program in terms of (1) goals, (2) design, (3) implementation, and (4) evaluation of the program.

On the other hand, Gary Griffin maintains that counting courses is a "linear activity," based on predetermined teaching tactics and prescriptions. It fails to take into account that teachers learn most of their teaching techniques, or at least reflect on and reshape them, on the job.[7] For Griffin and others, a good mentor system in the early years of teaching is more important than the number of education courses or competencies.

Education Courses: What Sequence?

Another content-related issue involves the sequencing of education courses. Should professional courses be introduced in the freshman, sophomore, or junior year? There is no agreement among institutions preparing teachers, and it often boils down to a teacher education committee at the institutional level making a decision which will not conflict with state guidelines and can be

---

7 Gary A. Griffin, "The Future of Teachers and Teaching," *Peabody Journal of Education* (Spring 1988), pp. 74-87.

supported by one of the reform "waves" in teacher education. Some institutions even advocate putting off education courses until the senior year, when the students have finished their general or liberal education and are free to devote themselves full time to a year of professional study, as is the current situation in a few experimental programs. Others suggest a fifth year, a master's in teaching, when the students would begin their professional training. This idea is gaining popularity among many deans of education at research-based universities such as the Holmes Group.

There are advantages and disadvantages to each of these various sequences. If students are introduced to education at an early stage in college, their professional training can be integrated with a general or liberal education. Such students would also get an early taste of education and would have time to switch careers if they so desired or to alleviate anxieties related to teaching. A disadvantage is that if students are introduced to professional courses from the start of their education, they may have invested too much of their college time to quit or change courses if they discover, in their third or fourth year of school, that teaching is not for them.

A fifth-year program has two advantages: first, it increases the number of academic-oriented and -educated teachers; and, second, it delays entry of new teachers into the job market, therefore, increasing the demand for teachers (and hopefully increasing salaries). The main disadvantage is that many teacher education students may not be able to afford another year without income and may be discouraged from pursuing a teaching career or attending a college that has a five-year program.

ISSUES RELATED TO TEACHING

Few, if any, activities are as crucial in schooling as teaching; and, as elusive and complex as teaching may be, research toward its understanding must continue. Most of the research on teaching, however, is not read by the most important group, that is, by teachers, who can and should benefit by knowing, understanding, and integrating the ideas, concepts, and conclusions of the research. Another problem is that we are unable to define precisely what a good teacher is so that the preparation of teachers and the definition of teacher competency are open to widely varying interpretation.

Teaching: Science versus Art

One problem with preparing teachers, and examining teaching principles and practices, is that we cannot agree on whether teaching is a science or an art. Some readings say that this is a hopeless dichotomy, because the real world rarely consists of neat packages and either/or situations. Nate Gage uses this distinction between teaching as a science and as an art to describe the elements of predictability in teaching and what constitutes "good" teaching. A science of teaching is attainable, he contends, because it "implies that good teaching will some day be attainable by closely following rigorous laws that yield high predictability and control." Teaching is more than a science, he observes, because it also involves "artistic judgment about the best ways to teach." When teachers leave the laboratory or textbook and come face to face with students, "the opportunity for artistry expands enormously." No science can prescribe successfully all the subtle interactions as teaching unfolds, or as teachers respond with "judgment, sudden insight, sensitivity, and agility to promote learning." These are expressions of art which depart from the science of "rules, formulas, and algorithms."[8]

Is such a limited scientific basis of teaching even worthwhile to consider? Yes, but the practitioner must learn as a teacher to draw not only from his or her professional knowledge (which is grounded in scientific principles), but also from a set of personal experiences and resources that are uniquely defined and exhibited by the teacher's own personality and "gut" reaction to classroom events (which form the basis for the art of teaching). Indeed, the hunches, judgments, and insights of the teacher, as he or she responds spontaneously to events in the classroom, are as important, and perhaps even more important, than the science of teaching. The use of hunches and gut feelings is quite common among classroom teachers. Many choices and responses must be made intuitively and instantly because of the rapid pace of teaching.

To some extent, the act of teaching must be considered intuitive and interactive, not prescriptive or predictable. According to Elliot Eisner, teaching is based primarily on feelings and artistry, not scientific rules. In an age of science and technology, there is a special need to consider teaching as an "art and craft." Eisner condemns the scientific movement in psychology, especially behaviorism, and the scientific movement in education, especially in school management, as reducing the teaching act to trivial specifications. He regards teaching as a "poetic metaphor" more suited to satisfying the soul than informing the head, more concerned with the whole than with a set of discrete skills or stimuli. Our role as teachers, he claims, should not be that of a "puppeteer," "engineer," or manager; rather, it is "to orchestrate the dialogue (as the conductor of a symphony) moving from one side of the room to the other."[9] The idea is to perceive patterns in motion, to improvise within the classroom, and to avoid mechanical or prescribed rules.

Louis Rubin has a similar view of teaching—that effectiveness and artistry go hand in hand. The interplay of students and teacher is crucial and cannot be predetermined with carefully devised strategies. Confronted with everyday problems that cannot be predicted in advance, the teacher must rely on intuition

---

8 N. L. Gage, *The Scientific Basis of the Art of Teaching* (New York: Teachers College Press, Columbia University, 1978), pp. 15, 17.

9 Elliot W. Eisner, "The Art and Craft of Teaching," *Educational Leadership* (January 1983), p. 8. Also see Elliot W. Eisner, "What Really Counts in School," *Educational Leadership* (February 1991), pp. 10–17.

and on "insight acquired through long experience."[10] Rubin refers to such terms as "with-it-ness," "instructional judgments," "quick cognitive leaps," and "informal guesses" to explain the difference between the effective teacher and the ineffective teacher. Recognizing limits to rationality, he claims that for the artistic teacher a "feel for what is right often is more productive than prolonged analysis." In the final analysis, Rubin compares the teacher's pedagogy with the "artist's colors, poet's words, sculptor's clay, and musician's notes"[11]—in all of which a certain amount of artistic judgment is needed to get the right mix, medium, or blend.

Harry Dawe is most extreme in his analysis of teaching solely as an art, providing romantic accounts and tales of successful teaching and teaching strategies, described in language that could hardly be taken for social science research. He considers the act of teaching akin to drama and feels that those who wish to teach should audition in a teaching studio with teachers trained as performing artists. Good teaching is likened to good theater, and a good teacher is likened to a good actor.[12] Sometimes practitioners inform us that the best teachers are "actors" and "hams" and excel at improvisation and imagery. They have few, or no, prescriptive formulas and allow for adaptation to unexpected events and the demands of reality. Such teachers tend to defy the science of pedagogy and the techniques that have been found effective in the research.

Blending Science and Art

The more we consider teaching as an art, packed with emotions, feelings, and excitement, the more difficult it is to derive rules or generalizations. If teaching is more of an art than a science, then principles and practices cannot be easily codified or developed in the classroom or easily learned by others. Hence, there is little reason to offer teacher method courses in education. If, however, teaching is more of a science, or at least partly a science, then pedagogy is predictable to that extent; it can be observed and measured with some accuracy, and the research can be applied to the practice of teaching (as a physician applies scientific knowledge to the practice of medicine) and learned in a university or on the job.[13]

Balance is Needed

The more we rely on artistic interpretations or on old stories and accounts about teachers, the more we fall victim to fantasy, wit, and romantic rhetoric, and the

10 Louis J. Rubin, *Artistry in Teaching* (New York: Random House, 1985), p. 61.

11 Ibid., pp. 60, 69.

12 Harry A. Dawe, "Teaching: Social Science or Performing Art?" *Harvard Educational Review* (February 1984), pp. 111–114.

13 Allan C. Ornstein, "A Difference Teachers Make," *Educational Forum* (Fall 1984), pp. 109–118; Ornstein, "A look at Teacher Effectiveness Research—Theory and Practice," *NASSP Bulletin* (October 1990), pp. 78–88.

more we depend on hearsay and conjecture in evaluating teacher competency rather than on social science or objective data. On the other hand, the more we rely on the scientific interpretation of teaching, the more we overlook those commonsense and spontaneous processes of teaching and the sounds, smells, and visual flavor of the classroom. The more scientific we are in our approach to teaching, the more we ignore what we cannot accommodate to our empirical assumptions or principles. What sometimes occurs, according to Eisner, is that the educationally significant but difficult to measure or observe is replaced by what is insignificant but comparatively easy to measure or observe.[14]

It is necessary to blend artistic impressions and relevant stories about teaching—because good teaching involves emotions and feelings—with objective observations and measurements and precise language. There is nothing wrong with considering good teaching to be art, but we must also consider it to lend itself to a prescriptive science or practice. If it does not, then there is little assurance that new teachers can be trained—told what to do, how to instruct students, how to manage students, and so forth—and experienced teachers will be extremely vulnerable to public criticism and to people outside the profession telling them how and what to teach.

True knowledge of teaching is achieved by practice and experience in the classroom. According to one researcher, the "knowledge that teachers came to have the most faith in and used most frequently to guide their [teaching] is consistent with traditions that have worked in . . . the classroom arena." Although it seems to be "more everyday and common-sensical, both in form and structure, than highly specialized and theoretical," the process still includes teaching a prescribed curriculum with planned methods.[15] There are technical skills that can be taught to teachers and that can be designed and developed in advance and based on sound research and objective data. Such skills are rooted in college-based teacher education programs.[16]

In this connection, the information in this text attempts to apply the science of teaching (what some educators might call "conceptual" or "theoretical"), while recognizing that much of teaching deals with feelings and emotions— what some might say is the art of teaching (and still others might call the "humanistic" side). The science of teaching can be taught; the art of teaching is based more on personality.

The Teacher You Choose to Be

If you intend to make teaching a career, it makes sense to do some serious thinking about the kind of teacher you wish to become, the subjects and grade

---

14 Eisner, "The Art and Craft."

15 Arthur S. Bolster, "Toward a More Effective Model of Research on Teaching," *Harvard Educational Review* (August 1983), pp. 294-308.

16 David H. Gliessman et al., "Variables Influencing the Acquisition of a Generic Teaching Skill," *Review of Educational Research* (Spring 1988), pp. 25-46.

levels you wish to teach, and how you intend to teach. You need also to ask yourself why you want to teach and whether you have the commitment to work with children and youth who need dedicated teachers.

One overriding factor is that teachers must face themselves and be honest about themselves and what they are trying to achieve in the classroom. To teach moral values, learning skills, critical thinking, or creativity calls for a teacher who has these skills and has a healthy self-concept. Teachers must be willing to ask themselves tough questions that deal with feelings, attitudes, and behaviors. More than 35 years ago Arthur Jersild, a well-known psychologist, asked teachers to deal with crucial issues of personal and professional life— such issues as striving, conflict, anxiety, loneliness, self-doubt, alienation, hostility, guilt, anger, and despair. He asked teachers to search for meaning, to go beyond surface facts and behaviors and analyze motives.[17]

More recently, Heck and Williams stressed the importance of a healthy self-concept which translates to positive feelings and behaviors toward others. The only way a teacher can be warm, open, and humane with students is to be an "actualized" person who is trusting enough in life situations and carries that trust into the teaching act.[18]

To gain knowledge of oneself as a teacher and person, and to face the looking glass to see how others view one, requires courage and humility. All of us should be able to analyze our strengths and weaknesses as teachers and our anxieties and aspirations as people. We cannot run from our feelings or mask them for long. They affect our relations with others, especially our students. A teacher who is not timid and not fearful, who has a realistic and positive self-concept, can help others understand themselves, which is at the core of teaching. Learning to deal with one's feelings is a profound and personal experience. Teachers must be willing to take risks, to allow students to see their humaneness and humanity. They can show weakness, concern, and empathy with students; they can allow students to get to know them and still maintain authority as a teacher.

Similarly, our students have personal problems of growing up, problems with parents, siblings, and peers, that eventually affect their schoolwork and behavior. Most teachers ignore these problems, for many of us are afraid to deal with the feelings and emotions of our students. We prefer dealing with subject matter, not the realities of life. But to teach children and youth today calls for a psychologically healthy learning environment and a mentally healthy teacher. Teachers must not only teach students, they must also learn to nurture them. The research data suggest that recognition and rewards for student accomplishments are a proven way of raising children's

17 Arthur T. Jersild, *When Teachers Face Themselves* (New York: Teachers College Press, Columbia University, 1955).

18 Shirley F. Heck and C. Ray Williams, *The Complex Roles of the Teacher* (New York: Teachers College Press, Columbia University, 1984).

self-esteem[19] Not only young children, but also adolescents and even adults need to be praised and stroked, and need to feel good about themselves. Sticking to the facts, and nothing more than the facts, as in the "good" old days (which were not really all that good for most students), while ignoring obvious social or personal problems among students that surface in class, is an unrealistic teaching strategy in the world we live in. Ignoring the problem(s) of adolescence will not make them go away; teachers must face these problems as well as their own personal problems.

Teachers Make a Difference

A good deal of well-publicized and large-scale research has promoted the idea that teachers and schools contribute little to student achievement; that IQ, family life, peer groups, and social class are the most important variables and that all other variables are secondary or irrelevant. This line of reasoning is based on the Coleman and Jencks studies on equality, Project Talents longitudinal studies, the International Achievement studies that extend over 20 years, and the recent results of the National Assessment for Educational Progress. The data from these studies are impressive and the message is clear: what teachers and schools do has minimal impact, and where positive impact is evidenced it tends to "fade out," that is, what positive effects do occur are not sustained for long.[20]

The other side of the coin is that in the last 15 years impressive research also indicates that teachers and schools do make a difference. The **teacher effectiveness research**, exemplified by the works of David Berliner, Jere Brophy, Walter Doyle, Carolyn Evertson, N. L. Gage, Thomas Good, Barak Rosenshine, and Herb Walberg, has shown, mainly through correlational studies, that teacher behaviors and teaching methods consistently relate to student achievement. (Most of this research will be discussed in Chapter 12.)

The problem is, however, that many teacher behaviors and teaching methods that seem to have an effect in one situation may be ineffective and inappropriate in another. The same teacher behaviors and methods have different effects on different students, in different grades, different subjects, and different classroom groups and school settings. Compounding the problem is the fact that variables such as socioeconomic status, personality traits, and human behaviors mean different things to different researchers.[21] Also, it is

---

19 Robert Abrell, "The ABC's of Teaching," *Kappa Delta Pi Record* (Fall 1989), pp. 31-32; Gloria Ryan, "Nurture Students to Attain Success," *PTA Today* (October 1989), p. 12.

20 James S. Coleman, "Families and Schools," *Educational Researcher* (August-September 1987), pp. 32-38; Christopher Jencks, "Inequality in Retrospect," *Harvard Educational Review* (February 1973), pp. 102-108; and Allan C. Ornstein, "In Pursuit of Cost-Effective Schools," *Principal* (September 1990), pp. 28-30.

21 Allan C. Ornstein, "Research on Teaching: Issues and Trends," *Journal of Teacher Education* (November-December 1985), pp. 27-31; Ornstein, "How Good Are Teachers in Effecting Student Outcomes?" *NASSP Bulletin* (December 1982), pp. 61-70.

often difficult to isolate teacher effects from the effects of other agents (parents, peer group, and other teachers), and we are unable to assess accurately changes in learning in short-term intervals.[22] Our instruments, for the greater part, are not sensitive enough to accurately assess small changes in learning over short periods of time, and standardized tests that are often used to show these changes in student learning were not developed with this purpose in mind.

Despite these and other measurement problems the findings clearly show that teachers can make a difference (positive or negative). Teachers and schools influence achievement. And if they did not make a difference, then there would be (1) minimal need for teacher preparation, since there would be little of value in well-prepared teachers; (2) minimal need for concern about teacher competence, since it would not matter much; and (3) little justification for holding teachers accountable for student performance.

Part of the shift in the idea of an effective teacher is due to the progress of what we now know about teaching and learning. From the post-Sputnik era to the 1970s, teaching theories were for the most part "subject domain" related; good teaching attempted to characterize general principles and methods that were hypothetically applicable to different subject areas. The effective secondary teacher was described as a scholar in his or her subject, then called a discipline. The teacher taught in terms of the *structure* of the subject, that is, the theories, principles and specific methods of the subject such as mathematics, science, history, English, etc. Each subject had its own structure and thus secondary methodology courses at the college level were subject related.

Recent cognitive research on teaching and learning diverges from the particulars of a subject and puts greater emphasis on the thinking process, that is general strategies and skills that can be used in many different learning situations or subjects, not specific knowledge or curricula. The idea is to teach students the "domain of thinking," or what some educators now call metacognitive knowledge. Students are no longer expected only to remember information they have to read from a text, but now they must engage in general thinking strategies when they read and use problem-solving behaviors or answer text-related questions. The emphasis is on cognitive processes, not on subject knowledge.

Identifying Effective Teaching

To describe what **effective teachers** do in the classroom, Levine and Ornstein have reviewed ten years of research and hundreds of research studies. The research reviewed deals primarily with low-achieving students in inner-city schools, but it applies to many other student types and many grade levels and subjects.

---

22 Samuel Messick, "Meaning and Values in Test Validation," *Educational Researcher* (March 1989), pp. 5-11; Marilyn Cochran-Smith and Susan Lytle, "Research on Teaching and Teacher Research," *Educational Researcher* (March 1990), pp. 12–17.

1. *Classroom management.* Effective teachers develop good managerial techniques. They make sure students know what they expect; they make certain that students know what to do if they need help; they follow through with reminders and rewards to enforce rules; and they do not respond to discipline problems emotionally.

2. *Direct instruction.* Effective teachers have a clear, systematic method of teaching, called *direct instruction* or *explicit teaching.* They proceed in small steps, provide ample review and explanation before proceeding to the next step, ask questions and check for understanding, and provide systematic feedback and correction.

3. *Time on task.* Effective teachers provide students with relevant academic activities and see to it that students spend an adequate amount of time actually engaged in these learning activities.

4. *Questioning.* Effective teachers ask appropriate questions in a manner that ensures participation and facilitates mastery of academic content. Questioning focuses on both facts and abstract thinking.

5. *Comprehension instruction.* Effective teachers emphasize independent learning and learning to learn. They teach students to apply concepts, solve problems, and monitor their own comprehension.

6. *Level of cognitive instruction.* Most instruction for low-achieving students emphasizes mechanical rote learning. Effective teachers try to move toward high-order thinking skills and independent learning by motivating students to learn and by using appropriate materials and activities.

7. *Grouping.* Effective teachers are able to group students for individualized and small-group instruction. They are able to work with more than one student or group at time.[23]

In the same connection, Porter and Brophy have also reviewed ten years of research on effective teaching. The two researchers claim that good teachers do have long-term effects on student achievement and that their behaviors and routines help students activate (1) information-processing strategies and (2) commonsense strategies that promote academic achievement. Effective teachers are

1. Clear about their goals and/or objectives.
2. Knowledgeable about their subject matter or content.
3. Able to communicate to their students what is expected of them.

23 Daniel U. Levine and Allan C. Ornstein, "Characteristics of Effective Classrooms and Schools," *Urban Review* (June 1989), pp. 81–94; Allan C. Ornstein and Daniel U. Levine, "School Effectiveness And Reform," *Clearing House* (November– December 1990), pp. 115-118.

4. Knowledgeable about their students' abilities, needs, and interests, and they adapt instruction to the students.
5. Knowledgeable about various instructional materials that enrich the content.
6. Able to integrate metacognitive (learning) strategies with the content and give students opportunities to master these strategies.
7. Frequently monitoring students' work and providing feedback.
8. Able to integrate their subject with other subject areas.
9. Willing to accept responsibility for student outcomes.
10. Thoughtful and willing to modify their practice.[24]

The two models of effective teaching apply more to middle and secondary school teachers, since these models stress subject matter as an essential ingredient in good teaching. Teacher behaviors and routines are considered natural, not contrived, developed through prior experience and automatically activated in relevant situations. Originally, some of these behaviors or routines were developed as part of teacher preparation (and other training sessions) and through modeling cooperating teachers (while student teaching) or colleagues (while teaching in their early years). The highlights or characteristics of effective teachers suggest that teachers can and do learn from preparation or training, as well as from experience. See Tips for Teachers 1.1.

CLASSROOMS: WHAT HAPPENS, WHAT WORKS

Classrooms are where the action is, where all the participants involved in teaching and learning interact. This is the place where the lessons are taught, where instructional methods and materials are introduced by the teacher, where students learn the subject matter, and where they are evaluated by the teacher. Classrooms can be organized or disorganized, the climate can be positive or negative, and students can experience success and pleasure or frustration and tension in dealing with the teaching and learning process.

Change in Classrooms

If we take a broad, long view of classrooms—that is, a *macro* view—we can observe noticeable changes in classrooms over time. Historically, according to Philip Jackson, "one has only to think of wooden benches and planked floors of the early American classroom as compared with plastic chairs and tile flooring in today's suburban schools to note changes."[25] We can strengthen the

---

24 Andrew C. Porter and Jere Brophy, "Synthesis of Research on Good Teaching," *Educational Leadership* (May 1988), pp. 74–85.

25 Philip W. Jackson, *Life in Classrooms* (New York: Holt, Rinehart & Winston, 1968), p. 6.

Tips for Teachers 1.1

Rewarding Effective Teachers

Real changes in teacher pay are in the offing. A growing number of school districts have taken the position that merit pay (a supplement to a teacher's base salary) is a cost-effective way of rewarding effective teachers and encouraging excellence in teaching. Below are ten recommendations for implementing a merit-pay program.

1. Teachers must be evaluated objectively on clear and agreed-upon standards.
2. Teacher raters, those who evaluate teachers, must receive training in the use of objective measures.
3. Teachers must be afforded appeal procedures, but those procedures cannot be time consuming.
4. A mechanism must exist for policing or ensuring that the merit procedures are void of politics and ethnic favoritism.
5. Teachers should receive assistance to meet the standards for merit.
6. Public disclosure of merit awards should be minimized since it often humiliates nonrecipients before students, parents, and colleagues.
7. The expense of incentive pay should not be offset by lowered annual salaries.
8. Both administrators and teachers must believe they can make competent judgments about the worth of teaching and the individual performance of teachers.
9. The administration, school board, and community must be willing to accept the fact that teaching is a full-fledged profession, and that highly rated teachers should have the opportunity to earn up to $100,000 by the mid-1990s.
10. By raising the lid on teacher salaries and by making distinctions based on merit, we will raise the prestige of teachers, attract brighter students into teaching, and increase the professionalism of teachers.

Source: Allan C. Ornstein, "The Evolving Teaching Profession: New Trends, New Policies," *Kappa Delta Pi Record* (Fall 1989), p. 25.

contrast by looking back to the one-room schoolhouse. Students of many ages were crowded in one room: The teacher stood behind the pulpit (like the church minister) preaching the daily lessons; no chalkboards or chalk were used; the desks and chairs were bolted down; the sun was the major source of light and firewood was the main source of heat.

The content and methods of teaching, up to the turn of the twentieth century, stressed basic-skill acquisition, timeless and absolute values, first religious and then social and moral conformity, faith in authority, rote learning and memorization. It was based on the Protestant ethic and notion of child depravity (play was idleness and child's talk gibberish), and thus the teacher needed to apply constant discipline. The child's mind was similar to an empty vessel, and the teacher was expected to fill their empty heads with facts—actually what turned out to be isolated bits of knowledge.

If we look at classrooms during our lifetime—that is, a *micro* view—say, from the time when we were attending elementary school, we note that changes have been minimal. Surface changes, small and isolated innovations in teaching and a lack of comprehensive approaches to changes in learning (with the exception of perhaps the computer) have characterized the schools.[26]

Although the research in education may be impressive in quantity, very few noticeable changes have resulted in schools and classrooms since our days as students. We are basically using the same teaching methods in the classroom that we were using fifty years ago. On the other hand, the changes and improvements in science, technology, and medicine within the last five years have been impressive, and they have affected almost all of our lives in some way. "Had Rip Van Winkle been a teacher and slept for fifty years, he could return to the classroom and perform relatively well; the chalk, eraser, blackboard, textbook, and pen and paper are still, today, the main tools for most teachers, as they were a half a century ago—or longer." If, however, Mr. Van Winkle's occupation "had been related to one of the other three fields, and had he dozed off for five years, he would be unable to function effectively for his knowledge and skills would be dramatically dated."[27]

We might expect educational aims and subject matter to change as society imposes new social and political demands on the schools and as new knowledge is created. And they do! However, we should not expect the structure and organization of schools or classrooms to change dramatically. This is why Rip Van Winkle could function in most schools after sleeping for so long or why many teachers, after ten or twenty years of retirement, could, if they wanted, go back into the classroom and still be effective.

---

26 Michael Fullan, *The Meaning of Educational Change* (New York: Teachers College Press, Columbia University, 1982); Ann Lieberman, ed., *Rethinking School Improvement* (New York: Teachers College Press, Columbia University, 1986).

27 Allan C. Ornstein, *Urban Education* (Columbus, Ohio: Merrill, 1972), p. 50.

We must understand that schools are slow moving, conservative, and traditional institutions that operate with standardized norms of behavior, written rules and regulations, and well-defined tasks dispersed among administrators, teachers, and students. As parents and/or teaches who were once students, we can return to school and readily cope with and recognize the features of the classroom immediately, because the behaviors and tasks, the rituals, rules, and regulations have not changed much since we were children.

Thus a set of routines and rules becomes part of the climate of schools and classrooms, for both students and teachers. Hoy and Miskel describe this process: "The school is a system of social interaction; it is an organized whole comprised of interacting personalities bound together in an organized relationship." The school is "characterized by an interdependence of parts, a clearly defined population . . . a complex network of social relationships, and its own unique culture.[28] The outcome is a host of institutional norms and patterns of behaviors that students and teachers must learn—and which influence their interaction in class. Thus educators use the term "institutional realities," "structures of schooling," and "circumstances of teaching" to describe the process of teaching and learning, and changes in classrooms and schools are usually piecemeal and slow.[29]

Classroom Interactions

According to Philip Jackson, a large portion of teaching is spontaneous and intuitive, not easily predictable. Teachers engage in more than "200 to 300 interpersonal interchanges every hour of [the] working day."[30] Although some of these interchanges are somewhat repetitive, Jackson contends that "the content and sequence of these interchanges cannot be predicted or preplanned with any exactitude." Paul Gump's observations are similar. He concludes that there are approximately 1300 teacher acts in one day. Most of these interactions involve minor and repetitive decisions and behaviors, but they tend to be swift and predominantly teacher initiated (in 73 percent of the cases) and centered on the main goal of promoting student activity.[31] In short, the spontaneity and speed of classroom events involving the interaction of teaching and learning

---

28 Wayne K. Hoy and Cecil G. Miskel, *Educational Administration: Theory, Research, and Practice,* 3rd ed. (New York: Random House, 1987), p. 58.

29 Walter Doyle, "Academic Work," *Review of Educational Research* (Summer 1983), pp. 159-199; John I. Goodlad, "A Study of Schooling: Some Findings and Hypotheses," *Phi Delta Kappan* (March 1983), pp. 465-470; and Allan C. Ornstein and Francis P. Hunkins, "Implementing Curriculum Changes—Guidelines for Principals," *NASSP Bulletin* (November 1989), pp. 67–72.

30 Jackson, *Life in Classrooms,* p. 149.

31 Paul V. Gump, "Environmental Guidance of the Classroom Behavioral System," in B. J. Biddle and W. J. Ellena, eds., *Contemporary Research on Teacher Effectiveness* (New York: Holt, Rinehart & Winston, 1964), pp. 165-195; Gump, "Social Settings and Their Keeping," In D. Duke, ed., *Helping Teachers Manage Classrooms* (Alexandria, Va.: Association for Supervision and Curriculum Development, 1982), pp. 98–114.

principles seem somewhat metaphysical, not always to be taken literally, and research generalizations must be tempered by the context of the situation.

Classroom Instruction

In a study of more than 1,000 elementary and secondary classrooms, John Goodlad and his colleagues provide comprehensive data on the general patterns of instruction which he characterized as "widespread" and of "extraordinary sameness" among grade levels in varied schools. (1) The dominant pattern of classroom organization is a group that the teacher treats as a whole. This pattern seems to arise from the need to "maintain orderly relationships" among the students in a relatively small space. (2) The teacher is the dominant figure in the classroom and makes virtually all the decisions regarding instructional materials and methods. (3) There is much praise and correction of students' performance. (4) Enthusiasm, joy, anger, and other emotions are kept under control; the emotional tone of the classroom is "flat" or "neutral." (5) Most student work involves listening to the teacher, answering the teacher, or writing answers to questions in all grade levels and subjects. (6) Students rarely learn from one another, and there are few "hands-on activities." (7) The teacher-to-child pattern of interaction overwhelmingly pervades to the point that it becomes a monotonous recurring piece of data. (8) Textbooks and workbooks are the main forms of instruction. (9) These instructional patterns increasingly dominate classrooms as students proceed through the grades.[32]

In short, classroom patterns suggest boring and repetitive interactions between the teacher and students—instructional activities divorced of human feelings and emotions. Little wonder that many teachers often lose their students' interest after 10 or 15 minutes of instruction, that student doze off, stare out the window, or stare past the teacher, while others doodle, pass notes, or throw "spitballs"—or just pass time in classrooms. What remedy or behavior do you as a student exhibit when you are bored? Do you expect your students to be any different? What changes in instruction would you make to improve the classroom situation? To reduce boredom?

The classes described by Goodlad (and by the author) differ markedly from the classes observed during Dunn and Griggs' visits to grades 6 through 12 in more than 100 schools (rural, suburban, and urban; private and public).

In the classes, they describe,

1. The focus for teaching and learning was the individual student.
2. Patterns within the classroom reflected pairs, small groups, or individuals working alone.
3. Teaching was compatible with the students' assessed learning style preference.

---

32 John I. Goodlad, *A Place Called School* (New York: McGraw-Hill, 1984).

4. The room design was cheerful and innovative, with formal and informal areas.
5. Students assumed a major responsibility for learning.
6. Students created their own hands-on resources.
7. The emotional tone of the classroom was supportive.
8. A wide range of instructional materials and methods was used in class (such as graphs, charts, computers, films, videotapes, graphics, games, dramatizations, and experiments).[33]

The schools observed by Dunn and Griggs were exemplary schools participating in an innovative program dealing with learning styles. Nevertheless, the results of the study indicate that classroom patterns can improve when teachers and administrators work together with a common focus in mind. Indeed, classrooms and schools can be appealing for students, and learning can be encouraged, when the cognitive, motivational, and physiological elements that affect each student's learning environment are considered.[34]

Classroom Tasks

Instructional tasks are the core of the classroom setting. Most teachers maintain control over instructional tasks by making the decisions about what is to be taught, what materials and methods are to be used, and how much students are to be allowed to interact. There are teachers, however, who do permit student input in planning content and activities. Secondary school classrooms tend to be more controlled settings than elementary school classrooms.[35] The key variable, of course, is the teacher and not the grade level. When the teacher has complete control over instruction, it is likely that most students, if not all, will be engaged in a single classroom task and work toward the same goal with the same content. When students have input, it is likely that they will work on different classroom tasks.[36]

Teacher control over tasks affects the social setting and nature of evaluation. Under single-task conditions with high teacher control, students usually

---

33 Rita Dunn and Shirley A. Griggs, *Learning Styles: Quiet Revolution in American Secondary Schools* (Reston, Va.: NASSP, 1988).

34 Rita Dunn and Shirley A. Griggs, "Learning Styles: Key to Improving Schools and Student Achievement," *Curriculum Report* (January 1989), pp. 1–4.

35 Goodlad, *A Place Called School*; Sara Lawrence Lightfoot, *The Good High School* (New York: Basic Books, 1983).

36 Ronald W. Marx and John Walsh, "Learning from Academic Tasks," *Elementary School Journal* (January 1988), pp. 207–219; Mary J. Partridge, Roger Gehlbach, and Ronald W. Marx, "Social Contingencies, Physical Environment, and Prosocial Behavior in Children's Play," *Journal of Research and Development in Education* (Summer 1987), pp. 25–29; and Penelope L. Peterson et al., "Students' Cognition and Time on Task During Mathematics Instruction," *American Educational Research Journal* (Fall 1984), pp. 487–516.

Students often work at skills and tasks they enjoy without the assistance of teachers.

work alone, and evaluation of academic abilities and achievement is based on comparison to others in the class or to standardized achievement levels. Under multiple-task conditions with low teacher control, there is more social interaction and cooperative learning, and evaluation is made more on the basis of individual progress than by comparison to others.[37]

Most **classroom tasks** are initiated by the teacher; students usually act in response to the teacher's expectations. Such tasks are procedural in nature and concentrate on the acquisition and comprehension of knowledge as well as practice. Basically, classroom tasks that are initiated by the teacher fall into four categories: (1) *incremental tasks,* which focus on new skills or ideas and require recognition; (2) *restructuring tasks,* which involve the discovery of an idea or pattern and require some reorganization of data; (3) *enrichment tasks,* which involve application of familiar skills and ideas to new problems; and (4) *practice tasks,* which are aimed at making new skills and ideas automatic so they can be used in other task situations and cognitive processes.[38]

In order to facilitate learning, the teacher must learn to match appropriate tasks with the students' abilities and background knowledge. Matching becomes more difficult as students get older and have the potential to learn more. It is also more difficult in heterogeneously grouped classrooms because of the range in abilities and interests. The teacher must consider which tasks contribute most to students' learning, and when it is appropriate to introduce these tasks so students gain new insights and skills.

37 Susan J. Rosenholtz and Carl Simpson, "The Formation of Ability Conceptions: Developmental Trend or Social Construction," *Review of Educational Research* (Spring 1984), pp. 31-63.

38 Neville Bennett and Charles Desforges, "Matching Classroom Tasks to Students' Attainments," *Elementary School Journal* (January 1988), pp. 221-234.

Success in matching can be judged by student performance. The more errors that students make in working on the tasks, the greater the mismatch. Fewer errors mean that students are capable of working on the tasks, but not necessarily that a good match has been made, because the tasks may be too easy to contribute to learning.

In observing 17 different math and language art classes, Bennett and Desforges observed 600 different classroom tasks and found that approximately 40 percent of all instructional tasks were matched, 28 percent were too difficult, and 26 percent were too easy (remaining tasks were not characterized). Students with different abilities had different experiences. High achievers were underestimated on 41 percent of the tasks assigned to them, and low achievers were overestimated on 44 percent of the tasks.[39]

This pattern of over- and underestimation of tasks was found in another study of 21 middle grade classes in math, language arts, and social studies. In this study 500 academic tasks were analyzed, and the extent of mismatching was greater for both high- and low-achieving students.[40]

In both studies teachers were more concerned with overestimating than underestimating tasks. In fact, no teacher saw any task as too easy. Actually, both types of mismatching lead to failure to meet the needs of the students. When tasks are underestimated, too many students are not learning up to potential, and they also may become bored. When tasks are overestimated, too many student fail to learn because they don't understand what they are being asked to do and they are likely to become discouraged. Furthermore, the research cited studied elementary and middle grades. If the assumption that matching becomes more difficult in the upper grades is correct, then mismatching may help explain why so many students drop out of school at adolescence.

Improving Success Rates on Classroom Tasks

The nature of school learning requires students to cope with moderate stress as they engage in classroom tasks. Moderate errors in classroom tasks can have a *positive* influence on learning when the norms of the class emphasize understanding of tasks and when errors are followed by immediate feedback. The number of errors that students can cope with is not perfectly clear or linear, but is more associated with the students' prior achievement and self-concept. Each student is obviously different, however. Researchers have argued that students' perception of environmental contingencies (sometimes called "classroom contexts," "classroom climate," or "classroom conditions") and their belief that they have control over the environment and the outcomes of the tasks are

---

39 Ibid.

40 Neville Bennett et al., "Task Processes in Mixed and Single Age Classes," *Education* (Fall 1987), pp. 43-50.

important factors for learning.[41] Students who feel they have control over conditions believe that events are predictable and can be attributed to consistent causes, and feel they are personally competent to resolve tasks and can deal with more errors as well as with more difficult tasks. See Tips for Teachers 1.2.

High success rates on classroom tasks are associated with teachers who structure information about task performance (how things are to be performed) and provide information for student self-regulation.[42] Also, it is important for teachers to present clear rules and procedures on what is expected of students. In this connection, effective classroom managers are a requirement for students' task-related performance, but teachers must go beyond management and maximize student time-on-task and teach as if they expect students to understand how, why, and when tasks are performed. They need to instill in students the belief that they are capable task performers.

Gaea Leinhardt points out that good task performance in class is associated with behaviors that students can do "quickly, accurately, flexibly, and inventively under several types of processing constraints" or situations; moreover, they can explain what they are doing and why. Students enter almost all learning situations with some level of prior knowledge and the idea is for the teacher to link the students' knowledge with what is being taught.[43]

Leinhardt distinguishes four types of knowledge for conducting classroom tasks: (1) *intuitive* or real-life, circumstantial knowledge, which often has little to do with specific instruction and is sometimes disorderly or idiosyncratic; (2) *concrete*, basic knowledge portrayed by texts and teachers, or what is often called information; (3) *computational*, that is numerical as well as verbal and related to procedures used for solving problems; and (4) *conceptual*, underlying knowledge that facilitates deductive operations and becomes a bridge for transferring relationships from one context to another.[44] These four types of knowledge are basically more independent than interrelated, but as a core or whole they form the "connections" that lead to understanding and task performance.

Because **intuitive knowledge** tends to be personal or at least highly contextualized, it is difficult to teach and for the teacher to build upon. Nevertheless, it is probably the most powerful form of knowledge (and the one that distinguishes an "A" student who does not study from an "A" student who must study), and the one least utilized in the teaching process or tested by the teacher.

41 John R. Weisz and Alan S. Cameron, "Individual Differences in the Student's Sense of Control," in C. Ames and R. Ames, eds., *Research on Motivation in Education*, vol. 4 (New York: Academic Press, 1985), pp. 93–140; Merlin C. Wittrock, "Students' Thought Processes," in M. C. Wittrock, ed., *Handbook of Research on Teaching*, 3rd ed. (New York: Macmillan, 1986), pp. 297–314.

42 Barry K. Beyer, *Practical Strategies for the Teaching of Thinking* (Needham Heights, Mass.: Allyn and Bacon, 1991).

43 Gaea Leinhardt, "Getting to Know: Tracing Students' Mathematical Knowledge From Intuition to Competence," *Educational Psychologist* (Spring 1988), pp. 119-144.

44 Leinhardt, "Getting to Know." Also see Gavriel Salomon and David N. Perkins, "Rocky Roads to Transfer," *Educational Psychologist* (Spring 1989), pp. 113-142.

Tips for Teachers 1.2

Task Difficulty and Teaching

According to much research on teaching and classroom tasks, a low error rate is associated with reading achievement. This is not always the case. A deeper analysis of factors indicates the following:

1. Moderate errors (say 10 to 15 percent) in classroom tasks produce moderate tension which increases attention and instills deeper cognitive processing or effort to gain meaning. However, higher error rates will create frustration and inhibit learning.
2. High achievers can tolerate more classroom errors without becoming frustrated and ceasing to pay attention.
3. Students performing difficult tasks will make more mistakes; thus, higher error rates are expected when classroom tasks are difficult.
4. If classroom tasks are too easy for students, then time is wasted by allowing students to short-circuit thinking required to master material. The need is to challenge students with tasks appropriate to their level of thinking.
5. Increased learning takes place when errors are followed by immediate feedback, but not when feedback follows correct responses. Correct responses should be followed by moderate praise or recognition that the student is correct.
6. Error rates on classroom tasks over an extended period of time, say a term, reflect students' level of understanding of subject matter and in many cases are more accurate in judging their comprehension than are standardized tests or other "one-shot" instruments.

Source: Richard C. Anderson et al., "Do Errors on Classroom Reading Tasks Slow Growth in Reading?" *Elementary School Journal* (January 1988), pp. 268–280.

As students grow, and as subjects become more advanced, intuitive knowledge should converge with computational and conceptual knowledge to form the basis from which the teacher could then employ his or her teaching methods. Although all this is somewhat speculative, the bottom line is that teachers need to connect the students' prior or existing knowledge with new concepts, skills, or tasks to facilitate instruction.

Classrooms are places where most students learn; but, learning requires appropriate student responses, or what might be called "adaptive strategies"

Table 1.1   ADAPTIVE STRATEGIES STUDENTS AND TEACHERS CAN PERFORM WITH DIFFICULT CLASS-
ROOM TASKS

Adaptive Responses by Students	Adaptive Responses by Teachers
Change Task	*Change Task*
1. Simplify task	1. Simplify task
2. Reread directions	2. Divide into parts
3. Gather more knowledge	3. Relate to something familiar
4. Divide into parts	4. Reassign student to a different task
5. Relate to something familiar	5. Require more practice
6. Practice more	6. Provide coaching
Change Situation	*Change Situation*
1. Seek assistance from peers or teacher	1. Provide assistance (i.e., peers or tutors)
2. Remove distractions	2. Assign or supplement with instructional resources (i.e., computer)
3. Remove self from task; ask to do something else	3. Assist student; complete work for student
4. Go on to another task; return to task later	4. Model adaptive student responses
	5. Ask student to make adaptive responses
	6. Substitute or change task

Source: Adapted from Lynn Corno, "What It Means to be Literate About Classrooms," *Classrooms and Literacy* (New York: Ablex Publishers, 1989), pp. 29-52.

or "moves," in performing classroom tasks; it also requires teachers to modify classroom tasks so that students can cope with and regulate or control their learning (i.e., by understanding instructions, making good use of homework or study time, knowing to raise a hand and ask for help when confused, etc.). Table 1.1 shows a range of adaptive strategies that students and teachers can use to promote learning. The categories are organized by *task* and *situation*. For example, a student may modify a task by slowing it down or speeding up the pace. A student may modify the situation by taking a break or changing study time; the situation can be changed by seeking assistance or working alone. A teacher uses other adaptive strategies, by changing a *task* or *situation*. The changes shown are based on the teacher's perception of the task or situation, whether it is too difficult or too easy; the idea is to respond to students' errors in ways that are encouraging to them and help them correct themselves.

Perhaps the most important thing to remember is that there are limits to the number of and difficulty of tasks that students can attend to and process effectively. When too much new information or too many new skills are presented at once, our strategies for dealing with classroom tasks break down and we are unable to process them or to function effectively. Consequently, teachers need to teach appropriate amounts of information or skills processed into what learning theorists call "short term" or "working" memory.

Depending on age and ability, students need to rehearse, review, summarize, and elaborate the major points of the tasks we are trying to teach. This is best achieved by active participation of students, especially among low and average achievers, which is facilitated by the teacher asking questions that highlight important information: presenting important points clearly and sometimes in outline form, requiring students to explain main points, tutoring or providing additional time for those who have difficulty in understanding, and modeling the information or skills. Such structured learning need not be the basis for all students, especially high achievers, who can analyze and abstract and do independent work. Often, they prefer to see the "big picture," and then concentrate on the details or specifics.

Guidelines for Teaching Classroom Tasks

Fourteen techniques are recommended below for helping students perform classroom tasks. In general, teachers who are successful in improving students' success with tasks analyze or break down task demands clearly, maintain high levels of attention, encourage students when they have a task problem, and provide general strategies that work in several task-related contexts. More specifically such teachers

1. Help students cope with moderate stress, when they do not understand a specific task.
2. Permit students to respond in a flexible manner in solving tasks.
3. Do not waste time; maintain high levels of attention.
4. Provide adequate amounts of practice.
5. Provide informative explanations on how to perform tasks; explain common strategies and rules for understanding task demands.
6. Explicitly relate examples and specific strategies or rules to broader concepts or principles; explain how parts are related to the whole and how the whole is related to parts.
7. Create opportunities for students to monitor their own task performance, to check their work, and to make modifications if necessary.
8. Monitor students' performance on tasks; take time out to discuss common problems.
9. Clarify standards of behavior and accountability for task performance; students know what is expected of them and what to do when one task is completed.
10. Create smooth transitions from one task to another.

11. Instill in students a sense of control over tasks and task outcomes; create general understanding of their behavior as they perform tasks.
12. Help students learn how to organize or plan steps in solving tasks that carry over to other tasks.
13. Reduce students' focus on knowing the right answer (which only counts for one task or problem); reorient them to the process that will have meaning for many related tasks and problems.
14. Encourage students to deal with ambiguity or vagueness, or not knowing the answer, without getting upset or frustrated; teach them to backtrack in the text, ask questions, seek help (from a peer, parent, or teacher).

Altering Instructional Variables

Researchers are focusing on elements of the classroom that teachers and schools can change, or what some call **alterable environments**, for purposes of measuring the effect they have on student achievement. According to Robert Slavin, there are four components of instruction: (1) *quality* of instruction, (2) *appropriate* level of instruction, (3) *incentives* to work on instructional tasks, and (4) *time* needed to learn tasks.[45] He concludes that all four components must be adequate for instruction to be effective. For example, if the quality of instruction is low, it matters little how much students are motivated or how much time they have to learn. Each of the components "is like a link in a chain, and the chain is only as strong as its weakest link."[46]

Benjamin Bloom lists 19 teaching and instructional variables based on a summary of several hundred studies conducted during the past half century. His research synthesizes the magnitude of effect these variables have on student achievement. The five most effective ones in rank order are: (1) tutorial instruction (1:1 ratio), (2) instructional reinforcement, (3) feedback and correction, (4) cues and explanations, and (5) student class participation. The next most effective variables for student achievement are (6) improved reading and study skills, (7) cooperative learning, (8) graded homework, (9) classroom morale, and (10) initial cognitive prerequisite.[47]

Bloom concludes that the *quality* and *quantity* of instruction (teacher performance and time devoted to instruction) are the most important factors related to teaching and learning. Moreover, most of the instructional variables that are effective tend to be emphasized in individualized and small-group instruction (see Chapter 10). Bloom assumes that two or three variables used together

---

45 Robert E. Slavin, "A Theory of School and Classroom Organization," *Educational Psychologist* (Spring 1987), pp. 89-128.

46 Ibid., p. 92

47 Benjamin S. Bloom, "The 2 Sigma Problem: The Search for Methods of Group Instruction as Effective as One-to-One Tutoring," *Educational Researcher* (June-July 1984), pp. 4-16.

especially among the first five rankings contribute more learning than any one of them alone." [48]

According to Herb Walberg's review of hundreds of studies, nine general factors influence student achievement: (1) ability, (2) stage of development, (3) motivation, (4) instruction quality, (5) instruction quantity, (6) home environment, (7) classroom social group, (8) peer group, and (9) use of out-of-school time[49] (see Table 1.2). Walberg (with Waxman) lists 23 variables under instructional quality. The variables are similar to Bloom's. For Walberg, teacher reinforcement (reward for correct performance) has the largest overall effect on student achievement, slightly more than one standard deviation; it ranked second with Bloom. Reading training (programs designed to help students improve reading) was ranked third by Walberg and sixth by Bloom. The variable labeled "cues, participation, and feedback" was ranked fourth by Walberg; it was split in two and ranked third and fourth by Bloom. Graded homework and cooperative learning ranked fifth and sixth for Walberg and ninth and tenth for Bloom. The only major differences within the top rankings are tutorial instruction, which ranked first with Bloom and tenth with Walberg; and instructional acceleration, which Bloom did not rank and was second with Walberg.

The general conclusion is that the classroom environment, that is, both the quality and quantity of instruction, can be modified for the students' benefit. The instructional variables discussed by Bloom and Walberg provide excellent guidelines for improving instruction. They seem to be effective across school districts, ethnicity and gender, grade level, classroom size, and subject area. They deal mainly with improving the process, not increasing inputs or spending. It suggests that throwing money into schools is not always prudent; changing instruction, that is the process, can enhance output.

ACADEMIC TIME IN SCHOOLS

Time in school can be divided into four categories relating to academic work. (1) *Academic mandated time* is the number of days and hours in the school calendar specified by state and school district laws. (2) *Academic allocated time* is the portion of time in school allocated to different subjects and other activities in academic and nonacademic areas. Allocation is often suggested in state guidelines and is influenced by attitudes and interests of the local community and school superintendent. (3) *Academic instructional time* is the time the teacher actually spends in class giving instruction by various means in particular

---

48 Ibid, p. 6. Also see Benjamin S. Bloom, "Helping All Children Learn," *Principal* (March 1988), pp. 12-17.

49 Herbert J. Walberg, "Improving the Productivity of America's Schools," *Educational Leadership* (May 1984), pp. 19-27; Walberg, "Synthesis of Research on Teaching," in M. C. Wittrock, ed., *Handbook of Research on Teaching*, 3rd ed. (New York: Macmillan, 1986), pp. 214-229.

Table 1.2   INSTRUCTIONAL FACTORS RELATED TO LEARNING

Factor	Mean correlation or effect
Ability (IQ)	.71
Developmental (Piagetian stage)	.47
Motivation	
Motivation	.34
Self-concept	.18
Instructional quality	
Reinforcement	1.17
Acceleration	1.00
Reading training	.97
Cues, participation, and feedback	.97
Graded homework	.79
Cooperative learning	.76
Reading experiments	.60
Personalized instruction	.57
Adaptive instruction	.45
Tutoring	.40
Higher-order questions	.34
Diagnostic prescriptive methods	.33
Individualized instruction	.32
Teacher expectations	.28
Computer-assisted instruction	.24
Sequenced lessons	.24
Advanced organizers	.23
Direct instruction	.23
Homogeneous groups	.10
Class size	.10
Praise	.08
Programmed instruction	−.03
Mainstreaming	−.12
Quantity of instruction	
Instructional time	.38
Assigned homework	.28
Home environment	
Home interventions	.37
Home environment	.50
Socioeconomic status	.25
Classroom social group (class morale)	.60
Peer group	.24
Use of out-of-school time (leisure-time television)	−.05

Source: Hersholt C. Waxman and Herbert J. Walberg, "Teaching and Productivity." *Education and Urban Society.* (February 1986), p. 214.

Teachers need to make effective use of classroom time. This means students need to attend to academic tasks or content.

subjects and skills. It is influenced by class size, student abilities and interests, program tracking, and instructional level. (4) *Academic engaged time* is the time the students spend in performing academic work. It is influenced by routine practices, classroom management, student motivation, and instructional quality.[50]

Academic Mandated Time

Academic mandated time averages about 178 days per year and about 5 hours and 8 minutes per day. The longer school term and days of Japan (220 days and more than 6 hours per day), the Soviet Union, and western European nations (200-215 days) lead some educators to conclude that one reason for poor performance of U.S. students is the shorter time in school. But research indicates that increasing time in school by itself, without changing other aspects of instruction, does not result in increased achievement.[51] Nonetheless, common sense suggests that if instructional quality is kept constant, then extra instructional quantity should have positive effects. Students who have more time to study specific knowledge, skills, or tasks should learn more than students who have less time. Increasing school time in U.S. public schools about 40 minutes per day would add 119 hours in one school year, about 290 school days over 12

50 Nancy Karweit, "Time on Task: The Second Time Around," *NASSP* (February 1988), pp. 31-39; Allan C. Ornstein, "Private and Public School Comparisons: Size, Organization, and Effectiveness," *Education and Urban Society* (February 1989), pp. 192-206.

51 Gene V. Glass, "What Works: Politics and Research," *Educational Researcher* (April 1987), pp. 5-11; Nancy Karweit, "Should We Lengthen the School Term?" *Educational Researcher* (June 1985), pp. 9-15.

years, and 1 $^2/_3$ extra years of schooling.[52] This is an important point that has future consequences in terms of American human capital, productivity, and, in turn, our standard of living for all age groups.

Academic Allocated Time

Academic allocated time is the portion of the school day (or school year) the school assigns to academic and nonacademic instruction. About 60 to 80 percent of the school day is allocated to academic content. Secondary schools are subject-oriented and allocate more time to academic content than do elementary schools. The younger students need more time for socialization and personal growth.

More than half of the states make recommendations and some have requirements for allocating time in curriculum content at the elementary and middle grades. School districts can and usually do modify the recommendations or requirements upward, especially in math and English (perhaps because of the recent publicity given to the results of statewide programs to test performance in math and reading). Modifications of allocated time in schools also reflect the philosophy of the local community, district superintendent, and school principal: for example, a "progressive" educator might allocate more time for socialization than an "essentialist," who might put more emphasis on the three R's and subtract time from a sports or music/art program.

Although state policies vary, as illustrated in Table 1.3, English (reading) receives the most allocated time in the early grades, after which the time decreases. Math receives the second most attention and remains relatively constant throughout the grades. Note, however, that the difference in recommendations among the states for allocated time in English is 102 minutes per day in the third grade and 75 minutes in the sixth grade. In math the difference is as much as 45 minutes. The time allocated to science and social studies increases from the early grades to grade 8, when it is equal to the time for other subjects (except in Illinois). If standardized testing in grades 3 to 6 included science and social studies, then there would most likely be more allocated time for them in those grades. The states that do not establish time allocations (such as California, Florida, and New York) focus on instructional objectives and test for performance in subject areas.

At the secondary level allocated time is better defined and is influenced by the nature of the students' program (academic, technical, vocational). In response to national demands for upgrading academic requirements and increasing academic productivity, the curriculum was changed in the 1980s to put more emphasis on such core subjects as English, social studies, math, and science—and academic course requirements for graduation were also increased.

---

52 Allan C. Ornstein, "Academic Time Considerations for Curriculum Leaders," *NASSP Bulletin* (September 1989), pp. 103–110.

Table 1.3   ALLOCATED TIME BY SUBJECT AND GRADE LEVEL

Subject	Grade	Illinois (minimum recommendations)	Michigan (minimum recommendations)	Texas (minimum requirements)
Math	3	50	15	60
	6	49	15	60
	8	47	15	45
Science	3	26	9	20
	6	39	9	45
	8	44	15	45
English	3	142	40	120
	6	107	32	90
	8	87	15	45
Social	3	45	4	20
Studies	6	42	9	45
	6	42	9	45
	8	44	15	45

Source: Based on telephone conversations with curriculum specialists from the respective State Departments of Education, January 27, 1989.

Table 1.4 shows that there has been a marked increase in required course work for public high school graduation in all major academic subjects, especially in math and science, between 1981 and 1988. Graduation requirements in English and social studies for public schools are now only slightly below the recommendations of the National Commission on Excellence in Education; they are still substantially below the recommended levels in math, science, and, especially, foreign languages. Moreover, the proportion of high school seniors who completed more than three years of course work in English was 26 percent in 1980 and 87 percent in 1987; in mathematics, 8.5 percent in 1980 and 36 percent in 1987; in science, 6 percent in 1980 and 23 percent in 1987; in social studies, 10 percent 1980 and 12 percent in 1987.[53]

Considering that we live in a highly technological society and in a world in which the push of a button can have enormous impact on our lives, the small

53 *The Condition of Education 1983* (Washington, D.C.: U.S. Government Printing Office, 1984), Table 1.11, p. 34; "High School Transcript Study of Percentage of Graduates Earning Various Number of Credits, Carnegie Units," Preliminary Data for Educational Research and Improvement (Washington, D.C.: U.S. Department of Education, 1988), Table 2, p. 42; and Ornstein, "Private and Public School Comparisons: Size, Organization, Effectiveness," Table 7, p. 203.

Table 1.4   AVERAGE YEARS OF COURSE WORK REQUIRED FOR PUBLIC HIGH SCHOOL
GRADUATION

School year	Subject area				
	Mathematics	Science	English	Foreign languages	Social studies
1981-1982	1.6	1.5	3.6	[a]	2.6
1984-1985	1.9	1.8	3.8	.1	2.8
1987-1988[b]	2.3	2.0	3.9	.2	2.9
Recommendations of National Commission on Excellence in Education[c]	3.0	3.0	4.0	2.0[d]	3.0

[a]Less than 0.05 year.

[b]Expectations as of fall 1985 about requirements for seniors graduating in 1988.

[c]Another half year of course work was recommended in computer science. Almost no school districts had requirements in this area in 1981-1982. That situation changed by 1984-1985, when the average for all school districts was 0.1 year of course work required for graduation in computer science; the expected average for 1987-1988 was 0.2 year.

[d]The Commission's recommendations about foreign languages applied only to the college-bound, not to all students. The figures for actual requirements represent requirements for all graduates.

Source: The Condition of Education 1987 (Washington, D.C.: U.S. Government Printing Office, 1987), Table 1.3B, p. 84.

enrollments in science and mathematics have serious implications for our future. A similar concern was voiced nearly thirty years ago, when our standard of living was increasing more rapidly, when we were more influential as a superpower, and when we were jolted by the Soviet Union's rapid advances in space. Then, James Conant stressed that our educational programs needed more emphasis on science, mathematics, and foreign languages.[54] Our failure to heed Conant's warning may be viewed as one reason for our decline as the political and economic giant of the world, the general decline of our manufacturing capability and standard of living, and the urgency of the problem today.

Consider that Japanese students are required to take 23 percent of their total junior high school curriculum in science and mathematics. In high school they are required to take 1.25 science courses per year and 1.5 math courses per year (including calculus and statistics). As a point of comparison, American graduating high school seniors average a total of 2.3 years in math and 2.0 years in science. Because 94 percent of Japanese attend high school, their requirement

---

54 James B. Conant, *The American High School Today* (New York: McGraw-Hill, 1959).

produces a more scientifically literate public than ours.[55] In addition, Japanese students have continuously outperformed United States students in science and mathematics on the International Association for the Evaluation of Educational Achievement (IEA) study since comparisons were started in the mid-1970s. In fact, according to recent comparisons of student achievement in math and science, Americans score slightly below the mean among 14 industrial nations and more than 15 percent below Japanese scores in both subject areas.[56]

Academic Instructional Time

Whereas allocated time is the maximum possible time (or opportunity time) that might be spent in subject areas, **academic instructional time**, sometimes referred to as "academic learning time" or "content covered," is the actual amount of time the teacher spends on specific content.

Goodlad and Klein observe that teachers devote most academic learning time to reading activities at all elementary and middle grade levels (except kindergarten). This includes related activities in phonics instruction, listening to stories, and discussion of library books and elements of language. In terms of time allocation, this curriculum area is followed by "independent activities," such as filling in workbooks, looking up words in the dictionary, writing in journals, spelling words, and attending to class projects (almost all of which deal with language and have a reading component). Mathematics was the third most popular activity.[57]

According to David Berliner, the academic instructional time in reading per day over a school year at the fifth-grade level ranged from 68 to 137 minutes (or a difference of 69 minutes per day). There were similar ranges in mathematics: 20 to 73 minutes (or a difference of 53 minutes per day) in the fifth grade. These data are shown in Table 1.5. Thus one teacher may spend two to three times more academic learning time per day on reading and math than another teacher. Over a school year this difference in instructional time affects achievement.

Even in junior and senior high schools, where departmentalization forces time allocating for each subject, teachers must still make decisions on actual time for lesson units or topics. How much time should be spent on subjects such as creative writing that achievement tests don't usually test? One fifth-grade teacher spent 29 minutes all year on linear measurements, while another spent

55 Allan C. Ornstein, "Sources of Change and the Curriculum," *High School Journal* (April-May 1988), pp. 192–199; Kay M. Troost, "What Accounts for Japan's Success in Science Education?" *Educational Leadership* (December-January 1984), pp. 26-29.

56 *Digest of Education Statistics 1988* (Washington, D.C.: U.S. Government Printing Office, 1988), Tables 289–290, pp. 342–343.

57 John I. Goodlad and Francis Klein, *Behind the Classroom Door* (Worthington, Ohio: Jones Publishers, 1970); Goodlad, *A Place Called School.*

Table 1.5   ACADEMIC INSTRUCTIONAL TIME FOR READING AND MATHEMATICS IN GRADE 5 CLASSES

Reading		Mathematics	
Class	Allocated minutes per day	Class	Allocated minutes per day
6	68	3	20
27	88	9	36
1	102	6	58
23	121	25	64
12	137	24	73

Source: David C. Berliner, "Recognizing Instructional Variables," in D. E. Orlosky, ed., *Introduction to Education* (Columbus, Ohio: Merrill, 1980), p. 203. Originally adapted from Marilyn Dishawi, *Descriptions of Allocated Time to Content Areas for the A-B Period, Technical Notes IV-11a and IV-11b of the Beginning Teacher Evaluation Study* (San Francisco: Far West Laboratory for Education Research and Development, 1977).

500 minutes. One teacher spent 399 minutes on fractions, while another teacher spent no time. See Table 1.6.

Vast differences in time were also noted in seven language arts classrooms at the sixth grade. One teacher spent 63 minutes during the entire school year on library skills while another spent 886 minutes. One teacher spent 124 minutes on creative writing and another spent 967 minutes. In grammar the ranges were 261 to 1486 minutes, and in reading vocabulary it was 112 to 991 minutes.[58] Thus, within the same subject area, and in the same school district, when we analyze specific content the ranges among teachers are wide over the entire school year—as much as seven to ten times more in content areas related to fifth-grade math and sixth-grade language arts.

Obviously, the students who have no instruction in fractions or only 71 minutes for spelling during the entire year are at a disadvantage compared with students at the same grade level who received considerable instruction. One must also ask what content was taught in lieu of fractions or spelling—and whether this time was overkill (too much practice in a specific content area), wasteful (disciplinary problems surfaced), or put to good use. Then we might ask, how much time should be spent in areas such as library skills or creative writing that achievement tests don't usually test?

Two cautionary observations should be noted. First, we do not conclude that "more is always better." Quality is crucial, and there is a point at which

58 Allan C. Ornstein, "Time Considerations for Curriculum Leaders," *NASSP Bulletin* (September 1989), pp. 103-110.

Table 1.6   ALLOCATED TIME IN MATHEMATICS (GRADE 5) AND LANGUAGE ARTS (GRADE 6)

	Minutes per year	
	Least	Most
Mathematics (Grade 5)		
Computations, speed tests	31	232
Fractions	0	399
Word problems	109	416
Linear measurements	29	400
Language Arts (Grade 6)		
Library skills	63	886
Spelling	71	216
Creative writing	124	967
Grammar	261	1486
Reading		
Vocabulary	112	991
Comprehension	444	1841

Source: Adapted from David C. Berliner, "Recognizing Instructional Variables," in D. E. Orlosky, ed., in *Introduction to Education* (Columbus, Ohio: Merrill, 1982), p. 204; Allan C. Ornstein, "Time Considerations for Curriculum Leaders," *NASSP Bulletin* (September 1989), p. 107.

"more" becomes boring. On the other hand, teachers must allocate sufficient time for their students to learn the required material.

Second, teachers vary in how efficiently they use time. A good portion of classroom time that seems to be devoted to instruction is often wasted on clerical and housekeeping activities and managerial problems. According to researchers, no more than 50 to 60 percent of an elementary school day and 30 to 45 percent of a high school day is devoted to academic instruction.[59] The rest of the time is spent on nonacademic subjects, recess, lunch, and/or study time, transitions between classes, announcements, and procedural and maintenance tasks.

Also, there is a problem of absenteeism, and in many inner-city schools the absenteeism among students is high. When a student is absent or late, it does

---

59 Walter Doyle, "Academic Work," *Review of Educational Research* (Summer 1983), pp. 159-199; Allan C. Ornstein, "Emphasis on Student Outcomes Focuses Attention on Quality of Instruction," *NASSP Bulletin* (January 1987), pp. 88-95; Ornstein, "Private and Public School Comparisons: Size, Organization, and Effectiveness"; and Richard A. Rossmiller, "Time on Task: A Look at What Erodes Time for Instruction," *NASSP Bulletin* (October 1983), pp. 45-49.

not matter how much time the teacher devotes to instruction. A student who is not present receives no instruction.

To increase academic learning time, teachers should have a system of rules and procedures that facilitate noninstructional tasks and reduce disruptions and disciplinary problems. Similarly, the schools need to implement policies that decrease absenteeism and lateness. See Tips for Teachers 1.3.

Academic Engaged Time

Academic engaged time is the time a student spends attending to academic tasks or content. For some educators, it also means that students must perform the tasks or be engaged in the content with a high success rate (80 percent or more).[60] Although actual classroom instructional time is a more important variable than engaged time in the sense that is shows a higher correlation with improved performance, there is more data on engaged time because it is easier to measure. Moreover, different teachers use different materials and methods to cover the same content, and they focus on different aspects of content. Since researchers have not developed a way to code content in such situations, they often turn to academic engaged time as a proxy for instructional time, or content covered.[61]

Recently, Susan Stodolsky studied 20 mathematics classes and 19 social studies classes in 11 Chicago city and suburban school districts. She identified 15 instructional formats or activities—ways in which teachers chose to instruct. Mathematics teachers emphasized skill development in terms of content and used 47 percent of their instructional time for seatwork (mostly uniform seatwork) and another 31 percent on recitation. Students spent 6 percent of their time checking or reviewing their work. Other instructional activities occurred infrequently.[62] These instructional formats in mathematics are shown in Table 1.7, along with the instructional formats for social studies.

Social studies classes were more varied in content and instruction. The content drew from many disciplines such as history, economics, government, and sociology, and encouraged not only recall of information—dates, names, or events—but also concepts, problem solving, and research skills.

Stodolsky found in social studies that a much greater amount of time was spent on group work (11 percent), student reports (7 percent), and audiovisual materials (7 percent) than in mathematics (.01, 0, 0 respectively). Although

---

60 James H. Block, Helen E. Efthim, and Robert B. Burns, *Building Effective Mastery Learning School* (New York: Longman, 1989); Benjamin S. Bloom, *Human Characteristics and School Learning* (New York: McGraw-Hill, 1976).

61 Ornstein, "Emphasis on Student Outcomes Focuses Attention on Quality of Instruction"; Barak Rosenshine, "Content, Time, and Direct Instruction," in P. L. Peterson and H. J. Walberg, eds., *Research on Teaching: Concepts, Findings, and Implications* (Berkeley, Calif.: McCutchan, 1979), pp. 28–56.

62 Susan Stodolsky, *The Subject Matters* (Chicago: University of Chicago Press, 1988).

Tips for Teachers 1.3

Increasing Academic Time

Too much instructional time is wasted in today's classrooms. Two educators contend that as much as 50-60 days or nearly one-third of the school year may be wasted but can be regained without increasing the school day or school year simply by improving or changing some procedures. Here are some major time wasters to resolve.

1. *Working on homework during the school day.* It is not uncommon to find teachers allocating 20-30 minutes in class for students to work on homework assignments. This is equivalent to about 10 school days if only one teacher per day is guilty of this practice. *Action to be taken*: Time used for homework in class should be converted to instructional time. Teachers should still explain the homework assignment and review common problems, but not permit work on homework in class.

2. *Excessive viewing of films.* Too many teachers use too many films, especially on Fridays. Viewing films for one hour per week uses up 36 hours or 7 days. *Action to be taken*: Use of instructional tools should be justified in terms of student results. A cumulative record of film time used by teachers should perhaps be kept.

3. *Changing and beginning classes.* In most middle and secondary schools, students move from room to room. It is not unusual for teachers to use 5 or 10 minutes per class to take attendance and make announcements. If only 5 minutes were used, 75 hours or 15 days would be saved. *Action to be taken*: Teachers need to devise systems, such as assigned seats, printed lists, or diagrams, to show quickly who is absent from class.

4. *Teacher absences.* Learning suffers when teachers are absent (the average teacher is absent three to five times a year), since most substitute teachers are unable to reach desired academic objectives. *Action to be taken*: Excellent substitute teachers need to be identified by the school principals. Also, the regular teacher needs to make available the lesson plan for the day, along with related materials, when he or she expects to be absent.

5. *Registration and testing.* About 3 days a year are lost on registration and another 3 on schoolwide testing. In both cases students are often free for portions of the day. *Action to be taken*: Registration should be scheduled prior to the school year. Schoolwide and standardized testing should be incorporated into the regular class time, not treated as a separate testing day.

(continues)

6. *Extracurricular activities.* Although it is impossible to state the exact number of days lost by students who are dismissed early for athletic events, school tournaments, community and state activities, music and dance workshops, band, and other activities, a good estimate is 5 to 10 days. *Action to be taken:* Students must be encouraged to make up their academic work. Special events should be scheduled on activity days, not regular academic days, or after school hours (in the afternoon, evenings, or on weekends), not during class time.

Source: Adapted from Robert Lowe and Robert Gervais, "Increasing Instructional Time in Today's Classroom," *NASSP Bulletin* (February 1988), pp. 19–22.

students in both subjects spent a similar amount of time on recitation, they spent no time on individualized seatwork in social studies.

In general, in math the source for new knowledge, and for learning how to learn, was the teacher. Math teachers were expected to present new materials and explain how to do problems. In contrast, social studies students were expected to learn on their own by reading the text and other materials. They were supposed to develop research skills by gathering and using information from many sources, whereas math students were expected to first learn the fundamentals and then become problem solvers.

In the final analysis, both the quantity and quality of academic engaged time (as well as actual instructional time) are considered to be important in improving the outcomes of student learning, although quantity is easier to agree upon and measure.

Students of teachers who provide more academic engaged time (as well as actual instructional time) learn more than students of teachers who provide relatively less time. In a review of more than 20 different studies, the correlations between student achievement in reading and mathematics and learning time was between .40 and .60.[63]

Since academic time, both instructional and engaged, seems to be a scarcer commodity than most of us probably realized, what we might focus on in the future is how teachers can better utilize their time when they are actually

---

63 Benjamin S. Bloom, *Human Characteristics and School Learning* (New York: McGraw-Hill, 1976); Charles W. Fisher et al., "Teacher Behaviors, Academic Learning Time and Student Achievement," in C. Denham and A. Lieberman, eds., *Time to Learn* (Washington, D.C.: National Institute of Education, 1980), pp. 27–45.

Table 1.7 DISTRIBUTION OF INSTRUCTIONAL ACTIVITIES IN MATHEMATICS AND SOCIAL STUDIES

Format	Mathematics			Social Studies		
	N	% Segments	% Time	N	% Segments	% Time
Uniform seatwork	144	26.9	29.8	69	12.7	21.8
Individualized seatwork	59	11.0	13.7	—	—	—
Diverse seatwork	14	2.6	3.8	26	4.8	6.1
Recitation	155	28.9	30.9	96	17.6	28.1
Group work	1	.2	0.1	183	33.6	10.7
Contest, game	44	8.2	6.2	8	1.5	1.5
Checking work	42	7.8	5.9	12	2.2	2.4
Giving instructions/task preparation	33	6.2	1.7	58	10.9	5.4
Student reports	—	—	—	20	3.7	6.9
Discussion	2	0.4	0.4	19	3.5	3.1
Test	18	3.4	5.1	10	1.8	3.9
Lecture/Demonstration	15	2.8	1.9	12	2.2	2.5
Film/Audiovisual	—	—	—	24	4.4	6.8
Tutorial	8	1.5	0.2	—	—	—
Stocks	—	—	—	8	1.5	0.8
Totals	535	100.00	100.00	545	100.0	100.0

Source: Susan Stodolsky,"How Content Changes Teaching,," *University of Chicago Education News*, Annual ed., 1989, p. 9.

teaching (instructional time) and how students can better utilize their time when on task (engaged time).

SUMMARY

1. There is wide variation among states, as well as among institutions of higher learning in the same state, concerning the number of education courses required to prepare teachers.
2. The general trend is to reduce the number of education courses; the average number of credit hours in education required for elementary teachers is 24 and for secondary teachers it is 18.
3. Teaching combines science and art. Good teaching incorporates sound principles and methods (the theoretical and scientific elements of

teaching) and the use of judgment and insight (the practical and artistic elements of teaching).

4. The kind of teacher you choose to be is based in part on your reasons for teaching, professional knowledge, and pedagogical skills.

5. Teachers do make a difference in student achievement. However, the differences vary with classroom and school conditions and are not easy to discern.

6. Effective teachers are good classroom managers, provide direct instruction, keep students on task, ask appropriate questions, emphasize comprehension monitoring and learning-to-learn skills, and provide small group and individualized instruction.

7. Classrooms are places where students think and learn; the quality of learning that occurs is largely influenced by teacher-student interactions and the tasks students perform.

8. Most classroom tasks performed by students are either too easy or too difficult.

9. The quality and quantity of academic instructional and engaged time affect student performance.

10. Most teachers and schools waste precious academic time with changes between classes, administrative announcements, clerical tasks, disciplinary tasks, and excused student absences for extracurricular activities.

CASE STUDY

Problem

When speaking to an experienced teacher, a beginning seventh grade teacher complained that she (1) did not have enough academic time for practice or drill and (2) did not have enough academic time for reviewing explanations of previously taught subject matter with which some students were having difficulty. (Furthermore, when students entered and left the classroom, the lack of order took away from academic time since the teacher needed to re-establish order.)

Suggestion

An experienced teacher knew of studies that showed that too much classroom time is spent on students' random behavior (1) when starting and ending classes and (2) each time materials and equipment need distribution. The teacher suggested that routines for entering, leaving, distributing materials, turning in homework, needed to be clearly explained, practiced, and followed consistently. Her first suggestion was that the beginning teacher *set* these procedures, *practice* them, and have *consistent* implementation. In the beginning of the semester, classroom routines would take priority over concentration on instruction alone so that later, as the routines saved organizational time, more time could be given to academic time.

The teacher also suggested structuring review and drill *into* the formal lessons by presenting lessons in a series of academic sequences. Each sequence would have "break" points, rather than there being one continuous lesson. At the break point the teacher would review that sequence, allow for drill or questioning, make certain the material was understood, and then present the next sequence. When all the sequences were presented in this manner, the teacher "tied" them together for a *final* presentation/review/practice that included the basic academic work. Through the inclusion of once segmented activities, the teacher maximized academic time.

Discussion Suggestion

At another school, one teacher met the problem of maximizing academic time by the productive use of "dead space." Such use helped in classroom management, created productive practice, drill time and academic time. When students were leaving for lunch or home, the teacher would end the formal lesson to allow for an *orderly* retrieval of coats and putting away of personal and classroom materials. This allowed for about ten minutes, or more, of "dead space," between the wait for dismissal and the completion of the lesson. The process was not hurried and was practiced first.

While waiting these ten minutes or so, the teacher structured in academic time through *systematic* verbal drill by individual students, either asking them for facts about the subject or appropriate problem-solving activities from a number of subject matter areas. The difficulty of the questions matched the student's abilities. This was done with a "light" approach and teacher/student interaction had an air of camaraderie, even allowing the students to give some comments to the teacher.

The teacher had laminated "review cards" which were kept at students' desks with "grease" pencils attached. While waiting, the students gave written answers which they could then easily erase.

Discussion Questions

1. How do these suggestions agree or disagree with suggestions or models in this chapter?
2. Can these suggestions be used successfully with other, less structured, approaches?
3. What kinds of modifications, if any, would you plan for different grades?
4. If these suggestions work, how would you justify their use to principals or supervisors who might criticize "rote" learning or drill?
5. How do you feel about the initial concentration on practice or routine instead of on academic time for instruction?

QUESTIONS TO CONSIDER

1. In what way do schools and education differ?
2. Why is it important for teachers to be willing to face themselves? How can this be accomplished at the preservice level? In-service level?
3. To what extent do teachers make a difference in student achievement? Which of your teachers made the most difference to you? Why?
4. What teaching methods can be used to improve students' success in performing classroom tasks?
5. How would you improve academic instructional time and academic engaged time as a teacher?

THINGS TO DO

1. Debate in class: What is the proper mix of general or liberal arts courses, specialized courses, and education courses?
2. Interview two or three successful teachers. Ask them to take a position: Is teaching a science or an art? Report to the class.
3. Make a list of the characteristics of good teachers you remember as a student in grades 5–12. How do they compare (contrast) with the characteristics of an effective teacher described in this chapter?
4. Observe two or three teachers at work in the classroom and try to describe the classroom interactions taking place. Why do things happen in the classroom?
5. Speak to a local school principal or teacher to find out the school's allocated time by subject and grade level. Compare this with Table 1.3. Try to explain the reasons for whatever differences may exist.

RECOMMENDED READINGS

Apple, Michael W. *Teachers and Texts*. New York: Routledge & Kegan Paul, 1988. Examines the culture of teaching and politics of texts.

Cooper, James. *Classroom Teaching Skills*, 4th ed. Lexington, Mass.: D. C. Heath, 1990. A book of readings and guide to better teaching and instruction.

Dillion, J. T. *Personal Teaching*. Lanham, Md.: University Press of America, 1990. A personal approach to teaching based on engaging the student in the learning process and showing humane and supportive feelings.

Good, Thomas L. and Jere E. Brophy. *Looking in Classrooms*, 5th ed. New York: Harper-Collins, 1991. The authors describe what happens in classrooms and how teachers influence students' learning.

Jackson, Philip W. *The Practice of Teaching*. New York: Teachers College Press, Columbia University, 1986. Personal reflections and insights by the author about teaching.

Rosenholtz, Susan J. *Teachers' Workplace*. New York: Longman, 1989. A study of school as a workplace—and where teachers and students interact and grow.

Waxman, Hersholt and Herbert J. Waxman, eds. *Contemporary Research on Teaching*. Berkeley, Calif.: McCutchan Press, 1991. An up-to-date analysis of the research on teaching described by several prominent thinkers in the teaching field.

KEY TERMS

Holmes Group
Cognitive psychology
Professional knowledge base
Teacher effectiveness research
Effective teachers
Classroom tasks

Alterable environments
Academic mandated time
Academic allocated time
Academic instructional time
Academic engaged time
Intuitive knowledge

Chapter
2

Learning: A Developmental Approach

FOCUSING QUESTIONS

1. How do the cumulative effects of growth and development affect future learning?

2. Why is socialization a lifelong process? Why are the adolescent years more important than the adult years in terms of how people develop?

3. How do the Erikson and Havighurst models of development differ? In what ways are they similar?

4. What are the differences between moral knowledge, moral character, and moral development? How does value clarification foster moral thinking?

5. How can students learn how to learn? Which cognitive processes contribute to learning?

6. What is critical thinking? Can teachers teach critical thinking? How?

7. How would you define creativity? How can creativity in the classroom be enhanced?

*T*his chapter first addresses learning issues related to development and growth, in particular social development during preadolescence and adolescence. Next, we discuss the school's responsibility in transmitting values and beliefs through moral education. We examine the differences between moral knowledge, moral character, moral values, and moral development. Finally, we look at different cognitive processes that students can learn: learning to learn, critical thinking, and creative thinking.

DEVELOPMENTAL NEEDS OF ADOLESCENTS

A number of theories focus on the global aspects of human growth and development. Behavior can be studied as a totality, these theories suggest, starting with infancy and extending into adulthood. **Developmental theories** address the cumulative effects of change, and the interaction of environment and heredity, that occur as a consequence of learning or failing to learn appropriate tasks during each of the critical stages of life.

Shifts from one stage to the next are based on maturation but are subject to variations as a result of cumulative differences in the quantity and quality of experiences over long spans of time. (Stages in maturation tend to set certain upper limits at given points in the developmental process.) Each stage is built on earlier stages of development. Failure to learn an appropriate task at a given stage of development tends to have detrimental effects on the developmental sequence to follow.

Erikson: The Eight Stages of Growth

Erik Erikson describes eight stages of human development, each containing a crisis of identity which is brought on by physiological changes to which the individual must adapt. He describes both positive and negative responses to these crises and asserts that elements of both exist in most people. When things go well, the maturing individual works out solutions to these "identity crises" (the term he uses) and the result is a stable identity.[1]

Erikson's eight stages are briefly listed in Table 2.1; they connote a sequence of the life cycle and how the person integrates each stage (when things go right or wrong), as well as the predominant setting of each stage. The student populations we are concerned with is in the three stages examined below.

---

1 Erik H. Erikson, *Childhood and Society* (New York: W. W. Norton, 1950).

Table 2.1   ERIKSON'S EIGHT STAGES OF LIFE

Age	Stage	Predominant social setting
Infancy	Trust vs. Mistrust	Family
Early childhood	Autonomy vs. Shame and Doubt	Family
Ages 4–5	Initiative vs. Guilt	Family
Ages 6–12	Industry vs. Inferiority	School
Adolescence	Identity vs. Role Confusion	School; peers
Early adulthood	Intimacy vs. Isolation	Couple
Adulthood and middle age	Generativity vs. Stagnation	New family, work
Old age	Integrity vs. Despair	Couple or retirement

Source: Adapted from Erik H. Erikson, Childhood and Society (New York: W. W. Norton, 1950), pp. 47–74.

Industry versus Inferiority (School Age)

As the social setting shifts from the home to the school and larger community, children enter the impersonal world of unrelated children and adults. They learn to win recognition by producing things, by participating and winning in various activities, and by adjusting themselves to the tool world; ideally they take pride in *industry*. However, if they fail to do well in school or if they are rejected because of their race, religion, or class (or performance in school), they tend to develop a sense of *inferiority*.

Identity versus Role Confusion (Adolescence)

At this stage childhood has ended, and a sense of *identity* develops if the youth has confidence in himself or herself, if past experiences have been derived from a sense of sameness and continuity, and if there is a future purpose. If a person cannot integrate his or her various roles into a clear identity, then the self remains diffuse and there is *role confusion*.

Intimacy versus Isolation (Early Adulthood)[2]

The young adult is willing to fuse his or her identity with others, to make a commitment, to enter into close friendships or marriage. Young people who are sure of themselves will be able to develop *intimate* relationships; those without a clear identity will keep to themselves or move from one short-lived relation-

---

2 The legal definition of a young adult varies according to state and federal law; at 16 most youth can drive cars, at 17 they can enlist in the army without parental consent, and at 18 they drink in many states and vote in state and federal elections.

ship to another. They may feel safe, but they develop a sense of loneliness or *isolation*.

Each of the **critical stages** is systematically related to the others, and all depend on the proper development of the previous stage. While the tempo and intensity of each stage will vary, depending on one's experiences, failure to integrate one of the eight stages will have a modifying influence on all later stages and may impair psychosocial development. Each culture develops a particular style of integrating these stages, but for the stages of industry and identity, and to a lesser extent intimacy, teachers and schools must be prepared to help youth resolve their problems and find solutions that coincide with the norms and values of society. This is one role teachers have as professionals, and we sometimes fail our students by ignoring their problems, not trying to understand their view of the world, or not making time to work with and help them cope with their growing pains. Youth catch on very quickly—that adults who work with them sometimes don't have time or want to be bothered by them.

Havighurst: Developmental Tasks

Robert Havighurst has identified six periods in human development: (1) infancy and early childhood, (2) middle childhood, (3) adolescence, (4) early adulthood, (5) middle age, and (6) late maturity. **Developmental tasks** are defined as "the tasks the individual must learn" for the purpose of "healthy and satisfactory growth in our society."[3] They are what a person must learn in order to be reasonably happy and successful.

The school years begin in the middle of the first period (early childhood) and generally end in period three (adolescence); periods two and three correspond with the scope of this book.

1. Early Childhood
   a. Forming concepts and learning language to describe the social and physical reality.
   b. Getting ready to read.
   c. Learning to distinguish right from wrong and beginning to develop a conscience.
2. Middle Childhood
   a. Learning physical skills necessary for ordinary games.
   b. Building wholesome attitudes toward oneself.
   c. Learning to get along with age-mates.
   d. Learning societally accepted male and female roles.
   e. Developing fundamental skills in reading, writing, and mathematics.

---

3 Robert J. Havighurst, *Human Development and Education* (New York: Longman, 1953), p. 2.

    f. Developing concepts for everyday living.
    g. Developing morality and a set of values.
    h. Achieving personal independence.
    i. Developing (democratic) attitudes toward social groups and in-
       stitutions.
3. Adolescence
    a. Achieving new and more mature relations with age-mates of both
       sexes.
    b. Achieving a masculine or feminine social role.
    c. Accepting one's physique and using the body effectively.
    d. Achieving emotional independence of parents and other adults.
    e. Preparing for marriage and family life.
    f. Preparing for an economic career.
    g. Acquiring a set of values and an ethical system to guide behavior.
    h. Achieving socially responsible behavior.[4]

The Havighurst classification scheme is a classic model that stresses the development of the whole student and includes psychological, social, moral, civic, physical, and productive (or economic) dimensions of learning. Although first developed in the 1950s, it still makes sense today, in the 1990s, even in an era of extremes—where adolescent tennis players are trained through instructional videotapes, a high-speed cameras, and computers while other young people are downing crack or cheap wine on our mean streets.

Student Stress

Stress among our students is common and symptomatic of the problems of an urban/technological and fast-changing society. The old values and social structures break down in a rapidly changing culture. Children entering middle school or junior high have to deal with new students, dating, body changes, and increased peer, parental, and school pressures. The term "over-programmed" kids is very common within middle- and upper middle-class cultures. By the time students reach the "eighth grade, questions about drugs, sexual relationships, and [peer] values can become overwhelming concerns." Eighth grade (in some places it's the ninth grade) is also the last time in which youth are in a protected learning environment, where they feel on top. Once these students enter high school, they must "start at the bottom of the totem pole again."[5] They are forced to survive in a larger, more bureaucratic setting

---

4 Robert J. Havighurst, *Developmental Tasks and Education*, 3rd ed. (New York: Longman, 1972), pp. 14–35, 43–82.

5 "Transitions—Coping with School Day Blues," *The Capable Kid Report* (Fall 1989), p. 1. Also see Ernest Boyer, "Civic Education for Responsible Citizens," *Educational Leadership* (November 1990), pp. 4–7.

and also compete in a stiffer arena. Some never make it back to the top of the totem pole—eventually falling into the cracks or dropping out of school.

Adults take it for granted that adolescents will just go to school—and behave. "We all had to do it. We survived." Well, we shouldn't be so quick to underestimate the effects of rapid change, the predictions of environmental or nuclear disaster, televised sex and violence, overstressed and working moms, the breakdown of the traditional family, the influence of drugs on the adolescent world, and the growing indifference of bigness, bureaucracy, and computerized big-brother devices on children and youth.

Harold Shane reports some depressing statistics that may be criticized as one-sided but highlight some of the outcomes when adolescents feel isolated or can no longer cope.

1. Among twelve- to seventeen-year-olds, suicide is attempted by 18 percent of the girls and 10 percent of the boys. (It is much more prevalent among middle- and upper middle-class youth.)
2. Teen pregnancy in the U.S. continues at the highest rate of all developed countries; one in ten teenage girls will become pregnant.
3. Alcohol consumption involves 100,000 elementary schoolchildren and 500,000 secondary youth who get drunk at least once a week.
4. Gonorrhea and syphilis among teenagers has tripled since 1965, with 2.5 million adolescents each year contracting a sexually transmitted disease.
5. Drugs affect more than 3.5 million twelve- to seventeen-year-olds who have tried marijuana and one-third who are regular users; a half-million young people have tried cocaine—half of these are regular users.
6. In 1950 youths between fourteen and seventeen years of age had an arrest rate of four per thousand. In 1985, the arrest rate was 118 per thousand.
7. The dropout rate in the U.S. currently stands at 30 percent.
8. The poverty rate for young people six to seventeen years old living in families with incomes below the poverty line was 13 percent in 1969 and increased to 20 percent in 1985. (It is expected to increase to 25 percent by 1995.)[6]

We know what stress in adolescent (or adult) culture can lead to: drugs, alcohol, satanic cults, suicide, or just dropping out—of school or society. The need is to head off these problems and to deal with the early signs of stress: (1) academic regression, (2) belligerent behavior, (3) unpredictability, (for example), high-low swings, (4) moodiness, (5) noncommunication, (6) frequent outbursts, (7) lack of sleep (actually inability to sleep), and (8) sudden nail-

---

6 Harold G. Shane, "Improving Education for the Twenty-First Century," *Educational Horizons* (Fall 1990), pp. 11–15.

biting. It is at the early stage where intervention is much easier, and where a sensitive teacher who understands students can spot the early signs and take appropriate action—which involves the home and guidance counselor.

Adolescent Concerns

When I close my eyes and go back to my early adolescence, the problems that occupied my time were making the first string in basketball and baseball and "making out" with Kate. Some of my friends were concerned about their physical development and used to lift weights and look in the mirror. Still others were concerned about being " cool" or "tough." My sister and her girlfriends seemed more concerned about their breasts and about boyfriends, and they did a lot of talking over the phone. These were the days of "Father Knows Best" and "Ozzie and Harriet." In 1955, when I was in the ninth grade, two-thirds of U.S. households consisted of two or three kids, a working father, and a wife and mother who stayed home and cooked dinner. There was no white picket fence or dog in our household, since we lived in the city in a three-room flat, but the school yard and ballfield were always open—where we could play out our fantasies and aggressions.

By 1985, when some of the readers were in high school, only 7 percent of American families could be described as above: where there was no divorce and Mom was still home waiting for the kids to come out of school.[7] In 1990, the divorce rate in this country was nearly 60 percent and about 50 percent of mothers with children in school or even younger worked:[8] Today, before and after school care have become as important as school care.

Most important, we might contrast the concerns of 13– and 14–year-olds today as reported in a 1987 nationwide poll.

1. Kidnapping (76 percent very concerned; 16 percent sort of concerned).
2. Nuclear war (65 percent very concerned; 20 percent sort of concerned).
3. AIDS (65 percent very concerned; 20 percent sort of concerned).
4. Drugs (52 percent very concerned; 25 percent sort of concerned).
5. Air/water pollution (47 percent very concerned; 38 percent sort of concerned).
6. Having to fight a war (47 percent very concerned; 26 percent sort of concerned.)
7. Divorce (39 percent very concerned; 33 percent sort of concerned).[9]

7 Harold Hodgkinson, *Infancy to Adolescence: Opportunities for Success* (Washington, D.C.: U.S. Government Printing Office, 1989).

8 Shane, "Improving Education for the Twenty-First Century."

9 Roper Organization, *The American Chicle Youth Poll* (Morris Plains, N.J.: Warner-Lambert, 1987). Also see Judith A. Brough, "Changing Conditions for Young Adolescents," *Educational Horizons* (Winter 1990), pp. 78–81.

Three observations should be noted. The "sort of concerned" rating may reflect the respondent who sits on the fence, plays it safe or "cool" in answering these type of questions, but may really have anxieties that unravel when confronted in a peer, parental, or counseling discussion. The concerns expressed are also adult concerns; in fact, these are the kinds of concerns we would expect parents to express. The fact that young adolescents expressed them probably reflects the growing influence of television (and the decline of youth-adult demarcations of knowledge and authority) and the middle-level, junior high school curriculum that is increasingly responsive to social issues confronting the nation's youth. Finally, the concerns expressed by young adolescents suggest a much more complex world than the world the author knew 30 or 40 years ago, especially in terms of adolescent or peer relationships, so that the developmental models of Erikson, Havighurst, and others may need modification. The sense of identity versus role confusion outlined by Erikson, the stage of adolescence as described by Havighurst, (and the notions of self-concept and self-actualization developed by Maslow) may have to be further analyzed in terms of today's boy-girl relations, working women (mothers), family breakup, drug culture, and electronic/video media.

To be sure, all these social factors lead to increased personal stress. The end of a marriage involves fighting and custody battles in which children often feel theat they are the cause and, therefore, have a sense of guilt. The new electronic media, their violence and speed that bombard youth, are much more intimidating and violent than my rebellious world of "Blue Suede Shoes" and James Dean. There were no suggestions of sadism or suicide in my rock music, no raw sex or blood pouring in slow motion with James Dean's struggle for manhood. Our adolescents live in an era in which many adults who work with them just do not understand them. My major decisions, and the decisions of most of the adults who teach youth today, did not have to be made until we were a junior or senior in high school. Sixth and seventh graders, today, must often make decisions about sex, drugs, gangs, or which parent they are going to live with. Almost every middle school and high school, especially in rural and suburban areas, must deal with cult groups—although there is a tendency to deny the problem since recruitment usually occurs outside school grounds—at rock concerts, video parlors, and parties. See Tips for Teachers 2.1.

Latchkey Students

Less than 40 percent of all children and youth today in the United States live with both natural parents, and more than 60 percent (ages 6 to 16) are **latchkey students**, who return to empty homes after school and either sit by the television (with pretzels or potato chips) or roam the streets.[10]

---

10 Freya L. Sonenstein and Charles A. Calhoun, "Child Support Compliance: Who Pays and Why," *Urban Institute Policy and Research Report* (Winter 1988), p. 4–5; Edward A. Wynne, "Youth Alienation: Implications for Administrators." *NASSP Bulletin* (February 1989), pp. 86–91.

Tips for Teachers 2.1

Characteristics of Cults

Teachers and administrators must learn, today, to distinguish normal adolescent rebellion from *cult behavior*: suggested by abnormal behavior, arson, vandalism, extreme cruelty to animals, dangerous role-playing, and deep involvement in military, sexual, or drug-related activities or heavy metal rock music—and *cult victimization*: physically neglected or abused, drug addicted, withdrawn, lacking in creative energy and play. In helping to decide if a youngster is just going through an adolescent phase or is seriously involved in cult activities (satanist, paramilitary, pornographic groups, etc.) some common characteristics of cults are worth noting.

1. Members submit to an authoritarian, all-powerful leader or leaders whose decisions cannot be questioned and who discourage rational thought.
2. Cults use deceptive recruiting techniques. For example, they may not identify the group immediately, explain what the group is really about, or reveal how much time, energy, or money must be given.
3. Leaders weaken the followers psychologically by undermining other support systems such as friends, families, and clergy. Members may be cut off from their pasts—from schools, jobs, families, and friends—and from information from newspapers, radio, and television.
4. Cult members are told the outside world is evil, that the cult and its members are "good" and the outside world is "bad" or even "satanic."
5. Every career or life decision may be made by the cult leaders, including whether members should go to school, keep their jobs, marry, or bear children. Cults control their members' time.
6. Followers work long, exhausting hours either recruiting or raising money for the group or working for low wages in cult-owned businesses. They often must contribute large sums of money to the group. (This money generally goes to the group or its leaders, and not to improve the world, as they claim. Many cults are wealthy.)
7. Cults generally force followers to break relations with their families outside the cult. If the entire family is inside the cult, leaders weaken or destroy family ties so that all affection and loyalty can go to them and to the group.
8. Members may be psychologically, physically, or sexually abused. Women and children are especially mistreated. Leaders skillfully

(continues)

manipulate the followers through sexual humiliation and general fear.

9. Some groups are heavily armed and train their members—even small children—to use weapons. Cult leaders claim they need weapons because the outside world is against them. Because of their hostile behavior, this often becomes a self-fulfilling prophecy.

10. Cults hold outside society and its laws and social mores in contempt because they believe they have "the truth" and are working for the good of the world or spiritual salvation, so their goals justify even deceptive means.

Source: Marcia R. Rudin, "Cults and Satanism: Threats to Teens," *NASSP Bulletin* (May 1990), p. 48.

Nationwide it is estimated that among mothers with children in junior and senior high, approximately two-thirds work full time and another 20 percent work part time.[11] In a sample of 362 randomly selected junior and senior high school students whose mothers worked, the unattended teens surveyed were unsupervised an average of three hours per day. Latchkey adolescents exhibited more academic and social problems; they were more fearful, lonely, and bored and more susceptible to peer pressure to commit antisocial acts than youth who had parental supervision at home.[12]

Because of economic factors, mainly the need for women to work (including those who are married), a mother who is home to greet her children at 3 p.m. is becoming a luxury only possible for the upper 5 to 10 percent of the nation's income bracket. And, many of these upper-class mothers, for purposes of identity and fulfillment, prefer the world of work to the home.

Like it or not, schools need to help students with their developmental problems—academic, social, and psychological—in the absence of parents (mothers) who have to work or who are no longer married. Whether it is a "breakfast club" mixed with emergency tutoring (i.e., "homework I did not understand," "questions for today's quiz") by peers or classmates during the school week, an afternoon (3–6 P.M.) formal study skills-homework center, an informal enrichment (computer club, SAT study group, etc.), or remediation

---

11 Daniel Duke, "The Wake of the Summit: The Crusade for Youth and the Quest for Consensus," *NASSP Bulletin* (March 1990), pp. 57–69; Hodgkinson, *Infancy to Adolescence.*

12 Lynette Long and Thomas L. Long, "Latchkey Adolescents: How Administrators Can Respond to Their Needs," *NASSP Bulletin* (February 1989), pp. 102–108.

program (reading, writing, etc.), the dividends are immense: increased self-esteem, improved attitudes toward school, greater class and school participation, increased attendance and reduced lateness, higher test scores, and reduced dropout rates.[13] Although the focus might be on latchkey students, since this group is most at risk and represents the majority of today's students, the larger student population would be served, too.

How Teachers and Schools Can Respond

Supporting students' psychological, social, moral, and cognitive development means that school people find ways to help them learn to resolve their problems and interact with others and to become socially responsible in a complex world. "Just as the life of all growing things is based on the concept of expansion," healthy human development "leads beyond a narrow focus on 'me' to the ever-widening perspective of 'we,' our family, community, country, and world." Concern and respect for others are signs of a socially mature and psychologically healthy youngsters but a goal the public schools usually do not sufficiently emphasize.[14]

In order to facilitate our students' growth and development, as teachers we must have knowledge of age-appropriate needs and expectations and implement developmentally appropriate practices. This is only half of our responsibility; equally important is knowledge of what is individually appropriate for each student in a classroom. Although universal and predictable stages of human development exist, each student is unique and has an individual personality, learning style, sense of self-worth, and set of expectations and abilities. Developmentally appropriate teachers are flexible in their expectations about when and how students will acquire various competencies in class. Recognition of individual differences among students is essential and results in a variety of teaching methods, grouping patterns, classroom tasks, and school assignments. A uniform, lockstep method of teaching is inappropriate.

Schools must provide supportive, nurturing experiences for students. They must be composed of teachers, administrators, support staff, and community representatives who find ways to help students interact well with peers and adults. Schools need to help compensate for the fact that an increasing percentage of children and youth today in the United States do not live with both natural parents, and even if they do many are latchkey students. In short, schools need to help students' development in the absence of parents who have to work or are no longer married. See Tips for Teachers 2.2.

---

13 Daniel U. Levine and Allan C. Ornstein, "Research on Classroom and School Effectiveness," *Urban Review* (July 1989), pp. 81–95; Michael P. Wolfe, Glenna L. Howell, and Judy A. Charland, "Energizing The School Community," *Clearing House* (September 1989), pp. 29–32.

14 "Summertime: Still a Learning Time," *Tribes Trail* (Spring 1989), p. 1.

Tips for Teachers 2.2

Teaching Latchkey Students

According to a recent Harris poll, teachers feel latchkey youngsters are the number-one social problem facing schools—surpassing problems such as truancy, discipline, and drugs. Teachers and schools can no longer ignore the needs of these youngsters. It is another responsibility they must deal with, like it or not. Below are ten suggestions that school people might implement.

1. *Check up on absent students.* Calls home might have to be followed by calls to the parents' workplace.
2. *Provide instruction on how to care for young children.* Adolescents need information on how to care for younger siblings, as well as how to constructively organize and fill their time.
3. *Sponsor a phone support service developed and staffed by school students.* Set up a telephone hotline for youngsters who are home alone; high school students can provide such services under the supervision of counselors.
4. *Advise parents how to monitor homework effectively.* Homework assignments can be improved if parents check it regularly; however, many parents need written instructions or a workshop to properly assist their children.
5. *Help students and parents become selective television viewers.* Since television plays an important part in the life of youngsters, and is considered detrimental for learning when excessively viewed, teachers need to take time out to teach students how to make maximum use of television programming.
6. *Establish after-school programs.* Schools can provide effective, well-supervised after-school activities; coordinate ways for students who lack transportation to obtain a ride home; and develop a buddy system for walking home after the activities end.
7. *Initiate school-sponsored trips or related school activities for half days or for those days school is not in session.* Many parents would gladly pay for an interesting trip or activity for their children.
8. *Assist students who are unattended during summer vacations.* Increase summer and holiday activities; coordinate summer jobs for students who are age 15 or younger.
9. *Start a guest house program for adolescents who may be unattended overnight.* Work with the community to organize a drop-off system for leaving children or youth overnight.

(continues)

10. *Make before-school facilities available.* Provide a study hall for students who have failed to complete their homework the night before. Provide interesting social or athletic activities for "early birds," such as weight lifting, an exercise room, aerobics, computer activities, etc. Many youngsters would also benefit from having breakfast in school before classes begin.

Source: Adapted from Lynette Long and Thomas L. Long, "Latchkey Adolescents—How Administrators Can Respond to Their Needs," *NASSP Bulletin* (February 1989), pp. 102–108.

Adolescents, needing to feel wanted, need adults who are willing to provide understanding, guidance, and love. When parents fail them, they need substitute adults, such as teachers, to fill in. This does not always happen and sometimes the results are disastrous.

We can raise the question whether teachers or schools should be burdened with this new role. But the schools that seem to be the worst offenders, where "the intellectual and emotional needs of youth will go unmet," according to a recent Carnegie report, *Turning Points*, are the large schools, "which function as mills that contain and process endless streams of students. Within them are masses of anonymous youth." Large for a middle grade or junior high school is defined as a school exceeding 1,000 students and for high schools exceeding 2,000 students.[15] Most students in these schools fall into the cracks. They change class six or seven times a day and encounter teachers who have little time to understand or get to know them. If an idea in class is confusing, there is little time for explanation; students have learned not to ask questions, not to seek help, to keep their problems to themselves.[16]

After a review of several studies, Gregory and Smith point out that large secondary schools are preoccupied with control and order, and anonymity works against sharing ideas and working together. The authors contend that in small schools the organization of space, time, and people, what they term "structure," are more supportive and positive to human functioning. There is

---

15 *Turning Points: Preparing American Youth for the 21st Century*, Report of the Carnegie Task Force on Education of Young Adolescents (Washington, D.C.: Carnegie Council on Adolescent Development, 1989). Also see Allan C. Ornstein, "School Size and Effectiveness: Policy Implications," *Urban Review* (September 1990), pp. 239–245.

16 Ibid.

also a sense of "community"—commitment and morale among students, teachers, and parents and the feeling of having a stake in the school.[17] According to Ornstein, there is greater identification and sense of belonging in small schools, especially for those students who lack prestige among favored cliques and would regularly fall into the cracks of large secondary schools; in small schools there is more opportunity for student leadership roles and participation in activities.[18]

The Carnegie report makes the following recommendations for humanizing schools and for meeting the developmental needs of adolescent students: (1) There must be opportunity for students and teachers to get to know each other, to share ideas and common educational purposes, ideally through an extended homeroom period. (2) Subject matter must be integrated. (3) The instability of the peer group must be reduced through school activities that reach all students (not just 10 or 15 percent, the "social" or "power" cliques). (4) Every student must be able to rely on a small, caring group of adults (teachers, counselors, parent volunteers) who work closely with each other to provide meaningful educational experiences. (5) Teachers must have the opportunity to know their students, to understand and to teach them as individuals. (6) Every student must have the opportunity to know a variety of peers, some of them well (through a classroom and school climate that is conductive to sharing and working together).[19]

FOCUS ON MIDDLE SCHOOLING

There is recognition today that the attention and motivation of 10- to 15-year-olds are frequently diverted from their school work because they are going through a time of rapid growth and development. Enormous variability exists among these **preadolescents**, even of the same age and in the same classroom. One administrator points out that these middlegrade students "experience the greatest change in their minds and bodies." Averages have little meaning at this time of development. One student "may be 6'2" and 237 lbs." and his classmate "may be 4'3" and 84 lbs."[20] One boy may be the next Tip O'Neill or Mark Spitz or be unaware what the Bill of Rights guarantees or afraid of water above his knees. One girl may be the next Jessica Savitch or a high fashion model or be unable to pronounce the difference between foe, for, and fowl or may never have heard of Yves St. Laurent.

---

17 Thomas B. Gregory and Gerald R. Smith, *High Schools as Communities: The Small School Reconsidered* (Bloomington, Ind.: Phi Delta Kappa Foundation, 1987).

18 Allan C. Ornstein, "School District and School Size: Is Bigger Better?" *PTA Journal* (October 1989), pp. 16–17.

19 *Turning Points: Preparing American Youth for the 21st Century.*

20 Alan Knight, "The Magic Word for Middle Level Educators," *NASSP Bulletin* (November 1988), p. 99.

The need to be sensitive to this age group is compounded by the fact that secondary school teachers have been trained in subject areas and prefer teaching at the high school level—where subjects are well defined. Very few secondary teachers have been trained to work with middle school or junior high school adolescents, or expected to work at this level when they prepared to teach. Many are unaware or unwilling to provide the nurturing and guidance that preadolescents need from their teachers, because they are too academically oriented. Driven by content, they overlook the sociopsychological process. They sometimes fail to understand that students who are rapidly growing, or who are in growth transition periods, have multiple confusing and threatening experiences. Suddenly, these children have concerns (sometimes overwhelming concerns) they did not have at a younger age and in a more protected elementary school environment.

Preadolescent students do not need scholars or overly academic teachers; rather they need understanding, flexible, and humane teachers—one or two roles removed from a mom or dad. Their support and understanding is crucial for these children. However, according to one authority, "telling traditional, secondary-oriented teachers that their role includes a guidance-advisory function . . . has caused violent eruptions . . . in staff development meetings."[21] Violent disruptions may be an overstatement, but the point is that many preservice secondary teachers prefer and think they will be working in the high school and give little thought about middle grade or junior high schools.

These preservice teachers do not recognize, and they are rarely told in their preparatory programs, that the majority of them will get their first job in a middle or junior high school—where most of the secondary school vacancies exist. Consequently, the majority of teachers in these schools are not totally prepared for their assignment, much less told about the philosophy or goals of these schools. They have little idea how to match teaching and intervention strategies with the learning needs and developmental levels of their students. Most are professionally illiterate and ill-trained for teaching preadolescents. Of course, there are beginning teachers who are committed to middle and junior high schools, and have some preservice training in this area—but the numbers are few compared to elementary-trained and high school-trained teachers.

For the greater part, we continue to train our upper elementary teachers and secondary teachers as if the middle or junior high did not exist. Only a limited number of colleges make the distinction in their preparatory programs. Best available data, from institutions who are willing to provide information, indicate that nationwide 25 percent of preservice teachers have had some preparation in middle level teaching (ranging from class discussions, school observations, or a specific course) and 33 percent of teacher preparation institu-

21 Paul George, "Which Way the Middle School?" *Education Digest* (January 1989), p. 15. Also see Paul George, "From Junior High to Middle School—Principal's Perspectives," *NASSP Bulletin* (February 1990), pp. 86–94.

tions have specialized courses (not always required) for middle grade teachers.[22]

Organization of Middle Schools

The grade span commonly referred to as **middle school** is 6, 7, and 8. In the United States and Canada about 70 percent of all middle schools represent these grade levels, although another 25 percent in the U.S. is represented by grades 5–8 and 17 percent in Canada is represented by grades 7–9[23] (what we call the junior high school). Nonetheless, grades 6, 7, and 8, according to research findings, are found in 34 different school grade configurations (K-6, K-7, K-8, 1–6, 1–7, 1–8, 2–8, 3–6, 3–7, 3–8, etc.) and middle schools (5–7, 5–8, 6–7, 6–8, 7–8, etc.). See Table 2.2.[24] This reflects our national lack of consensus about the best type of school for the preadolescent or the 6, 7, 8 grade level. Adding the fifth grade, where some middle-grade schools start, would increase the configurations to more than 50 possibilities.

One reason for the confusion about middle schools is they were originally established for administrative reasons, such as to alleviate overcrowded facilities or to help desegregate schools. Only recently (mid-1980s) have the social and psychological factors been introduced in the professional literature—that is, to design a special program to meet the special needs of the ten- to fourteen-year-old student. The schools with clearly defined goals along these lines tend to be more effective than similar grade schools that were designed for administrative reasons.[25]

Another reason for confusion is that the differences between middle school (grades 5–8, 6–8, or 7–8) and junior high school (grades 7–9 and 8–9) are subtle but important. The differences deal in the degree of emphasis on socialization vs. academics, "exploratory" subjects vs. traditional subjects, the extent of interdisciplinary teacher planning, and the amount of advisory student time. Middle schools tend to be more progressive, therefore, stress more socialization, "exploratory" subjects, interdisciplinary team organization, and advisory group time. Table 2.3 highlights some major differences based on a 1988 national survey.

---

22 William A. Alexander and C. Kenneth McEwin, *Preparing to Teach at the Middle Level* (Columbus, Ohio: National Middle School Association, 1988).

23 Jim Fasano, "Canada's Schools: Focus on the Middle," *Middle School Journal*, (September 1989), p. 8; Gene I. Maeroff, "Getting to Know a Good Middle School," *Phi Delta Kappan* (March 1990), pp. 504–511.

24 *Making Schools Work for Young Adolescents* (Chapel Hill, N.C.: Center for Early Adolescence, University of North Carolina-Chapel Hill, 1987).

25 William M. Alexander, *A Survey of Organizational Patterns of Reorganized Middle Schools* (Gainesville, Fla.: University of Florida, 1964); William M. Alexander and C. Kenneth McEwin, *Schools in the Middle: Status and Progress* (Columbus, Ohio: National Middle School Association, 1989); and Maeroff, "Getting to Know a Good Middle School."

Table 2.2   MIDDLE GRADE PATTERNS, 1988

GRADE ORGANIZATION	Percent of Schools[b]	Percent of Students
Elementary-middle combinations (K-8)	32.1	9.3
Elementary-middle-high combinations (K-12)	10.5	2.4
Middle school (6-8)[a]	25.3	39.3
Middle school (7-8)	11.0	24.6
Junior high school (7-9)	8.4	17.4
Middle-high combinations (7-12)	12.7	7.0

[a]Middle school 5-8 not reported.
[b]Based on a sample of 1,753 public schools.
Source: Joyce L. Epstein and Douglas J. MacIver, "The Middle Grades: Is Grade Span the Most Important Issue?" *Educational Horizons* (Winter 1988), p. 89.

Middle School Characteristics

In Canada, the Middle Years Association describes the guiding beliefs of middle years as when (1) students experience a distinct developmental stage different from the primary or secondary student; (2) students require teachers who understand their physical, social, emotional, and academic needs as a group; (3) students require a school atmosphere that enhances self-concept, self-expression, and personal growth; (4) students require a flexible program that deals with their special needs; and (5) students require societal understanding and support.[26]

The Association for Supervision and Curriculum Development, as a result of a nationwide survey of 672 schools, contends that schools should provide the following program to meet the needs of preadolescent students (aged 10–15):

1. *Guidance.* A guidance system should provide an adult who has time for each student, assuring familiarity and continuity in providing advice on personal and school matters.
2. *Transition.* A smooth transition between elementary and high school should minimize distress for newly arriving middle grade (junior high school) students; make special efforts to provide orientation activities, and invite parents to visit teachers and classes.

---

26 Eleanor Campbell, "In Saskatchewan—Its' Middle Years," *Middle School Journal* (September 1989), pp. 11–12.

Table 2.3 MIDDLE SCHOOLS VS. JUNIOR HIGH SCHOOLS, 1988

1. Middle schools were more recently established and more often established for student-related reasons than were junior high schools.

2. Middle schools offer more exploratory subjects than do junior high schools.

3. Middle schools utilize more random assignment for grouping students for instruction than do junior high schools.

4. Middle schools utilize flexible scheduling more often than do junior high schools.

5. Middle schools teach all the basic subjects daily to all students more often than do junior high schools.

6. The interdisciplinary team organization plan is utilized more frequently in middle schools than in junior high schools.

7. The "newer" exploratory subjects of creative writing, sex education, health, and computers are offered in larger percentages of middle schools than junior high schools.

8. Departmentalization is found more often in junior high schools than in middle schools.

9. Foreign languages are offered more often in junior high schools than in middle schools.

Source: Adapted from William M. Alexander and C. Kenneth McEwin, *Schools in the Middle: Status and Progress* (Columbus, Ohio: National Middle School Association, 1989). Also see C. Kenneth McEwin, "How Fares Middle Level Education?" *Educational Horizons* (Winter 1988), pp. 100-104.

3. *Block Time Schedule.* The daily schedule should feature blocks of instructional time—that is, combining periods and varying lengths of periods, to accommodate team teaching, interdisciplinary teaching, and short or long class periods based on the nature of classroom tasks.

4. *Varied Teaching Strategies.* A variety of teaching strategies are needed, since students of this age often have limited attention spans and learning styles. Among the teaching strategies most often used are mastery learning, cooperative learning, direct instruction, critical thinking skills, and independent learning. (More emphasis should be put on tutoring and computer-assisted instruction.)

5. *Exploratory Subjects.* Schools need to offer a wide range of elective courses for students to develop their own interests and to be exposed to different ideas.

6. *Core Curriculum.* A core of subjects should be required of all students, and students should be encouraged to master learning skills they will need for future learning.[27]

27 Gordon Cawelti, "Middle Schools a Better Match With Early Adolescent Needs," *ASCD Curriculum Update* (November 1988), pp. 1–12.

Based on recent research, the author adds the following characteristics or activities for schools that cater to the middle school/junior high school group:

1. *Team Teaching.* Teachers of the basic academic subjects should form interdisciplinary groups or teams to plan curriculum around the needs of 125 to 150 students and to frequently discuss special problems or needs of the group and of individual students.

2. *Extended Advisory.* Every preadolescent needs a "home base," a place and time (20 to 30 minutes daily) for a teacher to serve as an advisor and support person. (The homeroom period should not be wasted on clerical duties and administrative record keeping.) In addition, a guidance counselor program should be provided for all students on a weekly basis to discuss personal, social, and academic problems. For this period, boys and girls should be separated.

3. *Intramural Sports.* Notwithstanding the importance of intrascholastic sports and despite criticism of excessive competition and high rates of injuries among ten- to fourteen-year-olds involved in sports, intramural sports should be expanded. The need is to offer a wide range of sports—not only baseball, basketball, and soccer—so all (boys and girls) can participate in at least two or more sports.

4. *Curriculum.* With the advent of the many social and personal problems these youngsters experience—which are compounded by the pressures of the peer group, television viewing of sex, violence, and drugs, and parents who seem to have less time for them than in the past—subjects such as drug education, sex education, environmental education are necessary and may have to be substituted in lieu of a fifth academic subject. These multidisciplinary subjects can be taught by various subject teachers and are urged in addition to the "exploratory" subjects (such as computer science, drama, creative writing or journalism, enriched reading study skills, etc.) that have been already mentioned.

5. *Grouping Patterns.* Most middle and junior high schools have *some* form of homogeneous grouping either between or within classes. According to research data, fewer than 10 percent of these schools have *no* classes grouped homogeneously.[28] The recommendation is that all subjects that build on a base of knowledge, skills, or concepts (such as math, science, language arts, and foreign language) should have homogeneous grouping to make it easier for instruction. Where subject matter, that is, units or topics, is independent, and not built on a structure or foundation, grouping should be heterogeneous to promote integration among student groups and abilities. This pattern

28 Joyce L. Epstein and Douglas J. MacIver, "The Middle Grades: Is Grade Span the Most Important Issue?" *Educational Horizons* (Winter 1988), pp. 88–94.

would involve subjects such as social studies, "exploratory" subjects, and minor subjects such as music, art, and physical education.

Most middle schools are adopting positions that coincide with the first three characteristics, since they are student oriented and recognize the importance of student-centered programs. We can expect student-oriented middle schools to possibly adopt characteristic four and more subject-oriented middle schhols to adopt characteristic five.

Guidelines for Meeting Preadolescent Developmental Needs

All students need to be taught according to their developmental needs and unique individual abilities and interests. The guidelines below are for teaching adolescents, grades 5 through 12.

1. *Instructional Diversity.* Teachers need to match the varied abilities, needs, and interests of students with an equally diverse classroom setting through a variety of teaching styles, methods, and materials and flexible scheduling and grouping patterns.

2. *Self-Understanding.* Teachers need to help students understand, appreciate, and integrate their own capabilities, interests, and relationships into a sense of who they are by focusing on social/moral issues, career guidance, family relations, cultural values, and sexuality.

3. *Social Responsibility.* Teachers must emphasize that students are responsible for their own actions and behavior; they must learn to get along with others, communicate effectively, act humane and civil, make proper decisions, care about and help others (especially the less fortunate), and say "no" to negative influences.

4. *Meaningful Participation in School and Community.* Teachers need to offer opportunities for students to become involved in school and community activities. This can be achieved by emphasizing the strengths and interests of each student in student-initiated projects, school improvement projects, and service to others through community agencies.

5. *Positive Interaction with Peers and Adults.* Teachers can encourage positive interaction with peers by offering small-group instructional activities, cooperative learning, and peer-tutoring. Teachers can engage in increased adviser-advisee relationships, periodic rap sessions, monthly breakfast meetings, and informal, after-school activities.

6. *Respect for Others.* Teachers must encourage students to respect the views and rights of others, to appreciate differences among classmates and schoolmates, and to respect different cultural, ethnic, and religious groups. No one has a lock on being the best or the brightest, and it is important that students understand that yardsticks and judgments are often colored by social or subjective lens.

7. *Competence and Achievement.* Teachers must have positive expectations about their students' learning abilities and offer high quality instruction. They must provide honest rewards and praise and opportunities for students to increase their social and academic independence and responsibility. It is the teacher's role to assure that each student can be successful at something.

8. *Structure and Clear Limits.* Teachers should establish rules and expectations that are understood and accepted by students. Students need the security provided by clear limits to learn and grow during a period of rapid change. They need to take responsibility for their work in the classroom and be held accountable for performing assigned tasks.

9. *Classroom Climate.* Teachers must work to build the sense of "community" in the classroom. They should encourage the students to care for and help each other, as well as to share and express their feelings. Each student should have a classroom partner to help with classroom tasks, to share ideas, and to make decisions and choices together.

10. *Teacher-Parent Involvement.* Teachers must regularly communicate with parents and provide opportunities to meet with them in supporting the healthy development of all students. Teachers must provide methods for parents to assist their children in the learning process, especially at home when they are studying, and clarify the goals of the curriculum and the responsibilities of each child in meeting those goals.[29]

MORAL EDUCATION

How a person develops morally is partially, if not predominantly, based on the way he or she interacts with family, schools, and society—more precisely, on the roles and responsibilities he or she learns and deems important based on contact with people who are considered important.

Schools have traditionally been concerned with the moral education of children. In the nineteenth century moral education became linked to obedience and conformity to rules and regulations. Standards of moral behavior were enforced by rewards and punishments and were translated into grades in what at different times was called morals and manners, citizenship, conduct, or social behavior.

---

29 "Developmental Needs of Young Adolescents: How Can Schools Respond," report prepared for the Center of Early Adolescence, University of North Carolina-Chapel Hill, 1987; "Skills for Adolescence," report prepared by Lions International and Quest International, Granville, Ohio, undated.

Until the middle of the nineteenth century public schools typically exhibited a strong, nonsectarian Protestant tone, which was reflected in activities such as Bible readings, prayers, and the content of instructional materials such as the McGuffey readers. By the turn of the century the schools shifted the notion of moral education to purely secular activities such as student cooperation in class, extracurricular activities, student councils, flag salutes, assembly rituals, and school service. In short, schools have never ignored moral education, but teachers have often avoided the teaching of morality because of its subjective nature and its potential overlap with religious indoctrination.

Moral Knowledge

It is possible to give instruction in moral knowledge and ethics. We can discuss philosophers such as Socrates, Immanuel Kant, and Jean-Paul Sartre, religious leaders such as Moses, Jesus, and Confucius, and political leaders such as Abraham Lincoln, Mohandas Gandhi, and Martin Luther King. Through the study of the writings and principles of these moral people, students can learn about moral knowledge. For young readers there are "Aesop's Fables" and "Jack and the Beanstalk." For older children, there are *Sadako, Up from Slavery,* and the *Diary of Anne Frank.* And for teenagers, there are *Of Mice and Men, A Man for all Seasons,* and *Death of a Salesman.* All these books deal with moral and value-laden issues. Whose morality? Whose values? There are agreed-upon virtues, such as honesty, integrity, civility, caring, and so forth, that represent an American consensus. It is there if we have sufficient moral conviction to find it.

According to Philip Phenix, the most important sources of moral knowledge are the laws and customs of society, and they can be taught in courses dealing with law, ethics, and sociology. However, moral conduct cannot be taught; rather it is learned by "participating in everyday life of society according to recognized standards of society."[30] Although laws and customs and obedience to them are not always morally right, accepted standards do provide guidance for conduct and behavior.

The content of moral knowledge, according to Phenix, covers five main areas: (1) human rights, involving conditions of life that ought to prevail, (2) ethics concerning family relations and sex, (3) social relationships, dealing with class, racial, ethnic, and religious groups, (4) economic life, involving wealth and poverty, and (5) political life, involving justice, equity, and power.[31] The way we translate moral content into moral conduct defines the kind of people we are. It is not our moral knowledge that counts; rather it is our moral behavior in everyday affairs with people that is important.

---

30 Philip Phenix, *Realms of Meaning* (New York: McGraw-Hill, 1964), pp. 220–221.

31 Ibid.

Moral Character

A person can have moral knowledge and obey secular and religious laws but still lack moral character. **Moral character** is difficult to teach because it involves patterns of attitudes and behavior that result from stages of growth, distinctive qualities of personality, and experiences. It involves a coherent philosophy and the will to act in a way consistent with that philosophy.

To have moral character also means to help people, to accept their weaknesses without exploiting them, to see the best in people and to build on their strengths, to act civilly and courteously in relations with classmates, friends, or colleagues, to express humility, and to act as an individual even if it means being different from the crowd. Perhaps the real test of moral character is to cope with a crisis or setback, to deal with adversity, and to be willing to take risks (that is, possible loss of jobs, even life itself) because of one's convictions. Courage, conviction, and compassion are the ingredients of character. What kind of person do we want to emerge as a result of our efforts as teachers? We can engage in moral education and teach moral knowledge, but can we teach moral character? See Tips for Teachers 2.3. The world is full of people who understand the notion of morality but take the expedient way out or follow the crowd. Who among us (including our colleagues) possesses moral character? Who among our students will develop into morally mature individuals? To be sure, moral character cannot be taught by one teacher; rather it takes concerted effort by the entire school and involves the nurturing of children and youth over many years.

Moral Values

Good moral character requires a clear set of values. The values a person holds depend on many factors, including environment, education, and personality. Teachers and schools are always transmitting values to students, both consciously and unconsciously. Sometimes the transmission occurs through what educators call the "hidden curriculum," the unstated meanings conveyed by teacher attitudes and behavior, class routines, school policies, and the curriculum in general.[32] **Value clarification** (sometimes called *value building*) is now considered part of the teaching-learning process. Advocates of value clarification have a high regard for creativity, freedom, and self-realization. They prefer that learners explore their own preferences and make their own choices.

Confusion over values can result in apathy, uncertainty, inconsistency, extreme conformity, or extreme dissension. Value clarification is designed to help persons overcome value confusion and become more positive, purposeful, and productive, as well as to have better interpersonal relationships. There are

---

32 Allan C. Ornstein, "The Irrelevant Curriculum: A Review from Four Perspectives," *NASSP Bulletin* (September 1988), pp. 26–32; Clark Power and Lawrence Kohlberg, "Moral Development: Transforming the Hidden Curriculum," *Curriculum Review* (September–October 1986), pp. 14–17.

Tips for Teachers 2.3

The Morally Mature Person

The Association for Supervision and Curriculum Development has tried to write a description of the morally mature person. The characteristics it lists offer teachers a framework for classroom discussion and classroom interaction.

I. *Respects human dignity*, which includes
1. Showing regard for the worth and rights of all persons
2. Avoiding deception and dishonesty
3. Promoting human equality
4. Respecting freedom of conscience
5. Working with people of different views
6. Refraining from prejudiced actions

II. *Cares about the welfare of others*, which includes
1. Recognizing interdependence among people
2. Caring for one's country
3. Seeking social justice
4. Taking pleasure in helping others
5. Working to help others reach moral maturity

III. *Integrates individual interests and social responsibilities*, which includes
1. Becoming involved in community life
2. Doing a fair share of community work
3. Displaying self-regarding and other-regarding moral virtues—self-control, diligence, fairness, kindness, honesty, civility—in everyday life
4. Fulfilling commitments
5. Developing self-esteem through relationships with others

IV. *Demonstrates integrity*, which includes
1. Practicing diligence
2. Taking stands for moral principles
3. Displaying moral courage
4. Knowing when to compromise and when to confront
5. Accepting responsibility for one's choices

V. *Reflects on moral choices*, which includes
1. Recognizing the moral issues involved in a situation
2. Applying moral principles (such as the Golden Rule) when making moral judgments
3. Thinking about the consequences of decisions

(continues)

4. Seeking to be informed about important moral issues in society and the world

VI. *Seeks peaceful resolution of conflict*, which includes
1. Striving for the fair resolution of personal and social conflicts
2. Avoiding physical and verbal aggression
3. Listening carefully to others
4. Encouraging others to communicate
5. Working for peace

In general, then, the morally mature person understands moral principles and accepts responsibility for applying them.

Source: ASCD Panel on Moral Education, "Moral Education and the Life of the School," *Educational Leadership* (May 1988), p. 5.

many ways of teaching value clarification. *Inculcation* is teaching accepted values with the support of common law. *Moral development* is highlighting moral and ethical principles and applications. *Analysis of issues* is the examination of situations involving values. *Action learning* is trying and testing values in real-life situations. *Valuing* is a method of choosing, prizing, and acting among alternatives.[33]

Louis Raths and his colleagues have outlined the major components in a process of value clarification (see Chapter 7). They developed various strategies, employing dialogue, writing, questioning, and other activities, for teaching the process of valuing. The value activities are not intended to impart specific values to students, but to probe their thoughts and feelings so that they make choices.[34]

How might the teacher engage students in the clarification of values that have moral overtones (that is, that deal with right and wrong)? Merrill Harmin makes five general recommendations.

1. *Speaking up for morality.* Teachers sometimes do not express moral indignation, claiming that they should maintain value neutrality. On

---

33 Ronald C. Doll, *Curriculum Improvement: Decision Making and Process,* 8th ed. (Needham Heights: Allyn & Bacon, 1989/1992).

34 Louis E. Raths, Merrill Harmin, and Sidney B. Simon, *Values and Teaching,* 2nd ed. (Columbus, Ohio: Merrill, 1978), pp. 27–28.

important issues teachers should voice their concerns or take a stance in front of the class.

2. *Stating personal positions.* Students should be encouraged to express their position or viewpoint on controversial issues. They should not feel that it is best to avoid stating a personal viewpoint.

3. *Explaining rules.* Sometimes teachers merely state classroom or school rules without explanation. Giving the reasons for required behavior may help teachers gain respect, trust, and cooperation among students.

4. *Speaking forthrightly.* There is no reason why teachers cannot be honest with students; indeed, such honesty has a positive influence on student behavior. When teachers speak forthrightly for their values, without condemning others who have different values, they advance understanding of their values and respect for free speech and a free press, which our society demands.

5. *Increasing moral experience.* Sometimes a gap exists between words and deeds. If teachers want people to speak truthfully, be tolerant of others, and keep an open mind, then they must monitor their own behavior to see if they exemplify these characteristics.[35]

Moral Development: Piaget and Kohlberg

While some self-control of behavior may be seen in the preschool years, researchers agree that not until the child is about 4 years old do moral standards begin to develop at a rapid rate. During the period when the child begins to abandon behavior governed by whatever he or she wants to do at a particular moment, conscience tends to be erratic, largely confined to prohibitions against specific behaviors and based on external sanctions. Before age 5, morality does not exist for children because they have little or no conception of rules. From about 5 to 6 years, conscience becomes less confined to specific behaviors and begins to incorporate more generalized standards; it becomes determined less by external rewards or punishments and more by internal sanctions.[36]

Piaget's Theory of Moral Development

Piaget's theory was based on techniques of investigation that included conversing with children and asking them questions about moral dilemmas and events in stories. For example, he might ask a child, "Why shouldn't you cheat in a game?" Piaget's observations suggest that from age 5 to 12, children's concept of justice passes from a rigid and inflexible notion of right and wrong, learned

---

35 Merrill Harmin, "Value Clarity, Higher Morality: Let's Go for Both," *Educational Leadership* (May 1988), pp. 24–30; Harmin, "The Workshop Way to Student Success in School," *Educational Leadership* (September 1990), pp. 43–47.

36 Paul H. Mussen, John J. Conger, and Jerome Kagan, *Child Development and Personality* (New York: Harper & Row, 1969).

The ability to understand other's thoughts and feelings is an essential skill that positively influences moral development.

from parents, to a sense of equity in moral judgments. Eventually, it takes into account specific situations or circumstances.

As children grow older, they become more flexible and realize that there are exception to rules. As they become members of a larger, more varied peer group, rules and moral judgments become less absolute and rigid and more dependent on the needs and desires of the people involved. Wrote Piaget, "For very young children, a rule is a sacred reality because it is traditional; for the older ones it depends upon a mutual agreement."[37]

On the basis of numerous studies, Piaget concluded:

> . . . There are three great periods of development of the sense of justice in the child. One period, starting at age 5 and lasting up to age 7–8, during which justice is subordinated to adult authority; a period contained approximately between 8–11, and which is that of progressive equalitarianism; and finally a period that sets in

37 Jean Piaget, *The Moral Development of the Child* (New York: Free Press, 1965), p. 192.

toward 11–12, and during which purely equalitarian justice is tempered by consideration of equity.[38]

Kohlberg's Theory of Moral Reasoning

More recently, Lawrence Kohlberg studied the development of children's moral standards and concluded that the way people think about moral issues reflects their culture and their stage of growth. He outlined six developmental stages of moral judgment grouped into three moral levels that correspond roughly to Piaget's three stages of cognitive development.

    I. *Preconventional level.* Children have not yet developed a sense of right or wrong. The level comprises two stages: (1) children do as they are told because they fear punishment, and (2) children realize that certain actions bring rewards.

    II. *Conventional level.* Children are concerned about what other people think of them, and their behavior is largely other-directed. The two stages in this level are (3) children seek their parents' approval by being "nice," and (4) children begin thinking in terms of laws and rules.

    III. *Postconventional level.* Morality is based not only on other people's values but also on internalized precepts of ethical principles and authority. This level also includes two stages: (5) children view morality in terms of contractual obligations and democratically accepted laws, and (6) children view morality in terms of individual principles of conscience,[39] as well as a higher being (if I may add).

Unless a reasonable degree of moral development takes place during childhood and adolescence, that is, unless standards of right and wrong are established, the child, and later the adult, is likely to engage in a social and/or antisocial behavior. On the other hand, if the acceptance of others' standards or the internalization of standards and prohibitions is unduly strong, guilt may develop in association with a wide variety of actions and thoughts. Ideally, individuals work out an adequate sense of morality and at the same time avoid self-condemnation, in the context of the culture in which they live.

Kohlberg's theory has been widely criticized on the grounds that moral reasoning does not necessarily conform to development and involves many complex social and psychological factors, that particular moral behaviors are not always associated with the same reasoning (and vice versa), that his prescriptions are culture-bound and sexist. However, he has made researchers

---

38 Ibid., p. 314.

39 Lawrence A. Kohlberg, "The Development of Children's Orientations Toward a Moral Order, I: Sequence in the Development of Moral Thought," *Vita Humana*, (vol. 6 1963), pp. 11–33; Kohlberg, "Development of Moral Character and Moral Ideology," in M. L. Hoffman and L. W. Hoffman, eds., *Review of Child Development*, vol. 1 (New York: Russell Sage Foundation, 1964), pp. 383–431.

and practitioners aware of moral reasoning and provides a theory, along with Piaget's, to guide teaching.

To put Piaget and Kohlberg into a classroom perspective, it seems likely that teachers need to discuss various viewpoints in class and accept divergent answers on essay examinations as long as the arguments are logical and well supported. Teachers should be willing to encourage dialogue and give-and-take in classroom discussions. They must become informed and stay informed about good teaching practices for purposes of improving their effects on students. Here we might argue for the need to become more concerned about the human quality of teaching and less concerned about the academic quantity or outcomes of teaching.

Educators in the Baltimore County schools maintain that the great issues must be discussed in class and demonstrated through school policy: rule by law, due process, equity and justice, courtesy, compassion, loyalty and patriotism, responsibility, tolerance and truth.[40] According to educators in Syracuse, NY., there is need for teachers to become involved in moral dilemma discussions and debates at staff development meetings, and to learn how they can incorporate values and ethics in academic subjects. The schools need to evaluate their own policies in context with moral criteria, and teachers need to apply moral literature and practices in their methodologies and modeling behaviors.[41] With a little introspection and self analysis, many of us might be surprised about our existing (or nonexisting) moral policies and practices in schools and classrooms. Actual behaviors versus lipservice might be examined.

What practical strategies can teachers use to promote moral education? The strategies listed below fall into three categories: teacher actions that set the stage for learning, general cognitive strategies, and specific cognitive strategies. The cognitive strategies of the latter two categories combine critical thinking skills and moral reasoning skills.

I. Teacher Actions
 1. Trying to establish a clear understanding of what morality is
 2. Focusing on the group (the school, classroom) in initial discussions before proceeding to individual students
 3. Involving all students in making rules and enforcing them
 4. Speaking up as an advocate of justice, reason, and enlightenment in the classroom and in school meetings
 5. Assuring that advocacy does not become a form of indoctrination or self-assertiveness[42]

---

40 Bonnie S. Copeland and Mary Ellen Saterlie, "The Baltimore County Model: Designing and Implementing a Values Education Program," *NASSP Bulletin* (October 1989), pp. 46–49.

41 Fritz Hess and Scott Shablak, "The Schools of Character Project," *NASSP Bulletin* (October 1989), pp. 50–57.

42 Clark Power and Lawrence A. Kohlberg, "Moral Development: Transforming the Hidden Curriculum," *Curriculum Review* (September–October 1986), pp. 14–17.

II. General Cognitive Strategies
   6. Avoiding oversimplification of moral issues
   7. Developing one's moral perspective
   8. Clarifying moral issues and claims
   9. Clarifying moral ideas
   10. Developing criteria for moral evaluation
   11. Evaluating moral authorities
   12. Raising and pursuing root moral questions
   13. Evaluating moral arguments
   14. Generating and assessing solutions to moral problems
   15. Identifying and clarifying moral points of view
   16. Engaging in Socratic discussion on moral issues
   17. Practicing dialogical thinking on moral issues
   18. Practicing dialectical thinking on moral issues
III. Specific Cognitive Strategies
   19. Distinguishing facts from moral principles, values, and ideals
   20. Using critical vocabulary in discussing moral issues
   21. Distinguishing moral principles or ideals
   22. Examining moral assumptions
   23. Distinguishing morally relevant from morally irrelevant facts
   24. Making plausible moral inferences
   25. Supplying evidence for a moral conclusion
   26. Recognizing moral contradictions
   27. Exploring moral implications and consequences
   28. Refining moral generalizations[43]

COGNITIVE LEARNING: CRITICAL THINKING AND CREATIVITY

It is important for teachers to understand the ways students learn and the components of critical and creative thinking. Learning is a reflective process, whereby the learner either develops new insights and understanding or changes and restructures his or her mental process. So, constructed learning combines both inductive thought (fact gathering) and deductive thought (elaborate ideas). Whereas learning connotes a general process, critical thinking and creativity connote specific aspects of learning.

Principles of Learning

There have been three major schools of learning theories in the last hundred years. (1) Behavioral theories see learning in terms of changing what we do.

---

43 Richard W. Paul, "Ethics Without Doctrination," *Educational Leadership* (May 1988), p. 12.

They emphasize behavioral modification through conditioning by means of reinforcements. (2) Field and gestalt theories consider how the individual perceives the learning environment or situation. They emphasize observational learning, imitation, and modeling. (3) Cognitive theories consider how the learner thinks, reasons, and transfers information to new learning situations.

In the last 15 years or so the cognitive theories have had the greatest impact on educational thought, but at the same time some ideas from the three schools have been fused. The new development in the theories about how learners process information is called "cognitive psychology" or "cognitive science." The following list discusses principles of learning of contemporary cognitive psychology that have implications for teachers today.

1. Learning by doing is good advice. But teachers should also understand that students learn by direct and indirect means, by observing others (peers and teachers), by obtaining corrective feedback, and through encouragement to try again or to go to the next task or skill level.

2. One learns to do what one does. If students are unwilling to read or play tennis, they will not learn how to read or play tennis. Students who do not study are not going to learn as much as students who do. What students already know influences what and how they learn.

3. The amount of reinforcement necessary for learning is relative to the students' needs and abilities. An important part of teaching is to know who needs additional practice and who is ready to learn new tasks.

4. The principle of **readiness** is related to the learners' stage of development and their previous learning. The teacher must consider the students' age in presenting certain content and in expecting certain cognitive processes. (A third grader can deal with concrete operations but cannot make inferences.) The teacher should also periodically assess the current skills of students and adjust instructional objectives, subject matter, and cognitive expectations accordingly.

5. The students' self-concept and beliefs about their abilities are extremely important. Teachers sometimes forget that these personal factors affect learning and that teachers' attitudes toward students influence the students' perceptions of themselves.

6. Teachers should provide opportunities for meaningful and appropriate practice (rehearsal). Practice tasks should be varied to engage students fully and to take advantage of learning the same thing.

7. Transfer of learning to new situations can be horizontal (across subject matter) or vertical (increased complexity of the same subject).

8. Learning should be goal-directed and focused. Teachers must assist students to become task-oriented, purposive, and efficient in their use

of time for learning and studying. Teachers should discourage students from memorizing facts and encourage them to focus on "big" ideas or concepts. New information is made more meaningful to students through relating it in a meaningful way to knowledge they already know.

9. Positive feedback, realistic praise, and encouragement are motivating in the teaching process. Teachers must also consider situation factors (home and classroom environment), basic human needs (a hungry child or one who lacks love is concerned with things other than learning), and personal factors (student self-concept).

10. **Metacognition** is an advanced cognitive process whereby students acquire specific learning strategies and also sense when they are not learning or having trouble learning. Teachers need to help students learn how to organize their thoughts, how to assess their own thinking, and how to study. They also need to assist students to make meaningful connections between prior knowledge or experiences and new information, as opposed to teachers drilling facts or the "basics" without indicating the connections. These processes are more important than the immediate acquisition of particular content or teaching basic facts or tasks. To apply these new principles may require teachers who are test- and results-oriented to rethink their approach and methods.[44]

Learning-to-Learn Skills

The concept of learning in this text differs from the notion that the learner merely remains passive, reacts to stimuli, and waits for some reward. Here the learner is regarded as active and able to monitor and control cognitive activities. He or she processes new information through assimilation and integration with old information. Without this integration, new information is lost to memory and task performance dependent on the information is unsuccessful.[45] Learning new information results in modification of long-term memory. The responsibility for engaging in learning, including control, direction, and focus, belongs to the individual.[46] The teacher can facilitate the process through

---

44 Stephen F. Foster, "Ten Principles of Learning Revised in Accordance with Cognitive Psychology," *Educational Psychologist* (Summer 1986), pp. 235–243; Wilbert McKeachie, "Learning, Thinking, and Thorndike," *Educational Psychologist* (Spring 1990), pp. 127–142; and Allan C. Ornstein "Problem Solving: What is It? How Can We Teach It?" *NASSP Bulletin* (November 1989), pp. 113–121.

45 David P. Ausubel, Joseph D. Novak, and H. Hanesian, *Educational Psychology: A Cognitive Perspective* (New York: Holt, Rinehart & Winston, 1978); John Flavell, *Cognitive Development*, 2nd ed. (Englewood Cliffs, N.J.: Prentice-Hall, 1985).

46 Penelope L. Peterson, "Making Learning Meaningful: Lessons from Research on Cognition and Instruction," *Educational Psychologist* (Fall 1988), pp. 365–374; Lauren B. Resnick and Leopold E. Klopfer, "Toward the Thinking Curriculum," in L. B. Resnick and L. E. Klopfer, eds., *Toward the Thinking Curriculum: Current Cognitive Research*, 1989 ASCD Yearbook (Alexandria, Va.: Association for Supervision and Curriculum Development, 1989), pp. 1–18.

explicit or direct instruction and by linking new information with existing relevant and related information.

Cognitive structures are searched when students want to identify, categorize, and process new information. If the cognitive structures are disorganized, unclear, or not fully developed (for the person's age), then new information will not be clearly identified, categorized, and assimilated. To be sure, new learning based on previous learning should be meaningful to students—in context with prior knowledge and real-life experiences—regardless of whether the students are low or high achieving. The difference is that low-achieving students have a more limited knowledge and cognitive base than high-achieving students.

From a review of the literature, Charles Letteri has compiled a list of seven comprehension or thinking skills that students can develop to enhance the way they process and integrate information. They are skills that teachers should understand and help students acquire.

1. *Analysis* (sometimes called field dependence-independence), the ability to break down complex information into component parts for the purpose of identification and categorization.
2. *Focusing* (scanning), the ability to select relevant or important information without being distracted or confused by the irrelevant or secondary information.
3. *Comparative analysis* (reflective-impulsivity), the ability to select a correct item from among several alternatives; the ability to compare information and make proper choices.
4. *Narrowing* (breadth of categorization), the ability to identify and place new information into categories through its attributes (physical characteristics, principle, or function).
5. *Complex cognitive* (complexity-simplicity), the ability to integrate complex information into existing cognitive structures (long-term memory).
6. *Sharpening* (sharpening-leveling), the ability to maintain distinctions between cognitive structures (including old and new information) and to avoid confusion or overlap.
7. *Tolerance* (tolerant-intolerant), the ability to monitor and modify thinking; the ability to deal with ambiguous or unclear information without getting frustrated.[47]

A cognitive framework proposed by Weinstein and Mayer consists of eight comprehension or thinking strategies.

1. *Basic rehearsal strategies*, the ability to remember names or words and the order of things.

---

47 Charles A. Letteri, "Teaching Students How to Learn," *Theory into Practice* (Spring 1985), pp. 112–122.

2. *Complex rehearsal strategies*, making appropriate choices or selections (such as knowing what to copy when the teacher explains something or what to underline or outline while reading).

3. *Basic elaboration strategies*, relating two or more items (such as nouns and verbs).

4. *Complex elaboration strategies*, analyzing or synthesizing new information with old information.

5. *Basic organizational strategies*, categorizing, grouping, or ordering new information.

6. *Complex organizational strategies*, putting information in hierarchical arrangements (such as in outlining notes or homework).

7. *Comprehension monitoring*, checking progress, recognizing when one is on the right track or confused, right or wrong.

8. *Affective strategies*, being relaxed yet alert and attentive during a test situation and studying.[48]

All of these learning skills combined represent knowledge about and control over cognitive processes, what some educators refer to as metacognition. The specific strategies deal with the identification, categorization, and integration of information.

Of all the specific strategies discussed, **comprehension monitoring** is often considered the most important. This skill permits the student to monitor, modify, and direct his or her cognitive activities. The student remains focused on the task, is aware of whether he or she is getting closer to or farther away from an answer, and knows when to choose alternative methods to arrive at the answer. A student with good comprehension monitoring has developed self-correcting cognition processes, including how to determine what part of a problem needs further clarification, how to relate parts of a problem to one another, and how to search out information to solve the problem. In short, the student is able to identify what has to be done, focus attention, cope with errors, and make modifications in steps to work out a solution—all without losing control, getting frustrated, or giving up.

Learning-to-learn skills are basic thinking skills that are used in most content areas. Although some of these learning skills are generic and can be taught solely as general strategies, without reference to content, it is impossible to avoid a certain amount of subject matter,[49] especially in the upper (secondary) grades. Many average and high-achieving students develop these skills on their own, yet the skills can be taught to all students. It is the bottom half of

48 Claire E. Weinstein and Richard E. Mayer, "The Teaching of Learning Strategies," in M. C. Wittrock, ed., *Handbook of Research on Teaching*, 3rd ed. (New York: Macmillan, 1986), pp. 315–327.

49 Ron Brandt, "On Learning Research: A Conversation with Lauren Resnick," *Educational Leadership* (December-January 1989), pp. 12–16.

the bell-shaped curve that needs to be taught learning skills; failure to learn these basic skills correlates with academic failure.

Learning skills can be incorporated into regular classroom activities or taught as a special course that incorporates content from several subjects and focuses on cognitive processes that cut across subjects. The classroom activities or special course should be designed to make all students independent learners in all subjects. The training should begin early in the elementary grades, say around the third or fourth grade. It should continue thereafter with additional time devoted to these skills, perhaps twice the time by the sixth or seventh grade, when students must gather and organize increasing amounts of subject-related information. It cannot be postponed until high school, when the job of learning how to learn has become more difficult because of increasing academic deficiencies.

Guidelines for Teaching Learning Skills

How do teachers help students learn different learning skills? The teacher's role is essentially fivefold: (1) Teachers do not merely mention a particular learning skill; they direct and explain what a particular skill is and how to use it. (2) Teachers provide progressively more difficult items for students to practice on until students can complete the tasks on their own. (3) Teachers determine whether students can perform the task and use related skills and then give the students opportunities to apply the skills to new and different learning situations. (4) Teachers identify the processes or thinking operations students use to perform tasks or solve problems by asking appropriate questions and listening to students' responses. (5) Teachers learn to use diagnostic and assessment tools to make appropriate connections between learning skills and concepts or problems being taught in the particular subject.[50]

All too often teachers are more interested in whether students know the facts or can complete tasks than in whether they understand the skill for performing the task; they are more concerned with test scores than with the development of cognitive process. Teachers have to redirect their efforts to focus on teaching students how and when to employ different learning skills. This type of teaching has immense potential for students in all subjects and grade levels.

---

50 Richard E. Mayer, "Aids to Text Comprehension," *Educational Leadership* (Winter 1984), pp. 30–42; P. Peterson, "Making Learning Meaningful: Lessons from Research on Cognition and Instruction"; and Weinstein and Mayer, "The Teaching of Learning Strategies."

One instructional framework for enhancing students' learning strategies is based on a form of direct instruction and consists of six components.

1. *Modeling* (sometimes called *introduction*). The teacher identifies the skill required and shows how it is used. In effect, the teacher "shares a cognitive secret" of how to execute a strategy.

2. Guided practice. Teachers and students work together on a skill or task and figure out how to apply the strategy. The teacher stays in the background but guides students by asking such questions as why they have rejected some information or some specific strategy.

3. *Consolidation* (sometimes called *extension*). The teacher helps students to consider a skill in relation to several examples and to determine when the skill should not be used. The teacher corrects imperfect examples of the skill. He or she may also test the students' skills by the technique of providing misinformation or irrelevant information to see how students cope.

4. *Independent practice*. The students complete assignments by themselves, first in class with the teacher present to provide aid if necessary, and then at home or on their own without the assistance of the teacher. The teacher checks the students' work, then gives the students an opportunity to consolidate and modify the skill to prevent patterns of failure, if they exist.

5. *Application*. The teacher asks students to apply the skill to a new problem.

6. *Review*. The teacher periodically reviews the when, why, and how of the skill. It is incorporated into classroom and homework assignments over an extended period. It is discussed and integrated into new tasks until students have mastered it and integrated it into the learning of new skills. Test results are used for assessing the amount of review needed.[51]

According to Barry Beyer, instruction in each skill should occur 10 to 15 times a year in the subject in which it was introduced. When previously learned skills are being reinforced and applied in new contexts, the number of practice or application lessons can be reduced. A curriculum guide should provide the teacher with content and activities for integrating them into the subject.[52] Either the curriculum by itself or the instructional leader should see to it that the same skills or strategies are taught horizontally across subjects or by more than one teacher at the same grade level as well as vertically in each subject, to ensure review of old strategies and integration with new ones. See Tips for Teachers 2.4.

---

51 Barry K. Beyer, *Teaching Thinking Skills* (Needham Heights, Mass.: Allyn & Bacon, 1991).

52 Barry K. Beyer, *Practical Strategies for the Teaching of Thinking* (Boston: Allyn & Bacon, 1987).

Tips for Teachers 2.4

Enhancing Learning Skills

Here is a teaching inventory for enhancing learning skills among students. The first part is what the school can do; the second part is what the teacher can do.

I. The school district or school should have:
1. A list of major learning skills to be taught throughout the system
2. Agreement among all subject areas that these skills should be taught throughout the system
3. A curriculum document that clearly specifies which learning skills are to be taught at each grade level in each subject area
4. A curriculum document that presents skills to be taught in a developmental sequence based on the cognitive development of learners
5. A learning skills curriculum that provides for continuing instruction in key thinking skills across many grade levels and subjects
6. Detailed descriptions of the operating procedures, rules, and distinguishing criteria of each major skill to be taught
7. Appropriate learning skill descriptions available to every teacher and administrator
8. Provisions for instruction in each skill with a variety of media in a variety of settings, and for a variety of goals

II. The teacher should:
1. Use a common terminology and instructional language to describe the learning skills they are required to teach
2. Provide instruction in learning skills when these skills are needed to accomplish subject matter learning goals
3. Understand the major components of the skills they are teaching
4. Provide continuing instruction in each skill through stages of introduction, guided practice, extension, practice, and application
5. Introduce learning skills as explicitly as possible by explaining and modeling each skill and having students apply the skill with their guidance
6. Provide frequent guided practice in each skill with appropriate instructive feedback
7. Require students to reflect on and discuss how they make each skill operational
8. Use instructional materials appropriate to learning the skills

(continues)

> 9. Test on their own unit tests the learning skills or strategies they are responsible for teaching
>
> *Source:* Barry K. Beyer, "Teaching Thinking Skills," *NASSP Bulletin* (January 1985), pp. 82-83.

Critical Thinking

One of the most important things a teacher can do in the classroom, regardless of subject or grade level, is to make students aware of their own thinking processes—to examine what they are thinking about, to make distinctions and comparisons, to see errors in what they are thinking about and how they are thinking about it, and to make self-corrections.

It is now believed that **critical thinking** is a form of intelligence that can be taught. The leading proponents of this school are Matthew Lipman, Robert Sternberg, and Robert Ennis.

Lipman's program was originally designed for elementary school grades but is applicable to all grades. He seeks to develop the ability to use (1) concepts, (2) generalization, (3) cause-effect relationships, (4) logical inferences, (5) consistencies and contradictions, (6) analogies, (7) part-whole and whole-part connections, (8) problem formulations, (9) reversibility of logical statements, and (10) applications of principles to real-life situations.[53]

In Lipman's program for teaching critical thinking, children spend a considerable portion of their time thinking about thinking and about ways in which effective thinking differs from ineffective thinking. After reading a series of stories, children engage in classroom discussions and exercises that encourage them to adopt the thinking process depicted in the stories.[54] Lipman's assumptions are that children are by nature interested in such philosophical issues as truth, fairness, and personal identity, and that children can and should learn to explore alternatives to their own viewpoints, to consider evidence, to make distinctions, and to draw conclusions.

Lipman distinguishes between *ordinary thinking* and *critical thinking*. Ordinary thinking is simple and lacks standards; critical thinking is more complex and is based on standards of objectivity, utility, or consistency. He wants teachers to help students change (1) from guessing to estimating, (2) from preferring to evaluating, (3) from grouping to classifying, (4) from believing to

---

53 Matthew Lipman, "The Culturation of Reasoning through Philosophy," *Educational Leadership* (September 1984), pp. 51–56.

54 Matthew Lipman et al., *Philosophy for Children*, 2nd ed. (Philadelphia: Temple University Press, 1980).

assuming, (5) from inferring to inferring logically, (6) from associating concepts to grasping principles, (7) from noting relationships to noting relationships among relationships, (8) from supposing to hypothesizing, (9) from offering opinions without reasons to offering opinions with reasons, and (10) from making judgments without criteria to making judgments with criteria.[55]

Sternberg seeks to foster many of the same skills, but in a different way (see Table 2.4). He points to three categories of components of critical thinking: (1) *meta-components*, high-order mental processes used to plan, monitor, and evaluate what the individual is doing; (2) *performance components*, the actual steps the individual takes; and (3) *knowledge-acquisition components*, processes used to relate old material to new material and to apply to new material.[56] Sternberg does not specify how to teach these skills; rather he gives general guidelines for developing or selecting a program.

Robert Ennis identifies 13 attributes of critical thinkers. They tend to (1) be open-minded, (2) take a position (or change a position) when the evidence calls for it, (3) take into account the entire situation, (4) seek information, (5) seek precision in information, (6) deal in an orderly manner with parts of a complex whole, (7) look for options, (8) search for reasons, (9) seek a clear statement of the issue, (10) keep the original problem in mind, (11) use credible sources, (12) remain relevant to the point, and (13) be sensitive to the feelings and knowledge level of others.[57]

Some educators contend that teaching a person to think is like teaching someone to swing a golf club; it requires a holistic approach, not a piecemeal effort, as implied by Lipman, Sternberg, and Ennis. "Trying to break thinking skills into discrete units may be helpful for diagnostic proposals," say Sadler and Whimbey, "but it does not seem to be the right way to move in the teaching of such skills." Critical thinking is too complex to be divided into small processes; teaching must involve "a student's total intellectual functioning, not . . . a set of narrowly defined skills."[58]

Perhaps the major criticism of thinking skills programs has been raised by Sternberg. He cautions that the kinds of critical thinking skills stressed in school and the way they are taught "inadequately prepares students for the kinds of problems they will face in everyday life."[59]

---

55 Matthew Lipman, "Critical Thinking—What Can It Be?" *Educational Leadership* (September 1988), pp. 38–43.

56 Robert J. Sternberg, "How Can We Teach Intelligence?" *Educational Leadership* (September 1984), pp. 34–48; Robert J. Sternberg and Joan B. Baron, "A Statewide Approach to Measuring Critical Thinking Skills," *Educational Leadership* (October 1985), pp. 40–43; and Robert J. Sternberg et al., "Practical Intelligence for Success in School," *Educational Leadership* (September 1990), pp. 35–39.

57 Robert H. Ennis, "A Logical Basis for Measuring Critical Thinking Skills," *Educational Leadership* (October 1985), pp. 44–48; Ennis, "A Taxonomy of Critical Thinking Skills," in J. B. Barron and R. J. Sternberg, eds., *Critical Thinking* (New York: Freeman, 1987), pp. 19–26.

58 William A. Sadler and Arthur Whimbey, "A Holistic Approach to Improving Thinking Skills," *Phi Delta Kappan* (November 1985), p. 200.

59 Robert J. Sternberg, "Teaching Critical Thinking: Possible Solutions," *Phi Delta Kappan* (December 1985), p. 277.

Table 2.4   CRITICAL THINKING SKILLS UNDERLYING INTELLIGENT BEHAVIOR

1. Recognizing and defining the nature of a problem

2. Deciding upon the processes needed to solve the problem

3. Sequencing the processes into an optimal strategy

4. Deciding upon how to represent problem information

5. Allocating mental and physical resources to the problem

6. Monitoring and evaluating one's solution processing

7. Responding adequately to external feedback

8. Encoding stimulus elements effectively

9. Inferring relations between stimulus elements

10. Mapping relations between relations

11. Applying old relations to new situations

12. Comparing stimulus elements

13. Responding effectively to novel kinds of tasks and situations

14. Effectively automatizing information processing

15. Adapting effectively to the environment in which one resides

16. Selecting environments as needed to achieve a better fit of one's abilities and interests to the environment

17. Shaping environments so as to increase one's effective utilization of one's abilities and interests

Source: Robert J. Sternberg, "How Can We Teach Intelligence?" *Educational Leadership* (September 1984), p. 40.

Further caution is needed. Thinking skills programs often stress "right" answers and "objectively scorable" test items; therefore, they are removed from real-world relevance. Most problems and decisions in real life have social, economic, and psychological implications. They involve interpersonal relationships and judgments about people, personal stress and crisis, and dilemmas involving responsibility and survival. How a person deals with illness, aging, or death or with less momentous events such as starting a new job or meeting new people has little to do with the way a person thinks in class or on critical thinking tests. But such life situations are important matters. In stressing cognitive skills, educators tend to ignore the realities of life. Being an A student in school guarantees little after school and in real life. There are many other factors associated with the outcomes of life—and many of them have little to do with metacognition. Thus, we need to keep in mind social, psychological and moral components of learning, as well as "luck," or what some of us might call the unaccounted for variables, in the outcomes of life.

Guidelines for Teaching Critical Thinking

Teachers must understand the cognitive processes that constitute critical thinking; be familiar with the tasks, skills, and situations to which these processes are applied; and employ several classroom activities that develop these processes. Ennis provides a framework for such instruction. He divides critical thinking into four components, each consisting of several specific skills that can be taught to students.

I.　Defining and clarifying
　　1.　Identifying conclusions
　　2.　Identifying stated reasons
　　3.　Identifying unstated reasons
　　4.　Seeing similarities and differences
　　5.　Identifying and handling irrelevance
　　6.　Summarizing
II.　Asking appropriate questions to clarify or challenge
　　1.　Why?
　　2.　What is the main point?
　　3.　What does this mean?
　　4.　What is an example?
　　5.　What is not an example?
　　6.　How does this apply to the case?
　　7.　What difference does it make?
　　8.　What are the facts?
　　9.　Is this what is being said?
　　10.　What more is to be said?
III.　Judging the credibility of a source
　　1.　Expertise
　　2.　Lack of conflict of interest
　　3.　Agreement among sources
　　4.　Reputation
　　5.　Use of established procedures
　　6.　Known risk to reputation
　　7.　Ability to give reasons
　　8.　Careful habits
IV.　Solving problems and drawing conclusions
　　1.　Deducing and judging validity

2. Inducing and judging conclusions
3. Predicting probable consequences[60]

In general, teachers must ask students a great many questions; require students to analyze, apply, and evaluate information; take opposing sides to tease and test students; and require them to support their answers or conclusions. Supplementary materials, beyond the workbook and textbook, will be needed; it is recommended that teachers work together to develop such materials. David and Roger Johnson point out that students must learn to respect and value one another, so they can learn from each other. Students must feel secure enough to challenge each other's ideas and reasoning, and they must be encouraged to engage in controversial discussions, debates, problem-solving activities, and decision-making activities.[61] By varying instructional activities, ensuring that groups are heterogeneous in skills, distributing relevant materials, and giving instruction in constructing logical arguments, teachers can help students to learn to think critically in a variety of academic situations.

No one teacher can do the job alone. It is a process that takes years to develop. It behooves the school administration to establish the tone and instill in its teachers of all subjects and grades the need for cooperation to make students aware of what it means to be a critical thinker.

Creative Thinking

Standardized tests do not always measure creativity accurately; in fact, we have difficulty agreeing on what creativity is and who is creative. All children who are normal are potentially creative, yet many parents and teachers impose so many restrictions on their natural behaviors that the children learn that creativity gets them into trouble and earns them disapproval. Parents often react negatively to children's inquisitiveness and "messing around." Teachers impose rules of order, conformity, and "normalcy" to suit themselves, not the children.

There are many types of **creativity**—artistic, dramatic, scientific, athletic, manual—yet we tend to talk about creativity as an all-encompassing term and usually limit the term to cognitive or intellectual endeavors. Educators tend to assess people as smart or dumb based on their performance in one or two areas of intelligence, say, linguistic or mathematical ability. Because of this narrow view of human abilities and this insensitivity to how individuals differ, schools often prevent the development of a positive self-concept in young children who have creative abilities other than in the cognitive domain. The potential talents of many creative children are lost because of our fixation on specific and limited kinds of knowledge.

---

60 Ennis, "A Logical Basis for Measuring Critical Thinking Skills."

61 David W. Johnson and Roger T. Johnson, "Critical Thinking Through Structured Controversy," *Educational Leadership* (May 1988), pp. 58–64.

Creative students are often puzzling to teachers. They are difficult to characterize, their novel answers are threatening, and their behavior often deviates from what is considered normal or proper. Creative students have a certain freedom of spirit and unwillingness to be bound by conventional norms or rules; they posses a dimension of imagination which many of us do not possess, and they tend to be more inquisitive and venturesome than most of us. A person's propensity to act or think in an unusual way can certainly get that person in trouble, especially in classrooms that are run on the basis of control and conformity. These students are often considered difficult to teach, partially because we are unable to recognize and appreciate fundamental differences in the way students learn.

Curriculum specialists tend to ignore the creative students in their plans, and teachers usually ignore them in their program and classroom assignments. Little money is earmarked to support special programs and personnel for them. Even if creativity is recognized, educators often lump "gifted" children together without distinguishing between intellectual and talented students or among different types of creativity.

Because cultural values and creativity are interwoven, we sometimes lose sight in our own middle-class schools that many lower-class and inner-city students may possess creative characteristics and potential quite different from our middle-class standards. Authorities have continuously hoped that our education programs would awaken and build on the potentialities of these students: their (1) ability to express feelings and emotions, (2) ability to improvise with common materials, (3) expressive role playing and story telling, (4) enjoyment of music, drama, and dance, (5) participation skills in informal group activities, (6) responsiveness to concrete and kinesthetic activities, (7) richness of informal language, (8) frankness and responsiveness to people, (9) expressiveness of human and body language, and (10) ability to size up and manipulate their environment.[62] Most of these behaviors are not rewarded in school; in fact, lower-class culture is often in conflict with the school's middle-class culture. But on our asphalt city streets, these lower-class behaviors often lead to practical and even imaginative solutions to problems.

Characteristics of Creativity

In a classic cross-cultural study, E. P. Torrance investigated elementary and secondary teachers' concepts of the "ideal" creative personality.[63] He sampled from 95 to 375 teachers in each of five countries: United States, Germany,

---

62 Frank Riessman, *The Culturally Deprived Child* (New York: Harper & Row, 1962); Riessman, "Overlooked Positives of Disadvantaged Groups," *Journal of Negro Education* (Summer 1964), pp. 225–231; and E. P. Torrance, *The Creative Teacher at Work* (Lexington, Mass.: Ginn, 1972). Also see David N. Perkins, *The Mind's Best Work: A New Psychology of Creative Thinking* (Cambridge, Mass: Harvard University Press, 1983).

63 E. P. Torrance, *Rewarding Creative Behavior: Experiments in Classroom Creativity* (Englewood Cliffs, N.J.: Prentice-Hall, 1965).

Greece, India, and the Philippines. Cultural values are reflected in definitions of creativity. For example, teachers in the United States and Germany (technologically developed countries) gave high ratings to independent thinking, industriousness, curiosity, and independent judgment; these traits were not regarded as important by teachers in the less-developed countries. Greek and Philippine teachers valued remembering, but many American teachers considered this type of thinking to be uncreative. Teachers in the three less-developed countries linked creativity with obedience, courtesy or sincerity, being well liked, and having self-confidence, but many of these traits were associated with conformity by American teachers.

Robert Sternberg identified 6 attributes associated with creativity from a list of 131 mentioned by laypeople and professors in the arts, science, and business: (1) lack of conventionality, (2) intellectuality, (3) esthetic taste and imagination, (4) decision-making skills and flexibility, (5) perspicacity (in questioning social norms), and (6) drive for accomplishment and recognition.[64] He also makes important distinctions among creativity, intelligence, and wisdom. Although they are mutually exclusive categories, they are interrelated constructs. **Wisdom** is more clearly associated with intelligence than is creativity, but differs in emphasis upon mature judgment and use of experience with difficult situations. Creativity overlaps more with intelligence than it does with wisdom; with creativity, there is more emphasis on imagination and unconventional methods, while intelligence deals with logical and analytical absolutes.

According to Carl Rogers, the essence of creativity is novelty, and, hence, we have no standard by which to judge it. In fact, the more original the product, the more likely it is to be judged by contemporaries as foolish or evil.[65] The individual creates primarily because creating is self-satisfying and because the behavior or product is self-actualizing. (This is the humanistic side of creativity, even though the process and intellect involved in creating are cognitive in nature.)

Erich Fromm defines the creative attitude as the willingness to be puzzled (to orient oneself to something without frustration), the ability to concentrate, the ability to experience oneself as a true originator of one's acts, and the willingness to accept the conflict and tension caused by the lack of tolerance for creative ideas.[66]

The above studies show that there is little agreement on a definition of creativity except that it represents a quality of mind and is associated with

---

64 Robert J. Steinberg, "Intelligence, Wisdom, and Creativity: Three Is Better Than One," *Educational Psychologist* (Summer 1986), pp. 175–190.

65 Carl Rogers, "Toward a Theory of Creativity," in M. Barkan and R. L. Mooney, eds., *Conference on Creativity: A Report to the Rockefeller Foundation* (Columbus, Ohio: Ohio State University Press, 1953), pp. 73–82.

66 Erich Fromm, "The Creative Attitude," in H. H. Anderson, ed., *Creativity and Its Cultivation* (New York: Harper & Row, 1959), pp. 44–54.

intelligence. For teachers, the definition of creativity comes down to how new ideas have their origin. We are dealing with processes that are both logical and unconscious and both observable and unrecognizable. Because unconscious and unrecognizable processes are difficult to deal with in the classroom, there is often misunderstanding between teachers and creative students.

Teachers generally require "reactive" thinking from their students; that is, they expect them to react to questions, exercises, or test items and give a preferred answer. They tend to discourage "proactive" thinking, that is, generating novel questions and answers. This is the way most teachers were taught, and they feel uneasy about not having "right" answers. Some teachers do try to develop critical thinking in their students, but they need to go beyond reaction thinking and even beyond critical thinking and encourage learners to generate ideas. Society needs generative thinkers to plan, to make decisions, to deal with social and technological problems. Teachers need to let students know that having the right answer is not always important, that depth of understanding is important, and that different activities require different abilities. Teachers need to understand that nearly all students have the potential for creative thinking. The need is to encourage the creative spark, which may differ among all individuals.

In order to stimulate creative thinking, teachers should encourage students to make inferences and to think intuitively, and use inquiry-discovery teaching techniques. Three types of inferences have creative potential: (1) elaboration of characteristics, categories, or concepts (for example, a student is told some of the objects in a category are "right" and some are "wrong"; the problem is to infer from this information the definition of the category); (2) elaboration of causality (What were the causes of World War I? Why did the compound turn into gas?); and (3) elaboration of background information (making inferences about possible effects of events and facts from past events and facts in order to make decisions and solve problems).[67]

Intuitive thinking is a cognitive process that has been discouraged because traditional teaching relies on facts and rote. A good thinker, according to Jerome Bruner, is creative and has an intuitive grasp of subject matter. Intuition is part of the process of discovery; investigating hunches and playing with ideas can lead to discoveries and additions to the storehouse of knowledge. The steps involved in intuitive thinking often cannot be differentiated or defined; intuition involves cognitive maneuvers "based on implicit perception of the total problem. The thinker arrives at an answer, which may be right or wrong, with little, if any, awareness of the process by which he reached it."[68]

---

67 John H. Clarke, *Patterns of Thinking* (Needham Heights, Mass.: Allyn & Bacon, 1991); David N. Perkins, *Knowledge as Design* (Hillsdale, N.J.: Erlbaum, 1986). Also see Robert J. Marzano and Daisy E. Arredondo, "Restructuring Schools Through the Teaching of Critical Skills," *Educational Leadership* (May 1986), pp. 20–26.

68 Jerome S. Bruner, *The Process of Education* (Cambridge, Mass.: Harvard University Press, 1959), p. 57.

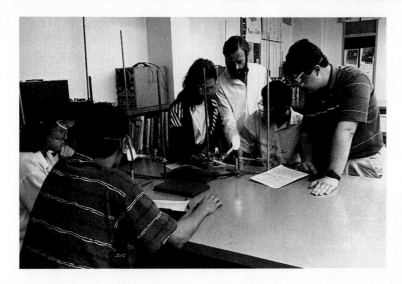

The problem solving/discovery approach to learning combines traditonal laboratory methods with intuitive, commonsense processes.

Teaching Creativity

Teachers must encourage students to make educated guesses, to follow hunches, and to make leaps in thinking. Not having a clear account of how we obtain an answer is sometimes secondary; understanding the nuances and larger concepts is more important.

In inquiry-discovery techniques of teaching, students are not presented with subject matter in its final form; questions, answers, solutions, and information are devised and derived by the students. The techniques can be adapted to students of all ages. In this connection, Ronald Bonnstetter has summarized the most desirable teacher behaviors observed over a five-year period in more than one thousand exemplary science programs across the country. These behaviors were considered most effective in fostering inquiry-discovery skills among students in science courses. In general, the list of behaviors in Table 2.5 encourages students to "mess about," to explore, to experiment, to appreciate new techniques, to respect differing (as well as novel) ideas, to make mistakes and learn from them. Students taught by teachers who exhibit these behaviors tend to be more creative, more innovative, and more at ease with themselves as well as their peers and teachers than students taught by teachers who exhibit more conventional methods of teaching.

Most people would agree that it is tremendously important to society that the creative abilities of our children and youth be identified and developed— important for the welfare of our civilization. Torrance, who is probably the best known expert on the subject, points out that students can be taught in such ways that their creative thinking abilities are nourished. Teachers need to

Table 2.5   TEACHING BEHAVIORS THAT CORRELATE WITH STUDENT
INQUIRY-DISCOVERY BEHAVIORS

The teacher

1. Accepts student ideas
2. Develops student interests and creative potential
3. Recognizes personal limitations of students
4. Provides a stimulating and accepting environment
5. Has high expectations of students
6. Views learning beyond classroom boundaries
7. Develops effective communication skills
8. Wants students to apply knowledge
9. Puts more emphasis on process of learning than outcomes
10. Stimulates in-depth learning of subject
11. Allows students to pursue activities, thus students decide the point of closure
12. Creates in students a sense of ownership in learning
13. Permits student choices and decisions concerning classroom activities
14. Designs learning experiences around students' life experiences, needs, and interests
15. Encourages risk-taking and a questioning attitude
16. Reduces classroom anxiety
17. Encourages divergent thinking and new ideas
18. Encourages frequent self-evaluation by students
19. Provides sufficient structure for students to understand goals, rules, and routines without stifling creative behavior
20. Provides students with an awareness of the interrelationships of science, technology, and social science

Source: Adapted from Ronald J. Bonnstetter, "Teacher Behaviors That Facilitate New Goals," *Education and Urban Society* (November 1989), pp. 31–32.

recognize that highly creative children learn in different ways than do children who have high IQ's but are not highly creative, and there are social pressures in school and outside of school that interfere with the development of their creative abilities.[69]

The teacher needs to recognize that students can learn in both active and quiet environments. Important ideas occur to some people in the heat of activity

---

69 J. Pansy Torrance, ed., *Over the Years: Research Insights of E. Paul Torrance* (Athens, Ga.: University of Georgia, Department of Educational Psychology, 1984).

as well as in quiet periods of relaxation. As for the teacher, he or she must have the courage and maturity to accept the original answers of these students and be willing to accept some degree of nonconforming behavior—not an easy concept for some teachers to accept. To be sure, teachers are better able to free and develop the creative capacities of their students so long as their own behavior and values support creativeness.

In the final analysis, teachers are going to have to learn to accept an inquiring and divergent mind—one that questions and challenges common thinking and is willing to avoid the ordinary and think of the unusual. The information age is upon us, and those who can digest, assimilate, and question data and see different perspectives and opportunities when they are confronted with problems will be better able to cope with the future. Managers and executives of business and industry, even the government and military, are going to have to learn to deal with creative people—who can creatively deal with complex information—in order to stay ahead. The quicker teachers come to realize that a narrow classroom mold, one that breeds conformity, complacence, and rote learning, is old fashioned and out of tune with the future, the better off will be our students, schools, and society.

Guidelines for Teaching Creativity

The teacher must provide, and give credit, for self-initiated learning. Creative kids are sometimes mislabeled as lazy or as daydreamers because they spend some of their time sitting and thinking—not visibly busy; sometimes their thoughts are interrupted, their questions rejected, their daydreams ridiculed; their ideas go unexpressed and their judgments are unsought. Even worse, because they don't always fit the conventional mold in the classroom, they are increasingly labeled as "disabled learners" and funneled into an educational wasteland. Teachers must wake up to the unused talents of these students, and how we sometimes mislabel them "learning disabled" or "behavioral disabled." They must also awaken their own creative juices and thinking. Below are ten recommendations for stimulating the teacher's own creativity, then fifteen recommendations for enhancing the students' own creative processes in class.

Facilitating the Teacher's Creativity

1. Approach personal and professional problems with a *holistic view*; avoid the trees and look at the forest.
2. Avoid single-category or single-effect thinking for multi-cause or *multi-effect thinking*; avoid step-by-step formulas and rely on contexts and processes that suggest whole scenarios.

3. Think in terms of *risk-reward behavior*. Be willing to take risks as long as there is a "safety net" for failure and/or the rewards are significant (more than the risks).

4. *Balance* personal and professional commitments in order to develop a mentally healthy attitude. Hobbies, vacations, and sports contribute to renewal and help decrease burnout or stagnation on the job.

5. *Reduce stress* by proper diet, exercise, and relaxation. In particular, physical exercise helps promote relaxed consciousness and better mental and physical health. Remember not to take too many things too seriously—a philosophical attitude helps to cope with stress.

6. Take time out to *meditate*. There are a variety of ways to meditate, such as reading, listening to soft music, worshipping, yoga, zen, transcendental meditation. Meditation fosters a balanced, integrated state of being which fosters creative thinking.

7. Allow problems to *incubate*. Don't react immediately. Allow ideas to germinate through passive self-exploration, relaxation, and leisure activities. Come back to problems and build on prior ideas.

8. Stimulate *nonverbal thought* through music, visual art, or dance. Autistic expressions of others develop imagination and relativity in thought of the beholder or viewer.

9. *Imagine and daydream*. Have faith in yourself. Be willing to let your imagination and dreams influence your thinking. Channels for imagery and dreaming can involve the general senses, relaxation, meditation, and exercise.

10. Accept and be guided by your own *intuition*. It is one key to creativity that should be developed, mastered, and enhanced. Many people are afraid to let go, or to be guided by their feelings, subconscious, or general senses.[70]

Facilitating the Students' Creativity

1. Make students more sensitive to their environment.
2. Encourage manipulation of objects and ideas.
3. Develop tolerance toward new ideas.
4. Encourage students to explore, test, search, and predict.
5. Resist one acceptable answer or a set pattern.
6. Teach skills for avoiding peer sanctions.
7. Teach students to value their own creativity.
8. Encourage self-initiated and independent learning.

---

70 These recommendations are intermixed with the author's own views and M. Kent Gregory, "Facilitating Creativity: Techniques for Educational Leaders," *Kappa Delta Pi Record* (Spring 1990), pp. 85–87.

9. Look and listen carefully; stir up the uninspired; don't accept superficial answers.
10. Make available different resources for working out ideas.
11. Encourage the habit of working out the full implication of ideas.
12. Provide active and quiet places—where students can "mess around" or "do their thing"; however, provide guidance and direction.
13. Integrate knowledge in a variety of subjects.
14. Keep alive the excitement of learning and thinking; encourage, stimulate, motivate.
15. Develop adventure and spirit in the classroom.[71]

SUMMARY

1. Educators describe different stages of human development, ranging from infancy to old age. Both Erikson and Havighurst set forth ideas to help explain preadolescent and adolescent behavior and the role of the school as a social institution for helping students socially develop.
2. Teachers and schools must provide more humane and supportive settings for students who are in their critical years of development. Teachers and schools must implement developmentally appropriate practices, while recognizing that all students are individuals with their own sets of needs and expectations.
3. Moral knowledge can be acquired through academic content, but moral character takes many years to develop and reflects the whole person.
4. Whereas Piaget concludes there are three stages of moral development, Kohlberg adds to our knowledge of moral thinking by specifying six stages grouped into three moral levels of the way people think about moral issues. Both Piaget and Kohlberg view moral development as a socialization process that can be shaped, in part, by the schools.
5. Students can be taught learning-to-learn skills, critical thinking skills, and creative thinking skills.
6. Differences among creativity, intelligence, and wisdom are examined. Creativity tends to overlap with divergent thinking, and intelligence tends to deal with logical or convergent thinking. Wisdom comes with years of experience and reflects mature judgment.

---

71 Torrance, *Over the Years.*

CASE STUDY

Problem

Dissension had arisen between some faculty members in a high school social studies department over aspects of "moral" education curriculum that they were to develop. A first group tended toward a "secular humanist" viewpoint that defined "morals" in totally secular terms. A second group argued a need to teach "moral" education that included some kinds of absolute standards in conduct and belief. The first group implied that the second wanted a curriculum more suitable to religious or political groups and attributed present social problems to judgmental and inflexible social policies. The second group argued for some absolute standards that would not shift with popular definitions of "moral." They cited the present problems as being related to the relativistic, "secular humanism," and a breakdown of the family and decline of influence of church-related agencies. The first group threatened to bring in the ACLU if any "absolute" standards, religious or otherwise, were included. The other group threatened trouble over infringement on their academic freedom, which included a "censorship" of absolutes from the curriculum.

Suggestion

Neutral teachers suggested the development of a course of instruction that examined morals and ethics from a historical and social perspective. Instead of defining morals in a way applicable only to current problems and discussions, these teachers urged an examination of how various social and cultural forces merge to determine how various people and groups have developed "moral" ideas throughout history; how there have always been various starting points, both absolute and relativistic, at similar times throughout human history. They also compared religious absolutes of the past to "social absolutes" or political absolutes of today, such as the absolutes of a "prohibition" on sexist or racist language in the present society. There was an attempt to show that "absolutes" or "relatives" are a matter of history and of their times.

Discussion Suggestion

Suggested by other members of the faculty, but not accepted, was the idea of inviting social science professors and socially oriented philosophers to the classes, along with theologians and various groups holding "absolutist" views. The guests would discuss both approaches in class and would be videotaped for future classes. Students would then choose points of view to defend in debate topics and would be responsible for analysis of current social problems as they would be dealt with within each approach; absolute, relativistic, or a combination of both.

Discussion Questions

1. Which "side," if any, would you have taken during the faculty debate? Why? How would you have argued your position?

2. Why do you think the suggestion to bring in a guest speaker was voted down? (You may want to review the chapters dealing with teaching-learning problems and nonacademically related influences).

3. What might be your "biases" toward "absolutes," or toward "secular absolutes"? How might these biases, or lack of biases, affect your teaching, planning, and approaches to moral or ethical training?

4. Do you think morals or ethics have a place in the public school curriculum? Why or why not?

5. What groups in the community might you interview to see how they would include morals and ethics in a public school curriculum? (Do not leave out groups such as home schooling groups, ACLU, or nonmainline religious groups or groups with social action agendas such as animal rights or feminist groups).

QUESTIONS TO CONSIDER

1. How can teachers help students in the socialization process?
2. Why are small (or large) schools more effective in helping students cope with their stages of growth and development?
3. What are the best methods for teaching about moral character?
4. What teaching methods can be used to improve students' thinking skills?
5. What are the attributes of critical thinking and creative thinking? Which type of thinking is more important for students to develop in school? Why?

THINGS TO DO

1. Observe two or three teachers at work in their classrooms and try to describe the social (peer) interactions taking place. How do the peer interactions differ from the teachers' expectations?
2. Spend a morning in a local school observing the social interactions of the students. Observe in the hallways, yard, cafeteria, homeroom, and auditorium. How does the school socialize students? How does the school help students cope with the problems of growing up?
3. Some observers argue that Piaget and Kohlberg ignored women in developing their moral theories. What books would you include in the curriculum to ensure the voice of women in moral education?
4. School success is partially based on the students' ability to think critically. Identify the things teachers can do to foster critical thinking among students.

5. Speak to one or two teachers to find out their views about the characteristics of intelligent and creative students. Which type of students would you prefer to teach? Why?

RECOMMENDED READINGS

Beyer, Barry K. *Teaching Thinking Skills*. Needham Heights, Mass.: Allyn & Bacon, 1991. Explains the thinking process, including critical thinking, information processing, problem solving, and decision making, and gives guidelines for improving thinking skills programs.

Havighurst, Robert J. *Developmental Tasks and Education*, 3rd ed. New York: Longman, 1972. A detailed discussion of developmental tasks to be mastered for achieving a scale of values, a philosophy of life, and successful living.

Johnson, David W. and Roger T. Johnson. *Learning Together and Alone*, 3rd ed. Englewood Cliffs, N.J.: Prentice-Hall, 1991. Practical guides for learning together and alone, as well as learning skills needed to apply knowledge in practical situations.

Kohlberg, Lawrence. *Psychology of Moral Development*. New York: Harper & Row, 1984. A theory of moral reasoning in relation to cognitive abilities and age of children.

Piaget, Jean. *The Equilibration of Cognitive Structures*, trans. and rev. ed. Chicago: University of Chicago Press, 1985. Theory of cognitive development, intelligence, and cognitive processes involved in thinking.

Raths, Louis E., Merrill Harmin, and Sidney Simon. *Values and Teaching*, 2nd ed. Columbus, Ohio: Merrill, 1978. An important text on how teachers can help students clarify values and thinking, with instructional strategies discussed in detail.

Rogers, Carl. *Freedom to Learn*, 2nd ed. Columbus, Ohio: Merrill, 1983. Methods of building freedom and choice in classrooms and developing person-centered (humanistic) teachers.

KEY TERMS

Developmental theories

Developmental tasks

Critical stages

Developmental tasks

Latchkey students

Preadolescents

Middle school

Moral character

Value clarification

Readiness

Metacognition

Comprhehension monitoring

Learning-to-learn skills

Critical thinking

Creativity

Wisdom

Intuitive thinking

Chapter 3

Classroom Management and Discipline

FOCUSING QUESTIONS

1. Why is classroom management an integral part of teaching?

2. What are some approaches to classroom management? Which ones best fit your personality and philosophy?

3. What is the best way to decide on which approach best fits your classroom management goals?

4. What are some characteristics of successful classroom managers? How many of these characteristics coincide with your management behaviors?

5. How can preventive disciplinary measures improve classroom management? Which ones best fit your personality and philosophy?

6. How can you analyze your strengths and weaknesses as a classroom manager? What means or techniques would you use to evaluate your management abilities?

*I*n order to teach, you must be able to manage your students. No matter how much potential you have as a teacher, if you are unable to control the students in your classroom, little learning will take place. Classroom management is an integral part of teaching, and techniques of managing students can and must be acquired by the teacher.

Inadequate classroom management and discipline are widely considered by the public to be the major educational problem, even though the media has spotlighted school busing, school financing, declining test scores, and student drugs. In annual Gallup polls of parents since 1970, student discipline, or the lack of it, has been listed as the number one or number two school problem each year for the last 20 years.[1]

According to a recent NEA teacher opinion poll, 90 percent of teachers maintain that student misbehavior interferes with their teaching, and nearly 25 percent claim that it greatly interferes. The same poll revealed that approximately 100,000 teachers suffer personal attacks from students annually, most often in front of other students in the classroom.[2]

The problem of discipline is persistent, especially in inner-city schools, because (1) many students lack inner control and are unwilling to defer to teacher authority, (2) many teachers lack systematic methods for dealing with discipline problems, and (3) many school administrators do not provide adequate support for teachers. According to the same NEA poll, the four major reasons the public gives for disciplinary problems in schools nationwide are parents' failure to discipline youth in the home (84 percent), increased use of drugs and alcohol (83 percent), breakup of traditional family values (72 percent), and schools' lack of authority to deal with the problem (67 percent).

APPROACHES TO CLASSROOM MANAGEMENT

Your personality, philosophy, and teaching style will directly affect your managerial and disciplinary approach. There are many approaches, but the one you adopt must be comfortable for you and coincide with your personal characteristics.

The seven approaches, or models, that are considered below are grounded in research and are applicable to classrooms. Although they are presented as distinct approaches, they do share common features. All are based on a mixture of psychology, classroom experience, and common sense. All blend elements of prevention with techniques for intervention. They recommend somewhat

1 The annual poll is published in the September or October issue of *Phi Delta Kappan*. The twenty-third survey was published in *Phi Delta Kappan* (September 1991, pp. 17–30).

2 *Public and K-12 Teacher Members* (Washington, D.C.: National Education Association, 1988).

similar measures. They differ as to the relative importance of prevention and intervention, the degree of control and supervision exercised by the teacher, and the relative emphasis on tasks and personalities. They form a continuum from firm, direct, and business-like to flexible, indirect, and democratic.

Assertive Approach

The **assertive approach** to classroom management expects teachers to specify rules of behavior and consequences for disobeying them and to communicate these rules and consequences clearly. The classroom is managed in such a way that students are not allowed to forget who is in charge of the classroom. According to Duke and Meckel, "Students come to realize that the teacher expects them to behave in a certain way in class." Teachers hold students accountable for their actions. Students who disobey rules receive "one warning and then are subjected to a series of increasingly more serious sanctions."[3] The ideas is for the teacher to respond to a student's misbehavior quickly and appropriately; mild misbehavior is matched by mild sanctions, but if the misbehavior continues, the sanctions toughen. The approach assumes that misbehavior is contagious and will snowball unless checked early. If misbehavior is ignored or not stopped at an early stage, it will eventually become uncontrollable and more and more students will become disruptive.[4]

The assertive approach is based on Lee and Marlene Canter's model of discipline in which teachers insist on responsible behavior by their students. The teacher takes charge of the classroom immediately, sets the ground rules, and interacts with students in a calm yet forceful way.[5] The teacher is expected to combine clear expectations, active response to misbehavior, and consistent follow-through with warmth and support for all students. The approach assumes that students expect this insistence on responsible behavior, that parents want it, and that the educational process comes to a halt without it.

The approach assumes that firm classroom management liberates students because it allows them to develop their best traits, skills, and abilities and provides them with psychological security in the classroom and an effective learning environment. It also assumes that good teachers can handle discipline problems on their own and that teaching failure is directly related in many classrooms to the inability to maintain adequate classroom discipline. Success, if not predicated on, at least correlates with, good discipline. The approach probably is most effective at the secondary level and in inner-city classrooms where chronic student behavior problems often exist.

---

3 Daniel L. Duke and Adrienne M. Meckel, *Teacher's Guide to Classroom Management* (New York: Random House, 1984), p. 23.

4 Allan C. Ornstein, "Techniques and Fundamentals for Teaching the Disadvantaged," *Journal of Negro Education* (Spring 1967), pp. 136–145.

5 Lee Canter and Marlene Canter, *Assertive Discipline* (Los Angeles: Canter Associates, 1979).

This type of approach was criticized in the 1960s as "authoritarian," "repressive," "militaristic," and "prejudicial" against minority students. Its acceptance today is due in part to the student disruptions of the 1970s and the general public demand in the 1980s for firmer discipline and higher academic standards for all students.

The Canters make the following suggestions for teachers applying assertive discipline:

1. Clearly identify desired behaviors and consistently point students toward those behaviors through *positive reinforcement* and recognition.
2. Apply *negative consequences* when inappropriate behavior is evidenced.
3. Take a position (Say, "I like that" or "I don't like that").
4. Use a firm tone of voice.
5. Use eye contact, gestures, and hand gestures to supplement verbal messages.
6. Say no without guilt feelings.
7. Give and receive compliments genuinely.
8. Place demands on students and enforce them.
9. Set limits on students and enforce them.
10. Indicate consequences of behavior and why specific action is necessary.
11. Be calm and consistent; avoid emotion or threats.
12. Follow through regularly.
13. Persist; enforce minimum rules; don't give up.
14. Establish positive expectations for student behavior; eliminate negative expectations about students.
15. Gain confidence and skills in working with chronic behavior problems in the classroom.[6]

The last point relates to the impact that assertive discipline has on the teacher. Teachers who are able to apply assertive discipline techniques not only have more confidence in their own abilities as teachers but also get along better with students. The assumption is that a nonassertive approach is typical of teachers who have given in to students or feel it is wrong to place demands and limitations on students. Nonassertive teachers are basically powerless to control students and often passively accept what students do or react with sarcasm, hostility, or idle threats.

The assertive model holds that teachers must establish firm management at the beginning of the year by (1) clarifying appropriate expectations of responsible behavior, (2) identifying existing or potential discipline problems, (3) deciding on negative and positive consequences of behavior that fit the

6 Ibid.

students and situation, and (4) learning how to follow through and implement these consequences. The plan is best achieved through mental rehearsal (having a good idea of what do before something occurs) and practice (learning from mistakes). In general, according to Lee Canter, "teachers need to set firm and consistent limits in their classrooms." These limits, however, "must be fair, and the consequences must be seen as outcomes of behaviors that students have chosen." The approach helps students accept responsibility for their behavior and provides "a plan that explains what will happen when students choose to misbehave."[7]

The assertive teacher does not ignore minor behavioral infractions; he or she stops the lesson to deal with inappropriate behavior, so that students learn that inappropriate behavior will be dealt with promptly. One might expect this practice to have a negative effect on academic work; tentative findings indicate the opposite. Writes one educator: "When teachers stop class immediately to deal with behavioral problems, more time-on-task is ultimately devoted to academic lessons."[8] Also, it is easier to deal with small infractions, rather than ignore them and wait until they get bigger and louder.

According to Tom Savage, novice teachers often worry about survival in the classroom and have not yet developed a successful management style. Canter's approach provides the basis for gaining control of the classroom, provides the teacher with a set of rules, and gives some security in what to do or how to react to discipline problems.[9] The problem is, the approach may not be appropriate for all inexperienced teachers and the range of recommended rules and consequences for breaking rules may not be appropriate for all students. Basically, there are more rules to enforce, and consequences for breaking rules, than most novice teachers can handle. A modified assertive approach, personalized to fit the needs of the teacher and students, is probably more feasible.

Business-Academic Approach

Well-run classrooms free from disruptions, where students behave in an orderly manner and are highly involved in learning, are not accidental. They exist where teachers have a clear idea of the type of classroom conditions (arrangement, materials), student behaviors (rules, procedures), and instructional activities (assignments, tasks) they wish to produce. The **business-academic approach**, developed by Emmer and Evertson, emphasizes the organization and management of students as they engage in academic work.[10] Task orienta-

---

7 Lee Canter, "Assertive Discipline—More than Names on the Board and Marbles in a Jar," *Phi Delta Kappan*, (September 1989), p. 59.

8 Ray Petty, "Managing Disruptive Students," *Educational Leadership* (March 1989), p. 26.

9 Tom V. Savage, *Discipline for Self-Control* (Englewood Cliffs, N.J.: Prentice-Hall, 1991).

10 Edmund T. Emmer and Carolyn M. Evertson, *Classroom Management for Secondary Teachers*, 2nd ed. (Englewood Cliffs, N.J.: Prentice-Hall, 1989).

tion, that is, focusing on the businesslike and orderly accomplishment of academic work, leads to a clear set of procedures for students and teachers to follow.

Emmer and Evertson divide organizing and managing student work into three major categories: establishment and communication of work assignments, standards, and procedures; monitoring of student work; and feedback to students.

I. *Clear communication of assignments and work requirements.* The teacher must establish and explain to students work assignments, features of the work, standards to be met, and procedures.

1. *Instruction for assignments.* Explanations should be made in both oral and written forms. In addition to telling the students about assignments, teachers should post assignments on the chalkboard or distribute duplicated copies. Students should be required to copy assignments posted on the chalkboard into their notebooks.

2. *Standards for form, neatness, and due dates.* Before students start, they should be given general rules for all assignments: type of paper and writing material to use (pencil, pen, typewriter), page numbering system, form for headings, due dates, and so forth. Students will then know what is expected of them without having to be told each time.

3. *Procedures for absent students.* Routines should be established for makeup work for absent students. These must include meeting briefly with students at a set time before or after school, assigning class helpers who will be available at particular times of the day (usually during seatwork activities) to help the students, and having a designated place where students can pick up and turn in makeup work.

II. *Monitoring student work.* Monitoring student work helps the teacher to detect students who are having difficulty and to encourage students to keep working.

1. *Monitoring group work.* Before helping any individual student with work, the teacher must be sure that all students start to work and are able to do the assignment; otherwise, some students will not even start the assignment and others may start incorrectly.

2. *Monitoring student work.* Work can be monitored several ways, including circulating around the room and giving feedback where needed, having students bring their work to the teacher one at a time at some designated point during an activity, and establishing due dates that correspond with stages in an assignment.

3. *Monitoring completion of work.* Procedures for turning in work must be established and enforced. When all students are turning in work at the same time, the best procedure is to have the work

passed in a given direction with no talking until all the work is collected.

4. *Maintaining records of student work.* It is important for teachers to keep a record of the students' work and to incorporate it as part of the grade. The record should be divided into several headings, such as workbook assignments, major assignments or projects, daily homework, and quizzes and tests.

III. *Feedback to students.* Frequent, immediate, and specific feedback is important for enhancing academic monitoring and managerial procedures. Work in progress, homework, completed assignments, tests, and other work should be checked promptly.

1. *Attention to problems.* It is important for teachers to pay careful attention at the beginning of the year to completion of classroom and homework assignments. The first time a student fails to turn in an assignment without a good reason is the time to talk to the student. If the student needs help, the teachers should provide it, but should insist at the same time that the student do the work. If the student has persistent problems completing work, then parental communication may be needed. The teachers should not wait until the grading period is over to note the problems that exist.

2. *Attention to good work.* Part of giving feedback is to acknowledge good work. This may be done by displaying the work, giving oral recognition, or writing comments.[11]

According to Emmer and Evertson, an effective manager incorporates 11 managerial methods, all of which have been shown to correlate with improved student achievement and behavior. These methods are listed in Table 3.1.

The general approach and methods used by Evertson and Emmer are appropriate for both middle and high school teachers. The approach coincides with various instructional techniques, especially Rosenshine's direct instruction (see Chapter 10), Bloom's mastery learning (Chapter 10), Ryans's pattern Y teacher (Chapter 12), and Good and Brophy's methods of effective teaching (Chapter 12).

The business-academic approach involves a high degree of "time on task" (and "academic engaged time") for students. The idea is that when students are working on their tasks, there is little opportunity for discipline problems to arise. The teacher organizes students' work, keeps them on task, monitors their work, gives them feedback, and holds them accountable by providing rewards and penalties. It is a no-play, no-frills approach, corresponding to old-

---

11 Ibid.

Table 3.1   METHODS OF EFFECTIVE CLASSROOM MANAGERS

1. *Readying the classroom*. Classroom space, materials, and equipment are ready at the beginning of the year. Effective managers have better arranged rooms, and they have coped more effectively with existing constraints.

2. *Planning rules and procedures*. Teachers make sure students understand and follow rules and procedures; they spend more time in the beginning of the year explaining and reminding students of rules.

3. *Teaching rules and procedures*. Rules and procedures are systematically taught (i.e., lining up, turning in work, etc.) and reinforced. Most of these teachers have taught their students to respond to certain cues or signals, such as a bell or the teacher's call for attention.

4. *Consequences*. Consequences for not following rules and procedures are clearly established by the teachers; there is consistent follow through.

5. *Beginning of school activities*. The first few days are spent getting students ready as a coherent and cooperative group. Once established, these teachers sustain a whole-group focus.

6. *Strategies for potential problems*. Strategies for dealing with potential problems are planned in advance. With these strategies teachers can deal with misbehavior more quickly than can less effective managers.

7. *Monitoring*. Student behavior is closely monitored; the teacher does not lose audience contact; student academic work is also monitored.

8. *Stopping inappropriate behavior*. Inappropriate or disruptive behavior is handled promptly and consistently—before it worsens or spreads.

9. *Organizing instruction*. Teachers organize instructional activities at suitable levels for all students in the class. There is a high degree of student success and content is related to student interests.

10. *Student accountability*. Procedures have been developed for keeping students accountable for their work and behavior.

11. *Instructional clarity*. Teachers provide clear instructions; these help keep students on task and allow them to learn faster, while reducing discipline problems. Directions are clear, thus confusion is minimized.

Source: Edmund T. Emmer and Carolyn M. Evertson, "Synthesis of Research on Classroom Management," *Educational Leadership* (January 1981), pp. 342-347; Emmer et al., "Effective Classroom Management at the Beginning of the School Year," *Elementary School Journal* (May 1980), pp. 219-231; and Evertson and Emmer, "Effective Management at the Beginning of the School Year in Junior High School Classes," *Journal of Educational Psychology* (vol.4, 1982), pp. 485-498.

fashioned "three Rs" and now packaged as part of the "academic productivity" movement in education.

Behavioral Modification Approach

Behavioral modification is rooted in the classic work of James Watson and the more recent work of B. F. Skinner. It involves a variety of techniques and methods, ranging from simple rewards to elaborate reinforcement training. Behaviorists assume that behavior is shaped by environment and pay little attention to the cause of problems.

Teachers using the **behavior modification approach** spend little time on the personal history of students or on searching for the reasons for a particular problem. They strive to increase the occurrence of appropriate behavior through a system of rewards and reduce the likelihood of inappropriate behavior through punishments. According to Albert Bandura, teachers would ask the following questions: (1) What is the specific behavior that requires modification (increase, reduction, elimination)? (2) When does the behavior occur? (3) What are the consequences of the behavior? Or, what happens in the classroom when the behavior is exhibited? (4) How do these consequences reinforce inappropriate behavior? How can the consequences be altered? (5) How can appropriate behavior be reinforced?[12]

The basic principles of the behavioral modification approach are as follows:

1. Behavior is shaped by its *consequences,* not by root causes in the history of the individual or by group conditions.
2. Behavior is strengthened by immediate reinforcers. *Positive reinforcers* are praise or rewards. *Negative reinforcers* take away or stop something that the student doesn't like.[13]
3. Behavior is strengthened by *systematic reinforcement* (positive or negative). Behavior is weakened if not followed by reinforcement.[14]
4. Students respond better to positive reinforcers than they do to punishment (aversive stimuli). Punishment can be used to reduce inappropriate behavior, but sparingly.
5. When a student is not rewarded for appropriate or adaptive behavior, inappropriate or maladaptive behavior may become increasingly dominant and will be utilized to obtain reinforcement.

12 Albert Bandura, *Principles of Behavioral Modification* (New York: Holt, Rinehart & Winston, 1969); Bandura, *Social Foundations of Thought and Action: A Social-Cognitive Theory* (Englewood Cliffs, N.J.: Prentice-Hall, 1986).

13 B. F. Skinner, "The Evolution of Behavior," *Journal of Experimental Analysis of Behavior* (March 1984), pp. 217–222; Skinner, "Cognitive Science and Behaviorism," *British Journal of Psychology* (August 1985), pp. 291–301.

14 Gordon H. Bower and Ernest Hilgard, *Theories of Learning,* 5th ed. (Englewood Cliffs, N.J.: Prentice-Hall, 1981).

6. *Constant reinforcement*—the reinforcement of a behavior every time it occurs—produces the best results, especially in new learning or conditioning situations.

7. Once the behavior has been learned, it is best maintained through *intermittent reinforcement*—the reinforcement of a behavior only occasionally.

8. Intermittent reinforcement schedules include (a) *variable ratio*, supplying reinforcement at unpredictable intervals, (b) *fixed ratio*, supplying reinforcement after a preselected number of responses, and (c) *fixed interval*, supplying reinforcement at preselected intervals.[15]

9. There are several types of reinforcers, each of which may be positive or aversive (examples of positive reinforcers are given); (a) *social reinforcers*, such as verbal comments ("Right," "Correct," "That's good"), facial expressions, and gestures, (b) *graphic reinforcers*, such as written words of encouragement, gold stars, and checks, (c) *tangible reinforcers*, such as cookies and badges for young students and certificates and notes to parents for older students, and (d) *activity reinforcers*, such as being a monitor or sitting near the teacher for young students and working with a friend or on a special project for older students.

10. *Rules* are established and enforced. Students who follow rules are praised and rewarded in various ways. Students who break rules are either ignored, reminded about appropriate behavior, or punished immediately. The response to rule-breaking differs somewhat in different variations of the behavioral modification approach.[16]

Each teacher has an undetermined value as a potential reinforcing agent for each student. This value is assigned initially by students on the basis of past experiences, and it changes as a result of the teacher's actions. The teacher must realize that this evaluation process is going on with the students and that a positive relationship with the students will enhance his or her potential for influencing their behavior in class. Moreover, the teacher is one of many adults who serve as reinforcing agents in the students' life. In order to facilitate the classroom management process the teacher may have to enlist the support of others.

There are a number of systems or variations of behavioral modification that are applicable to classroom management. They basically build limits and consequences into behavior and employ various rules, rewards, and punishments.

---

15 Robert F. Biehler and Jack Snowman, *Psychology Applied to Teaching*, 6th ed. (Boston: Houghton Mifflin, 1990).

16 John P. Houston, *Fundamentals of Learning and Memory*, 4th ed. (San Diego: Harcourt Brace Jovanovich, 1991); Ellen P. Reese, "Learning About Teaching from Teaching About Learning," in V. P. Makosky, ed., *The G. Stanley Hall Lecture Series*, vol. 6 (Washington, D.C.: American Psychological Association, 1986), pp. 65–128.

A well-known system utilized in various social learning situations is termed **modeling**.

Models are effective in modifying behavior to the degree that they capture attention, hold attention, and are imitated. Effective models may be parents, relatives, teachers, other adults (community residents), public figures (sports people, movie stars), and peers. The best models are those that individuals can identify with on the basis of one or more of the following traits: (1) sex, (2) age, (3) ethnicity, (4) physical attractiveness, (5) personality attractiveness, (6) competence, (7) power, and (8) ability to reward imitators. Teachers who want to use modeling in classroom management should recognize that the first five are personal characteristics that are hard to change, but the last three are institutional and role characteristics that are easier to manipulate to increase their effectiveness as models.

Building good discipline through modeling includes the following:

1. *Demonstration*. Students know exactly what is expected. In addition to having expected behavior explained to them, they see and hear it.
2. *Attention*. Students focus their attention on what is being depicted or explained. The degree of attention correlates with the characteristics of the model (teacher) and characteristics of the students.
3. *Practice*. Students are given opportunity to practice the appropriate behavior.
4. *Corrective feedback*. Students receive frequent, specific, and immediate feedback. Appropriate behavior is reinforced; inappropriate behavior is discouraged and corrected.
5. *Application*. Students are able to apply their learning in classroom activities (role playing, modeling activities) and other real-life situations.[17]

The teacher's role in modeling includes (1) selecting behavior to be learned, (2) ensuring that the behavior is modeled clearly and accurately, (3) helping students focus attention on what is being modeled, (4) providing suitable practice of the behavior, (5) providing corrective feedback during student re-enactment, and (6) providing reinforcement following desired behavior.[18]

Group Managerial Approach

The **group managerial approach** to discipline is based on Jacob Kounin's research. He emphasizes the importance of responding immediately to group

17 Albert Bandura et al., "Representing Personal Determinants in Causal Structures," *Journal of Personality and Social Psychology* (June 1985), pp. 406–414; Shelby R. Cohen, "Models Inside and Outside the Classroom: A Force for Desirable Learning," *Contemporary Education* (Summer 1980), pp. 186–188; and B. F. Skinner, "The Evaluation of Verbal Behavior," *Journal of Experimental Analysis of Behavior* (January 1986), pp. 115–122.

18 C. M. Charles, *Building Classroom Discipline*, 3rd ed. (New York: Longman, 1989); Vernon F. Jones and Louise S. Jones, *Comprehensive Classroom Management* (Needham Heights, Mass.: Allyn & Bacon, 1990).

student behavior that might be inappropriate or undesirable in order to prevent problems rather than having to deal with them after they emerge. He describes what he calls the "ripple effect."[19] If a student misbehaves, but the teacher stops the misbehavior immediately, it remains an isolated incident and does not develop into a problem. If the misbehavior is not noticed, is ignored, or is allowed to continue for too long, it often spreads throughout the group and becomes more serious and chronic.

Kounin analyzes classroom activities for purposes of management by dividing them into categories of pupil behavior and teacher management behavior (see Table 3.2). Major categories of pupil behavior are work involvement and deviancy. Major categories of teacher behavior are desist techniques, movement management, and group focus.

Work involvement is the amount of time students spend engaged in assigned academic work. (Other researchers call it "time on task" or "academic engaged time.") Students who are involved in work (writing in a workbook, reciting, reading, watching a demonstration) exhibit fewer disciplinary problems than students who are not involved in any assigned task. If the teacher keeps students involved in work, there is less chance that boredom and discipline problems will arise.

Deviancy ranges from no misbehavior to serious misbehavior. *No misbehavior* means the student is not purposefully misbehaving, but nevertheless is upsetting another student or teacher or is slightly off task. *Mild misbehavior* includes such actions as whispering, making faces, teasing, reading a comic, passing notes. *Serious misbehavior* is aggressive or harmful behavior that interferes with others or violates school or social codes. The point is not to permit mild misbehavior to degenerate into serious misbehavior by dealing with mild misbehavior as soon as it occurs. See Tips for Teachers 3.1.

Desist techniques are teacher actions taken to stop misbehavior. Kounin feels that they depend on two abilities. *With-it-ness* is the ability to react on target (react to the proper student) and in a timely fashion. It also involves communicating to students that one knows what is happening, or as Kounin puts it, that one "has eyes in the back of one's head." *Overlapping* behavior refers to the teacher's ability to handle more than one matter at a time. He or she can attend to more than one student at the same time—say, a student who is reciting and another student who is interrupting with a question or comment.

Movement management is the organization of behavior in transitions from task to task within and between lessons. Movement may be characterized as smooth or jerky. *Smoothness* is an even and calm flow of activities. It involves uninterrupted work periods and short, fluid transitions that are made automatically and without disruption. In particular, the teacher (1) avoids unnecessary announcements and interruptions when students are busy doing work, (2)

---

19 Jacob S. Kounin, *Discipline and Group Management in Classrooms* (New York: Holt, Rinehart & Winston, 1970); Kounin, *Discipline and Classroom Management* (New York: Holt, Rinehart & Winston, 1977).

Table 3.2   KOUNIN'S BEHAVIORS AND CATEGORIES FOR OBSERVING CLASSROOM MANAGEMENT

Categories of pupil behavior	
I. Work Involvement	*II. Deviancy*
A. Encourage	A. No misbehavior
B. Permit	B. Mild misbehavior
C. Discourage	C. Serious misbehavior

Categories of teacher management behavior	
I. Desist Techniques	*III. Group Focus*
A. "With-it-ness"	A. Alerting
1. Target student	1. Encourage suspense
2. Timely fashion	2. Pick reciter randomly
B. Overlapping	3. Call on nonvolunteers
1. Multiple behaviors	4. Present new materials
	5. Ignore group in favor of reciter
II. Movement Management	6. Select reciter before asking question
A. Smoothness-Jerkiness	7. Ask question, then call reciter
1. Stimulus-bounded	B. Accountability
2. Thrust	1. Ask students to hold up props
3. Dangle	2. Actively attend to mass unison response
4. Truncation	3. Call on others
5. Flip-flop	4. Ask for volunteers
B. Momentum	5. Check products of nonreciters
1. Overdwelling	6. Require student to demonstrate performance
2. Fragmentation	7. Review frequently

Source: Adapted from Jacob Kounin, *Discipline and Group Management in Classrooms* (New York: Holt, Rinehart & Winston, 1970), Chaps. 3, 7.

finishes one activity before starting on the next, and (3) doesn't abruptly end or start an activity. *Jerkiness* is a disorderly flow of activities. It may result if the teacher tries to do too many things at once or does not make clear to students procedures for ending one task and changing to a new one. The teacher may have to shout during transitions, disorder may arise as students have to ask questions about what to do, and unengaged students may create disruptions. In order to prevent jerkiness, five subcategories of behavior should be avoided.

> **1.** *Stimulus-bounded.* The teacher is so immersed in a small group of students or activity that he or she ignores other students or misses an event that is potentially disruptive.

Tips for Teachers 3.1

Dealing with Student Emotions

Young adolescents tend to exhibit great variation in moods and emotions. Some students tend to be hostile, defiant, or angry; others tend to be nervous, excitable, and hyperactive; still others tend to be awkward, withdrawn, and overanxious to please.

An effective classroom manager must be able to deal with the emotions of students. Below are ten suggestions written by a dean of students to assist teachers.

1. *Try to have contact with students before a disciplinary situation arises.* Eating with students in the lunchroom, watching them perform in athletic or theatrical events (and commenting later), or engaging in a conversation with them in the schoolyard builds rapport with students and can be utilized during a disciplinary situation.

2. *Listen to the student before you speak.* Not only does this tactic ensure greater trust, it also gives the teacher the opportunity to better understand and evaluate the student's attitude toward the offense; it gives the teacher opportunity to determine whether the student was acting deliberately or out of emotion, or possibly from some unexpected motivation.

3. *Be consistent.* One must give roughly the same penalty for similar offenses; likewise, one cannot "change the rules in the middle of the game."

4. *Never try to force a student to tell a lie.* The teacher should be open and honest with the student; he or she should expect the same from the student.

5. *Never react with anger or emotion.* While all teachers have emotions, they should remain calm even under stressful conditions and not act or react out of anger or emotion in meting out punishment.

6. *Be firm and don't retreat because the student becomes angry.* Students sometimes project anger toward teachers, especially when frustrated. Avoid reacting to the anger and remain focused on the student's behavior. Do not let the student's anger, which often cannot be controlled, diminish your relationship.

7. *Concentrate on the lesson to be learned, not the punishment.* Understanding why the student did what he did and helping him learn how to avoid future behavior that will result in serious consequences helps determine whether the incident will be a learning experience for the student.

(continues)

> 8. *Try to find something positive to say.* A student's self-image is often at stake, when the student is exhibiting strong emotions; it is important for the teacher to find something positive in the student's recent behavior or performance that deserves a compliment.
> 9. *Find a way to bring closure to the situation.* Youngsters expect to be punished when they are wrong, but they don't want to be continuously reminded of their past mistakes. After the incident, or punishment, forget the situation and be sure the student feels he or she has a new lease or clean bill of health.
> 10. *Communicate with parents.* Let the student know that the parents will be told, but be sure the communication is not intercepted by the student.
>
> *Source:* Adapted from Raymond P. Deering, "Discipline: Dealing with Emotions," *NASSP Bulletin* (February 1988), pp. 105-106.

2. *Thrust.* The teacher bursts into activities without assessing student readiness and gives orders, statements, or questions that only confuse the students.
3. *Dangle.* The teacher ends an activity or drops a topic before it is completed.
4. *Truncation.* The teacher ends an activity abruptly.
5. *Flip-flop.* The teacher terminates one activity, goes to another, and then returns to the previously terminated activity. The teacher lacks clear direction and sequence of activities.

Movement management also involves *momentum*, that is, keeping activities at an appropriate "pace." Momentum is slowed or impeded if the teacher engages in overdwelling or fragmentation. *Overdwelling* may take the form of giving explanations beyond what is necessary for most students' understanding, or lecturing, preaching, nagging, overemphasizing, or giving too many directions. *Fragmentation* takes the form of giving too much detail, breaking things down into too many steps, or duplicating or repeating activities. For example, a teacher who calls students to the desk to read, one by one, when one student can read aloud while the others listen, is engaging in fragmentation.

Group focus is keeping the students focused on the group activity or task. It can be achieved by what Kounin calls *alerting.* Alerting activities include creating suspense, presenting new material, choosing reciters randomly, and selecting reciters (see Table 3.2 for other methods Kounin lists). Group focus can also be achieved by using *accountability.* This involves such methods as asking students to hold up props, circulating to check the products of nonreciters, and requiring students to perform and checking their performance (see Table 3.2).

Kounin believes that work involvement, smoothness, and momentum are enhanced by instructional techniques that facilitate learning. Student *satiation* (boredom) can be avoided in three ways: by providing a feeling of *progress*, providing *challenges*, and adding *variety* to the lessons.

In summary, Kounin believes that student engagement in lessons and activities is the key to successful classroom management. Students are expected to work and behave. The successful teacher monitors student work in a systematic fashion, clearly defines acceptable and unacceptable behavior, and exhibits with-it-ness and overlapping abilities. The successful teacher has a clear sense of direction and sequence for tasks. Smooth transitions are made from one activity to another, so that student attention is turned easily from one activity to another. Similarly, lessons are well paced.

Almost all of the major theorists of classroom management—Brophy, Doyle, Emmer, Evertson, and Good—have been influenced by Kounin. Most of what they say, today, was said by Kounin 20 years ago.

Group Guidance Approach

The **group guidance approach** is based on manipulating (a better word is "changing") the surface behavior of the students on a group basis. Since teachers have few opportunities to work with students on an individual basis, they must learn to work with groups of students and to maintain group focus on the content and tasks of the group. Discipline and classroom control are produced through the group atmosphere and enhanced through group rapport.

The work of Fritz Redl and his colleagues with delinquent and disruptive students is the basis for much of the group guidance approach. He holds that disciplinary problems have three causes.

1. *Individual case history.* The problem is related to the psychological disturbance of one child; disruptive behavior in class is part of the child's larger emotional problem. The surface problems are repetitive since they arise from the individual case history.
2. *Group conditions.* The problem reflects unfavorable conditions in the group. It is easier to resolve than a problem produced by a case history.
3. *Mixture of individual and group causes.* The problem centers on an individual but is triggered by something in the group. A remedy must consider both elements.[20]

---

20 Fritz Redl and David Wineman, *Children Who Hate* (New York: Free Press, 1951); George V. Scheviakov and Fritz Redl, *Discipline for Today's Children and Youth* (Washington, D.C.: National Education Association, 1957).

According to Redl's research, 10 percent of all cases of school discipline are simple cases of individual disturbances, about 30 percent involve group conditions or inadequacies, and 60 percent seem to include both individual and group factors. This means 90 percent of all discipline cases indicate a need for group remediation, or what he refers to as "group psychological engineering."[21]

In analyzing a disciplinary situation, Redl contends that teachers must ask themselves to what extent problems reflect elements of the group, the teacher's own behavior, and the behavior of the students. To maintain good discipline, the teacher must understand the group—its needs and interests—and be able to manipulate the surface behavior of the group. Group elements to be considered include the following:

1. *Dissatisfaction with classroom work.* The work is too easy or too difficult. The work load is too light or too heavy. Assignments are poorly planned or poorly explained. Assignments are considered unfair by students because they have not been prepared for them. Learning experiences emphasize verbalization, omitting motor skills and manipulative activities. Work is badly scheduled, badly sequenced, or confusing.

2. *Poor interpersonal relations.* Problems are caused by friendships or tensions among individuals, cliques, or subgroups; by badly filled group roles (for example, teacher assistant, tutor-tutoree); and by student-teacher friction.

3. *Disturbances in group climate.* The climate is punitive, tinged with partiality (certain children can do no wrong, others are accused of almost anything); too competitive (leading to hostile or defeatist attitudes); too exclusive (the group rejects individuals who don't fit).

4. *Poor group organization.* The group is characterized by too much autocratic pressure or too little supervision and security. Standards for group behavior are too high or too low. The group is too highly organized (too many rules) or too unstructured. The group organization is out of focus with the age, developmental maturity, social background, needs, or abilities of the group members.

5. *Sudden changes and group emotions.* The group is experiencing a high level of anxiety (for example, just before exam period). Contemporary events lead to unusual depression, fear, or excitement. Students are bored (there is lack of interest or emotion).[22]

According to Redl and his colleagues, boredom is one of the major causes of disciplinary problems, and it leads to withdrawal, frustration and irritability, or aggressive rejection of the entire group on the part of the students.[23] When-

---

21 Scheviakov and Redl, *Discipline for Today's Children and Youth.*

22 Fritz Redl and David Wineman, *Controls from Within* (New York: Free Press, 1952); Scheviakov and Redl, *Discipline for Today's Children and Youth.*

23 Ibid.

The fact that adolescents need to be accepted by their age-mates gives the peer group great influence and must be considered in managing students.

ever something is wrong with the organizational composition (for example, in relation to student needs, abilities, or age), discipline problems are inevitable.

Perhaps one of the most difficult managerial tasks for the teachers is dealing with a hostile or aggressive group. Such a classroom group subtly and overtly defies the teacher and disrupts instructional activities. Among the symptoms that reveal this condition are:

1. Continual talking, lack of attention when instructional tasks are presented.
2. Constant disruptions that interfere with teaching.
3. Overall nonconformity to classroom rules or school practices.
4. Overt challenges and refusal to obey.
5. Group solidarity in resisting the teacher's efforts.[24]

24 Anne M. Bauer and Regina H. Sapona, *Managing Classrooms to Facilitate Learning* (Englewood Cliffs, N.J.: Prentice-Hall, 1991); James S. Cangelosi, *Classroom Management Strategies* (New York: Longman, 1988).

A class group with these symptoms usually continues to be aggressive and resistant long after the cause of the behavior is removed. When group members act together to defy and resist the teacher's efforts, the teacher may react by trying to match force with force. In some cases the teacher's behavior is the source of the problem—being inconsistent in enforcing rules, yelling or making idle threats, displaying frequent outbursts of emotion, giving assignments that lack challenge, variety, or interest. In such situations teachers often mistakenly identify the ringleaders or the entire group as causes of the problem rather than looking to their own behavior.

In other cases the problem can be traced to the students' attitudes toward authority, and has little to do with the teacher. Here the teacher must be able to change the students' feelings of hostility to trust and confidence. According to educators, this difficult task of developing a positive working relationship with the students on an individual and group basis involves reacting with sensitivity to the needs and feelings of students, making an effort to understand students' individual problems, showing trust and respect for them, listening to and observing them, diagnosing what has to be done to manipulate their surface behavior in a group, providing meaningful work, and encouraging on-task behavior.[25]

Of course, if teachers do not diagnose management problems correctly, especially group managerial problems, the problems will persist and increase. When such problems exist, having group discussions with students can be helpful for exploring differences and identifying causes of conflict. But the teacher needs human-relation skills in working with groups. A safer and more conservative strategy is for the teacher, alone or with colleagues, to analyze how his or her own behavior affects the group, how individual student case histories create difficulties, and how group factors are reflected in the problem.

Acceptance Approach

The **acceptance approach** to discipline is rooted in humanistic psychology and maintains that every person has a prime need for acceptance. Students, like everyone else, strive for acceptance. They want to belong and to be liked by others who are important to them more than they want to learn. Similarly, they would rather behave than misbehave. The acceptance approach is also based on the democratic model of teaching in which the teacher provides leadership by establishing rules and consequences, but at the same time allows students to participate in decisions and to make choices.

Rudolph Dreikurs is noted for a disciplinary approach based on the need for acceptance.[26] He maintains that acceptance by peers and teachers is the prereq-

---

25 Arlene Breckenridge, "Performance Improvement Program Helps Adminstrators Assess Counselor Performance," *NASSP Bulletin* (February 1987), pp. 23–28; Jere E. Brophy, "Educating Teachers About Managing Classrooms and Students," *Teaching and Teacher Education* (vol. 4 (1988), pp. 1–18; and Fred T. Wilhelms, "The Gentlest Need," *Educational Leadership* (September 1990), pp. 51–52.

26 Rudolph Dreikurs, *Psychology in the Classroom*, 2nd ed. (New York: Harper & Row, 1968); Rudolph Dreikurs and Pearl Cassel, *Discipline Without Tears*, rev. ed. (New York: Dutton, 1988).

uisite for appropriate behavior and achievement in school. People try all kinds of behavior to get status and recognition. If they are not successful in receiving recognition through socially acceptable methods, then they will turn to mistaken goals that result in antisocial behavior. Dreikurs identifies four mistaken goals:

1. *Attention getting.* When students are not getting the recognition they desire, they often resort to attention-getting misbehavior. They want other students or the teacher to pay attention to them. They may act as the "class clown," ask special favors, continually seek help with assignments, refuse to work unless the teacher hovers over them. They function as long as they obtain their peers' or teacher's attention.

2. *Power seeking.* Students may also express their desire for recognition by defying adults to achieve what they perceive as power. Their defiance is expressed in arguing, contradicting, teasing, temper tantrums, and low-level hostile behavior. If the students get the teacher to argue or fight with them, they win because they succeed in getting the teacher involved in a power struggle.

3. *Revenge seeking.* Students who fail to gain recognition through power may seek revenge. Their mistaken goal is to hurt others to make up for being hurt or feeling rejected and unloved. Students who seek revenge don't care about being punished. They are cruel, hostile, violent toward others. Simple logic doesn't work with them. Being punished gives them renewed cause for action. The more trouble they cause for themselves, the more justified they feel.

4. *Withdrawal.* If students feel helpless and rejected, the goal of their behavior may become withdrawal from the social situation rather than confrontation. They guard whatever little self-esteem they have by removing themselves from situations that test their abilities. Such withdrawal displays their feelings of inadequacy. If not helped, they eventually become isolated.[27]

The first thing teachers need to do is to identify students' mistaken goals. The type of misbehavior indicates the type of expectations students have for their mistaken goal.

1. If students stop the behavior and then repeat it, their goal is *getting attention*.
2. If students refuse to stop or increase their misbehavior, their goal is *power seeking*.
3. If students become hostile or violent, their goal is *getting revenge*.
4. If students refuse to cooperate or participate, their goal is *withdrawal*.

---

27 Rudolph Dreikurs, Bernice B. Grunwald, and Floyd C. Pepper, *Maintaining Sanity in the Classroom*, 2nd ed. (New York: Harper & Row, 1982); Rudolph Dreikurs and Loren Grey, *Logical Consequences: A New Approach to Discipline* (New York: Dutton, 1988).

After teachers identify the mistaken goals, they need to confront the students with an explanation of what they are doing. Dreikurs maintains that by doing this in a friendly, nonthreatening way, teachers can get students to examine—even change—their behavior. The teachers should then encourage students in their efforts to recognize their mistaken goals and to change their behavior. Dreikurs sees an important distinction between encouraging and praising. *Encouragement* consists of words or actions that convey respect and belief in students' abilities. It tells students they are accepted; it recognizes efforts, not achievements. *Praise*, on the other hand, is given when a task is achieved. It promotes the idea that an action is worthless unless it receives praise. (This concept contradicts Brophy, who believes in realistic praise; see Chapter 7.)

Finally, the teacher needs to be sure the students are aware of and understand the consequences of inappropriate behavior. The consequences must be as closely related to the misbehavior as possible, and the teacher must apply them consistently, immediately, and in a calm manner, displaying no anger or triumph. For example, failing to complete a homework assignment means staying after school and finishing it. Disturbing others in class results in isolation from the group for a short period. Students gradually learn that poor choices result in unpleasant consequences, which are nobody's fault but their own. Eventually, students learn to control their actions and to make better decisions, and thus they reach a point where their behavior is controlled by self-discipline.

Dreikurs suggests several strategies for working with students who exhibit mistaken goals to encourage them and to enforce consequences. These points are listed in Table 3.3.

Success Approach

The **success approach**, like the acceptance approach, is rooted in humanistic psychology and the democratic model of teaching. However, instead of dealing with inappropriate behavior and the consequences of such behavior, it deals with general psychological and social conditions. William Glasser, most noted for this approach, which he calls reality therapy, insists that although teachers should not excuse bad behavior on the part of the student, they need to change whatever negative classroom conditions exist and improve conditions so they lead to student success.[28]

Glasser's view about discipline is simple but powerful. Behavior is a matter of choice. Good behavior results from good choices; bad behavior results from bad choices. A teacher's job is to help students make good choices. Students make choices according to whether they see the results of those choices as desirable. If bad behavior gets them what they want, they will make bad choices.

---

28 William W. Glasser, *Reality Therapy: A New Approach to Psychiatry* (New York: Harper & Row, 1965).

Table 3.3 STRATEGIES FOR CARRYING OUT THE ACCEPTANCE APPROACH

To encourage students	To enforce consequences
1. Be positive; avoid negative statements.	1. Give clear directions.
2. Encourage students to improve, not to be perfect.	2. Establish a relationship with each student based on mutual trust and respect.
3. Encourage effort; results are secondary if students try.	3. Consequences must be logical; a direct relationship between misbehavior and consequences must be understood by students.
4. Emphasize strengths; minimize weaknesses.	
5. Teach students to learn from mistakes.	4. Put behavior in its proper perspective; avoid making issues out of trivial incidents.
6. Stimulate motivation; do not exert undue pressure.	
7. Encourage student independence.	5. Permit students to assume responsibility for their own behavior.
8. Exhibit faith in student's abilities.	6. Treat students as social equals.
9. Offer to help overcome student's obstacles.	7. Combine friendliness with firmness; students must see the teachers as a friend, but limitations must be established.
10. Encourage cooperative or team effort among students.	
11. Send positive notes home; note improvement.	8. Distinguish between the deed and doer. React to the behavior, not the person.
12. Show pride in student's work; display it.	9. Set limits at the beginning, but work toward a sense of responsibility on the part of the student.
13. Be optimistic, enthusiastic, supporting.	
14. Set up situations that lead to success for all.	10. Keep demands or rules simple.
15. Use encouraging remarks: "I know you can"; "Keep trying"; "Thatta boy."	11. Mean what you say; carry out your rules.
	12. Close an incident quickly; revive good spirits; mistakes are corrected, then forgotten.

Source: Adapted from Rudolf Dreikurs, *Maintaining Sanity in the Classroom,* 2nd ed. (New York: Harper & Row. 1982).

Students who have feelings of positive self-worth and experience success will make good choices most of the time. The road to positive self-worth and to success begins with a good relationship with people who care. For some students school may be the only place where they meet people who genuinely care for them. Yet, some students resist entering into positive relationships with adults, especially teachers. Teachers, therefore, must show that they care and are positive, and they must be persistent about both. The emphasis is on helping—exactly what the teaching profession is about—and therefore the approach is attractive to many educators.

Glasser makes the following suggestions:

1. *Stress students' responsibility for their own behavior continually.* Since good behavior comes from good choices, their responsibility for their choices and behavior must be explored and clarified on a regular basis.

2. *Establish rules.* Rules are essential, but they should be established and agreed upon early in the term by the teacher and students. Rules should facilitate group achievement and group morale. Rules can be evaluated and changed, but as long as they are retained, they must be enforced.

3. *Accept no excuses.* The teacher should not accept excuses for inappropriate behavior as long as the student is able to distinguish right from wrong. This is especially true if the student has made a commitment to a rule.

4. *Utilize value judgments.* When students exhibit inappropriate behavior, the teacher should call on them to make value judgments about their behavior. This enhances the students' responsibility to make better choices.

5. *Suggest suitable alternatives.* Alternatives to inappropriate behavior should be suggested by the teacher. The students should make the choice, one which reinforces their responsibility.

6. *Enforce reasonable consequences.* Reasonable consequences must follow whatever behavior the students choose. The consequences of inappropriate behavior should not be erratic, emotional, sarcastic, or physically punishing. The consequences of good behavior should be satisfying to students. The teacher should never manipulate events or make excuses so that reasonable consequences do not occur after a behavior is exhibited.

7. *Be persistent.* The teacher must repeatedly and constantly make sure that students are committed to desirable behavior. The teacher must always help students make choices and have them make value judgments about bad choices.

8. *Continually review.* Topics and issues relevant to these procedures should be discussed and developed during a classroom meeting separate from academic activities. This is the time for students and teacher to seek plausible solutions to problems. Students should never be allowed to find fault with or place blame on others, to shout or threaten. If attention is directed to real matters of concern, a bonding or caring attitude between teacher and students may have a chance to take form.[29]

Glasser makes the point that teachers must be supportive and meet with students who are beginning to exhibit difficulties, and they must get students involved in making rules, making commitments to the rules, and enforcing them. School must be a friendly, warm place, especially for students who have previously experienced failure in school. Student misbehavior is often intertwined with academic problems. The failing student, frustrated by an inability to function in the classroom, frequently expresses uneasiness by acting out. To

---

29 William R. Glasser, *School Without Failure* (New York: Harper & Row, 1969).

correct an academic problem, the student, teacher, and school must make a specific commitment to overcome the problem. Too often the student is unaware of how to deal with the problem, the teacher is too burdened with other problems, and the school lacks the resources for helping the student and teacher.[30]

For Glasser, school reform is not linked to stimulating teachers and students to work harder. People, including students, will not be more productive unless what is being asked of them is psychologically satisfying. We have to change school not by changing the length of the school day or year or the amount of homework, but by making it more satisfying to students and more consistent with their interests, so that they gain a sense of power, fulfillment, and importance in the classroom. Solutions to the problems of discipline and achievement are related and based primarily on making students feel that someone listens to them, thinks about them, cares for them, and feels they are important.[31]

Although Glasser is somewhat vague on just what teachers can do in dealing with academic or behavior problems, most of his ideas involve time set aside for therapeutic sessions, encounter groups, or other forms of group discussion. For this reason, more elementary and junior high school teachers use this approach than high school teachers. The high school teachers are not expected to deal with social or psychological problems of students on a regular basis, and they tend to be more concerned with subject matter. His approach also involves a certain amount of warmth, genuineness, and concern for the whole child, his or her social, psychological, and cognitive needs. For this reason, progressive educators tend to adapt many of Glasser's ideas without even knowing that they are his, since many of his ideas also coincide with classic progressive thinkers from Pestalozzi and Frobel to Parker and Washburne.

Guidelines for Implementing Alternative Approaches to Classroom Management

---

All seven approaches have elements of prevention and intervention, and all, regardless of how firm or flexible they appear to be, deal with a set of rules, limitations, and consequences of behavior. In all the approaches students must complete academic work and they are held accountable for their behavior and work. A brief overview of the seven approaches is shown in Table 3.4.

Whereas all the approaches advocate having clear and well-communicated *rules*, the firmer approaches expect the teacher to assert more power and

---

30 William R. Glasser, *Control Theory in the Classroom* (New York: Harper & Row, 1986).

31 Pauline B. Gough, "The Key to Improving Schools: An Interview with William Glasser," *Phi Delta Kappan* (May 1987), pp. 656–662.

Table 3.4 OVERVIEW OF CLASSROOM MANAGEMENT MODELS

I. Canter Model
1. Firm, assertive approach
2. Insistence on appropriate behavior
3. Clear limits and consequences
4. Taking action promptly
5. Follow through, checking, and reinforcing rules

II. Emmer-Evertson Model
1. Identifying and enforcing school and class-room rules
2. Procedures for seatwork, teacher-led activities, transition between activities
3. Purposeful academic instruction, student accountability
4. Procedures for assignments and monitoring student work

III. Skinner-Bandura Model
1. Reinforcement through rewards
2. Constant and then intermittent reinforcement produces the best results
3. Shaping desired behavior quickly and strongly
4. Modeling appropriate behavior
5. Use of verbal comments, observations, practice, prizes, etc.

IV. Kounin Model
1. Group focus and group management
2. On task, work involvement
3. With-it-ness, overlapping, smoothness, and momentum
4. Variety and challenging instruction
5. Teacher alertness, student accountability

V. Redl Model
1. Group manipulation and group rapport
2. Curtailing misbehavior at early stages
3. Student self-control and self-discipline

VI. Dreikurs Model
1. Acceptance of and belonging to a group
2. Student recognition and praise
3. Routines and limitations
4. Firmness and friendliness
5. Teacher leadership, corrective action by teacher

VII. Glasser Model
1. Student success and achievement
2. Reasonable rules with reasonable consequences
3. Student responsibility and self-direction
4. Good choices result in good behavior
5. Teacher support, fairness, and warmth

authority with students. The more flexible approaches rely more on mutual trust and respect between teacher and students. The more assertive approaches look to the teacher to take control of the classroom and quickly establish rules. The more humanistic approaches emphasize positive expectations of students; they have more faith in the students' ability to exhibit self-control and to work out the rules with their peers and the teacher.

Although all the approaches establish *limitations*, the flexible approaches permit greater latitude in enforcing rules and allow the students to share power with the teacher. In the firmer approaches the teacher asserts authority, takes charge, and tends to intervene immediately and automatically in all cases of misbehavior, even mild ones (on the theory that this will prevent more serious problems).

All the approaches rely on *consequences*. The difference is that the firm approaches advocate stricter imposition of generally more severe sanctions as a consequence of disobedience. Punishment for inappropriate behavior is permissible as long as it is logical and related to the severity of the disturbance. The flexible approaches impose sanctions, but emphasize making students aware that their behavior influences others, helping them to examine their behavior, and helping them to identify the consequences of their misbehavior.

All the approaches hold students *accountable* for academic work. The firmer approaches limit students' socializing and group activities, determine academic tasks, and demand that they complete assignments. Students are told what is expected of them and little time is spent in any activities other than academic work. The classroom is organized so that students' engagement in academic work is continuous. In the more flexible approaches students are still accountable for academic work, but they participate in planning the curriculum, and socializing is tolerated. Engagement in academic tasks is less intense and work is often performed on a cooperative or group basis.

Regardless of the approach, the real test is its use by teachers in the classroom. In contemplating any model of discipline, one educator asserts that it must be judged in terms of five general criteria; it must be (1) philosophically sound, (2) pedagogically defensible, (3) psychologically appropriate, (4) pragmatically feasible, and (5) professionally evaluated.[32]

There are few absolutes in dealing with difficult discipline problems, but teachers need a systematic way to respond to discipline problems; also, they need criteria (like the five above) to guide their options or potential strategies.

In choosing an approach, teachers must be objective about their personality and philosophy and what they are trying to accomplish. It is important that they be honest about themselves—their strengths and weaknesses. To be sure, teachers vary in their ability to handle discipline problems; but regrettably, teacher-educators often make it sound easy to manage students and often provide novice teachers with a host of strategies that conflict with the personality or philosophy of the teacher. It is also essential to understand, according to Tom Lasley, that the efficacy of any approach depends on the classroom context, that is, the student group and individual student. It is silly to expect to set the same rules for all students, or expect the same reaction from all students. Teachers need to identify their own predispositions and match them with the students' developmental levels and needs before employing specific management techniques.[33] To help determine the approach that is best, Duke and Meckel have constructed a series of questions that try to identify teacher goals and values and also consider specific student and school criteria, such as the age of students and established school policies (see Table 3.5).

---

32 Thomas R. McDaniel, "The Discipline Debate: A Road Through the Thicket," *Educational Leadership* (March 1989), pp. 81–82.

33 Tom Lasley, "A Teacher Development Model for Classroom Management," Phi Delta Kappan (September 1989), pp. 36–38. Also see Theodore A Chandler, "Why Discipline Strategies are Bound to Fail," *Clearing House* (November-December 1990), pp. 124–126

Table 3.5   QUESTIONS TO HELP DETERMINE WHICH CLASSROOM MANAGEMENT
APPROACHES TO ADOPT

Teacher criteria: consider your goals and values

1. What are my primary goals in classroom management?

2. Which classroom management approaches address these goals?

3. What are my values or beliefs concerning classroom management?

4. Which classroom management approaches consider these values and beliefs?

5. Which classroom approaches are consistent with my goals and values?

Student criteria: consider their needs and problems

1. What are the age and maturity of my students?

2. Which classroom management approaches are best suited to my students?

3. What is the past disciplinary record of my students?

4. Which classroom management approaches are best suited to my students' past disciplinary record?

5. What are the backgrounds of my students?

6. Which classroom management approaches are most suited to my students' background?

7. What are the abilities and interests of my students?

8. Which classroom management approaches are most suited to my students' abilities and interests?

9. How much support can I expect from my students' parents?

10. Which classroom management approaches are best suited to the expected level of parental support?

School criteria: consider its policies and procedures

1. How much support can I expect from the school administration?

2. Which classroom management approaches coincide with the administrative philosophy or policy?

3. What aspects of each approach coincide to school district or school guidelines?

4. What aspects of each approach conflict with school district or school guidelines?

5. Which classroom management approaches coincide most and conflict least with school district or school guidelines?

Source: Adapted from Daniel L. Duke and Adrienne M. Meckel, *Teacher's Guide to Classroom Management* (New York: Random House, 1984), pp. 123-125, 127.

Still another point to consider is that some educators are quick to package programs that are discussed in the professional literature or advertised as "reform" or a "quick fix." It is wrong to assume that a process as complicated and multidimensional as managing students can be understood by reading a list of do's and dont's or attending a two-day workshop.[34]

Certain rules are central to all the models, but they are conceptual and must be modified according to the classroom situation and personalities involved. The models should not be construed as lockstep or set in stone; for example, "Raise your hand when you wish to speak." There are many gray areas involved in managing students that involve common sense and maturity by the teacher. The models, if taken literally, limit teacher discretion and judgment and in some cases only offer one option for teachers when a rule is violated.

The point is, teachers need to be flexible and examine the models in relationship to their own classroom situation and personality. But, according to experts, the models are supported by research and they provide an effective strategy for teachers to use, as well as a way to respond to real discipline problems.[35] They are the best we have now, and teachers do need an effective strategy now to apply in the classroom.

In considering what is best for you, you must consider your teaching style, your students' needs and abilities, and your school's policies. As you narrow your choices, remember that approaches overlap and are not mutually exclusive. Also remember that more than one approach may work for you. You may borrow ideas from various approaches and construct your own hybrid. The approach you finally arrive at should make sense to you on an intuitive basis. Don't let someone impose his or her teaching style or disciplinary approach on you. Remember, what works for one person (in the same school, even with the same students) may not work for another person.

PUNISHMENT

Educators disagree as to the extent to which misbehavior should be ignored. Although it seems contrary to the teacher's normal tendency, some researchers have found repeatedly that the best procedure is to ignore undesirable behavior while paying attention to and reinforcing desirable behavior.[36] If this is the case,

---

34 Richard L. Curwin and Allen N. Mendter, "Packaged Discipline Programs: Let the Buyer Beware," *Educational Leadership* (October 1988), pp. 68–71; Gary F. Render et al., "What Research Really Shows About Assertive Discipline," *Educational Leadership* (March 1989), pp. 72–75.

35 Lee Canter, "Let the Educator Beware," *Educational Leadership* (October 1988), pp. 71–73; M. Carol Tama and Kenneth Peterson, "Achieving Reflectivity Through Literature," *Educational Leadership* (March 1991), pp. 22–24.

36 Daniel O'Leary and Susan G. O'Leary, *Classroom Management: The Successful Use of Behavior Modification*, 2nd ed. (New York: Pergamon, 1977); Ian Mallinson, *Guide to the Children's Act* (Rutherford, N.J.: Cassell, 1991).

then teachers have been undermining their own managerial purposes by scolding, shaming, threatening, or punishing students from misbehavior.

Brophy and Evertson are skeptical about avoiding or ignoring inappropriate behavior. They contend that certain misbehaviors are too disruptive or dangerous to be ignored.[37] Ignoring such behavior leaves students with the impression that the teacher is unaware of what is going on or is unable to cope with it. Still others may take the middle stance: that undesirable behavior can be ignored by the teacher when it is momentary, not serious, unlikely to be disruptive, and attributable to a student who is usually well behaved.

Robert Slavin makes still another distinction. Many forms of misbehavior are motivated by the desire for peer attention and approval. Students who disobey the teacher are usually (consciously or unconsciously) weighing the effect of their defiance on their standing among classmates; this is especially true as students enter adolescence. Slavin concludes that ignoring misbehavior is ineffective if it is reinforced or encouraged by peers. Such behavior cannot be ignored, for it will worsen and attract more peer support.[38]

Ornstein makes still another distinction among misbehaving students. He asserts that emotionally disturbed children and children who lack healthy ego development pose a special challenge. Their inability to get along with normal children makes them isolated and rejected. Often, they are unaware of their responsibility for or contribution to events. They have almost no feelings of guilt and are not responsive to others' feelings. When they realize they are wrong, they tend to withdraw. He claims that "by threatening or punishing, the teacher makes the mistake of appearing hostile; in turn, these children feel they have a right to hate the teacher and be 'bad.' " It is advisable, Ornstein asserts, for the teacher "to be sympathetic," not overly assertive, and even "make special allowances." The other children know these disturbed children are different and will accept the fact that concessions are made "or rules are modified to accommodate their special needs."[39]

For situations in which it is decided that punishment is appropriate and will be effective, the teacher must decide on its form and severity. The teacher should establish criteria for using it. Punishment is construed by behaviorists as an unpleasant stimulus that an individual will try to avoid. Common punishments, according to Gage and Berliner, are *soft reprimands* (heard only by the student concerned); *reprimands* coupled with praise, social isolation (detention, missed recess), point loss in academics; and *severe reprimands* being reported to someone outside the classroom (disciplinarian, principal, parent).[40]

37 Jere E. Brophy, "Classroom Organization and Management," *Elementary School Journal* (March 1983), pp. 265–286; Carolyn Evertson et al., "Effective Classroom Management," Final Report for the Natioanl Institute of Education, *Improving Classroom Management* (June 1985). Also see Brophy and Evertson, *Student Characteristics and Teaching* (New York: Longman, 1981).

38 Robert E. Slavin, *Cooperative Learning* (Englewood Cliffs, N.J.: Prentice-Hall, 1990) Slavin, *Educational Psychology: Theory into Practice*, 3rd ed. (Englewood Cliffs, N.J.: Prentice-Hall, 1991).

39 Allan C. Ornstein, "Teaching the Disadvantaged," *Educational Forum* (January 1967), p. 221.

40 N. L. Gage and David C. Berliner, *Educational Psychology*, 5th ed. (Boston: Houghton Mifflin, 1992).

Corporal punishment should not be used; the negative side effects outweigh the temporary advantages of quashing inappropriate behavior. It tends to demoralize the class. Although it may keep young and physically immature students in check, it creates anger and resentment in them. If it is to have any effect, the teacher will at some point have to use it with physically stronger students, and the teacher who backs down loses face and authority. Moreover, it is outlawed in many states.

One researcher, who refers to punishment as "management strategies," has assessed 24 common strategies employed by junior high school teachers.[41] The sample consisted of 281 students and 80 teachers who were asked to rate the severity of each strategy. As shown in Table 3.6, those with a mean rating of 5 or 4 were classified as "very severe," those with a rating of 3 were classified as "moderately severe," and those with a rating of 2 or 1 were classified as "relatively unsevere."

The data reveal that teachers tend to employ as many relatively unsevere strategies as moderately severe and very severe strategies combined. Relatively unsevere strategies involve task assignments or removal of privileges. Moderately severe strategies impose constraints on students' freedom or time. Very severe strategies involve removal or transfer of the student or conferring with another authority about the problem.

Although there were significant differences between student and teacher mean ratings for about half the items, their rank orderings of the strategies were similar (correlation of .84), implying comparable perceptions of the severity of punishment.

In using punishment, it is important to match the misbehavior with appropriate consequences—not to overreact to mild infractions and not to understate serious misbehavior; the teacher must learn to fit the punishment with the infraction. Punishment should not be based on obedience to authority or on a power relationship between the teacher and students; punishment should be used to encourage respect and responsibility toward classmates (and the teacher).

Understanding the student is essential for good discipline; students can be classified into various problem types. Rohrkemper and Brophy have identified 12 problem student types, which can be classified into three broad types: *hyperactive, aggressive,* and *defiant*; they tend to be the most difficult for teachers to deal with, especially the defiant, who resist authority and are willing to engage in power struggles with teachers.[42]

Emotional, impulsive, and unpredictable students, not described in their research, also tend to be very difficult to deal with. In most cases, a firm, structured approach is necessary to control their impulses and moods. How-

41 Moshe Zeidner, "The Relative Severity of Common Classroom Management Strategies: The Student's Perspective," *British Journal of Educational Psychology* (February 1988), pp. 69–77.

42 Mary M. Rohrkemper and Jere E. Brophy, "Teacher Thinking About Problem Students," in J. M. Levine and M. C. Wang, eds., *Teacher and Student Perceptions* (Hillsdale, N.J.: Erlbaum, 1983), pp. 67–88.

Table 3.6 MEAN RATINGS OF COMMON CLASSROOM MANAGEMENT STRATEGIES

Strategies	Student (N = 281) M	Teachers (N = 80) M
1. Permanent suspension from school	4.78	4.60
2. Shaming or personally insulting student	4.32	3.14
3. Permanent removal from class	4.30	4.18
4. Parent-principal conference	4.21	3.14
5. Temporary demotion to lower grade	4.03	3.91
6. Withdrawal or denial of special privileges	4.00	3.74
7. Communicating problem to parents	3.46	3.34
8. Lowering school mark	3.46	4.03
9. Throwing student out of class	3.40	3.65
10. Learning material by heart	3.22	2.90
11. Summons of student to principal's office	3.17	2.80
12. Surprise quiz	3.09	3.06
13. Busy work	2.93	2.63
14. Detention after class	2.90	3.00
15. Teacher-student conference	2.70	3.08
16. Additional monitor duty	2.70	2.66
17. Cleaning up school grounds	2.60	2.59
18. Shortening recess	2.59	2.41
19. Reporting early to school	2.52	2.55
20. Teacher's aversive nonverbal communication	2.49	2.93
21. Verbal reprimand	2.47	2.88
22. Additional homework	2.22	2.22
23. Being placed in corner	1.90	2.70
24. Special classroom seating	1.73	2.16

Source: Moshe Zeidner, "The Relative Severity of Common Classroom Management Strategies: The Student's Perspective," *British Journal of Educational Psychology* (February 1988), p. 73.

ever, when punishing these students, the wrong reaction or punishment by the teacher can worsen the classroom situation.

In dealing with difficult students (especially the above three problem types), it is important for teachers to feel confident and comfortable with themselves and have realistic perceptions of themselves, the students, and the general classroom situation. Good classroom managers remain calm in a crisis. They can act and react without becoming defensive, authoritarian, or emotional. They can cope with the student "games," defiance, or moods without creating resentment on the part of the students. They know when to punish, how to punish—and when not to punish. They know how to integrate rules into a workable system and apply the system with patience and persistence. All these characteristics connote what we refer to as maturity and confidence in a person.

A few problem students in a class can create great anxiety, battle fatigue, and even fear for some teachers. But the student who may be the teacher's "biggest problem," if handled correctly, can become the teacher's "best friend." The knowing teacher devotes extra time to the student to get to the root of the student's problem before it comes to a head in class. He or she seeks out information and advice from parents, former teachers, guidance counselors, and supervisors. The idea is to get to know the student and the cause of the student's poor work and behavior quickly. Serious incidents do not just happen; anxieties collect and build up. The teacher who has common sense, emotional maturity, and good professional training can translate the student's inappropriate behavior into better efforts before his or her behavior becomes threatening or uncontrollable and before direct action is needed. See Tips for Teachers 3.2.

Guidelines for Using Punishment

Table 3.7 lists guidelines for using punishment. The first column, based on the work of O'Leary and O'Leary, lists seven principles that coincide with behavioral modification theory; punishment is combined with reinforcement of desired behavior. The second column is based on the work of Good and Brophy. These measures are stopgap measures to suppress overt misbehavior, but they do not change the underlying desires to misbehave or the causes of misbehavior. There are similarities between the columns; both lists represent firm approaches to discipline.

The 12 guidelines listed below can be used for all disciplinary approaches. Underlying the guidelines is the idea that punishment should be flexible and tailored to the specific student and situation.

Table 3.7   GUIDELINES FOR PUNISHING STUDENTS

O'Leary and O'Leary	Good and Brophy
1. Use punishment sparingly.	1. Threat of punishment is usually more effective than punishment itself especially when phrased in such a way that there are unknown consequences.
2. Make it clear why the student is being punished.	
3. Provide student with alternative means of obtaining some positive reinforcement.	2. Punishment should be threatened or warned before implemented. This is done in a way that the teacher hopes it will not be used and the students are responsible if it has to be used.
4. Reinforce student behaviors which are incompatible with those you wish to weaken or eliminate. For example, if you punish for being off task, reward for being on task.	3. The punishment should be accompanied with positive statements of expectations and rules, focusing on what the students should be doing.
5. Avoid punishing while you are angry or emotional.	4. Punishment should be combined with negative reinforcement, so that students must improve to escape punishment. For example, the students will lose a privilege until behavior improves.
6. Punish when inappropriate behavior starts rather than when it ends.	
7. Avoid corporal punishment.	5. Punishment should be systematic and deliberate; avoid emotional reaction or provocation to reaction when punishing.
	6. Do not punish an entire class or group because of the misbehavior of an individual.
	7. Avoid excessive punishment, since this may unite the students in sullen defense against the teacher.

Source: Adapted from K. Daniel O'Leary and Susan G. O'Leary, *Classroom Management: The Successful Use of Behavior Modification*, 2nd ed. (New York: Pergamon, 1977); Thomas L. Good and Jere E. Brophy, *Looking into Classrooms*, 5th ed. (New York: HarperCollins, 1991); and Good and Brophy, *Educational Psychology: A Realistic Approach*, 4th ed. (New York: Longman, 1992).

1. *Learn what type of punishment school authorities allow.* Different schools have different guidelines for punishment and punish students for infringement of different rules.
2. *Don't threaten the impossible.* Make sure the punishment can be carried out. Telling a student to stay after class at 3:00 P.M. when you have a 3:30 appointment with the dentist illustrates that you reacted hastily and cannot follow through.
3. *Don't punish when you are at a loss for what else to do or in an emotional state.* Sometimes it is best to delay action, that is, to tell the student to see you after class. The delay gives you time to think and be more

Tips for Teachers 3.2

Strategies for Managing Problem Students

Below are general strategies for dealing with problem students, some-times called "difficult" students, based on the experience of teachers. Al-though originally developed for junior high school inner-city students, the strategies apply to most school setting and grade levels.

1. *Accept the students as they are*, but build on and accentuate their positive qualities.
2. *Be yourself*, since these students can recognize phoniness and take offense at such deceit.
3. *Be confident*; take charge of the situation, and don't give up in front of the students.
4. *Provide structure*, since many of these students lack inner control and are restless and impulsive.
5. *Explain your rules and routines* so students understand them. Be sure your explanations are brief; otherwise you lose your effectiveness and you appear to be defensive or preaching.
6. *Communicate positive expectations* that you expect the students to learn and you require academic work.
7. *Rely on motivation* and not on your prowess to maintain order; an interesting lesson can keep the students on task.
8. *Be a firm friend*, but maintain a psychological and physical distance so your students know you are still the teacher.
9. *Keep calm*, and keep your students calm, especially when conditions become tense or upsetting. It may be necessary to delay action until after class, when emotions have been reduced.
10. *Size up the situation*, and be aware of undercurrents of behavior, since these students are sizing you up and are knowing man-ipulators of their environment.
11. *Anticipate behavior*; being able to judge what will happen if you or a student decide on a course of action may allow you to curtail many problems.
12. *Expect, but don't accept, misbehavior.* Learn to cope with misbehavior, but don't get upset or feel inadequate about it.

Source: Adapted from Allan C. Ornstein, "Teaching the Disadvantaged," *Educational Forum* (January 1967), pp. 215-223; Ornstein, "The Education of the Disadvantaged," *Educational Research* (June 1982), pp. 197-221.

rational. All things being equal, the quiet, cool approach is more effective than the angry, emotional approach.

4. *Don't assign extra homework as punishment.* This creates dislike for homework as well as the subject.

5. *Be sure the punishment follows the offense as soon as possible.* Don't impose punishment two days after the student misbehaves.

6. *Be sure the punishment fits the misbehavior.* Don't overreact to mild misbehavior or underplay or ignore serious misbehavior.

7. *Be consistent with punishment.* If you punish one student for something, don't ignore it when another student does the same thing. However, students and circumstances differ, and there should be room for modification.

8. *Don't use double standards when punishing.* You should treat both sexes the same way, and low-achieving and high-achieving students the same way. (Perhaps the only allowance or difference can be with emotionally disturbed children.) Avoid having teacher "pets."

9. *Give the student the benefit of doubt.* Before accusing or punishing someone, make sure you have the facts right.

10. *Don't hold grudges.* Once you punish the student, put the incident behind you and try to start with a clean slate.

11. *Don't personalize the situation.* React to misbehavior, not the student. Do not react to the student's anger or personal remarks. He usually doesn't mean them and is reacting out of emotion. Stay focused on the deed, remind the student he doesn't mean what he is saying and that things will worsen unless he calms down. When the student is out of control, the main thing is to get him to calm down. Punishment comes later, if it is required, after the student is calm.

12. *Document all serious incidents.* This is especially important if the misbehavior involves sending the student out the room or possible suspension.[43]

PREVENTIVE DISCIPLINE

Preventive discipline refers to establishing control systems in the classroom and avoiding the breakdown of controls. It involves a series of strategies to modify the surface behavior of the students so they are engaged in appropriate classroom tasks. It also involves preventing schools from getting out of control by reacting to small, manageable incidents before they become big and unmanageable. Preventive discipline permits the teacher to cope

---

43 Allan C. Ornstein, "A Difference Teachers Make: How Much?" *Educational Forum* (Fall 1984), pp. 109–117; Ornstein, "Techniques and Fundamentals for Teaching the Disadvantaged."

Classroom management can be enhanced by teachers who spend time after class with students

with student adjustment problems in class while helping students cope with their feelings.

The task is to establish ways of dealing with behavior that do not disrupt the group but still may be helpful to the students. It involves making judgments as to when to *tolerate* certain student behaviors (without approving them), when to *modify* behaviors, and when to *interfere* with behaviors in order to allow learning to take place. Indeed, a certain amount of common sense and emotional maturity on the part of the teacher are important in managing and modifying behavior.

General Preventive Measures: For All Teachers

Redl and Wineman established 21 specific techniques for working with aggressive boys in treatment centers. They later developed 12 of these for managing students in regular classrooms. They are classic techniques, based on clinical psychology and diagnostic insight into student behavior. They seek to enhance psychological protection of students on an individual and group basis. They attempt to avoid conflict, to enhance the comfort of the individual with himself, and to enhance cooperation with group members. Most important, the 12 techniques seem to apply to all disciplinary approaches.

1. *Planned ignoring.* Much inappropriate behavior has limited influence and will exhaust itself, especially if it is low level or mild. If it appears that the behavior will not spread to others, it is sometimes best to ignore it and not feed the student's secondary need for attention.

2. *Signal interference.* A variety of signals can be used to communicate disapproval to the student. Signals such as eye contact, hand gestures, snapping fingers, clearing one's throat, facial expressions, and body gestures are effective in handling the beginning stages of inappropriate behavior.

3. *Proximity control.* In some cases teacher proximity acts as a deterrent against misbehavior, and in other cases it can operate as a source of protection, strength, and identification. Some students need to have a teacher stand close by before they are able to control their impulses. (However, caution is recommended; in some cases proximity can spark a child to lose control or to get further out of control.)

4. *Interest boosting.* When a student shows signs of restlessness or boredom, it is often helpful for the teacher to show genuine interest in the student's work or incorporate his or her personal interest (for example, in athletics or music) into the discussion.

5. *Humor.* Almost everyone is aware that humor can defuse a tense situation and that it can make students relax. It is also an excellent way of showing that the teacher is secure during a stressful incident. (However, the teacher must be careful to distinguish between humor and sarcasm. Sarcasm should not be viewed as a technique, since it means that there is a winner and a loser.)

6. *Hurdle lessons.* Sometimes students misbehave because of frustration with a particular assignment. Students who do not understand the work may translate their frustration into disruptive behavior. The teacher should try to provide academic assistance before students get to the stage of not paying attention or disturbing others.

7. *Restructuring the program.* The classroom schedule may have to be modified because of some circumstances or problems. Tension levels may have to be reduced before the class can involve itself in the regular assignment. If students do not understand parts of the lesson, they may have to be retaught, or parts may have to be skipped because retracking would only increase student frustration.

8. *Routine.* Some degree of routine and structure makes most students feel comfortable and secure. Those who lack inner control need more routine and structure. Daily schedules of activities provide the kind of routine that eliminates aimless behavior while students wait for teachers to announce the next activity.

9. *Direct appeal.* Overreacting or intervening severely in order to demonstrate authority can backfire. An alternative technique is to appeal to values that the students have internalized regarding their

image ("Gentlemen don't engage in that kind of behavior. You know better"), the teacher-student relationship ("Have I been unfair to you?"), group codes or peer reaction ("You know I can't allow this behavior to go unnoticed"). The trick is to learn what appeal works with what students.

10. *Removing seductive objectives.* Certain objects elicit a particular type of behavior that leads to problems. For example, a water gun, flashlight, or ball may set off impulsive or mischievous behavior that disrupts the class. The objects to be eliminated in the classroom are determined by the age, maturity, and inner controls of the students.

11. *Antiseptic bouncing.* If a student's behavior reaches a point where he or she cannot be controlled, it is best to have the student removed from the room—either for a few minutes (for example, getting a drink or delivering a message) or for a full period (waiting in the guidance counselor's office). The intent of antiseptic bouncing is to protect and help the student and the group get over their immediate feelings of anger, disappointment, emotion, or silliness. It is not meant as punishment, which would defeat the original purpose of prevention.

12. *Physical restraint.* A student who loses control or threatens others must be restrained. The student should be held firmly but not roughly. Once again, the intent is protection, not punishment. The teacher substitutes a control system until the school's controls are operating again. (Punishing a student who lost complete control is not a solution; it adds to the student's anguish and can make him or her more enraged.) If the teacher is unable to restrain the student, one of the other students should be sent out to get help from a colleague or administrator.[44]

Preventive Measures: Firm to Moderate

From a review of the literature on classroom order and management, Walter Doyle has compiled a series of "management functions" for successful teachers.[45]

These functions, which coincide with our term *preventive measures*, tend to stress clear rules and routines, group cooperation and participation, as well as academic accountability. Taken as a whole, they correspond with most classroom disciplinary approaches, especially the group managerial and group guidance approaches and the business-academic approach.

For Doyle, preventive discipline is a matter of understanding events in the classroom—how processes evolve and how people interact. He claims that classroom order is fragile, a condition that can be easily disrupted by mistakes,

44 Fritz Redl an d David Wineman, *The Aggressive Child* (New York: Free Press, 1957); Redl and Wineman, *Children Who Hate.*

45 Walter Doyle, "Classroom Order and Management," in M. C. Wittrock, ed.: *Handbook of Research on Teaching*, 3rd ed. (New York: Macmillan, 1986), pp. 392–431.

intrusions, and unpredictable events. Order is not something that is achieved once and for all so that teaching can take place; rather, there is permanent pressure on the classroom life, and a teacher must be vigilant in preventing disorder. The managerial functions are important for enhancing the inherent delicacy of classroom order. Such functions correlate, according to Doyle, with being an effective manager at both the elementary and secondary levels.

1. *Establishing classroom activities*. The early class sessions of a school year are critical. During this period order is defined and procedures for sustaining order are put into place.
2. *Rules and procedures*. Life in classrooms must be governed by rules and procedures, with specific formats for opening, closing, and conducting lessons. Rules should be focused on behavior that is likely to disrupt activities, such as lateness, talking during lessons, gum chewing, being unprepared, or fighting.
3. *Academic work and activities*. Students are told what to do, beginning the first day in class, so that little time is lost finding seats, getting organized, or waiting between activities. Warm-up activities have a simple, whole-class instructional structure, and the work is familiar and easy to accomplish. Effective teachers establish a procedure for maintaining whole-group focus on academic work and protect it from intrusion and disruption.
4. *Routines*. Routinization makes classroom activities less susceptible to breakdowns and interruptions because students know the normal sequence of events and what is expected of them. The more familiar the "lesson contexts," that is, classroom processes, schedules, and structures, the more stable and predictable the student behavior. Establishing routines is also somewhat of a prerequisite for performing academic work.
5. *Enacting processes*. Rule systems are complex and vary with lesson contexts or distinctive phases of a class session. For example, quiet talk is often permitted among peers during entry and seatwork, but not during teacher presentations or question-answer recitation. Students know the difference, with little explanation needed, in well-controlled classes. With older children, rules often do not have to be explicitly articulated but are part of commonsense knowledge and past experience.
6. *Hidden curriculum*. Emphasis on authority, responsibility, orderliness, and task orientation is common in well-run classrooms. There is a heavy emphasis on following directions, accepting responsibility, and working quietly and diligently. Students are socialized to the world of work, that is, to modern bureaucracy, in classrooms; institutional constraints prevail over student preferences.
7. *Monitoring*. Monitoring operates on three levels. First, effective managers watch *groups*; they attend to what is happening in the entire room, while

they attend to individual students. Second, they watch *conduct or behavior*, that is, they are quick to react to misbehavior before it spreads. Third, they monitor the *pace, rhythm, and duration* of classroom events (avoiding what Gump calls "hesitations" and "lags" and emphasizing what Kounin calls "smoothness" and "momentum").[46]

8. *Maintaining group lessons.* Instructional strategies, such as grouping and questioning, ensure that all students in the class stay involved in the lesson, even when one or two students are performing. Materials and activities provide a group focus. In many classrooms the teacher sets specific limits on the type and amount of student participation. For example, the teacher sets the topics, formulates narrow rather than open-ended questions, and calls on students to secure a "right answer" to keep a planned discussion going.

9. *Seatwork.* Seatwork is well organized and monitored by the teacher. The teacher is available to work with students and circulates around the room to see how students are doing. The extent of whole-class supervision decreases when the teacher focuses attention on a small group, but the rest of the class works independently.

10. *Transitions.* Transitions are made with minimal loss of momentum or time. The teacher monitors them closely to see that students move from one task to another and provides considerable direction.

11. *Engaged time.* Opening routines are established, and enough work is assigned to fill the scheduled time. The opening routines—for example, copying down the assignments or writing in a journal—engage students immediately in work. Well-planned assignments mean that students do not run out of work, so they remain engaged throughout the period.

12. *Cueing.* Teachers and students adjust to the unfolding processes of the classroom. Order is maintained, even during disruptions by unforeseen events, by means of cues and messages (verbal and nonverbal) that teachers use to tell students what is happening or to announce a transition. (This is similar to Kounin's "signal systems.")

13. *Maintaining academic work.* Academic work can be used to achieve order by selecting tasks that are easy for students. The more demanding the academic work, the greater the risk that classroom routines will be slowed down or disrupted. Thus some teachers often simplify task demands and lower the risk of mistakes. When academic work is demanding, teachers often break down the work into small, sequenced tasks and heavily prompted increments.

14. *Cooperative learning teams.* Small groups in which students work together on assignments have positive effects on achievement, so long as instruc-

46 Paul Gump, *The Classroom Behavior Setting* (Washington, D.C.: Government Printing Office, 1967); Gump, *Ecological Psychology and Children* (Chicago: University of Chicago Press, 1975); and Kounin, *Discipline and Group Management in Classrooms.*

tion is carefully structured; individuals are accountable for performance, and a well-defined reward system is used. The effect on discipline is unclear, although it is assumed that cooperation among students enhances group morale and group rapport, which in turn has a positive effect on the organization and management of the classroom.

15. *Subject matter as procedure.* For purposes of control, subject matter is sometimes presented with an emphasis on practice and drill. Academic work is reduced by the teacher to completing one assignment or exercise and then going on to the next exercise. Neither teacher nor students talk much about the meaning or purpose of the work or the processes involved in doing the work. Although there is an appearance of engaged time, the work is often faked or performed without real understanding. So long as there is some feedback or evaluation, students are willing to spend time on these activities.

16. *Teacher expectations.* Some teachers appear to solve the problem of order in large group instruction by excluding low-ability students from participation in classroom activities. From a management perspective, such action is reasonable because it avoids conditions that lead to breakdown in momentum, pacing, and rhythm; it also avoids confusion and slowing down (hesitations, lags) of content flow and activities. From a teaching perspective, however, such actions restrict the opportunities of low-ability students.[47]

Preventive Measures: Moderate to Flexible

David Johnson has witten several books that deal with interpersonal relations, cooperation, and self-actualization. His methods of enhancing self-awareness, mutual trust, and communication among people serve as excellent preventive strategies. Johnson's methods correspond with democratic approaches to discipline such as the group, acceptance, and success approaches. They might be used by anyone who wishes to build a humanistic classroom based on student rapport and understanding, The specific methods can be applied on a one-to-one basis or on a group basis in which teachers emphasize interpersonal relations and cooperative processes.

Building Self-Awareness Through Feedback

Feedback tells students what effect their actions are having on others. It is important for the teacher to provide feedback in a way that does not threaten the student. The more threatened and defensive the student becomes, the more likely it is that he or she will not understand the feedback correctly. Increasing a student's self-awareness through feedback gives the students a basis for making informed choices in future behavior.

---

47 Doyle, "Classroom Order and Management."

1. *Focus feedback on behavior, not on personality.* Refer to what the person does, not to what you believe her traits to be. The former is a response to what you see or hear, and the latter is an inference or interpretation about character.

2. *Focus feedback on descriptions, not on judgments.* Refer to what occurs, not to your judgments of right or wrong, good or bad. ("You are not spelling the word correctly" or "We cannot hear you," rather than "You are a terrible speller" or "You don't know how to speak up in public.")

3. *Focus feedback on a specific situation, not on abstract behavior.* Feedback tied to a specific situation leads to self-awareness. Feedback that is abstract is open to interpretation and is often misunderstood.

4. *Focus feedback on the present, not on the past.* The more immediate the feedback, the more effective it is. ("You are becoming angry now as I talk to you," rather than "Sometimes you become angry.")

5. *Focus feedback on sharing feelings, not giving advice.* Sharing feelings gives people the opportunity to make a choice in light of their own needs and perceptions. Giving advice or telling people what to do limits their freedom and responsibilities.

6. *Do not force feedback on a person.* Feedback must be presented as an offer, not as something being forced on the receiver.

7. *Do not give more feedback than can be understood at one time.* Don't overload receivers with feedback; it reduces the chances they will understand or use it. When you give feedback that cannot be understood or used, you are satisfying your own needs and not the needs of others.

8. *Focus feedback on action that the person can change.* It does little good to tell a person that you don't like the color of his eyes. This is something that cannot be changed.

Developing and Maintaining Trust

To build a healthy relationship among students and between students and teacher, a climate of mutual trust must grow and develop. Fears of rejection or betrayal must be reduced, and acceptance, support, and respect must be promoted. Trust, like order, is not something that can be built once and forgotten about; it constantly changes and constantly needs nourishment.

1. *Building trust.* Trust begins as people take the risk of disclosing more and more of their thoughts and feelings to each other. If they do not receive acceptance or support, they back off from the relationship. If they receive acceptance or support, they will continue to risk self-disclosure, and the relationship continues to grow.

2. *Being trusting.* The level of trust that develops between two people is related to both individuals' willingness and ability to be trusting. Each must be willing to risk the consequences of revealing herself to and depending on the other person. Each must be openly accepting and supporting of the other to ensure that the other experiences beneficial consequences from the risk taken.

3. *Trusting appropriately.* A person must be able to size up a situation and make a wise judgment about when, whom, and how much to trust. Trust is appropriate when a person is reasonably confident that the other person will not react in a way that will be harmful.

4. *Trusting as a self-fulfilling prophecy.* Assumptions made about another person or a situation affect an individual's behavior. That behavior often elicits the expected reactions from the other person. The assumptions become a self-fulfilling prophecy. If you make other people feel they can trust you, they will often do so.

Communicating Effectively

All behavior conveys messages. A person sends messages to evoke a response from the receiver. The messages and responses are verbal and nonverbal. Effective communication takes place when the receiver interprets the sender's messages in the way that was intended; effective communication enhances understanding and cooperation among individuals. Ineffective communication arises when there is a discrepancy between what the sender meant and what the receiver thought the sender meant. This reduces understanding and cooperation. Mutual trust enhances the possibility of effective communication; distrust is a primary cause of miscommunication. Skill in sending messages can increase communication between teachers and students.

1. *Use the first person singular.* Take responsibility for your own ideas or feelings. People doubt messages that use terms like "most people," "some of your classmates."

2. *Make messages complete and specific.* People often make incorrect assumptions about what their listeners know, leave out steps in describing their thinking, and do not mention specific items or ideas that are necessary if their intentions are to be conveyed to their listeners.

3. *Make verbal and nonverbal messages congruent.* Communication problems arise when a person's verbal and nonverbal messages are contradictory.

4. *Be redundant.* Use more than one means of communication, such as verbal and nonverbal cues, to reinforce your message.

5. *Ask for feedback.* The only way to learn how a person is actually receiving and interpreting your message is to seek feedback from the receiver.

6. *Consider the listener's frame of reference.* The same information might be interpreted differently by a child and by an adult. It may be necessary to use different words or different nonverbal cues depending on the listener's age, maturity level, educational level, and cultural background.

7. *Make messages concrete.* It is important to be descriptive, to use verbs (I like *working*), adverbs (Your homework is due *tomorrow*), and adjectives (Johnnie is an *excellent* student) to communicate your feelings clearly.

8. *Describe behavior without evaluating it.* Describe the student's behavior ("You are interrupting Johnnie") rather than evaluating it ("You are self-centered and won't listen to anyone else's ideas").[48]

Guidelines for Implementing Preventive Measures

The preventive disciplinary measures discussed above range widely—from firm to flexible. No teacher will use all these measures. It is up to each to pick and choose according to what coincides with teaching style, personality, philosophy, and teaching situation.

In developing your approach to preventive strategies as one aspect of classroom management, you must know yourself, be capable of learning from your own mistakes, and know where to go for assistance. One way to improve your classroom management skills is to analyze sample cases presented on video-tapes of actual and role-play teacher situations. You can work on your own by reading on the subject or enrolling in an appropriate in-service or staff development course to benefit from group discussion and analysis. Other suggestions are given in Tips for Teachers 3.3.

Most important, don't be afraid to admit to disciplinary problems, to seek advice, or to think about transferring to another school if your disciplinary problems persist. Remember, if you wish to teach, if you expect to be an effective teacher, and if you want your students to learn, you will have to be an effective manager. For most of us, this should come with experience. For those of us who are unable to teach difficult students, a transfer is perhaps the most practical remedy. If this is the case, do it early in your career. Don't hang on in a school where you are unable to control the students or where you feel intense pressure, sense serious inabilities in yourself, or are afraid.

To move from the theory to the practice of good management and discipline, you must grasp the answers to some common, important questions and be able to translate those answers into action.

I. How do I encourage students to behave and work with me in the class?
1. Act as if you *expect students to be orderly* from the first day on.
2. *Expect everyone's attention* before you start teaching. Stop when there is noise. Don't teach over individual or group chatter.
3. *Don't talk too much.* After a while, you lose the students' attention. Involve the students in activities, ask questions, pose problems, etc.

---

48 David W. Johnson, *Reaching Out: Interpersonal Effectiveness and Self-Actualization,* 4th ed. (Englewood Cliffs, N.J.: Prentice-Hall, 1990).

Tips for Teachers 3.3

Suggestions for Analyzing Preventive Measures

Some of the causes of misbehavior are beyond your control. Knowing what measures to take to avoid common discipline problems and to handle problem student behaviors will increase your time for teaching and general teacher effectiveness. Below are suggestions for analyzing your measures.

1. Obtain private counseling to better understand your own emotional reactions to student behavior.
2. Organize rap sessions with students to better understand their concerns and emotional needs.
3. Meet privately with other teachers to discuss problems and successful strategies.
4. Identify and analyze the strengths of colleagues in dealing with discipline problems.
5. Determine which supervisors and administrators will provide support when necessary.
6. Ask another teacher, supervisor, or administrator to visit your classroom on a regular basis to analyze your classroom management.
7. Communicate with parents on a regular basis to learn about their management philosophies for purposes of support and follow-up in the class.
8. Keep informed on current legal issues concerning discipline. Read education journals, state law digests; talk to union representatives.
9. Document carefully all serious student behavior problems.
10. Evaluate your expectations about your disciplinary measures and what you ought to accomplish.

Source: Adapted from Daniel L. Duke and Adrienne M. Meckel, *Teacher's Guide to Classroom Management* (New York: Random House, 1984).

4. *Hold students accountable* for abiding by rules.
5. *Be businesslike but friendly.* It is important to establish reasonable limits and enforce them. It is also important to smile, to have a sense of humor, and to be warm and supportive.
6. *Maintain your dignity.* Students should know there are limitations in a teacher-student relationship. You may wish to establish an imaginary line or keep a psychological distance from your students.
7. *Treat minor disturbances calmly.* Small incidents can be ignored verbally; a stern look or gesture will suffice. Know when to pass over a situation quickly without making a fuss.

II. How do I handle group infractions or misbehavior?
1. *Don't wait until a class is out of control.* When students are restless, change the activity. When students are beginning to engage in disturbances, take measures to stop the behavior in the initial stages.
2. *Focus on the individual* rather than the class. Try to divert individuals by asking questions, assigning tasks, or reminding them they are wasting class time or spoiling it for the entire group.
3. *Don't punish the group* when you are unable to deal with the individual or to discover which individual is causing a disturbance.
4. *Maintain your temper and poise.* Students will test their teacher to see how far they can go; they are not being personal. Don't overreact; maintain your poise.
5. *Avoid threats,* but if you make one, carry it out. Don't threaten the impossible. Think before you threaten. Follow through on a threat.
6. *Analyze your own behavior for possible causes of misbehavior,* especially if the difficulty continues. Look at your mannerisms, speech, attitudes. Analyze your rules and routines. Is your teaching interesting? Organized? Suitable to the level of the students? Be objective in your analysis.
7. *Seek help from others.* Check with another teacher, guidance counselor, disciplinarian, or supervisor. All of them have different roles with regard to the schools and will give different views. Don't wait until a situation is beyond control.

III. How do I deal with individual offenders in the classroom?
1. When a student is involved in a minor infraction (whispering, annoying a neighbor, calling out), use nonverbal signals such as facial expressions or gestures while you continue to teach. If the infraction stops, don't reprimand the student.
2. If these signals fail, *move closer* to the student while you continue to teach. If this stops the student, don't reprimand any further.
3. If proximity fails, quietly *talk to the student* while the rest of the class continues to work.
4. *Avoid physical contact,* especially in a tense situation.

IV. How do I deal with discipline problems that cannot be resolved in class?
   1. *Talk to the offender in private,* before or after class. Try to determine causes of the problem. Try to reach an understanding or agreement with the student.
   2. If you have to punish, *make the punishment fit the misbehavior.* The first offense, unless it is quite serious, need not be punished.
   3. Leave the misbehaving student with the feeling that he is *ruining things for himself and the group.*
   4. Ignore a student's claims that she "doesn't care." This is usually a defensive reaction. *Remind the student that she really does care.*
   5. Give the student a *chance to redeem himself.*
   6. *Use the resources at your disposal.* For example, use student records, suggestions from other teachers and the guidance counselor, advice and authority of the dean of discipline or a supervisor.
   7. Communicate with the parents (by telephone or letter). Most parents will support the teacher in matters of discipline involving their children.
   8. *Analyze your methods.* What are you doing wrong, or how are you contributing to the problem?
   9. If you have to *refer the student* to a counselor, disciplinarian, or supervisor, be specific. Avoid subjective remarks. Stick to the facts.
   10. Don't rely too much on others to *solve your classroom problems.* Eventually this diminishes your authority. Save only the major discipline problems, the ones you really have trouble handling, for others to resolve.[49]

V. How do I develop and maintain a positive approach to classroom management (whatever discipline approach I wish to adopt)?
   1. *Be positive.* Stress what should be done, not what should not be done.
   2. *Use praise.* Give praise according to merit. Show that you appreciate hard work and good behavior.
   3. *Trust.* Trust students, but don't be an easy mark. Make students feel you believe in them as long as they are honest with you and don't take advantage of you.
   4. *Express interest.* Talk to individual students about what interests them, what they did over the weekend, how schoolwork is progressing in other areas or subjects. Be sensitive and respectful about social trends and styles and school events that affect the behavior of the group. Be aware that peer group pressure affects individual behavior.
   5. *Be fair and consistent.* Don't have "pets" or "goats." Don't condemn an infraction one time and ignore it another time.

---

49 *Getting Started in the Secondary School,* rev.ed. (New York: Board of Education of the City of New York, 1986). The author's own ideas are intermixed with this source.

6. *Show respect; avoid sarcasm.* Be respectful and considerate toward students. Understand their needs and interests. Don't be arrogant or condescending or rely on one-upmanship to make a point.

7. *Establish classroom rules.* Make rules clear and concise and enforce them. Your rules should eventually be construed as their rules.

8. *Discuss consequences.* Students should understand the consequences for acceptable and unacceptable behavior. Invoke logical consequences, that is, appropriate rewards and punishment. Don't punish too often; it loses its effect after a while.

9. *Establish routines.* Students should know what to do under what conditions. Routine procedures provide an orderly and secure classroom environment.

10. *Confront misbehavior.* Don't ignore violations of rules or disruptions of routines. Deal with misbehavior in a way that does not interfere with your teaching. Don't accept or excuse serious or contagious misbehavior, even if you have to stop your teaching. If you ignore it, it will worsen.

11. *Guide.* There is a different between guidance, whereby you help students deal with problems, and discipline, whereby you maintain order and control by reacting to student surface behavior. Your main goal should be guidance rather than discipline. Good guidance will serve as a preventive measure, whereby you can establish order and control without having to assert authority.

12. *Avoid overcontrolling.* Assert your authority only when you need to and without overdoing it. Be confident without being condescending or egotistical. The need is to show you are in control of the classroom without overcontrolling students.

13. *Reduce failure, promote success.* Academic failure should be kept to a minimum since it is a cause of frustration, withdrawal, and hostility. When students see themselves as winners and receive recognition for success, they become more civil, calm, and confident; they are easier to work with and teach.

14. *Set a good example.* Model what you preach and expect. For example, speak the way you want students to speak; keep an orderly room if you expect students to be orderly; check homework if you expect students to do the homework.

15. *Be willing to make adjustments.* Analyze your disciplinary approach and preventive strategies by yourself and with the help of experienced colleagues. Be objective about your abilities. Learn to compensate for your weaknesses by making adjustments in your disciplinary approach and preventive measures. Be sure your disciplinary approach and managerial techniques fit your own teaching philosophy and personality. See Tips for Teachers 3.4.

Tips for Teachers 3.4

Handling Continuing Student Behavior Problems

You are bound to run into some students who continually exhibit behavior problems that you must deal with for the sake of maintaining control. Here are some additional questions to ask yourself to alleviate the problem(s).

Ideally you should be able to say "yes" to all 30 questions below. This will probably not be the case, if you have a problem with the student(s). More than 5 "no" responses suggests you are contributing to your own problem or that the problem is serious.

I. *Background Information*
   1. Do I know the student's personal needs?
   2. Have I examined the student's records?
   3. Have I spoken to colleagues (other teachers) about the student?
   4. Is the student's home life psychologically safe and secure? (Does he or she eat a good breakfast, sleep enough, have a quiet place to work, etc.?)
   5. Do I know which peers influence the student and what students he or she influences?

II. *Attitude*
   6. Do I interact positively with the student?
   7. Do I listen to the student?
   8. Do I show respect toward the student?
   9. Do I provide helpful feedback?
   10. Do I communicate high expectations to the student?
   11. Do I compliment or praise the student when it is appropriate?
   12. Do I recognize (call on the student) in class?
   13. Do I emphasize the strengths of the student in front of the class?

III. *Routines and Procedures*
   14. Have the routines or rules been clearly stated to the student?
   15. Are the routines appropriate and succinct?
   16. Is there consistent routine in the classroom that the student can understand and model?
   17. Are the routines enforced equally with all students, including the student exhibiting inappropriate behavior?
   18. Have I been clear about the consequences of inappropriate behavior?
   19. Are the consequences fair and consistent with the misbehavior?
   20. Do I remain calm when the student exhibits inappropriate behavior?

(continues)

IV. *Instruction*
  21. Are the instructional demands appropriate to the ability and needs of the student?
  22. Is the student interested in the classroom tasks?
  23. Does the student understand the homework?
  24. Are special academic provisions (enrichment, tutorial) made for the student?

V. *Preventive Measures*
  25. Have I followed through with my warnings to the student?
  26. Have I changed the student's seat?
  27. Have I spoken to the student privately?
  28. Am I willing to spend extra time talking to and getting to know the student outside of class?
  29. Have I communicated to the student's parent(s)? Is there consistent follow-up with the parent(s)?
  30. Have I spoken to the guidance counselor or dean of discipline for advice about the student?

SUMMARY

1. Seven approaches to establishing and maintaining good discipline are presented. All establish clear rules and expectations, all include recommendations for preventive measures, and all are positive and practical. They differ as to the degree of control exercised by the teacher and the emphasis on tasks.

2. The approaches are the *assertive approach*, based on firm rules and forceful intervention and control by the teacher; the *business-academic approach*, based on an emphasis on work requirements and assignments and an organization of instructional activities to enhance discipline; the *behavioral modification approach*, based on the systematic reinforcement of good behavior and punishment of inappropriate behavior; the *group managerial approach*, based on the teacher's maintaining group focus and group participation and holding all members of the group accountable; the *group guidance approach*, based on manipulating the surface behavior of students as individuals and groups; the *acceptance approach*, based on the assumption that when students are given such acceptance by the teacher and peers, behavior and achievement improve; and the *success approach*, based on the teacher's helping students make proper choices by experiencing success.

3. Which approach or combination of approaches a teacher adopts largely depends on the teacher's philosophy, personality, teaching style, and teaching situation.
4. Punishment is sometimes necessary to enforce rules and regulations. Punishment should fit the situation and take into consideration the developmental stage of the student. It should also be in line with school policy.
5. Preventive measures for maintaining and enhancing discipline are based on the need to curtail classroom problems before they become disruptive and affect teaching.
6. To proceed along the road to good discipline, you must understand the answers to relevant questions. Five major questions were asked. You must learn to apply those answers to actual practice.

CASE STUDY

Problem

An experienced teacher, returned to teaching, was assigned to an eighth-grade class in a low-income school shortly after the semester had begun. His class of 35 students had already "gotten rid" of two other teachers. The class was bordering on anarchy, having kicked a 15–inch-diameter hole in the lower part of the back wall, thrown books out the third floor window, scratched profanities into the blackboard, and been generally out of control.

Suggestion

The teacher began immediately to restructure the classroom. He removed *all* things in the room related to the previous teachers; revamped the room with *his* own things, including window shades and a set of encyclopedias; covered up all signs of past defiance and failure such as the profanities and the hole; put up new bulletin boards; structured, controlled, and practiced movement in, out, and around the room; identified key trouble makers and isolated them through selective sanctions; provided rationales for all rules relating to the students' welfare; gave priority to room control; assigned structured and segmented written work with high success levels through practice and review activities; "modeled work" and circulated to check written work so success was structured; provided for display of students' work, especially for many who had never had success previously; refused to accept less than quality work; mailed quality work home to parent with a congratulatory note; had fellow teachers come into the room to comment on the favorable changes; arranged for some academic and non-academic projects to be reported in the community newspaper; and *handled all discipline problems himself.*

Discussion Suggestion

The principal, who was active in the community, added another dimension by pointing out that classroom management must also include *affective* approaches to balance the firm, structured ones. There are, he said, two approaches: *in-school* factors, which the teacher was addressing, and *nonschool* factors, which he could address. Nonschool factors included parents, community, adults important to students, out-of-school contact with students, PTA, church, community newspapers, and the like. He suggested the teacher supplement his structured classroom approach with the following more personal techniques.

Write letters introducing himself to all parents, followed by telephone calls; visit the Boy's Club and other places, where students played and observe the games; shop with his wife in neighborhood supermarkets during highly visible times, thereby meeting students with their parents; attend neighborhood churches; join the community group; have his students assist in PTA activities; invite parents to observe instruction or "teach" a lesson, modifying subject matter to match parents' skills; attend church/sports banquets or awards; volunteer to speak to PTA or community groups.

By midsemester actual teaching was taking place, with the principal being asked to visit the class for periodic congratulatory "visits." By semester's end the class had its own "government" and was assisting in various neighborhood and school projects. The teacher was actually able to leave the room without chaos ensuing.

Discussion Questions

1. Compare and contrast the techniques used by this teacher to the models in the chapter. Can the models be used as a whole or in separate parts and be as effective as the teacher's/principal's approach?
2. Could this teacher's techniques be used in other types of schools? How do the suggestions in the chapter relate to teacher's techniques in the case?
3. How do the techniques resemble the theories of classroom management as mentioned in the chapter?
4. Analyze the dynamics of these techniques by using segments from the chapter.
5. Are the principal's suggestions realistic for all teachers? Why do you think the principal suggested this teacher implement the "nonschool" approaches at the same time as the "in-school" approaches?

QUESTIONS TO CONSIDER

1. What goals do you expect classroom management to achieve?
2. What approaches to classroom management do you prefer? Why?
3. How do a teacher's personality characteristics affect his or her disciplinary strategies?
4. Which preventive measures discussed in the chapter seem to coincide best with your personality and philosophy?
5. Which key questions at the end of the chapter seem most relevant? How is your own attitude and behavior related to the answers to the questions?

THINGS TO DO

1. Arrange a conference with a teacher who is known as a "good" disciplinarian. Which of the approaches described in the chapter does

the teacher's approach resemble? What are the constructive or positive factors in the teacher's methods and strategies?

2. Arrange to visit a nearby school to observe a teacher. Does that teacher have any special "tricks of the trade" for preventing disorder or confusion? What methods do you like? Dislike? Why?

3. Invite a guidance counselor, dean of discipline, or supervisor to the classroom. Discuss the procedures used at his or her school for handling discipline cases.

4. Prepare a list of preventive disciplinary techniques and common errors of discipline. Discuss the preventive techniques and common errors in class. Which common errors could have been prevented with which preventive techniques?

5. Discuss in class how you would respond as a teacher to the following classroom situations: (a) student constantly calls out; (b) student refuses to do work; (c) student uses improper language as an affront against a classmate; (d) student begins to argue with another student.

RECOMMENDED READINGS

Bauer, Anne M. and Regina H. Sapona, *Managing Classrooms to Facilitate Learning.* Englewood Cliffs, N.J.: Prentice-Hall, 1991. An emphasis on group processes and activities for managing students.

Canter, Lee and Marlene Canter. *Assertive Discipline: A Take Charge Approach for Today's Educator.* Los Angeles: Canter & Associates, 1976. A tough-minded approach to discipline.

Emmer, Edmond T., et al. *Classroom Management for Secondary Teachers,* 2nd ed. Englewood Cliffs, N.J.: Prentice-Hall, 1989. A business-academic approach to organizing and controlling students, including several practical techniques for secondary teachers.

Getting Started in the Secondary School: A Manual for New Teachers, rev.ed. New York: Board of Education of the City of New York, 1986. An excellent manual for meeting the needs of beginning teachers.

Glasser, William. *Schools Without Failure.* New York: Harper & Row, 1969. A classic book on discipline that emphasizes humanitarian and democratic strategies and a positive approach to discipline.

Kounin, Jacob S. *Discipline and Group Management in Classrooms.* New York: Holt, Rinehart & Winston, 1970. A classic piece of research emphasizing group discipline problems.

Savage, Tom V. *Discipline for Self-Control.* Englewood Cliffs, N.J.: Prentice-Hall, 1991. An analysis of several discipline problems and how to deal with them as a teacher.

KEY TERMS

Assertive approach	Group guidance approach
Business-academic approach	Acceptance approach
Behavior modification approach	Success approach
Modeling	Preventive discipline
Group managerial approach	

Testing Students

FOCUSING QUESTIONS

1. What does it mean when we say a test is reliable? Valid?

2. What are the most common methods for testing reliability? Validity?

3. What are the differences between norm-reference measurements and criterion-reference measurements?

4. How can criterion-reference tests be improved?

5. How can classroom tests be improved?

6. What short-answer test questions generate the most controversy? Why?

7. How can the teacher improve the writing and scoring of essay test questions?

8. What test-taking skills can be taught to students? When was the last time you taught these skills to your students?

*E*valuation is a process in which we put a value on or assign worth to something. The essential characteristic of evaluation is judgment. Measurement is quantitative. It describes something in terms of specific numbers or percentages. In evaluation a judgment is made in attaching a value or a qualitative description to a measurement derived from a test.

For example, a student scores 65 on a test. This score is a measurement. However, the number does not indicate if the score should be judged good or poor, high or low. If most students score over 65, we may decide that the score is low and indicates poor performance. If most students score in the 60s, we may decide that the score is not so low. Measurement provides us with test data (numbers, percentages); judgment interprets the numbers and turns them into evaluations.

Evaluation is a two-step process. The first step is measurement, in which the data are obtained by the use of one or a series of tests. Once the measurement has been made, judgments are made about the adequacy of the performance, usually in the context of instructional objectives.

Problems in test content, sampling (norming), and procedures can result in errors in measurement, and all evaluations are subject to error, since human judgment is involved. The best we can hope for is to reduce the chance for and margin of error by careful measurement and evaluation procedures. In this chapter, we will focus on testing; in the next, on evaluation.

CRITERIA FOR SELECTING TESTS

Two major criteria for selecting tests are reliability and validity. No matter what type of test you use, it should be reliable and valid. By **reliability** we mean that the test yields similar results when it is repeated over a short period of time or when a different form is used. A reliable test can be viewed as consistent, dependable, and stable. By **validity** we mean that the test does measure what it is represented as measuring. An invalid tests not measure what it should. For example, a pen-and-pencil test is not suitable for measuring athletic abilities.

Reliability

Test reliability can be expressed numerically. A coefficient of .80 or higher indicates high reliability, .40 to .79 acceptable reliability, and less than .40 low reliability. Many standardized tests comprise several subtests or scales and thus have coefficients to correspond to each of the subtests, as well as the entire test. For example, reliability for a reading test might be reported as .86 for comprehension, .77 for vocabulary, .91 for analogies, and .85 for the test as a whole.

There are three basic methods for determining test reliability. In the method called *test-retest* a test is administered twice, usually with 10 to 30 days between tests.[1] The rank ordering of individual test scores on the two tests is compared. If the rank ordering of scores is exactly the same, then the correlation coefficient is 1.00, or perfect reliability. A correlation of .86 indicates that the test is highly consistent over time.

A number of objections have been raised to the test-retest method. If the same items are used on both tests, the respondents' answers on the second test may be influenced by their memory of the first test and by discussions about the items with classmates or teachers between tests. If the interval between tests is too short, memorization is a factor. If the interval is too long, scores may change as a result of learning. The two test conditions might also differ. Lack of interest on the student's part during one of the test situations, a change in a student's health or diet, a change in the mood of the student or the test administrator may affect the scores.

To overcome the problems introduced by repeated test items in the test-retest method, the *parallel forms* method may be used. Two different but equivalent forms of the test are produced, and students are given both forms of the test. The correlation between scores on the two tests provides a good estimate of reliability. One drawback to this method is that parallel forms are not always available, especially with teacher-made tests, but even with many standardized tests. The two forms are not always equivalent and may differ in difficulty.[2] Also, the parallel forms method does not address the problem of differing test conditions.

The difficulties associated with the test-retest and parallel forms methods have led to the development of the *split-half* reliability method. A single test is split into reasonably equivalent halves, and these two subtests are used as if they were two separate tests to determine reliability coefficients. One common method of splitting a test is to score the even-numbered and odd-numbered items separately. Of course, splitting a test in half means that the reliability scores are determined by half the number of items. Too few items in calculations can lead to greater distortions and more change effects.

Test reliability can be improved by the following factors.

1. *Increased number of test items.* Reliability is higher when the number of items is increased, because the test involves a larger sample of the material covered by the test.
2. *Heterogeneity of the student group.* Reliability is higher when test scores are spread over a range of abilities. Measurement errors are smaller than from a group that is more homogeneous in ability.

---

1 Anne Anastasi, *Psychological Testing*, 6th ed. (New York: Macmillan, 1988); Lee J. Cronbach, *Essentials of Psychological Testing*, 5th ed. (New York: HarperCollins, 1990).

2 Jum C. Nunnally, "Reliability of Measurement," in M. C. Wittrock, ed., *Encyclopedia of Educational Research*, 5th ed. (New York: Macmillan, 1982), pp. 1589–1601.

3. *Moderate item difficulty.* Reliability is increased when the test items are of moderate difficulty because this spreads the scores over a greater range than a test composed mainly of difficult or easy items.

4. *Objective scoring.* Reliability is greater when tests can be scored objectively. With subjective scoring, the same responses can be scored differently on different occasions, even if the scorer is the same person. A machine-scored test is more reliable than a hand-scored test because it is less subject to error.

5. *Limited time.* A test in which speed is a factor is more reliable than a test that students can complete in their own time.[3]

Validity

A great many different types of validity exist. Basically, we try to determine whether we are measuring what we think we are measuring. Depending on a person's knowledge of research and reason for administering the test, an individual can choose from several different types of validity.

Content Validity

When constructing a test for a particular subject, we must ask whether the items adequately reflect the specific content of that subject. If test items can be answered on the basis of basic intelligence, general knowledge, or test wiseness, the content of a course or knowledge of a subject is not being tested adequately. The test lacks content validity.

Of all the forms of validity, content validity is perhaps the most important one. An eighth-grade science test should measure scientific knowledge and skills taught in eighth grade, not reading comprehension, not mathematics, and not tenth-grade science.

Curricular Validity

A standardized test that covers a good sample of a subject, but not the subject or course as taught in a particular school, would have content validity, but not curricular validity. A test that reflects the knowledge and skills presented in a particular school's curriculum has curricular validity. In such a test the items adequately sample the content of the curriculum the students have been studying.[4]

The problem of curricular validity arises more often with standardized (or norm-reference) tests than with teacher-made (or criterion-reference) tests.

---

3 Lewis R. Aiken, *Psychological Testing and Assessment,* 7th ed.(Englewood Cliffs, N.J.: Prentice-Hall, 1991); Cronbach, *Essentials of Psychological Testing;* and William A. Mehrens and Irwin J. Lehmann, *Measurement and Evaluation in Education and Psychology,* 3rd ed. (New York: Holt, Rinehart & Winston, 1984).

4 Samuel Messick, "Validity," in R. L. Linn, ed., *Educational Measurement,* 3rd ed. (New York: Macmillan, 1989), pp. 13–103; Richard M. Wolf, "Validity of Tests," in M.C. Wittrock, ed.*Encyclopedia of Educational Research,* 5th ed. (New York: Macmillan, 1982), pp. 1991–1998.

Many standardized tests have excellent content validity on a nationwide or statewide basis, but the items are not matched on a local school basis.

Construct Validity

Construct validity is the extent to which the test measures the attributes or "constructs" it is supposed to measure. If we are using an aptitude test, we ask if we are really measuring the construct aptitude. If it is measuring something else—general intelligence, reading comprehension, or creativity—then it is not measuring what it claims to measure.

A construct—for example, scientific aptitude, mechanical ability, or IQ—can be defined as a measurable quality that exists and explains some behavior or performance. When we interpret test scores in terms of a construct, say, mechanical ability, we make the assumption that there is an attribute or quality that we can properly call mechanical ability and that it can be measured by some objective means.

Criterion Validity

Criterion validity is the extent to which a particular test correlates with some other acceptable and valid test or measure of performance. Suppose, for example, a test for creativity is given to students. Scores of the test are compared with scores on another test or measure of creativity that is accepted as valid.[5] If there is a high correlation between the high and low scores of the new and established test, then the new test is considered to have criterion validity. In effect, the test scores are related to a criterion that is independent of the test but is established as measuring what it purports to measure.

Predictive Validity

Predictive validity is concerned with the relation of test scores to performance at some future time. For example, valid aptitude tests, administered in the twelfth grade or first year of college, can predict success in college. This is what the Scholastic Aptitude Tests (SATs) that students take in high school are supposed to do. Information on how a student is likely to perform in an area of study or work can be helpful in counseling students and in selecting students for different programs. (It is important to consider other factors as well, including previous grades and letters of recommendation.)

---

5 Anne Anastasi, "Coaching, Test Sophistication, and Developed Abilities," *American Psychologist* (October 1981), pp. 1086–1093; Samuel Messick, "Test Validity and the Ethics of Assessment," *American Psychologist* (November 1980), pp. 1021–1028; and Robert L. Linn, *Intelligence: Measurement Theory and Public Policy* (Urbana, Ill.; University of Illinois Press, 1988).

STANDARDIZED AND NONSTANDARDIZED TESTS

A **standardized test** is an instrument that contains a set of items that are administered and measured according to uniform scoring standards. The test has been pilot tested and administered to representative populations of similar individuals to obtain normative data. Most standardized tests are published and distributed by testing companies (such as Educational Testing Service and Psychological Corporation); publishing companies (such as Houghton Mifflin and Macmillan), which usually publish reading and math tests to accompany their textbooks; and universities (such as Iowa University and Stanford University), which have developed and validated specific achievement and IQ tests.

Standardized tests are widely used in schools, and you most certainly have taken a number them throughout your academic career. Standardized tests usually have high reliability coefficients and good validity, since they have been tested on representative sample populations. The unreliable or invalid test items have been eliminated through pilot testing over the years. Normative data are useful in interpreting individual test scores and in ranking individual scores within a comparative population. However, normative data are less useful in special school or class situations in which the students have abilities, aptitudes, needs, or learning problems that are quite different from the normative population. The content of standardized tests does not always coincide with the content in a particular school or classroom—that is, the tests may lack curricular validity for that school or classroom.

Nonstandardized tests, usually referred to as teacher-made tests or classroom tests, have not been tested on several sample populations and therefore are not accompanied by normative data. These test scores cannot indicate an individual's position with reference to a standard or larger sample. Standardized tests are usually administered only once or twice a year; teacher-made tests provide more frequent evaluations. Teacher-made tests are more closely related to the school's and/or teacher's objectives and content of the course. Who knows better than the teacher what content was covered and emphasized and hence should be tested? Who knows better than the teacher what are the needs, interests, and strengths of the students, when to test, and when, based on test outcomes, to proceed to the next instructional unit?[6]

The relative advantages and disadvantages of standardized and nonstandardized tests are listed in Table 4.1. These advantages and limitations are analyzed in terms of our previous discussion of reliability and validity.

---

6 Tom Kubiszyn and Gary Borich, *Education Testing and Measurement*, 3rd ed. (Glenview, Ill.: Scott, Foresman, 1990); W. Bruce Walsh, *Tests and Measurements*, 4th ed. (Englewood Cliffs, N.J.: Prentice-Hall, 1989).

Table 4.1 ADVANTAGES AND DISADVANTAGES OF STANDARDIZED AND NONSTANDARDIZED TESTS WITH RESPECT TO RELIABILITY AND VALIDITY

Standardized	Advantages	Limitations
1. Reliability	For best tests, fairly high—often .85 or more for comparable form.	High reliability is no guarantee of validity. Also, reliability depends upon range of ability in group tested.
2. Validity		
a. Curricular	Careful selection by competent persons. Fits typical situations.	Inflexible. Too general in scope to meet local requirements fully, especially in unusual situations.
b. Statistical	With best tests, high.	Criteria often inappropriate or unreliable. Size of coefficients dependent upon range of ability in group tested.
Nonstandardized (essays)	Advantages	Limitations
1. Reliability		Reliability usually quite low.
2. Validity		
a. Curricular	Useful for English, advanced classes; affords language training. May encourage sound study habits.	Limited sampling. Bluffing is possible. Mixes language factor in all scores.
b. Statistical		Usually not known
Nonstandardized (objective)	Advantages	Limitations
1. Reliability	Sometimes approaches that of standardized tests.	No guarantee of validity.
2. Validity		
a. Curricular	Extensive sampling of subject matter. Flexible in use. Discourages bluffing.	Narrow sampling of tested functions. Negative learning possible.
	Compares favorably with standard tests.	May encourage piecemeal study.
b. Statistical		Adequate criteria usually lacking.

Source: Julian C. Stanley, *Measurement in Today's Schools*, 4th ed. (Englewood Cliffs, N.J.: Prentice-Hall, 1964). pp. 304–305. Also see Kenneth D. Hopkins, Julian C. Stanley, and B. R. Hopkins, *Educational and Psychological Measurement and Evaluation*, 7th ed. (Englewood Cliffs, N.J.: Prentice-Hall, 1990).

Norm-Reference Tests (NRT)

Standardized tests are **norm-referenced**—that is, the performance of sample populations has been established and serves as a "basis for interpreting a [student's] relative test performance. A norm-reference measure allows us to compare one individual with other individuals."[7] The idea of norms, especially if the norms are based on a larger population, say, nationwide or statewide, is to compare the score of a student on a test with students from other schools. Suppose, for example, on a statewide achievement test Jack's score places him in the 98th percentile in his school, but in the 58th percentile in the state. Although Jack's score is extremely high when compared with scores of students in his school, it is barely above average compared to scores of a large pool of students. Students who attend inner-city schools may exhibit excellent performance when compared with classmates or peer groups, but poor performance on a national or statewide basis. If their scores are compared only with other inner-city schools or even with the city norms rather than statewide or national norms, their percentile scores are likely to be higher since the norm group is different.

Norm-reference tests tend to have high estimates of reliability and validity because the norms are based on large populations. The test manual usually reports reliability and validity data obtained for various sample populations. A test manual should provide a comprehensive description of procedures in establishing normative data. Although norms can be reported for almost any characteristic (sex, ethnicity, geographical setting, and so forth), such data are usually not shown or are incomplete for students who have special characteristics or backgrounds.

Criterion-Reference Tests (CRT)

Sometimes an educator is not concerned with how well a student performs compared to other students, but whether the student exhibits progress in learning. The educator establishes a set of objectives with corresponding proficiency or achievement levels and then determines whether the student can achieve an acceptable proficiency or achievement level.[8] Rather than compare the student to other students, the teacher assesses the student only on the basis of a predetermined standard. Scores can demonstrate progress (or minimal progress) in learning over time.

Criterion-reference tests measure individuals' ability in regard to a criterion, that is, a specific body of knowledge or skill. The tests are used to

---

7 N. L. Gage and David C. Berliner, *Educational Psychology*, 4th ed. (Boston: Houghton Mifflin, 1988), p. 572.

8 Norman E. Gronlund, *How to Construct Achievement Tests*, 4th ed. (Englewood Cliffs, N.J.: Prentice-Hall, 1988); W. James Popham, *Criterion-Referenced Measurement* (Englewood Cliffs, N.J.: Prentice-Hall, 1978).

Some students prefer to study for tests by themselves while others prefer to work in small groups or still others in a "buddy" system.

determine what students know or can do in a specific domain of learning rather than how their performance compares with other students.

Criterion-reference tests are usually locally developed and sometimes teacher-made. Norm-reference tests usually have better overall reliability and validity, since they have been constructed by test experts and tested on larger sample populations.[9] However, the criterion-reference tests allow the teacher to judge students' proficiency in specific content areas, and therefore they usually have better curricular validity than norm-reference tests.

Criterion-reference measurements may be practical in areas of achievement that focus on the acquisition of specific knowledge (for example, the Civil War in history or gas laws in physics) and in special programs such as individually prescribed instruction, mastery learning, and adaptive instruction.[10] It is important to note that it is difficult to develop reliable or valid criterion measurements, since most instructional units and special programs deal with specific information. See Tips for Teachers 4.1.

9 William A. Mehrens and Robert L. Ebel, "Some Comments on Criterion-Referenced and Norm-Referenced Tests," *Measurement in Education* (August 1979), pp. 43–53; W. James Popham, "Can High-Stakes Tests Be Developed at the Local Level?" *NASSP Bulletin* (February 1987), pp. 77–84.

10 Edward Haertel, "Construct Validity and Criterion-Reference Testings," *Review of Educational Research* (Spring 1985), pp. 47–86; W. James Popham, "Measurement Driven Instruction: It's on the Road," *Phi Delta Kappan* (May 1985), pp. 628–634; and Herbert C. Rudman, "Classroom Instruction and Tests," *NASSP Bulletin* (February 1987), pp. 3–22.

Tips for Teachers 4.1

Constructing Criterion-Reference Tests

In criterion-reference tests (1) performance is related to a set of behavioral objectives or referents, (2) the test items represent samples of actual performance or behavior, and (3) performance can be interpreted in terms of predetermined cutoff scores or achievement levels (such as low, average, high). If, for example, the test is on grammar, we must have some basis for saying that a student knows grammar, and what kinds of questions can be answered (dealing with nouns, verbs, adjectives, and so forth).

To construct a criterion-reference test, the following steps are recommended.

1. Prepare a content outline of the knowledge or skills that the test will measure. This should coincide with the course or unit outline.

   Example: Classifying singular nouns
   Classifying possessive nouns
   Classifying adjectives
   Classifying verbs
   Identifying pronouns
   Identifying adverbs
   Placing commas
   Placing semicolons
   Placing colons

2. Restate the knowledge or skills in behavioral terms—that is, identify the required performances. Include an *action* word and performance *criteria.*

   Example: *Action:* Write commas in appropriate places.
   Criteria: Use a comma to separate parts of compound sentence; after an adverbial clause; before a conjunction connecting the last two elements in a series of three or more.

3. To increase the content validity of the test, write test items to cover particular domains or areas, with at least two items per objective.

   Example: *Domain:* Compound sentences
   Objective: Given a short paragraph containing compound sentences, place all necessary commas properly.
   Test item: In the paragraph below insert five missing commas in the appropriate places.

(continues)

Test item: The paragraph below contains several sentences. Change two simple sentences to compound sentences, placing commas in the appropriate places in the sentences.

4. Validate the fact that the knowledge and skills measured by the test are prerequisite for moving to the next objective. This is based on judgment. To validate your assumption, give the test items to a group of experts or colleagues or obtain actual data by giving the test to a group of students who have overall proficiency to see which test items are more difficult than others.

5. Decide upon scores to indicate proficiency levels (below average, average, above average).

Source: Adapted from Bruce W. Tuckman, *Testing for Teachers*, 2nd ed. (San Diego: Harcourt Brace Jovanovich, 1988), pp. 44–46, 197. All examples and test items are this author's; the steps are based on Tuckman.

Differences Between Norm-Reference and Criterion-Reference Tests

The norm-reference test measures a student's level of achievement at a given period or time compared to other students elsewhere. Scores from a criterion-reference test do not indicate a relative level of achievement or produce standards because no comparisons are made. The test indicates how proficient a student is in terms of a specific body of learning. It can measure changes in learning over time, but it cannot produce meaningful comparisons or standards.

According to researchers, the norm-reference test is valuable for measuring higher and abstract levels of the cognitive domain, whereas the criterion-reference test is valuable for measuring lower and concrete levels of learning. The norm reference is valuable for heterogeneous group in which the range of abilities is wide and a test is intended to measure a wide range of performance. The criterion-reference test is more useful in homogeneous groups in which the range of abilities is narrow and a test is intended to measure a limited or predetermined range of objectives and outcomes. With norm-reference tests external standards can be used to make judgments about a student's performance, whereas criterion-reference tests lack uniform standards, and the interpretation of the scores is only as good as the process used to set the proficiency levels.[11]

Gronlund and Linn point out five differences: (1) Whereas the norm-reference test covers a *large or general domain* of learning tasks, with only a few items measuring each task, the criterion-reference test covers a *limited or specific domain*, with a relatively large number of items measuring each task. (2) The norm reference emphasizes *discrimination* among students in terms of relative levels of learning or achievement, whereas the criterion reference focuses on *description* of what learning tasks students can or cannot perform. (3) The norm-reference test favors *average difficulty* and omits easy or difficult items; the criterion-reference test *matches* item *difficulty* to the difficulty of learning tasks and does not omit easy or difficult items. (4) The norm-reference test is used for *survey or general testing*, while the criterion-reference test is used for *mastery or specific test situations*. (5) Interpretation of a norm-reference score is based on a *defined group*, and the student is evaluated by his or her standing relative to that group. Interpretation of a criterion-reference score is based on a *defined learning domain*, and the student is evaluated by items answered correctly.[12]

Criterion-reference tests are usually teacher-made and are used by teachers to tailor tests to their objectives, to develop more efficient and appropriate teaching strategies, and to fit the needs of the classroom population. Because norm-reference tests are prepared for many different school districts, with different curricular and instructional emphases, they are unable to do these individualized things. Criterion-reference tests better coincide with the actual teaching-learning situation of a particular class or school. The problem is that local school officials and teachers often lack the expertise in test construction needed to develop criterion-reference tests. Thus, it is recommended that teachers develop these tests in a group, where they can exchange information with colleagues and perhaps with a test consultant. Table 4.2 provides an overview of the difference between norm-reference and criterion-reference tests. Norm-reference tests are usually more carefully constructed than criterion-reference (teacher-made) tests, since the former are developed by test experts and test items are pilot tested and revised. The advantage of criterion-reference tests is that the teacher (or school) has more control over the content of the test.

---

11 Ronald K. Hambleton et al., "Criterion-Referenced Testing and Measurement: A Review of Technical Issues and Developments," *Review of Educational Research* (Winter 1978), pp. 1–47; Robert L. Linn, "Educational Testing and Assessment," *American Psychologist* (October 1986), pp. 1153–1160; and Craig G. Schoon et al., "An Alternative Criterion-Reference Passing Point Method," paper presented at the annual meeting of the American Educational Research Association, New Orleans, April 1988.

12 Norman E. Gronlund and Robert L. Linn, *Measurement and Evaluation in Teaching*, 6th ed. (New York: Macmillan, 1990).

Table 4.2   COMPARISON OF NORM-REFERENCE AND CRITERION-REFERENCE TESTS

Characteristic	Norm-reference test	Criterion-reference test
1. Major emphasis	Measures individual's achievement (or performance) in relation to a similar group at a specific time	Measures individual's change in achievement (or performance) over an extended period of time
	Survey test, achievement test	Mastery test, performance test
2. Reliability	High reliability; usually test items and scales are .90 or better	Usually unknown reliability; when test items are estimated, they are about .50 to .70
3. Validity	Content, construct, and criterion validity usually high	Content and curricular validity usually high if appropriate procedures are used
4. Usability	For diagnosing student difficulties; estimating student performance in a broad area; classifying students; and making decisions on how much a student has learned compared to others	For diagnosing student difficulties; estimating student performance in a specific area; certifying competency; and measuring what a student has learned over time
	Administration procedures are standardized and consistent from class to class	Administration procedures usually vary among teachers or schools
	Large group testing	Small group, individual testing
5. Content covered	Usually covers a broad area of content or skills	Typically emphasizes a limited area of content or skills
	School (or teacher) has no control over content being tested	School (or teacher) has opportunity to select content
	Linked to expert opinion	Linked to local curriculum
6. Quality of test items	Generally high	Varies, based on ability of test writer
	Test items written by experts, pilot tested, and revised prior to distribution; poor items omitted before test is used	Test items written by teachers (or publishers); test items are rarely pilot tested; poor items omitted after test has been used
7. Item selection	Test items discriminate among individuals to obtain variability of scores	Includes all items needed to assess performance; little or no attempt to deal with item difficulty

Table 4.2 (Continued)

Characteristic	Norm-reference test	Criterion-reference test
	Easy and confusing items usually omitted	Easy or confusing items are rarely omitted
8. Student preparation	Studying rarely helps student obtain a better score, although familiarity with the test seems to improve scores	Studying will help student obtain a better score
	Students are unable to obtain information from teachers about content covered	Students are able to obtain information from teachers about content covered
9. Standards	Norms are used to establish a standard or to classify students	Performance levels are used to establish students' ability
	Intended outcomes are general, relative to performance of others	Intended outcomes are specific, relative to a specified level
	Score is determined by a ranking, average, or stanine	Score is determined by an absolute number, e.g., 83 percent right

Types of Standardized Tests

There are basically four types of standardized tests. The scores from these tests will appear in the student record, often called the *cumulative record*.

Intelligence Tests

An **intelligence test** provides a *general* measurement as opposed to a specific measurement, of understanding abstract relations and complex reasoning abilities. Intelligence tests were once thought to measure innate abilities not subject to change. This assumption is invalid since the characteristic or score is based on interaction factors related to heredity and environment (the latter which can be modified and affect outcomes). There is some evidence, for example, that continuing education raises IQ test scores.[13] To avoid the implica-

---

13 Alan S. Kaufman, *Assessing Adolescent and Adult Intelligence* (Englewood Cliffs, N.J.: Prentice-Hall, 1990); Gilbert Sax, *Principles of Educational and Psychological Measurement and Evaluation*, 3rd ed. (Belmont, Calif.: Wadsworth, 1989).

tions of innateness, many test makers today prefer to use the term "potential learning ability" or "aptitude."

Intelligence tests have come under attack in recent years and many school systems use them sparingly or mainly for special testing or placement of students. The two most commonly used IQ tests are the Stanford-Binet (SB) and the Wechsler Intelligence Scale for Children (WISC). The SB was originally developed in 1905, and it has been continuously revised (1911, 1937, 1960, 1986). Unlike previous editions, the latest revision includes special norms for minority groups. The test is administered on a group basis and consists of 15 test items that measure four cognitive areas (see Table 4.3): (1) verbal reasoning, (2) abstract/visual reasoning, (3) quantitative reasoning, and (4) short-term memory. The SB is a very good predictor of school performance, and the reliability of test items ranges from the mid .80s to mid .90s, with reliability scores higher for older students (which is common for most standardized tests).[14]

The Wechsler Intelligence Scale for Children (WISC), originally published in 1949, was revised in 1974 and 1981 and is designed for children between 6 and 15. The test consists of two general areas and ten tests: *Verbal* (1) information, (2) similarities, (3) arithmetic, (4) vocabulary, and (5) comprehension; *Performance* (6) picture completion, (7) picture arrangement, (8) block design, (9) object assembly, and (10) coding. The test is administered on an individual basis and like the SB, has test item reliability of around .90.[15]

Both IQ tests have separate adult versions. The SB adult level starts at age 15 and the tasks are spaced at one-year intervals. The Wechsler adult test starts at age 16, and items are arranged by separate subtests rather than by ages. Whereas the SB uses a separate form of the same test to test adults, the Wechsler has a separate test, the Wechsler Adult Intelligence Scale (WAIS).

Achievement Tests

The use of **achievement tests** has increased in recent years, replacing intelligence testing as the prime source of information for educators about students and how they perform in comparison to each other and to students elsewhere. Every elementary student is exposed to a series of reading, language, and mathematics standardized tests to evaluate performance at various grade levels. There are several types of achievement tests, as stated below.

1. The most common *survey* or *general achievement tests* are the Stanford Achievement Tests (grades 2 through 9) and the Iowa Test of Basic Skills. The National Assessment of Educational Progress (NAEP)

---

14 Robert L. Thorndike, Elizabeth P. Hagen, and Jerome M. Sattler, *Stanford-Binet Intelligence Scale Technical Manual*, 4th ed. (Chicago, Ill.: Riverside, 1986).

15 Oscar K. Buros, ed., *Ninth Mental Measurement Yearbook* (Highland Park, N.J.: Gryphon Press, 1985).

Table 4.3   COGNITIVE AREAS TESTED ON THE STANFORD-BINET INTELLIGENCE TEST, 1986 EDITION

I. Verbal Reasoning	III. Quantitative Reasoning
1. Vocabulary	9. Quantitative
2. Comprehension	10. Number series
3. Absurdities	11. Equation building
4. Verbal relations	IV. Short-Term Memory
II. Abstract/Visual Reasoning	12. Bead memory
5. Pattern analysis	13. Memory of sentences
6. Copying	14. Memory of digits
7. Matrices	15. Memory of objects
8. Folding and cutting	

Source: Adapted from Robert L. Thorndike, Elizabeth P. Hagen, and Jerome M. Sattler, *Stanford-Binet Intelligence Scale Technical Manual*, 4th ed. (Chicago: Riverside, 1986), pp. 52–53.

exams are designed to measure the knowledge and skills of American students in 10 subject areas (with emphasis in the arts, science, math, and career development) at ages 9, 13, and 17.

The periodic release of results (which is often published in local newspapers) attracts wide attention and has become known as the "Nation's Report Card." As a nation, our trend in achievement compared to other industrialized nations is disturbing (and is now linked to one reason for our economic decline).

2. Many students are required to take *diagnostic tests*, usually in the basic skills and in study skills, to reveal strengths and weaknesses for purposes of placement and formulating an appropriate instructional program. The California Achievement Test (CAT) is an excellent example of an achievement test that can be used for diagnostic purposes for all students. It goes beyond reporting numerical scores and percentiles, that is, global achievement scores, and describes and interprets a student's skills and knowledge in particular subject areas, such as reading, language, math, and study skills.

A report goes to the school and then the parent. Sections of each test are graphed for easy interpretation, whereby the student scores on subtests are shown in relationship to national standards, and in a corresponding box an analysis is written for each text; for example, the student "is strongest in differentiating between forms of understanding, understanding the meaning of words, and identifying missing words by their context. Further help is needed in identifyingmultimeaningwords."[16] Both the teacher and parent are told specific knowledge of what the student has mastered or not mastered in a particular subject area.

3. An increasing number of students in many school systems must pass *competency tests* to prove they are competent in reading, language, and math. Students who fail are usually provided with some type of remediation. In some cases the tests are used as "break points" or "gate guards" between elementary, junior high, and high school and as a requirement for graduation from high school. Students in some states are denied promotion or a diploma until they pass the examinations.[17]

4. *Subject exit tests* are used in a few school systems at the high school level. Students must pass tests to graduate, to receive a particular diploma, or to enroll in certain programs. For example, New York State uses the Regents examinations in basic academic subject areas (English, history, science, mathematics, foreign language) as a screen for eligibility to matriculate full time in a state college or university; the student must also pass these examinations to receive an academic diploma. Actually, these exams may be considered competency tests.

Aptitude Test

The difference between aptitude and achievement tests is that **aptitude tests** predict achievement, while achievement tests provide information about present achievement or cumulative past learning.

Whereas achievement tests deal with content that the schools teach (or should be teaching), aptitude tests may stress what is not taught in schools. The most common aptitude tests are briefly discussed below.

1. Most students who wish to go on to college have to take a number of *general aptitude tests* to provide information to college admissions officers. You probably took the Scholastic Aptitude Tests (SAT) or the American College Testing Program (ACT) exam. Students applying to graduate school may take the Miller Analogies Test (MAT) or the Graduate Record Examination (GRE). The MAT is a general aptitude test in logic and language skills. The GRE is a general aptitude test, but the advanced parts are considered a *professional aptitude test*.

2. *Special* or *talent aptitude tests* are frequently administered as screening devices for students who wish to enroll in a special school (such as

---

16 Based on an actual report of a student, test date April 19, 1990, from the reading section of the California Achievement Test.

17 Allan C. Ornstein, "Accountability Report from the USA," *Journal of Curriculum Studies* (December 1985), pp. 437–439; Ornstein, "National Reform and Instructional Accountability," *High School Journal* (October-November 1990), pp. 51–56.

music, art, or science), a special course (such as an honors or a college credit course) or a special program (such as creative writing or computers).

Personality Tests

Personality tests are generally used for special placement of students with learning or adjustment problems. Most students in school are not tested for personality. The most commonly used personality tests are the California Test of Personality, the Pinter Personality Test, and the Thematic Apperception Test, all intended for use in primary grades through college and designed to measure various aspects of social and personal adjustment.

Three additional categories of personality tests are listed below:

1. A number of general *attitudinal scales*, which estimate attitudes in diverse economic, political, social, and religious areas, are available; among the more common ones are the Allport Submission Reaction Study and the Allport-Vernon-Lindsey Study of Values.
2. Among *occupational attitudinal tests*, the Occupational Interest Inventory is suitable for students with at least a sixth-grade reading level, and the Kuder Preference Record is designed for high school and college students.
3. The most popular *projective test* is the Rorschach Inkblot Test. The test has some reliability and validity problems, especially in prediction from trait scores to behavioral situations, but it is still widely used in many schools.

Trends in Standardized Testing

Test are sometimes misused or misinterpreted by teachers and counselors. To the extent the school curriculum coincides with middle-class values, tests will usually reflect these values. While the middle-class bias of standardized tests is often criticized in the professional literature, these values reflect our evolving society, which is technological, bureaucratic, information-based. This is the nature of our present society, and there is little need to romanticize the culture of poverty or to argue that catching fish or hunting game is more important than learning how to read or use computers.

However, as critics point out, there is a need to (1) train teachers and counselors to properly administer and interpret test scores, (2) understand that scores are not fixed but correlate with changes in environment (and schooling) and conditions in the home, (3) evaluate each student in the context of a pluralistic society, and (4) use separate norms for different subgroups when we identify, classify, or make decisions about students.[18] The purpose of testing is

---

18 Ronald Samuda, *Psychological Testing of American Minorities* (New York: Dodd, Mead, 1975); Sandra Scarr, *IQ: Race, Social Class, and Individual Differences* (Hillsdale, N.J.: Erlbaum, 1981).

to help each student (or individual) develop his or her fullest potential by diagnosing present problems and strengths and placing the student in an appropriate program with appropriate instruction, so that each student can overcome problems and excel. The idea is to help the students, not to hammer them over the head or discourage them, with results of test scores.

It is also important to recognize that a student's placement and progress in school, from grades 1 to 12, is largely determined by his or her scores on achievement tests in reading and math and, later on, aptitude tests of general knowledge or literacy. On a practical basis most standardized tests, at all grade levels (with the exception of personality tests), focus on declarative or simple content and not on high-level cognitive processes which cut across subject matter and are useful for critical thinking in several subjects.

Testing and Cognition Levels

As many as 22 cognitive processes have been identified by thinking skills theorists. However, in a review of 6,942 test items on standardized tests, Marzano and Costa found that only nine cognitive processes were involved in answering the items. Two were involved in some way in answering every item: retrieving information from long-term memory, and comparing different pieces of information. The seven other processes, with corresponding percentage of use, were: referencing, or identifying explicit or implicit information (17 percent); visual matching, or relating a picture or symbol to a linguistic term (8.5 percent); inferring, or deducing unstated information (6.5 percent); ordering, or ranking or sequencing data (5.5 percent); representing, or devising a graphic or pictorial representation of information (5 percent); transposing, or translating information from one source to another (5 percent); and summarizing, or combining information (3 percent). The remaining 13 high-order thinking skills were considered absent on standardized tests.[19]

Until standardized tests are revised to reflect important cognitive processes such as extrapolating, synthesizing, verifying, and predicting, teachers will continue to stress these nine cognitive processes during teaching and instructional practices to prepare students for the tests they must take. To be sure, curriculum and instruction are test driven. It behooves test developers to improve their tests if they wish teachers to upgrade and incorporate critical thinking or problem solving in the content or subject matter.

So long as school authorities focus their attention on test results and not on how students think, standardized tests will continue to emphasize low-level cognitive operations. Some states, for example, Illinois and Michigan, are

---

19 Robert J. Marzano and Arthur L. Costa, "Question: Do Standardized Tests Measure General Cognitive Skills? Answer: No," *Educational Leadership* (May 1988), pp. 66–71.

Tests come in many formats, but most high school students are well aware of the SATs and their importance.

beginning to develop standardized tests in reading that attempt to determine how well readers process information.[20] To assess readers' processes—that is, the way they think—is a step toward providing information about how students read. This information is much more important than reading results if we are going to help students become better readers. The same is true in math, science, and other subject areas.

Coaching and College Admission Scores

The Scholastic Aptitude Test (SAT) is a measure of a student's potential for success in college. It assesses verbal and mathematical reasoning skills developed over time both in and out of school. It is not a curriculum-based test; rather it measures both school and nonschool experiences. In particular, the verbal part of the SAT depends in part on vocabulary and language skills

---

20 Roger Farr, "New Trends in Reading Assessment: Better Tests, Better Uses," *Curriculum Review* (September-October 1987), pp. 21–23; Sheila W. Valencia et al., "Theory and Practice in Statewide Reading Assessment," *Educational Leadership* (April 1989), pp. 57–63.

developed through outside reading.[21] Despite high reliability and validity, the test is criticized for being biased against minority and lower-class students.

Because the test is not curriculum based, some colleges are beginning to consider the American College Test (ACT)—which comprises reading and three achievement tests (English, science, and math) and which stresses mastery of the high school curriculum—in lieu of the SAT. The maximum score for the ACT is 36 with an average score representing 18 for the last five years (1986–1990); the maximum SAT score is 1600; the average is 426 for the verbal and 476 for the math for the last five years.

Despite its limitations, the public and news media often use the SAT scores as a barometer to measure the effectiveness of individual high schools. Administrators are under pressure to raise score averages; in turn, teachers are often forced in class to spend time preparing students for the test. The reason is simple: More than 1.6 million students annually take the SAT and some 2,600 colleges and universities use the test as part of their admission process and also award a limited number of scholarships on the basis of such scores.

Although the Educational Testing Service, which developed the SAT, and the American College Testing Program, which developed the ACT, have long claimed that coaching does little to raise scores, controversy has surfaced around the question of coaching. Not only has ETS abandoned its original opposition to coaching and now advises students to prepare for the tests, the association of 2,600 colleges and universities that uses the SAT in their admission process are now selling computer software to help students study for the test.[22] To add more confusion to the coaching issue, the ACT still claims that a "cram" course is unlikely to help and that the best procedure is to take a full course in the subject area in which one is weak.[23]

To what extent coaching influences test outcomes for the SAT varies according to the specific study. One reason is that *coaching* is used to refer to a wide variety of test preparation activities undertaken by students to improve test scores: (1) focusing on content and ability areas measured by the test; (2) reducing test anxiety by increasing familiarity with directions, format, pacing; and (3) improving test-taking skills and answer-selection strategies.[24]

The length of the coaching period is often associated with score improvement, although the relationship is not linear but levels off after 30 hours. For example, one review shows verbal scores on the SAT increase an average of 8 points after 10 hours, 16 points after 30 hours, and 24 points after 100 hours.

21 Jim Montagne, "Beyond the SAT," *American School Board Journal* (June 1990), pp. 31–33.

22 Gary L. Peltier, "Empowering Students to Improve Their College Admission Test Scores," *Clearing House* (December 1989), pp. 163–165.

23 *Preparing For the ACT Assessment* (Iowa City, Iowa.: ACT, no date).

24 Betsy J. Becker, "Coaching for the Scholastic Aptitude Test," *Review of Educational Research* (Fall 1990), pp. 373–417; Peltier, "Empowering Students to Improve Their College Admission Test Scores."

Math scores rise 12 points after a 10–hour course, 25 points after 30 hours, and 30 points after 100 hours.[25] The length of the program also is a factor in determining the method of coaching. For example, longer coaching periods (10 weeks or more) focus on content-related items and broad cognitive skills; short-term programs focus on test-taking strategies.[26]

Other factors that interact with test outcomes are the size of the class, the selectivity and motivation of the students who enroll in these coaching programs, the effects of growth and development of the students, and the statistical regression effects (namely, students who score below their potential on test 1 will statistically score higher on test 2 without coaching, and students who score above their potential on test 1 will tend to show minimal improvement even with coaching). Also, "practice makes perfect," as the old axiom goes. The average student may raise his test score about 50 points simply by retaking the test and being familiar with it, without coaching. When private companies announce 100 to 150 point increases, they are not considering the first 50 points that usually goes along with simple retake. (Another 50 points may be attributed to sustained review—even without private coaching—and the motivation factor pertaining to anyone who would become involved in a lengthy review.)

The mean point gains on the SAT have varied dramatically—from as low as 10 points on the verbal and 15 points on the math, says the ETS, to as many as 150 points on the verbal and math tests, if we believe the claims made by some of the private coaching organizations, such as the Kaplan and Princeton Review programs. The Kaplan Education Center requires 40 to 50 hours in class and another 30 hours of homework. It has about 125 permanent locations and another 200 temporary sites across the country and offers test reviews in many other professional areas. The program takes the long-term approach and focuses on content and prepares about 20,000 students a year for the SATs. Their fees are $565.

The Princeton Review program is a six-week program taught in 45 cities (mainly in schools and community agencies) and prepares about 15,000 students a year. It takes the short-term approach and focuses on test anxiety and test-taking strategies. Both approaches review and analyze old SAT tests and claim the test has a definite format that changes little from test to test and can be learned. Their fees run approximately $600 per student.

The Kaplan Center also prepares students for the ACT, but the Princeton Review does not—contending that the ACT recently has changed the format of its test and provides insufficient data to explicitly state what to study. The test is mainly taken in the Midwest and the Review is an Eastern–based company—another reason for the Review's slow movement in reviewing the

25 M. Elias, "SAT Preps: Math Scores Benefit Most," *USA Today*, January 19, 1989, p. 10.

26 James A. Kulik et al., "Effectiveness of Coaching for Aptitude Tests," *Psychological Bulletin* (March 1984), pp. 179–188.

ACT. It also tentatively takes the ACT's position that the sum total of the knowledge or content being tested cannot easily be changed in a specific subject area, at least not in a short period of time.

In addition to these two popular programs, coaching courses are offered at schools on weekends and during summer, for free, and at YMCAs and community colleges. A slight advantage of school-based programs over commercial coaching may exist. Stronger coaching effects seem also to exist for the math test than the verbal test.[27] Such findings are contrary to expectations about the effects of student motivation in commercial coaching programs. Much of the variation in results arises from studies without comparison groups,[28] meaning that growth and development over a one-year period and regression effects (scoring low on the first test and higher on the second) are not controlled, which would account for some of the gains without any treatment (or coaching).

When it comes down to it, the best test strategies for the SAT and ACT seem to be based on common sense. ("Never" or "always" suggests a false or wrong answer.) Minority groups are favorably discussed in reading passages so that the answers are positive (i.e., The author views Hispanic Literature with [a] indifference, [b] despair, [c] distaste, or [d] admiration. Without reading the passage, the answer is d.). The SAT test items for each section (except reading passages) are in order of difficulty (which suggests that students should devote more time to the first questions in a section), while the ACT spreads the difficult items and therefore, the testee should skip the difficult questions: "After answering all of the easy questions, go back and answer the more difficult questions."[29] The SAT deducts 1/4 point for guessing so it is more important to eliminate incorrect answers and then take educated guesses; with the ACT, the score is based on the number of correct responses, with no penalty for guessing, so that it is important to answer every question. Whereas most average students will finish the SAT, and must resist the urge to blindly guess, it is still better to guess in the beginning (when the questions are easy) than at the end. If an answer to a question at the end seems obvious it is probably wrong, because the test items become increasingly more difficult and subtle. Almost the reverse is true with the ACT, where speed is important and the difficulty of the questions are intermixed. Whereas the SAT is known for tricking students at the end, the ACT questions should be taken more literally.

So with all this new information, is it still worth spending money to be coached? Well, perhaps it depends on how hard students are "driven" or how hard parents push kids.

---

27 Lloyd Bond, "The Effects of Special Preparation on Measures of Scholastic Ability," in R. L. Linn, ed., *Educational Measurement*, 3rd ed. (New York: Macmillan, 1989), pp. 429–444; Elias, "SAT Preps: Math Scores Benefit Most."

28 Becker, "Coaching for the Scholastic Aptitude Test."

29 *Preparing for the ACT Assessment*, p. 1. Also see *The Enhanced ACT Assessment* (Iowa City, Iowa.: ACT, 1989).

Questions to Consider in Selecting Tests

Hundreds of standardized tests exist, and selecting an appropriate one is difficult. Individual classroom teachers usually do not have to make this choice, but you may be called upon to make selections if you serve as a member of a test or evaluation committee for your school district. Below are 12 questions to assist you in selecting an appropriate standardized test. They are based on criteria formulated by W. James Popham.

1. *Is the achievement test in harmony with course instructional objectives?* An achievement test should correspond with the objectives of the course, and it should assess the important knowledge, concepts, and skills of the course.
2. *Do the test items measure a representative sample of the learning tasks?* The test items cannot measure the entire course or subject matter, but they should cover the major objectives and content.
3. *Are the test items appropriate for measuring the desired outcomes of learning?* The test items should correspond to behaviors or performance levels consistent with the course level.
4. *Does the test fit the particular uses that will be made of the results?* For example, a diagnostic achievement test should be used for analyzing student difficulties, but an aptitude test should be used for predicting future performance in a given subject or program.
5. *Is the achievement test reliable?* The test should report reliability coefficients for different types of students, and they should be high for the student group you are testing.
6. *Does the test have retest potential?* Equivalent forms of the test should be available so that students can be retested if necessary. There should also be evidence that the alternative forms are equivalent.
7. *Is the test valid?* Standardized tests usually have poor curricular validity, but the test should have good construct validity and good criterion validity.
8. *Is the test free of obvious bias?* It is difficult to find a test that is totally free of bias toward all student groups, but teachers should look for tests that are considered culturally fair or at least sensitive toward minority groups and that provide normative data (reliability and validity data) for minority groups.
9. *Is the test appropriate for students?* The test must be suitable for the persons being tested in reading levels, clarity of instructions, visual layout, and so forth. It must be at the appropriate level of difficulty for students of a given age, grade level, and cultural background.
10. *Does the test improve learning?* Achievement tests should be seen as part of the teaching and learning process. This means a test should provide feedback to teachers and students and be used to guide and improve the teacher's instruction and the student's learning.

11. *Is the test easy to administer?* Tests that can be administered to large groups are more usable than tests that can only be given to small groups or individuals. Tests that require less time and are still reliable are more usable than lengthy tests.

12. *Is the cost of the test acceptable?* The total cost of the test, including the time involved in administering and scoring it, should be commensurate with the benefits to be derived. If similar information can be obtained by some other method that is just as reliable and valid, and less costly, then that method should be considered.[30]

Improving Tests

The types of questions on a test influence the way students study; research suggests that recall test questions encourage cramming and memorization of text material and classroom notes in the days immediately before the examination. It has been argued that such examinations (and studying) may actually serve to clear from the student's short-term memory the knowledge involved, rather than strengthen it. It is also possible that this kind of study behavior results in test anxiety (from cramming and memorizing isolated pieces of information), which in turn detrimentally affects future learning and test taking.

Although most educators call for students to analyze, synthesize, critically think, and problem solve, our statements about teaching and learning do not coincide with our testing polices. Although many researchers and test experts see serious limitations to our testing practices, and caution educators about misuse of tests and the fact that most test items are poor indicators of what students learn in class, most school people seldom show concern about these matters. They continue to be driven by tests and use tests for sorting and tracking students—and sometimes as a weapon to control or undercut students.

The common belief is that high-level thinking activities cannot be easily tested as a whole process, and perhaps the only method is to break thinking into a collection of facts, subactivities, and tiny observable behaviors that can be taught and tested. But once we start breaking down thinking into small tasks so we can measure it, we often discourage critical thinking, problem solving and creativity. However, teachers engaged in teaching higher levels of thinking usually do not worry much about tests, correctly assuming their students will do well on them.[31] Teachers who are behaviorist or task oriented often try to modify thinking and learning activities in class so they fit prevailing assessment

---

30 W. James Popham, *Modern Educational Measurement*, 2nd ed. (Englewood Cliffs, N.J.: Prentice-Hall, 1990).

31 Rexford Brown, "Testing and Thoughtfulness," *Educational Leadership* (April 1989), pp. 31–33.

criteria. The result is a teacher who is knowledge oriented—who teaches and tests by asking: What is the capital of Chile? What is the formula for salt?

The prevailing assumption about testing is that knowledge is objective and concrete and can easily be tested. High-order thinking is somewhat personal and abstract—and its application shifts with the problem at hand or the context of the situation—so it cannot easily be tested.[32] Thoughtful thinking involves inquiry, discovery, and activity—all "messy" testing situations. Although we talk a good game about thinking strategies and learning how to learn, we may need to change the whole concept of testing, to move from its present focus on objective and isolated knowledge to subjective and active exam tasks.

In this connection, tomorrow's tests need to provide more than scores or correct or incorrect marks; a student should be told why an answer was correct or incorrect or perhaps be asked to justify an answer. A test should provide a "progress map," that is, a big picture of what students have learned, what knowledge and skills they have mastered, and what still needs to be mastered. Using such a map, or detailed report, the teacher and students would be able to assess their progress and gauge their cognitive growth. With this test approach, teaching and learning could highlight progress as well as proficiency in a given subject area.[33]

Another idea for improvement is to present tasks and questions on tests that relate to the real world of thinking and problem solving—which frequently takes place under unclear or changing conditions. Such test items are difficult to construct, and suggest greater reliability problems since the conditions might differ. But such tests can be constructed, given our computer-based knowledge, and they offer an improved method of testing broad thinking skills that cut across subjects.

An important consideration is that educators give greater emphasis to the knowledge, skills and tasks they perceive as important and be sure they test them. Some of our important objectives may be hard to test and evaluate, especially when we move from low-level to high-level thinking, as well as to the affective domain of teaching and learning, but it is important that we find ways to assess them. If we cannot measure what we think is important, then we are lowering our academic expectations and subsequently the teaching and learning process.

Finally, greater efforts are needed to make teachers aware of the role of testing in teaching and in assessing learning. More experience with basic principles of testing and measurement must be provided to teachers, and they must learn how to interpret different assessment devices, including norm-reference tests, criterion-reference tests, and judgmental instruments.

---

32 Brown, "Testing and Thoughtfulness"; Ruth Garner and Patricia A. Alexander, "Metacognition: Answered and Unanswered Questions," *Educational Psychologist* (Spring 1989), pp. 143–158.

33 Michael E. Martinez and Joseph I. Lipson, "Assessment of Learning," *Educational Leadership* (April 1989), pp. 73–75.

CLASSROOM TESTS

Teachers are expected to write their own classroom tests. Most of these tests will be subject-related, will focus on a specific domain of learning, and will assess whether a subject has been mastered and it is time to move on to a new area. In this context classroom tests are criterion-reference measurements.

Two researchers report that the majority of teachers develop more than half the tests used in class. About a third of the teachers surveyed estimate they spend between 11 and 20 percent of their professional time on developing and correcting teacher-made tests, and slightly more than a third estimate they spend more than 20 percent of their time on such tests.[34] William Mehrens estimates that a student may take as many as 400 to 1,000 teacher-constructed tests prior to high school graduation.[35]

It may be said that teachers and schools are in the business of testing and that they are highly influenced (sometimes hypnotized) by test scores. However, according to researchers, the bulk of the testing is done with teacher-made tests that have unknown or low reliability, and most teachers do not know how to check for reliability or how to ensure appropriate weighting of content (which impacts on validity).[36] Analysis of teacher-made tests reveals that about 80 percent of test questions emphasize knowledge or specific content, that tests frequently do not give adequate directions or explain scoring, and that about 15 to 20 percent contain grammatical, spelling, and punctuation errors.[37]

In spite of these limitations, classroom tests still serve important and useful purposes. They provide information related to (1) formulating and refining objectives for each student, (2) deciding on curriculum content, (3) evaluating and refining instructional techniques, and (4) evaluating the degree to which learning outcomes have been achieved. One study states that classroom tests are used by teachers (1) to group or place students initially, (2) to decide on what to teach and how to teach it to students of different abilities or achievement levels, (3) to monitor student progress, (4) to change student grouping and placement, (5) to guide changes in their teaching approach, and (6) to evaluate students on their performance.[38]

---

34 Deena C. Newman and W. M. Stallings, "Teacher Competency in Classroom Testing, Measurement Preparation, and Classroom Testing Practices," paper presented at the annual meeting of the National Council on Measurement in Education, March 1982.

35 William A. Mehrens, "Educational Tests: Blessing or Curse?" unpublished, 1987.

36 William A. Mehrens and Irwin J. Lehmann, "Using Teacher-Made Measurement Devices," *NASSP Bulletin* (February 1987), pp. 36–44; Popham, "Can High-Stakes Tests Be Developed at the Local Level?"

37 Margaret Fleming and Barbara Chambers, "Teacher-Made Tests: Windows in the Classroom," in W. E. Hathaway, ed., *Testing in Schools* (San Francisco: Jossey-Bass, 1983), pp. 29–38.

38 D. W. Dorr-Bremme, "Assessing Students: Teacher's Routine Practice and Reasoning," paper presented at the annual meeting of the American Educational Research Association, New York, March 1982.

A classroom test should be considered a learning tool for students and a measuring tool for teachers. If used as a learning tool, then the teacher cannot retrieve copies of the test for the purpose of reusing it the following term. The procedure has great advantage for the teacher, saving time in devising a new test, but then the test functions almost exclusively as a measuring instrument. Some teachers, who rely on short-answer tests, tend to collect all copies of the test each time it is used, since a good deal of time was consumed in the construction of tests. But the ideal situation is to permit students to review the test results (keep it if they want to study for the final examination) and to create separate forms of the test. Another reason for students keeping their test is that it can be used a second time as a posttest—providing opportunities for them to practice problems and to study to improve their answers.

A good test can assist teaching and learning, but it needs to be clear and test the learning goals we think are important. It must be challenging, yet not too difficult; fair and provide useful information about what students have or have not learned, yet allow flexibility in the way students learn and think. In some cases (especially in math and science), the answer is not as important as the process involved in responding to the question. The test must consider the context of the subject matter, measuring useful knowledge, depth, and complex thinking; it should not measure esoteric information or simple acquisition of knowledge. Table 4.4 presents an overview of the characteristics of a good test for classroom (or schoolwide) use.

Differences Between Short-Answer and Essay Tests

Most classroom tests fall into two categories: *short-answer tests* (multiple choice, matching, completion, and true-false), sometimes called *objective tests*, and *essay* (or *discussion*) *tests*, sometimes called *free-responsive tests*. **Short-answer tests** require the student to supply a specific and brief answer, usually in one or two words; essay tests require the student to organize and express an answer in his or her own words and do not restrict the student to a list of responses.

An **essay test** usually consists of a few questions, each requiring a lengthy answer. A short-answer test consists of many questions, each taking little time to answer. Content sampling and reliability are likely to be superior in short-answer tests. Essay tests provide an opportunity for high-level thinking, including analysis, synthesis, and evaluation. Most short-answer items emphasize low-level thinking or memorization, not advanced cognitive operations.

The quality (reliability and validity) of an objective test depends primarily on the skill of the test constructor, whereas the quality of the essay test depends mainly on the skill of the person grading the test. Short-answer tests take longer to prepare but are easier to grade. Essay tests may be easier to prepare but are difficult to grade. Short-answer items tend to be explicit, with only one correct answer. Essays permit the student to be individualistic and subjective; the answer is often open to interpretation, and there is more than one right answer. Short-answer tests are susceptible to guessing and cheating; essay tests are susceptible

Table 4.4   CHARACTERISTICS OF GOOD TESTS

I. *Intellectual Standards*

1. *Essential*—is not needlessly intrusive or arbitrary or developed to "trick" students.
2. *Enabling*—is constructed to assess sophisticated learning skills.
3. *Contextualized*—tests complex academic challenges, not tiny tasks or isolated outcomes.
4. *Useful*—requires students' use of knowledge, application of content.
5. *Comprehensive*—assesses students' habits and repertoires, not mere recall or simple skills.
6. *Representative*—emphasizes depth more than breadth.
7. *Clear*—is not ambiguous or ill-conceived (disjointed) tasks or problems.

II. *Scoring Standards*

1. *Important criteria* are assessed.
2. *Performance* is based on a clear criterion.
3. *Self-assessment* is included as part of overall assessment.
4. *Multifaceted scoring system* is achieved; not one aggregate grade.
5. *Harmony* with schoolwide goals is attained.

III. *Fairness*

1. *Hidden strengths* of the student are identified.
2. *Balance* is maintained between prior achievement or skills and new content or skills.
3. *Comparisons* among students are minimized.
4. *Learning styles* that differ among students are considered.
5. *Scaffolded up*, not watered down; yet tests are attempted by all students.
6. *Accountability* is directed at the teacher as well as the students.
7. *Follow-up* procedures for items missed; weaknesses are identified.

Source: Adapted from Grant Wiggins, "Teaching to the Authentic Test," *Educational Leadership* (April 1989), p. 45.

to bluffing (writing "around" the answer).[39] Table 4.5 provides an overview of some reasons for selecting short-answer and essay tests. The relative advantages of the two types of tests are suggested by the characteristics noted in the table.

39 Robert L. Ebel and David A. Frisbie, *Essentials of Educational Measurement,* 2nd ed. (Englewood Cliffs, N.J.: Prentice-Hall, 1991); R. L. Linn, ed., *Educational Measurement,* 3rd ed. (New York: Macmillan, 1989); and Anthony Nitko, *Educational Tests and Measurements* (San Diego, Calif.: Harcourt Brace Jovanovich, 1983).

Table 4.5   REASONS FOR SELECTING SHORT-ANSWER OR ESSAY TESTS

Short answer (multiple choice, matching, completion, true-false)	Essay
1. Provides good item pool	1. Calls for higher levels of cognitive thinking
2. Samples objectives and broad content	2. Measures student's ability to select and organize ideas
3. Is independent of writing ability (quality of handwriting, spelling) and verbal fluency	3. Is easy and quick to prepare
4. Discourages bluffing by writing or talking "around the topic"	4. Tests writing ability
5. Is easy and quick to score	5. Eliminates guessing or answering by process of elimination
6. Scoring and grading are reliable procedures	6. Measures problem-thinking skills
7. Scoring is objective	7. Encourages originality and unconventional answers
	8. Is practical for small groups of students, older students, and high-achieving students

According to Mehrens and Lehmann, there are six factors to consider in choosing between short-answer and essay tests.

1. *Purpose of the test.* If you want to measure written expression or critical thinking, then use an essay. If you want to measure broad knowledge of the subject or results of learning, then use short-answer items.
2. *Time.* The time saved in preparing an essay test is often used up in grading the responses. If you are rushed before the test and have sufficient time after it, you might choose an essay examination. If you must process the results in two or three days, you should use short-answer items—provided you have sufficient time to write good questions.
3. *Numbers tested.* If there are only a few students, the essay test is practical. If the class is large or if you have different classes, short-answer tests are recommended.
4. *Facilities.* If typing and reproduction facilities are limited, the teacher may be forced to rely on essay tests. Completion and true-false questions can be administered by reading the question aloud, but it is best that all short-answer tests be typed, reproduced, and put in front of students to respond to at their own pace.
5. *Age of students.* Not until about the fifth or sixth grade should students be required to answer essay questions. Older students (sixth grade and above) can deal with a variety of types of short-answer items, but

Essay tests are probably the best classroom teacher-made test for requiring higher cognitive levels of thinking.

younger students are confused by changing item formats and accompanying directions.

6. *Teacher's skill.* Some types of items (true-false) are easier to write than others, and teachers tend to prefer one type over another. However, different types should be included. Test writing is a skill that can be improved with practice.[40] See Tips for Teachers 4.2.

SHORT-ANSWER TESTS

Short-answer questions include multiple-choice, matching, completion, and true-false. Writing the test questions generally involves finding the most appropriate format for posing problems to students. Test questions often ask for the recall of information—facts, terms, names, or rules—but they can also involve higher-order cognitive abilities. (It is easier to devise multiple-choice questions for testing advanced cognitive abilities; it is more difficult with the other short-answer types.) A number of suggestions should be considered when preparing and writing short-answer tests.

1. The test items should measure all the important objectives and outcomes of instruction.
2. The test items should reflect the approximate emphasis given the various objectives and content of the subject or course. They should

---

40 Mehrens and Lehmann, *Measurement and Evaluation in Education and Psychology.* (The fifth point is based, in part, on the author's ideas about testing students at various ages.).

Tips for Teachers 4.2

Constructing and Using Classroom Tests

Teacher-made tests are the major source for evaluating students' progress in school. Below are some tips for preparing and using tests to measure the performance or achievement of your students.

I. *How is the test to be used?*
   1. The test should be used both as a learning tool for students and an assessment tool for teachers.
   2. Decide on the nature of the test: short quiz, review, major exam, etc.
   3. Provide ample time to study if the test is a major exam.

II. *How many tests are appropriate?*
   1. Frequent testing has the advantage of providing a more reliable and valid basis for evaluation.
   2. Preparing, administering, and scoring tests is time consuming.

III. *What type of test (short-answer or essay) is appropriate?*
   1. Short-answer tests take longer to prepare but are easy to score.
   2. Essay tests are easier to prepare but more time consuming and subjective to grade.
   3. More emphasis should be on short-answer tests for low-achieving and/or younger students.
   4. More emphasis should be on essay tests for high-achieving and/or older students.
   5. In general, strive for a variety of test questions.

IV. *What test items should be emphasized?*
   1. The test items should reflect important objectives and content.
   2. The test items should sample a wide background of information.
   3. The test items should draw from the required text or material without attempting to use trick questions or esoteric information.

V. *How long should the test be?*
   1. The majority of students should have ample time to answer all questions under normal rates of speed.
   2. The achievement level and age of students place a limit on the number (and type) of test questions and the time needed to answer the questions.
   3. The larger the pool of test items (and the more homogeneous the population being tested), the more accurate the test score is as a measurement of performance.

(continues)

VI *How difficult should the test be?*
1. A good test should include various levels of thinking, from simple to complex.
2. Test items that measure high-level thinking, or complex tasks, are difficult and time consuming to write; the best answer is sometimes uncertain.
3. The questions should be within the grasp of most students; the majority of the questions should be geared to low-achieving students (or the bottom third of the class) so they can pass the test.
4. The test items should be stated clearly so they are understood by all students.
5. The test should become progressively more difficult, especially if short-answer items are used.

VII. *What should be done after the tests are scored?*
1. The test should be scored and returned as soon as possible; delay in returning the test discourages students and increases their anxiety.
2. Whatever evaluative comments or judgments are made on the test should be in terms of the student's own performance, not the performance of others.
3. Low-achieving and younger students need more praise and words of encouragement on their returned papers.
4. Students should be permitted to review the test results and discuss the questions they missed on the test.
5. Common problems or test items missed by many students should be discussed when the tests are returned.
6. Each student should recognize his or her errors and understand the correct answers when discussed in class.
7. Be prepared to review or reteach portions of the content so that students fully comprehend all the questions they missed.

VIII. *How do the tests affect grades?*
1. Scores obtained from classroom tests serve as a significant basis for the grades to be entered on report cards.
2. The assigned grades will be as reliable and valid as the scores obtained from the tests used.
3. Students should understand how grades are determined and what percentage of the report card grade is based in test scores.
4. Use supplementary evaluative sources to help determine grades.
5. Educators disagree to what extent a student's grades should be determined on the basis of individual progress and/or in relation to the achievement of other students in the class.

not focus on esoteric or unimportant content and not overemphasize one aspect of instruction.

3. The test items should be clearly phrased so that a knowledgeable person will not be confused or respond to a wrong choice. The test items should not contain clues that might enable an uninformed person to answer correctly.

4. Trick or trivia test items should be avoided since they may penalize students who know the material and benefit students who rely on guessing or chance.

5. Every test item should separate students who know the material from those who do not.

6. Test items should not be included just to add length to the test or be used if most students will answer them correctly (too easy) or incorrectly (too difficult).

7. Test items should not be interrelated. Knowing the answer to one item should not furnish the answer to another.

8. Test items should be grammatically correct.

9. Test items should be appropriate to the students' age level, reading level, and cognitive and developmental levels.

10. Test items should not be racially, ethnically, or sexually biased.

11. Test items should have a definitely correct answer, that is, an answer that all experts (other teachers) can agree on.

12. The number of test items should be appropriate to the abilities of the student group as well as to the time available for testing; low-achieving students should have fewer test items or more time to answer than high-achieving students.

13. The test should consider the physical conditions under which the test is administered—heat, ventilation, lighting, noise, and other physical conditions.

14. Tests should not be the only basis for evaluating the students' classroom performance or for deriving a grade for a subject.

In order to write an appropriate test the teacher must obviously know the course content (specific knowledge, skills, concepts, common misconceptions, difficult areas, etc.). But knowledge of content is not enough. The teacher must be able to translate the objectives of the course into test items that will also distinguish between students who know the material and those who do not, and that will measure qualitative differences (preferably in higher-order thinking) related to the course.

Multiple-Choice Questions

These are the most popular objective test items, especially at the secondary level, and some students think they are fun to answer because they see the task almost as a puzzle, putting pieces together: doing easy pieces first and hard pieces last. The basic form of the **multiple-choice** item is a *stem or lead*, which defines the problem, to be completed by one of a number of alternatives or choices. There should be only one correct response, and the other alternatives should be plausible but incorrect. For this reason the incorrect alternatives are sometimes referred to as "distractors." In most cases four or five alternatives are given.

The idea in writing the question is to have the knowledgeable student choose the correct answer and not be distracted by the other alternative; the other alternatives serve to distract the less knowledgeable students. The effect of guessing is reduced, but not totally eliminated, by increasing the number of alternatives. In a 25 item four-alternative multiple-choice test, the probability of obtaining a score of at least 70 percent by chance alone is 1 in 1,000. To achieve a similar freedom from the effect of guessing in a true-false test requires 200 items.[41]

The use of plausible distractors helps the teacher to control the difficulty of the test. They should not be tricky or trivial. The major limitation of the multiple-choice format is that the distractors are often difficult to construct, particularly as the number of choices increases to five.[42] Unless the teacher knows the content of the course well, he or she is usually limited in the number of good multiple test items that can be constructed.

Following are three examples of multiple-choice questions. The first tests simple knowledge, the second the application of a formula, and the third the application of a concept.

1. Henry Kissinger is a well-known (a) corporate lawyer, (b) avant-garde playwright, (c) surrealist artist, (d) international statesman, (e) pop musician.
2. What temperature, in degrees Fahrenheit, is equivalent to 10° Centigrade? (a) 0°F, (b) 32°F, (c) 50°F, (d) 72°F, (e) 100°F
3. Based on the map provided, which product is most likely to be exported from Bango (a fictitious country for which longitude, latitude, and topography are shown)? (a) fish, (b) oranges, (c) pine lumber, (d) corn.

Guidelines for Writing Multiple-Choice Questions

Below are some suggestions for writing multiple-choice questions.

1. The central issue or problem should be stated in the stem. It should be a singular statement, topic, or problem.

---

41 David A. Payne, *The Assessment of Learning* (Lexington, Mass.: Heath, 1974); William Wiersma and Stephen G. Jurs, *Educational Measurement and Testing*, 2nd ed. (Needham Heights, Mass.: Allyn & Bacon, 1990).

42 Gronlund, *How to Construct Achievement Tests*; Bruce W. Tuckman, *Testing for Teachers*, 2nd ed. (San Diego: Harcourt Brace Jovanovich, 1988).

2. In the stem a direct question is preferable to an incomplete statement. A direct question will result in less vagueness and ambiguity, especially among inexperienced test writers.

3. Include in the stem any words that might otherwise be repeated in the alternative responses. This reduces wordiness in the alternatives and increases clarity in the stem.

4. Negative statements in the stem and alternatives should be avoided, since they lead to confusion.

5. Use numbers to label stems and letters to label alternatives.

6. Avoid absolute terms ("always," "never," "none"), especially in the alternatives; a test-wise person usually avoids answers that include them.

7. Avoid using items directly from the text or workbook, since this practice encourages memorization.

8. Arrange alternatives in some logical order—for example, alphabetically or chronologically.

9. Alternatives should be parallel in content, form, length, and grammar. Avoid making the correct alternative different from wrong alternatives; longer or shorter, more precisely stated, having a part of speech others lack.

10. Correct responses should be in random order. Do not use one particular letter more often than others or create a pattern for the placement of correct responses.

11. Alternatives should be mutually exclusive. Overlapping or similar responses permit the student to eliminate two or more alternatives in one choice or result in poor discrimination of the correct alternative.

12. Alternative responses should be plausible to less knowledgeable students.

13. The answers should be objectively correct; that is, other teachers who might grade the test should agree on the correct answers.

14. The alternatives "All of the above" and "None of the above" should be used sparingly, since the test writer may fail to take into consideration all the nuances in the choices or the test taker may see other nuances. Moreover, these items are too tricky for most students.

Matching Questions

In a **matching test** there are usually two columns of items. For each item in one column, the student is required to select a correct (or matching) item in the other. The items may be names, terms, places, phrases, quotations, statements, or events. The basis for choosing must be carefully explained in the directions.

Matching questions have the advantages of covering a large amount and variety of content, being interesting to students (almost like a game), and being easy to score. Matching questions may be considered a modification of multiple-choice questions in which alternatives are listed in another column instead of in a series following a stem. The questions are easier to construct than multiple-choice questions, however, since only one response item has to be constructed for each stem. One problem with matching tests, according to test experts, is finding homogeneous test and response items that are significant in terms of objectives and learning outcomes. A test writer may start with a few good items in both columns but may find it necessary to add insignificant or secondary information to maintain homogeneity. [43]

Another problem is that matching questions often require recall rather than comprehension and more sophisticated levels of thinking. Higher levels of cognition may be called for in matching questions that involve analogies, cause and effect, complex relationships, and theories, but such items are hard to construct.[44]

Below is an example of a matching exercise.

Famous American presidents are listed in column A, and descriptive phrases relating to their administration are listed in column B. Place the letter of the phrase that describes each president in the space provided. Each match is worth 1 point.

Column A: Presidents
1. George Washington
2. Thomas Jefferson
3. Abraham Lincoln
4. Woodrow Wilson
5. Franklin Roosevelt

Column B: Descriptions or Events
a. Civil War president
b. "New Deal"
c. First American president
d. Purchased Louisiana territory
e. "New Frontier"
f. World War I president

Guidelines for Writing Matching Questions

The following are suggestions for the construction of matching questions:

1. The directions should briefly and clearly indicate the basis for matching items in column A with items in column B.
2. An entire matching question should appear on a single page. Running the question on two pages is confusing and distracting for students.
3. Wording of items in column A should be shorter than those in column B. This permits students to scan the test question quickly once or twice.

---

43 Gronlund and Linn, *Measurement and Evaluation in Teaching*; Mehrens and Lehmann, *Measurement and Evaluation in Education and Psychology.*

44 Benjamin S. Bloom, J. Thomas Hastings, and George F. Madaus, *Evaluation to Improve Learning* (New York: McGraw-Hill, 1981); Kenneth D. Hopkins, Julian C. Stanley, and B. R. Hopkins, *Educational and Psychological Measurement and Evaluation*, 7th ed. (Englewood Cliffs, N.J.: Prentice-Hall, 1990).

4. Column A should contain no more than 10 test items; 5 or 6 items is probably ideal. Longer lists confuse students.

5. There should be more alternatives in column B than there are items in column A to prevent answering the last one or two items by simple elimination. Column B should contain 6 or 7 items if column A contains 5. A list of 10 items in column A should be accompanied by about 12 items in column B.

6. Column A items should be numbered, as they will be graded as individual questions, and column B items should be lettered.

7. Column B items should be presented in a logical order, say alphabetically or chronologically (but not one that gives away the answer), so the student can scan them quickly in search of correct answers.

8. Items in each column should be similar in terms of content, form, grammar, and length. Dissimilar alternatives in column B result in irrelevant clues that can be used to eliminate items or guess answers by the test-wise student.

9. Negative statements (in either column) should be avoided, since they confuse students.

10. Many multiple-choice questions can be converted to a matching test; therefore, many of the suggestions are applicable to both.

Completion Questions

In the **completion test**, sentences are presented from which certain words have been omitted. The student is to fill in the blank to complete the meaning. This type of short-answer question, sometimes called a *free response* or *fill-in-the-blank* question, is suitable for measuring a wide variety of content. Although it usually tests recall of information, it can also demand thought and ability to understand relationships and make inferences. Little opportunity for guessing and for obtaining clues is provided, as with other short-answer questions. The major problem of this type of test question is that the answers are not always entirely objective, so the scoring for the teacher is time consuming and the grading may vary subjectively with the grader. Combining multiple-choice and completion is an effective method for reducing ambiguity in test items and making scoring more objective. However, this combination does restore the opportunity for guessing.

The examples below illustrate how guessing is reduced. To answer the completion item (question 1), the student must know the capital of Illinois. To arrive at an answer to the multiple-choice question (question 2), the student may eliminate alternatives through knowledge about them or simply choose one of them as a guess.

1. The capital of Illinois is_____.
2. The capital of Illinois is (a) Utica, (b) Columbus, (c) Springfield, (d) Cedar Rapids.

Guidelines for Writing Completion Questions

General suggestions for writing completion items are listed below.

1. The direction "Fill in the blanks" is usually sufficient, but the student should be informed about how detailed the answer should be.
2. Do not use questions or statements that are copied from the textbook or workbook, since this encourages memorization.
3. Fill-in items should be clearly worded to avoid unexpected responses.
4. The completion part should be near the end of the item.
5. It is simpler and clearer to write the completion item as a question then as a statement.
6. There should only be one possible correct answer, even though students are expected to make their own response rather than choose among given responses.
7. If more than one answer is correct, equal credit should be given to each one.
8. The fill-in should be plausible to the knowledgeable student; it should not be based on trivia or trick data.
9. The correct response should not be part of a particular grammatical form, common expression, or well-known saying. An item such as "Give me liberty or give me _____" is a famous American revolutionary slogan which should be avoided.
10. Use one blank, or certainly no more than two, in any item, since more than two blanks leads to confusion and ambiguity.
11. The required completion should be a specific term (person, place, object, concept), since an item requiring a more general phrase may elicit more subjective responses and be harder to score.
12. When combining multiple-choice and completion formats, the alternative responses should be homogeneous in form, length, and grammar to avoid clues.

True-False Questions

Of all types of short-answer questions used in education, the **true-false** question is the most controversial. Advocates contend that the basis of "logical reasoning is to test the truth or falsity of propositions" and that "a student's command of a particular area of knowledge is indicated by his (or her) success in judging the truth or falsity of propositions related to it."[45]

---

45 Ebel and Frisbie, *Essentials of Educational Measurement*, pp. 164–165.

The main advantages of true-false items are their ease of construction and ease of scoring. A teacher can cover a large content area, and a large number of items can be presented in a prescribed time period. This allows the teacher to obtain a good estimate of the student's knowledge. If the items are carefully constructed, they can also be used to test understanding of principles.

Critics assert that true-false items have almost no value, since they encourage, and even reward, guessing, and measure memorization rather than understanding. Others note that true-false questions tend to elicit the response set of acquiescence, that is, the response of people who say yes (or "true") when in doubt.[46] The disadvantages of true-false questions may outweigh their advantages unless the items are well written. Precise language that is appropriate for the students taking the test is essential so that ambiguity and reading ability do not distort test results.

Here are a few examples of ambiguous true-false questions. True or false:

1. Australia, the island continent, was discovered by Captain Cook.
2. Early in his career, Ben Franklin said: "A penny saved is a penny earned."
3. At age seven, the majority of students are capable of performing hypothetical problems.

In question 1 two statements are made, and it is unclear whether the student is to respond to both or only one; moreover, the meaning of *island* and *continent* is also being tested. In question 2 is the student being asked whether Franklin made the statement early or late in his career or whether this is the exact statement? A test-wise person might say false, because there are two ways of being wrong in this question, but the person would be wrong in this case. Question 3 tests knowledge of Piaget's principle of formal operations, not understanding of the principle. A test-wise student should know the correct answer is false, simply by using common sense or by having a younger sibling at home.

Guessing is the biggest disadvantage to true-false tests. When students guess, they have a fifty-fifty chance of being right. Clues in the items and being test-wise improve these odds. The purpose of the test is to measure what students know, not how lucky or clever they are. This disadvantage can be compensated for to some extent by increasing the number of test items and by penalizing (deducting a quarter or one-third point) for an incorrect answer. True-false items should be used sparingly for older students, who are more test-wise and able to sense clues in questions. They are more appropriate for younger students, who respond more to the content than to the format of questions.

---

46 Gage and Berliner, *Educational Psychology.*

Guidelines for Writing True-False Questions

Here are some suggestions for writing true-false items.

1. Each true-false item should test an important concept or piece of information, not just a specific date or name. The knowledge being tested should be significant.
2. True-false statements should be completely true or false, without exception.
3. The intended correct answer should be clear only to a knowledgeable person. The true-false item should not test general knowledge or experience, and its answer should not be given away by unintentional clues.
4. Avoid specific determiners and absolute statements ("never," "only," "none," "always"), since they are unintentional clues. Most important, do not use them in statements you want to be considered true.
5. Avoid qualifying statements and words that involve judgment and interpretation ("few," "most," "usually"). Most important, do not use them in statements you want to be considered false.
6. Avoid negative statements and double negatives, since they confuse students and may cause knowledgeable students to give the wrong answer.
7. Avoid verbatim textbook and workbook statements, since use of such statements promotes memorization.
8. Use the same form and length for true and false statements. For example, do not make true statements consistently longer than false statements; test-wise students will recognize a pattern.
9. Present a similar number of true and false items.
10. Use simple grammatical structure. Avoid dependent clauses and compound sentences, since they may distract the student from the central idea. There is also a tendency for the knowledgeable student to see a more complex item as a trick question or to read more into the meaning than is intended.
11. Be clear and concise. Avoid unfamiliar language and wordiness, since they confuse the student and test reading comprehension rather than knowledge.
12. Place the idea being tested at the end of the statement. Most students focus more attention on the last portion of the item; thus the teacher's intent and student's attention will coincide.

Overview of Short-Answer Questions

Table 4.6 summarizes many of the points we have discussed. The different types of short-answer tests all have advantages and disadvantages, and some teachers will eventually prefer certain types and avoid others. Although each has features that make it useful for specific testing situations, the different types can be used together to add variety for the test taker and to test different types and levels of knowledge.

Table 4.6   ADVANTAGES AND LIMITATIONS OF SHORT-ANSWER TEST QUESTIONS

Question Type	Advantages	Disadvantages	Precautions
Multiple choice	1. Flexibility in measuring objectives or content 2. Well-constructed items have potential to measure high-level thinking 3. Guessing can be minimized by a built-in penalty 4. Easy to score; little interpretation to count correct responses 5. Requires knowledge of test construction and subject to constructing plausible incorrect answers	1. The stem or alternatives are sometimes too long, confusing, or vague 2. A correct answer can sometimes be determined without knowledge of content 3. Susceptible to guessing and eliminating incorrect choices 4. Time consuming to write 5. Sometimes there is more than one possible correct answer	1. Write short, parallel stems and alternatives 2. Avoid clues based on longer or shorter alternatives or incorrect grammar 3. Use plausible choices or alternatives 4. Avoid textbook language or direct phrases 5. Be sure there is only one correct answer
Matching	1. Relatively easy to write, easy to score 2. Well suited to measure associations 3. Amenable to testing a large body of content; many options available 4. Fun for students to take, especially for those who enjoy puzzles 5. Guessing can be minimized by a built-in penalty	1. Necessary to use single words or short phrases 2. Cannot be used to assess all types of thinking; lists or individual pieces of information can only assess limited situations 3. Directions are sometimes confusing; students are not always told clearly how to respond 4. Harder to write than other short-answer items because all items must fit together and distinguish from each other 5. By eliminating choices, last few questions are susceptible to guessing	1. Avoid trivia information; avoid textbook language 2. Be sure the choices are parallel; avoid clues within items; avoid additional or modifying words 3. Attend to complete directions and mechanical arrangement of choices 4. Provide consistency in classification of items for each set; place all test items and choices on the same page 5. Provide extra choices, say 6 or 7 per 5 test items; avoid too many choices because of confusion

Table 4.6   (Continued)

Question Type	Advantages	Disadvantages	Precautions
Completion	1. Easy to write test items 2. Minimal guessing; clues are not given in choices or alternatives 3. Amenable to what, who, where, and how many 4. No distractors, options, or choices to worry about	1. Difficult to score 2. Some answers are subjective or open to interpretation 3. Usually measures simple recall or factual information 4. Test items are sometimes confusing or ambiguous; constrained by grammar	1. Consider scoring convenience; require one word 2. Be sure there is only one correct answer 3. Avoid too many blanks, or long sentences, to avoid confusion 4. Keep test items brief; avoid instances where grammar helps in answering question
True-false	1. Easiest test items to write; easy to score 2. Comprehensive sampling of objectives or content 3. Guessing can be minimized by a built-in penalty 4. No distractors to worry about, highly reliable and valid items	1. Sometimes ambiguous o too broad 2. Simplicity in cognitive demands; measures low-level thinking 3. Susceptible to guessing 4. Dependence on absolute judgments, right or wrong	1. Ensure a single correct answer, true or false; avoid "trap" or "tricky" items 2. Avoid long sentence structure, double negatives or "not," in order to avoid confusion 3. Avoid clues such as absolute terms ("always," "never," "all") 4. True items are easier to construct than false items; use approximately equal true and false items

Multiple-choice questions are the most difficult and time-consuming items to construct. However, they can be used more readily to test higher levels of learning than other short-test items. Matching questions and answers are also difficult and time consuming to write, but they are interesting for students and can be used for variety. Completion questions are open to subjective interpretation and scoring, but they can be used also to test higher levels of learning. True-false questions tend to focus on trivia, but they are easy to construct and score. See Tips for Teachers 4.3.

ESSAY QUESTIONS

Short-answer questions, no matter how well formulated, cannot measure divergent thinking, subjective or imaginative thought. To learn how a student thinks,

Tips for Teachers 4.3

Overview of Writing Test Items

Here are some don't's in formulating short-answer tests which serve as an overview.

MULTIPLE-CHOICE ITEM
1. Don't choose *distractors* (that is, incorrect choices) that do not fit the kinds of mistakes students are likely to make.
2. Don't choose distractors that are actually correct or plausible answers.
3. Don't make distractors stand out from the correct answer either by length or by grammar.
4. Don't use language your students won't understand.
5. Don't use statements that have multiple meanings.
6. Don't use absolute terms such as *always*, *never*, and *all*.
7. Don't build clues into the item statement.
8. Don't test more than one point per item.
9. Don't always assign the correct choice the same letter.
10. Don't let one item clue the answer to another.
11. Don't write long answer choices.
12. Don't write overlapping answer choices.

MATCHING ITEM
1. Don't include elements of more than one category.
2. Don't build clues into your response choice.
3. Don't write long responses.
4. Don't write overlapping responses.
5. Don't write implausible responses.
6. Don't write responses that distinguish between points other than the one being measured by the item.
7. Don't write items that require information not contained within them.
8. Don't build in systematic response patterns.
9. Don't mix stems and options.

COMPLETION ITEM
1. Don't leave out so much as to create ambiguity.
2. Don't leave out so little as to provide clues.
3. Don't let sentence grammar serve as a clue.

(continues)

4. Don't let the length of the blank space serve as a clue.
5. Don't have more than one correct answer.
6. Don't require that the student write too much.
7. Don't have more than one blank per item.

TRUE-FALSE ITEM
1. Don't use absolute terms like *always* and *never*.
2. Don't write only trues or only falses.
3. Don't put all the trues or all the falses together.
4. Don't measure more than one idea per item.

Source: Bruce W. Tuckman, *Testing for Teachers*, 2nd ed. (San Diego: Harcourt Brace Jovanovich, 1988), pp. 75-76.

attacks a problem, writes, and utilizes cognitive resources, something beyond the short-answer test is needed. Essay questions, especially where there is no specific right answer, produce evaluation data of considerable value.

Authorities disagree on how structured and specific essay questions should be. For example, some authorities advocate using words such as "why," "how," and "what consequences." They claim questions worded in this way (which we call type 1 essay questions) call for a command of essential knowledge and concepts and require students to integrate the subject matter, analyze data, make inferences, and show cause-effect relations.[47] Other test specialists urge words such as "discuss," "examine," and "explain," claiming that this wording (type 2 essay questions) gives the student less latitude in responding, but provides an opportunity to learn how the student thinks.[48] Although more restricted than the first type, this type of question may still lead to tangential responses by some students. It is useful when the object is to see how well the student can select, reject, and organize data from several sources. Other test specialists advocate more structure or precision through

---

47 Phyllis C. Blumenfeld and Judith L. Meece, "Task Factors, Teacher Behavior, and Students' Involvement and Use of Learning Strategies in Science," *Elementary School Journal* (January 1988), pp. 235–250; Thomas P. Carpenter and Penelope L. Peterson, "Learning Through Instruction," *Educational Psychologist* (Spring 1988), pp. 79–86; and Allan C. Ornstein, "Questioning: The Essence of Good Teaching," *NASSP Bulletin* (February 1988), pp. 72–80.

48 Gage and Berliner, *Educational Psychology*; John R. Hayes and Linda S. Flower, "Writing Research and the Writer," *American Psychologist* (October 1986), pp. 1106–1113; and Charles D. Hopkins and Richard L. Antes, *Classroom Testing*, 2nd ed. (Itasca, Ill.: Peacock, 1989).

the use of words such as "identify," "compare," and "contrast."[49] (We call these type 3 questions.) They feel that in addition to giving more direction to the student, such wording demands that the student select and organize specific data. Thought processes elicited by different essay questions are listed in Table 4.7. They are arranged from simple to complex thinking.

In effect, we are talking about the degree of freedom permitted the student in organizing a response to a question. All types have their disadvantages. The first two types of essay questions allow an "extended response;" they can lead to disjointed, irrelevant, superficial, or unexpected discussions by students who have difficulty organizing their thoughts on paper. The third type of essay question is the easiest to answer and suggests a "focused response;" it can lead to simple recall of information and mass of details. In fact, unless the teacher reinforces critical thinking in testing and grading, most essay responses become lengthy enumerations of memorized facts and events; students tend to be right-answer oriented and often turn divergent questions into convergent answers. Even *Why* questions (i.e., Why did the U.S. defend Kuwait against Iraq?) often become converted to *What* answers (that is, a list of reasons in paragraph form).

Essay questions can be used effectively for determining how well a student can analyze, synthesize, evaluate, think logically, solve problems, and hypothesize. They can also show how well he or she can organize thoughts, support a point of view, and examine ideas, methods, and solutions. The complexity of the questions, and the complexity of thinking expected of the student, can be adjusted to correspond to students' age, abilities, and experience. Another advantage is the ease and short time involved in constructing an essay question. The major disadvantages of essay questions are the considerable time to read and evaluate answers and the subjectivity of scoring. (The length and complexity of the answer, as well as the standards for responding, can lead to reliability problems in scoring.)

Some studies report that independent grading of the same essay by several teachers results in appraisals ranging from excellent to failing. The variation illustrates a wide range in criteria for evaluation among teachers. Even worse, studies show that the same teacher grading the same essay at different times gave the essay significantly different grades.[50] It has also been demonstrated that teachers are influenced by such factors as penmanship, quality of composition, and spelling, even when they are supposed to grade on content alone.[51]

---

49 Gronlund and Linn, *Measurement and Evaluation in Teaching;* Bruce W. Tuckman, *Measuring Educational Outcomes,* 2nd ed. (San Diego: Harcourt Brace Jovanovich, 1985).

50 Howard B. Lyman, *Test Scores and What They Mean,* 5th ed. (Needham Heights, Mass.; Allyn & Bacon, 1991); Albert E. Meyers, Carolyn McConville, and William E. Coffman, "Simplex Structure in the Grading of Essay Tests," *Educational and Psychological Measurement* (Spring 1966), pp. 41–54; and Ernest W. Tiegs, *Educational Diagnosis* (New York: McGraw-Hill, 1952).

51 Ray Bull and Julia Steens, "The Effects of Attractiveness of Writing and Penmanship on Essay Grades," *Journal of Occupational Psychology* (April 1979), pp. 53–59; Jon C. Marshall and Jerry M. Powers, "Writing Neatness, Composition Errors, and Essay Grades," *Journal of Educational Measurement* (Summer 1969), pp. 97–101.

Table 4.7   SAMPLE THOUGHT QUESTIONS AND COGNITIVE LEVELS OF THINKING

1. Comparing
   a. Compare the following two people for . . .
   b. Describe the similarities and differences between . . .
2. Classifying
   a. Group the following items according to . . .
   b. What common characteristics do the items below have . . .
3. Outlining
   a. Outline the procedures you would use to calculate . . .
   b. Discuss the advantages of . . .
4. Summarizing
   a. State the major points of . . .
   b. Describe the principles of . . .
5. Organizing
   a. Trace the history of . . .
   b. Examine the development of . . .
6. Analyzing
   a. Describe the errors in the following argument . . .
   b. What data are needed to . . .
7. Applying
   a. Clarify the methods of . . . for purposes of . . .
   b. Diagnose the causes of . . .
8. Inferring
   a. Whyd did the author say . . .
   b. How would (person X) more likely react to . . .
9. Deducing
   a. Formulate criteria for . . .
   b. Based on the premise of . . . , propose a valid conclusion.
10. Synthesizing
    a. How would you end the story of . . .
    b. Describe a plan for . . .
11. Justifying
    a. Provide a rationale for . . .
    b. Which alternatives below do you agree with? Why?
12. Evaluating
    a. What are the reasons for . . .
    b. Based on the following criteria . . . , assess the value of . . .
13. Predicting
    a. Describe the likely outcomes of . . .
    b. What will most likely happen if . . .? Why?
14. Creating
    a. Develop a theory of . . .
    b. Propose a solution for . . .

Source: Allan C. Ornstein, "Essay Tests: Use, Development and Grading," *Clearing House* (In print 1992).

One way to increase the reliability of an essay test is to increase the number of questions and restrict the length of the answers. The more specific and restricted the question, the less ambiguous it is to the teacher and the less affected by interpretation subjectivity in scoring.

An entire test composed of essay questions can cover only limited content because only a few questions can be answered in a given time period. However, this limitation is balanced by the fact that in studying for an essay test high-achieving students are likely to look at the subject or course as a whole and at the relationships of ideas, concepts, and principles.

The essay answer is affected by the student's ability to organize written responses. Many students can comprehend and deal with abstract data but have problems writing or showing that they understand the material in an essay examination. Students may freeze and write only short responses, write in a disjointed fashion, or express only low-level knowledge. One way of helping to alleviate this problem is to discuss in detail how to write an essay question. Sadly, few teachers take the time to teach students how to write essay examinations. They expect English teachers to perform this task, and English teachers may be so busy teaching grammar, spelling, and literature that they do not teach the mechanics of essay writing.

On the other hand, there are students who write well but haven't learned the course content. Their writing ability may conceal their lack of specific knowledge. It is important for the teacher to be able to distinguish irrelevant facts and ideas from relevant information. Even though essay questions appear to be easy to write, careful construction is necessary to test students' cognitive abilities, that is, to write valid questions. Many essay questions can be turned around by the student so that he or she merely lists facts without applying or integrating information to specific situations and without showing an understanding of concepts. "What were the causes of World War II?" can be answered by listing specific causes without integrating them. A better question would be "Assume that Winston Churchill, Franklin Roosevelt, and Adolf Hitler were invited to speak to an audience on the causes of World War II. What might each of them say? What might each select as the most important causal factor? On what points would they agree? Disagree?"

Factors to be considered in deciding whether to use essay questions are the difficulty and time involved in grading essays, the low reliability of grading, the limited sampling of content, and the validity of the essay itself versus the ease in formulating questions, the testing of advanced levels of cognition, and the fostering of the integration of the subject as a whole. Many teachers take advantage of what both short-answer questions and essay questions have to offer by writing tests consisting of both, perhaps 40 to 60 percent short-answer and the remainder essay. This balance is to some extent determined by grade level. In the upper grades there is a tendency to require students to answer more essay questions since it is believed they should have the ability to formulate acceptable answers. According to Piagetian developmental stages, students should begin to be able to handle essays (actually short essays) at the formal operation stage, beginning at age 11. But given the number of poor readers and writers in this country, 11 may be pushing reality.

Guidelines for Writing Essay Questions

Here are suggestions for preparing and scoring essay tests.

1. **Make directions specific,** indicating just what the student is to write about. Write several sentences of directions if necessary.
2. **Word each question as simply and clearly as possible.** Use a vocabulary consistent with the student's level. Avoid excess verbiage since it may confuse the student.
3. **Prepare enough questions to cover the material of the unit or course broadly.** Write questions that are germane to the course and cover its major objectives.
4. **Allow sufficient time for students to answer the questions.** A good rule of thumb is for the teacher to estimate how long he or she would take to answer the questions, and then multiply this time by two or three, depending on the students' age and abilities. Suggest a time allotment for each question so students can pace themselves.
5. **Ask questions that require considerable thought.** Use essay questions to focus on organizing data, analysis, interpretation and formulating theories, rather than on reporting facts.
6. **Give students a choice of questions,** say, two out of three, so as not to penalize students who may know the subject as a whole but happen to be limited in the particular area asked about.[52]
7. **Determine in advance how much weight will be given to each question or part of a question.** Give this information on the test, and score accordingly.
8. **Ask questions that have an answer that is generally accepted by other teachers as better than other answers.**
9. **Increase the number of questions in order to increase the content coverage of the test and the reliability of the test score.** Asking only one essay question puts too much pressure on students and penalizes many who may know the material but not the answer to the specific question.

---

52 Many authorities (for example, Ebel, Gronlund, and Payne) recommend that students answer all questions and that no choice be provided because a common set of questions tends to increase reliability in scoring while options tend to distort results. However weighed against this advantage is the fact that being able to select an area they know well increases student morale, reduces test anxiety, and gives students a greater chance to show they can organize and interpret the subject matter.

10. Provide sample questions (which will not be on the test) to students before the test so they have an idea of what to expect and how to respond.
11. Explain your scoring technique to students before the test. It should be clear to them what weight will be given to knowledge, development and organization of ideas, grammar, punctuation, spelling, penmanship, and any other factor to be considered in evaluation.
12. Be consistent in your scoring technique for all students. Try to conceal the name of the student whose answer you are grading to reduce biases that have little to do with the quality of the student's response and more to do with the "halo effect" (the tendency to grade students according to impressions of their capabilities, attitudes, or behavior).
13. Grade one question at a time, rather than one test paper at a time, to increase reliability in scoring. This technique makes it easier to compare and evaluate responses to each specific question.
14. Write comments on the test paper for the student, noting good points and explaining how answers could be improved. Do not compare a student to others when making comments.

Discussion Questions

The **discussion question**, or short essay question, is an essay question that requires a short response. The response can be either oral or written. In a test situation it is usually written and requires an answer that may range from one or two sentences to one or two paragraphs (or a page at most).

The discussion question is excellent for examining the causes of an event, describing the advantages or disadvantages of techniques, for making comparisons, for briefly explaining concepts, and for evaluating data. Of crucial importance are the directions you give that specify the approximate detail and the approximate length expected in the response. Because of the brevity of the response, the quality of the answers depends heavily on the ability to phrase ideas, write, and select the most relevant data.[53]

The discussion questions should coincide with the objectives of the course, and focus on the most important content. It is common for teachers, especially at the secondary level, to use a number of short discussion questions to cover several important objectives and areas of content. Less important content can be covered by short-answer questions.

The advantages and disadvantages of discussion questions are similar to those of essay questions, but there are a few differences. Essays emphasize the integrative, subjective, and imaginative thought processes of students rather than their presentation of objective information. Discussion questions are more specifically focused on knowledge and short generalizations relating to a par-

---

53 Robert E. Slavin, *Educational Psychology: Theory into Practice*, 3rd ed. (Englewood Cliffs, N.J.: Prentice-Hall, 1991).

ticular topic. Compared to essay questions, the discussion question takes less time to answer and to evaluate, and therefore more can be included in a test. Following are some examples of discussion questions.

1. Briefly list the reasons why the United States entered World War I.
2. Evaluate the poem below in 200 words or less.
3. Identify two ways in which the Democratic party and the Republican party differ in their attitude toward social spending.
4. Explain three ways in which you can improve breakfast eating habits.

Guidelines for Writing Discussion Questions

Here some suggestions for writing discussion questions. Most of the suggestions for writing essay questions also apply.

1. Give clear and concise directions, indicating the length of response and amount of detail expected. "List at least three factors," "Describe the reasons," "Briefly evaluate" are more specific terms than "Discuss," "Tell about," and "Examine."
2. Ask questions that focus on important instructional objectives and course content.
3. Allow sufficient time for students to answer the questions. Estimate about two to three times longer than it takes the teacher to answer, depending on the age and abilities of the students.
4. Match questions and expected responses with the age and abilities of the students.
5. Use the same techniques and criteria for evaluating all the students' responses.

Every test, regardless of type, should be checked for errors before it is duplicated and distributed. Directions and time allotments should be clearly stated. Any errors, vagueness, or omissions should be corrected. Most important, the teachers should be clear on the reasons for using discussion questions, essays, or a combination. See Table 4.8.

With older or high-achieving students, there should be an increasing emphasis on discussion and essay examinations because they elicit critical thinking. This does not mean, however, that short-answer tests are suitable only for testing knowledge and recall. Given an appropriate command of the subject, the teacher should be able to develop short-answer questions that extend beyond knowledge and rote learning. The worth of a classroom test is based on how all the items relate to each other, integrate, and measure what has been taught by the teacher and, one hopes, learned by the students.

Table 4.8   WHEN TO USE DISCUSSION AND ESSAY TESTS

Mechanical

1. The group to be tested is small and the test will not be reused.

2. The teacher wishes to develop student's skill in writing.

3. The teacher is more interested in exploring the student's attitude than in measuring precise achievement outcomes.

4. The teacher is confident in his or her ability as a critical and objective reader.

5. The time available for test preparation is shorter than the time available for grading tests.

Cognitive

1. The teacher wishes to test critical thinking or problem solving.

2. The teacher wishes to test the student's ability to select and organize relevant facts or ideas.

3. The teacher wishes to encourage originality and unconventional answers.

4. The teacher wishes the student to apply principles or concepts, to integrate them into a complex solution.

5. The teacher wishes to test the student's overview of the subject.

Note: The first five items are based on Robert L. Ebel and David A. Frisbie, *Essentials of Educational Measurement*, 5th ed. (Englewood Cliffs, N.J.: Prentice-Hall, 1991); the next five items are the author's.

ADMINISTERING AND RETURNING TESTS

As early as possible in the term, it should be decided when and how often tests will be given. Teachers who consider testing important often give several short tests at short intervals of time. Those for whom testing is not so vital may give fewer tests. Teachers who prefer a mastery or competency approach to instruction generally give several criterion-reference tests for purposes of diagnosing, checking on learning progress, and individualizing instruction, as well as for grading. Those who prefer a broad, cognitive approach may rely more on standardized tests or fewer classroom tests that integrate the subject matter. Whatever their approach to testing, it is recommended that teachers announce tests well in advance. Discuss what will be covered, how it will be evaluated, and how much it will count toward a final grade. Be considerate in scheduling tests. It is unwise to schedule a test on the same day as or the day before a big game, dance, or student activity, on Friday afternoon, or before a major holiday such as the Easter or Christmas vacation.

Test-Taking Skills

Conditions other than students' knowledge can affect their performance on tests. One such factor is their general test-taking ability, completely apart from the subject matter of particular tests. Test-taking skills are important for all students. Almost any student who has taken a few tests and who has common sense can learn certain skills that will improve his or her scores. Developing good test-taking strategies should not be construed as amoral or dishonest. Rather it is a way of reducing anxiety in test situations. A number of test authorities contend that all students should be given training in test-wiseness.[54]

Table 4.9 lists important test-taking skills that can be taught to students. When students are given practice in diagnosing test questions and in strategies involved in taking tests, their test scores usually improve (although researchers differ as to the size of the effect).[55]

In addition to the strategies listed in the table, it is important to tell students that consistent studying or review over the course is more effective than cramming. Advise them to get a good night's sleep before the test. There is nothing wrong in telling students to chew gum or to nibble on candy (as long as they don't wrinkle papers or make a mess) if it will reduce their anxiety. Remind them to wear a watch if there is no clock in the room to help pace themselves and to come prepared with more than one pen or pencil.

Tips for Teachers 4.4 will help the teacher prepare students for test taking. Of course, one of the best strategies is for the student to see the teacher after class, just to make "points," to say hello, so the teacher gets to know the student by name and as an individual. Under these circumstances, most teachers will give the benefit of doubt to the student—what is often the difference between a B+ or an A as the final grade.

Test Routines

Both short-answer and essay tests must be administered carefully to avoid confusion. A routine should be established by the teacher for handing out the test questions and answer sheets, papers, or booklets. The answer sheets, papers, or booklets should be passed out first, for example, with the exact number for each row given to the first student in each row and then passed back along the row for distribution. Students should be instructed to fill out information required on the answer papers, such as their names and class. To avoid confusion the test should not be handed out until the answer papers or booklets

---

54 Robert F. Biehler and Jack Snowman, *Psychology Applied to Teaching*, 6th ed. (Boston: Houghton Mifflin, 1990); Randolph E. Sarnacki, "An Examination of Test-Wiseness in the Cognitive Test Domain," *Review of Educational Research* (Spring 1979), pp. 252–279.

55 Henry S. Dyer, "The Effects of Coaching for Scholastic Aptitude," *NASSP Bulletin* (February 1987), pp. 46–53; Samuel Messick, "Issue and Equity in the Coaching Controversy: Implications for Educational Testing and Practice," *Educational Psychologist* (Summer 1982), pp. 67–91.

Table 4.9 TEST-WISE STRATEGIES

1. Determine the basis upon which the responses will be scored. Will points be subtracted for wrong answers, punctuation, spelling, etc.?

2. Read each test item carefully.

3. Be aware that both human scores and machine scores place a premium on neatness and legibility.

4. Establish a pace that will permit sufficient time to finish; check the time periodically to see if the pace is being maintained.

5. Bypass difficult test questions or problems; return to them at the end of the test.

6. If credit is given only for the number of right answers, or if correction for guessing is less severe than a wrong response (i.e. −1/4 for a wrong response and +1 for a correct response), it is appropriate to guess.

7. Eliminate items known to be incorrect on matching or multiple choice questions before guessing.

8. Make use of relevant content information on other test items and options.

9. Consider the intent of the test constructor; answer the item as the test constructor intended; consider the level of sophistication of the test and audience for which the test is intended.

10. Recognize idiosyncracies of the test constructor that distinguish correct and incorrect options; for example, correct (or incorrect) options: (a) are longer or shorter, (b) are more general or specific, (c) are placed in certain logical positions within each set of options, (d) include or exclude one pair of diametrically opposed statements, and (e) are grammatically inconsistent or consistent with the stem.

11. Wording of a test item may imply that the correct response begins with a vowel or consonant, thus eliminating some alternatives.

12. True items may be longer than false items because they require qualifying phrases.

13. Words such as "always," "never," and "none" are associated with false items.

14. Words such as "usually," "often,," and "many" are associated with true items.

15. Some alternatives in a multiple-choice item may not be parallel with other alternatives, thus eliminating some alternatives; make sure all choices are grammatically consistent with the question, grammatically incorrect items are usually wrong.

16. Periodically check to be sure the item number and answer number match, especially when using an answer sheet.

17. Reflect on and outline an essay before starting to write; decide how much time you can afford for that question given the available time. In all cases, attempt an answer, no matter how poor, to gain some points.

18. Write short paragraphs for an essay; develop one idea or concept around each paragraph to make it easier for the reader (teacher) to discern. Include several short paragraphs as opposed to a few long paragraphs that tend to blend or fuse distinct ideas.

19. If time permits, return to omitted items, if any; then check answers and correct careless mistakes.

Tips for Teachers 4.4

Preparing Students for Tests

You should be able to help your students prepare for tests and take tests. Students who are prepared for tests—in terms of knowledge of content and an effective study plan, and know how to take tests, in terms of strategies—perform better in test situations than students who are not prepared or skilled in taking tests. Below are suggestions for helping your students become better test takers.

I. *Discuss the purpose of testing*
    1. Discuss your reasons for testing students. What do you hope to accomplish?
II. *Discuss the type of test*
    1. Provide sample test items.
    2. Discuss answers.
    3. Discuss methods of eliminating options in short-answer questions.
    4. If reviews are available, distribute and discuss them.
    5. Refer to practice tests in textbook. Encourage students to answer these tests on a regular basis to determine what they are weak in or need to study.
III. *Take time out to illustrate how to write an essay answer*
    1. Have students practice writing on a related topic, or sample questions used in previous years.
    2. Ask for student volunteers to share their written answers with other students; ask for volunteers to avoid embarrassment.
    3. Point out the need for clarity, organization, and overall effectiveness of writing.
    4. Point out the need to respond to abstract or general questions by focusing on hooks or anchors, familiar concepts, names, or events.
    5. Read essay questions more than once. Determine the number of parts in each essay question.
    6. Look for key verbs—compare, analyze, review, evaluate, etc., and do what the verb asks.
    7. If possible avoid questions such as "discuss" or "examine," since it is difficult to focus on the test answer. If a choice is given, answer "compare/contrast," "cause-effect," or "identification" questions, since the intent or focus of discussion is already stated.

continues

    8. Outline before writing; keep the discussion focused; avoid tangential discussions.

    9. Short paragraphs will help avoid tangential writing. Each paragraph should correspond with a major concept or point.

  10. Teach students to manage time wisely. If time permits, have them reread their answers and make corrections accordingly.

IV. *Suggest methods for studying for the specific test*

    1. Remind students not to cram before the test; it is more effective for the studying to be gradual than hurried.

    2. For memorizing factual details, intensive studying is probably effective and should be completed one or two days before the test.

V. *Discuss strategies for answering reading passages*

    1. Students should read the passage thoroughly and then answer each question, referring to the passage as needed. This is the most common strategy.

    2. Read the questions first to gain an idea of what is sought in them, then read the passage with the answers in mind. This strategy is effective for low-achieving students and/or those who lack knowledge of the content.

    3. Scan the passage quickly in order to gain an overview of the content, then answer each question by backtracking to the specific paragraph or line. This strategy tends to save time and is effective for high-achieving students who can scan, process, and integrate information and/or for students who are familiar with the content of the passage.

VI. *Reduce test anxiety*

    1. Discuss the scope (content to study) of the test.

    2. Suggest that students (with high anxiety) study in small groups or with friends.

    3. Assure students that everyone feels a certain amount of test anxiety before tests, and a reasonable amount can be helpful in keeping students focused, alert, and test-wise during the test.

    4. Discuss specific fears, needs, or concerns of students in private.

    5. Explain how test items will be weighted and scored.

    6. Point out that last minute cramming usually increases anxiety, as does staying up unusually late to study the night before the exam (since it disturbs routine and reduces needed sleep).

    7. Self-confidence is an excellent antidote to anxiety; help students increase self-confidence by (a) reviewing content without giving away test questions, (b) reminding them to practice test items in the text or study guide, (c) consulting with a guidance

continues

counselor if needed, and (d) following up by asking how the students felt taking the test.

VII. *Discuss strategies one day prior to the test*

1. Encourage students to continue their routines, moderate eating, and regular sleep up to the day of the test.
2. Advise students to come to class (or the test site) on time.
3. Remind them to follow all directions (oral and written).

VIII. *Discuss strategies for answering short-answer questions*

1. Pace the work by determining how many questions are in the test or subtests; estimate amount of time needed for each set or group of questions.
2. Read carefully; do not speed up pace by skimming directions or reading test items too quickly.
3. Mark short-answer items carefully and completely; to change an answer students need to entirely erase the old answer.
4. Remind students that if they skip a short-answer question, they must also skip the corresponding row of answer choices.
5. Encourage students to guess wisely, especially if there is no penalty for guessing.
6. For unsure choices, students should be taught to eliminate as many options as possible before selecting among the remaining choices.
7. Some questions call for calculations. It is sometimes appropriate to estimate correct answers, rather than use time performing detailed calculations.
8. Check for accuracy if time remains; be sure changed answers have been completely erased along with stray marks. This is especially important if the answer sheet is electronically graded.

have been distributed. In some cases, the answer paper can be inserted into the test so as to hand out the necessary papers in one step.

Before the test begins, be sure that students understand the directions and questions; that the test papers are clear, complete, and in proper order; and that students have any necessary supplies, such as pencil or pen, ruler, calculator, or dictionary. It is important for the teacher to have on hand extra copies of the test and extra supplies.

Establish a procedure for clarifying directions and test items during test time. Once the test begins, a student with a question should raise his or her hand without talking out loud or disturbing classmates. With young students, the teacher should go to the student's desk and both should whisper. Older students may be permitted to come to the teacher. If several students have the same question or a problem with the same item, the teacher should interrupt the students briefly to clarify it for all. This should be done sparingly to limit distractions.

To further reduce distractions or interruptions, the door to the hallway should be closed and a sign, "Testing—Do Not Disturb," should be posted on the door.

Late students will disturb the others no matter how quiet they are in picking up the test papers and getting seated. Unless they have a proper pass or excuse for being late, the teacher should not give them extra time to complete the examination. If students enter the room late for a standardized examination, they should not be permitted to take the exam since the norms are based partially on time allotments.

Pressure on students for good grades causes some to cheat. Short-answer tests are particularly vulnerable to cheating, because a student can easily see someone else's answer by glancing at his or her paper.[56] To reduce cheating, some teachers have students sit in alternate seats if sufficient seats are available, or have students sit at a distance from each other if seats can be moved. Using two versions of the same test or dividing the test into two parts and having students in alternate rows start on different parts also helps reduce cheating. One of the best deterrents to cheating is the teacher's presence. To what extent the teacher needs to police students during the test depends on how common cheating is. Even if there is no cheating problem, a teacher should stay alert and not bury his or her head in a book while the test is being administered.

Routines should be established for collecting tests at the end of the period. Students who finish early should be reminded to review their answers. When the test period ends, the papers should be collected in an orderly fashion, for example, with papers being passed forward to the first student in each row and then collected by the teacher.

Table 4.10 indicates some things a teacher can do to improve test conditions and help students. Most of these strategies are geared to limiting confusion and interruptions before and during the test, ensuring that students know what to do, curtailing their anxieties and nervousness, and motivating them to do their best.

In this connection, a review of 562 studies, involving more than 20,000 students, shows that test anxiety strongly correlates with feelings of academic inadequacy, helplessness, and anticipation of failure. After grade 4, students who exhibit high **test anxiety** (that is, emotions and worry) wish to leave the

---

56 Jean D. Grambs and John C. Carr, *Modern Methods in Secondary Education*, 5th ed. (New York: Holt, Rinehart and Winston, 1989); Samuel Messick, "Meaning and Values in the Test Validation: The Science and Ethics of Assessment," *Educational Researcher* (March 1989), pp. 5–11.

Table 4.10   TEST GIVER'S LIST OF THINGS TO DO

1. Before giving a standardized test:

   a. Order and check test materials in advance of the testing date.

   b. Be sure there are sufficient tests and answer sheets.

   c. Securely store all test materials until the testing date.

   d. Follow the testing instructions, including how to administer the test.

2. Before giving a teacher-made test:

   a. Check the questions for errors and clarity.

   b. Be sure there are sufficient tests and answer sheets.

   c. Be sure the test pages are sequenced properly.

   d. Securely store all test materials until the testing date.

   e. Announce testing date; avoid days that are before holidays or coincide with major events.

3. Be sure classroom conditions are adequate:

   a. Is there adequate workspace, desks, chairs?

   b. Is there sufficient light, heat, and ventilation?

   c. Is it a quiet location?

   d. Is there a wall clock that is visible to the students? If not, you will need your own watch to post the time or announce it at intervals.

   e. See that desks are cleared.

4. Study the test materials before the test:

   a. Are the directions clear?

   b. Are the time limits clear?

   c. Are the methods for indicating answers clear?

5. Minimize distractions and interruptions during the testing period:

   a. Decide the order in which materials are to be distributed and collected.

   b. Be sure that students have pencils or pens and other needed supplies. Have extra pencils or pens handy for students who are unprepared.

   c. Close the hallway door.

   d. Post a sign: "Testing in Progress: Do Not Disturb."

   e. Decide what students who finish early are to do.

6. Motivate students to do their best:

   a. Explain the purpose of the test.

   b. Ask students to do their best: "I will be pleased if you try your best," for example.

   c. Reduce test anxiety: "Take it easy." "Take a deep breath." "Shake your fingers and wrist." "Relax, it's only a test."

7. Reassure students; provide positive expectations and strategies:

   a. "Some test questions are difficult. Don't worry if you can't answer all of them."

   b. "It is all right to guess. Choose the answer you think is best. Don't blindly guess."

Table 4.10   (Continued)

   c. "If you don't finish, don't worry about it. Just try your best."

   d. "Don't work too fast, whereby you start making careless mistakes."

   e. "Don't work too slow, whereby you start falling behind. Work at a moderate pace."

   f. "Don't dwell on a difficult question; return to it when you finish and if there is time to do so."

   g. "Pay close attention to your work and to the time."

   h. "Good luck."

8. Follow directions and monitor time:

   a. Distribute materials according to predetermined time allotment.

   b. Read test directions, if permitted.

   c. Give signal to start.

   d. Do not help students during the test, except for mechanics (i.e., providing an extra pencil or answer sheet).

   e. Stick to the time schedule, especially if you are administering a standardized test.

   f. Periodically post or announce time; provide 5- to 10-minute time announcements during last 15 or 20 minutes of test.

9. Observe significant events:

   a. Pay attention to students; monitor the test situation.

   b. Make sure students are following directions and answering in the correct place.

   c. Replace pens or pencils if needed; provide extra test booklets, sheets, or papers if needed.

   d. Note if any student displayed behavior that might affect his or her test results; curtail cheating.

   e. Note any major distractions or interruptions that could affect the test results. If administering a standardized test, report these problems to the administration.

10. Collect test materials:

   a. Attend to students who finish early; remind them to check answers before handing in test.

   b. Collect materials promptly and without confusion.

   c. If administering a teacher-made test, perhaps provide a few minutes extra for slow students or students who walked in late. Use good judgment.

   d. Count and check to see that all materials have been turned in.

Source: Adapted from Norman E. Gronlund and Robert L. Linn, *Measurement and Evaluation in Teaching*, 6th ed. (New York: Macmillan, 1990); Charles Hopkins and Richard Antes, *Classroom Testing*, 2nd ed. (Itasca, Ill: Peacock, 1989); and David A. Payne, *The Assessment of Learning* (Lexington, Mass: Heath, 1974).

test situation and consistently score low on tests, thus reinforcing the negative view of themselves (A child's *original* view of self, before entering school, is likely to be positive). Performance on tests also strongly varies with students' perception of the test's difficulty, affecting average-achieving students more than other groups.[57]

The high test anxiety/low test performance cycle is difficult to reverse. Incentives, praise, rewards, and prompt feedback all have minimal benefits, as do frequent tests, detailed test instructions, and test reviews. What works best, according to the research, is to teach students study skills and test-taking skills.[58] However, it needs to be reaffirmed that good study skills and test skills are already associated with high achievement, although one might now argue these measures are possibly confounded by test anxiety.

Returning Tests and Feedback

Tests should be returned to students as quickly as possible. As the papers are returned the teacher should make some general comments to the class about awareness of the group effort, level of achievement, and general problems or specific areas of the test that gave students trouble.

Each question on the test should be discussed in class; questions that many students missed should be gone over in detail. If the missed test items are fundamental for mastery, then the teacher should take extra time to explain the material and provide similar but different exercises for students to review. Some teachers call on volunteers to redo and explain parts of the test that were missed, although this method may not always be the most profitable use of time.

For students who have achieved a good grade, especially an unexpectedly good grade, the teacher should provide approval. Students who have performed poorly should be given special help in the form of extra reading, selective homework, or tutoring. In some cases, teachers will retest them after they have restudied the material. The teacher should meet with students who have questions about their grades after class privately, or possibly in a small group if several students have the same question. Regardless of the type of test, the teacher should make some comments about the individual student's answers and progress, with more personal comments directed at younger children. Personal comments, so long as they are objective and positive, help motivate students and make them aware that they need to improve in specific areas.

---

57 Ray Hembree, "Correlates, Causes, Effects and Treatments of Test Anxiety," *Review of Educational Research* (Spring 1988), pp. 47–77.

58 Ibid.

SUMMARY

1. A good test is reliable and valid. Methods for establishing reliability are test-retest, parallel test forms, and split-half reliability. Forms of validity are content, curricular, construct, criterion, and predictive.
2. There are two major types of tests: norm-reference and criterion-reference. Norm-reference tests measure how a student performs relative to other students. Criterion-reference tests measure a student's progress and appraise his or her ability relative to specific criterion.
3. For general appraisal of an individual's performance or behavior, the standardized (norm-reference) test is an excellent instrument. There are four basic types of standardized tests: intelligence, achievement, aptitude, and personality.
4. Teacher-made tests may be short-answer or essay tests. Short-answer questions include multiple-choice, matching, completion, and true-false. Essay, or free-response, questions also include discussion questions.
5. Proper test administration reduces confusion, curtails students' anxieties, and motivates and helps them to do as well as possible.
6. Important test-taking skills can be taught to students.

CASE STUDY

Problem

A twelfth-grade teacher, in a lower-middle class school, had organized her room in a "democratic" fashion, using group decision making for constructing room rules, for making some curriculum decisions, and for deciding on units of study. In certain subject matter areas, she encouraged her students to challenge ideas and "traditional" viewpoints.

She was having a problem in the acceptance of test grades by her students. They would not accept the result without offering arguments (many irrelevant and supercilious). They also charged unfairness. The situation had reached a point where the teacher experienced so much argument and both covert and overt hostility after testing that she was about to give up academic evaluation and grade only on participation and general attitude, thereby almost assuring everyone a "good" grade. Yet she knew intuitively this was not fair to students in other classes where teachers were able to provide accurate evaluations.

Suggestion

The teacher's principal commented that her classroom "techniques" were in direct contradiction to the necessary, nondebatable outcomes of tests. The teacher was unaware that when students challenged the grades they were simply carrying on the process of debate and group decision and the challenging of traditional ideas that was encouraged in class. The principal pointed out that the classroom is a complex social system in which ideas and attitudes in one area cannot be separated from other areas. The democratic process and the adversarial teaching model was being carried over into challenging the role of the teacher. The principal suggested she clarify the distinction between teaching process and objective evaluation; modify the overemphasized challenges to tradition; not surrender a teacher's leadership role to a total democracy of the classroom; carefully check tests for ambiguous statements; make a systematic check to see the frequency of incorrect answers for some items; match the wording of the questions to the statements in the text; and for lengthy, or summary tests narrow the ambiguity by providing page numbers from which the questions will be drawn.

Discussion Suggestion

Another teacher suggested that the students' so-called "hostility" was actually anxiety. The students were not *used* to taking tests and needed assistance in mastering the *form* of the test. The teacher was urged to pay close attention to word construction and oral and written direction, and to provide some practice tests before the actual test. Further, since the students did poorly in placement tests for high schools when they took the IBM format, some classroom tests should be modeled on the form of the placement tests and the *word construction* of the placement tests. This could be done by using IBM sheets separate from question sheets, thereby giving the students *practice* in following *written* test instructions instead of only oral instructions; they could use the form of the more complicated placement tests, such as having separate questions matched to a separate text referred to by numbered lines.

The teacher making the suggestions said his students' placement scores improved and they reported beginning the placement tests with a comfortable security rather than with anxiety, which lost them time and points. He felt that if the teacher helped her students do well on placement, they would understand her attitude toward regular classroom evaluation: was preparation for their future.

Discussion Questions

1. Could the first teacher have used a type of evaluation other than tests and still remained credible to her colleagues and remained a democratic teacher to her student? What methods are suggested in this chapter for so doing?

2. In modeling his tests after placement tests, was the second teacher providing his students with an unfair advantage? Can this modeling method of testing be justified?

3. Do you agree with the principal when he suggested the first teacher modify her emphasis on a democratic classroom situation? Why? Why not?

4. Can you anticipate any objections from your colleagues to the modeling of tests? From curriculum consultants or parents? If so, what kinds of objections and how might you answer?

QUESTIONS TO CONSIDER

1. What are the most important factors to consider in choosing a test?
2. What are the advantages and disadvantages of a norm-reference test?
3. What are the advantages and disadvantages of a criterion-reference test?
4. What are the advantages of teacher-made tests over standardized tests? What are the advantages of standardized tests over teacher-made tests?
5. What strategies or principles should be considered in administering a test?

THINGS TO DO

1. Explain the differences between reliability and validity.
2. Visit a school and talk to a few teachers, the school counselor, or one of the administrators about the standardized tests the school uses. Try to find out which ones are used, and why. What are the advantages and disadvantages of the tests? Report back to the class.
3. Discuss in class five guidelines for constructing multiple-choice questions and five guidelines for constructing matching questions.
4. Develop five essay questions (in the subject you plan to teach or are teaching) that test critical thinking. Indicate in class what type of thinking these questions test.
5. Invite a test specialist to class to discuss strategies about how students can learn to increase their test-wiseness.

RECOMMENDED READINGS

Cronbach, Lee J. *Essentials of Psychological Testing*, 5th ed. New York: HarperCollins, 1990. An up-to-date treatment of testing with emphasis on reliability and validity.

Ebel, Robert L. and David A. Frisbie, *Essentials of Educational Measurement*, 5th ed. Englewood Cliffs, N.J.: Prentice-Hall, 1991. Emphasizes the advantages and disadvantages of different types of short-answer questions and essay questions.

Gronlund, Norman E. and Robert L. Linn, *Measurement and Evaluation in Teaching*, 6th ed. New York: Macmillan, 1990. Several suggestions for constructing various type of tests, including short-answer and essay tests.

Lehman, Irwin J. *Standard for Educational and Psychological Testing*, 2nd ed. Washington, D.C.: American Psychological Association, 1985. Testing standards and procedures adopted by the number-one psychological association.

Mehrens, William A. and Irwin J. Lehman. *Measurement and Evaluation in Education and Psychology*, 3rd ed. New York: Holt, Rinehart & Winston, 1984. A major text dealing with the basic principles involved in constructing , selecting, administering, and interpreting tests.

Popham, W. James. *Modern Educational Measurement*, 2nd ed. Englewood Cliffs, N.J.: Prentice-Hall, 1990. Describes the differences between norm-reference and criterion-reference tests and their application.

Tuckman, Bruce W. *Testing for Teachers*, 2nd ed. San Diego: Harcourt Brace Jovanovich, 1988. A brief text on testing, written for the practitioner, that puts measurement and evaluation in perspective.

KEY TERMS

Reliability

Validity

Standardized test

Nonstandardized test

Norm-reference test

Criterion-reference test

Intelligence test

Achievement test

Aptitude test

Personality test

Short-answer test

Essay test

Multiple-choice test

Matching test

Completion test

True-false test

Discussion test

Test anxiety

Chapter 5

Evaluating Students

FOCUSING QUESTIONS

1. Why should students be evaluated?

2. What is the difference between placement evaluation and diagnostic evaluation? Formative and summative evaluation?

3. What methods other than tests are available for evaluating students?

4. What are the advantages and disadvantages of absolute grade standards and relative grade standards?

5. When is it appropriate to grade students on the basis of contracts, mastery learning, and effort?

6. Why is it important to communicate with parents about their children's work and progress? How might communication with parents be improved?

7. How might the grading system in schools be changed to reduce student anxiety and student competition?

Testing of students, since it is based on quantifiable data, is more objective than evaluation. Evaluation is more subjective, involving human judgment. We make evaluations of people and their performance not only in school but also on the job and at home. Similarly, we make evaluations of consumer goods (food, clothing, cameras, televisions) and services (auto repair, insurance, medical treatment, legal advice). We use various kinds of information, including test data and other objective measurements. We weigh our information against various criteria and make an evaluation about people or products. As teachers, we strive to reduce the chance for misjudgment in the evaluation of students by carefully designing evaluation procedures.

REASONS FOR EVALUATION

According to Robert Slavin, there are basically five purposes for evaluating students.

1. *Motivation of students.* Evaluations, if properly conducted and presented to students, can motivate them. For example, high grades, gold stars, certificates of achievement, and prizes that are used as rewards for good work can stimulate further good work.
2. *Feedback to students.* Students need to know the results of their efforts. Regular evaluation can reveal strengths and weaknesses, and the teacher should relay this information to the students with recommendations for improvement. Explanations of grades and examination of performance are more helpful for students' learning than grades without explanations.
3. *Feedback to teachers.* Evaluation provides information to teachers on the effectiveness of their instruction, how well the students have learned the material, and to what extent they are improving. Evaluation data (student records and teacher evaluations) also provide information to other teachers who instruct the students in other classes or later grades.
4. *Information to parents.* School evaluations of many kinds—test papers, certificates, prizes, letters, report cards—provide information to parents. Evaluations should be sent to parents regularly, and parents should be instructed in home-based reinforcement and follow-up procedures.
5. *Information for selection.* Evaluations can be used to select and sort students for different types of instruction, such as homogeneous or

heterogeneous grouping in classrooms and special courses or programs.[1]

To be of any use to students, teachers, or parents, evaluation of students must be fair. Students must feel that the evaluation of their performance is objective and the same for all students. If students feel that some students are evaluated more leniently or more strictly than others, the effectiveness of the evaluation will be reduced.[2]

Students must feel that their academic efforts will lead to success. The evaluation process should motivate them; it should encourage them to set progressively higher goals for personal achievement. If students feel the evaluation process will lead to failure, or if they feel the process is unfair, then they will be discouraged by it.

The evaluation process should also be realistic. Students should be able to assess their own performance in relation to classmates and normative standards. In a class where most students cannot read well, a student who is an average reader may get an inflated impression about his or her real abilities. Evaluations are more effective when students are provided with valid norms of what constitutes success.

Every student, during his or her school career, will experience the pain of failure and the joy of success as a result of the evaluation process. The student must learn, according to Philip Jackson, "to adapt to the continued and pervasive spirit of evaluation that will dominate his school years." Although school is not the only place "where the student is made aware of his strengths and weaknesses," school evaluation happens most frequently and has the most lasting impact.[3]

The impact of school evaluation is profound because students are forming their identities during their school years, because they are going through their most critical stages of development, and because they lack defensive mechanisms to ward off extreme or continuous negative evaluations. Whether evaluation focuses on academic work, behavior, or personal qualities, it affects the student's reputation among his or her peers, confidence in his or her abilities, and motivation in work. The student's popularity, self-concept, personal adjustment, career goals, even physical and mental health are related to the judgments that others communicate to him or her throughout school.[4] We

1 Robert E. Slavin, *Educational Psychology: Theory into Practice*, 3rd ed. (Englewood Cliffs, N.J.: Prentice-Hall, 1991).

2 Gary Natriello and Stanford M. Dornbusch, *Teacher Evaluative Standards and Student Effort* (New York: Longman, 1984); Blaine R. Worthen, Walter R. Borg, and Karl R. White, *Measurement and Evaluation in the Schools* (New York: Longman, 1989).

3 Philip W. Jackson, *Life in Classrooms* (New York: Holt, Rinehart & Winston, 1968), p. 19.

4 Helen S. Farmer, "A Multivariate Model for Examining Gender Differences in Career and Achievement Motivation," *Educational Researcher* (March 1987), pp. 5–9; Robert J. Trotter, "Stop Blaming Yourself," *Psychology Today* (February 1987), pp. 31–39.

are what we see ourselves to be, and like it or not, we see ourselves as others perceive and evaluate us. The self is a social product that emerges as the child grows and interacts with others.

TYPES OF EVALUATION

There are four basic evaluation techniques that are appropriate for and commonly used in the classroom. (1) Placement evaluation helps to determine student placement or categorization before instruction begins. (2) Diagnostic evaluation is a means of discovering and monitoring learning difficulties. (3) Formative evaluation monitors progress. (4) Summative evaluation measures results at the end of instruction.

Placement Evaluation

Placement evaluation, sometimes called *preassessment*, takes place before instruction. The teacher wants to find out what knowledge and skills the students have mastered to establish a starting point of instruction. Sufficient mastery might suggest that some instructional units may be skipped or treated briefly. Insufficient mastery suggests that certain basic knowledge or skills should be emphasized. Students who are required to begin at a level that is too difficult or beyond their understanding will encounter frustration and will most likely be unable to gain new knowledge and skills. Students who are required to review old material they already know are wasting instructional time and may eventually become bored.

It is also important to find out how much a student knows and what his or her interests and work habits are in order to decide on the best type of instruction (group or independent, inductive or deductive), methods, and materials for that student.

A third reason for placement evaluation is to place students in specific learning groups. Although this procedure may lead to tracking, teachers find that grouping students by knowledge and skills facilitates teaching and learning. Placement evaluation is based on readiness tests, aptitude tests, pretests on course objectives, and observation.

At the middle school level, students are usually divided into groups according to ability, and groups of students may be created from several classes to form another group or special class. With high-school students, judgments about ability or achievement may be used as a basis for enrolling students in certain classes or programs, or for limiting enrollment in particular classes to those who meet specific criteria. Ability grouping has been generally upheld in the courts, despite widespread criticism by some educators, so long as assignments are made in a nonarbitrary and nondiscriminatory manner.

Diagnostic Evaluation

Diagnostic evaluation attempts to discover the causes of students' learning problems. If a student continues to fail a particular subject or is unable to learn basic skills in elementary school or basic content in secondary school, diagnosis of the cause of the failure may point to ways to remedy it. According to Bruce Tuckman, "where proficiency has not been demonstrated, remedial instruction aimed directly at those [deficiencies] can be instituted." Evaluation can "provide the kind of information that will make it possible to overcome failure."[5]

In many cases diagnostic and formative evaluation (discussed below) overlap. Formative evaluation is mainly concerned with progress, but the lack of progress may indicate a problem, which should then be investigated with more specific diagnostic evaluation. According to Gronlund and Linn, formative evaluation serves as a guide to general, everyday treatment, but diagnostic evaluation is necessary for detailed, remedial treatment.[6] Diagnostic evaluation is based on teacher-made and published tests and observational techniques.

Formative Evaluation

Formative evaluation and summative evaluation are terms coined by Michael Scriven in his analysis of program and curriculum evaluation.[7] **Formative evaluation** monitors progress during the learning process, while summative evaluation measures the final results at the end of an instructional unit or term. Benjamin Bloom and his associates describe formative evaluation as a major tool of instruction: "Too often in the past evaluation has been entirely summative in nature, taking place only at the end of the unit, chapter, course, or semester, when it is too late, at least for that particular group of students, to modify either ... the teaching [or] learning ... process."[8]

If evaluation is to help the teacher and student, it should take place not only at the end point of instruction, but also at various points during the teaching-learning process while modifications can be made. Instruction can be modified, based on the feedback that formative evaluation yields, to correct learning problems or to move ahead more rapidly.

Formative evaluation focuses on small, comparatively independent units of instruction and a narrow range of objectives. It is based on teacher-made and published tests administered throughout the term, homework and classroom

---

5 Bruce W. Tuckman, *Measuring Educational Outcomes*, 2nd ed. (San Diego: Harcourt Brace Jovanovich, 1985), p. 300.

6 Norman E. Gronlund and Robert L. Linn, *Measurement and Evaluation in Teaching*, 6th ed. (New York: Macmillan, 1990).

7 Michael Scriven, "The Methodology of Evaluation," in R. W. Tyler, R. Gagné, and M. Scriven, eds., *Perspectives on Curriculum Evaluation* (Chicago: Rand McNally, 1967), pp. 39–83.

8 Benjamin S. Bloom, J. Thomas Hastings, and George F. Madaus, *Handbook on Formative and Summative Evaluation of Student Learning* (New York: McGraw-Hill, 1971), p. 20.

performance of students, informal teacher observations of students, student-teacher conferences, and parent-teacher conferences.

Summative Evaluation

As the phrase implies, **summative evaluation** is an evaluation that takes place at the end of an instructional unit or course. It is designed to determine the extent to which the instructional objectives have been achieved by the students and is used primarily to certify or grade students.[9] It can also be used to judge the effectiveness of a teacher or a particular curriculum or program. Whereas formative evaluation provides a tentative judgment of teaching and learning, summative evaluation, coming when teaching and learning are over, is a final judgment.

Summative evaluation focuses on a wide range of objectives and relies on an accumulation of student work and performance. Although teacher-made tests can be used for this purpose, it is often based on formal observation scales or ratings and standardized tests.

Table 5.1 provides a summary of the four evaluation categories, which the teacher can use during the instructional process.

EVALUATION METHODS AND APPROACHES

Everyone is evaluated and makes evaluations on a daily and informal basis. Students and teachers are continuously evaluating each other in class on an informal basis. When teachers observe students at work or answer students' questions, they are engaging in **informal evaluation**. When they make a decision to assign one of two alternative books for students to read, they are also engaging in informal evaluation. Evaluation, when it is thorough and precise, is usually formal. When it is impressionistic or based on hunches it is informal.

Informal Evaluation

Testing is the most obvious method by which students are evaluated, but it is not the only one. In fact, evaluation without tests occurs on a daily basis and is considered by Philip Jackson to be more powerful and influential than tests. He asserts that students quickly come to realize "when things are right or wrong, good or bad, largely as a result of what the teacher tells them." The teacher

---

9 Norman E. Gronlund, *How to Construct Achievement Tests*, 4th ed. (Englewood Cliffs, N.J.: Prentice-Hall, 1988); Robert F. Mager, *Making Instruction Work* (Belmont, Calif.: Fearon, 1988).

Table 5.1   TYPES OF EVALUATION

Type	Function	Illustrative instruments used
Placement	Determines skills, degree of mastery before instruction to determine appropriate level and mode of teaching	Readiness tests, aptitude tests, pretests, observations, interviews, personality profiles, self-reports, videotapes, ancedotal reports
Diagnostic	Determines causes (cognitive, physical, emotional, social) of serious learning problems to indicate remedial techniques	Published diagnostic tests, teacher-made diagnostic tests, observations, interviews, ancedotal reports
Formative	Determines learning progress, provides feedback to refacilitate learning and to correct teaching errors	Teacher-made tests, tests from test publishers, observations, checklists, videotapes
Summative	Determines end-of-course achievement for grading or certification	Teacher-made tests, rating scales, standardized tests

Source: Adapted from Peter W. Airasian and George F. Madaus, "Functional Types of Student Evaluation," *Measurement and Evaluation in Guidance* (January 1972), pp. 221–233; Norman E. Gronlund and Robert L. Linn, *Measurement and Evaluation in Teaching*, 6th ed. (New York: Macmillan, 1990), p. 17.

"continuously makes judgments of students' work and behavior [and communicates] that judgment to the students in question and to others."[10]

A second source of daily evaluation is the judgment of peers. "Sometimes the class as a whole is invited to participate in the evaluation of a student's work, as when the teacher asks, 'Who can correct Billy?' or 'How many believe that Shirley read the poem with a lot of expression?'" At times an obvious error evokes laughter or destructive criticism, while outstanding performance wins "spontaneous applause."[11] Little urging on the part of the teacher is needed, although the teacher may consciously or unconsciously egg the students on.

A third source of daily evaluation is student self-judgment. Students appraise their own performance without the "intervention of an outside judge." This type of evaluation is more difficult to discern and describe, but it occurs throughout instruction, for example, when the student works on the chalkboard and knows that the work is correct or incorrect, although the teacher may not bother to indicate one way or another.[12]

10 Jackson, *Life in Classrooms*, p. 19.

11 Ibid., p. 20.

12 See Mary C. Ellwein, Gene V. Glass, and Mary L. Smith, "Standards of Competence: Propositions on the Nature of Testing Reforms," *Educational Researcher* (November 1988), pp. 4–9; Ray Hembree, "Correlates, Causes, Effects, and Treatments of Test Anxiety," *Review of Educational Research* (Spring 1988), pp. 47–78.

There are many other types of evaluation, according to Jackson, which are both *private*, such as IQ and personality test scores (that always follow the student and lead to labels) or certain communications to parents or other teachers about students; and *public*, such as the display of work for others to see or a teacher review for the class of someone's mistake. Evaluation in class and school never ceases.

Although critics make many negative comments about the evaluation process, evaluation is still necessary. Although it can be argued that tests are not always necessary for grading, classifying, or judging students, evaluation is. Teachers need to evaluate students' performance and progress; otherwise, they are surrendering an important role in teaching. On the other hand, the evaluation process should consider the students' feelings and self-concept; it should avoid labels that lead to traps, embarrassment, and despair among students whose performance is less than average. Not an easy task, given the nature of middle-class society.

Feedback

Evaluation in the form of feedback can take place through tests, classroom questions and answers, homework assignments that are collected or reviewed in class, and reading and writing assignments. Feedback serves to confirm correct answers or identify errors and help the student correct them. In most studies such feedback clearly improves understanding and subsequent performance on similar questions. However, there is evidence that feedback in programmed or computerized instruction has little effect on subsequent performance—except in special cases where the student has major doubts about the correctness of the answer.[13]

Effective feedback is associated with three variables: the correctness of the answer, the student's degree of confidence in the answer, and the difficulty of the task. If the answer is correct and knowledge based, then a simple confirmation of its correctness will suffice. If the answer is incorrect, the most efficient feedback is to provide the correct answer. If the question involves higher cognitive skills, more detailed feedback is desirable. Students who answer such questions incorrectly with high confidence need help to identify their source of misunderstanding. Students who answer the question incorrectly with low confidence need broad or conceptual help and to restudy selected materials.[14]

Research on feedback indicates negative effects when the questions asked or the materials being read are too difficult for the students. Low-achieving

---

13 Robert L. Bangert et al., "Effects of Frequent Classroom Testing," paper presented at the annual meeting of the American Educational Research Association, Washington, D.C., April 1988; Terrence J. Crooks, "The Impact of Classroom Evaluation Practices on Students," *Review of Educational Research* (Winter 1988), pp. 438–481.

14 Crooks, "The Impact of Classroom Evaluation Practices on Students"; John Fredericksen, "Implications of Cognitive Theory for Instruction in Problem Solving," *Review of Educational Research* (Fall 1984), pp. 363–407.

students tend to give up quickly, thus ignoring the feedback; and high-achieving students tend to focus on the main points of the feedback without always trying to understand the question or materials. In short, the research affirms that when error rates are high, learning from feedback is minimal.[15] Negative results can also occur when the feedback is readily available or available too soon, as in the back of a text or in some programmed or computerized materials. This allows the student to avoid careful analysis of the question or reading of the material.

In general, simple verbal praise or positive comments on papers are beneficial for learning and harsh criticism is harmful. Both the age and the ability of the students affect this generalization. Younger and low-achieving students benefit more from feedback with praise. For older students, praise should be linked to specific achievements, whereas general feedback (i.e., "good work") can be used more often with younger ones. The more specific the teacher is, however, the more valuable the feedback for the student.

A review of 53 studies indicates a modest advantage for delayed feedback as opposed to no feedback. For immediate versus delayed quiz feedback, the difference in achievement was significant in nearly half the studies. The results of all the studies on achievement were modest: .28 higher for immediate rather than delayed feedback. Feedback delayed more than 7 days after a test tends to negatively affect performance. Older students can tolerate more delay in feedback than younger students.[16] Beyond the data, it is also assumed that high-achieving students can tolerate and learn more than low achievers from delayed feedback. When feedback is provided in conjunction with a final exam or grade, the students tend to pay minimum attention and learn little from it. If students are given multiple tests or evaluation opportunities during the course, they usually pay closer attention to feedback.[17]

Frequent feedback helps students achieve. Questions in class and/or in conjunction with reading assignments encourage more active engagement in learning, provide practice or review of the material, consolidate student learning, help correct misconceptions, and clarify understanding. In addition, questions in class accompanied by feedback help students recognize what the teacher regards as important and thus is more likely to include in tests. Likewise, constructive evaluation is positively associated with student achievement because ideally it (1) consolidates knowledge or skills prior to introducing new material, (2) focuses attention on important aspects of the subject, (3)

---

15 Bangert, "Effects of Frequent Classroom Testing"; James A. Kulik and Chen-Lin C. Kulik, "Timing of Feedback and Verbal Learning," *Review of Educational Research* (Spring 1988), pp. 79–97; and Wilbert J. McKeachie, "Learning, Thinking, and Thorndike," *Educational Psychologist* (Spring 1990), pp. 127–142.

16 Kulik and Kulik, "Timing of Feedback and Verbal Learning."

17 James M. McPartland, "Changing Testing and Grading Practices to Improve Student Motivation," paper presented at the annual meeting of the American Educational Research Association, Washington, D.C., April 1987.

encourages active learning, (4) gives students opportunities to practice skills, (5) provides knowledge of results, (6) helps students to monitor their own progress, and (7) helps students feel a sense of achievement.[18]

Evaluation Other Than Testing

Student performance and progress can be measured through a variety of formal methods other than tests, although testing is the most common source of data and should be included as part of the total evaluation. The various other methods and approaches can be used to supplement test data.

Observation of Student Work

The teacher has the opportunity to watch students perform various tasks on a daily basis, under various conditions, alone and with different students. The teacher sees students more or less continually simply by virtue of being in the classroom, but he or she needs to know what to look for and to have some objective system for collecting and assessing data.

Although the teacher should observe all students, individuals who exhibit atypical behavior or learning outcomes are often singled out for special study. The keys to good observation are objectivity and documentation. Teachers cannot depend on memory or vague statements, such as "Johnny misbehaves in class." They must keep accurate, specific written records.

If observations are free from bias and tempered with common sense, this informal, nonstandardized evaluation method can provide more insightful information about a student than would test scores alone.

Group Evaluation Activities

Teachers can set aside a time to allow students to participate in establishing instructional objectives, to evaluate their strengths and limitations, and to evaluate their own progress in learning. Students can evaluate themselves or their classmates on study habits and homework, class participation, quizzes, workbook or textbook activities, and other activities. They can keep anecdotal reports or logs about their own work in which successes and difficulties are recorded and then discussed in class. They can check off assignments they complete and evaluate their work in group discussions.

Evaluation techniques such as these "make it possible for teachers to . . . diagnose [student] errors and to measure student progress. Teachers can also use these [activities] to show students how well they are getting on and what their faults and strengths are."[19]

---

18 Robert M. Gagné, *The Conditions of Learning,* 4th ed. (New York: Holt, Rinehart & Winston, 1985).

19 Leonard H. Clark and Irving S. Starr, *Secondary and Middle School Teaching Methods,* 5th ed. (New York: Macmillan, 1986), p. 355.

Class Discussions and Recitations

Many teachers consider a student's participation in class discussion an essential source of data for evaluation. Teachers are impressed by students who volunteer, develop thoughts logically, and discuss relevant facts and relationships. Answering the teacher's questions frequently and carrying out assignments in class are considered to be evidence of progress. The inability to answer questions and the inability to perform assignments in class are taken to be indications of learning problems or lack of motivation.

Homework

The teacher can learn much about students' achievements and attitudes by checking homework carefully. A good rule is not to assign homework unless it is going to be checked in some way, preferably by the teacher and in some cases by another student or by the student herself. The idea is to provide prompt feedback to the student, preferably emphasizing the positive aspects of work while making one or two major recommendations for improvement. As Herb Walberg points out, student achievement increases significantly when teachers assign homework on a regular basis, students conscientiously do it, and comments and feedback are provided when the work is completed.[20]

Notebooks and Note-Taking

Notebooks should be used as an assessment tool for evaluating the writing and understanding of subject matter for students in the middle grades and junior high school. Note-taking is more important for secondary school students, especially at the high school level. At this level students should begin to be able to take notes on some of the unanticipated ideas that emerge from the classroom discussions. According to William Rohwer, good note-taking consists of arranging information in a systematic form, focusing on major points of discussion, condensing material, and integrating new with old information.[21] Verbatim notes or simple paraphrasing or listing of information are not as effective.

Reports, Themes, and Research Papers

Written work serves as an excellent way to assess students' ability to organize thoughts, to research topics, to develop new ideas. In evaluating projects, the teacher should look to see how well students have developed their thoughts in terms of explanations, logic, and relationship of ideas; whether ideas are expressed clearly; whether facts are documented or distinguished from opinion; and what conclusions or recommendations are evidenced. Spelling and gram-

---

20 Herbert J. Walberg, "Homework's Powerful Effects on Learning," *Educational Leadership* (April 1985), pp. 76–79.

21 William Rohwer, "An Invitation to an Educational Psychology of Studying," *Educational Psychologist* (Winter 1984), pp. 1–14.

mar should not be the key to evaluating students; rather, emphasis should be on the thinking process of the students, the use of reference materials, and the ability to keep to the topic and develop it logically.

Discussions and Debates

Evaluating oral work is less reliable than evaluating written samples, but oral work may reveal creative and critical thinking that cannot be measured with other methods. Louis Raths and others point out that when students freely discuss topics that are of interest to them, their thinking is based on many skills, insights, and experiences not evidenced in a one-hour written test.[22]

Free discussion in groups brings values out in the open and forces students to think about other people's values. Analysis of problems and attempts to find solutions to problems through debates, panel discussions, or buzz sessions are valuable tools for teachers to use to understand how their students think and feel.

During discussions students can be rated not only on their mastery of and ability to analyze material, but also on several social and cognitive characteristics. According to Peter Martorella, such characteristics would include the way in which the student "(1) accepts ideas of others, (2) initiates ideas, (3) gives opinions, (4) is task oriented, (5) helps others, (6) seeks information, (7) encourages others to contribute, (8) works well with all members, (9) raises provocative questions, (10) listens to others, (11) disagrees in a constructive fashion, and (12) makes an overall positive contribution to the group."[23]

Portfolios

Student portfolios can consist of the student's work related to his or her academic achievements and interests. The portfolio is begun in the beginning of the term and continues until the end. It may consist of a written autobiography, a statement about work (including a résumé), an essay on ethics, a written summary of coursework (or life in school), a project or paper on a topic pertaining to the subject of the student's choice. The portfolio is an excellent way for the teacher to get to know the student as a person.[24]

Quizzes

Quizzes are brief exams. They provide an excellent basis for checking homework and for evaluating the progress of students. Some teachers give

---

22 Louis E. Raths et al., *Teaching for Thinking: Theory, Strategies, and Activities for the Classroom* (New York: Teachers College Press, Columbia University, 1985); Lauren B. Resnick, *Education and Learning to Think* (Washington, D.C.: National Academy Press, 1987).

23 Peter M. Martorella, *Elementary Social Studies* (Boston: Little, Brown, 1985), p. 247.

24 F. Leon Paulson, Pearl R. Paulson, and Carol A. Meyer, "What Makes a Portfolio a Portfolio?" *Educational Leadership* (February 1991), pp. 60–64; Dennie P. Wolf, "Portfolio Assessment: Sampling Student Work," *Educational Leadership* (April 1989), pp. 35–40.

unannounced quizzes at irregular intervals, especially quizzes related to specific assignments. Others give regular, scheduled quizzes to assess learning over a short period of time, say a week or two. Quizzes encourage students to keep up with the assignments and show them their strengths and weaknesses in learning.

Frequent and systematic monitoring of students' work and progress through short quizzes helps teachers improve instruction and learning. Errors serve as early warning signals of learning problems that then can be corrected before they worsen. According to researchers, student effort and achievement improves when teachers provide frequent evaluation and feedback on quizzes.[25] Quizzes are easy to develop, administer, and grade, thus providing an avenue for multiple and prompt evaluations.

Teacher Logs

In a notebook, a teacher can record almost anything—the student's behavior, conversations with a parent, anecdotal observations, comments, test scores, and so on. The information, although informal, is valuable and should be dated. The best time to make entries is probably right after school or after a specific incident. A check or asterisk next to a recorded entry might connote that a reference or sample of work is on file in the student's permanent folder or it was submitted to a specific supervisor. The information should be considered a private record for your own use as a teacher; it can be useful for a parents' conference or for writing a future letter of reference. See Tips for Teachers 5.1.

Teacher Judgments of Academic Performance

Teachers continuously judge the students' academic work in many ways. Because subjectivity and bias are often introduced in this evaluation process, teachers in this role will always be the potential target for criticism. Given the importance of grades and the consequent sorting process in our society, teachers need to make these judgments with care.

Even during the instructional process, teachers are always making decisions, including judgments about how well the students are comprehending. For example, in the *preinstructional phase* of teaching, teachers often formulate judgments about their students' reading and writing abilities in the middle (or junior high) schools and students' prior knowledge in the high schools;

---

25 *What Works: Research About Teaching and Learning* (Washington, D.C.: U.S. Government Printing Office, 1986); Benjamin S. Bloom, J. Thomas Hastings, and George F. Madaus, *Evaluation to Improve Learning* (New York: McGraw-Hill, 1981); and Eva L. Baker and Merlin C. Wittrock, *Testing and Cognition* (Needham Heights, Mass.: Allyn & Bacon, 1991).

Tips for Teachers 5.1

Time-Saving Grading Methods

Teachers need to adopt efficient methods of grading, especially at the secondary level where they usually teach 100 to 150 students per semester. Teachers should learn a wide variety of grading methods to reduce time spent on grading and record keeping. Here are some tips.

1. Students can discuss or read their own assignments or homework to a small group, or copies of the students' work can be made for other students to read. The group (or partner) must comment on the individual student's work. Each student makes a specific suggestion for improvement.

2. Students are randomly selected by the teacher to work out a problem or homework item at the blackboard. The work is discussed in class, and the individual student is graded.

3. Two or three students act as teacher helpers and grade class homework by using the teacher's instructor's manual or quizzes by using the test key. These students are given "pass" privileges to arrive thirty minutes before school begins and work in the teacher's homeroom (or advisory room).

4. Whenever students must study a list of questions from the text, instead of asking each student to hand in the entire assignment, have students place each question on a separate sheet of paper. The next day the teacher selects one question to turn in for grading.

5. Students can check their own homework or answers to each problem in class by referring to an answer key supplied by the teacher or posted on a bulletin board. Only one student at a time is allowed at the bulletin board. The answers to the last two are not posted, because the teacher will collect and check these.

6. Students grade their own homework or quizzes. One student puts the grade on a separate index card or on the back of the paper. As a double-check, another student then grades the paper and writes it on a separate index card or on the front. The second student then checks to see if the grades match. If they do, the homework or quiz is returned to the original student. If they do not, then the second student meets with the first student who graded the paper to work out the discrepancy.

7. Grade only the major paper or homework assignment per class per week. If you have organized student helpers, give the paper or assignment to them to grade. Periodically check the helpers' work to ensure accuracy and honesty.

(continues)

8. Grade only every fourth or fifth review item or exercise in a series of problems.

9. The teacher carries a clipboard or record book, with graph paper on it for easy observation and lining up, around the room as he or she monitors, checks, or marks the assignments students perform in class. At the end of the grading period, these grades for classwork are averaged as one component of the grade (say 20 percent).

10. The teacher can assign self-correcting or programmed worksheets for homework. The value of this is that students become responsible for their own learning—and pace of learning. Students are encouraged to ask questions about items that confuse them when students meet the next day as a group.

11. Instead of grading homework or review exercises, the teacher can ask students to discuss the work or give examples of what they have worked on.

12. The teacher grades only one major paper or activity per two or three papers or activities. The one that is graded is unannounced until the day of submission. The other papers are reviewed by another student, working in pairs, or read and/or discussed in class with feedback provided by the students and teacher.

Source: Adapted from Cathy Collins, "Grading Practices that Increase Teacher Effectiveness," *Clearing House* (December 1989), pp. 167–169; Allan C. Ornstein, "The Nature of Grading," *Clearing House* (April 1989), pp. 365–369.

these judgments often result in instructional grouping and tracking.[26] During the *interactive phase* of teaching, teachers make decisions about the materials, the kinds of subject-related questions they ask students and the answers they expect from them, as well as the level of the general discussion.

According to one researcher, as many as 61 percent of the teachers interviewed were clear about recalling their thoughts while teaching: their thoughts

---

26 Robert J. Shavelson and Paula Stern, "Research on Teachers' Pedagogical Thoughts, Judgments, Decisions, and Behaviors," *Review of Educational Research* (Winter 1981), pp. 455–498; Dan Wright and Martin J. Wiese, "Teacher Judgment in Student Evaluation: A Comparison of Grading Methods," *Journal of Educational Research* (September–October 1988), pp. 10–14.

centered on student comprehension as the content or tasks were unfolding (e.g., "I was thinking . . . that they don't understand what they are doing").[27] Other researchers also report that the majority of teachers are concerned with the thought processes of the students while they teach, as well as the level of sophistication of the students' responses to their questions.[28] And it is reasonable to assume that teacher judgments about student cognition are based on prior test data and/or evaluation of the students' academic work in class.

Despite criticism about teachers being poor judges of their students' abilities, a review of 16 studies where judgmental and test data were collected concurrently (that is, where teachers were asked to predict their students' performance on standardized tests) shows the correlation is high. This is true in two types of teacher judgments: (1) where teachers estimate the *specific* number of items on an achievement test that each student will solve correctly, and (2) when teachers are less specific and estimate the *total* score for each student on the test. Taken as a whole, the first group of studies (nine) yielded a median correlation of .62 and the second group (seven) yielded a median correlation of .69.[29] Teachers were more accurate in judging expected student achievement in reading and math than in science or social studies (probably because they spend more time teaching and testing the first two areas of knowledge and the curriculum in these two subjects is more precise or agreed upon; these are only hunches by the author that extend beyond the research review).

Evaluation Based on Test Outcomes

As a teacher you should know what test scores mean and how to interpret test data. The test scores are indices of measurement but mean very little by themselves; they must be understood and given meaning in some way, and they should be used for grading. Knowledge and skill in using and interpreting basic statistical techniques are necessary for adequate assessment of instruction and evaluation of student performance. Certain numerical facts, summarized in the form of statistical indices, assist in evaluating and making decisions about students.[30]

---

27 Lawrence Coker, "Teachers' Interactive Thoughts about Pupil Cognition," paper presented at the annual meeting of the American Educational Research Association, Chicago, April 1984.

28 Penelope L. Peterson, "Teachers' and Students' Cognitional Knowledge for Classroom Teaching and Learning," *Educational Researcher* (June/July 1988), pp. 5–14; Thomas J. Shnell, "Phases of Meaningful Learning," *Review of Educational Research* (Winter 1990), pp. 531–548.

29 Robert D. Hoge and Thedore Coladarci, "Teacher-Based Judgments of Academic Achievement," *Review of Educational Research* (Fall 1989), pp. 297–313.

30 Richard C. Sprinthall, *Basic Statistical Analysis* (Englewood Cliffs, N.J.: Prentice-Hall, 1990); Robert M. Thorndike et al., *Measurement and Evaluation in Psychology and Education*, 5th ed. (New York: Macmillan, 1991).

The Normal Curve

The **normal curve** illustrates a mathematical concept that is derived from a hypothetical bell-shaped distribution of scores, as shown in the top of Figure 5.1. Information derived from this curve can be applied to normal distributions that characterize many standardized tests. When the test maker uses the normal curve as guide, test items are carefully selected and their scoring adjusted to give a symmetrical arrangement of test scores like a bell-shaped curve. This means that the majority of students score at the middle of the scale and an increasingly smaller number score at the high and low ends.

When the distribution is badly skewed to the right, this means there are too many high scores and the test is too easy (middle of Figure 5.1). When it is skewed to the left this means there are too many low scores and the test is too difficult (bottom of Figure 5.1). When a test is skewed too much to the right (positively) or left (negatively), the test is not suitable for the group. A test should reflect scores that coincide with a bell-shaped curve.

Standard Deviation

The **standard deviation**, expressed by the symbol σ, is important to know when test scores coincide with the normal probability curve; it provides information concerning the way the individual's score falls around the mean score. We know, as shown in the top of Figure 5.2, that all test scores fall between three standard deviations above (plus) the mean and three standard deviations below (negative) the mean. We also know that approximately 34 percent of the test scores (actually 34.13 percent) are between the mean and one standard deviation (1σ) above the mean, and that 34 percent of the test scores are between the mean and one standard standard (-1σ) below the mean. The two halves of the curve are equal, and slightly more than two-thirds (68 percent) of the test scores are plus or minus one 1σ from the mean. We also know that 14 percent of the test scores fall between 1σ and 2σ in the normal curve, and about 2 percent between 2σ and 3σ. The same percentages (14 and 2) are true for the other side of the normal curve, and the mean divides the curve in half. While standardized test distributions almost always look vaguely normal in shape, they are usually slightly skewed to the left or right.

Suppose that on a math test administered to 3,000 children in the sixth grade of a large urban school district, the mean is 60 and the standard deviation is 9, and suppose further the test scores resemble the normal curve. Taking the normal curve as our base, we say that two-thirds of the scores (2,000) fall between 51 and 69 (60±9), about 14 percent of the scores (420) fall between 69 and 78 (between 1σ and 2σ), and another 14 percent fall between 42 and 51 (also between 1σ and 2σ). Moreover, about 2 percent (60) fall between 78 and 87 and another 2 percent fall between 33 and 42. These relationships are shown at the bottom of Figure 5.2. A student who scores 79 is in the highest two percent category for that particular test. Likewise, a student who has scored 55 is performing only slightly below the mean, or what we call the average.

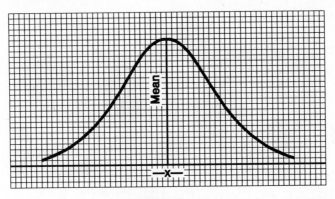

Normal Curve

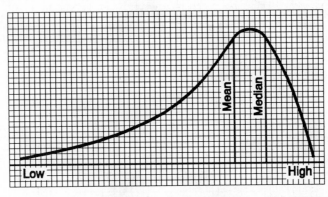

Positively Skewed Curve

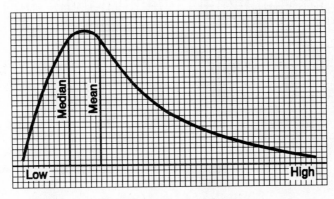

Negatively Skewed Curve

Figure 5.1 The Normal, Negative, and Positive Curves

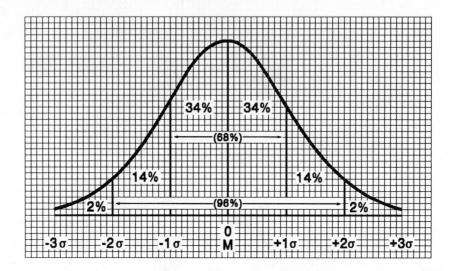

Areas Under the Normal Curve

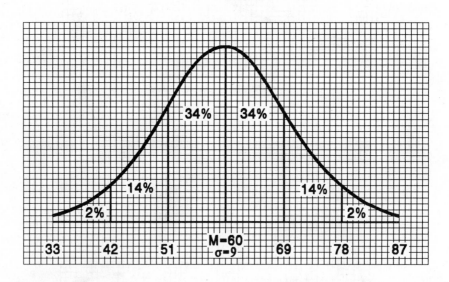

Distribution of Test Scores on a Hypothetical Math Test

Figure 5.2   Distribution of Test Scores in Terms of the Standard Deviation

Grade Equivalent Scores

The **grade equivalent score** is established by interpreting performance on a test in terms of a grade level. A student who has a reading score of 8.8 is performing at the eighth grade level and eighth month of the year. An eighth grader, at the beginning of the term, would be performing above grade level in terms of the norm; a ninth grader would be reading below grade level. One major problem with grade equivalents is that raw scores are used to translate to grade equivalents. A raw score gain of three or four points is usually sufficient to account for an improvement of a half to one grade level placement, say from 3.0 to 4.0, as measured by most popular batteries used by schools, because few items (less than 50) are used. Test-wise students, or students who are coached, can easily guess a few items correctly and significantly increase their grade level, even with highly reliable tests.

An underlying assumption of teachers who use this scale is that performance improves throughout the school year. For those subjects that are independent of others and "taught systematically and steadily through the grades such an assumption seems reasonable." However, the assumption begins to dwindle for most subjects beyond the seventh grade and comes to a halt in the upper grades because the "overlap is very large and the average differences between grades are small."[31] Linear growth in subject matter vanishes in the high school grades.

Rank Scores

The simplest way to view a student's test score in terms of other student scores is to arrange all scores in order from highest to lowest—what we call a **rank score**. This ordering of test scores gives meaning to a score by showing where it appears relative to other scores, above or below.

The rank number of an individual's test score in relation to his classmates is shown in Table 5.2. The highest score, in this case 95, receives a rank of one, the second score a rank of two, and so on. To make the ranking meaningful, the total number of scores should be given. If a score is tenth in a set of 30 scores, we know that the student is ranked in the highest one-third of the class for that test.

A rank score gives information needed to place each student in relation to all others based on order and gives a good indication of individual performance compared to general group performance. Referring to Table 5.2, if Johnnie receives a score of 82 on a hypothetical reading test, then we learn that he is ranked 9th out of 30. The problem is, a student can be above average but be competing with very bright students so that his or her ranking will only be average or even below average. This is a common problem in high-ranking academic high schools.

---

31 Donald R. Green, "A Guide for Interpreting Standardized Test Scores," *NASSP Bulletin* (February 1987), p. 32.

Table 5.2   A LIST OF TEST SCORES ASSOCIATED WITH RANKS

Raw score	Rank	
95	1	
93	2	
91	3	
88	4	
85	5.5	
85	5.5	
83	7.5	
83	7.5	
82	9	(Johnnie's score)
80	10	
79	11.5	
79	11.5	
78	13.5	
78	13.5	
77	15.5	
77	15.5	
76	18	
76	18	
76	18	
75	21	
75	21	
75	21	
72	23.5	
72	23.5	
70	25	
68	26	
65	27	
60	28	
54	29.5	
54	29.5	

A standardized test reports scores in terms of a **percentile rank**. This score indicates the percentage of students who are at and below the score of the student. A student with a percentile ranking of 80 did as well or better than 80 percent of the students who took the test, or who are part of the normative group being used. The percentile rank has one major disadvantage. The distribution is not an equal unit scale, but rather it is rectangular; that is, achievement differences among students clustered around the middle of the distribution are usually less than the differences among those at the extremes. The reason is that most scores cluster around the mean, or middle, of most distributions. The difference in raw scores between students at percentile ranks near the middle are much smaller than differences at the ends. At the 50th percentile, it may be one point or less. But the difference in raw scores between students with a percentile rank of 90 or 95 may be ten or more points in raw score. The one problem with percentiles is that teachers who refer to them, especially who compare percentiles at different points on the scale, can be misled unless they understand how percentiles are distributed.

Stanine Scores

A **stanine score** can have a value of 1 to 9, with stanines 1, 2, and 3 suggesting lowest, lower, and low; stanines 4, 5, and 6 suggesting low average, average, and high average; and stanines 7, 8, and 9 as high, higher, and highest. Stanines were often used to group students; those in the lowest three stanines were grouped in one category or class; students in stanines 4 to 6 in another category or class, and so on. This is no longer customary, since homogeneous tracking is discouraged in most school systems.

Stanines are derived from the normal probability curve, and they avoid pointing out small differences among scores and thus reduce the use of comparisons of one student to all students within the norm group. Norms of many standardized tests are available in stanines and are used to communicate general test performance.

Stanine scores are easy to calculate; each stanine score has a mean of 5 and a standard deviation of 2. As a result, each stanine, except the first and ninth, is half a standard deviation unit in length. (See Figure 5.2.) The scores can be normalized by a simple counting procedure as shown in Table 5.3. Similarly, raw scores can be converted to stanine scores by first converting them into a normal distribution as Figure 5.2 shows.

Improving Evaluation

Most people, including teachers, commit errors in judgment in one way or another and in various degrees. Limiting such errors is important for objective and fair evaluation, and the best way is to understand the various sources of contamination. Table 5.4 defines nine basic errors in evaluation, but only you can discover ways to control them. Many people (i.e., teachers) who engage in evaluation of others (i.e., students) make these errors, what are sometimes called **constant errors**; that is, they exhibit certain tendencies or predisposi-

Table 5.3 CONVERSIONS AMONG STANINE AND RAW SCORES AND PERCENTILES

Stanine score	Ranked raw scores in approximate percentages	Percentile
9	Top 4	96–99
8	7	89–95
7	12	77–88
6	17	60–76
5	20	23–39
4	17	40–59
3	12	11–22
2	7	4–10
1	Bottom 4	0–3

Table 5.4 COMMON EVALUATION ERRORS

1. *Inaccurate recall*. The tendency to forget relevant details, because of time passage.

2. *Halo effect*. The tendency to positively or negatively generalize from one characteristic of an individual to other characteristics.

3. *Contrast effect*. The tendency to compare people to each other rather than to preestablished standards or criteria.

4. *Stereotyping*. The tendency to classify or overgeneralize in a specific way because of particular characteristics or categories (i.e., race, religion, sex, etc.).

5. *Different standards*. The tendency to evaluate people on the basis of different experiences, expectations, or standards.

6. *Fixed impression*. The tendency to allow one observation or incident to influence indefinitely an overall evaluation of the person.

7. *Time effects*. The tendency to allow time proximity (most recent event or incident) to affect the evaluation.

8. *Projection*. The tendency to allow one's own values or characteristics to influence one's evaluation.

9. *Inference*. The tendency to confuse objective facts with internal thoughts so that the judgment of performance or behavior is assumed rather than based on what has actually occurred.

Source: Adapted from Stephen L. Cohen, "Keeping Your Data Clean," *Training and Development Journal* (August 1989), pp. 50–54.

tions. The need is to understand these errors, to admit they exist and contribute to misjudgments, and to control their influence when evaluating others.

The errors listed in the table lead to three problems in evaluation: (1) instability, (2) inconsistency, and (3) subjectivity. Instability can be reduced by frequent tests and evaluation (informal and formal). Inconsistency can be reduced by improving the measurement instruments and criteria for judgment. Subjectivity, which accounts for a considerable amount of error, can be reduced by standardized evaluation procedures and by using similar forms and methods of evaluation for all concerned.

GRADING

The purpose of grading is somewhat different for teachers at different grade levels. Some studies indicate that middle school teachers tend to say they give grades because the school district requires it, not because the function of grades as a yardstick is important to them. In contrast, high school teachers feel grades are necessary for informing students, other teachers, and colleges about performance.[32] The same studies showed that middle school teachers rely more on their observations of student participation in class, motivation, and attitudes than on tests. High school teachers assign grades mainly on the basis of test results. On average, no more than 15 percent of the grade is based on professional judgment.

Teachers need to recognize, also, that young students (grade 4 or lower) have little understanding of the meaning of grades and that understanding of grading concepts increases with age. It is not until grade 9 that most students understand complex schemes such as a grading curve, grade point average, and weighted grading. Students below grade 6 attach less importance to grades and consider external and uncontrollable factors to be important influences on grading; older students attach more importance to grades, see them as linked to internal and controllable factors, and are aware of the reasons for grading. However, older students are more likely to be critical of grading practices and less accepting of low grades received than are younger students.[33] Such findings indicate that teachers might consider postponing formal grading until grades 5 or 6, if school policy permits, and that teachers should expect concern and even criticism among older students, especially since they increasingly see grades as important for their future.

---

32 Fred Burton, *A Study of the Better Grade System and Its Effects on the Curriculum*, ERIC No. 238143 (March 1983); Gary Natriello and James McPartland, *Adjustments in High School Teachers' Grading Criteria* (Baltimore: Johns Hopkins University Press, 1988). Also see Thomas L. Good and Jere E. Brophy, *Educational Psychology: A Realistic Approach*, 4th ed. (New York: Longman, 1991).

33 Ellis D. Evans and Ruth A. Engleberg, "Student Perceptions of School Grading," *Journal of Research and Development in Education* (Winter 1988), pp. 45–54.

Researchers tend to list general purposes for grading: (1) certification, or assurance that a student has mastered specific content or achieved a certain level of accomplishment; (2) selection, or identifying or grouping students for certain educational paths or programs; (3) direction, or providing information for diagnosis and planning; and (4) motivation, or emphasizing specific material or skills to be learned and helping students to understand and improve their performance.[34]

Grades often result in the same group of students being "winners" or "losers" from grade to grade. Robert Slavin puts it this way: "In the usual, competitive reward structure, the probability of one student's receiving a reward (good grade) is negatively related to the probability of another student's receiving a reward."[35]

A demonstrable relationship exists between formal instruction and student performance at all grade levels, but constructing tests and grading accurately to reflect classroom tasks and intended learning are difficult for most teachers. Although teachers report that they feel they are able to interpret test results and transfer test scores into grades or grade equivalents, when teachers are tested on these abilities, the majority misinterpret concepts presented to them.[36]

Assigning grades to students' schoolwork is inherently subjective, regardless of the method used. Not only is a high degree of expertise required for being accurate in grading, one that eludes many teachers, but there is the false assumption that teacher-made tests reflect precisely what is being taught.[37] Teachers are required to make judgments, and few, if any, are purely objective; a few teachers even use grades as a weapon to control students or to "shape" them to their own beliefs or attitudes. What test items should be included and how the items should be weighted are matters of judgment. Should points be deducted for wrong answers? How many As or Bs or Fs should be awarded? Will grading be on a curve or absolute? And what about all those special cases ("I lost my notebook") and problems ("I was sick last week")? Are students to be allowed to retake an exam because the results deviate from past performance? Should extra credit assignments be used to modify grades and to what extent? If test modification, additional tests or credit assignments are introduced, then teachers are forced to be

34 Robert L. Linn, "Testing and Instruction: Links and Distinction," *Journal of Education Measurement* (Summer 1983), pp. 179–189; Gary Natriello, "The Impact of Evaluation Processes on Students," *Educational Psychologist* (Spring 1987), pp. 155–175.

35 Robert E. Slavin, "Classroom Reward Structure: An Analytical and Practical Review," *Review of Education Research* (Fall 1977), pp. 633–650; Slavin, "Synthesis of Research on Cooperative Learning," *Educational Leadership* (February 1991), pp. 71–82.

36 Herbert C. Rudman, "Classroom Instruction and Tests: What Do We Really Know about the Link?" *NASSP Bulletin* (February 1987), pp. 3–22.

37 Marv Nottingham, "Grading Practices—Watching Out for Land Mines," *NASSP Bulletin* (April 1988), pp. 24–28; Margot A. Olson, "The Distortion of the Grading System," *Clearing House* (November-December 1990), pp. 77–79.

decision makers. If a teacher fails to consider extraneous circumstances, possibly modifying the scoring results, then it can be argued that grades are being used as a weapon, certainly as a cold symbol of learning. It can also be argued that students are entitled to extra coaching and practice, but retaking exams or extra credit is unfair because it affects the grades of some, but not all, students.

Homework is another consideration. Who should grade the homework—students or teacher? Prompt scoring by students enables the teacher to decide promptly what material needs further analysis. When the teacher grades the homework, it increases his or her paper load, and feedback to students is delayed. But grading the homework adds to the teacher's information about the specific thinking skills and problems of the students. Moreover, researchers point out that when the teacher takes time to write encouraging and constructive comments on the homework (or other student papers) it has positive measurable effects on achievement.[38]

Homework may be important in the learning process, but there is a question about whether it should be counted in the grading system. Some educators say no. There are similar questions about lowering grades for minor discipline problems (for example, chewing gum), not typing a paper, not doing an assignment on time, and coming to class late. A student whose behavior is unacceptable must be held accountable, but most educators are against reducing grades as a deterrent.[39] Many teachers, however, take another view, especially when classroom discipline is at stake. There is also considerable disagreement about the value of using routine class activities, class participation, recitations, oral reading, chalkboard work, oral presentations, and even reports as part of the grade system. Although such practices broaden the base of information on student performance and also give students a chance to be evaluated on grounds other than tests, there are serious questions about the quality of information they provide. For example, some students "talk a good game" and know little, while others are introverted or shy but know the material. One educator maintains that grades should be divided into primary measures of performance (unit tests, term papers) and secondary measures (homework, quizzes). The secondary measures are considered less important and are given less weight, since their purpose is to prepare students to achieve the primary learning outcomes.[40]

38 Gary Natriello and Edward L. McDill, "Performance Standards, Student Effort on Homework and Academic Achievement," *Sociology of Education* (January 1986), pp. 18–31; Linda G. Stewart and Mary A. White, "Teacher Comments, Letter Grades and Student Performance," *Journal of Educational Psychology* (August 1976), pp. 488–500.

39 Gary Natriello, "The Impact of Evaluation Processes on Students," *Educational Psychologist* (Spring 1987), pp. 155–175; Nottingham, "Grading Practices—Watching Out for Land Mines."

40 Robert F. Madgic, "The Point System of Grading: A Critical Appraisal," *NASSP Bulletin* (April 1988), pp. 29–34.

Combining and Weighing Data

Some researchers recommend that grades at all levels be based on exams, 50 percent; class work, 30 percent; assigned papers, 10 percent; and homework, 10 percent.[41] Another group of experienced teachers maintains that grades should be based on tests and quizzes, 60 percent; class participation, 15 percent; written and oral projects, 15 percent; and notebook and homework, 10 percent.[42] Although researchers generally agree that grading should be based on several indicators that are directly related to the instructional program, there is less agreement on what should be included, and how the indicators should be weighted, and whether indicators not directly related to instruction, such as participation, effort, neatness, and conduct, are appropriate at all.[43]

Grades based on little information, say one or two tests, are unfair to students and probably invalid. Assigning too much importance to term papers or homework is also invalid and unwise because these indicators say little about whether the students have really learned the material. Relying more heavily on test data is preferred, especially at the secondary school level, as long as there are several quizzes or examinations and the tests are weighted properly.

There are a number of problems related to combining several test scores into a single measure (or grade) for each student, including the fact that test scores may have different significance. For example, a teacher who wishes to combine scores on two separate tests might consider that each contributes 50 percent to the composite score. However, this rarely is the case, especially if one test was more difficult than the other; the composite score is a function not only of the mean but also of the standard deviation.

Another question is whether scores from different sources, representing different learning outcomes and levels of difficulty, can be combined into a composite score. Although there are arguments for and against this procedure, it is acceptable as long as the composite score is based on several sources that are independent of each other. See Tips for Teachers 5.2.

Form of Grades

The most popular form in which grades are presented is the *letter grade*. According to David Payne, the letter grade "represents a translation from a number base, resulting from a combination of test scores, ratings, and the like . . . [and has a] common meaning for most people, and for this reason should probably be retained."[44]

---

41 Good and Brophy, *Educational Psychology: A Realistic Approach.*

42 Association of Teachers of Social Studies in the City of New York, *A Handbook for the Teaching of Social Studies*, 2nd ed. (Boston: Allyn & Bacon, 1985).

43 Natriello, "The Impact of Evaluation Processes on Students"; Herbert C. Rudman, "Classroom Instruction and Tests: What Do We Really Know about the Link?"; and Robert E. Slavin, "Separating Incentives, Feedback, and Evaluation," *Educational Psychologist* (Spring 1978), pp. 97–100.

44 David A. Payne, *The Assessment of Learning* (Lexington, Mass.: Heath, 1974), p. 425.

Tips For Teachers 5.2

Advantages and Disadvantages of Point System of Grading

Most teachers, especially from the middle grades onward, rely on a point system of grading whereby the teacher identifies points or percentages for various tests and class activities. Some teachers even post summaries at regular intervals so students can see their point total as the term progresses. The point system has advantages and disadvantages. Special caution is recommended with the problems associated with this system.

ADVANTAGES

1. Is fair and objective. The teacher is not apt to be swayed by subjective factors, and the need for interpretation is minimized.
2. Is quantifiable, explicit, and precise. Students and teachers know exactly what the numbers are and what they stand for.
3. Minimizes conflict over what grade a student should receive.
4. Facilitates the weighting of tests and class activities. For example, a teacher may choose 5 points for each quiz, 25 points for a special project, 25 points each for the midterm and final.
5. Is cumulative. The final grade can be determined by a single computation at the end of the grading period.
6. Facilitates grading by establishing clear distinctions. Once categories are weighted and points totaled, assigning the grade for each student is a straightforward task.

DISADVANTAGES

1. Emphasizes objectivity of scoring, not learning. Conveys the message that learning is equivalent to the accumulation of points, not the acquisition of skills and knowledge.
2. Presents an illusion of objectivity. Every test and assignment results from a series of subjective decisions by the teacher—what areas to cover, how to weigh particular answers or aspects of performance, and so forth.
3. Reduces teacher's judgment. A point system minimizes the teacher's professional judgment and results in a somewhat inflexible grading system.
4. Hides importance of patterns. Average or total scores at any point, rather than improvement or decline, are emphasized.
5. Gives undue weight to fine distinctions. A single point difference, which may represent only a small difference in learning, may be the difference between a B– and a C+.

(continues)

6. Leads to cumulative errors. A particular test score or classroom activity may not truly reflect the student's abilities or learning. The final total represents the sum of all such errors.
7. Is subject to misinterpretation. Without norms it is false to assume that a certain range (90 to 100) or number (93) represents a valid indicator (e.g., an A) of performance or that categories (breakpoints) can be decided in advance.

Source: Adapted from Robert F. Madgic, "The Point System of Grading: A Critical Appraisal," *NASSP Bulletin* (April 1988), pp. 29–34.

A disadvantage is that the conversion from numbers to letters to some extent distorts meaning and masks individual differences. Since a letter represents a range of numbers, different students may receive the same letter grade from the same teacher for different levels of performance. However, although the number system is more precise, the difference between two or three points for a final grade is often not that meaningful.

Most schools convert letters to an even more general statement of evaluation as follows:

A= superior, excellent, outstanding
B= good, above average
C= fair, competent, average
D= minimum passing, weakness or problems
F= failure, serious weakness or problems

The standards upon which grades are based vary considerably among school districts, so that a C student in one school may be an A student in another school. Hence schools and school districts eventually get reputations about how low or high standards are.

Absolute Grade Standards

Grades may be given according to fixed or **absolute standards**, as illustrated in Table 5.5. One disadvantage of this approach is that the standards may be subject to the *error of leniency*; that is, if students have an easy grader, many As and Bs will be assigned, or if they have a tough grader, many Cs and Ds will be

Table 5.5   EXAMPLES OF ABSOLUTE AND RELATIVE STANDARDS OF GRADING

Absolute standard		Relative standard	
		Percent of students*	Number of students (total = 32)
A = 90% or above	A =	7%	2–3
B = 80–89%	B =	24%	7–8
C = 70–79%	C =	38%	12–13
D = 60–69%	D =	24%	7–8
F = Below 60%	F =	7%	2–3

*Based on a normal curve.

Source: Adapted from Robert E. Slavin, *Educational Psychology: Theory into Practice*, 3rd ed. (Englewood Cliffs, N.J.: Prentice-Hall, 1991).

assigned.[45] Also, student scores depend on the difficulty of the tests given. In some tests a score of 65 percent may be above average, but with an absolute or fixed standard, as indicated in the table, this score would be a D. Hence, many students would be given a minimum passing grade under an absolute grading approach.

Despite these limitations, most teachers use this method of grading. It makes a great deal of sense as long as teachers have a firm idea of what students should be able to do and as long as standards are realistic and fair. The main advantage, according to Good and Brophy, is that "it puts control of grades in students' hands." If the standards are fair, students should work hard to earn good grades. "However, if standards are too high, students will give up."[46]

Absolute grading systems are best organized around specific objectives, competencies, or preestablished standards. The performance or behavior to be learned is specified in advance. Test items are matched with particular objectives, and test scores are reported in terms of whether and to what extent the objectives were attained. For example, a grade of A means 23 to 25 test items (related to particular objectives) were right. Most schools do not employ such a narrowly defined (some people would say rigid) criteria for teachers to follow in their grading policy: If you score 22, well you receive a B+ . . . too bad . . . but those are the specifications. Try harder next term.

45 Allan C. Ornstein, "How Good Are Teachers in Effecting Student Outcomes," *NASSP Bulletin* (December 1982), pp. 61–70; Ornstein, "Research in Teaching: Measurements and Methods," *Education and Urban Society* (February 1986), pp. 176–181.

46 Good and Brophy, *Educational Psychology: A Realistic Approach*, p. 793.

Relative Grade Standards

Grades may be given according to how a student performs in relation to others. If a student scores 80 on an examination, but most others score above 90, the student has done less than average work. Instead of receiving a B under the relative, or norm-reference, method of grading, the student might receive a C. If a student scores 65, but most others score below 60, he or she has done well and might receive a B instead of a D.

Relative grading can be based on a curve, either a normal bell-shaped curve or a curve derived from a simple ranking system. In a normal curve few students receive As or Fs, the majority receive Cs (midpoint of the curve), and many receive Bs and Ds. This is also shown in Table 5.5, which uses a 7–24–38–24–7 percent grade distribution. In a ranking system, which is almost as common, the teacher determines in advance percentage equivalents for each letter grade: for example, the top 25 percent will receive A, the next 30 percent B, the next 25 percent C, and the next 20 percent D or F. The grading on this curve is not always as precise as with the normal curve, and it tends to be a little easier for students to score higher grades.

Grading on a curve and other relative grading practices assure that grades will be distributed on the basis of scores in relation to one another, whatever the difficulty of the test. However, according to research, this can create competition among students, inhibit them from helping each other, and affect social relations.[47]

Relative grading assumes that human performance is normally distributed among the population and that scores should be normally distributed about the mean score for a class. This assumption, of course, is usually incorrect.[48] The numbers in a class of 20 to 30 are too small to achieve normality. One way to compensate for this problem is to grade students across all similar classes rather than one class to increase the numbers for normal distribution. The possibility of a total sample for all of the same courses would satisfy the original assumption even better; this would involve cooperation among teachers (for example, all eighth-grade social studies teachers) in the school.

Contracting for Grades

A few schools permit teachers and students considerable flexibility in formulating grading standards. Teachers and students come to an agreement early in the term concerning grades for specific levels of performance or achievement

---

47 Carole Ames, Russell Ames, and Donald W. Felker, "Effects of Competitive Reward Structure and Valence of Outcome on Children's Achievement Attributions," *Journal of Educational Psychology* (February 1977), pp. 1–8; David W. Johnson and Frank P. Johnson, *Joining Together*, 4th ed. (Englewood Cliffs, N.J.: Prentice-Hall, 1991).

48 Jon J. Denton, "Selecting an Appropriate Grading System," *Clearing House* (November 1989), pp. 107–110; Penelope Engel, "Tracking Progress Toward the School Readiness Goal," *Educational Leadership* (February 1991), pp. 39–42.

on various tasks. Maximum, average, and minimum standards or performance levels are usually established for those who wish to receive passing and progressively higher grades. In effect, the teacher promises to award a specific grade for specified performance; a **contract** is established. With this approach students know exactly what they have to do to receive a certain grade; depending on the amount of work they wish to do, they can receive a particular grade.

The plan seems suited to criterion-reference learning and to teaching and learning by a set of objectives. The approach is not recommended for elementary school students because of their lack of maturity and their inability to engage in independent work for a sustained period of time and to follow through on individual activities. The contract can be implemented at the middle school level (grade 5 or higher) if great care is taken to match student maturity and abilities with performance requirements. Different standards will be needed with different students.

Revised contracts can be designed for students whose work is not satisfactory or who expected a higher grade than they received. This grading system provides more latitude for teachers in responding to unsatisfactory work and gives students a chance to improve their work and their grade.

Mastery and Continuous Progress Grading

Many elementary schools and a few middle and junior high schools now stress **mastery grading and continuous progress grading**. Both approaches require that teachers maintain specific records for each student and report on the student's progress. Schools using these approaches usually do not use grades, but rather evaluate the student in terms of expected and mastered skills and behaviors.[49] Reports for the student and parents describe how the student is performing and progressing without any indication of how the student is doing in relation to others. Although a judgment is made about the student, the absence of a standard for comparison reduces some pressure related to grades. In mastery learning situations and continuous progress reporting, grades are usually based on criterion-reference measurements. In more traditional situations grades are also based on normative data.

Grading for Effort or Improvement

To what extent should teachers consider effort or improvement as part of the grade? This question surfaces with most teachers when they grade their students. Problems with considering effort are that bright students may show the

---

49 Benjamin Bloom, "The 2 Sigma Problem: The Search for Methods of Instruction as Effective as One-to-One Tutoring," *Educational Researcher* (June/July 1984), pp. 4–16; Robert E. Slavin, "On Mastery Learning and Mastery Teaching," *Educational Leadership* (April 1989), pp. 77–79.

least improvement and effort and that by raising the grade or average of low-achieving students to reflect effort rather than achievement, you are to some extent lowering the value of the grade given to high-achieving students.[50] Also, low-achieving students have more opportunity to improve by simple regression toward the mean.

Most teachers leave some room for judgment in grading. The more effort and improvement are considered in deciding on final grades, the more subjective and the more biased the grades are likely to be. The teacher must examine his or her perceptions for accuracy. If the teacher feels strongly about a judgment, then the movement in a grade from a B+ to a B or an A or A– is acceptable. A major change in a grade, say from a C to an A, cannot be justified on the basis of the student's effort or teacher's hunches about the student.

Grade Inflation

Grade inflation is another problem. Not only does the same grade mean different things to different teachers (and professors) but grade inflation can lead to the abandonment of clearly objective measurable scores.[51] For example, 55 means failure but since so many students received 55 or lower, we have to adjust our grades upward and pass our students to avoid pressure from students, administrators, or parents. Put in different terms, an "A" is sometimes really an "F"—but who wants to challenge grading hypocrisy?

Few of us would take comfort in widespread use of tests and grades as the major sorting instrument in our society. Certainly grades and test scores must be balanced with student work, letters of recommendation, motivation, and the like. We cannot simply give every student an A or B to avoid evaluation; nor can we ask students to grade themselves. The clarity, reliability, and validity of the SAT, ACT, and GRE test scores contrast sharply with the confusion over course grades, and yet these examinations are often criticized by educators (and parents) who wish to stifle the messenger who brings bad news. The politics of test information is a real concern given our multiethnic society, where not all groups perform equally in school, and where "winners" and "losers" are slotted and tracked very early in the schooling process. Also, as students get older, they are more willing to challenge their teachers' grading systems, and this kind of pressure puts teachers on the defensive.

---

50 Thomas L. Good and Rhona S. Weinstein, "Schools Make a Difference: Evidence, Criticisms, and New Directions," *American Psychologist* (October 1986), pp. 1090–1097; Allan C. Ornstein, "Evaluation of Students: A Practitioner's Perspective," *NASSP Bulletin* (in print 1992).

51 Dona M. Kagan, "How Schools Alienate Students at Risk," *Educational Psychologist* (Spring 1990), pp. 105–126; George F. Madaus, "The Distortion of Teaching and Testing," *Peabody Journal of Education* (Spring 1988), pp. 29–46; and Madgic, "The Point System of Grading."

Guidelines for Grading Students

Here are some suggestions for deriving grades.

1. *Explain your grading system to the students.* For young students (grades 5–7), explain your grading system orally and with concrete examples. Older students can read handouts that describe assignments, tests, test schedules, and grading criteria.
2. *Base grades on a predetermined set of standards.* For example, a student who is able to perform at a significantly higher performance standard than another student should receive a higher grade.
3. *Base grades on the student's degree of progress.* The student who comes to a class with poor skills and improves greatly might get a higher grade than a student who was slightly less than average when he came to class and showed no marked improvement.
4. *Base grades on the student's attitude, as well as achievement, especially at the middle or junior high school level.* Some educators argue this is unfair, and the citizenship or conduct grade, not the academic grade, should reflect attitude. Others argue that penalizing a disruptive child in the subject grade is a legitimate method of shaping behavior.
5. *Base grades on the student's relative standing compared to classmates.* The teacher needs to consider the student's work in relation to others in the class, not only for grading but also for grouping purposes.
6. *Base grades on a variety of sources.* The more sources of information used and weighted properly, the more valid is the grade. Although most of the grade should be based on objective sources, *some* subjective sources should also be considered. For example, a student who frequently participates in class may be given a slightly higher grade than her test average.
7. *As a rule, do not change grades.* Grades should always be arrived at after serious consideration, and only in rare circumstances should they be changed. Of course, an obvious mistake or error should be corrected, but if students think you will change grades, they will start negotiating or pleading with you for changes.
8. *Become familiar with the grading policy of your school and with your colleagues' standards.* Each school has its own standards for grading and procedures for reporting grades. Your standards and practices should not conflict with those of the school and should not differ greatly from those of your colleagues.
9. *When failing a student, closely follow school procedures.* Each school has its own procedures to follow for failing a student. You may be required to have a warning conference, to send a pending failure notice to parents, and so forth.

10. *Record grades on report cards and cumulative records.* Report cards usually are mailed to parents or given to students to give to parents every six to eight weeks. Cumulative records are usually completed at the end of the school year and remain at the school.[52]

Remember to use the evaluation procedures as a teaching and learning device, to be fair in your evaluation of students, to interpret evaluative data properly, and to give students the benefit of the doubt.

RECORDS AND REPORTS OF PERFORMANCE

There is usually a difference in the way student performance is recorded and reported in elementary and secondary school. Elementary teachers are usually more sensitive about the student's feelings, attitudes, and effort, and are willing to consider these factors in reporting performance. Elementary school report cards often contain a narrative or a combination of grades and narrative about the child's progress. The parents may be asked to write a reply, instead of merely signing the report card, or to schedule conferences perhaps two or three times a year during which the parent and teacher discuss the child's work.

Fewer middle grade and junior high schools have such elaborate reporting systems, and at the high school level this human (or social) dimension of reporting is almost nonexistent, partly because teachers have more students (perhaps 150 or more) and thus cannot easily write narratives and hold conferences for the parents of each student.

Report Cards

The teacher's judgments and scores on tests are communicated to students and parents by means of a report card. The reports should not come as a surprise to students. Both students and parents should know how marks or grades are to be computed and to what extent tests, class participation, homework, and other activities contribute to their overall grade. Many students and parents become anxious if they do not know the basis for the marks or grades on the report card.

At the elementary grade level (below grade 5), and to a much lesser extent at the middle school and junior high school levels, the school may use a progress or **mastery report card** on which a list of descriptors or categories is given and the teacher indicates what the student can do by checking off terms such as "yes" or "no" or "outstanding," "satisfactory," or "unsatisfactory." A middle school or junior high school that uses a mastery or progress approach is trying to stall the competitive nature of grading and is more than likely

---

52 Allan C. Ornstein, "The Nature of Grading," *Clearing House* (April 1989), pp. 365–369.

progressive in outlook. Below is a sample list of common reading descriptors for which "yes" or "no" must be indicated.

	Yes	No
1. Reads at appropriate level	_____	_____
2. Reads with comprehension	_____	_____
3. Identifies main ideas in stories	_____	_____
4. Recognizes main characters in stories	_____	_____
5. Finds details in stories	_____	_____
6. Draws conclusions from reading stories	_____	_____
7. Demonstrate appropriate vocabulary	_____	_____
8. Reads with appropriate speed	_____	_____
9. Skims with accuracy	_____	_____
10. Summarizes key concepts	_____	_____
11. Finishes reading assignments on time	_____	_____
12. Persists even if understanding does not come immediately[53]	_____	_____

Teachers can make up their own lists for any basic skill or subject. A mastery report might also involve descriptions of progress or problems rather than yes/no evaluations. At some levels and for some types of course content the list of descriptors or categories can be precise, with a date for achievement or mastery to be shown.

This mastery approach fits in with a criterion-reference system of evaluation and is useful for schools that wish to eliminate grades and put more emphasis on progress or mastery.

The same approach can be used for all subjects and grade levels. For example, the list below illustrates a progress report for junior high school students for almost any subject.[54] The descriptors are checked if the student shows strength in a specific area (absence of a check suggests need for improvement). A three- or five-point scale could also be used to give a more precise report.

Areas of strengths are checked below.

	First Quarter	Second Quarter	Third Quarter	Fourth Quarter
Obeys school and classroom rules	____	____	____	____
Completes homework	____	____	____	____
Follows directions	____	____	____	____

---

53 Ibid.

54 Adapted from Science Report Card, Miner Junior High School Progress Report, Aptakisic-Tripp Community Consolidated School District 102, Illinois, no date.

	First Quarter	Second Quarter	Third Quarter	Fourth Quarter
Brings materials to class	___	___	___	___
Completes work neatly and carefully	___	___	___	___
Works independently	___	___	___	___
Uses media equipment carefully	___	___	___	___
Participates in class discussions	___	___	___	___
Makes good use of class time	___	___	___	___
Seeks help when needed	___	___	___	___
Gets to class on time	___	___	___	___
Puts forth satisfacory effort	___	___	___	___
Listens attentively	___	___	___	___

The emphasis, by this author, is to postpone letter grades or percentages as long as possible, perhaps until the beginning of high school. This is obviously a progressive view, one that deemphasizes competition and comparisons among individual students. The student merely competes with himself and learning is evidenced in terms of progress, not comparisons. There is less labeling and tracking of the student with this approach.

Whereas the above list of criteria intermixes general cognitive and social skills, and can be used in many different subject areas, each subject can have its own report card. In this case the list of descriptors would be more content oriented. For example, eighth-grade math might consist of the following items: (1) positive and negative items, (2) solving equations, (3) geometric figures, (4) percentages and probability, (5) powers and roots, and (6) areas and volumes, etc.[55] Space should also be provided for the teacher's comments—permitting latitude for the teacher to talk about strengths, weaknesses, and recommendations. Again, there is less labeling and tracking with both type of report cards.

As a compromise, some schools might be willing to wait until the middle of the seventh grade or beginning of the eighth grade before introducing letter or percentage grades. The rationale is liked to the demands of the high school—the need for quantitative data for the purpose of sorting and selecting students into groups and programs. This being the case, however, it is still possible to avoid letter or percentage grades until the end of the seventh or eighth grades—just before the student enters high school—depending on the district's philosophy and the structure of its secondary schools. See Tips for Teachers 5.3.

Although educators can make a good case for normative comparisons and, therefore, the need for percentage or letter grades, postponing this until as late as possible limits the potential for students to develop negative self-concepts

---

55 Adapted from Mathematics Report Card, Grade 7, Wasburne Middle School, Winnetka, Illinois School District, no date.

Tips for Teachers 5.3

Innovative Practices for Reporting Student Performance

In lieu of traditional report cards, teachers might experiment with new reporting procedures for providing information on student performance and progress. A number of innovative ideas are listed below. Some are in practice in a few schools. Just how innovative you can be will depend to a large extent on your school's policy and philosophy about grading.

1. Consider more than a single grade or mark. Develop a progress report for each activity detailing specific instructional tasks and student performance.
2. List more than cognitive development and specific subjects. Include social, psychological, and psychomotor behaviors and creative, esthetic, and artistic learning as well as scientific and technical abilities.
3. Develop forms of report cards specifically suited to particular grade levels rather than using one form for the entire school.
4. Grade students on the basis of both an absolute standard and a relative standard.
5. Report each student's progress (based on his own ability and that of others).
6. Replace or use in addition to standard letter grades or categories—such as excellent, good, fair—new categories; or, write individual statements—such as "needs more time to develop," "advanced understanding for the child's age."
7. Stress strengths of the student. Point out only two or three weaknesses or problem areas, and specify ways for improving weak or problem areas.
8. Replace or supplement the standard card with a larger, more detailed folder, one that contains explanations for students and parents.
9. Provide space for comments by both teachers and parents, not just for their signatures.
10. Provide space for requests by both parents and teachers for parent-teacher conferences.
11. Organize committees of students, teachers, and parents to meet periodically (every three or four years) to improve the school district's standard report card.
12. Supplement report cards with frequent informal letters to parents, parent-teacher conferences, and student-teacher conferences.

Source: Adapted from Allan C. Ornstein, "The Nature of Grading," *Clearing House* (April 1989), pp. 365–369; and David A. Payne, *The Assessment of Learning*, p. 417.

and the sense of helplessness and futility about their academic performance; such students are less likely to exert effort on future tasks and thus they perform below their true capabilities. This effect of grades on students in early development is rarely mentioned in the literature, yet it may have powerful effects on why so many students are demotivated early in their academic careers, and why others fail to live up to their academic potential.

By the eighth grade (or sooner in the great majority of schools), most report cards merely report grades in terms of A, B, C, D and F (where the range is from excellent to failure) in the basic academic subjects (English, mathematics, science, social studies, and foreign language) and minor subjects (physical education, health education, music, and art). If there is emphasis on reading or language skills, as in most urban school districts, English might be divided into several categories on the report card, such as reading, writing, and even listening and speaking (with bilingual groups). Grades for citizenship, character, conduct, social habits, or work habits, depending on the district's current terminology, usually come as a separate category—not intermixed with academic grades. Some high schools completely omit citizenship (or its like descriptors). The term is divided into trimesters or quarters, with the three or four terms usually averaged for the final grade. Regardless of grade level, absenteeism and lateness (sometimes called tardiness) should be shown, too. Places for a parent's signature and parent or teacher requests for a conference to discuss the report are usually provided. Indeed, the report card can be an excellent vehicle or motivating factor for holding a student-parent-teacher conference.

Electronic Record Keeping

The need for careful record keeping is an important part of the teacher's job and has financial and legal implications for the school. Research shows that the average teacher, with the assistance of a calculator, takes 87 minutes to record grades for 30 students in a traditional record book. This time does not include actual grading; it includes (1) alphabetizing and entering names, (2) entering grades, (3) averaging grades for five categories, (4) performing statistical analysis, such as means or frequency distributions, and (5) providing progress reports. The same teacher with a computerized record keeper takes 15 minutes to do the same work—a saving of 62 minutes for one class during a single grading period.[56]

Secondary school teachers usually have three or four grading periods and four or five classes per semester or half year (a saving of up to 40 hours for the year or about one week's work). The savings in time for all teachers is further increased, considering that teachers are required to generate reports that include grades to school administrators weekly and monthly, and reports to parents about their children's progress. The **computerized record keeper** can generate school reports and parental reports, as well as customized letters and

---

56 Edward L. Vockell and Donald Kopenic, "Record Keeping Without Tears," *Clearing House* (April 1989), pp. 355–359.

printout lists concerning student grades by numerous categories, in 10 to 20 seconds per report, compared to an average of 20 minutes per report with traditional methods. Figuring on a minimum of one school report per week for 40 weeks and two customized letters or progress reports per year for 30 parents, the savings is another 33 hours.

Two researchers have listed 22 tasks that computerized record keeping can accomplish more effectively than a traditional record keeping book. Ten are listed below.

1. Permitting the teacher to make easy and quick modifications of recorded scores, to correct clerical errors, or to accommodate retest scores or new test scores.
2. Computing grade averages and applying weighted formulas to grade students on various categories: 40 percent for exams, 30 percent for weekly quizzes, 15 percent for homework, and 15 percent for class participation.
3. Converting numerical grades to letter grades according to specific standards.
4. Providing records of student performance by ranking, percentages, frequency, distributions, etc., for subgroups or the entire class.
5. Making comparisons of one student or subgroup on any recorded category for purpose of diagnostic, formative, or summative evaluation.
6. Providing printouts of student performance on specific tests or subtests for purposes of instruction.
7. Designating or flagging students according to specific levels of performance on specific tests (students who failed or who received 90 percent or higher).
8. Generating reports that include standardized comments for one student or groups of students.
9. Generating personal letters for individual students, including specific comments about grades.
10. Reusing names for different reports, labels, printouts, or another grading period; creating class lists for attendance, lateness, extra credit, phone numbers, addresses, etc.[57]

We must keep in mind that we are in the age of electronics, and the pen-and-pencil method of recording data is quickly becoming dated. It behooves teachers to manage information efficiently and use various data bases and spreadsheets for grading, evaluating, and reporting student performance. These methods provide many alternatives to help busy teachers take advantage of the tools of the twenty-first century.

---

57 Ibid.

Cumulative Record

Each student has a permanent record in which important data are filed during his or her entire school career. It contains information about subject grades, standardized test scores, family background, personal history, health, school service, parent and pupil interviews, special aptitudes, special learning, behavioral or physical problems, number of absences, and tardiness. A sample cumulative secondary school record is reproduced in Figure 5.3.

The **cumulative record** is usually stored in the main office or guidance office. Teachers are permitted access to the cumulative records of the students in their classes to obtain information about them. They are also required to add to the information at the end of the term to keep the records complete and up to date.

Although the information found in the cumulative records is extremely helpful, a major criticism of using these records is that the teacher may make prejudgments about students before even meeting them in class. For this reason, some educators argue that a teacher should not look at cumulative records until a month or more after the school year begins.

Since federal legislation (Records Law 93–830) permits the records of a child to be open to inspection and reviewed by the child's parents, most educators are reluctant to write statements or reports that may be considered controversial or negative, unless supported with specific data. Sometimes important information is omitted. When parents review information in cumulative records (they also have the right to challenge the information), a qualified employee of the school (principal's secretary or guidance counselor) should be present to give assistance.

COMMUNICATION WITH PARENTS

How the teacher can help the parents to improve the child's academic work and behavior is often the major concern among parents and teachers alike. According to Joyce Epstein, more than 85 percent of parents spend 15 minutes or more helping their child at home when asked to do so by the teacher. Parents claim they can spend more time, 40 minutes on the average, if they are told specifically how to help, but fewer than 25 percent receive systematic requests and directions from teachers to assist their children with specific skills and subjects.[58] Epstein further notes that parents become involved most often with reading activities at the lower grades: reading to the child or listening to the

---

58 Joyce L. Epstein, "Parents' Reactions to Teacher Practices of Parent Involvement," *Elementary School Journal* (January 1986), pp. 277–294; Epstein, "Parent Involvement: What Research Says to Administrators," *Education and Urban Society* (February 1987), pp. 119–136.

child read, taking the child to the library, and helping with teaching materials brought home from school for practice at home.[59] Parents of older students (grade 6 and above) become more involved with specific homework and subject-related activities. Research shows that children have an academic advantage in school when their parents support, participate, and communicate on a regular basis with school officials.[60] Schools typically communicate with parents in three ways: report cards (already discussed), conferences, and letters. Parents expect feedback from the teacher and school, and they usually welcome the opportunity to meet with the teacher and to stay in touch through phone calls and letters.

Letters to Parents

Letters to parents fall into three categories. First, letters are sent to make parents aware of or invite them to participate in certain classroom or school activities or functions. Second, letters may be sent out regularly, perhaps weekly or bimonthly, to keep parents up to date about their children's academic work and behavior. Parents are entitled to and appreciate this communication. Informing parents and seeking their input and support may help to stop minor problems before they become serious. Of course, letters can be about commendable behavior. Third, letters are written to address specific problems. In such letters problems are described, parents are asked for their cooperation in one or more ways, and a conference may be requested.

Parent Conferences

Scheduling parent-teacher conferences is becoming increasingly difficult because an increasing number of children have only one adult living at home, or have two parents in the work force, or have parents with more than one job. Few parents are able to attend school activities or conferences during normal school hours, and many have trouble scheduling meetings at all. Today's teacher must adjust to these new circumstances with greater efforts through letters and telephone calls to set up meetings and greater flexibility to accommodate the needs of the parents.

Usually both teachers and parents are a little apprehensive before a conference, want to impress each other favorably, and don't know exactly what to expect. Teachers can reduce their anxiety by preparing for the conference, assembling in advance all the information pertinent to the student and the subject to be discussed with parents. This might include information regarding

59 Joyce L. Epstein, "How Do We Improve Programs for Parent Involvement?" *Educational Horizons* (Winter 1988), pp. 58–59; Epstein, "Parent Involvement: What Research Says to Administrators."

60 Anne T. Henderson, "An Ecologically Balanced Approach to Academic Improvement," *Educational Horizons* (Winter 1988), pp. 60–62; Beth Sattes, "Parental Involvement in Student Learning," *Education Digest* (January 1989), pp. 37–39.

Conferences with students and parents encourage full explanations of teachers' evaluations and the exchange of information necessary for planning the student's progress.

the student's academic achievement, other testing results, general health, attendance and lateness, social and emotional relations, work habits, special aptitudes, or other noteworthy characteristics or activities. If the conference is about subject grades, the teacher should assemble the student's tests, reports, and homework assignments. If it is about discipline, he or she might have on hand written and detailed accounts of behavior.

The conference should not be a time for lecturing parents. If the teacher asked for the conference, the teacher will set the agenda, but should remain sensitive to the needs of the parents. The atmosphere should be unrushed and quiet. The information presented should be based on as many sources as possible. It is advisable to begin and end on a positive note, even if a problem has to be discussed. The idea is to encourage parents. The teacher should not monopolize the discussion, should be truthful yet tactful and constructive, and should remain poised. The teacher should be cautious about giving too much advice, especially with regard to the child's home life.[61] The average conference, unless there is an important problem, lasts 20 to 30 minutes. See Tips for Teachers 5.4.

The parent-teacher conference is helpful for both parties. The conference helps teachers (1) understand and clarify parents' impressions and expectations of the school program or particular classes, (2) obtain additional information about the child, (3) report on the child's developmental progress and suggest things the parents can do to stimulate development, (4) develop a working relationship with parents, and (5) encourage parents' support of the school.

---

61 J. Karen Chapman, "Advice for Parents," *PTA Today* (October 1988), pp. 9–10; Allan C. Ornstein, "The Parent-Teacher Conference," *PTA Today* (October 1988), pp. 8–9.

Tips for Teachers 5.4

Guide to Discussion During a Parent-Teacher Conference

During a conference the teacher can expect parents to ask about certain things. And if parents don't ask about them, the teacher should be prepared to introduce the topics into the discussion. Below is a list of questions (that may be introduced by the parent or teacher) that can guide your discussion.

1. How does the student behave in class? In school?
2. How does the student get along with classmates?
3. Is the student working up to full potential?
4. How does the student's progress compare with that of classmates?
5. What are the potential strengths of the student? In what skill area or subject?
6. What problems does the student have, if any? In what skill area or subject?
7. What interests or special abilities does the student demonstrate in class?
8. In what way has the student performed well?
9. How can the parent help the student?
10. How can the parent help the teacher?

Source: Adapted from Leonard H. Clark and Irving S. Starr, *Secondary and Middle School Teaching Methods*, 5th ed. (New York: Macmillan, 1986), p. 393; Allan C. Ornstein, "The Parent-Teacher Conference," *PTA Today* (October 1988), pp. 8–10.

The conference helps parents (1) gain a better understanding of the child's school program, (2) learn about school activities that can enhance the child's growth and development, (3) learn about the child's performance and progress, (4) learn about the school's faculty and support staff, (5) communicate concerns and ask questions about the child, and (6) both provide and receive information that can benefit the child's development in school and at home.[62]

---

62 Jeffrey L. Gelfer and Peggy B. Perkins, "Effective Communication with Parents," *Childhood Education* (October 1987), pp. 19–22; Howard Margolis and Kenneth J. Tewel, "Resolving Conflict with Parents," *NASSP Bulletin* (March 1988), pp. 1–8.

Guidelines for Conducting Parent-Teacher Conferences

All parents have the right to know how their children are progressing in school and how the teacher evaluates this progress. Such information should be communicated to the parent(s) on a regular basis. The parent conference is one important vehicle for providing such information. Below are some guidelines for communicating with parents at the conference.

Mechanics of the Meeting with the Parent

1. Make an appointment for the conference well in advance.
2. Provide two or more options for the parent's visit.
3. Greet the parent courteously using his or her proper name. Stand up to greet the person.
4. Take the parent's wraps and show him or her to a comfortable chair.
5. If the parent is upset or emotional, allow for expression of feelings without interruptions. Do not become defensive; remain calm.
6. Be objective in analyzing the child's progress; also, show interest in the child's development, growth, and welfare.
7. Never get trapped into criticizing another teacher or the principal.
8. Explain how you and the parent can work together to help the student.
9. Set up a date for a follow-up conference, if needed.
10. Walk with the parent to the door, if possible; end on a positive note.

Discussion about the Child

1. Begin on a positive note.
2. Be truthful and honest.
3. Accept the parent's feelings.
4. Emphasize the child's strengths.
5. Be specific about the student's learning difficulties/strengths.
6. Have ready samples of the student's class work and homework as well as a record of his or her test scores, attendance, etc.
7. Be receptive to the parent's suggestions.
8. Let the parent have the opportunity to voice concerns.
9. Avoid arguments; avoid pedantic language.
10. Provide constructive suggestions.
11. Be willing to explain activities or changes in the school curriculum that meet the needs of the child.
12. Close on a positive note, and with a plan of action.[63]

---

63 Allan C. Ornstein, "Parent Conferencing: Recommendations and Guidelines," *Kappa Delta Pi Record* (Winter 1990), pp. 55–57.

SUMMARY

1. The reasons for evaluating students include motivating students, providing feedback to students and teachers, informing parents, and making selection decisions.
2. Four types of evaluation are placement, diagnostic, formative, and summative.
3. Sources of information for evaluation in addition to tests include classroom discussion and activity, homework, notebooks, reports, and quizzes.
4. Knowledge of basic statistical terms is important for assessing test results, especially standardized tests; these terms are the normal curve, standard deviation, grade equivalent score, rank score, and stanine score.
5. Grades are based on absolute or relative scales. Alternative grading practices include contracts, mastery grading, and grades for effort and progress.
6. The conventional report card emphasizes basic subject areas and uses letters to designate grades; more contemporary methods of reporting include mastery and progress reports and statements about process.
7. The cumulative record is a legal document that includes important data about the students' performance and behavior in school; it follows the students throughout their school career.
8. Communication with parents takes place in the form of report cards, conferences, and letters.

CASE STUDY

Problem

An experienced ninth-grade math teacher, in a high school changing from highly academically oriented to average to low academic, was determined to maintain strict "standards" in evaluation. He chose to retain the evaluation process used with his former students. Over time, his new students became sullen and discipline problems surfaced after the grading periods. Almost a third of the class failed and another third received a C, which the teacher said is nothing to be ashamed of since it means they are doing average work for their age and grade.

Suggestion

Another experienced teacher, newly transferred into the school, suggested his colleague might maintain standards while having an evaluation process that reflected the students' accomplishments in learning. The math teacher was to choose only one class with which to try the new method of evaluation. He was first to gather baseline data on his students. Then he could either (1) separate the class into groups within a range of skills or (2) use the data for developing a baseline for each student. The students would then be evaluated by their improvement within their own group of students of equal or near-equal ability, or be evaluated by competition with themselves using some predetermined standard of improvement. Later in the semester he could then shift to a fixed standard method once students showed improvement by groups or individuals. This change would require some individualizing of instruction. Later, he could extend this evaluation process to his other classes.

The teacher began the method and used it for the semester. The class he worked with showed an improvement in attitude and a bit more incentive to work. Their grades improved. However, the teacher transferred to another high school similar to his original situation. He now said the last evaluation method was not fair to other students, was too much work, and degraded the purpose of evaluation by providing students with false measures of their abilities, therefore leading to future disillusionment.

Discussion Suggestion

The transferred teacher implemented the method of evaluation in his new school. However, he did modify it based on his last experiences. While holding students to a fixed standard, he began to take an assessment of the students' abilities before designing his units and lessons. Each unit would then have a preevaluation for a specific needed review and for the planning of instruction. After concentrating on the needs identified by the preevaluation he would then evaluate the students at the end of each lesson. There was also a cumulative evaluation at the end of the unit. In this way he felt he met the needs of students in his academically oriented class. Since all his final evaluations were of the fixed standard type, he felt he had maintained the integrity of his evaluation process.

Discussion Questions

1. Was the math teacher being realistic in his expectations in a changing school situation? If not, what will happen to an educational system in which standards vary from school to school, teacher to teacher? What would you have done?
2. Do you feel the math teacher transferred from the school for the reasons he cited? How would you react to a colleague such as this if he were team teaching with you or your supervisor?
3. What models for evaluation in this chapter seem promising for you? What kinds of modifications would you implement in a changing school situation?
4. Give the pros and cons of the idea of evaluating by fixed standards rather than by relative scales or on a curve.
5. Could the math teacher have used the method devised for his academically oriented students as effectively with his nonacademically oriented students? Why? Why not?

QUESTIONS TO CONSIDER

1. Can a teacher be objective in evaluating student performance? Explain.
2. How would you distinguish between placement, diagnostic, formative, and summative evaluation?
3. How might you improve your own grading practice compared to that of teachers you had in school?
4. What are the differences between absolute and relative standards in grading? Which do you prefer? Why?
5. Why is it desirable to use several sources of data when arriving at a grade for a student?

THINGS TO DO

1. From your past school experiences, list some examples of inappropriate evaluation techniques.
2. Discuss with your classmates the meaning of the normal curve, standard deviation, and stanine score. Provide examples by using the test scores of a recent class examination.
3. List and discuss criteria for good grading.
4. Outline a grading procedure you expect to follow as a teacher.
5. Visit local schools, obtain sample report cards, and discuss their major characteristics in class. Analyze how various report cards differ.

RECOMMENDED READINGS

Bloom, Benjamin S., J. Thomas Hastings, and George F. Madaus. *Handbook of Formative and Summative Evaluation of Student Learning.* New York: McGraw-Hill, 1971. A mammoth-size text that can serve as an excellent source for technical questions about evaluation.

Gronlund, Norman E. and Robert L. Linn. *Measurement and Evaluation in Teaching*, 6th ed. New York: Macmillan, 1990. An appreciation of the advantages and disadvantages of various tests and evaluation procedures.

Guba, Egon G. and Yvonna S. Lincoln. *Fourth Generation Evaluation.* Newbury Park, Calif.: Sage, 1990. A practical discussion of the ethics, politics, and methodology of evaluation.

Hopkins, Kenneth D., Julian C. Stanley, and B. R. Hopkins. *Educational and Psychological Measurement*, 7th ed. Englewood Cliffs, N.J.: Prentice-Hall, 1990. A practitioner's perspective for testing and evaluating students.

Popham, W. James. *Modern Educational Measurement*, 2nd ed. Englewood Cliffs, N.J.: Prentice-Hall, 1990. Various models and strategies for evaluating student outcomes.

Thorndike, Robert M. et al., *Measurement and Evaluation in Psychology and Education*, 5th ed. New York: Macmillan, 1990. An important reference on testing and evaluation that is comprehensive but easy to read.

Worthen, Blaine R., Walter R. Borg, and Karl R. White. *Measurement and Evaluation in Schools*. New York: Longman, 1989. Helps the reader assess the quality and function of evaluation tools and how to interpret them; advises how to set up schoolwide evaluation programs.

KEY TERMS

Placement evaluation	Stanine score
Diagnostic evaluation	Constant error
Formative evaluation	Absolute grades
Summative evaluation	Relative grades
Informal evaluation	Contract grading
Normal curve	Mastery grading
Standard deviation	Continuous progress grading
Grade equivalent score	Mastery report card
Rank score	Computerized record keeper
Percentile rank	Cumulative record

Instruction

Chapter
6

Instructional Objectives

FOCUSING QUESTIONS

1. What should the school teach?

2. How are aims, goals, and objectives formulated?

3. How do aims, goals and objectives differ?

4. How would you characterize the approaches to writing objectives by the following: Tyler, Bloom, Gronlund, Mager, and Gagné?

5. How does each approach differ? In what way should teachers use enabling objectives?

6. How specific should course objectives be? Classroom objectives?

Aims, *goals*, and *objectives* are terms that can be defined in many ways. We use the term **aims** to refer to broad statements about the intent of education. They are value-laden statements, written by panels, commissions, or policy-making groups, that express a philosophy of education and concepts of the social role of schools and the needs of children and youth. In short, they are broad guides for translating the needs of society into educational policy. Aims, sometimes called purposes, are written on a societal (or national) level. They are descriptive and vaguely written statements. For example, what does the phrase "preparing students for democratic citizenship" mean? What do we have in mind when we stress "citizenship preparation"?

Educators need to translate aims into statements that will describe what schools are expected to accomplish (which is more focused than saying what education is for). These translations are called **goals.** Goals are sometimes called *mission statements* or *guiding principles*. Goals make it possible to organize learning experiences in terms of what the state, school district, or school plans to stress on a systemwide basis. In effect, goals are statements that cut across subjects and grade levels and represent the entire school program. Goals are more definite than aims, but they are still nonbehavioral and therefore nonobservable and non-measureable. Goal provide direction for educators, but they do not specify achievement levels or proficiency levels. Examples of goals are "development of reading skills," "appreciation of art," and "understanding of mathematical concepts." Goals are written by professional associations and state and local educational agencies to be published as school and curriculum guidelines for what all students should accomplish over their entire school career.

Objectives are descriptions of what is eventually to take place at the classroom level. They specify content and the proficiency level to be attained. Objectives are stated in behavioral terms. They state specific skills, tasks, content, and attitudes to be taught and learned and give teachers and students a standard by which to judge if they are achieving the objectives. According to Hilda Taba, "The chief function of . . . objectives is to guide the making of . . . decisions on what to cover, what to emphasize, and what content to select, and what learning experiences to stress."[1] Because the possibilities of content, learning, and teaching are endless, teachers face the problem of selection: What content is most important? What learning activities are most appropriate? What unit plan is most effective? Objectives supply criteria for these decisions, according to Taba. No matter what its nature, the statement of objectives in terms of desired outcomes "sets the scope and limits for what is to be taught and learned."[2]

---

1 Hilda Taba, *Curriculum Development: Theory and Practice* (New York: Harcourt Brace Jovanovich, 1962), p. 197.

2 Ibid.

Naturally, objectives should be consistent with the overriding goals of the school system and state and the general educational aims of society. Each teacher, when planning for instruction, may contribute to these goals and aims in a different way. Recalling our three examples of goals, we can now give examples of objectives to be attained in their pursuit: (1) goal: development of reading skills; objective: to gain knowledge in word recognition; (2) goal: appreciation of art; objective: to recognize the paintings of major artists; (3) goal: understanding of mathematical concepts; objective: to understand mathematical proofs.

AIMS

Aims are important statements that guide our schools and give educators direction. However, we will discuss them only briefly because they are not written by teachers. Perhaps the most widely accepted list of educational aims in the twentieth century was compiled by the Commission on the Reorganization of Secondary Education in 1918. Its influential bulletin was entitled *Cardinal Principles of Secondary Education*. The seven principles, or aims, designated by the commission are listed below.

1. *Health.* The secondary school should . . . provide health instruction, inculcate health habits, organize an effective program of physical activities, regard health needs in planning work and play, and co-operate with home and community in safeguarding and promoting health interests.
2. *Command of fundamental processes.* The facility that a child of twelve or fourteen years may acquire . . . is not sufficient for the needs of modern life. (Further instruction in the fundamentals is urged.)
3. *Worthy home membership.* Worthy home membership as an objective calls for the development of those qualities that make the individual a worthy member of a family, both contributing to and deriving benefit from that membership.
4. *Vocation.* Vocational education should equip the individual to secure a livelihood for himself and those dependent on him, to serve society well through his vocation, to maintain the right relationships toward his fellow workers and society, and, if possible, to find in that vocation his own best development.
5. *Civic education.* Civic education should develop in the individual those qualities whereby he will act his part as a member of neighborhood, town or city, state, and nation, and give him a basis for understanding international problems.

6. *Worthy use of leisure.* Education should equip the individual to secure from his leisure the recreation of body, mind, and spirit, and the enrichment and enlargement of his personality.

7. *Ethical character.* In a democratic society ethical character becomes paramount among the objectives of the secondary school. Among the means for developing ethical character may be mentioned the wide selection of content and methods of instruction in all subjects of study and the social contacts of pupils with one another and with their teachers.[3]

The commission's work was the first statement of educational aims to address the need to assimilate immigrant children and to educate an industrial work force, reflecting events in the country at that period. The most important aspect of the document is that it emphasized the need to educate all students for "complete living," not to educate only students headed for college and not to develop only cognitive abilities. It endorsed the concept of the whole child, meeting the various needs of students, while it provided a common ground for teaching and enhancing American ideals and educating all citizens to function in a democratic society. These aims are still relevant for all levels of education and are still found in one form or another in statements of educational aims.

GOALS

Goals tend to reflect the developmental needs of children and youth. According to Peter Oliva, goals "are timeless, in the sense that no time is specified by which the goals must be reached," and at the same time they "are not permanent," in the sense that they "may be modified wherever necessary or desirable." Goals usually cut across subjects and grades and apply throughout the school. They do not delineate specific items of content or corresponding activities. Goals should be stated broadly enough "to be accepted at any level of the educational enterprise," but specifically enough to lead to desired outcomes. [4]

Increasingly, the schools are being burdened by the rest of society with roles and responsibilities that other agencies and institutions no longer do well or want to do. The schools are seen as ideal agents to solve the problems of the nation, community, and home. Many people and groups refuse to admit to their own responsibilities in helping children develop their capabilities and adjust to society. More and more, the schools are being told that they must educate and socialize all children, regardless of the initial input and support from home.

---

3 Commission on the Reorganization of Secondary Education, *Cardinal Principles of Secondary Education* (Washington, D.C.: U.S. Government Printing Office, 1918), pp. 11–15.

4 Peter F. Oliva, *Developing the Curriculum*, 2nd ed. (Glenview, Ill.: Scott, Foresman, 1988), p. 265.

The schools may now be attempting to accomplish too many things and therefore not performing many of them effectively.

Goal statements are sometimes written by professional associations for educators at the state and local level to modify and adopt. One of the more influential lists of goals was published by the Association for Supervision and Curriculum Development (Table 6.1). Many of the goals are interrelated, and the achievement of some facilitates the achievement of others. The acquisition of basic skills, for example, is prerequisite to all other goals. Anything that prevents the achievement of one goal may thereby restrict the attainment of other goals.

In preparing his classic study of schooling, John Goodlad surveyed the school goals that had been published by state and local boards of education across the country. From approximately 100 different statements of goals, he constructed 12 that represent the spirit of the total list (Table 6.2). He further defined each with subgoals and a rationale statement. The goals summarize what educators are expected to attend to and what they might be held accountable for.

It needs to be pointed out that Goodlad's study represents a blend of the most common goals (or mission statements) of school districts. Some school districts are much more traditional or conservative and focus on a host of cognitive or subject matter goals (dealing with reading, writing, and math skills, computer literacy, and core academic subjects) whereas other districts are more progressive and learner oriented. It should be noted, however, that school districts that discuss, as part of their mission, the students' self-concept, emotional well-being, and self-realization may or may not, in reality, do a good job of implementing these goals. They may merely give lip service to such goals.

One of the most progressive school districts in the United States, rooted in the philosophy of Francis Parker, John Dewey, and Carleton Wasburne, is in Winnetka, Illinois. Its eleven goals, on which curriculum and instruction are constructed, are (1) childhood protection, (2) global understanding, (3) community-school partnership, (4) consistent relationships (peer, teacher, and family role), (5) parent-school cooperation, (6) student-teacher planning, (7) learning and thinking skills, (8) developmental learning, (9) integrated learning (high-order thinking and creativity), (10) understanding technology, and (11) physical and emotional well-being.[5]

Note the direct emphasis on the learner (4 goals) in relationship to peers and parents (2 goals) and the local and international community (2 goals). Only three goals (7, 9, 10) deal with cognitive understanding. Of course, one must understand that Winnetka is an upper-class community and can afford to be progressive; its students have built-in home support systems and are high achievers.

---

5 "Winnetka: A Community of Learners," *Winnetka Schools* (March 1987), p.1.

Table 6.1   EDUCATIONAL GOALS OF THE ASSOCIATION OF SUPERVISION AND
CURRICULUM DEVELOPMENT

1. *Basic skills.* Acquires information and meaning through observing, listening, and reading, as well as through reflective thinking.

2. *Self-conceptualization.* Recognizes that self-concept is acquired in interaction with other people, and distinguishes between significant and nonsignificant others.

3. *Understanding others.* Bases actions and decisions on the knowledge that individuals differ but are similar in many ways, and that values and behaviors are learned and differ from one social group to another; acts on belief that each individual has value as a human being and should be respected as a worthwhile person in his or her own right.

4. *Using accumulated knowledge to interpret the world.* Applies basic principles and concepts of the sciences, arts, and humanities to interpret personal experiences; analyzes and acts upon public issues; understands natural phenomena; evaluates technological progress; and appreciates aesthetic events.

5. *Continuous learning.* Bases actions and decisions on the knowledge that it is necessary to continue to learn throughout life because of the inevitability of change.

6. *Mental and physical well-being.* Consumes a nutritionally balanced, wholesome diet, exercises sufficiently to maintain personal health; avoids, to the extent possible, consuming materials harmful to health, particularly addictive ones; behaves rationally based upon reasonable perceptions of self and society; and perceives self positively with a generally competent sense of well-being.

7. *Participation in the economic world of production and consumption.* Selects and pursues career opportunities consonant with social and personal needs and capabilities; makes informed consumer decisions based on appropriate knowledge of products, needs, and resources.

8. *Responsible societal membership.* Acts consonant with an understanding of the basic interdependence of the biological and physical resources of the environment; acts in accordance with a basic ethical framework incorporating those values contributing to group living, such as honesty, fairness, compassion, and integrity; assumes responsibility for own acts; works in groups to achieve mutual goals; and invokes law and authority to protect the rights of all persons.

9. *Creativity.* Generates a range of imaginative alternatives to stimuli; entertains and values the imaginative alternatives of others.

10. *Coping with change.* Works for goals on realistic personal performance standards; decides when a risk is worth taking; works now for goals to be realized in the future.

Source: Adapted from ASCD Committee on Research and Theory, *Measuring and Attaining the Goals of Education* (Alexandria, Va.: Association for Supervision and Curriculum Development, 1980), pp. 9–12.

Table 6.2   MAJOR GOALS OF AMERICAN SCHOOLS

1. *Mastery of basic skills or fundamental processes*. In our technological civilization, an individual's ability to participate in the activities of society depends on mastery of these fundamental processes.

2. *Career or vocational education*. An individual's personal satisfaction in life is significantly related to satisfaction with her or his job. Intelligent career decisions require knowledge of personal aptitudes and interests in relation to career possibilities.

3. *Intellectual development*. As civilization has become more complex, people have had to rely more heavily on their rational abilities. Full intellectual development of each member of society is necessary.

4. *Enculturation*. Studies that illuminate our relationship with the past yield insight into our society and its values; furthermore, these strengthen an individual's sense of belonging, identity, and direction for his or her own life.

5. *Interpersonal relations*. Schools should help every child understand, appreciate, and value persons belonging to social, cultural, and ethnic groups different from the child's own and to increase affiliation with and decrease alienation from them.

6. *Autonomy*. Unless schools produce self-directed citizens, they have failed both society and the individual. As society becomes more complex, demands on individuals multiply. Schools help prepare children for a world of rapid change by developing in them the capacity to assume responsibility for their own needs.

7. *Citizenship*. To counteract the present human ability to destroy humanity and the environment requires citizen involvement in the political and social life of this country. A democracy can survive only with the participation of its members.

8. *Creativity and aesthetic perception*. Abilities for creating new and meaningful things and appreciating the creations of other human beings are essential both for personal self-realization and for the benefit of society.

9. *Self-concept*. The self-concept of an individual serves as a reference point and feedback mechanism for personal goals and aspirations. Factors for a healthy self-concept can be provided by the school environment.

10. *Emotional and physical well-being*. Emotional stability and physical fitness are perceived as necessary conditions for attaining the other goals, but they are also worthy ends in themselves.

11. *Moral and ethical character*. Development of the judgment needed to evaluate events and phenomena as right or wrong and a commitment to truth, moral integrity, moral conduct, and a desire to strengthen the moral fabric of society are the values manifested by this goal.

12. *Self-realization*. Efforts to develop a better self contribute to the development of a better society.

Source: John I. Goodlad, *What Schools Are For* (Bloomington, Ind.: Phi Delta Kappa, 1979), pp. 44–52. Also see Goodlad, *A Place Called School* (New York: McGraw-Hill, 1984).

Given our growing technological society, computer literacy is a goal that the schools increasingly deem as important.

LEVELS OF OBJECTIVES

Instructional objectives help the teacher focus on what students should know at the end of a lesson, unit, or course and also help students know what is expected of them. They help the teacher plan and organize instruction by identifying what is to be taught. Instructional objectives are stated in observable and measurable terms (outcomes, proficiencies, or competencies). Their specificity enables the teacher to determine whether what was intended was achieved, and to what extent.

When we move from goals to instructional objectives, the role and responsibility of the teacher become evident. Objectives are behavioral in nature and are observable and measurable in some way. They are formulated on three levels with increasing specificity: program, course, and classroom. Objectives at the classroom level can be further divided into unit plan and lesson plan objectives.

Program Objectives

Program objectives stem from the goals of the school and are written at the subject and grade level. Although they do not state specific content or competencies, they do focus on general content and specific behaviors. Like goals, they refer to the accomplishments of all students, rather than to those of individual students or groups of students, or to specific achievement levels or outcomes.[6]

---

6 Ivor K. Davies, *Objectives in Curriculum Design* (New York: McGraw-Hill, 1976); Oliva, *Developing the Curriculum.*

Nearly every state and school district has an overview or set of program objectives at the subject and grade level to facilitate what teachers should be teaching. In most cases these instructional objectives are formulated by curriculum committees made up of administrative, teacher, and community (or parent) groups. Table 6.3 provides a detailed list of the instructional objectives for grades 8 and 12 in language arts for the Chicago Public Schools. (The original list included eight other subject areas, including mathematics, science, social studies, fine arts, physical education, health and safety.) The table helps the reader envision program objectives on a vertical basis, to see relationships that exist by subject and grade levels. Other schools might develop program objectives in terms of standards, expectations, and/or ideal outcomes. Such an approach is more behaviorist and precise than the Chicago approach—which provides direction but more room to operate.

Course Objectives

Course objectives are derived from program objectives: they categorize and organize content and sometimes concepts, problems, or behaviors, but do not specify the exact content to be examined or exact instructional methods and materials to be used. Course objectives are stated in the form of topics, concepts, or general behaviors.

Objectives stated as *topics* for an American history course might be "The Colonial Period," "The Revolutionary Period," "The Framing of the Constitution," "Manifest Destiny," "The Civil War Period," "The Reconstruction Period," "Industrialization and Colonialization," "Immigration and Nationalism," "World War I." Objectives stated as *concepts* for a science course might be "Science and Knowledge," "Science and Method," "Science and Humanity," "Science and Environment," "Science, Products, and Technology," "Science and Space." Examples of objectives stated as general *behaviors* (which are not easy to measure or observe) might be phrased "To develop critical thinking in . . .," "To increase understanding of . . .," "To have experience for . . . ."

Course objectives (as well as program objectives) help the teacher organize the content in terms of *scope* (topics, concepts, behaviors to be covered), *continuity* (recurring and continuing opportunity to teach important content and practice certain skills and tasks), *sequence* (cumulative development or successive treatment of topics, concepts, or behaviors that build upon preceding ones), and *integration* (relationships of content in one course to content in another course).[7]

7 David G. Armstrong, *Developing and Documenting the Curriculum* (Needham Heights, Mass.: Allyn & Bacon, 1989); Allan C. Ornstein and Francis P. Hunkins, *Curriculum: Foundations, Principles and Issues* (Englewood Cliffs, N.J.: Prentice-Hall, 1988); and Taba, *Curriculum Development: Theory and Practice.*

Classroom Objectives

Classroom objectives are usually formulated by the teacher, who divides course objectives into several units. Unit plan objectives usually encompass one to three weeks of instruction, organized in a sequence and corresponding to expectations for the entire class, not for particular individuals or groups. Unit plan objectives are then further divided to create lesson plan objectives, ideally organized around one day of instruction on a particular subject.

Unit Plan Objectives

Unit plan objectives are usually categorized into topics or concepts. Recall the history course objective, "The Framing of the Constitution." This *topic* might be divided into the following units: "To understand the system of American government," "To comprehend the rights of American citizens," "To identify characteristics of a democratic society," "To apply the principles of American government to classroom and school activities."

The science objective, written as a *concept*, "Science and Method," might be broken down into the following unit plan objectives: "To organize inductive, deductive, and intuitive methods in answering questions about the (a) biological world, (b) chemical world, and (c) physical world,"; "To organize scientific information according to (a) logic, (b) explanations, (c) causal relations, (d) hypotheses, and (e) projections"; "To gain understanding in the methods of (a) inquiry, (b) experimentation, and (c) problem-solving"; "To show interest in scientific hobbies or projects."

Unit plan objectives are sometimes called *general instructional objectives*. They should be specific enough to provide direction for instruction, but not so specific that they restrict the teacher's selection of instructional methods, materials, and activities. Almost any appropriate instructional technique—lectures, discussions, demonstrations, laboratory work, textbook assignments, additional readings—might be used to achieve the unit plan objectives.[8]

Lesson Plan Objectives

Lesson plan objectives, sometimes call *specific instructional objectives*, further define the unit objectives by providing clear direction for teaching and testing. Instructional objectives at the lesson plan level state (1) *expected behaviors*, in terms of specific skills, tasks, or attitudes, and (2) *content*. They may also state (3) *outcomes*, sometimes called *standards*, in terms of level of achievement, proficiency, or competency, and (4) *conditions* of mastery. There is currently debate on how detailed these objectives should be and whether too much specificity leads to concern with the trivial.

---

8 Norman E. Gronlund, *Measurement and Evaluation in Teaching*, 5th ed. (New York: Macmillan, 1985); Robert E. Mager, *Measuring Instructional Results* (Belmont, Calif.: Fearon, 1984); Allan C. Ornstein, "Effective Course Planning by Mapping," Kappa Delta Pi Record (Fall 1990), pp. 24–26.

Table 6.3   OVERVIEW OF PROGRAM OBJECTIVES OF THE CHICAGO PUBLIC SCHOOLS FOR LAN-
GUAGE ARTS: GRADES 8 AND 12

Grade 8

Reading

Read for various purposes and identify types of text that accomplish each purpose.

Infer meaning from context.

Use research sources.

Identify literary devices: flashback, foreshadowing, imagery, sarcasm. irony, humor, figurative language, and characterization.

Identify elements of short stories: setting, plot, characters, point of view, theme, and mood.

Provide rationale for predictions and questions before, during, and after reading.

Interpret symbolism.

Interpret poetry.

Compare themes.

Draw conclusions about author's point of view.

Infer word relationships in analogies.

Detect biased viewpoints.

Compare excerpts of literary works from different historical periods.

Develop reading skills by using materials written by authors representing different cultures as well as different countries.

Use functional information.

Infer conclusions.

Interpret parts of a play.

Recall, compare, and summarize information from two or more sources.

Synthesize information.

Understand the textual structure of a selection: vocabulary, content, organization, and author's purpose.

Listening

Recognize and identify cultural differences and similarities among people as expressed in their communication behaviors.

Listen critically to make judgments and inferences.

Listen attentively for a sustained period of time.

Understand the purposes and motivations of the speaker and evaluate the effectiveness and style of the spoken communication.

Identify facts, details, sequence, and other components of spoken communication.

Identify the organizational pattern of an oral selection.

Recognize the central theme or main idea in an oral presentation.

Exhibit appropriate listening behavior.

Listen courteously and respectfully to oral contributions of persons of all racial/ethnic backgrounds to gain information about, understanding of and appreciation for persons and their cultures.

Identify inconsistencies in verbal and nonverbal messages.

Demonstrate higher-level thinking skills in spoken communication.

Formulate concepts and generalizations presented orally.

Interpret oral presentations of literary selections.

Summarize information in an oral message.

Analyze criteria for evaluating oral communication.

Writing

Write appropriate heading on papers.

Use one central idea or topic when writing.

Use varied methods of paragraph development.

Use effective transitions within and between paragraphs to develop narrative, expository, descriptive, and persuasive forms.

Produce various types of public and personal writing.

Understand the functions of grammar and usage.

Write for diverse audiences and occasions.

Write résumés.

Research and write about various cultures and other countries.

Apply knowledge of sentence parts in writing.

Edit and revise written work, using conventional forms of Standard English.

Write in a well-organized manner around a central theme.

Write coherently.

Identify Latin roots and affixes.

Know double consonant spelling patterns.

Know vowel spelling patterns.

Utilize prefixes and suffixes.

Use a dictionary to check spelling.

Write legible letters in both manuscript and cursive writing.

Produce letters with the appropriate alignment.

Write with an acceptable degree of legibility and uniformity.

Write fluidly, quickly, and consistently.

Table 6.3 OVERVIEW OF PROGRAM OBJECTIVES OF THE CHICAGO PUBLIC SCHOOLS FOR LAN-
GUAGE ARTS: GRADES 8 AND 12 (Continued)

Grade 12

Reading

Adjust reading strategies to subject matter and purpose.

Utilize prior knowledge to make inferences.

Use textual information to verify inferences.

Research, analyze, and integrate information from a variety of sources to support conclusions.

Judge the value and reliability of material written by authors from various cultures.

Listening

Listen courteously to all speakers.

Exhibit sensitivity toward speaker, message, and cultural variations.

Differentiate purposes for listening.

Analyze the sequence of main ideas and supporting details from a variety of spoken messages.

Recognize the implications of verbal and nonverbal cues.

Distinguish among observations, inferences, and judgments.

Analyze the relationship between support data and central theme.

Evaluate the techniques used to accomplish a specific purpose.

Analyze the relationship between the speaker's point of view and the content of an oral message.

Judge the overall effectiveness of oral messages, including sufficiency of detail, credibility of sources, effectiveness of proposed solutions, and/or the validity of conclusions.

Writing

Research and write about various cultures and other countries.

Adapt language and style to purpose and audience.

Develop and maintain a focus.

Support and elaborate the thesis, main idea, or unifying event with suitable information.

Use a variety of organizational structures.

Employ the conventions of Standard written English.

Edit, revise, and proofread written work.

Use writing as a way to facilitate learning and clarify ideas.

Table 6.3   OVERVIEW OF PROGRAM OBJECTIVES OF THE CHICAGO PUBLIC SCHOOLS FOR LAN-
GUAGE ARTS: GRADES 8 AND 12 (Continued)

Grade 8

Speaking

Pronounce words clearly and distinctly.

Express ideas in a clear and understandable manner.

Demonstrate flexibility in the use of language.

Utilize voice variation for clarity and understanding.

Utilize language appropriate to the situation.

Refine oral presentation skills.

Speak courteously and respectfully to persons of all racial/ethnic backgrounds to share information, ideas, opinions, values, and points of view.

Extend debating skills.

Use an outline when making oral presentations.

Deliver a speech to describe, persuade, narrate, and explain.

Specify and limit a topic for an oral presentation.

Use different organizational patterns for oral messages.

Use a variety of sources to support ideas in an oral message.

Distinguish among statements of observation, opinion, and judgment.

Demonstrate flexibility in language usage.

Use Standard English when speaking.

Use physical movement, gestures, and eye contact to communicate interest and enthusiasm.

Identify the various purposes for communicating: informing, persuading, imagining, feeling, and socializing.

Use information effectively in an oral message.

Prepare and follow an agenda for a meeting.

Use organization of an introduction, a body, and a conclusion in an oral message or presentation.

Literature

Read selected works, representing males and females, diverse multicultural groups, and handicapped persons.

Read to identify examples of cultural differences and recognize their impact on literary works.

Read to understand and appreciate cultural variations in a literary work through focus on holidays, music, art, clothing, dance, and language.

Read to gain an understanding of people as individuals.

Read to develop an awareness of and pride in one's cultural heritage.

Read to identify how the values and beliefs of various historical periods influenced selected literary works.

Identify types of figurative language.

Identify the elements of nonfiction.

Recognize significant elements of fiction.

Know the characteristics of symbolism, allegory, and myth.

Identify the theme, idea, or meaning of a literary selection.

Formulate an opinion of literary works.

Compare literary themes to real-life situations.

Read and identify a variety of poetic forms and styles.

Identify terms and conventions unique to drama.

Recognize the difference between fictional prose and other literary forms.

Identify a variety of fictional forms.

Compare and contrast various types of factual literature.

Compare and contrast literary works from two different historical periods.

Recognize the perspectives of authors of selected works.

Compare and contrast the values, beliefs, or prejudices represented in several literary works.

Language

Understand the ways in which language has evolved.

Recognize the existence of various languages and language patterns.

Use Standard English grammar.

Recognize the advantages of the diversity of languages in a multicultural society.

Appreciate the contributions made to language by various cultural groups.

Table 6.3   OVERVIEW OF PROGRAM OBJECTIVES OF THE CHICAGO PUBLIC SCHOOLS FOR LAN-
GUAGE ARTS: GRADES 8 AND 12 (Continued)

Grade 12

Speaking

Speak courteously and respectfully to all persons.

Speak clearly and expressively for a variety of situations and audiences.

Demonstrate proficiency in extemporaneous speaking.

Organize oral presentations with suitable transitions and developmental techniques.

Use verbal and nonverbal techniques appropriate to topic, audience, and setting.

Use Standard English.

Analyze the communication process in public speaking.

Identify and describe the fallacies in an argument.

Critique and evaluate oral messages and speeches in accordance with established criteria.

Literature

Read selected works by and about males and females, including the handicapped, from diverse multicultural and international backgrounds.

Read to identify and understand cultural variations and recognize their impact on given literary works.

Read to gain an understanding of people as individuals.

Read to develop an awareness of and pride in one's cultural heritage.

Read selected works from various historical periods to examine diverse value systems and philosophies.

Compare and contrast content, structure, style, and themes of works from two different historical periods or literary movements.

Recognize and evaluate writers' techniques.

Analyze symbolism, allegory, and myth in selected literary works.

Evaluate selected works and support judgments with valid evidence.

Language

Describe the ways in which languages have evolved.

Summarize the advantages of diverse language backgrounds in a multicultural society.

Use Standard English.

Understand the grammatical systems of the English language.

Evaluate the use of language in print media.

Justify the need for global communication skills.

Source: Systemwide Objectives and Standards, Grades 7–8 (Chicago: Board of Education of the City of Chicago, 1990), pp.40–45; *Systemwide Objectives and Standards, Grades 9–12* (Chicago: Board of Education of the City of Chicago, 1990), pp. 20–22.
Note: The emphasis on language is worth noting; it is due to the large non-English-speaking student population.

Lesson plan objectives are more specific than unit plan objectives. Whereas lesson plan objectives may include outcomes and conditions for a specific instructional sequence, unit plan objectives do not. Whereas lesson plan objectives usually include specific methods, materials, or activities, unit plan objectives may or may not, and if they do they are more general. However, the two levels of objectives do have several characteristics in common. Such characteristics, as described by Taba, are listed in Table 6.4.

To illustrate the kind of specificity involved in the two levels of classroom objectives, consider the unit plan objective, stated as the concept, "To gain understanding of graphs." Lesson plan objectives for this unit might read:

1. To identify different types of graphs when using different types of data.
2. To identify important terms of a graph.
3. To discover practical application of graphs.

Some educators would feel that these lesson objectives are not specific enough, since they lack outcomes and mastery levels.[9]

They might rewrite the above instructional objectives in the following way.

1. All students will be required to identify which sets of data are best represented by a bar graph, line graph, and circle graph. Seventy-five percent of the class are expected to earn 75 percent or higher.
2. High-achieving students will be required to demonstrate understanding of five terms associated with graphs by (a) defining them and (b) supplying appropriate illustrations of each term. No more than one error will be permitted for moving to the next sequence of material.
3. All students will be required to read an annual corporate report and translate the narrative into at least three graphs to state the financial condition of the company: (a) income, (b) operating cost, and (c) assets and liabilities. A panel of three students must unanimously agree that the graphs are accurate.

METHODS AND MODELS FOR FORMULATING GOALS AND OBJECTIVES

In our discussion so far, we have been using several words—*aims, goals, objectives, standards, conditions, outcome*—that have subtle differences in meaning

9 James H. Block, Helen E. Efthim, and Robert B. Burns, *Building Effective Mastery Learning Schools* (New York: Longman, 1989); Robert E. Slavin, *Educational Psychology: Theory into Practice*, 3rd ed. (Englewood Cliffs, N.J.: Prentice-Hall, 1991).

Table 6.4   CHARACTERISTICS OF INSTRUCTIONAL OBJECTIVES AT THE CLASSROOM
LEVEL

1. A statement of objectives should indicate the expected behaviors and content or the context to which that behavior applies.

2. Complex objectives need to be stated logically and specifically so that there is little doubt as to the kind of behavior expected.

3. Objectives should be described so that it is clear what is required of learners to attain different behaviors.

4. Objectives are developmental, representing direction rather than terminal points.

5. Objectives should be realistic and should include only what can be implemented in the classroom.

6. The scope of objectives should be broad enough to encompass all types of outcomes for which the school or teacher is responsible.

Source: Adapted from Hilda Taba, *Curriculum Development: Theory and Practice* (New York: Harcourt Brace Jovanovich, 1962), pp. 200–205.

related to different levels of education (national to classroom) and different levels of abstractness. At one end of the continuum are the value-laden abstract aims of society; at the other end are concrete objectives describing a specific behavior. Most teachers tend to favor the middle of the continuum, where goals and objectives are observable but not necessarily clearly measurable, or, if they are measurable, they are stated without proficiency levels. They may use such terms as "list," "describe," and "identify" in writing their classroom objectives, but unless they are behaviorists or sensitive to preparing tests, they may not always incorporate precise outcomes and conditions of mastery.

Goals and Objectives: The Tyler Model

Ralph Tyler uses the term *purposes* when discussing what we call the goals of the school. He indicates that educators need to identify purposes (goals) by gathering data from three *sources*: learners, society, and subject specialists.[10]

Educators then filter their identified purposes (or goals) through two *screens*: philosophy and psychology. What results from the screening are more specific and agreed-upon objectives, or what he calls *instructional objectives* (Figure 6.1).

10 Ralph Tyler, *Basic Principles of Curriculum and Instruction* (Chicago: University of Chicago Press, 1949).

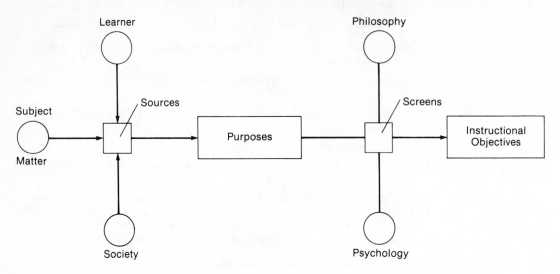

Figure 6.1 Tyler's method for formulating objectives.

Even though Tyler uses the term *instructional objectives,* he is not advocating narrow behavior objectives. For Tyler, objectives cannot be deduced from tiny bits of data or only from objective data. The formulation of objectives involves intelligence, insight, values, and attitudes of people involved in making decisions. Wise choices cannot be made without the most complete data available, but judgments must still prevail. We now turn to Tyler's three sources from which to select goals and two screens for refining goals into objectives.

1. *Studies of the learners.* The responsibility of the school is to help students meet their needs and develop to their fullest potential. Studies that focus on educational needs of students, that distinguish between what the schools do and what other social institutions do, that identify or distinguish gaps between students of the particular school (or school district) and students elsewhere, provide a basis for the selection of goals for the school program. It is possible to identify needs that are common to all students in school or to a certain group of students within a school or school district.

2. *Studies of contemporary life outside of school.* Educators must be aware of the tremendous impact of the increasingly rapid rate of change, the explosion of knowledge, and the increasing complexity of technology on our lives today and tomorrow. The trouble is that preparation for the future involves skills and knowledge that we may not fully understand today. As we analyze contemporary life, we might break it into manageable categories that are likely to result in implications for school goals.

Tyler emphasizes the need to study life at the community level in terms of needs, resources, and trends, but societal studies might also be extended to state, national, and international levels (which he seems to ignore). For example, in preparing students for the world of work, it is necessary to look at local conditions, but some students will move to other states or regions. Further, we live in a "global village," one that is strongly interconnected: state, national, and international conditions eventually affect conditions at the community level.

3. *Suggestions from subject specialists.* Every subject area has its professional association that lists goals and important knowledge in its field. What the subject specialists propose, however, is often too technical, too specialized, or inappropriate for goal setting that cuts across subject matter and is concerned with all students. The inadequacy of many of these lists for schools grows out of their misplaced emphasis. What schools need to ask is not what a specialist in a particular field needs to learn, but, according to Tyler, what the subject can contribute to the general education of young people who are not going to be specialists in the field.

As an example, in science, as a goal for all students in all schools we would not be as concerned with preparing scientists as with producing a scientifically literate citizenry that can understand and use science and technology. In the field of English literature, the idea is not to produce literary scholars, but rather to emphasize how reading and learning from literature can expand the ideas and experiences of young people, regardless of educational level, and to develop reading interests and habits that are satisfying and significant to students in general.

4. *The use of philosophy.* Once purposes have been identified from studies of the learner, society, and subject areas, the educator must review and refine them in light of philosophy and psychology, or as Tyler says, filter them through two screens. The first screen is *philosophy.* As a school tries to outline its educational program, "the educational and social philosophy of the school can serve as the first screen. The original list of [goals] can be culled by identifying those that stand high in terms of values stated or implied in the school's philosophy."[11]

For Tyler, goals should concern important values, be consistent with one another, and be clearly stated. We need not focus on unimportant goals or goals that create confusion or contradictory behavior. We should be aware of the values and way of life we are trying to preserve and what aspects of society we wish to improve. Goals should be consistent with the democratic values and ideals of our society, in all aspects of living, and not just politics. Education is for democracy, and this overriding philosophy must be reflected in our school goals.

5. *The use of psychology.* Goals must be in conformity with the psychology of learning, that is, the theories, concepts, and specific findings we accept. A psychology of learning includes a unified formulation of the processes in-

11 Ibid., p. 34.

Research indicates that students learn more when their academic subjects are integrated with real-life experiences.

volved, such as how learning takes place, under what conditions, and what mechanisms and variables operate. In formulating goals, teachers need to consider how appropriate they are in terms of what is known about learning—whether they can be achieved, how they can be achieved, and what the cost and time will be. Goals that conflict with an acceptable psychological viewpoint about learning should be rejected. Of course, there is more than one psychological viewpoint, and many theories, concepts, and even data are contradictory. However, even opposing theories of learning can agree on many of the same goals.

Moving beyond Tyler, when we formulate our goals, we might ask the following questions:

To what extent should our schools emphasize the needs of society and the needs of the individual?

Should schools emphasize excellence or equality?

Should we put equal emphasis on academic, vocational, and general education?

Should we put equal emphasis on cognitive learning or humanistic learning?

Which is more important—national commitment or a higher morality?

Should we educate students to their own ability level (and for some, that might mean an eighth-grade education) or should we push students beyond their aptitude and achievement level?

How should we apportion money to be spent on talented and gifted students, average students, and handicapped students?

How do we compare the payoff to society and the obligations of society in educating different student populations?

These questions are so tough and complicated that not only do educators disagree about them, but wars have been fought over them. Indeed, the way we answer these questions both reflects and determines the kind of people we are. Most people in this country readily say they believe in democracy, but how they answer these questions determines what democracy means and how it affects and controls our lives. Trying to resolve these questions, at least in this country, ideally involves a balancing act and sometimes the question as to whether our moral and legal restraints overrule our political and economic biases and whether needs of the group can be placed in perspective with the rights of the individual.

Taxonomy of Educational Objectives

Another way of formulating instructional objectives is to categorize the desired behaviors and outcomes into a system analogous to classification of books in a library, chemical elements in a periodic table, or divisions of the animal kingdom. Through this system, known as **taxonomy**, standards for classifying objectives have been established, and educators are able to be more precise in their language. The taxonomy is rooted in Tyler's ideas that all words in a scientific system should be defined in terms of observable events and that educational objectives should be defined operationally in terms of performances or outcomes. This method of formulating objectives can be used for writing objectives at the program and course level. By adding specific content, the objectives can be used at the classroom level, including the lesson plan level.

The educational taxonomy calls for the classification of learning into three domains: cognitive, affective, and psychomotor. The *Taxonomy of Educational*

Objectives, Handbook I: Cognitive Domain was developed by a committee of 36 researchers from various universities headed by Benjamin Bloom.[12]

The **cognitive domain** includes objectives that are related to recall or recognition of knowledge and the development of higher intellectual skills and abilities. The *Taxonomy of Educational Objectives, Handbook II: Affective Domain* was written by David Krathwohl and associates. The **affective domain** is concerned with aims and objectives related to interests, attitudes, and feelings.[13]

The description of the **psychomotor domain**, dealing with manipulative and motor skills, was never completed by the original group of researchers. A classification of psychomotor objectives by Anita Harlow closely resembles the intent of the original group.[14]

The fact that it was published by the same company that published the original two taxonomies adds to the validity of this version of the psychomotor domain. Below is a brief listing of the types of objectives of the three domains of learning.

Cognitive Domain

1. *Knowledge.* This level includes objectives related to (a) knowledge of specifics, such as terminology and facts; (b) knowledge of ways and means of dealing with specifics, such as conventions, trends and sequences, classifications and categories, criteria, and methodologies; and (c) knowledge of universals and abstractions, such as principles, generations, theories, and structures. *Example*: To identify the capital of France.

2. *Comprehension.* Objectives at this level relate to (a) translation, (b) interpretation, and (c) extrapolation of materials. *Example*: To interpret a table showing the population density of the world.

3. *Application.* Objectives relate to the use of abstractions in particular situations. *Example*: To predict the probable effect of a change in temperature on a chemical.

4. *Analysis.* Objectives relate to breaking a whole into parts and distinguishing (a) elements, (b) relationships, and (c) organizational principles. *Example*: To deduce facts from a hypothesis.

5. *Synthesis.* Objectives relate to putting parts together in a new form such as (a) a unique communication, (b) a plan of operation, and (c) a set of abstract relations. *Example*: To produce an original piece of art.

6. *Evaluation.* This is the highest level of complexity and includes objectives that relate to judging of (a) internal evidence or logical consis-

---

12 Benjamin S. Bloom et al., ed., *Taxonomy of Educational Objectives, Handbook I: Cognitive Domain* (New York: McKay, 1956).

13 David R. Krathwohl, Benjamin S. Bloom, and Bertram Masia, ed., *Taxonomy of Educational Objectives, Handbook II: Affective Domain* (New York: McKay, 1964).

14 Anita J. Harlow, *Taxonomy of the Psychomotor Domain: A Guide for Developing Behavioral Objectives* (New York: McKay, 1972).

tency and (b) external evidence or consistency with facts developed elsewhere. *Example*: To recognize fallacies in an argument.

Affective Domain

1. *Receiving.* These objectives are indicative of the learner's sensitivity to the existence of stimuli and include (a) awareness, (b) willingness to receive, and (c) selective attention. *Example*: To identify musical instruments by their sound.
2. *Responding.* This includes active attention to stimuli such as (a) acquiescence, (b) willing responses, and (c) feelings of satisfaction. *Example*: To contribute to group discussions by asking questions.
3. *Valuing.* This includes objectives regarding beliefs and evaluations in the form of (a) acceptance, (b) preference, and (c) commitment. *Example*: To argue over an issue involving health care.
4. *Organization.* This level involves (a) conceptualization of values and (b) organization of a value system. *Example*: to organize a meeting concerning a neighborhood's housing integration plan.
5. *Characterization.* This is the level of greatest complexity and includes behavior related to (a) a generalized set of values and (b) a characterization or philosophy of life. *Example*: To demonstrate in front of a government building in behalf of a cause or idea.

Psychomotor Domain

1. *Reflex movements.* Objectives relate to (a) segmental reflexes (involving one spinal segment) and (b) intersegmental reflexes (involving more than one spinal segment). *Example*: To contract a muscle.
2. *Fundamental movements.* Objectives relate to (a) walking, (b) running, (c) jumping, (d) pushing, (e) pulling, and (f) manipulating. *Example*: To run a 100–yard dash.
3. *Perceptual abilities.* Objectives relate to (a) kinesthetic, (b) visual, (c) auditory, (d) tactile, and (e) coordination abilities. *Example*: To distinguish distant and close sounds.
4. *Physical abilities.* Objectives relate to (a) endurance, (b) strength, (c) flexibility, (d) agility, (e) reaction-response time, and (f) dexterity. *Example*: To do twenty sit-ups.
5. *Skilled movements.* Objectives relate to (a) games, (b) sports, (c) dances, and (d) the arts. *Example*: To dance the basic steps of the waltz.
6. *Nondiscursive communication.* Objectives relate to expressive movement through (a) posture, (b) gestures, (c) facial expressions, and (d) creative movements. *Example*: to act a part in a play.

One point needs to be made about the cognitive domain. While Bloom acknowledges that the teaching of knowledge is essential, he asserts that "many teachers . . . prize knowledge . . . because of the simplicity with which it can be taught or learned."[15] Quite frequently we stop at the knowledge category, because it is easy to teach and test. Thus we ask our students: "What are three products of Brazil? What is the chemical formula for water?" Also, we tend to equate knowledge with intelligence. This is illustrated by our misconception that when someone can recall trivia information on a television quiz show, we often consider the person to be intelligent. It is not how much knowledge an individual possesses, but what the individual can do with the knowledge that characterizes intelligence.

Once we study the taxonomy, it becomes apparent that most teaching and testing we have been exposed to as students stressed knowledge—knowledge of facts, terms, conventions, classifications, categories, methods, and principles. As a teacher, you should not make the same mistake; rather you should advance into other cognitive dimensions that use knowledge for advanced teaching and learning.

Guidelines for Applying the Taxonomy of Educational Objectives

---

The categories of the three taxonomies describe levels of complexity from simple to more advanced. Each level is built upon and assumes acquisition of skills of the previous level. One must have knowledge of facts, for example, before one can comprehend material. The taxonomy as a whole is a useful source for developing educational objectives and for categorizing and grouping existing sets of objectives. Perhaps the greatest difficulty is deciding between adjacent categories, particularly if the objectives have not been clearly stated. To avoid becoming frustrated while categorizing objectives into appropriate categories, classroom teachers are advised to work in groups and share opinions. By studying and using the taxonomy, they may eventually appreciate it as a valuable tool for implementing objectives and formulating test items.

After you have decided you want to use the taxonomy and after you have determined what you want your students to learn, you might systematically review the major classifications of the various domains to make sure you are familiar with each classification. You might then ask the following questions when formulating objectives in the cognitive domain.

1. *Knowledge.* What specific facts do you want the students to learn? What trends and sequences should they know? What classifications,

---

15 Bloom, *Taxonomy of Educational Objectives: Handbook 1,* p. 34.

categories, and methods are important for them to learn? What general principles and theories should they learn?

2. *Comprehension.* What types of translation will students need to perform? What types of interpretation? What types of extrapolation?
3. *Application.* What will students be required to perform or do to show they can use the information in practical situations?
4. *Analysis.* What kinds of elements should students be able to analyze? What relationships? What organizational principles?
5. *Synthesis.* What kinds of communication should students be able to synthesize? What kinds of operation? What kinds of abstraction?
6. *Evaluation.* What kinds of evaluation should students be able to perform? Can they use internal evidence? Can they use external evidence?

When asking these questions and when formulating instructional objectives according to the taxonomy, the teacher should keep in mind that the classifications represent a hierarchy. Before students can deal with analysis, they must be able to function at the three previous levels, that is, knowledge, comprehension, and application. The same kinds of questions should be asked when writing objectives in the affective and psychomotor domains. The teacher needs to look at each level within the domain and ask what students are to be expected to achieve.

As an aid in writing and categorizing objectives, a list of key infinitives and direct objects for the cognitive, affective, and psychomotor domains are shown in Tips for Teachers 6.1, 6.2, and 6.3. In all of these examples, no specific content is described so as to keep them applicable to all subjects.

General Objective and Specific Learning Outcomes: The Gronlund-Linn Method

Gronlund and Linn have developed a flexible way of formulating instructional objectives whereby the teacher moves from a general objective to a series of specific learning outcomes, each related to the general objective. Their **general objectives** coincide with program (subject and grade) and course level objectives, and their **specific learning outcomes** coincide with unit plan and lesson plan objectives. They recommend that teachers start with general objectives because learning is too complex to be described in terms of specific behaviors or specific outcomes and because higher levels of thinking cannot be achieved by one specific behavior or outcome. To illustrate the difference between general objectives and specific learning outcomes, Gronlund and Link have prepared a list of general objectives that can be used for almost any grade, subject, or course.

1. Knows basic terminology
2. Understands concepts and principles
3. Applies principles to new situations
4. Interprets charts and graphs

Tips for Teachers 6.1

Key Words for the Taxonomy of Educational Objectives: Cognitive Domain

Taxonomy classification	Examples of infinitives	Examples of direct objects
1.0 Knowledge		
1.1 Knowledge of specifics	To define, to distinguish, to acquire, to identify, to recall, to recognize	Vocabulary terms, terminology, meaning(s), definitions, referents, elements, facts, factual information, (sources), (names), (dates), (events), (persons), (places), (time periods), properties, examples, phenomena
1.2 Knowledge of ways and means of dealing with specifics	To acquire, to identify, to recall, to recognize	Forms, conventions, uses, usage, rules, ways, devices, symbols, representations, styles, formats, actions, processes, movements, continuity, developments, trends, sequences, causes, relationships, forces, influences, areas, types, features, classes, sets, divisions, arrangements, classifications, categories, criteria, basics, elements, methods, techniques, approaches, uses, procedures, treatments
1.3 Knowledge of universals and abstractions in a field	To acquire, to identify, to recall, to recognize	Principles, generalizations, propositions, fundamentals, laws, principal elements, implications, theories, bases, interrelations, structures, organizations, formulations
2.0 Comprehension		
2.1 Translation	To translate, to transform, to give in own words, to illustrate, to prepare, to read, to represent, to change, to rephrase, to restate	Meanings, samples, definitions, abstractions, representations, words, phrases
2.2 Interpretation	To interpret, to reorder, to rearrange, to differentiate, to distinguish, to make, to draw, to explain, to demonstrate	Relevancies, relationships, essentials, aspects, new views, qualifications, conclusions, methods, theories, abstractions
2.3 Extrapolation	To estimate, to infer, to conclude, to predict, to differentiate, to determine, to extend, to interpolate	Consequences, implications, conclusions, factors, ramifications, meanings, corollaries, effects, probabilities

continues

Taxonomy classification	Examples of infinitives	Examples of direct objects
3.0 Application	To apply, to generalize, to relate, to choose, to develop, to organize, to use, to employ, to transfer, to restructure, to classify	Principals, laws, conclusions, effects, methods, theories, abstractions, situations, generalizations, processes, phenomena, procedures
4.0 Analysis		
4.1 Analysis of elements	To distinguish, to detect, to identify, to classify, to discriminate, to recognize, to categorize	Elements, hypotheses, conclusions, assumptions, statements of fact, statements of intent, arguments, particulars
4.2 Analysis of relationships	To analyze, to contrast, to compare, to distinguish, to deduce	Relationships, interrelations, relevance, relevancies, themes, evidence, fallacies, arguments, cause-effects, consistency, consistencies, parts, ideas, assumptions
4.3 Analysis of organizational principles	To analyze, to distinguish, to detect, to deduce	Forms, patterns, purposes, points of view, techniques, biases, structures, themes, arrangements, organizations
5.0 Synthesis		
5.1 Production of a unique communication	To write, to tell, to relate, to produce, to constitute, to transmit, to originate, to modify, to document	Structures, patterns, products, performances, designs, works, communications, efforts, specifics, compositions
5.2 Production of a plan or proposed set of operations	To propose, to plan, to produce, to design, to modify, to specify	Plans, objectives, specifications, schematics, operations, ways, solutions, means
5.3 Derivation of a set of abstract relations	To produce, to derive, to develop, to combine, to organize, to synthesize, to classify, to deduce, to formulate, to modify	Phenomena, taxonomies, concepts, schemes, theories, relationships, abstractions, generalizations, hypotheses, perceptions, ways, discoveries
6.0 Evaluation		
6.1 Judgments in terms of internal evidence	To judge, to argue, to validate, to assess, to decide	Accuracies, consistencies, fallacies, reliability, flaws, errors, precision, exactness
6.2 Judgments in terms of external criteria	To judge, to argue, to consider, to compare, to contrast, to standardize, to appraise	Ends, means, efficiency, economies, utility, alternatives, courses of action, standards, theories, generalizations

Source: Newton S. Metfessel, William B. Michael, and Donald A. Kirsner, " Instrumentation of Bloom's and Krathwohl's Taxonomies for the Writing of Educational Objectives," *Psychology in the Schools* (July 1969), pp. 227–231.

Tips for Teachers 6.2

Key Words for the Taxonomy of Educational Objectives: Affective Domain

Taxonomy classification	Examples of infinitives	Examples of direct objects
1.0 Receiving		
1.1 Awareness	To differentiate, to separate, to set apart, to share	Sights, sounds, events, designs, arrangements
1.2 Willingness to receive	To accumulate, to select, to combine, to accept	Models, examples, shapes, sizes, meters, cadences
1.3 Controlled or selected attention	To select, to posturally respond to, to listen for, to control	Alternatives, answers, rhythms, nuances
2.0 Responding		
2.1 Acquiescence in responding	To comply with, to follow, to commend, to approve	Directions, instructions, laws, policies, demonstrations
2.2 Willingness to respond	To volunteer, to discuss, to practice, to play	Instruments, games, dramatic works, charades, burlesques
2.3 Satisfaction in responding	To applaud, to acclaim. to spend leisure time in, to augment	Speeches, plays, presentations, writings
3.0 Valuing		
3.1 Acceptance of a value	To increase measured proficiency in, to increase numbers of, to relinquish, to specify	Group memberships, artistic productions, musical productions, personal friendships
3.2 Preference for a value	To assist, to subsidize, to help, to support	Artists, projects, viewpoints, arguments
3.3 Commitment	To deny, to protest, to debate, to argue	Deceptions, irrelevancies, abdications, irrationalities
4.0 Organization		
4.1 Conceptualization of a value	To discuss, to theorize on, to abstract, to compare	Parameters, codes, standards, goals
4.2 Organization of a value system	To balance, to organize, to define, to formulate	Systems, approaches, criteria, limits
5.0 Characterization by value or value concept		
5.1 Generalized set	To revise, to change, to complete, to require	Plans, behaviors, methods, efforts
5.2 Characterization	To be rated high by peers in, to be rated high by superiors in, to be rated high by subordinates in and to avoid, to manage, to resolve, to resist	Humanitarianism, ethics, integrity, maturity extravagances, excesses, conflicts, exorbitancy/exorbitancies

Source: Newton S. Metfessel, William B. Michael, and Donald A. Kirsner, "Instrumentation of Bloom's and Krathwohl's Taxonomies for the Writing of Educational Objectives," *Psychology in the Schools* (July 1969), pp. 227–231.

Tips for Teachers 6.3

Key Words for the Taxonomy of Educational Objectives: Psychomotor Domain

Taxonomy classification	Examples of infinitives	Examples of direct objects
1.0 Reflex movements	To flex, to stretch, to straighten, to extend, to inhibit, to lengthen, to shorten, to tense, to stiffen, to relax	Muscles
2.0 Fundamental movements	To crawl, to creep, to slide, to walk, to run, to jump, to grasp, to reach, to tighten, to support, to handle	Changes location, moves in space while remaining in one place, moves extremities in coordinated fashion
3.0 Perceptual abilities	To catch, to bounce, to eat, to write, to balance, to bend, to draw from memory, to distinguish by touching, to explore	Discriminates visually, discriminates auditory, discriminates kinesthetically, discriminates tactually, coordinates two or more perceptual abilities
4.0 Physical abilities	To endure, to improve, to increase, to stop, to start, to move precisely, to touch, to bend	Exerts tension, moves quickly, stops immediately, endures fatigue
5.0 Skilled movements	To waltz, to type, to play the piano, to plane, to file, to skate, to juggle, to paint, to dive, to fence, to golf, to change	Changes or modifies basic body movement patterns, uses a tool or implement in adaptive or skilled manner
6.0 Nondiscursive communication	To gesture, to stand, to sit, to express facially, to dance skillfully, to perform skillfully, to paint skillfully, to play skillfully	Moves expressively, moves interpretatively, communicates emotions, communicates aesthetically, expresses joy

Source: Adapted from Anita J. Harlow, *Taxonomy of the Psychomotor Domain: A Guide for Developing Behavioral Objectives* (New York: McKay, 1972).

---

5. Demonstrates skill in critical thinking
6. Writes a well-organized theme
7. Appreciates poetry, art, literature, dance, etc.
8. Demonstrates scientific attitude
9. Evaluates the adequacy of an experiment.[16]

---

16 Norman E. Gronlund and Robert L. Linn, *Measurement and Evaluation in Teaching*, 6th ed. (New York: Macmillan, 1990), pp. 41–42.

Note that the behavior (verb) in each statement is general enough to permit a host of specific learning outcomes. Such outcomes provide useful guides for teachers and students. There may be six or seven related specific outcomes for each general objective to clarify what students will do to demonstrate achievement of the general objective.

Guidelines for Applying Gronlund and Linn's Objectives

The two examples below illustrate how we move from general objectives (roman numbered) to a series of related, specific learning outcomes (arabic numbered).

I. Understands the meaning of terms
   1. Defines the terms in own words
   2. Identifies the meaning of a term in context
   3. Differentiates between proper and improper usage of a term
   4. Distinguishes between two similar terms on the basis of meaning
   5. Writes an original sentence using the term
II. Demonstrates skill in critical thinking
   1. Distinguishes between fact and opinion
   2. Distinguishes between relevant and irrelevant information
   3. Identifies fallacious reasoning in written material
   4. Identifies the limitations of given data
   5. Formulates valid conclusions from given data
   6. Identifies the assumptions underlying conclusions.[17]

The learning outcomes listed above are good examples of content-free objectives that can fit many different grade levels, subjects and courses. Because Gronlund and Linn feel it is important to keep specific learning outcomes content-free, they are not really applicable to the lesson plan level, which should be content-oriented.

The teacher can add content to objectives. For example, an objective might be to identify three causes of World War I or to differentiate between a triangle and a rectangle. Gronlund and Linn maintain that once a teacher identifies content, there is a risk of writing too many objectives for each general objective or topic. But instead of identifying the causes of World War I, as most teachers would do, they would say the objective is to identify important historical causes and events. Instead of differentiating between a triangle and a rectangle, the objective, for them, is to differentiate between geometric shapes. Their content-free specific outcomes can be used up to the unit plan level that focuses on concepts; only by including content can they be used at the lesson plan level.

---

17 Ibid., p. 43.

Table 6.5 STEPS FOR STATING GENERAL OBJECTIVES AND SPECIFIC LEARNING
OUTCOMES

Stating general instructional objectives

1. State each general objective as an intended learning outcome (i.e., pupils' terminal performance).

2. Begin each general objective with a verb (e.g., knows, applies, interprets). Omit "The pupil should be able to . . . "

3. State each general objective to include only one general learning outcome (e.g., not "Knows and understands").

4. State each general objective at the proper level of generality (e.g., it should encompass a readily definable domain of responses). Eight to twelve general unit objectives will usually suffice.

5. Keep each general objective sufficiently free of course content so that it can be used with various units of study.

6. State each general objective so that there is minimum overlap with other objectives.

Stating specific learning outcomes

1. List beneath each general instructional objective a representative sample of specific learning outcomes that describes the terminal performance pupils are expected to demonstrate.

2. Begin each specific learning outcome with an action verb that specifies observable performance (e.g., identifies, describes). Check that each specific learning outcome is relevant to the general objective it describes.

3. Include a sufficient number of specific learning outcomes to describe adequately the performance of pupils who have attained the objective.

4. Keep the specific learning outcomes sufficiently free of course content so that the list can be used with various units of study.

5. Consult reference materials for the specific components of those complex outcomes that are difficult to define (e.g., critical thinking, scientific attitude, creativity).

6. Add a third level of specificity to the list of outcomes, if needed.

Source: Norman E. Gronlund, *Measurement and Evaluation in Teaching*, 5th ed. (New York: Macmillan, 1985), p. 46.

Table 6.5 highlights Gronlund and Linn's steps for stating instructional objectives and can serve as a guide if you wish to adopt their method.

Specific Objectives: The Mager Method

Robert Mager is more precise in his approach to formulating instructional objectives. His objectives have three components.

1. *Behavior,* or performance, which describes what the learner is expected to do. *Example*: to know, to use, to identify.

A teacher's willingness to help students before or after class pays big dividends in achieving the desired outcomes of the lesson.

2. *Condition*, which describes under what circumstances or conditions the performance is to occur. *Example*: Given five sentences with adjectives . . ., Based on the statement . . .
3. *Proficiency level*, or criterion, which states an acceptable standard, competency, or achievement level. *Example*: 80 percent, 9 out of 10, judged correctly by the teacher.[18]

Mager is controversial in his approach to writing instructional objectives, and therefore it might be worthwhile to state some of the arguments for and against his approach. Some educators (including Tyler and Gronlund) claim that Mager's method produces an unmanageable number of objectives, leads to trivia, and wastes time. They also contend that the approach leads to teaching that focuses on low levels of cognitive and psychomotor objectives, emphasizes learning of specific bits of information, and does not foster comprehension and whole learning.[19]

---

18 Robert F. Mager, *Preparing Instructional Objectives*, rev. ed. (Belmont, Calif.: Fearon, 1984). The examples of each component are derived from the author.

19 Allan C. Ornstein and Francis P. Hunkins, *Curriculum: Foundations, Principles, and Issues* (Englewood Cliffs, N.J.: Prentice-Hall, 1988); Robert M. W. Travers, *Essentials of Learning*, 5th ed. (New York: Macmillan, 1982); and Bruce W. Tuckman, *Conducting Educational Research*, 3rd ed. (San Diego: Harcourt Brace Jovanovich, 1987).

Mager and other educators argue that the approach clarifies what teachers intend, what students are expected to do, and what to test to show evidence of learning.[20]

It provides a structured method for arranging sequences of skills, tasks, or content, provides a guide for determining instructional methods and materials, and adds precision for constructing tests. Most teachers prefer a less specific approach, corresponding more to the methods of Bloom or Gronlund.

Guidelines for Applying Mager's Objectives

Using Mager's approach, a teacher could write hundreds of objectives for each unit, certainly for each course. If we decide on his approach, we would first ask ourselves to identify or describe what the learner will be *doing*. Next we would identify or describe the *conditions* under which the behavior is to occur. Finally, we would state the *performance* criteria or achievement level we expect the learner to meet.

Here are some examples. The behavior, condition, and proficiency levels are identified.

1. *Given six primary colors, students will be able to identify five.* The behavior is to identify, the condition is given six primary colors, and the proficiency level is five out of six.
2. *Based on the reading passage in Chapter 7, students will compare the writing styles of Ernest Hemingway and John Steinbeck. Performance will be judged pass-fail by the teacher.* The behavior is to compare, the condition is after reading the passage in Chapter 7, and the proficiency level is to pass, a subjective judgment by the teacher.
3. *From the required list of 10 words, students will correctly spell 9 of them.* The behavior is to spell, the condition is the required list of words, and the proficiency level is 90 percent (9 out of 10).
4. *From the foul line, students will make 6 out of 10 baskets.* The behavior is to throw a basketball, the condition is from the foul line, and the proficiency level is 60 percent (6 out of 10).
5. *The student will be able to complete a 100–item multiple-choice examination on the topic of pollution, with 80 items answered correctly within 60 minutes.* The behavior is to complete an exam, the condition is 60 minutes, and the proficiency level is 80 percent (80 out of 100).

---

20 Robert J. Kibler, Larry L. Baker, and David T. Miles, *Behavioral Objectives and Instruction*, 2nd ed. (Boston: Allyn & Bacon, 1981); W. James Popham, *Criterion-Referenced Measurement* (Englewood Cliffs, N.J.: Prentice-Hall, 1978); and Paul D. Plowman, *Behavioral Objectives* (Chicago: Science Research Associates, 1971).

Mager lists eight words or phrases that he considers "fuzzy" and to be avoided in formulating objectives: to know, to understand, to appreciate, to grasp the significance of, to enjoy, to believe, to have faith in, and to internalize. He lists nine words or phrases that are open to fewer interpretations and are more appropriate to use: to write, to recite, to identify, to sort, to solve, to construct, to build, to compare, and to contrast.[21]

Performance Objectives: The Gagné Method

Robert Gagné is just as precise as Mager in his formulation of objectives. He contends that there are five basic types of **learned capabilities** that can be observed and measured in terms of exhibited performances. The five capabilities overlap the three domains of the taxonomy of educational objectives. (The first three capabilities mainly fall within the cognitive domain.)

1. *Intellectual skill.* The capability first to use symbols for learning how to read, write, and use numbers and later to distinguish, combine, tabulate, classify, analyze, and quantify objects, events, and other symbols. Intellectual skill is divided into five subcategories: (1) discrimination, (2) concrete concept, (3) defined concept, (4) rule, and (5) higher-order rule (problem solving).
2. *Cognitive strategy.* This involves tasks related to problem solving and independent learning. It involves searching for applicable information and values to arrive at solutions to problems and to understand how a solution applies to other instances. The learner has internalized various techniques to remember the main points of a lecture or text— search for relationships, analyze problems, and determine approaches to solving problems.
3. *Information.* The capability to state a fact or a set of events by using oral speech, written language, or pictorial or symbolic representation. The learner is able to retrieve, restate, and recount ideas and events.
4. *Motor skills.* The capability to execute simple to complex motor acts and movements. Complex acts, such as playing golf or driving an automobile, involve organized and comprehensive movements.
5. *Attitude.* What influences the learner's response to situations and choice of actions. It is a mental state that affects performance rather than a specific performance, unlike the other learned capabilities.[22]

The mental "operation" involved in each of the five capabilities is different. Writes Gagné, "Learning intellectual skills requires a different design of instructional events from those required for learning verbal information or from

---

21 Mager, *Preparing Instructional Objectives.*

22 Robert M. Gagné, *The Conditions of Learning,* 4th ed. (New York: Holt, Rinehart & Winston, 1985).

those required for learning motor skills, and so on."[23] The five categories underlie different types of performance and outcomes and are assessed differently. According to Gagné, the verb in the sentence describes performance and gives full meaning to the objective. For example, a student engaging in an *intellectual skill*, the first category, usually discriminates, identifies, classifies, or demonstrates. It doesn't matter much whether he or she is discriminating or identifying French sounds of "u" and "ou" or cities on the map. It is the verb that tells us what is happening. Similarly, in the last category, *attitude*, it is what the learner chooses to do or how he or she responds that illustrates attitude; and any number of activities can be used to represent learning capability or level of sophistication—such as reading a book, listening to music, or painting a landscape.

For Gagné, the ultimate aim of school is to equip learners with learning capabilities whereby they can apply what they learn in class to situations outside of class. In other words, learners learn how to learn on their own and to apply what they learn to everyday problems. Gagné implies that intellectual skill and cognitive strategy are more important learned capabilities than the others, although he never states there is a hierarchy.

Task Analysis and Enabling Objectives

As part of his system of formulating objectives, Gagné introduces the concept of **task analysis**, which is a common procedure used in business, industry, and the military. A task is broken down into the logical sequence of steps necessary to achieve an intended outcome. By analyzing a learning task into skills required, a teacher can pinpoint problem areas, make appropriate corrections, and make sure students have the necessary skills and subskills to complete the task. For example, an assignment to report on information found in the library involves the following separate skills:

1. Knowing how to look up words alphabetically
2. Using the card catalog system
3. Using tables of contents and indexes
4. Understanding the concepts of the topic
5. Reading and comprehending material
6. Getting the main idea from material
7. Distinguishing facts and opinions
8. Drawing conclusions or summarizing
9. Organizing or outlining a report
10. Knowing and applying basic rules of spelling, punctuation, and usage.[24]

---

23 Ibid., p. 245.

24 See Anita E. Woolfolk and Lorraine McCune-Nicolich, *Educational Psychology for Teachers*, 4th ed. (Englewood Cliffs, N.J.: Prentice-Hall, 1990).

Of course, all verbal tasks can be broken down into subtasks all the way back to letter recognition. The point is that the teacher must be aware of the tasks involved in learning a new skill or concept and must be certain that students know what they need to know to succeed. This may mean reviewing certain tasks or even teaching something new that students should have learned years earlier. Task analysis recognizes the importance of what the learner brings to a learning situation, or what Glaser calls the "entering behavior" of the learner.[25] And Gagné says, "Previously learned capabilities provide necessary support for new learning, regardless of what is being learned. For example, cognitive strategies of one kind or another must be brought to bear upon [various] phases of the learning process."[26] Intellectual skills learned many years ago can support new learning situations, and previously learned motor skills become refined and part of new advanced skills, which may lead in turn to a set of still more advanced motor skills.

Gagné calls the prerequisites for learning **enabling objectives**. Some prerequisites make sense as separate tasks, each of which the learner might perform by itself. Other prerequisites function only to facilitate the objective. For example, in learning to add double-digit numbers, one of the enabling objectives is to add single-digit numbers. This is by itself a useful task to be learned. In contrast, the enabling objective of carrying numbers to the second column is useful only for the operation of adding double- (or triple-, etc.) digit numbers and is not useful for other purposes.

Guidelines for Applying Gagné's Objectives

According to Gagné, learning can be enhanced by analyzing an objective into its enabling objectives. These tasks may have been learned a few minutes or long ago; nevertheless, at the time the new learning takes place, they must be retrieved by the learner.

Following are some examples of task analysis.

I. To solve subtraction problems
   1. To arrange sets of numbers to be subtracted
   2. To add numbers
   3. To identify plus and minus signs
   4. To recognize the meaning of numbers
   5. To write numbers

25 Robert Glaser, "Trends and Research Questions in Psychological Research on Learning and Schooling," *Educational Researcher* (November 1979), pp. 6–13.

26 Gagné, *The Conditions of Learning*, p. 268.

II. To evaluate statements made by government officials concerning the economy
1. To know economic principles and relationships
2. To know national and international events
3. To distinguish between evidence and opinion
4. To identify limitations of evidence
5. To draw conclusions from evidence
6. To know how to read with comprehension

III. To identify musical instruments
1. To identify an instrument by its appearance
2. To differentiate between instruments of an orchestra and band when pictures of each are displayed
3. To identify an instrument by its sound
4. To differentiate between instruments of an orchestra and band when each is played on a recording
5. To state the differences between the instruments of an orchestra and of a band

IV. To shoot a bow with accuracy
1. To estimate the balance point of a bow
2. To gauge string pressure
3. To place the arrow in the bow correctly
4. To hold the arrow and the bow correctly
5. To achieve balance when arching the bow
6. To aim, estimating distance and required angle of arrow flight

Task analysis is appropriate for many behavioral learning theories. It appears in the step-by-step frames of programmed instruction and computer-assisted instruction and in various mastery learning and adaptive learning programs that present subskills or tasks leading to the acquisition of more complex skills or tasks. For many experienced teachers it is second nature, and they do it as part of the teaching process without using the terms "task analysis" and "enabling objectives." On the other hand, task analysis is not suited for whole to part thinkers, or for those who appreciate the "big picture" or who are abstract, intuitive, or creative.

DEVELOPING GOALS AND OBJECTIVES

Writing goals and objectives for a school district, school, program, or course usually falls to a school committee. Individual classroom teachers are usually responsible for developing unit plans or lesson plans. If you are a member of a district or school committee, it is advisable to consult the following sources to be sure that your list corresponds to prescribed educational goals and objectives.

1. Federal and state mandates and legislation

2. National and state commission reports that identify aims and goals
3. Professional association reports that identify goals and objectives
4. Community concerns voiced by state and local business organizations and pressure groups
5. Parental concerns expressed in parental advisory committees, parent-teacher associations, and individual letters from parents
6. Professional literature on theories of learning and child development
7. Professional literature on student needs, assessments, and career choices
8. Books and reports on college and employee requirements
9. Teacher reports and comments
10. Subject specialist reports and comments
11. Evaluation reports about school programs and curriculum
12. Reports and studies about trends in society.[27]

It is also advisable to consult already published lists of goals and objectives. Most deal with the cognitive domain; only a few concern the affective and psychomotor domains. Lists can be obtained from government agencies (state departments of education and regional educational agencies), professional agencies (Association of Supervision and Curriculum Development, Phi Delta Kappa), publishing companies, universities, and school districts. Government and school district lists can be obtained free of charge; professional agencies may charge a nominal fee.

Several techniques are available for assigning priorities to goals and objectives. These techniques can assist both committee members formulating school goals or program and course objectives and teachers formulating unit plan and lesson plan objectives. A summary of these methods, with advantages, disadvantages, and recommendations, is given in Table 6.6. It should be noted that the first three methods involve sampling from a pool of objectives, while the remaining two use ratings based on people's opinions. Rating techniques have many advantages, but they are more complex and difficult to develop. They should be used for establishing priorities of goals or objectives, however, because of their greater objectivity.

In formulating classroom-level objectives—either unit or lesson plans—eight general rules should be kept in mind.

1. They should be related to the developmental needs and tasks of the learners, which in turn are related to the age and experiences of the students.

---

27 Lynn L. Morris and Carol T. Fitz-Gibbon, *How to Deal with Goals and Objectives* (Beverly Hills, Calif.: Sage, 1978); Allan C. Ornstein, "The National Reports on Education: Implications for Directions and Aims," *Kappa Delta Pi Record* (Winter 1985), pp. 58–64.

2. They should be an outgrowth of diagnostic data (achievement, aptitude, personality, behavioral tests) and student records.
3. They should be consistent with professional and subject specialist opinions.
4. They should be consistent with teaching and learning theories and procedures.
5. They should build on student interests and strengths, not on adult interests and student weaknesses.
6. They should foster higher-order thinking skills, rather than focus on busywork.
7. They should be based on subject- and grade-level objectives.
8. They should be flexible enough to keep pace with changing educational and social situations.

Theoretically sound and practical recommendations concerning the content and form of objectives are given in Table 6.7.

Finally, no matter how carefully you plan your objectives, there are likely to be some unintended outcomes of instruction. These outcomes may be desirable or undesirable, and most are likely to fall into the affective domain of attitudes, feelings, and motivation about learning. For example, as a result of a language arts lesson on a Tolstoy novel, some students may become more interested in reading novels on their own or be motivated to read more books by Tolstoy. Other students may become bored with language arts or uninterested in reading novels. Teachers may fail to notice or may ignore such side effects, because they result more from the method than from the content of instruction, more from the teacher's behavior than from students' attitudes.

Guidelines for Writing Objectives

Instructional objectives can be written at two levels of specificity: general and precise. Behaviorists prefer the precise level and view general objectives as fuzzy, resulting in hard-to-measure learning outcomes and difficult evaluation procedures. Cognitive developmentalists prefer the general approach and argue that precise objectives lead to a host of checklists that trivialize teaching and learning and result in lockstep instruction. Recommendations for writing general and precise objectives are shown below. The method you wind up using will probably depend upon your own theory of learning and that of your immediate supervisor.

Table 6.6 ASSIGNING PRIORITIES TO OBJECTIVES

Method	Summary	Advantages	Disadvantages	Recommendations
Sampling objectives	Objectives randomly selected from the total set	Can be done by evaluator alone (without cooperation from others) Quickest, simplest method Treats all program objectives (on the test or not) as instructionally important	Risk of missing important objectives of items thus reducing the credibility of the evaluation	Highly recommended when all objectives are of about equal importance
Sampling important objective	Pool of most important objectives chosen by two or three raters Objectives randomly chosen from pool, or all objectives rated as important used	Fairly fast Gives raters a say in the evaluation Unlikely that important objectives will be missed	Focuses evaluation on a small number of objectives Depends on cooperation of raters Raters' choices perhaps not representative of other concerned persons	Highly recommended when credible raters are available, objectives are not all of equal importance, and there are many objectives
Matrix sampling	All objectives assigned to parts of a test, and each part given to a randomly selected group of students	Can be done by evaluator alone (without cooperation from others) All objectives tested, albeit with samples of students rather than all students	Somewhat involved procedure Data not entirely appropriate for use with some statistical tests	Only method by which all objectives are assessed Due to procedure's complexity, however, best to use only when testing all objectives or items cannot be avoided

Ratings of objectives (retrospective needs assessment)	All objectives rated by about 15 raters on 5-point scale, with priorities determined by mean ratings	Yields accurate assessment of priorities of interest groups represented by the raters Involves raters in evaluation and is therefore likely to increase credibility	Focuses evaluation on a small number of objectives Depends on cooperation of raters Time-consuming for evaluators and raters	Recommended if time is available and enough raters will cooperate Especially recommended when acceptance of evaluation by various education or lay groups is a major concern
Objective hierarchies	Objectives grouped into content areas, then charted from simple to complex, with most complex or "terminal" ones receiving highest priority	Can be done by evaluator alone (without cooperation from others)	Assigns priority to most complex objectives, avoiding attention to simple ones	Relatively time-consuming, depending on the number of objectives May not be desirable to test only terminal, difficult objectives

Source: Lynn L. Morris and Carol T. Fitz-Gibbons, *How to Deal with Goals and Objectives* (Beverly Hills, Calif.: Sage, 1978), pp. 50–51.

Table 6.7   RECOMMENDATIONS FOR STATING OBJECTIVES: CONTENT AND FORM

Content	Form
1. Objectives should be appropriate in terms of the level of difficulty and prior learning experience (of students).	1. Objectives should be stated in the form of expected pupil changes.
2. Objectives should be "real," in the sense that they describe behaviors the teacher actually intends to act on in the classroom.	2. Objectives should be stated in behavioral or performance terms.
3. A useful objective will describe both the content and the mental process or behavior required for an appropriate response.	3. Objectives should be stated singly.
4. The content of the objectives should be responsive of the needs of the individual and society.	4. Objectives should be parsimonious [and] trimmed of excessive verbiage.
5. A variety of behaviors should be stated, since most courses attempt to develop skills other than "recall" [or simple motor or affective skills].	5. Objectives should be grouped logically, so they make sense in determining units of instruction and evaluation.
	6. The conditions under which the expected pupil behavior will be observed should be specified.
	7. If possible, the objective should contain criteria for acceptable performance. Criteria might involve time limits or a minimum number of correct responses.

Source: Adapted from Allan C. Ornstein and Francis P. Hunkins, *Curriculum: Foundations, Principles, and Issues* (Englewood Cliffs, N.J.: Prentice-Hall, 1988); David A. Payne, *The Assessment of Learning: Cognitive and Affective* (Lexington, Mass.: Heath, 1974), pp. 43–45.

General objectives

1. Determine the major objectives you wish to stress. (You may wish to arrange them in order of importance.)
2. Be sure the objectives are related to the goals of the school.
3. Be sure the objectives are related to sound principles of learning.
4. Be sure the objectives are realistic in terms of the students' abilities and the time and facilities available.
5. Be sure the objectives are related to important learning outcomes.
6. Arrange the objectives according to domains of learning or high-order/low-order cognitive, social, or psychological categories.
7. Arrange the content and activities of the subject, course, etc., so they correspond with the objectives.

8. Be sure the objectives satisfy or at least do not conflict with the views of the parents and community.

Precise objectives

1. Make a clear and precise determination of what you want the learner to accomplish.
2. Decide on *who* is to perform the desired behavior (e.g., the student).
3. Detail through an action word the actual *behavior* to be employed in demonstrating mastery of the objective (e.g., to write, to describe).
4. Establish the limiting and/or facilitating *conditions* under which the learner is to do what is asked (e.g., in one hour, with the textbook open).
5. Describe the *product* or *performance* of the behavior to be evaluated to determine whether the objective is achieved (e.g., an essay, a report, a speech).
6. Decide on a *standard* or achievement level that will be used to evaluate the success of the product or performance (e.g., 80 percent correct).

SUMMARY

1. Aims are broad statements about the intent of education as a whole. Goals are general statements about what schools are expected to accomplish. Objectives specify content and proficiency level to be achieved at some level of instruction (program, course, grade, classroom).
2. Objectives are written at several levels, including program, grade, subject, course, classroom, unit plan, and lesson plan, and at several degrees of specificity, from broad to precise.
3. The most popular approaches to formulating objectives are based on the work of Tyler, Bloom, Gronlund, Mager, and Gagné. Tyler identifies purposes and then interprets them in the light of philosophical and psychological concerns to arrive at instructional objectives.
4. Bloom's work (taxonomy of educational objectives) entails three domains of learning: cognitive, affective, and psychomotor.
5. Gronlund and Linn distinguish between general objectives and specific learning outcomes.
6. Mager relies on three major characteristics for writing objectives: behavior, condition, and proficiency level.
7. Gagné defines types of learned capabilities and stresses the importance and the identification of enabling objectives.
8. A number of recommendations for developing objectives are provided to facilitate teacher planning and instruction.

CASE STUDY

Problem

A student teacher assigned to the tenth grade had carefully constructed a series of objectives for a week-long lesson on the stars and astronomy. She had completed her search for supplementary materials, finding excellent children's and commercial books, good filmstrips, movies, and magazine materials. However, little in the content of the material would coincide with the objectives she had so laboriously culled from the students' text, her college text, and notes from her physical science class. She herself eventually constructed all the supplementary materials to match her objectives. She told her cooperating teacher that if as a "regular" teacher she had to follow this procedure for every subject she would have no time to teach or have a family.

Suggestion

The cooperating teacher suggested that in some cases the construction of objectives could be reversed: Rather than find materials to fit objectives, construct objectives to fit available materials. First examine the range of teaching materials—text, films, videotapes, records, magazine articles, etc.—to see if they suggest objectives that are valuable enough. Then design the objectives from the materials.

Discussion Suggestion

An experienced teacher, seeing the confusion of preservice teachers in attempting to choose between what the *students were to learn* and what the *teacher wished to teach*, suggested she construct *two* sets of objectives: those for the teacher and those for the students. Using this method the teacher would work with only *five* objectives. These would be (1) to introduce, (2) to develop, (3) to strengthen, (4) to maintain or review, and (5) to enrich. The students' objectives would be "productive," such as : to write, to explain, or to identify, to choose, or to contrast. An example for the stars and astronomy unit would be:

Teacher: *To introduce* the names of the planets
Student: *To write* the names of the planets

Teacher: *To develop* an understanding of the telescope
Student: *To explain* the parts of a functioning telescope

Teacher: *To strengthen* the distinction between stars and planets
Student: *To list* characteristics of stars and planets

Teacher: *To review* the content
Student: *To choose teams and compete in a review game* concerning concepts
    of light years, black holes, old and new stars

Teacher: To enrich understanding by a field trip to the planetarium
Student: To contrast the planetarium trip to learning in the text

Discussion Questions

1. As a beginning teacher, how much time do you expect to devote for lesson plan preparation?
2. Have you considered the possibility that you may be teaching three or four different subjects during the same term? How might this situation impact on your lesson preparation?
3. As a teacher, do you expect to fit objectives to materials? Or materials to objectives? Defend your choice.
4. Is there merit in organizing most of your lessons around the five teacher objectives, as suggested by the experienced teacher? Why? Why not?
5. Is there merit in in organizing most of your lessons around the five student objectives, as suggested by the experienced teacher? Why? Why not?

QUESTIONS TO CONSIDER

1. In terms of aims and goals, why is the question "What are schools for?" so complex?
2. Why is it important for aims and goals to change as society changes?
3. What sources of information does Tyler recommend in formulating his objectives? Which source is most important? Why?
4. How do Gronlund and Linn distinguish between general objectives and specific learning outcomes?
5. What are the three components of Mager's objectives?

THINGS TO DO

1. Find a list of school goals in a textbook or curriculum guide and revise them to conform to the guidelines in writing objectives at a particular subject and grade level.
2. Arrange the six categories of the cognitive domain into a hierarchy from simple to complex. Give an example of an instructional objective for each category.
3. Arrange the five categories of the affective domain into a hierarchy from simple to complex. Give an example of an instructional objective for each category.

4. Formulate ten unit plan objectives in your area of specialization. Use either Gronlund and Linn's or Bloom's method to write these objectives. Give an example of an instructional objective for each category.
5. Write six objectives for the subject you wish to teach at the lesson plan level. Use the method of Bloom, Mager, or Gagné to write these objectives.

RECOMMENDED READINGS

Bloom, Benjamin S. et al. *Taxonomy of Educational Objectives: Handbook I: Cognitive Domain.* New York: McKay, 1956. Describes six categories of the cognitive domain and objectives and test items related to knowledge and problem-solving skills.

Gagné, Robert M. *The Conditions of Learning,* 4th ed. New York: Holt, Rinehart & Winston, 1985. How to plan and write objectives based on learned capabilities and task analysis.

Gronlund, Norman E. *Stating Objectives for Classroom Instruction,* 3rd ed. New York: Macmillan, 1985. Step-by-step procedures for writing and using objectives for instruction and testing.

Harlow, Anita J. *Taxonomy of the Psychomotor Domain.* New York: McKay, 1972. Examines six categories of the psychomotor domain and presents sample objectives and test items in the domain.

Krathwohl, David R., Benjamin S. Bloom, and Bertram Maisa. *Taxonomy of Educational Objectives, Handbook II: Affective Domain.* New York: McKay, 1964. Describes five categories of affective domain and objectives and test items related to feelings, attitudes, and values.

Mager, Robert F. *Preparing Instructional Objectives,* rev. ed. Belmont, Calif.: Fearon, 1984. Describes objectives that specify behavior, condition, and proficiency.

West, Charles K., James A. Farmer, and Philip M. Wolf. *Instructional Design: Implications from Cognitive Science.* Needham Heights, Mass.: Allyn & Bacon, 1991. The implications of cognitive strategies for instructional design.

KEY TERMS

Aims
Goals
Objectives
Program objectives
Course objectives
Classroom objectives
Unit plan objectives
Lesson plan objectives
Taxonomy of educational objectives

Cognitive domain
Affective domain
Psychomotor domain
General objectives
Specific learning outcomes
Learned capabilities
Task analysis
Enabling objectives

Chapter 7

Instructional Methods

FOCUSING QUESTIONS

1. When is the method of practice and drill useful?

2. How can practice and drill be made most effective?

3. Why is the method of questioning crucial to good instruction?

4. What are the characteristics of well-formulated questions?

5. What factors should be considered in preparing a lecture?

6. Why should lecture and explanation times be limited?

7. What are good strategies for the problem-solving method?

To appreciate instruction, we need to make a distinction between teaching and instruction. Teaching is the behavior of the teacher during the instructional process. Instruction is the specific methods and activities by which the teacher influences learning. Whereas teacher behavior suggests an established pattern or personality, a teacher should have a repertoire of instructional techniques. A teacher who only has one instructional technique is like a baseball pitcher with only one pitch or a piano player who can play only one tune.

In this chapter we will explore four basic, traditional instructional methods: (1) practice and drill, (2) questioning, (3) lecturing and explaining, and (4) problem solving. The effectiveness of these methods is supported by many years of research and practice.

PRACTICE AND DRILL

The mention of practice and drill summons up images of the old-fashioned schoolmaster, the drillmaster who made learning a repetitive response whereby students either memorized their lessons or experienced his wrath. However, it is an intructional method that does serve certain purposes well and can be used to advantage in classrooms today.

Applications of Practice and Drill

Practice and drill is a common method used by elementary teachers to teach the fundamentals, especially to young children. The method is also employed by secondary teachers who teach students still lacking basic skills or knowledge of academic subject matter before asking them to move on to other tasks or transfer their learning to a new situation. Some teachers believe lots of practice is essential in order to learn a basic skill or task; most teachers are less drill-oriented and more open to other instructional approaches.

Busywork

A major problem with the practice and drill method is that although it is supposed to enhance student knowledge, it can turn into busywork, especially if the tasks are either too easy or too difficult for the majority of students, or if it supplants other methods. This is true whether the teachers use published practice and drill material or design the material themselves.[1]

---

1 Jean Osborn, "Do Workbooks Reflect the Rest of the Work?" paper presented at the annual meeting of the American Educational Research Association, San Francisco, April 1986; Barak V. Rosenshine, "Teaching Functions in Instructional Programs," *Elementary School Journal* (March 1983), pp. 335–351.

Teachers who emphasize routine and structure or who feel the need for a quiet and ordered environment sometimes disregard the classroom nuances or activities that produce those conditions and substitute busywork for meaningful practice and drill. According to one review of the research, about 25 to 30 percent of teachers[2] (especially new teachers who need a safe environment) fall into this category.

Seatwork Activities

Elementary school students spend about 70 to 85 percent of their time engaged in seatwork activities, and practice and drill take up about two-thirds of this time for students involved in learning the basic skills of reading, writing, and arithmetic.[3] High school students spend more time in seatwork activities, but the activities are more varied and challenging and involve less practice and drill;[4] this is the case regardless of whether the high school teachers are experienced or beginning teachers.

Back-to-Basics Approach

Because of the dramatic decline in SAT scores over the past 20 years, and because many high schools have permitted functional illiterates to graduate, there has been a popular cry to return to the basics—the so-called three Rs at the elementary school level, and "essential" academic subjects (math, science, English, history, foreign language) at the high school level.

The proponents of back to the basics argue that students should be drilled until they acquire basic knowledge in the three Rs and academic subjects; then they can become involved in inquiry-discovery learning. The real question is not whether they like reading or math, but whether they can read or compute.[5]

Behaviorist Approaches

Thorndike's **law of exercise**, which states that the more often a stimulus-response connection is made the stronger it becomes, and Skinner's finding that

---

2 Louis M. Heil, "Personality Variables, an Important Determinant in Effective Elementary School Instruction," *Theory into Practice* (February 1964), pp. 12–15.

3 John I. Goodlad and Frances M. Klein, *Behind the Classroom Door* (Worthington, Ohio: Jones, 1970); Barak V. Rosenshine, "How Time Is Spent in Elementary Classrooms," in C. Denham and A. Lieberman, eds., *Times to Learn* (Washington, D.C.: National Institute of Education, 1980), pp. 107–126.

4 Eric J. Cooper, "Toward a New Mainstream of Instruction in American Schools," *Journal of Negro Education* (Winter 1989), pp. 102–116; John I. Goodlad, *A Place Called School* (New York: McGraw-Hill, 1984); Jane A. Stallings, "Using Time Effectively: A Self-Analytic Approach," in K. K. Zumwalt, ed., *Improving Teaching*, 1986 ASCD Yearbook (Alexandria, Va.: Association for Supervision and Curriculum Development, 1986), pp. 15–28.

5 Allan C. Ornstein, "Curriculum Contrasts: A Historical Overview," *Phi Delta Kappan* (February 1982), pp. 404–408; Clare E. Weinstein et al., "Helping Students Develop Strategies for Effective Learning," *Educational Leadership* (December 1988–January 1989), pp. 17–19.

reinforcement of a response increases the likelihood of its occurrence, both provide some basis for the old maxim that practice makes perfect.[6]

Practice and drill can be provided by instructional techniques, such as teaching machines and computerized instruction, that rely on a schedule of reinforcement. Instructional materials are arranged in logical order and broken down into units, called *frames*, that lead students through the program in small steps from the simplest to the most complex material. A program may have hundreds or thousands of frames. Repetition is used to maximize correct responses and to prevent misconceptions. Continuous reinforcement is supplied by getting answers right, and the program presents material in a way designed to enable students to have a high rate of success. From time to time, frames review previous material or present the same material in different contexts. Practice is essential when the learner makes a mistake and before advancing to another level of difficulty.[7]

Mastery Learning Methods

Instruction that is arranged in a logical, progressive order and that matches materials and activities to individual needs and abilities is most effective in fostering achievement. The basis of mastery learning, and similar forms of teaching such as adaptive instruction and individualized instruction, is to make certain that adequate learning and mastery of certain concepts and skills have taken place, usually through practice and drill, "before progressing to more complex concepts and skills."[8] Mastery instruction, especially when it is individualized as opposed to group-based, accommodates varying rates of learning among students. A student who has difficulty in attaining a specific level of performance, or mastery, can improve by working on the necessary prerequisites through practice and drill.[9]

Where learning tasks are arranged in sequential order, mastery of the first task is a prerequisite of the second task, and all subsequent tasks build on preceding tasks. Uncorrected difficulties in a task are likely to create and to be compounded by further difficulties on following tasks. According to Bloom, the early tasks in the sequence are the most critical, since if these are not adequately learned, the student is likely to have difficulty with most later tasks. Practice and drill is important for teaching the early tasks.[10]

---

6 See Ernest R. Hilgard and Gordon H. Bower, *Theories of Learning*, 5th ed. (Englewood Cliffs, N.J.: Prentice-Hall, 1981).

7 Albert Bandura, *Social Learning Theory* (Englewood Cliffs, N.J.: Prentice-Hall, 1977); B. F. Skinner, *The Technology of Teaching* (New York: Appleton-Century-Crofts, 1968).

8 Robert Glazer, *Adaptive Education: Individual Diversity and Learning* (New York: Holt, Rinehart & Winston, 1977), pp. 77).

9 John H. Block, Helen E. Efthim, and Robert Burns, *Building Effective Mastery Learning Schools* (New York: Longman, 1989); Benjamin S. Bloom, *Human Characteristics and School Learning* (New York: McGraw-Hill, 1976).

10 Bloom, *Human Characteristics and School Learning*, p. 35.

Remedial Instruction

Low-achieving (and at-risk) students need more practice and drill than high-achieving students before they can move on to subsequent tasks. The teacher may have to reduce the breadth of the work for more depth and reduce the pace and difficulty of the material.[11] The teacher will need to monitor the practice and drill closely, providing corrective feedback to help students grasp the material and avoid confusion or frustration.

Much of teaching for low-achieving students will be remedial in nature. Students with learning problems need extra practice and drill and a variety of learning experiences that relate new learning with prior learning; they cannot easily keep up with more advanced students yet should not be allowed to become embarrassed or defensive. In heterogeneous classes, teachers must challenge high-achieving students and let them move on to other content. Practice and drill, and other direct forms of instruction, have limited value for these students.[12] But at the same time teachers must be sure that slower students learn the basic material thoroughly, in some cases only a limited amount, instead of racing through a large amount of material with little comprehension and retention.

Caution

Sensitivity, even caution, is needed to make teachers aware that too much emphasis on practice and drill, or repeated teaching of basic skills, for any group of students, even low achievers, leads to boredom, low-level thinking, and rote learning. "The big secret in American education," according to Stanley Pogrow, "is that at-risk students love to learn and be challenged with sophisticated [learning] tasks."[13] Pogrow's five years of research, involving 170 schools in a High-Order Thinking Skills (HOTS) program, shows that low achievers who are encouraged to "reflect" or think in subject courses score higher on standardized tests than comparison groups who are taught only by means of traditional drilling.[14]

Students who are encouraged to think, as opposed to learn through rote methods, have improved self-concepts, are more willing to think when posed with learning problems, and subsequently learn more than students with low self-concepts. The assumption is that students of all ages and all abilities prefer the opportunity to be challenged and learn in a reflective classroom setting.

---

11 Larry Cuban, "The 'At-Risk' Label and the Problem of Urban School Reform," *Phi Delta Kappan* (June 1989), pp. 780–784; Allan C. Ornstein and Daniel U. Levine, "Social Class, Race, and School Achievement," *Journal of Teacher Education* (September–October 1989), pp. 17–23.

12 Beau F. Jones and Lawrence B. Friedman, "Active Instruction for Students at Risk," *Educational Psychologist* (Summer 1988), pp. 299–308; Weinstein et al., "Helping Students Develop Strategies for Effective Learning."

13 Quote by Stanley Pogrow in Barbara Bell, "Educator Blasts Repeated Drilling in Basic Skills," *Leadership News* (April 15, 1989), p. 11.

14 Stanley Pogrow, 'Challenging At-Risk Students: Findings from the HOTS Program," *Phi Delta Kappan* (January 1990), pp. 389–397.

Moreover this does not mean that practice and drill has minimal place in the teaching and learning process; rather, too much emphasis on this instructional method, or any other method, leads to student boredom and off-task behavior.

Similarly, in a review of effective classroom teaching techniques for at-risk students, Levine and Ornstein point out that cognitive levels of instruction must not include constant drill—since it will turn into mechanical, rote learning—but also "thinking and high-order skills." However, this will require manageable class sizes for the teacher, availability of suitable learning materials, emphasis on students' self-monitoring, and nurturing of student performance—what the two researchers call "active/enriched" learning.[15]

In short, practice and drill is an excellent instructional method for teaching basic knowledge, and in tutorial and remedial situations, but teachers must utilize varied methods—including thinking and problem-solving instruction—instead of constantly reteaching what students did not learn the first time, second time, etc. The effective teacher must learn to use a mixture of instructional methods—and practice and drill is only one such method.

Functions of Practice and Drill

The main goal of practice and drill is to make sure that students understand the prerequisite skills for the day's lesson. Practice and drill activities include (1) reviewing the previous day's work and homework, (2) presenting skills and concepts necessary for new content, (3) providing student practice and checks to evaluate student responses, (4) receiving feedback from student work and questions and reteaching common problems, (5) providing students with methods for independent practice, and (6) conducting weekly or monthly reviews in test or nontest forms. These activities are presented in greater detail in Table 7.1.

In secondary grades the technique of beginning a lesson by checking or reviewing the previous day's assignment is common in many mastery learning and direct instructional approaches. In a 45–minute period in mathematics, for example, Thomas Good recommends that daily practice and drill be used to start the lesson, that it consist of approximately 8 minutes, and that it be related to homework assignments and computation exercises. He also recommends practice as part of seatwork activity, when students are engaged in learning new concepts and skills.[16] Practice and drill varies by subject and grade level; the data suggest that it occurs in 50 to 60 percent of the classes, less at the high

---

15 Daniel U. Levine and Allan C. Ornstein, "Research on Classroom and School Effectiveness and Its Implications for Improving Big-City Schools," *Urban Review* (June 1989), pp. 81–94; Levine, "Creating Effective Schools: Findings and Implications from Research and Practice," *Phi Delta Kappan* (January 1991), pp. 389–393.

16 Thomas L. Good, Douglas A. Grouws, and Howard Ebermeier, *Active Mathematics Teaching* (New York: Longman, 1983).

Table 7.1   PRACTICE AND DRILL ACTIVITIES

1. *Daily review, checking previous day's work, and reteaching (if necessary)*:

   Checking homework

   Reteaching areas where there were student errors

2. *Presenting new content/skills*:

   Provide overview

   Proceed in small steps (if necessary), but at a rapid pace

   Give detailed and redundant instructions and explanations, if necessary

   Phase in new skills while old skills are being mastered

3. *Initial student practice*:

   High frequency of questions and overt student practice (from teacher and materials)

   Prompts provided during initial learning (when appropriate)

   All students have a chance to respond and receive feedback

   Teacher checks for understanding by evaluating student responses

   Continue practice until students are firm

   Success rate of 80% or higher during initial learning

4. *Feedback and correctives (and recycling of instruction, if necessary)*:

   Feedback to students, particularly when they are correct but hesitant

   Feedback of students' errors to teacher that corrections and/or reteaching are necessary

   Corrections by simplifying question, giving clues, explaining or reviewing steps, or reteaching last steps

   When necessary, reteaching using smaller steps

5. *Independent practice so that students are firm and automatic*:

   Seatwork

   Unitization and automaticity (practice to overlearning)

   Need for procedure to ensure student engagement during seatwork (i.e., teacher or aide monitoring)

   95% correct or higher

6. *Weekly and monthly reviews*:

   Reteaching, if necessary

Source: Barak V. Rosenshine, "Teaching Functions in Instructional Programs," *Elementary School Journal* (March 1983), p. 338.

Learning is enhanced if practice and drill is distributed in short periods over an extended period of time.

school than middle grade level and more in mathematics and English than in social studies or science.[17]

Guidelines for Implementing Practice and Drill

In order to acquire many basic skills—such as arithmetic, grammar, and foreign languages—certain things need to be learned to the point of automatic response, such as simple rules of grammar and speech, word recognition, and mathematical calculations (adding, subtracting, multiplying). These things are needed for more advanced learning and are best learned through practice and drill.

Although practice and drill is accepted in theory, realistic guidelines need to be applied to the classroom setting. Below is a recommended list, based on practice and research.

---

17 Carolyn M. Evertson et al., "Relationship Between Classroom Behaviors and Student Outcomes in Junior High School Mathematics and English," *American Educational Research Journal* (Spring 1980), pp. 43–60; Thomas L. Good and Douglas A. Grouws, "The Missouri Mathematics Effectiveness Project," *Journal of Educational Psychology* (June 1979), pp. 355–362; and Herbert J. Walberg, "Improving School Science in Advanced and Developing Countries," *Review of Educational Research* (Spring 1991), pp. 25–70.

1. *Practice must follow understanding and can enhance understanding.* Students will learn more easily and remember longer if they practice what they understand or have learned through prior classroom experiences.[18]At the same time understanding can be further increased through practice and drill.

2. *Practice is more effective if students have a desire to learn what is being practiced.* Students will practice what they believe has value and if they are motivated. For these reasons, it is important for the teacher to provide situational variety (repetition can become boring), interesting aspects of a particular skill as well as interesting drill items, situations in which students can use the skill or knowledge in other phases of learning, drill items related to students' experiences and interests, and explanations of the relationship between the skill or knowledge being learned and more advanced learning.

3. *Practice should be individualized.* Exercises should be organized so that each student can work independently at his or her own level of ability and rate of learning. In this way low-achieving or slow students can devote more time to items that are difficult for them, and high-achieving or bright students can advance without waiting for the others.

4. *Practice should be specific and systematic.* A drill exercise should be related to a specific objective or skill, and students should know in advance what is being practiced. Drill on specific skills in which students need practice will produce better results than indiscriminate drill. Digressions should be avoided.[19] A systematic, step-by-step procedure fits well with all learners, especially low-achieving students.

5. *Practice should be intermixed with different materials and parts of the lesson.* Drill items can constitute part of chalkboard exercises, mimeographed materials, workbook and textbook exercises, homework, and reviews for tests.[20] Drill may also be used in conjunction with independent seatwork, small learning groups, or student learning teams.

6. *There should be much practice on a few skills rather than a little practice on many skills.* It is best to focus on one or two skills at a time and practice those.

7. *Practice should be organized so that students experience high rates of achievement.* Effective drill is characterized by high rates of correct

18 Neville Bennett, "The Search for a Theory of Pedagogy," *Teaching and Teacher Education* (no. 1, 1988), pp. 19–30; David E. Somerville and David J. Leach, "Direct or Indirect Instruction," *Educational Research* (February 1988), pp. 46–53.

19 Block, Efthim, and Burns, *Building Effective Mastery Learning Schools*; Robert M. Gagné, Leslie J. Briggs, and Walter W. Wager, *Principles of Instructional Design*, 3rd ed. (New York: Holt, Rinehart & Winston, 1988).

20 Gaea Leinhardt and William Bickel, "Instruction's the Thing Wherein to Catch the Mind that Falls Behind," *Educational Psychologist* (Spring 1987), pp. 177–207; Barak V. Rosenshine, "Explicit Teaching and Teacher Training," *Journal of Teacher Education* (May–June 1987), pp. 34–38.

responses. Correct responses serve as reinforcement. When students discover that their answers are correct, they are encouraged to go to the next question or item. This is especially important for slow learners. Research suggests that most students need at least a 90 percent rate of correct response while doing practice and drill activities (also for completing homework) in material that has supposedly been learned.[21] Success rates can be as low as 70 percent with students who will not become overly confused or frustrated, as long as the teacher is available to correct their work immediately.[22]

8. *Practice should be organized so that students and teacher have immediate feedback.* Drills should be either self-scoring or teacher-scored, with correct answers provided as soon as possible. The teacher needs to know scores or results in order to know if he or she can proceed to the next point or skill.[23] The student, especially the low-achieving student, needs to know the correct responses here and now, not next week or when the teacher has had time to mark the papers. Based on a review of 53 students, for best results tests should be returned within one or two days, and for lists (or items) to be learned the feedback time should be 4 to 10 seconds. Classroom practice should also be graded each day, with teacher suggestions given for what to do for wrong answers. Such feedback helps students to recall facts and concepts and supports further learning.[24]

9. *Practice material should be used for diagnostic purposes.* Drill items should be constructed to reveal individual problem areas. Much practice material can be used for diagnostic purposes as long as the teacher knows what skills each student is working on or has mastered.[25] Studying and keeping a record of students' performance can help the teacher recognize and treat problems before they become habits, seriously affect later work, or cause students to be branded as "remedial" or having a "learning disability."

21 Bloom, *Human Characteristics and School Learning*; Rosenshine, "Teaching Functions in Instructional Programs."

22 Thomas L. Good and Jere E. Brophy, *Looking into Classrooms*, 5th ed. (New York: Harper & Row, 1991); Richard S. Marliave and Nikola N. Filby, "Success Rate: A Measure of Task Appropriateness," in C. W. Fisher and D. C. Berliner, eds., *Perspectives on Instructional Time* (New York: Longman, 1985), pp. 217–236.

23 James A. Kulik and Chen-Lin C. Kulik, "Timing and Feedback and Verbal Learning," *Review of Educational Research* (Spring 1988), pp. 79–97.

24 Penelope Engel, "Tracking Progress Toward the School Readiness Goal," *Educational Leadership* (February 1991), pp. 39–42; Velma I. Hythecker, Donald F. Dansereau, and Thomas R. Rocklin, "An Analysis of the Processes Influencing the Structured Dyadic Learning Environment," *Educational Psychologist* (Winter 1988), pp. 23–37.

25 Stephen F. Foster, "Ten Principles of Learning Revised in Accordance with Cognitive Psychology," *Educational Psychologist* (Summer 1986), pp. 235–243; David E. Somerville and David J. Leach, "Direct or Indirect Instruction."

10. *Practice material should provide progressive continuity between learning tasks.* Too often a skill is taught and left without testing. To foster continuous mastery and systematic recall, there should be a whole sequence of practice for a specific unit or course, making certain that there is intermittent drill at desirable intervals. Practice should be given frequently; it should cover tasks in order of difficulty, and the range of items should be wide enough to connect prerequisite learning tasks with new learning tasks. Such practice systems help build learning "maps" in the sense they reinforce and display the concepts or "big picture" of what students have learned.[26] See Tips for Teachers 7.1.

QUESTIONING

Good teaching involves good questioning, especially when large groups of students are being taught. Skillful questioning can arouse the students' curiosity, stimulate their imagination, and motivate them to search out new knowledge. It can challenge the students, make them think, and help clarify concepts and problems related to the lesson. The type and sequence of the questions and how students respond to them influence the quality of classroom discussion and the effectiveness of instruction. Good teachers usually have skill in striking a balance between factual and thought-provoking questions and in selecting questions to emphasize major points and to stimulate lively discussion.

Types of Questions

Questions can be categorized in many ways: (1) according to thinking process, from low level to high level or (according to the cognitive taxonomy) from knowledge to evaluation; (2) according to type of answer required, namely convergent or divergent; (3) according to the degree of personal exploration, or valuing, they elicit, and (4) according to descriptive categories of questions.

Low-Level and High-Level Questions

Low-level questions emphasize memory and recall of information. When was the Declaration of Independence signed? Who won the Civil War? Where is the Statue of Liberty? These questions focus on facts and do not test understanding or problem-solving skills. They correspond to lower cognitive processes—what J. P. Guilford calls *information*, Jerome Bruner calls *concrete operations*, and Arthur Jensen calls *level-one thinking*.

---

26 The ten recommendations for practice and drill are based on Allan C. Ornstein, "Practice and Drill: Implications for Instruction," *NASSP Bulletin* (April 1990), pp. 112–116.

Tips for Teachers 7. 1

Improving Practice and Drill

Here are several recommendations for improving practice and drill and other seatwork activities to enhance academic learning.

1. *Have a clear system of rules and procedures for general behavior.* This allows students to deal with personal needs (for example, permission to use the bathroom pass) and procedural routines (sharpening or borrowing a pencil) without disturbing classmates engaged in academic work.

2. *Move around the room to monitor students' seatwork.* Students should feel that the teacher is aware of their behavior and alert to difficulties they may encounter. The extent of monitoring is correlated with the students' academic ability and the demands they make for the teacher's attention.

3. *Provide comments, explanations, and feedback.* The more recognition or attention students receive, the more they are willing to pursue seatwork activities. Watching for signs of confusion by students and dealing with them quickly increases students' willingness to persist and helps teachers to know how students are doing and to plan the next instructional task. Common problems should be explained immediately by interrupting the practice exercise if the problems are serious, or after the practice if they can wait.

4. *Spend more time teaching and reteaching the basic skills.* Young and low-achieving students should be exposed to heavy doses of skills learning, which requires practice and drill. When students have difficulty with basic skills, it is important to instruct in small steps to the point of overlearning.

5. *Use practice during and after learning.* Practice and drill should be used sparingly for initiating new learning, rather in conjunction with and after the learning. Practice activities can be mixed with other activities such as demonstrations, explanations, and questions—depending on the students' age and abilities. Games and simulations for young children, and field trips and buzz sessions for older students are not as effective for learning basic skills as practice and drill and other paper-and-pencil activities.

6. *Provide variety and challenge in practice and drill.* Practice can easily drift into busywork and frustrate or bore students if it is too easy, too difficult, or too monotonous. The teacher should motivate the students to work at optimum levels of their ability, gradually shifting into different activities to interest and challenge them.

continues

7. *Keep students alert and focused on the task.* Teachers need to keep students on task—occasionally questioning them, calling on both volunteers and nonvolunteers, elaborating on incorrect answers (preferably by asking other students to do so).

8. *Maintain a brisk pace.* There should be little confusion about what to do during practice and drill, and activities should not be interrupted by minor disturbances or environmental conditions. A snap of the finger, eye contact, or other "signal" procedures should help in dealing with inattentive or disruptive students without stopping the lesson.

High-level questions go beyond memory and factual information and call for complex and abstract thinking. Low-level questions have their place; they are used to assess readiness for the high-level questions that require analysis, synthesis, and problem solving. The ideal is to reach a balance between the two types of questions. The trouble is that many teachers do not progress beyond the knowledge-oriented questions. In fact, according to researchers, it is not uncommon to find that 60 to 90 percent of the questions teachers ask are low level.[27] One study indicates that 93 percent of the questions asked by teachers are knowledge based or at the literal level of comprehension, and 88 percent of students' answers—regardless of grade level—are at the lowest cognitive skill level.[28] Teachers seem unaware of the extent to which they are omitting meaningful, high-order questions.

Criticism of the use of low-level questions is complicated by recent research that indicates that low-level and narrowly defined questions characterize an effective instructional program for inner-city and low-achieving learners.[29] Teachers who ask high-level questions and encourage student-in-

27 Michael J. Dunkin and Bruce J. Biddle, *The Study of Teaching* (New York: Holt, Rinehart & Winston, 1974); David A. Payne, *The Assessment of Learning* (Boston: Heath, 1974); Meredith Gall, "Synthesis of Research on Teachers' Questioning," *Educational Leadership* (January 1984), pp. 40–47; and William W. Wilen, "Implications of Research on Questioning for Teacher Education," *Journal of Research and Development in Education* (Winter 1984), pp. 31–35.

28 Robert J. Kloss, "Toward Asking the Right Questions," *Clearing House* (February 1988), pp. 245–248; Imogene Ramsey et al., "Questioning: An Effective Teaching Method," *Clearing House* (May 1990), pp. 420–422.

29 Richard S. Prawat, "Promoting Access to Knowledge, Strategy, and Disposition in Students," *Review of Educational Research* (Spring 1989), pp. 1–41; Barak V. Rosenshine, "Content, Time, and Direct Instruction," in P. L. Peterson and H. J. Walberg, eds., *Research on Teaching: Concepts, Findings, and Implications* (Berkeley, Calif.: McCutchan, 1979), pp. 28–56.

itiated comments are least effective with these types of students,[30] the reason being that these students lack a knowledge base and need more low-level questions and feedback from teachers before they can move to problem-solving skills and high-level questions. The problem is that teachers often become set in their use of low-level questions and thus keep these students permanently in a cognitively second-rate instructional program.

Low-level questions can foster learning, especially with students who lack prerequisite knowledge and who are developing a knowledge base and need to experience simple questions to build their confidence in learning. According to researchers, low-order questioning is effective for such students when it is used for instructional activities involving basic reading and math. The new low-order information must be related in a meaningful way to knowledge the learner already has.[31] But we would expect teachers to progress to asking as many high-level questions as possible. Using the subjects of our three examples of low-level questions, here is a series of sample high-level questions: What were the reasons for signing the Declaration of Independence? What other alternative courses of action were available to the revolutionists? How would these other actions have affected history? What economic, political, and social events led to the Civil War? Why did the North win the Civil War? How did the results of the war affect black-white relations for the remainder of the nineteenth century? Or this century? What does the Statue of Liberty mean to you? To an immigrant arriving in America by ship in 1920? To a Vietnamese political refugee today? To a Hispanic worker today crossing the Rio Grande in search of a job?

These questions are obviously more advanced, more stimulating, and more challenging, and in many cases there are no right or wrong answers. As the questions become more advanced, they involve more abstractions and points of view. Writing high-level questions demands patience and clear thinking on the part of the teachers; creating appropriate timing, sequencing, and phrasing is no easy task for even the experienced teacher.

Benjamin Bloom's cognitive taxonomy can be related to the categories of low-level and high-level questions just described. Low-level questioning and knowledge correspond to the knowledge category of the taxonomy, what Bloom calls the "simplest" form of learning and the "most common educational objective."[32] High-level questioning and problem-solving skills correspond to

---

30 Walter Doyle, "Effective Teaching and the Concept of the Master Teacher," *Elementary School Journal* (September 1985), pp. 27–34; Donald S. Medley, "The Effectiveness of Teachers," in Peterson and Walberg, eds., Research On Teaching, pp. 11–27; and Jane Stallings and David H. Kaskowitz, *Follow Through Classroom Observation Evaluation* (Menlo Park, Calif.: Stanford Research Institute, 1974).

31 Penelope L. Peterson, "Making Learning Meaningful: Lessons from Research on Cognition and Instruction," *Educational Psychologist* (Fall 1988), pp. 365–373; Patricia A. Herman, "Incidental Requisition of Word Meaning from Expositions with Varied Text Features," *Reading Research Quarterly* (Summer 1987), pp. 263–284.

32 Benjamin S. Bloom, ed., *Taxonomy of Educational Objectives, Handbook I: Cognitive Domain* (New York: McKay, 1956), p. 28.

the remaining five categories of the taxonomy—comprehension, application, analysis, synthesis, and evaluation. This is shown in Table 7.2. As we saw in Chapter 6, the six categories of the cognitive taxonomy form a hierarchy of levels of complexity from simple to more advanced, with each level dependent upon the acquisition of skills at the lower levels. The sample questions in the table correspond to the cognitive categories of the taxonomy.

Convergent and Divergent Questions

Convergent questions tend to have one correct or best answer. For this reason they are often mistakenly identified as low-level and knowledge questions, but they can also be formulated to demand the selecting of relevant concepts and the working out of problems dealing with steps and structure. Convergent questions can deal with logic and complex data, abstract ideas, analogies, and multiple relationships. According to research, convergent questions can be used when students work on and attempt to solve difficult exercises in math and science, especially analysis of equations and word problems.[33]

Divergent questions are often open-ended and usually have many appropriate, different answers. Stating a "right" answer is not always most important; rather it is how the student arrives at his or her answer. Students should be encouraged by the teacher to state their reasoning and to provide supporting examples and evidence. Divergent questions are associated with high-level thinking processes and can encourage creative thinking and discovery learning. Often convergent questions must be asked first to clarify what students know before advancing to divergent questions. But the ideal is to ask fewer convergent questions, especially low-level ones, and more divergent questions. The mix of convergent to divergent questions will reflect the students' abilities, the teacher's ability to phrase such questions, and the teachers' comfort in handling varied responses.

Convergent questions usually start with *what, who, when* or *where;* divergent questions usually start with *how* or *why. What* or *who* questions followed by *why,* are really divergent questions that are introduced by *what* to get to the *why* aspect of the question. (For example, "Who won the Civil War?" leads to the ultimate question: "Why?") The differences are highlighted by the sample questions in Table 7.3. Most teachers ask far more *what, who, when,* and *where* questions than *how* or *why* questions; the ratio is about 3 or 4 to one.[34] This is because the convergent questions are simple to phrase and to grade; they help

---

33 Barry K. Beyer, *Teaching Thinking Skills* (Needham Heights, Mass.: Allyn & Bacon, 1991); Lauren B. Resnick and Leopold E. Klopfer, eds., *Toward the Thinking Curriculum: Current Cognitive Research,* 1989 ASCD Yearbook (Alexandria, Va.: Association for Supervision and Curriculum Development, 1989).

34 J. T. Dillon, "Research on Questioning and Discussion," *Educational Leadership* (November 1984), pp. 50–56; Gall, "Synthesis of Research on Teachers' Questioning." Also see J. T. Dillon, *Questioning and Teaching* (New York: Teachers College Press, Columbia University, 1988).

Table 7.2 QUESTIONS RELATED TO THE COGNITIVE TAXONOMY

Category	Sample question
1.0 Knowledge	
1.1 Knowledge of specifics	Who discovered the Mississippi River?
1.2 Knowledge of ways and means of dealing with specifics	What word does an adjective modify?
1.3 Knowledge of universals and abstractions in a field	What is the best method for calculating the circumference of a circle?
2.0 Comprehension	
2.1 Translation	What do the words *hasta la vista* mean?
2.2 Interpretation	How do Democrats and Republicans differ in their views of spending?
2.3 Extrapolation	Given the present birthrate, what will be the world population by the year 2000?
3.0 Application	How has the *Miranda* decision affected civil liberties?
	Given a pie-shaped lot 120 ft. x 110 ft. x 100 ft., and village setback conditions of 15 ft. in all directions, what is the largest size one-story home you can build on this lot?
4.0 Analysis	
4.1 Analysis of elements	Who can distinguish between fact and opinion in the article we read
4.2 Analysis of relationships	How does Picasso organize colors, shapes, and sizes to produce images?
4.3 Analysis of organizational principles	How does John Steinbeck use his characters to discuss the notion of friendship in *Of Mice and Men*?
5.0 Synthesis	
5.1 Production of a unique communication	Who can write a simple melodic line?
5.2 Production of a plan or proposed set of operations	How would you go about determining the chemical weight of an unknown substance?
5.3 Derivation of a set of abstract relations	What are the common causes for cell breakdown in the case of mutations, cancer, and aging?
6.0 Evaluation	
6.1 Judgment in terms of internal evidence	Who can show the fallacies of Hitler's *Mein Kampf*?
6.2 Judgment in terms of external evidence	Who can judge what is wrong with the architect's design of the plumbing and electricity?

Source: Allan C. Ornstein, "Questioning: The Essence of Good Teaching," *NASSP Bulletin* (May 1987), pp. 73–74.

Table 7.3 SAMPLE CONVERGENT AND DIVERGENT QUESTIONS

Subject and grade level	Convergent questions	Divergent questions
Social Studies, 5th–7th	Where did the Boston Tea Party take place?	Why did the Boston Tea Party take place?
		Why did it take place in Boston, not New York or Philadelphia?
Social Studies, 7th–9th	What are the three major products of Argentina?	How does wheat production in Argentina affect wheat export in our country?
English, 5th–7th	What is the verb in the sentence, "The girl told the boy what to do."?	How do we rewrite the present and future tenses of the verb in the sentence, "The girl told the boy what to do."?
English, 10th–11th	Who wrote *A Farewell to Arms*?	How does Hemingway's experience as a news reporter affect the story *A Farewell to Arms*?
Science, 5th–6th	Which planet is closest to the sun?	How would you compare living conditions on Mercury with those on Earth?
	Who was the first American astronaut to travel in space?	What planet, other than Earth, would you prefer to visit, if you were an astronaut? Why?
Science, 9th–11th	What are two elements of water?	How is water purified?
Math, 8th–11th	What is the definition of a triangle?	How have triangles influenced architecture?
Math, 6th–8th	What is the shortest distance between two points?	What is the best air route to take from New York City to Moscow? Why?

keep students focused on specific data; and they give many students a chance to participate. Convergent questions thus make good questions for practice and review. Divergent questions require more flexibility on the part of the teacher. For the student they require the ability to cope with not being sure about being right and not always getting approval from the teacher. In general, the pace of questioning is slower. There is more opportunity for students to exchange ideas and differing opinions. There is also more chance for disagreement among students and between students and teacher—which is often discouraged or viewed as tangential by teachers.

Right Answers Count

In the majority of classrooms, teachers ask convergent questions, which entail a "right" answer, and students are expected to give the answer—often resulting in teacher approval. These questions and answers, coupled with the students'

Teacher-student interaction has an advantage over the teacher glued to his or her desk (or chalkboard) as a method of instruction.

need for approval (especially at the elementary grade level) permit teachers to dominate classroom interaction and students learn to give the answer expected of them. According to Jules Henry, students "learn the signal response system called docility and thus obtain approval from the teacher." Indeed, right answers count in school, not necessarily how you arrived at the answer, because teachers are keyed to and approve right answers.[35]

For low-achieving students, and for students who need teacher approval, the magic word from the teacher is often "yes" or "right." The teacher determines what is right in the classroom, and the easiest way to test students is to ask convergent questions. Divergent questions, on the other hand, lead to novel responses, responses that the teacher does not always expect and responses that take up class time (or time out from the formal curriculum). This may be difficult to deal with for students who have come through the educational system being right-answer–oriented, or for teachers who have been trained to provide and then look for correct answers.

John Holt points out that as students become right-answer oriented, they become *producers*, producing what teachers want, not *thinkers*. It is only the rare student who is willing to play with ideas, not caring whether the teacher confirms an answer is right. But the average child must be right. "She cannot bear to be wrong. When she is wrong . . . the only thing to do is to forget it

35 Jules Henry, "Docility, or Giving Teacher What She Wants," in J. H. Chilcott, N. C. Greenberg, and H. B. Wilson, eds., *Readings in the Socio-Cultural Foundations of Education* (Belmont, Calif.: Wadsworth, 1969), p. 249.

as quickly as possible."[36] Under these circumstances, divergent questions, which may not have right answers, only prolong the child's agony in the classroom.

Asking questions to which there is only one right answer fosters a highly convergent mind, even an authoritarian mind—one that looks for simple "right" answers and simple solutions to complex problems, one that relies on authority rather than on rational judgment to find the "right" answer. It also breeds a rigid and narrow mind that fails to recognize or is unwilling to admit that facts and figures are screened through a filtering process of personal and social experience and interpretation.[37]

Valuing Questions

A number of educators and psychologists have advocated different ways of enhancing the creative and human potential of students. Some of these procedures and techniques stress **valuing**—a process in which students explore their feelings and attitudes, analyze their experiences, and express their ideas. The emphasis is on the personal development of the learner through clarifying attitudes and making choices.

A teacher can stimulate valuing through probing questions. Keep in mind, however, that a 10–year-old cannot be probed for feelings or attitudes in the same way as a 16–year-old. The teacher must also consider how far to get students to express themselves (or to reveal their inner thoughts) in the classroom, especially in front of their peers, and avoid unexpected, unintended, or extreme emotional reactions.

Louis Raths and his colleagues have developed a model for clarifying the values of learners. For him, valuing consists of seven components in three levels: *choosing*—(1) choosing freely, (2) choosing from alternatives, (3) choosing after considering the consequences of each alternative; *prizing*—(4) cherishing the choice, (5) affirming the choice to others; and *acting*—(6) doing something with the choice, (7) repeating the action.[38] Raths has also developed several general questions that can be used in any classroom to encourage students to clarify their values along his model. A sample of these questions is shown in Table 7.4.

Descriptive Categories of Questions

Several authorities have formulated their own categories and models of questions that correspond to the basic types we have just described. James Gallagher sorts questions into four categories.

---

36 John Holt, *How Children Fail* (New York: Pitman, 1964), p. 12.

37 Allan C. Ornstein, "Questioning: The Essence of Good Teaching," *NASSP Bulletin* (May 1987), pp. 71–79.

38 Louis E. Raths, Merrill Harmin, and Sidney B. Simon, *Values and Teaching*, 2nd ed. (Columbus, Ohio: Merrill, 1978).

Table 7.4   QUESTIONING STRATEGIES FOR THE VALUING PROCESS

1. *Choosing freely*

   a. Where do you suppose you first got that idea?

   b. How long have you felt that way?

   c. What would people say if you weren't to do what you say you must do?

2. *Choosing from alternatives*

   a. What else did you consider before you picked this?

   b. How long did you look around before you decided?

   c. Was it a hard decision? What went into the final decision? Who helped? Do you need any further help?

3. *Choosing thoughtfully and reflectively*

   a. What would be the consequences of each alternative available?

   b. Have you thought above this very much? How did your thinking go?

   c. This is what I understand you to say . . . [interpret statement].

4. *Prizing and cherishing*

   a. Are you glad you feel that way?

   b. How long have you wanted it?

   c. What good is it? What purpose does it serve? Why is it important to you?

5. *Affirming*

   a. Would you tell the class the way you feel?

   b. Would you be willing to sign a petition supporting that idea?

   c. Are you saying that you believe . . . [repeat the idea]?

6. *Acting upon choices*

   a. I hear what you are for; now, is there anything you can do about it? Can I help?

   b. What are your first steps, second steps, etc?

   c. Are you willing to put some of your money behind this idea?

7. *Repeating*

   a. Have you felt this way for some time?

   b. Have you done anything already? Do you do this often?

   c. What are your plans for doing more of it?

Source: Louis E. Raths, Merrill Harmin, and Sidney B. Simon, *Values and Teaching*, 2nd ed. (Columbia, Ohio: Merrill, 1978), pp. 64–66.

1. *Cognitive-memory* questions require students to reproduce facts or remember content through processes such as rote memory or selective recall. For example, "What is the capital of France?"
2. *Convergent* questions require students to recall information that leads to a correct or conventional answer. Given or known information is usually the expected response; novel information is usually considered incorrect. For example, "Summarize the author's major points."
3. *Divergent* questions require students to generate their own data or a new perspective on a given topic. Divergent questions have no right answer; they suggest novel or creative responses. For example, "What might the history of the United States have been if the South had won the Civil War?"
4. *Evaluative* questions require students to make value judgments about the quality, correctness, or adequacy of information, based on some criterion usually set by the student or by some objective standard. For example, "How would you judge the art of Picasso?"

Gallagher found that in classrooms with gifted students, cognitive-memory questions comprised more than 50 percent of the total questions asked. It is assumed that teachers ask even more cognitive-memory questions with average or low-achieving students. Convergent questions were the second most frequently used category. Few divergent and evaluative questions were asked. Gallagher surmises that teacher-student discussions can operate normally if only the first two categories of questions are used.[39]

Hilda Taba categorized questions according to cognitive operations pertaining to high-level thinking or what some have termed *reflective thinking*. The questions are designed to engage the learner in levels of cognitive tasks: (1) concept formation, (2) generalizing and inferring, and (3) application of principles.[40]

The cognitive tasks are defined in terms of overt activities (see Table 7.5). These cognitive tasks, overt activities, and eliciting questions form a hierarchy in which each is prerequisite to the next. As students proceed through the steps in each cognitive task, qualitative transformations occur in the thought process.

According to Taba's model, the teacher formulates appropriate questions for the cognitive activities within each task. The questions elicit from students

39 James J. Gallagher, "Expressive Thought by Gifted Children in the Classroom," in *Language and the Higher Thought Processes* (Champaign, Ill.: National Council of Teachers of English, 1965), pp. 56–65; James J. Gallagher and Mary J. Aschner, "A Preliminary Report on Analyses of Classroom Interaction," *Merrill Palmer Quarterly* (July 1963), pp. 183–194.

40 Hilda Taba, *Teaching Strategies and Cognitive Functions in Elementary School Children*, Cooperative Research Project No. 2404 (San Francisco: San Francisco State College, 1966); Hilda Taba and Freeman F. Elzey, "Teaching Strategies and Thought Processes," *Teachers College Record* (March 1964), pp. 524–534.

Table 7.5 COGNITIVE OPERATIONS AND LEVELS OF QUESTIONS

Overt activity	Eliciting questions
Cognitive task 1: Concept formation	
1. Enumeration and listing	What did you see? Hear? Note?
2. Groups together	What belongs together? On what criterion?
3. Labeling, categorizing	What would you call these groups? What belongs under what?
Cognitive task 2: Generalizing and inferring	
1. Identifying points	What did you note? See? Find?
2. Explaining identified items of information	Why did so-and-so happen? Why is so-and-so true?
3. Making inferences or generalizations	What does this mean? What would you conclude? What generalizations can you make?
Cognitive task 3: Application of principles	
1. Predicting consequences, explaining unfamiliar phenomena, hypotheses	What would happen if . . . ?
2. Explaining and supporting predictions and hypotheses	Why do you think this would happen?
3. Verifying predictions and hypotheses	What would it take for so-and-so to be true? Would it be true in all cases? At what times?

Source: Hilda Taba, *Teaching Strategies and Cognitive Functions in Elementary School Children*, Cooperative Research Project No. 2404 (San Francisco: San Francisco State College, 1966), pp. 39–40, 42.

different levels of complexity and abstraction. Taba relies heavily on divergent questions. The nature of the activities dictates the type of question to be used.

Dillon classifies research questions, or what we might also refer to as high-level questions, into four types.

1. *Theoretical*: Examples: How are the principles (or methods) consistent with the underlying rationale? What are the rationale and principles of the scheme?
2. *Reliability*: Examples: How precisely has each of the categories been defined? What is the definition of the thing whose kinds are being classified? How consistent is the performance?
3. *Logical*: Examples: What characteristics do these categories exhibit? What principle has been identified? What relationship exists among the categories exhibited?

4. *Utility*: Examples: For what use has the plan been designed? How well does it satisfy these uses? What kinds of action does the scheme permit?[41]

Unquestionably, these are tough questions that deal with abstractions and scholarly research. They are the kinds of questions that are appropriate mainly for high-achieving students who can deal with reflective questions and who are not concerned with right answers. The key, here, is the student's willingness to play with ideas and not have to impress the teacher with the right answer.

Formulating Questions

Through appropriate strategies in formulating questions the teacher can help students understand content and formulate ideas, concepts, relationships, and principles. Several different approaches to formulation have been suggested.

A teacher can formulate basic questions as he or she prepares each lesson. At this stage the teacher can reduce the number of questions to four or five, sometimes called **pivotal questions**, that relate to the major objectives or parts of the lesson. These questions can be used to introduce and clarify major ideas and to motivate students. The questions are written in advance, as part of the lesson plan, because they evolve naturally from the lesson plan; the teacher will have them available to use at appropriate places during the classroom discussion.

As the lesson proceeds and teacher-student interaction occurs, it is necessary for the teacher to formulate other questions, called **emerging questions**. These questions cannot be prepared in advance, since it is impossible to know exactly what discussion will lead to, but they are crucial for keeping the flow of ideas alive.

Some researchers suggest examining questions in terms of five major characteristics.

1. *Conciseness.* Questions should be simple and easily understood by all students. Good questions center on one specific point related to an objective topic or concept. Vague questions and multiple questions can lead to student confusion and frustration.

2. *Challenge.* Good questions promote inquiry-discovery learning. Questions that repeat subject material or facts in the text are not thought provoking. Challenging questions are conceptual, analytical, evaluative, divergent, and valuing. They lead to student participation, student problem formulation, and student explanation of problems. They encourage students to support their responses, express opinions, and use their own experiences.

3. *Group orientation.* Classroom questions are addressed to an entire class or group of students, not an individual. (Students should not receive

---

41 J. T. Dillon, "The Classification of Research Questions," *Review of Educational Research* (Fall 1984), pp. 327–361.

any indication as to who will be called upon to respond; this helps keep students alert.) Using the words *we* and *us* rather than *I* and *me* enhances group spirit and unites the class in working toward common goals: "Can *we* identify the reasons for . . . ?" rather than "Can anyone tell *me* the reasons for . . . ?"

4. *Appropriateness to age and ability of students*. Questions should push students to think and imagine, but they must be within their comprehension. Easier questions allow low-ability students to participate, and difficult questions can challenge high-achieving students. While it is important not to embarrass or frustrate students by asking them questions in class that they cannot handle, it is just as important not to track low-achieving students by asking them only the easy questions. (After a while the students will sense you are dividing the class into low and high achievers by the way you direct questions.) Slower students need more background information, more time to respond, and more convergent questions, but they should also be challenged and expected to stretch their thinking and imagination.

5. *Variety*. Depending on the objectives of the lesson and the age and ability of the students, questions should be mixed in terms of type (who, what, how, and why), difficulty, (low and high level), direction (convergent and divergent), and subjectivity (objective and valuing). The effective teacher utilizes several different kinds of questions and knows when and how to use which kind to achieve instructional objectives and increase student participation.[42]

Two researchers prescribe six steps in questioning: (1) Prepare questions in advance; (2) adapt questions to various student skill levels; (3) word questions so as to involve all students or as many as possible; (4) encourage students to take time to answer; (5) question students in a way that causes them (not the teacher) to answer; and (6) use questions to get feedback on students' learning and how they think.[43]

Still another point to consider is that most questioning sequences have two major purposes—instruction and diagnosis. **Instructional questioning** is generally convergent and tends to be used in new learning and practice situations. **Diagnostic questioning** is generally divergent and is designed to elicit information from students about their understanding of the topic. It usually results in a natural dialogue between teacher and students.[44] There are often right or preferred responses to instructional questions; diagnostic responses are

---

42 Allan C. Ornstein, "Questioning: The Essence of Good Teaching: Part II," *NASSP Bulletin* (February 1988), pp. 72–80.

43 Dorothy McCullough and Edye Findley, "How to Ask Effective Questions," *Arithmetic Teacher* (March 1983), pp. 8–9.

44 Donald M. Fairbairn, "The Art of Questioning Your Students," *Clearing House* (September 1987), pp. 19–22.

not labeled as right or wrong, but are viewed as information for the teacher. Both types of questions can give the teacher information about students' knowledge and level of cognitive development, but diagnostic questions permit more exploration of students' thought processes.

How Many Questions/To Whom

Although many teachers base curriculum pacing on student performance on weekly or unit tests, research suggests that when teachers assess mastery on a lesson-by-lesson basis, rather than weekly or more often, achievement is increased. Effective teachers do this by asking students a range of questions during the lesson—and do so for several reasons: to activate background knowledge, to stimulate interest, and to challenge students or make them think. For example, Carolyn Evertson found that the most effective junior high school teacher averaged 24 questions within a 50-minute period while the less effective teachers asked only 8.6 questions per period.[45] Other research shows that 80 percent of academic instruction is related to the teacher asking questions and students responding to them, and that on average high school teachers ask 395 questions per day in five class periods (quite different from Evertson's junior high school teachers).[46]

Some observers argue that a teacher cannot rely on questions to assess how well all students in a group understand a concept or skill, and that testing or reviewing based on several written questions is more efficient. With a class of 30 students, even 15 to 20 students, it is not feasible to ask a sufficient number of students questions to see if all students have mastered new learning. Moreover, research strongly suggests that students do not get equal opportunity to respond, and that most teachers favor bright students. Low-achieving students, who should provide the information of when to move to another concept or skill, often provide the least input.[47]

A related questioning problem is, how does the teacher know when to move on to the next part of the lesson? Asking students, "Are there any other questions?" usually gets little or no response, since there is insufficient direction (who should respond) and probing (not focused enough) and content

45 Carolyn M. Evertson et al., "Relationship Between Classroom Behaviors and Student Outcomes in Junior High Mathematics and English Classes," *American Educational Research Journal* (Spring 1980), pp. 43–60.

46 Dale Dean, "Questioning Techniques for Teachers: A Closer Look at the Process," *Contemporary Education* (Summer 1986), pp. 184–185; Meredith D. Gall, "The Use of Questions in Teaching," *Review of Educational Research* (December 1970), pp. 707–721. Also see Milbrey W. McLaughlin, Joan E. Talbert, and Nina Bascia, *The Contexts of Teaching in Secondary Schools* (New York: Teachers College Press, Columbia University, 1990).

47 Thomas L. Good and Jere E. Brophy, *Looking into Classrooms*, 5th ed. (New York: HarperCollins, 1991); Alan Hofmeister and Margaret Lubke, *Research into Practice: Implementing Effective Teaching Strategies* (Needham Heights, Mass.: Allyn & Bacon, 1991).

(lacks an anchor to hook on to). Thus the unsettling question is: when is it appropriate to move on?

Awareness of these problems has led educators to advocate several questioning strategies, usually based on direct or explicit instructional approaches, each with its own flaws.

1. *Call On Students Randomly.*[48] There is no guidance on just how many students should be called on—many students are "forgotten" or not included, especially low achievers.

2. *Use Ordered Turns.*[49] This often ensures better participation of low achievers, or prevents high achievers from dominating classroom instruction, but it also frustrates the latter group who want to respond and show they understand the questions. Also, if students know who is going to be called on, they often do not attend to the question or discussion until it is their turn.

3. *Encourage Choral-Group Responses.*[50] The research is mixed on requiring group responses to questions. In some studies it produces greater attention and higher achievement, and in others it creates confusion, management problems, and a negative effect on achievement. One might assume that it is probably more effective with younger students and in smaller classes where the noise level and excitement are more manageable.

4. *Organize Reciprocal-Peer Questioning.*[51] The class is divided into smaller groups, and each student is provided with the same set of generic questions to answer for most lessons. Students spend a portion of the lesson in the group asking and answering selected questions. The teacher signals when group discussion time is over, and brings the class together to share and discuss the same questions. This technique provides two opportunities (small-group and whole-group sessions) to clarify new learning and puts more of the responsibility and activity for learning onto students. The disadvantage is that the technique is time consuming and holds back high achievers who initially understood the concept and don't need all this practice.

48 Barak V. Rosenshine and Robert Stevens, "Classroom Instruction Reading," in P. D. Pearson, ed., *Handbook of Reading Research* (New York: Longman, 1984), pp. 745–797.

49 Linda M. Anderson, Carolyn M. Evertson, and Jere E. Brophy, "An Experimental Study of Effective Teaching in First-Grade Reading Groups," *Elementary School Journal* (March 1979), pp. 193–222; Meredith Gall et al., "Instructional Correlates of Effective Algebra Instruction," paper presented at the annual meeting of the American Educational Research Association, Washington, D.C., April 1987.

50 Jere E. Brophy and Carolyn M. Evertson, *Learning from Teaching: A Developmental Perspective* (Boston: Allyn & Bacon, 1976); Rosenshine and Stevens, "Classroom Instruction Reading."

51 Alison King, "Reciprocal Peer-Questioning: A Strategy for Teaching Students How to Learn from Lectures," *Clearing House* (November–December 1990), pp. 131–135.

5. *Rely on a Steering Group.*[52] Without letting students know, the teacher selects students in the bottom 10 to 25 percentile and determines the class is ready to move on when this group of 3 to 6 students (in a class of 20 to 30 students) can answer the discussion questions. The assumption is that when low-achieving students have mastered the concept, the whole class can move on. The problem is, after a while these students feel "picked on" and other students feel ignored.

6. *Computer-Managed Questions.*[53] Sometimes called "computer networking," this requires a keyboard for each student at his or her seat. Students answer a series of review questions (say 10) immediately following the teaching of the new concept or skill; this is similar to the notion of "guided practice." A monitor at the teacher's desk indicates the proportion of students who answer each question. If the proportion is less than an established criterion (say 80 percent), the teacher can provide additional review. The problems are whether the hardware is available for all students in the class, and whether questions can be devised on a daily basis that go beyond knowledge-based and low-level thinking for the purpose of grading right or wrong.

There is no sure method to know when to move on. The teacher must make the decisions about whether the group as a whole can or cannot move to the next concept or skill. These decisions are subjective. Teachers cannot wait to make sure every student in the group comprehends the material; if so, instruction will slow down and become extremely boring. However, if the teacher moves too quickly frustration and eventual failure will characterize a growing portion of the students.

The general rule is to involve as many students as possible, high and low achievers, and to insure that students take turns in asking and answering questions—without any one individual or group of students dominating the discussion. The teacher needs to recognize when students do not understand and additional review, remediation, or reteaching is appropriate—despite the time constraints imposed upon the curriculum. High school teachers tend to be driven by curriculum constraints more than junior high school teachers, and they often move to the next chapter or assignment too quickly in a heterogeneous class.

In the final analysis, teachers must be learn to determine when to move on: how many questions to ask, what types of questions, and to whom. Although teachers must develop skillful questioning strategies, preservice and in-service

---

52 Cecil M. Clark and Penelope L. Peterson, "Teachers' Thought Processes," in M. Wittrock, ed., 3rd ed. *Handbook of Research on Teaching*, (New York: Macmillan, 1986), pp. 255–296.

53 Nancy Golden, Russell Gersten, and John Woodward, "Effectiveness of Guided Practice: An Application of Computer-Managed Instruction," *Elementary School Journal* (January 1990), pp. 291–304; John Woodward et al., "Using Computer Networking for Feedback," *Journal of Special Education Technology* (Summer 1987), pp. 28–35.

teaching training devotes minimal time and energy to cultivating this method. Thus, many teachers have minimal understanding of which teaching and learning factors determine the students' and teacher's rate of instructional progress.

Guidelines in Asking Questions

Good questioning is both a methodology and an art; there are certain rules to follow that have been found to apply in most cases, but good judgment is also needed. See Tips for Teachers 7.2 and 7.3 for some review of formulating questions and for some recommendations for procedures in asking questions.

In preparing and asking questions in class, a number of instructional strategies have been shown to be effective with a large number of different teachers and students. Most of these instructional strategies come from educational psychology and the teacher effectiveness movement, not from the curriculum, instruction, or teaching method schools, which one might think would contribute to this field of knowledge.[54]

Wait-Time

The interval between asking a question and the student response is referred to as **wait-time**. One study by Mary Rowe indicated that the average amount of time teachers wait is 1 second. Increasing the wait-time to 3 to 4 seconds has several beneficial effects on student responses: (1) length of response increases, (2) unsolicited but appropriate responses increase, (3) failures to respond decrease, (4) confidence (as reflected in an affirmative, rather than a questioning, tone of voice) increases, (5) speculative responses increase, (6) student-to-student responses increase, (7) evidence-inference statements increase, (8) student questions increase, and (9) responses from students graded by teachers also increase.[55]

In a study of sixth- and seventh-grade language arts and math classes the use of teacher wait-time of 3 to 5 seconds in whole-class instruction was associated with improvements in student-teacher interaction: (1) fewer teacher utterances, (2) shorter length of teacher utterances, (3) fewer teacher interruptions of students, (4) increased student responses to teacher questions, (5)

---

54 Allan C. Ornstein and Francis P. Hunkins, *Curriculum: Foundations, Principles, and Issues* (Englewood Cliffs, N.J.: Prentice-Hall, 1988). Also see Francis P. Hunkins, *Teaching Thinking Through Effective Questioning* (Needham Heights, Mass.: Gordon, 1989).

55 Mary B. Rowe, "Wait-Time and Reward as Instructional Variables," *Journal of Research in Science Teaching* (February 1974), pp. 81–97. Also see David C. Berliner, "Laboratory Settings and the Study of Teacher Education," *Journal of Teacher Education* (November–December 1985), pp. 2–9.

Tips for Teachers 7.2

Don'ts in Asking Questions

Good questioning techniques have to be developed slowly and over the years. They must become second nature, a habit. Just as you can form good or bad habits in driving a car or swinging a golf club, you can develop good and bad habits in questioning. Try to eliminate the *don'ts* in asking questions before they become ingrained as habits and to practice the *do's*. Below is a list of things a teacher should *not* do.

1. *Ask "yes" or "no" questions or questions that allow a 50–50 chance of getting the right answer.* Example: Did Orwell write *Animal Farm*? Who won the Civil War? These kinds of questions encourage guessing, impulsive thinking, and right-answer orientation, not conceptual thinking or problem solving. If the teacher accidentally asks this kind of question, he or she should follow up immediately with a why or how question.

2. *Ask indefinite or vague questions.* Example: What are the important cities of the United States? How would you describe the sentence? Such questions are confusing and often must be repeated or refined. Questions should be clearly worded and coincide with the intent of the teacher.

3. *Ask guessing questions.* Guessing questions can also be "yes" or "no" questions, indefinite or vague questions. Ask students to explain ideas and show relationships, rather than searching for detailed or trivial information.

4. *Ask double or multiple questions.* Example: What is the chemical formula for salt? What is its chemical weight? Before students can respond to the first question, the second is asked. As a result, they don't know which question the teacher wants them to answer and they respond to the question they feel more knowledgeable about.

5. *Ask suggestive or leading questions.* Example: Why was Andrew Jackson a great president? The question really calls for an opinion, but a position or judgment is already stated.

6. *Ask fill-in questions.* Example: "The New Frontier occurred during whose presidency?" The question is embedded in the statement rather than being clearly expressed. "Which president implemented the New Frontier?" is a better wording of the question.

7. *Ask overload questions.* Example: In connection with pollution factors and the sun's rays, what conclusions can we come to about the future water level? How did Manifest Destiny lead to imperialism and colonialism, while enhancing the industrialization of the

continues

country? These questions are indefinite, multiple, and wordy. Trim excess verbiage, use simple rather than overly formal or obscure vocabulary, and ask clear, simple questions to avoid concealing the meaning of your question and confusing the student.

8. *Ask tugging questions.* Example: What else? Who else? These tug at the student and do not really encourage thought.

9. *Ask cross-examination questions.* You may be able to assist a student by asking a series of questions to draw out information. However, this should be distinguished from asking many or rapid questions of the same student. Also, the rest of the class tends to be neglected.

10. *Call the name of a student before asking a question.* As soon as students know that someone else is responsible for the answer, their attention lessens. First ask a question, pause to allow comprehension, and then call on someone to answer it.

11. *Answer a question asked by a student if students should know the answer.* Turn the question back to the class and ask "Who can answer that question?"

12. *Repeat questions or repeat answers given by students.* Reiteration fosters poor work habits and inattentiveness. A good practice is to say "Who can repeat that question or that answer?"

13. *Exploit bright students or volunteers.* The rest of the class becomes inattentive and loses contact with the discussion.

14. *Allow choral response or hand waving.* Both are conducive to undesirable behavior.

15. *Allow improper speech or incomplete answers to go unnoticed.* Youngsters are quick to cultivate wrong habits. Supply the correction without stopping the recitation.

Source: Adapted from Allan C. Ornstein, "Questioning: The Essence of Good Teaching: Part II," *NASSP Bulletin* (February 1988), p. 77.

increased average length of student responses, and (6) increase in teacher probing after student responses. Most important, increased wait-time was associated with higher achievement in both subject areas.[56]

No negative side effects of increasing wait-time have been observed, and the positive effects are numerous. Yet, many teachers do not employ this

---

56 Kenneth Tobin, "Effects of Teacher Wait Time in Discourse Characteristics in Mathematics and Language Arts Classes," *American Educational Research Journal* (Summer 1986), pp. 191–200.

Tips for Teachers 7.3

Do's in Asking Questions

Now that you know what not to do, here is a list of things to do in questioning. Practice them so they become second nature in your instructional process.

1. *Ask questions that are stimulating* and not merely memory testing or dull. A good teacher arouses students and makes them reflect with thought-provoking questions. Questions that ask for information recall will not sustain the attention of a class and that's when discipline and management problems begin.

2. *Ask questions that are commensurate with students' abilities.* Questions that are dramatically below or above the abilities of students will bore or confuse them. Target questions, even on difficult subjects, within the ability level of the majority of the class.

3. *Ask questions that are relevant to students.* Questions that draw on their life experiences will be relevant.

4. *Ask questions that are sequential.* Questions and answers should be used as stepping-stones to the next question. This contributes to continuous learning.

5. *Vary the length and difficulty of questions.* Questions should be diversified so that both high- and low-achieving students will be motivated to participate. Observe individual differences and phrase questions so that all students take part in the discussion.

6. *Ask questions that are clear and simple.* Questions should be easily understood and trimmed of excess verbiage.

7. *Encourage students to ask questions of each other and to make comments.* This results in students' becoming active learners and cooperating on a cognitive and social level, which are essential for reflective thinking and social development. Good questions stimulate further questions, even questions by students. The idea is to encourage student comments and interaction among themselves, and to refer student questions and comments to other students to promote discussion, even when they are directed at the teacher.

8. *Allow sufficient time for deliberation.* Pausing for a few seconds until several hands go up gives everyone, particularly the slow learners, a chance to consider the question. As a result, everyone profits from the discussion, and learning takes place for all.

9. *Follow up incorrect answers.* Take advantage of wrong or marginal answers. Probe the student's mind. Encourage the student to think

continues

about the question. Perhaps the student's thinking is partially correct, even novel.

10. *Follow up correct answers*. Use a correct answer as a lead to another question. A correct answer sometimes needs elaboration or can be used to stimulate student discussion.

11. *Call on nonvolunteers and volunteers*. Some students are shy and need coaxing from the teacher. Other students tend to daydream and need assistance from the teacher to keep attentive. Distribute questions among the entire class so that everyone can participate.

12. *Call on disruptive students*. This stops troublesome students without having to interrupt the lesson.

13. *Prepare five or six pivotal questions*. Such questions test students' understanding of the lesson as well as give the lesson unity and coherence.

14. *Write the objective and summary of the lesson as a question, preferably as a problem*. Questions encourage the class to think. The students are made to consider the new work by presenting it as a question or problem.

15. *Change your position and move around the room*. Teacher energy and vitality induce class activity, rapport, and socialization. They also foster an active audience and prevent daydreaming and disciplinary problems.

Source: Adapted from Allan C. Ornstein, "Questioning: The Essence of Good Teaching: Part II," *NASSP Bulletin* (February 1988), p. 78.

instructional strategy. Other data suggest that asking one to four questions per minute is reasonable and that beginning teachers ask too many questions, averaging only 1 1/2 seconds wait-time.[57] Also, although all students need time to process information, low-achieving students need more time, and the data indicate that teachers tend to wait less for an answer from the students they perceive as slow.[58]

---

57 Paulette P. Harris and Kevin J. Swick, "Improving Teacher Communications: Focus on Clarity and Questioning Skills," *Clearing House* (September 1985), pp. 13–15.

58 Rowe, "Wait-Time and Reward as Instructional Variables"; J. Nathan Swift and C. Thomas Gooding, "Interaction of Wait-Time Feedback and Questioning in Middle School Science Teaching," *Journal of Research in Science Teaching* (August 1983), pp. 721–730; and Good and Brophy, *Looking into Classrooms*.

Directing

As mentioned earlier, the recommended strategy in directing questions to students is to ask the question and then call a student's name, because more students will think about the question. Research on classroom management also confirms that it is better to be unpredictable in calling on students to answer questions than to follow a predictable order.[59] On the other hand, a predictable order seems to be more effective when calling on students to read in the lower grades.[60] The reason is perhaps that predictability reduces anxiety, which is important for children who are reading in front of the class. This may also be true for middle grade students, especially low achievers who often lack confidence and exhibit anxiety when reciting in front of peers.

The research also indicates that calling on nonvolunteers can be effective as long as students who are called on can answer the question most of the time. It is a good idea to call on nonvolunteers when it is believed that students can respond correctly, but it is not wise to embarrass them with their inability to answer the questions.[61] This is probably true at all grade levels and subjects. It is acceptable, however, to call on nonvolunteers with the understanding that they may not be able to answer the question correctly, in order to curtail disruptive or inattentive behavior—than to link their inability to answer to their behavior.

Although the research indicates that middle grade teachers should call on nonvolunteers no more than 15 percent of the time,[62] practice indicates this figure may be too low. By emphasizing volunteers, there is a tendency to call on high-achieving students more often than low-achieving students. Calling on more nonvolunteers increases the likelihood that low-achieving students will be included in the discussion. It is generally a good idea to call on low achievers who usually do not volunteer, and they should periodically be called as nonvolunteers as long as they are likely to be able to answer the question correctly.

Redirecting and Probing

If student response to a question is incorrect or inadequate, an effective strategy for the teacher is not to provide the answer, but to redirect the question to another student or to probe for a better answer from the same

59 Jere D. Brophy, "Classroom Management Techniques," *Education and Urban Society* (February 1986), pp. 182–194; Carolyn M. Evertson et al., "Effective Classroom Management: An Exploration of Models," Final Report for the National Institute of Education, Washington, D.C., 1985; and Jacob Kounin, *Discipline and Group Management in Classrooms* (New York: Holt, Rinehart & Winston, 1970).

60 Anderson, Evertson, and Brophy, "An Experimental Study of Effective Teaching."

61 Thomas L. Good and Jere E. Brophy, "Changing Teacher and Student Behavior: An Empirical Investigation," *Journal of Educational Psychology* (June 1974), pp. 390–405; Howard Gardner, ed., *Varieties of Thinking* (New York: Routledge, 1990).

62 Alexis L. Mitman and Andrea Lash, "Students' Perceptions of the Academic Learning and Classroom Behavior," *Elementary School Journal* (September 1988), pp. 55–68; Jones and Friedman, "Active Instruction for Students at Risk."

student. Redirecting the question is better for middle-class students, but probing is better for low-achieving students. Middle-class students seem to be able to cope better with minor academic failure in front of their peers and thus are better able to accept redirection. Teacher persistence in seeking improved responses from low-achieving or at-risk students is also related to positive teacher expectations, which is important in trying to reach and teach such students.

In **probing**, the teacher stays with the same student, asking for clarification, rephrasing the question or asking related questions, and restating the student's ideas. It is important not to overdo it, lest the probing become cross-examination. On the other hand, if the teacher feels that the student was not paying attention, it is best not to probe and give the student a second chance; unwittingly, the teacher would be condoning the student's lack of attention. During the probing process the teacher may ask a series of easier questions that lead toward the answer to the original question. If the student answers correctly (either initially or in response to a rephrased question), the teacher may want to follow with a related question to pursue the implications of the answer and to ensure student understanding.

Probing is acceptable for all students. With high-achieving students it tends to foster high-level responses and discussion. With low-achieving students it tends to reduce the frequency of "no responses" or "incorrect responses." In both cases probing is positively correlated with increased student achievement.[63]

Commenting and Praising

While research on the use of praise is mixed, it is generally agreed that honest praise increases achievement and motivation. Positive reactions can simply mean a smile, nod of approval, or brief comment ("Good," "Correct," "That's true") indicating approval or acceptance. Phony praise or too much praise can have detrimental effects. See Table 7.6.

Most teachers do not use sufficient or genuine praise. A summary of 10 studies, for example, shows that teachers on the average use it no more than 6 percent of the total time in regular classrooms.[64] In another study it was observed that praise of good answers to questions or good work in general was used less than five times per hour at the elementary school level and considerably less at the secondary school level.[65]

---

63 Anderson, Evertson, and Brophy, "An Experimental Study of Effective Teaching"; Jere E. Brophy and Carolyn M. Evertson, "Process-Product Correlations in the Texas Teacher Effectiveness Study," Final Report for the Research and Development Center for Teacher Education, University of Texas, 1974; and Robert S. Soar, "An Interactive Approach to Classroom Learning," Report published for the School of Education, Temple University, 1965.

64 Dunkin and Biddle, *The Study of Teaching.*

65 Jere E. Brophy, "Teacher Praise: A Functional Analysis," *Review of Educational Research* (Spring 1981), pp. 5–32.

Table 7.6   GUIDELINES FOR GIVING PRAISE

Effective praise	Ineffective praise
1. Is delivered contingently	1. Is delivered randomly or unsystematically
2. Specifies the particulars of the accomplishment	2. Is restricted to global positive reactions
3. Shows spontaneity, variety, and other signs of credibility; suggests attention to the students' accomplishment	3. Shows a bland uniformity that suggests a conditioned response made with minimal attention
4. Rewards attainment of specified performance criteria (which can include effort criteria, however)	4. Rewards mere participation, without consideration of performance processes or outcomes
5. Provides information to students about their competence and the value of their accomplishments	5. Provides no information at all or gives students no information about their status
6. Orients students toward better appreciation of their own task-related behavior and thinking about problem solving	6. Orients students toward comparing themselves with others and thinking about competing
7. Uses own prior accomplishments as the context for describing present accomplishments	7. Uses the accomplishments of peers as the context for describing students' present accomplishments
8. Is given in recognition of noteworthy effort or success at difficult tasks (for *this* student)	8. Is given without regard to the effort expended or the meaning of the accomplishment
9. Attributes success to effort and ability, implying that similar successes can be expected in the future	9. Attributes success to ability alone or to external factors such as luck or task difficulty
10. Fosters endogenous attributions (students believe that they expend effort on the task because they enjoy the task and/or want to develop task-relevant skills)	10. Fosters exogenous attributions—students believe that they expend effort on the task for external reasons like pleasing the teacher or winning a competition or reward
11. Focuses students' attention on their own task-relevant behavior	11. Focuses students' attention on the teacher as an external authority figure who is manipulating them
12. Fosters appreciation of and desirable attributions about task-relevant behavior after the process is completed	12. Intrudes into the ongoing process, distracting attention from task-relevant behavior

Source: Jere E. Brophy, "Teacher Praise: A Functional Analysis," *Review of Educational Research* (Spring 1981), p. 26.

The research is also mixed about negative comments. While the research suggests that teachers use criticism and disapproval sparingly, even less than praise, criticism can have a detrimental effect on student achievement. Similarly, if used by a teacher in response to a student question or comment, it can curtail students' asking questions or responding to the teacher's questions.[66] While low achievers receive more criticism than high achievers, it is possible that low achievement causes teachers to use more criticism. While boys receive more criticism from teachers than girls, we also know that boys achieve less than girls in the school grades.[67] In other words, a correlation exists between criticism and achievement, but the cause and effect is unclear.

Finally, comments can be categorized as negative but be used in a supporting way or be followed by positive suggestions or peer group recognition, as illustrated by the italicized statements. (1) "You don't understand. *Let's see who can help you*"; (2) "Your response is wrong. *Try it again, you can answer it*"; (3) "That's not really right. *But it was a difficult question. Let's see how we can improve the answer*"; (4) "Johnny, please be quiet. *You are spoiling it for the entire class. Besides, you know better.*" Mild criticism, moreover, is justified when the answer is wrong or the behavior is interfering with the rules or procedures of the classroom. The point is that it is not only what you say that counts, but how you say it, why you say it, and how you follow up.

LECTURES AND EXPLANATIONS

Lectures can be divided into three types.

1. *Formal lectures* last for most of or the entire class session, student questions and comments are discouraged. Formal lectures should be used only at the advanced high school and college levels, where students are mature enough to sit for long periods of time and take notes on their own.
2. *Informal lectures* last about 5 to 10 minutes; student responses and questions are permitted but not encouraged.
3. *Brief lectures* last for less than 5 minutes; student responses are encouraged.

Formal and informal lectures generally require extensive preparation; brief lectures involve less preplanning, perhaps only a one- or two-sentence reminder in the lesson plan.

---

66 J. T. Dillon, "A Norm Against Student Questioning," *Clearing House* (November 1981), pp. 136–139.

67 Dunkin and Biddle, *The Study of Teaching*; Thomas L. Good, Bruce J. Biddle, and Jere E. Brophy, *Teachers Make a Difference* (New York: Holt, Rinehart & Winston, 1975).

Explanations take only a few moments of teacher talk and are focused on a specific problem, task, or activity. Explanations are spontaneous, not preplanned or outlined in advance.

Discussions can be an outgrowth of lectures or explanations. They are oral exchanges between the teacher and students or among the students. Discussions permit students to respond to teacher statements, to ask questions, and to clarify ideas. The more involved students are in discussion, the more effective the exchange of ideas is likely to be, since students' thoughts tend to wander as teacher talk increases. The implication is clear: teachers should make an effort to maintain student attention by limiting lecture and explanation time and increasing discussion time.

Problems of Lecturing and Explaining

During lectures and lengthy explanations delivered by a teacher, there is little give and take between the teacher and students and among students. Lecturing is often described as "unnecessary," "dull," and a "waste of time." One observer has pointed out that it increases student passivity and reduces the student's role to note taking instead of luring students into more active learning.[68] Another critic has noted that if a student misses a point or is lost, he or she cannot interrupt for a personal explanation or stop and review as with a book, computer program, or tape.[69]

For levels below senior high school these criticisms are valid for formal lectures, especially when teachers do not allow for student response and when the lectures are not adequately prepared and are repetitive or digressive. According to many researchers, young and low-achieving students become inattentive more readily than older and high-achieving students.[70] For the former, it is essential that teacher talk in any form (especially lecturing and explaining) be limited to a few minutes' duration at any one time and be intermixed with other, more concrete, instructional activities (audio, visual, and physical), and fewer verbal and abstract presentations.

Lectures can quickly lead to boredom because the audience is passive for a lengthy period. One method for helping high school students learn from lectures, and also engage actively, is for the teacher to prepare a series of questions about the content to be covered. This helps students identify main ideas, organize notes, and engage in critical thinking as opposed to recording pieces of the lecture and memorizing the information. Table 7.7 lists several generic questions that can function as anchors or help students identify relevant ideas

---

68 John McLeish, *The Lecture Method* (Cambridge, England: Cambridge Institute of Education, 1968).

69 William J. Seiler et al., *Communication in Business and Professional Organizations* (Reading, Mass.: Addison-Wesley, 1982).

70 Robert F. Biehler and Lynne M. Hudson, *Developmental Psychology*, 4th ed. (Boston: Houghton Mifflin, 1990); Robert E. Slavin, *Educational Psychology: Theory and Practice*, 3rd ed. (Englewood Cliffs, N.J.: Prentice-Hall, 1991).

Table 7.7   GENERIC QUESTIONS FOR STUDENTS DURING AND AFTER A LECTURE

What is the main idea of . . . ?

How does . . . affect . . . ?

What is the meaning of . . . ?

Why is . . . important?

Describe . . .

What is a new example of . . . ?

What do you think would happen if . . . ?

Explain why . . .

Explain how . . .

What conclusions can I draw about . . . ?

What is the difference between . . . and . . . ?

How are . . . and . . . similar?

Summarize . . .

How would I use . . . to . . . ?

What are the strengths and weaknesses of . . . ?

What is the best . . . and why?

Source: Alison King, "Reciprocal Peer-Questioning: A Strategy for Teaching Students How to Learn from Lectures," *Clearing House* (November–December 1990), p. 132.

and think about how these ideas relate to each other during the lecture. Students can answer these questions on their own or in small groups during or after the lecture. Other advantages of such questions are that students become more involved in processing information about the lecture, as opposed to sitting passively; they pay closer attention since they are required to answer questions, and they become more involved and responsible for learning.

Benefits of Lecturing and Explaining

Based on a review of several studies of the lecture method, Gage and Berliner feel that it is appropriate when (1) the basic purpose is to disseminate information, (2) the information is not available elsewhere, (3) the information needs to be presented in a particular way or adapted to a particular group, (4) interest in a subject needs to be aroused, (5) the information needs to be remembered for a short time, and (6) the purpose is to introduce or explain other learning tasks. They further state that the lecture method is inappropriate when (1) objectives other than acquisition of information are sought, (2) long-term learning is desired, (3) the information is complex, abstract, or detailed, (4) learner participation is important for achieving the objectives, (5) higher cognitive learning, such as analysis and synthesis, is sought, and (6) students are below average in ability.[71]

There are administrative and practical benefits of brief lectures and explanations. The methods are flexible and can be used in regular classrooms, in small or large groups. Few materials and pieces of equipment are needed, giving the methods the additional benefit of being economical. Teachers who travel or change classrooms need only to carry with them their lesson plans or notes. Although good lectures need considerable preparation, their delivery does not require elaborate advance planning to have materials ordered or media scheduled and moved about. The fact that teachers are not dependent on others to carry out the lecture, explanation, or discussion makes it easy and comfortable for them.

Guidelines for Presenting Lectures and Explanations

When preparing and presenting informal or brief lectures and providing explanations, you might consider the following steps and suggestions.

1. *Establishing rapport with students.* At the beginning of a talk you should take measures to establish rapport with students. (Periodically telling a story or joke helps maintain their interest in the subject and rapport with you.) Always keep in mind the need to maintain the interest of students and the fact that students will react to you first on a personal basis, then on a cognitive basis.

2. *Preparing lectures and explanations.* The major concepts or ideas should be outlined in advance. Corresponding activities and materials might be indicated—say, in the lesson plan—to introduce at a certain point. Except for short passages or quotations to make a point, you should not read from notes. You must know the material well enough to speak clearly and with animation and to speak extemporaneously as you sense the need of the moment and the interests of the students.

3. *Keeping lectures and explanations short.* Although there are exceptions, the less you talk and the more your students talk, the more effective you are as a teacher. The greatest danger is that by talking too much you will create a passive audience and lose their interest. Lectures and explanations of 5 to 10 minutes are acceptable at the middle grade and junior high school levels. High school students can tolerate up to 10 to 15 minutes of interesting teacher talk. Always try to limit your lecturing and explaining and use questions, discussions, various student activities, and media as supplementary tools of instruction.

---

71 N. L. Gage and David C. Berliner, *Educational Psychology,* 4th ed. (Boston: Houghton Mifflin, 1988).

4. *Motivating students to pay attention*. Relevant lectures motivate students. To achieve relevance, you should consider the students' age, ability, educational experiences, environment, interests, needs, perceived goals, and career aspirations. You can make the lesson more understandable and interesting by combining other methods, materials, and media with your talk. When students perceive the relevance of, understand, and are interested in the topic, they become *success-oriented* and acquire *intrinsic motivation*—that is, they pursue "the goal of achievement for the sake of achievement."[72]

5. *Structuring and sequencing your talk*. A disorganized talk confuses and bores its audience. Present major concepts and difficult ideas in a linear and logical fashion, with examples and questions to test students' understanding. Facts and concepts should be developed systematically and sequentially from statement to statement. The overall topic should be related to the topic of the previous lesson. Sentence structure and vocabulary must be appropriate for the students' level of development. Although this sounds obvious, many beginning teachers speak over the vocabulary and content level of their students.

Criteria of a structured lecture, according to one researcher, are (1) *continuity*, a sequenced arrangement of ideas expressed in intelligible and grammatically correct sentences, (2) *simplicity*, the absence of complex sentences and the use of language within the students' vocabulary range, and (3) *explicitness*, the identification and explanation of major concepts and relationships.[73]

Explanatory talk that is considered effective tends to correspond with what we often mean by *coaching*. The explanations can be *physical* through demonstrations; *visual* through pictures or models; or *verbal* through oral discussion or tapes. It is this kind of teacher talk by teachers of low-achieving students that was found to be effective. The more effective teachers engaged in highly structured explanations and were: (1) more responsive to student questions, (2) clearer in presenting content, (3) more complete in providing specific information, and (4) better in giving students feedback to help them learn.[74]

6. *Providing appropriate organizers*. Teachers can provide for students what David Ausubel terms "advanced organizers." They can provide means for the students to organize the ideas to be presented by telling them in advance what the lecture or explanation will focus on and how it will be structured. Gage and Berliner use the terms *hooks* and *anchors* to mean major topics or concepts around which teachers structure information.[75] Another technique is to outline the major topics or parts of the lesson, either orally

---

72 Robert M. W. Travers, *Essentials of Learning*, 5th ed. (New York: Macmillan, 1982), p. 436.

73 Elizabeth Perrott, *Effective Teaching: A Practice Guide to Improving Your Teaching* (New York: Longman, 1982).

74 Gerald G. Duffy, "Conceptualizing Instructional Explanation," *Teaching and Teacher Education*, no. 2 (1986), pp. 197–214.

75 David P. Ausubel, "In Defense of Advanced Organizers: A Reply to the Critics," *Review of Educational Research* (Spring 1978), pp. 251–259; Gage and Berliner, *Educational Psychology*.

or in writing (on the chalkboard), as they unfold (not in advance) during the discussion. This is especially helpful when students are listening to the teacher and must select, process, and assimilate information with which they are working.

7. *Avoiding vagueness.* Lectures and explanations that are free of vague language are easier to follow. Researchers have labeled nine kinds of vague terms: (1) *ambiguous designation*—"somewhere, somehow," (2) *approximation*—"about, almost, nearly, sort of," (3) *bluffing*—"anyway, as you know, so forth, to make a long story short," (4) *error admission*—"I'm not sure, I guess, perhaps," (5) *indeterminate amount*—"a couple, few, some, many," (6) *negated intensifiers*—"not many, not very much," (7) *multiplicity*—"aspects, kind of, type," (8) *possibility*—"chances are, perhaps, it seems, could be," and (9) *probability*—"frequently, generally, usually, often."[76]

Smith and Land point out that vague terms include what they call *mazes*—false starts, incomplete words and sentences, redundant words, and tangled words. The mazes are italicized in the following paragraph.

> This mathematics lesson *will enab* . . . will get you to understand *number, uh,* number patterns. Before we get to the *main ideas of the,* main idea of the lesson, you need to review *four conc* . . . four prerequisite concepts. The first *ideas, I mean, uh,* concept you need to review is positive integers. A positive *number* . . . *uh* integer is any whole *integer, uh,* number greater than zero.[77]

Another factor that leads to vagueness is discontinuous and irrelevant content. The content may be important at another time, but when introduced at an inappropriate time, it becomes distracting from the main ideas. In a clear lecture, the sequence of the flow of ideas from sentence to sentence is clear, and the language is free of ill-defined and redundant words.

8. *Combining instructional materials.* The use of audiovisual aids and special materials and activities can enliven a talk and reinforce its content. Varied stimuli are important for all learners, but younger students especially benefit from less verbalization and more illustrations and activities.

9. *Summarizing content.* The classroom discussion should always end with a **final summary** or conclusion, what some educators call postorganizers.[78] The lesson may also have **internal summaries**, what some educators call medial

---

76 Jack Hiller, Gerald A. Fischer, and Walter Kaess, "A Computer Investigation of Verbal Characteristics of Effective Classroom Lecturing," *American Educational Research Journal* (November 1969), pp. 661–675.

77 Louis Smith and Michael L. Land, "Low Inference Verbal Behaviors Related to Teacher Clarity," *Journal of Classroom Interaction* (April 1981), p. 38.

78 Robert B. Burns and Lorin W. Anderson, "The Activity Structure of Lesson Segments," *Curriculum Inquiry* (Spring 1987), pp. 31–53; Robert E. Mayer, "Elaboration Techniques that Increase the Meaningfulness of Technical Text," *Journal of Educational Psychology* (December 1980), pp. 770–784.

summaries or chunking strategies.[79] Medial summaries, with accompanying or matching activities and transitions, subdivide a lesson into clear parts. It is more important to incorporate medial summaries for low-achieving and younger students than high-achieving or older students.

The best type of summary (medial or final) briefly reviews the presentation and gives students a chance to see whether they understand the material by asking them to explain ideas, provide examples, evaluate data, and do some exercises. It lets them know what they have learned and helps identify major ideas of the lesson.[80]

After the final summary, the teacher should explain related homework and prepare students for any problems they may encounter in it. Also, the teacher might establish a connection between the just completed lesson and the next lesson.

If time is running short, it is best for the teacher to stop at some logical point (not in the middle of a thought or while a student is speaking), leaving enough time to give a quick summary. Each lesson should be concluded by the teacher, not by the bell or by the students' closing their books or walking out. Don't try to keep talking at this point, and be sure you dismiss them to maintain good discipline.

10. *Style of presentation.* Appropriate gestures, movements, and voice quality can improve a talk and make it more interesting and understandable. Without being overly theatrical, it is effective to match nonverbal communication (facial expressions, body movements, eye contact) with the objectives of the talk. Similarly, teacher enthusiasm and expectations during the talk are likely to affect student attitudes and achievement. It should be clear from the presentation that the teacher finds the content interesting and expects students to learn. However, unusual gestures or speech inflections, extreme nervousness, inappropriate dress, and other idiosyncratic characteristics are things that students notice, remember, and are distracted by.

Thorough preparation is essential. Check your lesson to be sure that you have followed these guidelines: (1) State the objectives at the beginning, (2) define new terms and concepts, (3) use relevant examples, (4) explicitly relate new ideas to familiar ones, (5) use alternative explanations when necessary, (6) go slowly through difficult materials, (7) provide occasional summaries and restatements of important ideas, (8) include questions to clarify information being presented, and (9) provide a final summary.[81] A teacher must study his or her own style, become aware of strengths and weaknesses in delivery, and try to eliminate or reduce the weaknesses. Someone who is uncomfortable in talking or standing in front of an audience is unable to communicate as effectively as someone who is relaxed. The less a teacher is able to overcome nervousness and distracting mannerisms, the

79 Thomas L. Good and Jere E. Brophy, *Educational Psychology: A Realistic Approach*, 4th ed. (New York: Longman, 1990); Ornstein, "Questioning: The Essence of Good Teaching."

80 *Getting Started in the Secondary School*, rev. ed. (New York: Board of Education of the City of New York, 1986).

81 Larry A. Braskamp, Dale C. Brandenburg, and John C. Ory, *Evaluating Teaching Effectiveness* (Berkeley, Calif: Sage, 1984); Perrott, *Effective Teaching*.

more he or she should use methods other than lectures, involve the students in talking, and engage them in other instructional activities. The kind of image the teacher projects will influence the teaching-learning process.

PROBLEM SOLVING

A great deal of literature since the beginning of the twentieth century has focused on problem solving and related thinking skills. Educators and psychologists have identified various methods to teach students how to problem solve since Charles Judd (at the University of Chicago) and Edward Thorndike (at Columbia University) showed that learning could be explained in terms of general principles of thinking and methods of attacking problems transferred to different situations.

John Dewey's process of **reflective thinking** was considered the classic model for problem solving from 1910 until the 1950s, when Piaget's work and other models employing various cognitive and information-processing strategies were introduced. Although Dewey's model is viewed as an oversimplification by cognition theorists, it is still considered practical, especially by science and math teachers. Since one of the chief functions of school, for Dewey, was to improve the reasoning process, he recommended adopting the problem-solving method for all subjects and grade levels. Reflective thinking involves five steps: (1) become aware of difficulty, (2) identify the problem, (3) assemble and classify data and formulate hypotheses, (4) accept or reject tentative hypotheses, and (5) formulate and evaluate conclusions.[82]

Dewey's model is based on a mixture of theory and practice, and many problem-solving models today are also based on the same ingredients. For example, Bransford and Stein outline the IDEAL method for problem solving: (1) *i*dentify the problem, (2) *d*efine it, (3) *e*xplore possible strategies, (4) *a*ct on the strategies, and (5) *l*ook at the effects of your efforts.[83]

A number of educators describe successful problem solving as relying on **heuristic thinking**, that is engaging in exploratory processes that have value only in that they may lead to the solution of a problem. Physicians often diagnose problems in this manner, for example, doing tests to eliminate what is not the problem in order to narrow the possibilities down to a few probable diagnoses of what is the problem.[84] According to Newell and Simon's method for dealing with a problem, the person first constructs a representation of the problem, called the "problem space," and then works out a solution that involves a search through the problem space. The problem solver may break

---

82 John Dewey, *How We Think* (Lexington, Mass.: Heath, 1910).

83 John Bransford and Barry Stein, *The IDEAL Problem Solver* (San Francisco: Freeman, 1985).

84 Good and Brophy, *Educational Psychology: A Realistic Approach*; Richard E. Mayer, *Thinking, Problem Solving, and Cognition* (San Francisco: Freeman, 1983).

Creative teaching methods come in many formats; each type has its own advantages and limitations.

the problem into components, activate old information from memory, or seek new information. If an exploratory solution proves to be successful, the task ends.[85] If it fails, the person backtracks, sidetracks, or redefines the problem or method used to solve it. This type of problem solving is not linear; the problem solver may jump around, skip, or combine steps.

Richard Cyert also suggests a heuristic model. It includes 10 steps: (1) keep the basic problem in mind without being distracted by details, (2) avoid early commitment to a particular hypothesis when several hypotheses are possible, (3) simplify the problem by using phrases, symbols, or formulas, (4) change an approach that is not working, (5) ask questions and attempt to answer them, (6) be willing to question assumptions, (7) work backwards if necessary to work out solutions, (8) keep in mind partial solutions that later may be combined, (9) use metaphors and analogies, and (10) talk about the problem.[86]

Successful and Unsuccessful Problem Solvers

An individual is confronted with a problem when he encounters a situation to which he must respond but does not know immediately what the response should be. Regardless of the method, the student needs relevant information to assess the situation and to arrive at a response, that is, to solve the problem.

---

85 Allen Newell and Herbert Simon, *Human Problem Solving* (Englewood Cliffs, N.J.: Prentice-Hall, 1972).

86 Richard M. Cyert, "Problem Solving and Education Policy," in D. Tuma and F. Reif, eds., *Problem Solving and Education: Issues in Teaching and Research* (Hillsdale, N.J.: Erlbaum, 1980), pp. 3–8.

Which strategies are used is related to the student's age and the specific problem. According to researchers, not all successful students will use the same strategy to solve the same problem, and often more than one strategy can be used.[87]

Even with simple addition or subtraction, students use different strategies in solving problems and therefore have a different framework about the relative difficulty of the problems. For example, John has 6 marbles and Sally has 8. How many marbles do they have together? In a *join strategy*, elements are added (6 + 6 = 12, 2 more is 14). With a *separate strategy*, elements are removed (8 + 8 = 16, 2 less is 14). A *part-part-whole strategy* involves undertaking two or more elements ("I tabulated both numbers by adding 1 and 6 and subtracting 1 from 8. That makes 7 + 7, which is 14.").[88] All three students are using correct strategies, although the latter may be a little more cumbersome.

Although teachers often stress one specific strategy to solve specific problems, students often use a variety of strategies, especially with more complex problems. In fact as the problems become more abstract so do their strategies. The teacher who insists on one strategy and penalizes students who use another appropriate strategy is discouraging their problem-solving potential. Teachers need to become aware of how students process information and what strategies they use to solve problems, in order to teach problem solving according to the way *students* think. They can do this by asking them questions, listening to their responses, and inspecting their work.

Some basic problem-solving strategies do seem to emerge, however. In a classic study Benjamin Bloom pointed out several differences between successful and unsuccessful students engaged in problem-solving activities. Although the subjects were college age, the findings apply to students of various ages so long as they have reached the developmental stage (between age 11 and 15) of logical thinking or what Piaget called "formal mental operations."

1. *Comprehending the problem*. Successful problem solvers reacted to selected cues and immediately began to work out a solution. Unsuccessful students missed cues and often misinterpreted the problem.
2. *Employing previous knowledge*. The successful group utilized previous knowledge to solve the problem. The unsuccessful students possessed the accessory information, but did not utilize it. They often did not know where or how to start.
3. *Style of problem-solving behavior*. Successful students were more active and could verbalize what they were doing. They simplified the problem, whenever possible, or broke it down into parts, if they could not

87 Michael Pressley, "The Relevance of the Good Strategy User Model to the Teaching of Mathematics," *Educational Psychologist* (Spring 1986), pp. 139–161; David N. Perkins and Gavriel Saloman, "Teaching for Transfer," *Educational Leadership* (September 1988), pp. 22–32.

88 Penelope L. Peterson, Elizabeth Fennema, and Thomas Carpenter, "Using Knowledge of How Students Think About Mathematics," *Educational Leadership* (December 1989), pp. 42–46.

deal with the whole. The unsuccessful students rarely were able to clarify or state concisely what they were doing. They often did not attempt to analyze the various parts.

4. *Attitude toward problem solving.* The successful students had confidence and viewed the problem as a challenge. The unsuccessful students lacked confidence, became frustrated, and gave up.[89]

There is a consensus today that metacognitive skills (or processes) are transferable competencies that play a significant role in problem solving and high-order thinking. Metacognitive skills represent knowledge of how to do something (usually involving a plan, set of steps, or procedures) as well as the ability to evaluate and modify performance. Based on a review of the research, some metacognitive skills that have been found to distinguish successful problem solvers and that can translate into instructional methods are:

1. *Comprehension monitoring.* Knowing when one understands or does not understand something; evaluating one's performance.
2. *Understanding decisions.* Understanding what one is doing and the reasons why.
3. *Planning.* Taking time to develop a strategy; considering options; proceeding without impulse.
4. *Estimating task difficulty.* Estimating difficulty and allocating sufficient time for difficult problems.
5. *Task presentation.* Staying with the task; being able to ignore internal and external distractions; maintaining direction in one's thinking.
6. *Coping strategies.* Staying calm, being able to cope when things are not going easily; not giving up or becoming anxious or frustrated.
7. *Internal cues.* Searching for context clues when confronted with difficult or novel problems.
8. *Retracking.* Looking up definitions, rereading previous information; knowing when to backtrack.
9. *Noting and correcting.* Using logical approaches; double-checking; recognizing inconsistencies, contradictions, or gaps in performance.
10. *Flexible approaches.* Willingness to use alternative approaches; knowing when to search for another strategy; trying random approaches that are sensible and plausible, when one's original approach has been unsuccessful.[90]

---

89 Benjamin S. Bloom and Lois J. Broder, "Problem-Solving Process of College Students," in *Supplementary Educational Monograph*, no. 73 (Chicago: University of Chicago Press, 1950).

90 Jere E. Brophy, "Research Linking Teacher Behavior to Student Achievement," *Educational Psychologist* (Summer 1988), pp. 235–286; David F. Lohman, "Predicting Mathemathanic Effects in the Teaching of High-Order Thinking Skills," *Educational Psychologist* (Summer 1986), pp. 191–208; and Richard K. Wagner and Robert J. Sternberg, "Alternative Conceptions of Intelligence and Their Implications for Education," *Review of Educational Research* (Summer 1984), pp. 179–224.

It should be noted that low-achieving and younger students have fewer metacognitive skills compared to high-achieving and older students.[91] The implication for teaching is that an increase in knowledge of subject matter does not necessarily produce changes in metacognitive skills. These skills in general reflect high-order thinking processes that cannot be learned or developed overnight or in one subject. Developmental age is crucial in limiting potential metacognitive skills among students. An 8-year-old student is capable of just so much and cannot be pushed beyond her cognitive stage. According to Piaget, not until age 11 is a child capable of employing many of these metacognitive skills (corresponding to formal mental operations), and not until age 15 is the child capable of fully performing all metacognitive skills efficiently.[92]

A direct relation between the amount of teacher control versus student autonomy and student problem solving does not exist. Rather the relationship may be described as *curvilinear*, varying with what the teacher is trying to accomplish, the age or developmental level of the students, their prior exposure to similar problems, and their prior experience with similar styles of teachers.[93]

A high level of control is associated with lower levels of problem-solving abilities in students. Too much teacher control seems to stifle student self-regulation, independence, and inventiveness in problem solving. However, too much student autonomy increases ambiguity and anxiety, causing disruptions and loss of comprehension in basic task demands. Teachers inclined toward this approach usually do not provide sufficient structure or focus for students to be effective problem solvers. Problem solving tends to flourish best in moderate autonomy-granting classrooms, where there is also sufficient structure for younger and/or low-achieving students.

In this connection, Walter Doyle notes the distinction between direct instruction (explicit instructions on how to accomplish the task) and indirect instruction (based on self-discovery). He contends that direct instruction (overlapping with our notion of control) is more suitable for younger and lower-ability students, and those who lack expertise or background information, whereas indirect instruction (overlapping with our notion of autonomy) is

91 Brophy, "Research Linking Teaching Behavior to Student Achievement"; Lyn Corno and Richard E. Snow, "Adapting Teaching to Individual Differences Among Learners," in M. C. Wittrock, ed., *Handbook of Research on Teaching*, 3rd ed. (New York: Macmillan, 1986) pp. 605–629; and Lohman, "Predicting Mathemathanic Effects on the Teaching of High-Order Thinking Skills."

92 Jean Piaget, *The Origins of Intelligence in Children* (New York: International University Press, 1952); Jean Piaget and Barbel Inhelder, *The Early Growth of Logical Thinking in the Child* (London: Routledge & Kegan Paul, 1964).

93 Stanley Harter, "A Model of Intrinsic Mastery Motivation in Children," in A. Collins, ed., *Minnesota Symposium on Child Psychology* (Hillsdale, N.J.: Erlbaum, 1982), pp. 215–255; Richard S. Prawat and Ariel L. Anderson, "Eight Teachers' Control Orientations and Their Students' Problem-Solving Ability," *Elementary School Journal* (September 1988), pp. 99–112.

more appropriate to older and higher-ability students, as well as those who have acquired basic knowledge structures and skills.[94]

Likewise, it is suggested that part-whole strategies of solving problems are easier for unsophisticated learners to understand—evident in math and science problems. Many students resort to guessing or inappropriate strategies until they learn to break down and analyze problems. As students learn to analyze part-whole relationships, they should be encouraged to move into more sophisticated whole-part problem solving. Understanding the big picture before tackling a problem provides many cues and guidelines for determining how to approach a specific problem. It provides a general framework for focusing, while omitting irrelevant or unnecessary stimuli.

To be sure, the whole is greater than any part, and when someone understands the whole—the various relationships and subparts that affect each other—then solving problems is easier and more efficient. This is how a physician usually analyzes a medial problem: he or she views the whole patient—physically and psychologically—knowing the circumstances of the environment and the person (including the person's medical history) before rendering a decision concerning what is wrong and what has to be done to correct or improve the situation.

The Relationship Among Study Skills, Subjects, and Problem Solving

Every instructional program incorporates study skills. At the elementary school level, study skills are often considered as a separate subject or content area. At the secondary level, they are blended into the curriculum as part of the subject matter.

Study skills can be divided into three categories: verbal, symbolic, and investigative (see Figure 7.1). Examples of verbal skills are listening, reading, using a dictionary or the library. Skills with symbols include facility with maps and graphs, measuring and estimating. Investigative skills include observing, describing, interpreting, questioning, experimenting, and the like. Secondary students often cannot engage in problem solving without facility in these study skills. Their deployment may be considered generic content for problem solving, regardless of the subject.

Problem-solving methods may be referred to as operations. Figure 7.1 lists 27 different problem-solving operations which cut across subject matter and are written in the order in which they would most likely be performed. The operations help teachers and instructional leaders discover relationships that exist among study skills, subject areas, and problem solving.

---

94 Walter Doyle, "Academic Work," *Review of Educational Research* (Summer 1983), pp. 159–199.

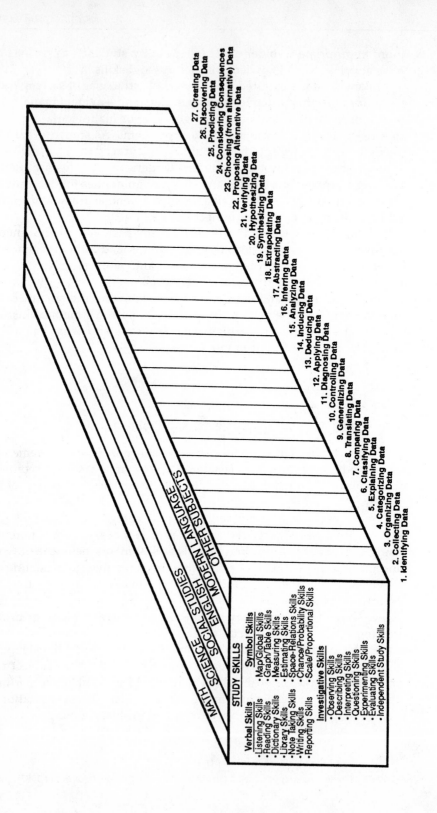

Figure 7.1 Problem Solving Operations with Related Study Skills and Subjects
Source: Allan C. Ornstein, "Problem Solving: What Is It? How Can We Teach It?" *NASSP Bulletin* (November 1989), p. 117.

According to Piagetian theory, students should be able to perform these problem-solving operations by age 14 or 15—when they enter into the formal operations stages of cognitive development.

Problem-Solving Processes

While most teachers acknowledge that problem solving is important, many have not learned how to incorporate it into their lessons. Others view problem solving as interfering with or taking time away from curriculum coverage, since many skills and processes are required. More important, problem solving does not express itself in easily observed behaviors and outcomes that can be simply listed in lesson plans, taught to students, and evaluated. Some teachers do not see problem solving as part of their instructional function. Rather they see it as a chore, not as a commitment, and in competition with, not complementary to, the teaching-learning process.

Good and Grouws have identified five problem-solving processes for mathematics, but they can be applied to the teaching-learning process in all subjects.

1. *Attending to prerequisites*. Solving new problems is based largely on understanding previously learned skills and concepts. The teacher should use the skills and concepts mastered by the students as a basis for solving problems.
2. *Attending to relationships*. Subjects comprise a large body of logical and closely related ideas; the teacher should emphasize meaning and interpretation of ideas.
3. *Attending to representation*. The more the student is able to represent a problem in context with concrete or real-world phenomena, the better able the student is to solve the problem.
4. *Generalizability of concepts*. Teachers need to explain the general applicability of the idea to students; skills and processes that apply to many settings should be practiced.
5. *Attending to language*. Teachers should use precise terminology of their subject, and students must learn basic terms and concepts of the subject.[95]

Matthew Lipman adds five other processes that cut across situational contexts and subject matter. Problem-solving teaching should take into account:

1. *Exceptional or irregular circumstances*. Certain things may be permissible under certain conditions and not under others.
2. *Special limitations or constraints*. Almost all theories, principles, and concepts have certain limitations or contingencies under which they don't apply or are not valid.

---

95 Thomas L. Good and Douglas A. Grouws, "Increasing Teachers' Understanding of Mathematical Ideas Through In Service Training," *Phi Delta Kappan* (June 1987), pp. 778–783.

3. *Overall configurations.* A concept or fact may be wrong or objectionable when taken out of context, but valid or proper in context.
4. *Atypical evidence.* Overgeneralizing from a small sample or one experiment is somewhat risky.
5. *Context-specific meanings.* There are terms and concepts for which there are no precise equivalents in other languages or subjects and whose meanings are therefore context-specific.[96]

In general, the improvement of students' thinking depends upon students' ability to identify good criteria for their opinions or solutions. The criteria should be based on one or more of the above processes, which can be taught. Students can also learn that for an opinion or solution to be good, it must be "relevant," "reliable," "coherent," and "consistent" with acceptable standards.[97] In this connection, the most characteristic feature of problem solving is that it discovers its own weaknesses and rectifies what is at fault in its procedures; thus, it is *self-correcting.* See Tips for Teachers 7.4.

The test for learning to problem solve is the ability to apply or use the strategies that have been learned in new, or at least a variety of, situations. Many times teachers think students have "mastered" relevant facts and procedures. In reality, according to Alan Schoenfeld, they have learned a strategy blindly and can use it only in circumstances similar to those in which they were taught. When given a slightly different version of a problem, or when they must make inferences or leaps in thinking, they are stymied.[98] Similarly, most of the problems found in textbooks, and those we assign for homework, are not problems in the true sense; they are exercises or tasks that reinforce specific, usually rote, procedures for solving a problem. In math, for example, most word problems are solved by students who rely on a key word without fully understanding the procedures involved. A real problem confronts a student with a difficulty, and the answer cannot be obtained by relying on rote procedures; it calls for relating or rearranging learned concepts or procedures with new ideas generated by the problem. It is not straightforward. A student's understanding of the procedures, and the transfer of understanding to new situations, is crucial. Most students cannot function in this arena, because our instructional methods tend to emphasize rote-mechanical procedures.

---

96 Matthew Lipman, "Critical Thinking—What Can It Be?" *Educational Leadership* (September 1988), pp. 38–43.

97 Robert H. Ennis, "A Taxonomy of Critical Thinking Dispositions and Abilities," in J. B. Baron and R. J. Sternberg, eds., *Teaching Thinking Skills* (New York: Freeman, 1987), pp. 9–26; Lipman, "Critical Thinking–What Can It Be?"

98 Alan H. Schoenfeld, "Teaching Mathematical Thinking and Problem Solving," in Resnick and Klopfer, eds., *Toward the Thinking Curriculum*, pp. 83–103.

Tips for Teachers 7.4

Applying Various Instructional Methods

Fourteen techniques are listed below to use in implementing the four instructional methods—practice and drill, questioning, lecturing and explaining, and problem solving—that have been described in this chapter.

1. Lessons are planned in advance by the teacher; student choices are limited within the boundaries established by the teacher.
2. Directions are clear, and students know what to expect and when to change activities. The pace of the lesson is brisk.
3. Materials and media are prepared in advance and incorporated without disturbing the momentum of the lesson.
4. The teacher is responsible for teaching the content of the lesson. The teacher explains, illustrates, and demonstrates what is to be learned.
5. The lesson proceeds in sequenced steps. Each academic task or skill builds on the preceding one. Students are helped to see relationships between previous and present learning.
6. In lecturing and explaining, the teacher matches style and content to students' abilities and interests, prepares and organizes content well, uses materials and media to clarify ideas, and asks questions to maintain student attention and to gauge student understanding and progress. Problem-solving activities are introduced as part of boardwork, seatwork, and homework.
7. In asking questions, the teacher makes sure all students have the opportunity to respond by using a variety of types of questions (low level and high level, convergent and divergent, valuing), allowing sufficient wait-time, calling on nonvolunteers as frequently as or more than volunteers, and calling on low achievers as frequently as or more than high achievers.
8. The teacher aims at a high success rate in student responses to questions. With low achievers, easier questions and factual questions may be emphasized to ensure high success rates and to build a knowledge base before proceeding to more difficult questions.
9. The teacher redirects incorrectly answered questions to other students or rephrases and probes for a better answer from the same student. Prompt comments and feedback are provided by the teacher, including appropriate praise. Correct answers are noted. Students who respond with no answer or a wrong answer are encouraged to try again to improve.

continues

10. The teacher uses practice and drill before and after other activities to ensure that students master required academic tasks. The drill may be incorporated into several parts of the lesson, including preliminary reviews and summaries.

11. Younger students and low-achieving students are provided with more practice and drill and less problem solving than older and high-achieving students. Practice exercises are checked and corrected promptly.

12. Problem-solving activities are reviewed in detail and at a much slower pace than practice and drill.

13. Homework is given frequently and returned promptly with corrective feedback. Gradually, problem solving is introduced into homework assignments, and it increasingly replaces practice and drill in higher grades.

14. All these instructional techniques must be modified to suit the classroom situation—age and academic abilities of the students, subject matter, teacher style, and student learning style.

Guidelines for Teaching Problem-Solving Strategies

Teachers need to provide students with good problem-solving strategies and practice in using such strategies. An extensive catalog of strategies is discussed below, all grounded in current research.

1. The problem-solving process in most cases is either *schema-driven*, with little search for solution procedures because appropriate procedures are activated by recognizing the particular problem type, or based on *search strategies*, in which the problem solver looks for or decides on a particular strategy before solution procedures are implemented.[99]

2. Experts and subject specialists possess schemata relevant to problems in their area of expertise or subject. Consequently, they rarely engage in search strategies as novices or students often do.

---

99 Mary L. Glick, "Problem-Solving Strategies," *Educational Psychologist* (Winter–Spring 1986), pp. 98–120.

3. In the absence of appropriate schemata, problem solvers proceed to a search strategy. Search strategies include, among others, means-ends analysis, analogies, matching, sequencing, and examining problems already worked out.

   a. *Means-ends* analysis is goal-based for a specific problem and requires that the problem solver eliminate differences between the current state and goal condition; this strategy usually leads to memory overload, and does not result in learning moves that can be used in different problems.

   b. *Analogies* are important for making the unfamiliar problem more familiar. Novice problem solvers are likely to engage in superficial analogies, as opposed to analogies that will help lead toward a solution.

   c. *Matching* involves selecting a plan of action and carrying it out accordingly; the process of matching plans and actions continues until the problem is solved.

   d. *Sequencing* strategies (step by step) is an integral part of training and can be used for solving straightforward problems.

   e. *Examining problems* already worked out results in general strategies for a similar set of problems. It does not prepare the problem solver for an atypical problem or a new set of problems.[100]

4. The use of different problem-solving strategies is influenced by the age and knowledge base of the problem solver and by the problem itself.

5. As students gain more knowledge in a subject area, they are better able to deal with problems without engaging in search strategies.

6. In analyzing a problem, students should be taught how to obtain a solution: where to begin, how to move forward, how to backtrack, how to combine parts of problems, and how to know when they have a satisfactory answer or solution.

7. Knowledge of when, where, and how to apply certain specific strategies is also crucial. The problem solver learns that errors are often the result of applying the incorrect strategies to problems, rather than lack of ability or effort.

8. Although some problem strategies cut across several objects, others are supported by a knowledge base. Without an adequate base in a given subject, it is nearly impossible to solve complex problems.

9. An extensive knowledge base permits both skipping and intermixing of strategies to solve problems.

---

100 Glick, "Problem-Solving Strategies"; Pressley, "The Relevance of the Good Strategy User Model to the Teaching of Mathematics."

10. In some advanced subjects, knowledge of when to apply certain strategies cannot be taught to students. Students must induce the knowledge indirectly or intuitively, sometimes by examining problems already worked out and making inductive leaps in thinking.

11. Perhaps the most fundamental problem-solving skill is monitoring progress—knowing when little is being achieved, when mistakes are being made, and when to modify strategies.

12. In working at solutions to problems, students should be taught by the teacher to compare, relate parts to the whole, decompose whole to parts, control variables, understand causal relationships, recognize inconsistencies in statements or findings, distinguish between bias and objective data, generalize from experience, generalize from findings, move from concrete to abstract, and then abstract to abstract. In all cases, there is need to stress objectivity of judgment and calm emotions in light of existing conditions.

13. Students should be taught to identify what they know and don't know, when new or extra information is needed, what new information will affect the unknown, and how to deal with incomplete information.

14. Students can learn to use specific strategies through consistent practice in a variety of settings so that eventually their strategies develop into broad schemata. Diverse opportunities to use strategies increase abstraction and strategy knowledge; abstraction of the above strategies broadens one's ability to cope with different problems.

15. Abstraction of strategies is less likely with low-achieving and younger students. More explicit teaching is necessary for these students.

16. Students need to learn that time and effort are important for problem solving. Time and effort should be matched with task situations; students should be cognizant of wasting time because of distractions or nonfocused behavior.

17. In general, problem solving should focus on (a) understanding concepts and procedures, (b) discerning relations, (c) reasoning logically, (d) making inferences, and (e) applying the concepts and procedures, relations, logic, and/or inferences in nonroutine situations.[101]

SUMMARY

1. Most instructional activities can be categorized as one of four instructional methods: practice and drill, questioning, lecturing and explaining, and problem solving.

---

101 Most of the guidelines are based on Allan C. Ornstein, "Problem Solving: What Is It? How Can We Teach It?" *NASSP Bulletin* (November 1989), pp. 113–121.

2. The method of practice and drill has applications for seatwork activities, back-to-basics approaches, behaviorist learning, individualized instruction, and remedial instruction.

3. Questioning is perhaps the most important instructional method used today in whole-group instruction. Types of questions include low-level and high-level, convergent and divergent questions, and valuing.

4. Lecturing and explaining is the oldest instructional method. Different types of teacher talks (formal, informal, and brief lectures and explanations) can be effective with different students, but in general the length, complexity, and frequency of teacher talks should be reduced for younger and slower students.

5. Problem-solving models and strategies were discussed. There is a need to increase problem solving in our instructional approach; likewise, teachers need to teach their students how to problem solve.

6. The instructional methods discussed in this chapter have broad application for most teachers, students, and classrooms.

CASE STUDY

Problem

An experienced eleventh-grade teacher became aware that in all the years he had taught, only a few students actually responded to questions asked in a general manner. He also realized that he called on only one-third of the students in every class because experience indicated that the other two-thirds would not provide an answer either because they were embarrassed or they seldom knew the answer. He decided to try modeling theory to help him involve all of the students in his class.

Suggestions

He began the modeling with one class to see if the idea would work. Rather than waiting until the end of the lesson for questions, he began to divide the lesson into segments, inserting questions so that the students could immediately model their answers on his just completed explanations.

The questions during the lesson were designed to be *specific* and *rote*, constructed as closely as possible to the *exact* words in the explanation. When asking the rote questions he first called on a student who he was confident would know the answer. He would model the answer by (1) acknowledging its correctness, (2) repeating the question, (3) again stating the answer. Then he (4) immediately called on a reluctant student and asked the *same* question. To encourage answering, the teacher circulated and "moved" toward the student in a friendly manner.

He then constructed questions in three categories: (1) *"hard,"* (2) *"average,"* (3) *"easy,"* to be used for the *end* of lesson questioning or the *final review*. He modeled the "hard" questions as given above. He modeled the easy questions by first asking the "reluctant" students and then asking the "participating" students the same question.

By the semester's end, the students became used to the pattern and more were participating. By the second semester, enough were participating so he did not need to model as intensely.

Discussion Suggestion

Another teacher felt participation was important but thought students should succeed or fail on their own, since both success and failure was a reality of school and of life. To gain full participation he had his students answer questions sequentially, either from front to rear or across by seating. In this manner each student knew when they were going to be asked. If they did not know the answer the next student responded.

The teacher prepared a list of mimeographed questions to follow each presentation. Before he would begin to teach, the students could see the questions and knew to look for the answers during the lesson.

Sometimes, after the lesson but before asking the questions, the teacher allowed the students to meet in groups to discuss the answers, and then they would answer by groups. Other times they answered individually after being given time to again look at the questions.

Discussion

1. Which method might, with adaption, be suitable for almost all subjects? Why?
2. How might the first and second teachers modify their techniques to account more for individual differences?
3. Would one of these methods be better for schools with high-achieving students and one with low-achieving students? If so, which methods for which kinds of students? Why?
4. How realistic is the modeling method for use by every teacher? Why?
5. What methods in the chapter might be better than those suggested? Why?

QUESTIONS TO CONSIDER

1. Why is practice and drill used more often in math than English?
2. What is the difference between convergent and divergent questions? Why do most teachers rely on convergent questions?
3. Why is the wait-time important in questioning?
4. When should different types of lecturing and explaining be used?

5. What are the advantages and disadvantages of problem solving as an instructional method?

THINGS TO DO

1. List ten recommendations for conducting practice and drill. Indicate any that you feel particularly comfortable or uncomfortable with as a teacher. Based on these preferences, what conclusions can you draw about how you will use practice and drill?
2. Outline ten do's and don'ts in asking questions. Discuss each one with your classmates.
3. Teach a short lesson to your class by asking questions. Refer to Tips for Teachers 7.2 and 7.3 as guides to see how well you performed.
4. Develop a checklist for improving the lecture method. In doing so, review the procedures for preparing a lecture and recommendations for lecturing.
5. Identify five characteristics of successful problem solvers. What characteristics coincide with your own problem-solving strategies? How can these strategies be used to enhance your problem-solving instruction?

RECOMMENDED READINGS

Baron, Joan and Robert J. Sternberg, eds. *Teaching Thinking Skills: Theory and Practice.* New York: Freeman, 1987. A discussion of strategies for critical thinking, problem solving, and strategic learning.

Dillon, J. T. *Questioning and Teaching.* New York: Teachers College Press, Columbia University, 1988. A concise guide to questioning, when and how to ask questions.

Good, Thomas L. and Jere E. Brophy. *Educational Psychology: A Realistic Approach*, 4th ed. New York: Longman, 1990. Examination of the research pertaining to practice and drill, questioning, and problem solving.

Hunkins, Francis P. *Teaching Thinking Through Effective Questioning.* Needham Heights, Mass.: Gordon, 1989. A practical approach to the technique of questioning.

Louden, William. *Understanding Teaching.* New York: Teachers College Press, Columbia University, 1991. A discussion of how teachers think, feel, and teach; the emphasis is on the processes and techniques of teaching.

McLeish, John. *The Lecture Method.* Cambridge, England: Cambridge Institute of Education, 1968. Perhaps the most comprehensive text on how and when to lecture, including advantages and disadvantages of lecturing.

Raths, Louis E., Merril Harmin, and Sidney B. Simon. *Values and Teaching*, 2nd ed. Columbus, Ohio: Merrill, 1978. An important book on how to use valuing and strategies for lecturing and questioning, among other instructional approaches.

KEY TERMS

Law of exercise

Low-level questions

High-level questions

Convergent questions

Divergent questions

Valuing questions

Pivotal questions

Emerging questions

Instructional questions

Diagnostic questions

Wait-time

Probing

Lectures

Explanations

Final summaries

Internal summaries

Reflective thinking

Heuristic thinking

Chapter
8

Instructional Materials

FOCUSING QUESTIONS

1. How can instructional materials enhance learning?

2. What are the best methods for incorporating instructional materials into lessons?

3. How can the value and appropriateness of commercially produced or teacher-made instructional materials be estimated?

4. What are the characteristics of a good textbook?

5. How is the reading level of textbooks determined?

6. Why are workbooks often criticized? How can they be improved?

7. What problems might the teacher encounter in providing journals, magazines, or newspapers in the class?

8. What are the best methods for incorporating simulations and games into lessons?

*R*eal-life experiences provide the most direct type of learning, but they are difficult to supply in the traditional classroom. Most experiences in the classroom occur through verbal symbolism—written and spoken words. These classroom experiences may be easier for teachers to supply, but they may be more difficult for many students to understand. Verbal symbolism depends on the ability to conceptualize and think in the abstract, while the impact of firsthand experience is immediate and concrete. Various multisensory **instructional aids**—texts, pictures, games, simulations—can substitute for firsthand experiences and enhance understanding, so they are an integral part of the learning activity.

In this chapter we survey the use of instructional aids in general and then focus on written instructional materials, with emphasis on textbooks and workbooks. In the next chapter we emphasize technological tools and media equipment such as films, slides, computers, and videotapes.

PURPOSE OF INSTRUCTIONAL AIDS

Regardless of the type of instructional aid to be used, a teacher must consider it in light of the purpose of the learning activity. The instructional aid must be suited to that objective or purpose—whether it be subject matter mastery, skills improvement, or valuing. Although materials and media can stimulate and maintain student interest, they are not meant merely to entertain the students; students need to understand this fact. Unless students are properly guided, they become distracted by the attention-getting aspects of the instructional aids and lose sight of their educational significance. For example, the students of a teacher who frequently starts the lesson with a political cartoon, picture, or film-strip may, after a while, look forward to these little aids as a way of delaying or avoiding discussion and critical thinking.

High-achieving students, especially those at the secondary level, are able to cope with large doses of **verbal symbolism**. It is with slow learners and younger students that the advantages of audiovisual and tactile experiences become apparent.[1] The more senses that are involved in the learning process, the easier it is for the student to learn. Differences in learning styles must also be taken into account. Some students can learn a body of information by simply reading an assignment or listening to the teacher; others need additional stimuli and experiences involving hearing, seeing, and manipulating the subject matter. The old saying "one picture is worth a thousand words" remains true, but

---

1 Robert Calfee, "Computer Literacy and Book Literacy: Parallels and Contrasts," *Educational Researcher* (May 1985), pp. 8-13; Robert E. Slavin, "A Theory of School and Classroom Organization," *Educational Psychologist* (Spring 1987), pp. 89-108.

today the picture can be a photograph, filmslide, motion picture, television program, or videotape.

Instructional aids can affect students in many ways, by:

1. *Motivating students.* For example, model cars, trucks, trains, boats, and airplanes can be used to introduce a unit on transportation.
2. *Contributing to understanding.* For example, graphs can be used to clarify fluctuations of the stock market.
3. *Providing varied learning experiences.* For example, a workbook or paperback novel can supplement the assigned textbook.
4. *Reinforcing learning.* For example, when students hear the music of a composer, they can better understand a discussion of his or her style.
5. *Allowing for different interests.* For example, various sections of a newspaper can be assigned, depending on the type of lesson or the learner.
6. *Encouraging participation.* For example, role-playing increases individual involvement.
7. *Providing experiences that might not otherwise be had.* For example, simulations allow students to feel and sense experiences in the classroom.
8. *Changing attitudes and feelings.* For example, a photograph can be used to increase the emotional impact of abstract concepts such as pollution, war, and poverty.[2]

The experienced teacher will be able to use a variety of materials in a multimedia approach in any subject to vary the learning experiences. All students have different interests and abilities that determine what they attend to and learn. But what they learn also depends on the ability of the teacher to capture their attention and spark their interest through the use of appropriate instructional materials and media.

The needs of each learning situation determine the materials and media the teacher uses. These are some general considerations, however, that can help in estimating their value and appropriateness.

1. *Interest* is the extent to which the learner's curiosity is aroused and sustained by the use of instructional aids.
2. *Relevance* is the degree to which the experience provided by the aids is related to the learner's personal needs or goals.
3. *Expectancy* is the degree to which the learner expects to succeed at learning and sees success as being under his or her control when using the aids.

2 Allan C. Ornstein, Harrier Talmage, and Anne W. Juhasz, *The Paraprofessional's Handbook* (Belmont, Calif.: Fearon, 1975).

4. *Satisfaction* is the level of outcome and the learner's satisfaction in performing the tasks.[3]

All of these factors influence students' performance with instructional aids.

Guidelines for Using Instructional Aids

Just what instructional aids a teacher uses depends on his or her knowledge and experience, the availability of the materials, the lesson assignment, the subject, and the students. There are some basic guidelines for their use, however, summarized below. Instructional aids are made for situations in general; it is the teacher's job to tailor them to the needs of the students.

1. *Purpose.* Ask yourself what you are trying to accomplish and why this instructional aid is important.
2. *Definition of objective.* Clearly defined objectives are essential for planning the lesson and selecting instructional aids.
3. *Flexibility.* The same instructional aid can satisfy many different purposes.
4. *Diversity.* Use a variety of materials, media, and resources to develop and maintain student interest.
5. *Development.* Instructional aids must be related to the age, maturity, ability, and interest of students.
6. *Content.* You must know the content of the instructional aids to determine how to make the best use of them.
7. *Focus.* Focus students' attention on specific things to attend to while viewing, listening, or reading the materials.
8. *Evaluation of results.* Check students' reactions and consider your own reactions to the instructional aids.[4]

SELECTING INSTRUCTIONAL MATERIALS

Selecting appropriate commercial materials, especially textbooks, is the responsibility of teachers and administrators acting in small professional groups (at

---

3 Walter Dick and Robert A. Reiser, *Planning Effective Instruction* (Englewood Cliffs, N.J.: Prentice-Hall, 1989); Nancy Roberts et al., *Integrating Telecommunications into Education* (Englewood Cliffs, N.J.: Prentice-Hall, 1990).

4 George W. Maxim, *Social Studies and the Elementary School* (Columbus, Ohio: Merrill, 1983); Charles F. Schuller, "Using Instructional Resources and Technology," in D. E. Orlosky ed., *Introduction to Education* (Columbus, Ohio: Merrill, 1982), pp. 400-429.

the district, school, department, or grade level), in professional-lay groups that include parents and community members, or as individuals. The professional-lay group, according to Elliot Eisner, is subject to controversy when lay members have particular views about what students should be exposed to or when they object to what teachers are teaching.[5] Although committees make decisions about purchase or adaptation of materials on a schoolwide or districtwide basis, the teacher still needs to make professional judgments about the appropriateness and worth of the materials, since he or she is closest to the students and should know their needs, interests, and abilities.

The evaluator (committee or individual) should examine as many available materials as possible. The following general questions should be considered.

1. *Do the materials fit the objectives?* Materials should fit the objectives of the course as well as unit plan and lesson plan. Given the general nature of published materials, some may fit only partially; or it may not be possible to find materials to cover all the objectives. In such cases teachers need to create all or some of their own materials. On the other hand, there may be times when the teacher expands the objectives or activities to include an outstanding set of instructional materials.

2. *Are the materials well organized?* Good instructional materials will relate facts to a few basic ideas or concepts in a logical manner.

3. *Do the materials prepare the students for the presentation?* The materials should include instructional objectives or advance organizers.

4. *Are the materials well designed?* The materials should be attractive; the size should be appropriate for the intended use; print should be readable, with adequate margins, legible typeface, and comfortable type size.

5. *Have the materials been presented in a technically appropriate manner?* The material should not be "overpresented," with too much emphasis on design, elaborate presentation for its own sake, decorative but uninformative illustrations, unnecessary type elements. Nor should it be "underpresented," so that it lacks useful guides to its organization and content. Visual presentations, side notes in margins, appropriate headings, graphics, and color should be incorporated into the material.

6. *Do the materials provide sufficient repetition through examples, illustrations, questions, and summaries to enhance understanding of content?* Young students and low-achieving students need more repetition, overviews, and internal summaries, but for all students the material

5 Elliot W. Eisner, "Why the Textbook Influences Curriculum," *Curriculum Review* (January/February 1987), pp. 11-13.

should be paced properly, and they should have sufficient time to digest and reflect on it.

7. *Is the material suitable to the reading level of the students?* Many teachers can make this type of judgment intuitively by reading through the material, and others can make the judgment after students experience the materials. The most reliable method for all teachers is to use a standard readability estimate.[6]

8. *Does the difficulty of the materials match the abilities of the students?* Research indicates that highly motivated students require a minimum success rate of 50 to 60 percent when working with reading materials (or on related tasks) to maintain motivation and interest. Materials for low-achieving students, especially seatwork and drill materials, require minimum success rates of 70 to 75 percent when the teacher is nearby to provide corrective feedback and 80 to 90 percent (depending on their confidence level) when students work independently.[7]

Some questions more specifically related to content than these general considerations are listed in Table 8.1. Committees and teachers should vary the questions they ask to suit their own goals. Too often, the materials selected reflect what is available rather than the intended scope and sequence of curriculum offering, or the goals of the school district. Also, the teacher may want to observe students using the materials for several weeks and use their reactions to them in making final judgments. See Tips for Teachers 8.1. It is also worthwhile to consult with students about the worth of textbooks, since they are the ultimate consumers of these books. They represent a fresh and a different perspective. With the proper guidance from the teacher, in the form of questions and comments, students can provide valuable insight into what texts they prefer (and why) and which texts they understand and consider more interesting.

Duplicating

The types of educational materials used most by teachers are written texts (textbooks, workbooks, pamphlets, magazines, newspapers), pictures and models, and material used in association with games. They may be **printed materials**, that is, prepared and published commercially, or **duplicated materials**, that is, prepared by the teacher or school. Duplicated materials are used when teachers produce their own materials or when they wish to copy

---

6 Allan C. Ornstein, "The Development and Evaluation of Curriculum Materials," *NASSP Bulletin* (in press 1992).

7 James H. Block, Helen E. Efthim, and Robert B. Burns, *Building Effective Mastery Learning in Schools* (New York: Longman, 1989); Thomas L. Good and Jere E. Brophy, *Looking into Classrooms*, 5th ed. (New York: HarperCollins, 1991).

Table 8.1　QUESTIONS TO CONSIDER IN SELECTING INSTRUCTIONAL MATERIALS

1. Is there a need for the material?
2. Does the material further the objectives of the lesson?
3. Does the material contribute meaningful content to the unit or lesson plan?
4. Does the material build on previous learning?
5. Does the material relate to present learning in other subjects?
6. Is the material current, accurate, and defensible?
7. Is the material appropriate for the age, maturity, and experience of the students?
8. Is the material suitable to the reading level of the students?
9. Is the material free from bias, stereotyping, sexism?
10. Are the ideas, concepts, and points of views well expressed?
11. Is the physical presentation of the material acceptable? Are there appropriate margins, headings, summaries, review exercises and questions?
12. Is the material presented at a pace that allows for reflection and review?
13. Is the material suited for individual and small-group instruction? Can the material be used for direct instruction or mastery instruction?
14. Are the physical conditions in the room conducive to using the materials?
15. Are the materials worth the time, effort, and expense?
16. Will the materials last over a period of time so the initial cost will be worth the investment?

Source: Allan C. Ornstein, "The Development and Evaluation of Curriculum Materials," *NASSP Bulletin*, in press 1992.

---

printed material not easily available to students. Table 8.2 outlines three duplicating processes: photocopying, mimeographing, and thermofaxing.

Many teachers supplement the required text or workbook with instructional materials obtained from various sources—library texts, magazines and journals, government reports, newspapers. They duplicate these materials sometimes without being aware that there is a **copyright law** that controls their use. The law, enacted in 1976, permits an educator to make a single duplication for scholarly or instructional purpose of the following: (1) a chapter from a book, (2) an article from a magazine, journal, or newspaper, (3) a short story, essay, or poem, and (4) a chart, graph, drawing, or table from a book, periodical, or newspaper.[8]

Multiple copies for students, not to exceed one copy per student for a course, may be made without permission providing the following requirements are met.

---

8 American Library Association, *The New Copyright Law: Questions Teachers and Librarians Ask* (Washington, D.C.: National Education Association, 1977).

Tips for Teachers 8.1

Selecting and Using Instructional Materials

How do instructional materials best serve students? Well-developed materials contain well-constructed tasks and important aspects of what is being taught. Below are some guides for selecting, using, and developing instructional materials, with emphasis on reading and subject-related tasks.

1. Materials should be relevant to the instruction that is going on in the rest of the unit or lesson.
2. A portion of the materials should provide for a systematic and cumulative review of what has already been taught.
3. Materials should reflect the most important aspects of what is being taught in the course or subject.
4. Materials should contain, in a form that is readily accessible to students and teachers, extra tasks for students who need extra practice.
5. The vocabulary and concept level of materials should relate to that of the rest of the subject.
6. The language used in the materials must be consistent with that used in the rest of the lesson and in the rest of the textbook.
7. Instructions to students should be clear, unambiguous, and easy to follow; brevity is a virtue.
8. The layout of pages should combine attractiveness with utility.
9. Materials should contain enough content so that there is a chance a student will *learn* something and not simply be *exposed* to something.
10. Tasks that require students to make discriminations must be preceded by a sufficient number of tasks that provide practice on components of the discriminations.
11. The content of materials must be accurate and precise; tasks must not present wrong information or be presented in language that contains grammatical errors and incorrectly used words.
12. At least some tasks should be fun and have an obvious payoff to them.
13. Student response modes should be consistent from task to task and should be the closest possible to reading and writing.
14. The instructional design of individual tasks and of task sequences should be carefully planned.
15. There should be a limit on the number of different materials so as not to overload or confuse students.
16. Artwork in the materials must be consistent with the text.

(continues)

17. Cute, nonfunctional, space- and time-consuming materials should be avoided.

18. When appropriate, materials should be accompanied by brief explanations of purpose for both teachers and students.

Source: Adapted from Jean Osborn, "The Purposes, Uses, and Contents of Workbooks and Some Guidelines for Publishers," in R. C.Anderson, J. Osborn, and R. J. Tierney, eds., *Learning to Read in American Schools* (Hillsdale, N.J.: Erlbaum, 1984), pp. 110-111.

1. *Brevity.* The material may be no more than 250 words from a poem; no more than 1,000 words or 10 percent, whichever is less, from a prose work; no more than 2,500 words from a complete story, article, or essay; and no more than one chart, graph, drawing, or table per book or periodical issue.

2. *Spontaneity.* The materials are considered necessary for scholarly or teaching effectiveness, and the time required to obtain permission would interfere with the scholarship or teaching.

3. *Cumulativeness.* No more than one entire source (story, article, essay, poem) or two excerpts may be copied from the same author. No more than three sources may be copied from the same collective work, magazine, or journal during one class term.

4. *Prohibition.* The duplicated material should not create a substitute for a text or compilation of works, nor should it restrict the consumption or purchase of a published work. No charge shall be made to the student beyond the actual costs of duplication.[9]

Teachers should be aware of the potential consequences of violating copyright law; ignorance is no defense. When in doubt, it is best to follow the school district's policy (if it has one) or request written permission from the publisher or copyright holder to use the work.

Developing Materials

Sometimes slight modifications or supplements to published materials will make them suitable to use. Other times totally different materials are needed.

---

9 Frederick G. Knirk and Kent L. Gustafson, *Instructional Technology: A Systematic Approach to Education* (New York: Holt, Rinehart & Winston, 1986).

Table 8.2 USING THREE SELECTED DUPLICATING PROCESSES

Characteristics	Steps to Follow	Suggestions for Use
Photocopying		
Automatic, rapid copying Simple to control (dial settings and paper loading) Collating often available Copying through photographing	1. Lift document cover and place original face down. 2. Close the cover and set dial to number of copies desired. 3. Press start button (watch controls for indication of problems in the system).	1. Remove staples and paper clips before copying. 2. Check originals for irregularities (e.g., dark copy, off size, or tissue-thin paper, bent or torn originals). 3. Run one copy first when making many copies of a document to ascertain best copying position. 4. Learn how to deal with problems (i.e., loading paper, clearing stuck paper, stopping printing). 5. Learn how to use special features (i.e., collating, printing on two sides, adjusting for light and dark originals).
Mimeographing		
Automatic, rapid copying Consists of four main elements: stencil, ink, paper, and mimeograph machine Stencils are handwritten, typed, drawn, or electronically produced Duplicates letter- and legal-size paper Copying through ink printing	1. Prepare stencil appropriately according to method used (i.e., handwritten, typed, drawn, electronically produced. 2. Check ink supply. 3. Clamp stencil face down to revolving drum with the backing sheet face up. 4. Tear off backing sheet and clamp lower portion of stencil to drum. 5. Load paper supply by adjusting paper feeder and start the run.	*Typing Stencils* 1. Shift typing ribbon so keys strike stencil directly (if no stencil setting, remove ribbon). 2. Place a cushion sheet between stencil and backing sheet with wax stencil side face up. 3. Align stencil and set margins within markings printed on stencil face. 4. Apply correction fluid to make corrections. *Running stencils* 1. Run a few trial copies to check for quality. 2. Stay near machine to fix paper jams or add ink when necessary. 3. Remove stencil and place in a folder for future use.

continued

Table 8.2   *continued*

Characteristics	Steps to Follow	Suggestions for Use
Thermofaxing		
Automatic, rapid copying Consists of three main elements: heat stencil, thermograph machine, mimeograph machine Inexpensive method for making multiple copies of charts, drawings, articles, and complex illustrations Copying through imprinting and ink printing	1. Place material to be copied face up between the backing and carbon sheets of the spirit master. 2. Remove the slip (protective) sheet 3. Insert the prepared stencil into the thermograph machine (in a few seconds the heat will cause a transfer of carbon to the master). 4. Carefully peel the master from the carbon sheet 5. Attach the now imprinted master to the mimeograph machine 6. Set the mimeograph machine and run the copies.	1. Make sure original material that is to be copied is clearly printed (preferably in dark black print). 2. Become familiar with the lightness and darkness settings on the thermograph machine. This is the key to producing masters that will copy well. 3. Place used masters in a folder, face down on the smooth slip sheet for future use.

Source: Joel M. Levine, *Secondary Education* (Needham Heights, Mass.: Allyn and Bacon, 1989), pp. 150-151.

If none of the printed materials seems usable, you have to consider making your own.

Before developing new materials, you should examine your present materials carefully. There must be sufficient "no" responses to the evaluating questions in Table 8.1 to warrant producing new materials. There must be a sufficiently greater number of "yes" responses for your new material to justify the time, effort, and cost of its development.

If you decide to produce your own, take factors of time and cost into consideration. It is suggested that you take no more than 1 to 1-1/2 hours to develop materials for each lesson; any more is not worth the time and effort, and you may eventually lose interest in producing your own materials. The materials should be of a type that can be duplicated, put on a transparency or computer disk, or used again. The overall cost per unit declines as the number of copies increases, which is related to the number of students that will use the materials. Too often teachers make their own instructional materials at a high cost to themselves and their schools. There may be better uses for the teacher's time and the school's money.

A team of specialists can sometimes produce a better product than the individual teacher. The group may consist of subject specialists, learning specialists, and evaluation experts, as well as teachers who will use the package

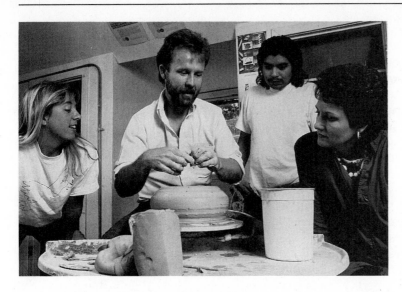

Students involved with diverse materials and activities are commonplace in good schools.

in the classroom. Estimates for the development of completely new material for a new program can run as high as 50 to 100 hours of development per hour of instruction.[10] Needs or problems must be addressed, objectives developed, methods and materials determined, tests and evaluation conducted, and parts of the program and the materials revised. The questions in Table 8.1. listed for evaluation of printed material apply as well to new materials. They can be taken as guidance for your own development of materials, as can the guidelines below in the event you work on a committee involved in selecting or developing materials.

Prepackaged Material

Prepackaged materials are a relatively new phenomenon (compared to the textbook), starting with the curriculum reform movement of the 1960s and the development of related government-funded curriculum projects. Evolving during the post-Sputnik era, the focus was on math and science and to a lesser extent on the social sciences and arts. The curriculum materials developed during this era took the form of prepackaged materials, reflecting a top-down model based on "experts" (usually the R&D community or professional associa-

---

10   Elizabeth G. Cohen, *Designing Group Work for the Classroom* (New York: Teachers College Press, Columbia University, 1986); Knirk and Gustafson, *Instructional Technology.*

tions) telling teachers what was best; that is, they developed the materials and expected the teachers to implement them on an "as is" basis.

The packaged materials often changed the way content was to be presented, how students were to be grouped, and what teaching techniques were to be used. The entire package was standardized and often described as "teacher proof"—meaning that teachers could not modify or change the materials.[11] The inference was that teachers were either incompetent or unable to develop their own materials or to change the materials to meet specific needs of their students. The materials were to be implemented as intended. Not only did such a philosophy exclude teachers, one reason for the demise of this reform movement, but also, according to Michael Apple, it deskilled teachers as professionals: it reduced their role in relation to the curriculum to a second-class status and altered their role in relation to students by encouraging everyone involved to see students as products.[12]

The current reform era has rethought the teacher's role and has included teachers in the developmental stage of packaged materials. Teachers are now seen by many "experts" or researchers as partners with whom they can work and by many school districts as playing a crucial role in curriculum making. Prepackaged materials do have much appeal and are still used today in elementary schools and in middle school or junior high school reading, math, and science programs. The difference is that teachers are now expected to help develop these materials and to transform them in the implementation stage to suit the experiences and needs of their students.

Guidelines for Selecting and Adopting Materials

Each school should have a curriculum committee to select and adopt instructional materials. At the secondary school level, this should be done by subject area. The trouble is, however, many selection/adoption committees are often unaware of how to proceed or create criteria for selecting materials. Many committee members, for example, are not afforded input for selecting criteria. An incomplete or irrelevant checklist is frequently imposed. In still other cases, only committee members are permitted input in the selection process. Others affected by the process who are not members of the committee feel left out.

Below are 16 guidelines for improving the selection process for instructional materials (including texts):

---

11 David Kirk, "School Knowledge and the Curriculum Package as Text," *Journal of Curriculum Studies* (September-October 1990), pp. 409-425.

12 Michael W. Apple, *The Politics of the Textbook* (Boston: Routledge & Kegan Paul, 1991); Apple, "The Politics of Curriculum and Teaching," *NASSP Bulletin* (February 1991), pp. 39-50.

1. The curriculum committee should comprise teachers, parents, and administrators; some schools might include students, too.
2. The committee should meet on a regular basis.
3. The committee should establish a mission or purpose in the early stages or meetings.
4. Needs and priorities should be established in relation to students and society.
5. School goals and objectives should be considered.
6. The committee should form subcommittees to consider each subject area comprised of teachers and members of each area.
7. Needs, priorities, and goals (numbers 4 and 5) should be the basis of establishing criteria for selecting materials (including texts) in each subject area.
8. Explicit directions for developing criteria (such as checklists) should be established.
9. The criteria should be easy to understand and reflect most of the items considered important by the school.
10. The criteria should be quantifiable in terms of a ranking system and/or qualitative in terms of specific advantages and disadvantages.
11. All teachers in a given subject area should have input, including the opportunity to review tentative decisions at selected points in the process.
12. The role of the sales representative should be considered; there should be safeguards that the criteria or outcomes of the evaluation are not being compromised or influenced by sales people.
13. If sales representatives are part of the selection process, each text/material representative should be given equal time and consideration.
14. The selection process should be considered ongoing and a continuous responsibility of subject area committee members; it should not be a five- or seven-year anniversary search, which is the case in many school districts.
15. The materials (or texts) should be evaluated to determine how well they really match the school's priorities and work out in the classroom. (This information is important for making modifications and future decisions about adoptions.)
16. Teachers should receive assistance or in-service education from either publisher, peers, or school district when new materials are implemented. (In particular, teachers need assistance in adopting new materials to the special needs of their students and classrooms.)[13]

13 Gerald D. Bailey, "Guidelines for Improving the Textbook/Materials Selection Process,"*NASSP Bulletin* (March 1988), pp. 87-92; Francis P. Hunkins and Allan C. Ornstein, "A Challenge for Principals—Designing the Curriculum, " *NASSP Bulletin* (September 1988), pp. 50-59.

PRESENTING MATERIALS

The teacher must incorporate instructional materials into the unit plan and lesson plan and modify them in a way that considers the students' developmental stages or age, needs and interests, aptitudes, reading levels, prior knowledge, work habits, learning styles, and motivation. The following factors should be considered when presenting materials (published or teacher-made).

Understanding

Understanding requires matching materials to the learner's abilities and prior knowledge. If students don't understand the materials, frustration sets in, making learning even more difficult. The teacher must know whether the materials are appropriate for the students to begin with and whether the students are understanding the material as it is being presented. The teacher must check for student understanding; this is especially important for younger and slower students and when teaching new information.

One educator suggests that teachers ask students or try to observe if they know *when* they understand and when they don't; if they know *what* they have learned; if they know what they *need* to know; if they know *how* to detect errors and improve.[14]

Structuring

Structuring, sometimes referred to as *clarifying*, involves organizing the material so it is clear to students. This means directions, objectives, and main ideas are stated clearly. Internal and final summaries cover the content. Transitions between main ideas are smooth and well integrated. Writing is not vague. Sufficient examples are provided. New terms and concepts are defined. Adequate practice and review assignments reinforce new learning.[15] Clarity is especially important when new subject matter is introduced and/or integrated into previous learning.

Sequencing

The teacher should arrange the material to provide continuous and cumulative learning and to give attention to prerequisite skills and concepts. According to two educators, there are four basic ways to sequence materials: (1) *simple to complex*—materials gradually increase in complexity and become broader and deeper in meaning; (2) *parts to whole*—parts of information are presented first to enable the student to grasp the whole; (3) *whole to parts*—whole concepts or

---

14 Jill Fitzgerald, "Helping Readers Gain Self-Control over Reading Comprehension," *Reading Teacher* (December 1983), pp. 249-254.

15 Velma I. Hythecker et al., "An Analysis of the Process Influencing the Structured Dyadic Learning Environment," *Educational Psychologists* (Winter 1988), pp. 23–38; Joseph L. McCaleb and Jacqueline A. White, "Critical Dimensions in Evaluating Teacher Clarity," Journal of Classroom Interaction (April 1980), pp. 27–30.

generalizations are presented first to facilitate organizing and integrating new and isolated items, and (4) *chronological* (which is a favorite organizer for many teachers)—topics, ideas, or events are studied in the order that they take place.[16]

Balancing

The materials need to be vertically and horizontally related or balanced. **Vertical relationships** refer to a building of content and experiences at the lesson, unit, and course levels. Ninth-grade math concepts build on eighth-grade concepts, the second unit builds on the first, and so on. **Horizontal relationships** establish a multidisciplinary and unified view of different subjects. The content of a social studies course is related to English and science.

Explaining

This refers to the way headings, terms, illustrations, and summary exercises are integrated and elucidate the content. Do the examples illustrate major concepts? Are the major ideas identified in chapter objectives and overviews? Do the headings outline a logical development of the content? Do the materials show relationships among topics, events, or facts to present an in-depth view of major concepts? The students should be able to discover important concepts and information and relate new knowledge to prior knowledge on their own through the materials. In short, the content of the materials should be explicit, related, and cumulative in nature.

Pacing

This refers to how much and how quickly material is presented. The volume or length of material should not overwhelm students, but there must be enough to have an effect. As students get older, the amount of material can increase, the presentation can be longer and more complex, and the breadth and depth can be expanded.

The rate at which the material is presented can be more rapid when old material is being reviewed than when the content is new. High-achieving and older students can tolerate more rapid pacing than low-achieving and younger students. The teacher should always build appropriate wait-time into his or her timing.

Elaborating

Learning is enhanced when the same material is presented in different ways. Teachers should to be taught to transform information from one form to another, and to apply new information to prior knowledge—by using various techniques such as comparing and contrasting, drawing analogies, drawing inferences, paraphrasing, summarizing, and predicting. A series of elaboration strategies helps students learn new materials. Students can be taught a broad

---

16 Allan C. Ornstein and Francis P. Hunkins, *Curriculum: Foundations, Principles, and Issues* (Englewood Cliffs, N.J.: Prentice-Hall, 1988).

list of questions representing different techniques (of comparing and contrasting, drawing analogies, etc.), or the teacher can raise the questions in class when discussing the materials: (1) What is the main idea of the story? (2) If I lived during that period, how would I feel? (3) What does this remind me of? (4) How can I use the information in the project I am working on? (5) How do I feel about the author's opinions? (6) How can I put this material in my own words? (7) What might be an example of this? (8) How can I explain this to my father, sister? (9) If I were to interview the author, what questions would I ask? and (10) How does this apply to my own life?[17]

Transferring

Instructional materials, according to Posner and Strike, may be transferred in that they are: (1) *concept-related*, drawing heavily on structure of knowledge, the concepts, principles, or theories of the subject; (2) *inquiry-related*, derived from critical thinking skills and procedures employed by learning theorists or scholars in the field; (3) *learner-related*, related to the needs, interests, or experiences of the students; and (4)*utilization-related*, showing how people can use them in real-life situations.[18] The first two organizers seem to work best with intrinsically motivated (self-motivated) students and the second two with students who need to be extrinsically motivated. Since most students need some extrinsic motivation, learner-related and utilization-related materials will be more effective with the majority of students.

TEXTBOOKS

The textbook is the most frequently used instructional tool beyond the primary grades, and in some cases it is the only one the teacher uses. "The textbook and its partner, the workbook," asserts Eisner, "provide the curricular hub around which much of what is taught revolves."[19] In terms of purchasing, it receives the highest priority, with the exception of costly hardware such as computers and copying machines. Textbooks can have a strong influence or even dominate the nature and sequence of a course and thus profoundly affect the learning experience.

Reliance on the textbook is consistent with the stress on written words as the main medium of education—as well as the way many teachers them-

---

17 Gaea Leinhardt and William Bickel, "Instruction's the Thing Wherein to Catch the Mind that Falls Behind,"*Educational Psychologist* (Spring 1987), pp. 177-207; Claire E. Weinstein et al., "Helping Students Develop Strategies for Effective Learning," *Educational Leadership* (December-January 1989), pp. 17-19.

18 George J. Posner and Kenneth A. Strike, "Categorization Scheme for Principles of Sequencing Content," *Review of Educational Research* (Fall 1976), pp. 401-406. Also see George J. Posner and Alan N. Rudnitsky, *A Guide to Curriculum Development for Teachers* (New York: Longman, 1986).

19 Eisner, "Why the Textbook Influences Curriculum," p. 111.

selves were educated. Dependence on the textbook is also linked to the time when a majority of teachers were poorly prepared in subject matter and read the text one day in advance of the students. Many of today's teachers, while better educated than their predecessors, may lack time or training to prepare new materials; thus they continue to rely on the textbook and workbook.

Advantages and Disadvantages

In many classes the textbook becomes the only point of view in the course. In effect, the course is based on the theories and biases of the author of the text. Even though the author may try to maintain objectivity, what is selected, what is omitted, and how the discussion is slanted reflect the author's views.

In order to have wide application and to increase potential sales, textbooks tend to be general, noncontroversial, and bland. They are usually written for a national audience, so they do not consider local issues or community problems. Because they are geared for the greatest number of "average" students, they may not meet the needs and interests of any particular group of students. Moreover, issues, topics, and data that might upset potential audiences or interest groups are omitted.[20]

Textbooks summarize large quantities of data and in so doing may become general and superficial and may discourage conceptual thinking, critical analysis, and evaluation. With the exception of those on mathematics, most textbooks quickly become outdated because of the rapid change of events; but because they are costly, they are often used long after they should be replaced.

Considering these criticisms, you might ask why teachers, when they have access to other instructional materials, rely so heavily on textbooks. The answer is, of course, they do have many advantages. A textbook (1) provides an outline that the teacher can use in planning courses, units, and lessons; (2) summarizes a great deal of pertinent information; (3) enables the students to take home in convenient form most of the material they need to learn for the course; (4) provides a common resource for all students to follow; (5) provides the teacher with ideas regarding the organization of information and activities; (6) includes pictures, graphs, maps, and other illustrative material, which facilitates understanding; (7) includes other teaching aids, such as summaries and review questions; and (8) relieves the teacher of preparing material for the course, thus allowing more time to prepare the lesson.[21]

---

20 Allan C. Ornstein, "Textbook Instruction: Processes and Strategies," *NASSP Bulletin* (December 1989), pp. 105-111.

21 George J. Posner and Kenneth A. Strike, "Categorization Scheme for Principles of Sequencing Content," *Review of Educational Research* (Fall 1976), pp. 401-406. Also see George J. Posner and Alan N. Rudnitsky, *A Guide to Curriculum Development for Teachers* (New York: Longman, 1986); Eisner, "Why the Textbook Influences Curriculum," p. 111.

Unless a curriculum committee or teachers can develop materials that are substantially better than a text in meeting evaluative criteria (see Table 8.1), there is little reason for them to spend time, effort, and money on "homemade" materials that are sometimes put together for the sake of throwing away the textbook. Given the facts that textbooks take several years to write and revise and that publishers often spend considerable effort developing and refining them through market analysis, subject and methods consultants, writing staffs, and copy editors, it makes little sense to condemn them as a whole as being ineffective or harmful to the educational process.

Good textbooks have many desirable characteristics. They are well organized, coherent, unified, relatively up to date, accurate, and relatively unbiased. They have been scrutinized by scholars, educators, and minority groups. Their reading level and knowledge base match the developmental level of their intended audience. They are accompanied by teacher's manuals, test items, study guides, and activity guides.[22] The textbook is an acceptable tool for instruction as long as it is selected with care and is kept in proper perspective so that it is not viewed as the only source of knowledge and it does not turn into the curriculum.

Stereotyping

Basic readers and textbooks began to be criticized in the 1960s and 1970s as irrelevant to the social realities of the inner-city and minority child. According to Fantini and Weinstein, our school books depicted "happy, neat, wealthy, white people whose intact and loving families live only in clean, grassy suburbs . . . Ethnic [and racial] groups comprising so much of our population are often omitted" or included only "as children from other lands."[23]

According to Ornstein, all American Indians were called "Big Horn" or "Shining Star"; people with Italian, Greek, or Polish names were likely to appear as peddlers or organ grinders, wearing red scarves and ragged clothes. Either there were no blacks or one black boy might be inserted in the background. Yellow or dark people were depicted in stories about China, India, and Africa, but they were always strangers and foreigners. Women were portrayed almost always as mothers, nurses, or teachers. Religion was rarely mentioned–except in relation to church attendance on Sunday morning. In short, the readers of these books were presented with a monocultural view of society; approximately 6.5 million non-white children were learning to read from books that either scarcely mentioned them, omitted them entirely, or represented them stereotypically.[24]

---

22 Thomas H. Anderson, "Content Area Textbooks," in R. C. Anderson, J. Osborn, and R. J. Tierney, eds., *Learning to Read in American Schools* (Hillsdale, N.J.: Erlbaum, 1984), pp. 193-226; Harold L. Herber, "Subject Matter Texts—Reading to Learn," in Anderson, Osborn, and Tierney, eds., *Learning to Read in American Schools*, pp. 227-234.

23 Mario D. Fantini and Gerald Weinstein, *The Disadvantaged: Challenge to Education* (New York: Harper & Row, 1968), p. 133.

24 Allan C. Ornstein, "The Irrevelant Curriculum: A Review from Four Perspectives," *NASSP* Bulletin, (September 1988), pp. 26-32; Ornstein and Hunkins, *Curriculum: Foundations, Principles, and Issues.*

Today, readers, workbooks, and textbooks exclude racial, ethnic, religious, and sexual stereotyping. (Obscenity, violence, and sexual topics are still generally avoided, as are such unpleasant issues as disease and death.) Major racial, ethnic, and minority groups, including the handicapped and elderly, tend to be well represented in story characters and pictures. Women are depicted as airplane pilots, police officers, construction workers, lawyers, and doctors. Blacks, Hispanics, and other minorities have professional and managerial jobs and are not all basketball players and musicians. Girls rarely play with dolls and boys rarely play baseball, at least not without girls.[25]

Finding good literature or good texts that meet all these requirements (and many more) is difficult. To accommodate some of the new criteria, many classic works of literature have been eliminated from the curriculum, and many bland texts and instructional materials have been included. Writes Connie Muther, "The idea is to please all and offend none (and thus) many textbooks (and related materials) have no clear point of view."[26] Although many new books portray the populace more accurately, they remain safe and in some cases they are boring.

Readability

Concern about student reading problems has prompted educators to identify textbooks and other reading materials that are suitable for specific student populations, especially below-average readers. **Reading formulas**, first devised in the 1920s to estimate the reading difficulty of a text, are now widely used by authors, publishers, teachers, reading consultants, and textbook adoption committees.

Some reading formulas count the number of syllables or the number of letters in a word, some count the number of words not on a specific word list, others measure sentence length, and still others remove words in a passage and test whether students can fill in the exact word that was removed.[27] Some formulas use graphs, regression statistics, and percentiles and range scores to calculate reading difficulty, and computer programs are now available for doing the counting and calculation chores involved in reading level determinations.[28]

---

25 Dennis Doyle, "The Unsacred Text," *American Education* (Summer 1984), pp. 3-13; Connie Muther, "What Every Textbook Evaluator Should Know," *Educational Leadership* (April 1985), pp. 4-8.

26 Muther, "What Every Textbook Evaluator Should Know," p. 7. Also see Connie Muther, "Reviewing Research When Choosing Materials,"*Educational Leadership* (February 1985), pp. 86-87.

27 Keith Kennedy, "Determining Readability with a Microcomputer," *Curriculum Review* (November-December 1985), pp. 40-42; Bonnie C. Konopak, "Development of a Prediction Scale for Text-Based Definitional Information," paper presented at the annual meeting of the American Educational Research Association, San Francisco, April 1986.

28 David L. Lillie, Gary B. Stuck, and Wallace H. Hannum, *Computers and Effective Instruction* (New York: Longman, 1989); Richard Venesky and Luis Osin, *The Intelligent Design of Computer-Assisted Instruction* (New York: Longman, 1991).

The best known reading formula was developed by Edward Fry. An estimate of the approximate grade level of the reading material is obtained by plotting on a graph the average number of sentences and the average number of syllables in three 100-word passages taken at random.[29]

The Raygor Reading Estimate, developed by Alton Raygor, is a graph procedure, too, but it is easier to use than the Fry method. Raygor's procedure is based on counting the number of words of six or more letters, instead of syllables. It has been validated with the Fry formula and is of equal accuracy.[30] There are many other reading formulas and methods for determining the reading level of instructional materials and textbooks.

Critics of the various reading formulas say that (1) they fail to consider students' prior knowledge, experience, and interests, all of which influence reading comprehension; (2) they assume that words with fewer syllables and shorter, simpler sentences are easier to comprehend than words with more syllables and longer sentences with subordinate clauses, which is not always true;[31] (3) publishers have reacted to these formulas by adjusting sentence and word length to give the appearance of certain levels of readability without necessarily providing them;[32] and (4) strict adherence to formulas robs prose of the connective words, vocabulary, and sentence structure that make it interesting and comprehensible and contribute to a style that makes the text worth reading.[33] In short, strict adherence to reading formulas often results in a boring and bland text.

Whatever their faults, reading formulas do help teachers to assess reading difficulty and to select printed material that is appropriate to the students' abilities. Since most teachers work with groups of students in which there is a range of abilities, it is advisable that the difficulty of the material not be more than one year below or above the average reading grade level of the group. If there is more than a 1-1/2- to 2-year spread in

29 Edward Fry, "Fry's Readability Graph: Clarification, Validity, and Extension to Level,"*Journal of Reading* (December 1977), pp. 242–252.

30 Alton L. Raygor and George B. Schick, *Reading at Efficient Rates*, 2nd ed. (New York: McGraw-Hill, 1980).

31 Suzanne Hidi, "The Effect of Information Salience on Text Comprehension and Recall: Lean, Salient, and Resolving Texts," paper presented at the annual meeting of the American Educational Research Association, San Francisco, April 1986; Taslina Rahman and Gay L. Bisanz, "Reading Ability and the Use of Story Schema in Recalling and Reconstructing Information," *Journal of Educational Psychology* (October 1986), pp. 323–333.

32 Alice Davidson, "Readability—Appraising Text Difficulty" in Anderson, Osborn, and Tierney, eds., *Learning to Read in American Schools*, pp. 121–139; Frank Smith, "Overselling Literacy," *Phi Delta Kappan* (January 1989), pp. 352–359.

33 Margaret T. Bernstein, "The New Politics of Textbook Adoption," *Education Digest* (December 1985), pp.12–15; Bernstein, "The Academy's Contribution to the Impoverishment of America's Textbooks," *Phi Delta Kappan* (November 1988), pp. 193–198.

reading ability in a group, the teacher should use more than one set of instructionalmaterials.

Comprehendability

Some educators now urge that **comprehendability**, not readability, is the major quality to consider when adopting a text. Teachers and textbook committees, for example, identify various textbook aids such as overviews, introductory objectives, summaries, and review exercises as devices that contribute to comprehendability. One reading expert lists more than 40 textbook aids that might be considered in selecting a text.[34]

In context with comprehension, textbook aids are sometimes called *structural signals*. Readers can use such aids or signals as key points throughout the text—in introductions, transitions, and conclusions. In a well-organized text, introductions foreshadow the main content, transitions link content across chapters and headings, and conclusions review content and point to significant implications. Signaling is particularly helpful for poor readers who need assistance in identifying content of the text, or what some educators call "anchoring" the content or using "graphic organizers." High-achieving students can function with few signals, or anchors, since they are integrating the material as they read it. In fact, integration of ideas is the key to reading.

Coherence also enhances comprehension. It suggests that readers organize text information according to either the text knowledge or their own background knowledge. Tighter linkages between text knowledge and the reader's background knowledge improve comprehension.[35] Texts that develop information through matrices, hierarchies, and categories are more coherent than texts that present information in topical, chronological, or list form.

Sequence connotes how students move from original understandings toward new understandings. A well-organized text moves the reader along a continuum from novice to expert. Linear sequences are much more common in texts than branching sequences (Figure 8.1).[36] Linear sequences are easier for readers to understand, but they lead to compartmentalization and isolation of information. Branching is more complex and appropriate for sophisticated or high-achieving students; this type of sequencing usually results in high-level or abstract understanding (how the expert thinks).

---

34 Robert A. Pavlik, "Tips on Texts," *Phi Delta Kappan* (September 1985), p. 86.

35 Bonnie B. Armbruster, Thomas H. Anderson, and Joyce Ostertag, "Teaching Text Structure to Improve Reading," *Reading Teacher* (November 1989), pp. 130-137; Meyer and Freedle, "Effects of Discourse Type on Recall."

36 Robert C. Calfee and Marilyn J. Chambliss, "The Structural Design of Large Texts," *Educational Psychologist* (Summer 1987), pp. 357-378; Marilyn J. Chambliss and Robert C. Calfee, "Designing Science Textbooks to Enhance Student Understanding," *Educational Psychologist* (Summer 1989), pp. 307-322.

Linear   Branching

Figure 8.1 Linear and Branching sequences

One of the most important factors in comprehension is the *match* between the text content and the readers' background. Good texts should be organized into coherent and explicit content that connects to the students' current knowledge and developmental level. Examples from the readers' own life experiences or environment are more effective than examples that contradict or are irrelevant to what the students know.

Perhaps just as important to comprehension are *transition words*, those little words and phrases (yet, also, next, etc.) that may seem unimportant to young students and low achievers, but provide cohesion within the text and suggest direction in thought. These words make up nearly 30 percent of the total words in a fifth/sixth grade social studies or science book and about 25 percent in a seventh/eighth grade social studies or science book.[37] Students must become aware of the importance of the linkage or direction they offer. Table 8.3 classifies these words into three types: "go," "caution," and "turn" signals. One might assume that certain subjects are more likely to have their own characteristic signal words or use certain signal words more often than other subjects.

Good reading requires that the student know when the cognitive actions being executed at a given point in time are permitting *progress* with respect to learning the content—that comprehension is occurring. If sufficient progress is being made considering the time and effort invested, the current reading is continued. If progress is slow or unsatisfactory, then behavior or text processing must be revised or abandoned in favor of another procedure (e.g., skimming first, taking notes, outlining, backtracking, checking the index to reread selected passages or terms).[38] In short, self-monitoring is at the heart of comprehension. It is an essential "executive" process, activating and deactivating various strategies as a function of the on-line evaluation of thought as reading evolves and understanding is generated. If the student is unable to accurately monitor himself, then most likely he or she will read with minimal comprehen-

---

37 Robert Hillerich, "The Value of Structure," *Teaching K-8* (March 1990), pp. 78–81.

38 Michael Pressley and Elizabeth S. Ghatala, "Self-Regulated Learning: Monitoring Learning from Text," *Educational Psychologist* (Winter 1990), pp. 19-33.

Table 8.3   CLASSIFICATION OF SIGNAL WORDS

"Go" signals indicate a continuation of the same line of thought:

for example	in addition	similarly
to begin with	for instance	then
finally	moreover	also
another	furthermore	likewise
first, second, etc.	next	not only but also

"Caution" signals indicate a conclusion or important point:

unquestionably	thus	therefore
hence	in conclusion	whenever
significantly	consequently	as a result
accordingly	in brief	without doubt

"Turn" signals indicate a change of direction or different view:

in contrast	but	even though
yet	otherwise	in spite of
on the contrary	although	despite
on the other hand	notwithstanding	meanwhile
conversely	however	nevertheless

Source: Robert L. Hillerich, "The Value of Structure," *Teaching K-8* (March 1990), p. 80.

sion. Students need to be taught to monitor themselves, to possibly change reading activities to improve comprehension, and to seek help when it is necessary (rather than close the book or throw it away in disgust or frustration).

Cognitive Task Demands

Critics have found that textbooks in nearly every subject and grade level cover too many topics, the writing is superficial, choppy, and lacking in depth and breadth (the phenomenon is called "mentioning"), and content wanders between the important and the trivial.[39] They fail to capture the imagination and

39 Harriet T. Bernstein, *A Conspiracy of Good Intentions: America's Textbook Fiasco* (Washington, D.C.: The Council for Basic Education, 1988); Marcy L. Stein, "Helpfulness of Context Plus Number Exposures," paper presented at the annual meeting of the American Educational Research Association, New Orleans, April 1988.

interest of the students or make students think, and they spurn current knowledge about cognitive information and linguistic processing.[40] The so-called best textbooks are often designed to entertain and to be decorative, but they provide only tidbits of information, lack adequate integration of subject matter, and do not stretch the student's mind. They unintentionally over-simplify and limit thinking!

Textbook adoption committees have contributed to the problem with their demands for topic coverage and easy-to-read prose. Special interest groups, with their passions and legal challenges, have added to the problem, causing publishers to become politically sensitive to the content at the expense of linguistic and cognitive processes. Teachers have done their part, too, since most teachers emphasize answers to be found, not problems to be solved or methods to be used.

Neville Bennett and his colleagues analyzed 417 language and math tasks assigned in texts by teachers and found that 60 percent were practice tasks, or content already known to the students. New tasks accounted for 25 percent, and tasks requiring students to discover, invent, or develop a new concept or problem made up 7 percent of the tasks.[41] In another study, approximately 84 percent of teachers rely on *textually explicit* instruction, a method of using printed material in which a correct answer can be obtained by selecting verbatim information from the textbook or workbook. Rarely do teachers employ *textually implicit* instruction, in which a correct answer requires students to make an inference from the textual information supplied. Even more rarely do they use *scripturally implicit* instruction, in which a correct answer requires students to go beyond the information given and call on prior knowledge and reasoning skills.[42]

Most teachers are right-answer–oriented in their teaching and testing. Hence, they are unwilling or unable to change from textbooks that are charac-terized by low-level cognitive demands and are divorced from how students think or reason. One might expect at least science teachers to exhibit textually implicit or scripturally implicit instruction, since they deal with scientific problems and laboratory experiments, yet the above conclusions were based on observations of seventh-grade science classes.

Teachers of mathematics, especially at the middle and junior high school grades, are not much different. Some data strongly suggest that many of these "teachers don't know mathematics. They assign the basic problems but skip word problems because word problems are harder to teach."[43] Students may learn to deal with simple right-answer problems (Which number is closest to

---

40 Rebecca Barr, *Reading Diagnosis for Teachers* (New York: Longman, 1985); Jill Bartoli and Morton Bofel, *Reading/Learning Disability* (New York: Teachers College Press, Columbia University, 1988).

41 Neville Bennett et al., *The Quality of Pupil Learning Experiences* (Hillsdale, N.J.: Erlbaum, 1984).

42 John R. Mergendoller et al., "Task Demands and Accountability in Middle-Grade Science Classes," *Elementary School Journal* (January 1988), pp. 251-265.

43 Ezra Bowen, "Flunking Grade in Math," *Time* June 20, 1988, p. 79. Also see Lyn Corno, "The Study of Teaching for Mathematics Learning," *Educational Psychologist* (Spring 1988), pp. 181-202.

27: 20, 31, 22, 35?), but they rarely learn how to think. (A better question would be: suppose you have seven coins and have at least one quarter, dime, nickel, and penny; what is the least amount of money you could have?) Kids who cannot handle this "penny-ante" problem are in trouble, but then some teachers may have trouble handling it—and that is trouble for the nation.

TEXTBOOK AND PEDAGOGICAL AIDS

Textbook aids, sometimes called *text-based aids, text features, textbook elements,* or *reader aids*, are designed to enhance understanding of the content. Aids that appear at the beginning of the chapter include overviews, instructional objectives, and focusing questions (prequestions). Aids that occur *throughout* the chapter include headings, key terms in special type, margin notes ("trigger items"), overview tables, outlines, discussions (point-counterpoint, pro-con), and illustrations such as graphs, charts, and pictures. Aids that come at the *end* of the chapter include summaries, discussion questions (postquestions), case studies, problems, review exercises, sample test questions, suggested activities, suggested readings, and glossaries.[44]

Pedagogical aids, sometimes called *instructional aids* or *teaching aids*, are materials designed for teacher use that are provided as supplements to the textbook. They include (1) teacher's manuals; (2) test questions; (3) skills books or exercise books; (4) transparencies or cutouts to duplicate; (5) reinforcement activities; (6) enrichment activities; (7) behavioral objectives; (8) lesson plans; (9) bulletin board displays; (10) supplementary tables, graphs, charts, maps; (11) parent involvement materials; (12) teacher resource binders; (13) computer software; and (14) audio- and videocassettes.[45]

Those aids used before students start to read the chapter acquaint them with the general approach and the information and concepts to be learned. The aids used while students are reading the chapter focus on organization of the content, provide examples, supply supplementary information, and repeat objectives. Those used after the chapter reinforce learning through summaries and exercises and encourage creative thinking through problems and activities. See Tips for Teachers 8.2.

The teacher may guide students with questions to facilitate comprehension: (1) Where is the information you need to know stated? (2) Can you find the information that makes the point? (3) Which words are unknown to you? (4) Where can you find a clue for understanding them? (5) How do the tables and graphs help you understand? (6) What do the margin notes tell you? (7) Does the order of summary (homework) questions correspond with the order of the topics? (8) Well, let's find out the answer to the fourth question, the ninth question, etc.

---

44 Ornstein, "Textbook Instruction: Processes and Strategies."

45 Sandra Conn, "Textbooks: Defining the New Criteria," *Media and Methods* (March-April 1988), pp. 30-31, 64.

Tips for Teachers 8.2

Student Use of Textbook Aids

Textbook aids (textbook elements) have continued to grow, as publishers and authors respond to growing needs of teachers and textbook criteria for selecting texts. Below is a list of features now commonly found in textbooks, with questions to ask the students to be sure they understand how to use these tools.

Features of Text: Sample Questions for Students

I. *Contents*
1. How do you use the table of contents?
2. What is the difference between major and minor headings?
3. In what chapters would you find information about____?

II. *Index*
1. What information do you find in an index?
2. On what pages would you find the following information____?
3. Why is the subject on _____cross-referenced?

III. *Opening material* (overview, objectives, focusing questions, outline)
1. What are the main points or topics of the chapter? How do we know?
2. Do the objectives correspond with the outline of the chapter?
3. In what section can we expect to find a discussion of ____?

IV. *Graphic material* (charts, graphs, diagrams) and *tabular material*
1. How does the legend at the bottom of the chart explain the meaning of data?
2. Based on the lines of the graph, what will happen in the year 2000? What do the dotted lines represent?
3. Where in the narrative does the author explain the table?

V. *Pictures*
1. Are the pictures relevant? Up to date?
2. What is the author trying to convey in this picture?
3. How do the pictures reveal the author's biases?

VI. *Headings*
1. What main ideas can you derive from the headings? Subheadings?
2. How are the subheadings related to the headings?
3. On what pages would you find a discussion of ____?

VII. *Information sources* (footnotes, references)
1. Where did the author get the information for the chapter
2. Are the footnotes important? Up to date?
3. What references might you use to supplement those at the end of the chapter?

(continues)

VIII. *Key terms in text*
   1. Which are the important terms on this page?
   2. Why are some terms in bold print? Why are other terms in italics?
   3. Where can you find the meaning of these terms in the text?
IX. *Margin notes* (or trigger items)
   1. Do the margin notes catch your eye?
   2. Why are these terms or phrases noted in the margin?
   3. Quickly find a discussion of the following topics____
X. *Supplementary discussion* (point-counterpoint tables, lists of suggestions, lists of issues)
   1. Why are the point-counterpoint discussions interesting? Which side do you take?
   2. What are the important issues on this topic?
   3. Which tips make sense to you? Why?
XI. *Summaries*
   1. If you could read only one page to find out what the chapter is about, which page would you read? Why?
   2. Where can we find a summary of the main ideas of the chapter?
   3. Does the summary correspond to the major headings?
XII. *End-of-chapter material* (review exercises, questions, activities, sample test items)
   1. Are the exercises meaningful? Do they tie into the text?
   2. Which discussion questions seem controversial? Why?
   3. Why should we do the activities?
   4. Take a practice test. Answer the sample test questions to see what we need to study.

The teacher can use the pedoggical aids of the text and teach the students to use the aids internal to the text. Students can be taught how to take notes, study, and integrate information in the text by learning to utilize textbook aids.

Textbook aids in particular can facilitate the development of cognitive processes. Table 8.4 lists four developmental stages of cognitive processes and corresponding cognitive operations, reader activities, outcomes, and their relationship to various textbook aids. The cognitive processes, operations, activities, and outcomes, in theory, each form an untested hierarchy in which one level is prerequisite to the next. The aids (last column) are not hierarchical, but they overlap in the sense that any one aid may facilitate learning at more than one level of the hierarchy.

Without good textbook aids, poor readers will learn little and capable readers will develop default strategies, or partially ineffective strategies for processing text

Table 8.4 LEVELS OF COGNITION AND READING, WITH IMPLICATIONS FOR USING TEXTBOOK AIDS

Cognitive process	Cognitive operations	Reader activities	Outcomes	Textbook aids
Identifying	Focusing on selective information Sequencing selective information	Copying Underlining Simple note-taking or discussion	Retention of target information	Overviews Instructional objectives Prequestions Key words or terms Margin notes Summaries Review exercises
Conceptualizing	Classifying main ideas of text Comparing main ideas of text	Logical or structured note-taking or discussion Distinguishing relevant information Relating points to each other	Retention of key concepts of text Internal connections (relations among ideas of text)	Headings Margin notes Point-counterpoint discussions Summaries Postquestions Problems Review exercises
Integrating	Analyzing main ideas of text Modifying ideas of text into variations or new ideas Deducing main ideas of text Expanding main ideas of text	Elaborate note-taking or discussion Making generalizations Hierarchical ordering of items Making inferences from text information	Understanding implications of text (explicit and implicit) External connections (relations between ideas of text and ideas outside of text)	Headings Graphs, tables Models, paradigms Postquestions Case studies Problems Activities (or things to do)
Transferring	Applying main ideas of text to problems Evaluating text information Verifying text information Going beyond text information Predicting from text information	Elaborate note-taking or discussion Evaluating, problem solving, and inferring based on text information Using text information to create new information	Establishing dimensions of a problem Understanding causal relations in text information Assessing the degree of universality of text information for predicting	Graphs, tables Models, paradigms Simulations Case studies Problems Activities (or things to do)

Source: Allan C. Ornstein, "Textbook Instruction: Processes and Strategies," *NASSP Bulletin* (December 1989), p. 109.

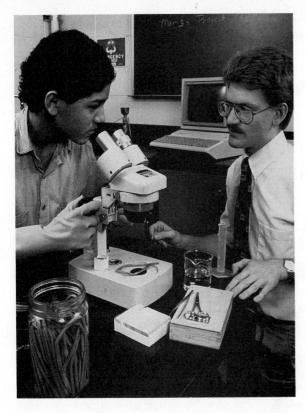

The best way to use a textbook is to go beyond it—to include various materials, experiences, and technology.

information. A default strategy is likely to involve focusing on topic sentences or unusual and/or isolated information, instead of main concepts and principles.[46]

A default strategy also leads to copying and memorizing long lists of information, rather than organizing, inferring, and transferring ideas of the text. All students who read engage in our four-step cognition sequence and reading sequence, according to Table 8.4; cognition and reading sequences are facilitated with appropriate textbook aids.

LEARNING TO READ

One does not become skilled at a sport simply by practicing various skills in isolation, but rather by learning how and when to apply them and by developing a positive mental attitude toward oneself as an athlete. Similarly, good

---

46 Richard E. Mayer, "Aids to Text Comprehension," *Educational Psychologist* (Winter 1984), pp. 30-42.

readers must not only possess important reading skills but also know how to apply them, and they need a positive attitude toward reading and themselves as readers. Based on this perspective, we define good readers as those who can integrate prior knowledge with present information. Good readers are not those who demonstrate mastery of isolated skills, but those who can apply their skills in a variety of reading situations.[47] Finally, good readers are those who enjoy reading and read as part of lifelong learning, not just to fulfill the demands of school.

The usual way to test reading has been to assign short pieces of text followed by multiple-choice questions that test comprehension. The current trend is to use longer text and test comprehension by asking students to respond critically and make appropriate inferences. Authorities today tend to agree on the following: (1) prior knowledge is an important determinant of reading comprehension, (2) well-written texts have structural and topical integrity, (3) inferential and critical reading are essential for comprehension, (4) reading involves the use of many skills and rules, (5) reading is systematic and self-directed, (6) the purpose of reading is to obtain meaning from the text, (7) reading involves conscious processing and awareness, (8) skilled readers apply metacognitive strategies to comprehend the text, (9) reading should be enjoyable, and (10) positive attitudes and habits go with reading for enjoyment and, in turn, reading achievement.[48]

Whereas research is mixed on whether whole learning experiences, student's own language, story readings, or basal reading approaches are more effective for young readers,[49] there is more agreement about helping secondary students become more proficient readers. Because of subject matter and text material, reading at this level consists of a series of complex interactions between *content schema* (prior knowledge) and *text structure* (features of the text that affect comprehension).[50] Most teachers of subjects emphasize content and overlook text structure, even though they rely on texts to teach the content; research strongly suggests the need to integrate both content schema and text structure.

Expository Text Structure

All things being equal, **narrative structure**, which deals with a broad theme and conveys information in story form, is easier for readers to understand than

---

47 Gay Su Pinnell, "Success for Low Achievers through Reading Recovery,"*Educational Leadership* (September 1990), pp. 17-21; Sheila W. Valencia et al., "Theory and Practice in Statewide Reading Assessment: Closing the Gap," *Educational Leadership* (April 1989), pp. 57-63.

48 Mark S. Meloth et al., "Teachers' Concepts of Reading, Reading Instruction, and Students' Concepts of Reading," *Journal of Teacher Education* (September-October 1989), pp. 33-39; Valencia et al., "Theory and Practice in Statewide Reading Assessment."

49 Steven A. Sahl and Patricia D. Miller, "Whole Language and Language Experience Approaches for Beginning Reading," *Review of Educational Research* (Spring 1989), pp. 87-116.

50 Marilyn M. Ohlhausen and Cathy M. Roller, "The Operation of Text Structure and Content Schema in Isolation and in Interaction," *Reading Research Quarterly* (Winter 1988), pp. 70-88.

expository structure, which the reader meets in textbooks. Children who learn to read in elementary school first learn through narratives. By the fourth or fifth grade, students begin to move into the more complex organizational patterns of the content areas which are conveyed through texts and expository structure. The emphasis on textbooks, and thus expository form, increases with the grade level: students who are unable to cope with this type of reading are bound to be low achievers.

Good texts are written with certain expository structures that can be taught to students; some of the common textbook structures are defined below.

1. *Response.* Sometimes referred to as "Question/Answer" or "Problem/Solution," these structures are most common and crucial for answering classroom or homework assignments. Often a problem is introduced, plan discussed, action presented, or outcome described. The teacher needs to help students become aware of what is being asked and where the solution can be found or how it can be worked out. In the middle grades and with low achievers, students as a group should discuss the difficulties encountered and what they did about them.

2. *Cause/Effect.* Students need to be taught to search for main ideas: (a) what is happening, (b) to whom, and (c) why. With this text form, the teacher needs to clarify the task or problem, present guided practice to the group, then independent practice. Whereas most texts usually deal in cause/effect relationships, especially science texts, the process is often reversed in social studies texts to effect/cause: an event is stated and the causes are explained.

3. *Comparison/Contrast.* This structure is common in most science and social studies texts. The author explains likenesses and differences—sometimes with tables, charts, or graphs. When tables or charts are used, the comparisons are usually given with categories and columns to help cluster the information. Students must be taught to slow down, deduce, and extrapolate data from the tables, charts, or graphs.

4. *Collection.* Texts often classify, enumerate, or list information. Although this text structure is easy for students to understand, the information is more difficult to recall because of overload (the list is too long) and the information is rarely integrated into larger concepts. Students must be taught to summarize or synthesize from long lists; most low achievers will attempt to memorize or write down long lists as opposed to conceptualizing the major points.

5. *Generalizations.* This structure is sometimes referred to as "Argument/Persuasion" in science texts and "Main Ideas" in social studies and English texts. The author presents concepts, summary data, or conclusions with supporting information. Students need to identify

the generalizations and their supporting information for each chapter. One method is to view major topics in relation to subtopics.[51]

6. *Topics and Subtopics.* Good textbooks sequence topics (sometimes called headings) in logical form and then integrate subtopics (or subheadings) within topics. Most middle school and junior high school texts contain between seven and fifteen pages per chapter; therefore, they should have three to four topics per chapter and two to four subtopics per topic. High school texts may have as many as twenty pages per chapter, although fifteen is the average. These texts should have four to five topics per chapter and the same number of subtopics per topic. More than four or five subtopics per topic will confuse or overload most readers.

7. *Whole-to-Part Organization.* Good texts are written with a whole-to-part strategy in mind, that is, the content is organized at several macro levels: whole book, parts, chapters, sections, subsections, and so on.[52] Content does not just evolve; it is organized with a larger purpose and themes in mind. The material converges, that is, it is organized in a way that is opposite to branching. Decisions of what content and how to focus on that content are made at each level of the text. Good text readers make use of similar macrostructures in their reading and thinking processes. However, all students must be encouraged to organize their expository reading around the overall organization of the text.

Students who have difficulty comprehending texts usually fall into two broad categories: concept unaware and data unaware.[53] The concept unaware reader can process the text adequately but has little prior knowledge or is unable to apply the knowledge while reading the text. The data unaware reader has adequate background knowledge but does not process the text adequately.

Most readers who lack comprehension are characterized as concept unaware, but there are numerous types of concept awareness and misdiagnosis can be damaging. For example, Anderson and Pearson describe two different dimensions of the problem: the most important one is reflected in the reader's general lack of background knowledge and experience; the other is evident in the reader's inability to recognize shifts in schema.[54] Also, some readers over-rely on a small domain of knowledge that seems to apply to a passage or section

---

51 Hillerich, "The Value of Structure." Headings two through five are based on Hillerich; discussions within each heading are the author's insights.

52 Chambliss and Calfee, "Designing Science Textbooks to Enhance Student Understanding."

53 Jon Shapiro and James D. Riley, "Overreliance on Data Processing in Reading," *Clearing House* (January 1989), pp. 211-215.

54 Richard C. Anderson and P. David Pearson, "A Schema-Theoretical View of Basic Processes in Reading Comprehension," in P. D. Pearson, ed., *Handbook of Reading Research* (New York: Longman, 1984), pp. 253-291.

and other readers overrely on the logic underlying a general concept without noting subtle differences that apply to the passage.

Techniques for assessing concept unawareness among readers can be performed by all teachers. These four questions can guide the analysis of the reader's performance:

1. *Are there miscues that are conceptually logical but inaccurate representations of the text*? For example, "Who discovered America?" Student's answer: "Columbus." Accurate answer for the passage: "The Vikings."

2. *In response to questions about a passage, does the reader tend to emphasize the same concept regardless of the emphasis and level of the question*? No matter what the question, the student's response includes a reference to Columbus and his three ships.

3. *In response to questions about the passage, is the student's response a representation of the logic of the concept rather than the logic of the passage*? For the student, Columbus is a hero, and in any situation about the discovery of America he must be included— and as a hero. The fact that he was searching for a shorter route to the East Indies and misjudged the route is insignificant to the student.

4. *When asked to reread the passage or section of the text, does the student become data aware and apply the appropriate concept*? In this case, the teacher can distinguish between concept unawareness and data unawareness by seeing whether the student can readjust his thinking to apply the appropriate concepts and logic of the text passages.[55]

All Teachers are Reading Teachers

All teachers, whatever the subject or grade level, are reading teachers in the sense that they should help their students read textbook material. Researchers suggest that students' comprehension of what they read is enhanced by (1) relating their knowledge and experience to the information in the text, (2) relating one part of the text to another, and (3) discussing the meaning of important new words.[56] Students need practice in inferential reasoning and other comprehension processes (see Table 8.3), but this may not occur because they are occupied with word recognition and vocabulary.[57]

Relating the text to students' experience can be done through asking their opinions, having them imagine themselves a part of the events described in the

55 James D. Riley and Jon Shapiro, "Overreliance on Prior Knowledge in Reading Comprehension," *Clearing House* (November-December 1990), pp. 119-123.

56 Bonnie B. Armbruster, "Schema Theory and the Design of Content Area Textbooks," *Educational Psychologist* (Fall 1986), pp. 253-268; Bruce K. Bromage and Richard E. Mayer, "Quantitative and Qualitative Effects of Repetition on Learning from Technical Text," *Journal of Educational Psychology* (August 1986), pp. 271-278.

57 Donald J. Leu, Linda J. DeGroff, and Herbert D. Simons, "Predictable Texts and Interactive Compensatory Hypotheses," *Journal of Educational Psychology* (October 1986), pp. 347-352.

text, or having them think of examples from their own experience. Relating parts of the text to one another can be achieved by asking students to summarize and analyze main points, to explain relationships and elaborate with examples, and to note main and minor headings, margin notes, key terms, and summary statements. Defining new terms can be accomplished by discussing in class selected terms that have conceptual meaning and encouraging students to use the dictionary and glossaries on their own. Providing repetitive sentence patterns and familiar words and concepts eases word recognition and comprehension tasks for students who have trouble reading. Paying close attention to instructional objectives or focusing questions, and answering review questions, helps students determine whether they understand the text material, and what sections need to be reread or skimmed.

Other methods for improving reading comprehension, as reported by Armbruster and Anderson, include the following:

1. Explain to students why it is important to know what they are studying so they can match the text to the task.
2. Teach students how to use the textbook aids.
3. Teach students to relate what they know to the text. Have students draw on their prior knowledge and experience to think of examples that relate to what they are reading.
4. Teach students how to outline and take notes on what they read.[58]

The notion of **advance organizers**, developed by David Ausubel to enhance conceptual thinking, can be used in teaching students how to read.[59] The advance organizers characterize the general nature of the text, the major categories into which it can be divided, the similarities and differences among categories, and examples within different categories. The organizers state the abstraction or generality under which data can be subsumed. To be useful, the organizers should be stated in terms that are familiar to the students and prior to their reading the text materials.[60] They are especially useful when the text is poorly organized or students lack prerequisite knowledge of the subject.

Although Ausubel and most other educators believe organizers should be presented before the text is read, others maintain that presenting them in the middle or after the text can also facilitate learning.[61] Other studies have shown that instructional objectives, overviews, prequestions, and specific instructions

---

58 Bonnie B. Armbruster and Thomas H. Anderson, "Research Synthesis on Study Skills," *Educational Leadership* (November 1981), pp. 154-156.

59 David P. Ausubel, "In Defense of Advance Organizers: A Reply to the Critics," *Review of Educational Research* (Spring 1978), pp. 251-257.

60 Michael P. Ford and Marilyn M. Ohlhausen, "Helping Disabled Readers in the Regular Classroom," *Educational Digest* (January 1989), pp. 48-51; Ornstein, "Textbook Instruction: Processes and Strategies."

61 Livingston Alexander, Ronald G. Frankiewicz, and Robert E. Williams, "Facilitation of Learning and Retention of Oral Instruction Using Advance and Post Organizers," *Journal of Educational Psychology* (October 1979), pp. 701-707; Mayer, "Aids to Text Comprehension."

prior to chapter reading facilitate learning of reading materials.[62] These textbook aids or cues are similar to advance organizers, because they provide advance information about the nature of the material to be learned. In addition, postquestions and summary activities that apply textbook material to concepts, problems, or creative things to do also enhance learning.

Teachers can help students gain facility in reading by encouraging them to think and by making them aware of the strategies needed to answer questions about the material they read. In this connection, researchers advocate the following introductory questions: (1) What does a good reader do when he or she reads? (2) What is the first thing you do when you are given a book or text to read? (3) What do you do when you come to a word you don't know? (4) What do you do when you cannot understand a sentence?[63] What should you do?

Claire Weinstein suggests nine specific questions to help students make sense of what they read: (1) What is the main idea of the story or chapter? (2) If you lived during this period, how would you feel about life? (3) If this principle were not true, what might happen? (4) What does this remind you of? (5) How can you use this information in the project you are working on? (6) How can you represent this in a diagram, a table? (7) How do you feel about the author's opinions? (8) How would you put this passage (heading) in your own words? (9) What might be an example of this?[64] The idea is to get students to elaborate on the strategies they use to process the information they read. Students use different strategies, and the need is to make students aware of what they are doing and how they can improve.

Teaching Text Structure

Text structure, sometimes called "macro structure," refers to the main ideas of the text, how information is organized, as well as the verbal and textual cues (or pedagogical aids) that help organize and bring unity to the text. Does teaching text structure to students increase learning? The research overwhelmingly indicates that students of all ages and abilities, and using texts in various subjects, improve their ability to learn from the text when taught to identify, summarize, and integrate text structure. Students' awareness of text structure improves (1) reading comprehension, (2) retention of information, and (3)

---

62 John A. Ellis et al., "Effect of Generic Advance Instructions on Learning a Classification Task," *Journal of Educational Psychology* (August 1986), pp. 294-299; James Harley and Ivor K. Davies, "Preinstructional Strategies: The Role of Pretest, Behavioral Objectives, Overviews, and Advance Organizers," *Review of Educational Research* (Spring 1976), pp. 239-265.

63 Eva Sivan, "Students' Concept of Reading: Their Metacognitive Awareness and Explicit Instruction," paper presented at the annual meeting of the American Educational Research Association, Boston, April 1987; Meloth, "Teachers' Concepts of Reading, Reading Instruction, and Students' Concepts of Reading."

64 Claire E. Weinstein et al., "Helping Students Develop Strategies for Effective Learning," *Educational Leadership* (December-January 1989), pp. 17-19.

written summaries of text material.[65] High-achieving students and skilled readers automatically abstract elaborate structures of the text.

Most learning in school depends on the ability to read and understand expository text. Students, in general have more difficulty with expository text than narrative text, because of insufficient prior knowledge, poor reading ability, lack of interest and motivation, and lack of sensitivity to how texts are organized.[66] In addition, a good many texts are poorly written, boring, and even confusing to students.

Well-written texts, however, have structural and topical integrity, and skilled readers make use of this integrity. Teaching structure does not add new information or content on a topic, but shows how the text is organized and how it can be read when the student is on his or her own—doing homework or studying for a test. See Tips for Teachers 8.2. This is essential for gaining mastery of the subject, since students must learn to read the text material on their own, without the teacher's assistance.

Teachers in all content areas need to foster awareness of text structure by having students make concrete representations of the ideas within the text. Such strategies are referred to as "mapping," "networking," and "graphing," and can involve (1) *diagramming*: students develop a diagram that represents basic concepts; (2) *outlining*: students use headings, subheadings, and paragraphs in the text; (3) *conventional classifications*: including (a) compare/contrast; showing similarities and differences; (b) problem/solution, showing a problem, attempted solutions and results; (c) cause/effect, describing stages of events and outcomes; (d) describe/enumerate, describing a major concept or theme, then listing supporting ideas for each concept, with details for each idea.[67]

These strategies are designed to provide more information about a topic, by presenting characteristics, specifics, explanations, and details. The skilled reader becomes sensitive to the author's text structure, including pedagogical aids, and uses them if they are well structured, along with his own prior

---

65 Bonnie B. Armbruster, Thomas H. Anderson, and Joyce Ostertag, "Does Text Structure/Summarization Instruction Facilitate Learning from Expository Text?" *Reading Research Quarterly* (Summer 1987), pp. 331–346; Lea M.McGee, "Awareness of Text Structure: Effects on Children's Recall of Expository Text," *Reading Research Quarterly* (Fall 1982), pp. 581-590; and Barbara M. Taylor and Richard W. Beach, "The Effects of Text Structure Instruction on Middle-Grade Students' Comprehension and Production of Expository Text,"*Reading Research Quarterly* (Winter 1984), pp. 136–146.

66 Armbruster, Anderson, and Ostertag, "Does Text Structure/Summarization Instruction Facilitate Learning from Expository Text?"; Gerald G. Duffy et al., "Effects of Explaining the Reasoning Associated with Using Reading Strategies," *Reading Research Quarterly*, (Summer 1987), pp. 347-367; and Marilyn M. Ohlhausen and Cathy M. Roller, "The Operation of Text Structure and Content Schemata,"*Reading Research Quarterly* (Winter 1988), pp. 70–88.

67 Beau F. Jones, Jan Pierce, and Barbara Hunter, "Teaching Students to Construct Graphic Representations," *Educational Leadership* (December-January 1989), pp. 20-25; Patricia A. Herman et al., "Incidental Acquisition of Word Meaning from Expositions with Varied Text Features,"*Reading Research Quarterly* (Summer 1987), pp. 263-284; and Ohlhausen and Roller, "The Operation of Text Structure and Content Schema."

knowledge of the topic, in helping to decide what information is important and how to integrate the new information. As for the teacher, it is important to stress one strategy at a time and have students practice and ask questions to fill in any gaps in understanding.

Guidelines for Using Textbooks

The following general guidelines should help increase the value of the text for students.

1. Do not become so hypnotized by the textbook that you follow it rigidly. Supplement the textbook with other instructional aids and printed materials (such as paperback books, for all students, and journals, magazines, and reports for middle and high school students).
2. Before they begin to read, question students about their knowledge of what is to be read. This helps them recognize what they know about the topic, what they need to know, and what they would like to know.
3. Adapt the textbook to the needs of the students and the objectives of the lesson. Do not allow the textbook to determine either the teaching level or the course content.
4. Organize guide sheets with definitions, questions, review exercises, supplementary readings, and assignments for each chapter.
5. Do not assign work in a textbook without referring to and assigning follow-up activities at the end of the chapter. Include assignments that call for understanding, evaluation, and critical thinking.
6. Teach older students how to analyze the textbook by noting when an author is editorializing, slanting the material, or over-generalizing.
7. Teach students how to interpret and use aids in the text, such as table of contents, headings, margin notes, illustrations, and index.
8. With another teacher or chairperson, learn to appraise the worth of the textbook. See Tips for Teachers 8.3.

Following is a list of more specific suggestions the teacher might make to students to improve their reading.

1. Try to be aware of how you gain understanding.
2. Reread unclear or difficult passages.

3. Change speeds—slow down when the material is difficult, go faster when it is easy.
4. Rely on imagery and expression of feelings to help illustrate passages.
5. Look for main ideas, what holds the passage together.
6. Look at the total format to identify and recognize key points.
7. Search for inconsistencies; ignore irrelevant information (for older students).
8. Use the context of the passage (for older students).
9. Modify and interpret as you read.

The following sequenced steps should help the teacher realize the goal of teaching text structure to students.

1. *Introduce.* Discuss with students why and when to use a particular text structure strategy.
2. *Choose.* Select a preferred strategy; present one strategy at a time.
3. *Demonstrate.* Show how to apply the strategy; present several examples of the completed strategy; summarize major points; introduce subtle variations.
4. *Group.* Have students work as a whole group, then in small groups to develop their strategy the first and second time.
5. *Involve students.* Encourage students to volunteer information, to share and compare with each other; make students explain what they did—and why.
6. *Feedback.* Provide ample feedback; help students understand different parts and procedures of the strategy.
7. *Review.* Ask questions; listen to student reactions.
8. *Individualize.* Provide several opportunities for students to practice on an individual basis; provide additional feedback.
9. *Reteach.* Teach specific parts that are still confusing to students.
10. *Shift responsibilities.* Shift responsibilities from the whole group to small groups to the individual; from the teacher to the students.

WORKBOOKS

At the lower grade levels, the workbook is often used separately to provide exercise for practice and drill in language arts, reading, and math; second only to the textbook, it dominates elementary school classrooms. In fact, in one study of 45 teachers, grades one to six, students spent as much time or more time alone with their workbooks as they did at other teacher-student activities.[68]

---

68 Jean Osborn, "The Purposes, Uses, and Contents of Workbooks and Some Guidelines for Publishers," in Anderson, Osborn, and Tierney, eds., *Learning to Read in American Schools*, pp. 45–111.

Tips for Teachers 8.3

Appraising the Worth of a Textbook

Here are some questions to keep in mind in assessing the worth of a textbook. The first group of questions deals with text content, the second with mechanics, and the third with overall appraisal.

CONTENT

1. Does the text coincide with the content and objectives of the course?
2. Is it up to date and accurate?
3. Is it comprehensive?
4. Is it adaptable to the students' needs, interests, and abilities?
5. Does it adequately and properly portray minorities and women?
6. Does it foster methodological approaches consistent with procedures used by the teacher and school?
7. Does it reinforce the type of learning (such as critical thinking and problem solving) sought by the teacher and school?
8. Does it provide the student with a sense of accomplishment, because it can be mastered and is still challenging?

MECHANICS

1. Is the size appropriate?
2. Is the binding adequate?
3. Is the paper of adequate quality?
4. Are the objectives, headings, and summaries clear?
5. Are the contents and index well organized?
6. Is there a sufficient number of pictures, charts, maps, and so on, appropriate for the students' level?
7. Does it come with instructional manuals and study guides?
8. Is it durable enough to last several years?
9. Is it reasonably priced relative to its quality? To its competitors?

OVERALL APPRAISAL

1. What are the outstanding features of the text?
2. What are the shortcomings of the text?
3. Do the outstanding features strongly override the shortcomings?

Source: Adapted from Allan C. Ornstein, "Textbook Instruction: Processes and Strategies," *NASSP Bulletin* (December 1989), p. 110.

At the secondary grade levels, workbooks are often used in different content areas keyed to or as a supplement (rarely independently) to the textbook for the purpose of practice. It sometimes exists, at the secondary grade level, in the form of a student's manual with drill exercises (sometimes problems) constituting most of the course content. Used in this context, students first engage in new learning derived from the textbook or another source. Then the workbook is used to reinforce the new learning; ideally, the exercises or problems are concrete examples of abstract learning. For this reason, many teachers view the workbook as a pedagogical aid and check with publishers to see whether a workbook accompanies the textbook.

Disadvantages

The value of the workbook depends on how the teacher uses it. The workbook is sometimes used as "busywork," to keep students occupied, or even worse, as a substitute for teaching. The workbook tends to overemphasize factual and low-level information. Students can spend hours, especially at the lower grade level, filling in blanks, completing sentences, recognizing correct words, and working on simple mathematical computations. According to critics, workbook exercises have little to do with and often discourage critical thinking or creativity, with learning the whole, abstract thought, or hands-on activities and materials.[69]

The teacher may assign workbook exercises in order to keep students busy while he or she grades papers, performs clerical functions, or confers with an individual student or group of students. The latter, in fact, often occurs at the middle and junior high school levels, when teachers divide students into reading or math groups. It is used, sometimes overused, in conjunction with seatwork activities—recommended by advocates of direct instruction and mastery teaching as a viable instructional approach. When workbooks are assigned either as busywork or merely to facilitate seatwork activities, and fail to link the exercises in a meaningful way to new information or to content coverage, the routine produces what critics call "management mentality" in both students and teachers, and such dependence "de-skills" teachers (they become ineffective) and curtails creative instruction.

Advantages

The merit of the workbook is that it performs the practice and drill function well and is helpful with young students who need to learn a knowledge base and with low-achieving students who need extra concrete activities to understand abstract learning and repeated exercises to integrate new learning. To the extent that the workbook is used in one of these instructional contexts, and that the exercises make learning more meaningful to students, it has value.

---

69 Richard L. Allington and Anne McGill-Franzen, "School Response to Reading Failure," *Elementary School Journal* (May 1989), pp. 529-542; Ruth Gardner and Patricia A. Alexander, "Metacognition: Answered and Unanswered Questions," *Educational Psychologist* (Spring 1989), pp. 143–158.

The criteria for judging that the workbook has merit include the following: (1) exercises (or problems) are related to abstract or new learning, (2) exercises are interesting and maintain students' interest, (3) exercises exist in proper quantity—not too many or too few, (4) students understand the directions (young students and low-achieving students often don't understand written directions), (5) students can perform or answer the majority of the exercises (if they cannot, frustration will mount and most students will no longer persist), (6)teachers provide needed direction and guided practice to help students learn the necessary skills and strategies for workbook comprehension or performance (the sheer ability to do something does not guarantee performance), and (7) teachers use the exercises discriminately (they supplement other instructional methods and materials).[70]

Workbooks are important for students for whom learning to read is difficult. Workbooks have good points and bad, and whatever bad points exist should be attended to, especially by those who write them and use them. For workbooks to be effective, Jean Osborn insists that they focus on a sequenced review of what has been taught, on the most important content, and on content that needs to be reinforced. Workbooks can provide students with (1) a means of practicing details of what has been taught, (2) extra practice for students who need it, (3) intermittent reviews of what has been taught, (4) ways for students to apply new learning with examples, (5) practice in following directions, (6) practice in a variety of formats that they will experience when they take tests, and (7) opportunity for students to work independently and at their own pace.[71]

Guidelines for Using Workbooks

In choosing, working with, or evaluating workbook materials, certain guidelines should be kept in mind. Below are a number of questions that should help make teachers aware if the workbook material is appropriate for their specific situation:

1. *Objectives.* Do the workbook materials meet the goals of the school? Which ones? Do the workbook materials meet the program objectives? Course objectives? Unit or lesson plan objectives?
2. *Readability.* What evidence is there that the workbook exercises coincide with the reading level of the students?

70 Patricia M. Cunningham, "What Would Make Workbooks Worthwhile?" in Anderson, Osborn, and Tierney, eds., *Learning to Read in American Schools*, pp. 113–120; Gail M. Inlow, *Maturity in High School Teaching*, 2nd ed. (Englewood Cliffs, N.J.: Prentice-Hall, 1970); and Bonnie J. Meyer, "Text Dimensions and Cognitive Processing," in H. Mandl, N. L. Stein, and T. Trabasso, eds., *Learning and Comprehension of Text* (Hillsdale, N.J.: Erlbaum, 1984), pp. 3–52.

71 Osborn, "The Purposes, Uses, and Contents of Workbooks."

3. *Utility.* What evidence is there that the workbook materials are helpful for the students? What evidence is there that students are interested in the exercises?

4. *Cognition.* Do the workbook exercises supplement or reinforce abstract thinking? Are the exercises intellectually stimulating? Are sample exercises or problems worked out, step by step?

5. *Content coverage.* Do the exercises cover the content in depth? Do they have balance in terms of scope and sequence of the content?

6. *Audiovisuals.* Is the workbook material user friendly? Are there a variety of appropriate illustrations—charts, tables, pictures, drawings, and so on—to facilitate learning?

7. *Learning theory.* Do the workbook exercises coincide (or conflict) with current learning theory? Which theory? In what ways do the exercises stimulate learning? In what ways are individual differences provided for?

8. *Pedagogical aids.* Is the workbook used independently or in conjunction with a text? Does a teacher's edition or instructor's manual accompany the workbook and is it valuable?

9. *Physical characteristics.* Is the workbook of quality material and binding? Is the workbook competitively priced? Can it be used more than once by students?

10. *Teacher training.* Are teachers trained in using the workbook (most need the training)? Does the training make any difference in how teachers use the workbook? How students integrate the materials?

JOURNALS, GENERAL MAGAZINES, AND NEWSPAPERS

These are primary sources and therefore excellent for developing thinking and research skills. Journals are the publications of professional and academic associations and as such are more technical then magazines and newspapers. The most popular general magazines used by teachers are *Time, Newsweek,* and *U.S. News & World Report,* although there are many others that can supplement or be the focal point of learning. (If you want to teach students how to read, Mad Magazine will stimulate many of them.)[72] It is appropriate to start students with the local newspaper at the middle grade and junior high school level, but the teacher should also consider the *New York Times, Washington Post,* or *Wall Street Journal* at the high school level. These papers are written at the tenth to twelfth grade reading level; therefore, the reading abilities of the student must be seriously considered.

---

72 Start children who are 9 or 10 years old on *Mad* and they will sharpen their reading and thinking skills—something to consider, although many educators object because they consider the views and material it contains questionable or even objectionable. Need a reason? The material is interesting to kids.

To enrich content, teachers in most subjects can encourage students to read journals, magazines, and newspapers. Many of these publications are interesting and more informative and up to date than the text. Gathering suitable magazine and newspaper materials can be delegated to the class or it can be done primarily by the teacher.

Journal and magazine articles have not been sanitized or toned down as textbooks have. They often express a point of view. Newspapers, in theory (not always in practice), deal in reporting, not analyzing or interpreting, data. It is up to the student to draw conclusions about and evaluate what is being reported. Editorials, department, "op-ed" columns, and letters to the editor are quite different from regular news stories, and students need to understand that this material is subjective. Although a youngster may understand that a particular point of view may be expressed in an article, he or she may be unable to identify distortions or biases and therefore accept the view as fact. In general, biases can be conveyed in eight ways: (1) through length, selection, and omission; (2) through placement; (3) by title, headline, or headings; (4) through pictures and captions; (5) through names and titles; (6) through statistics; (7) by reference source; and (8) by word selection and connotation.[73]

Although the teacher must use professional judgment in interpreting or assigning these instructional materials, students can learn to evaluate information contained in them by being trained to ask the following questions:

1. Is the account slanted?
2. Is important information treated accurately?
3. Are controversial topics discussed rationally?
4. Is there a clear distinction between fact and opinion?
5. Do the headlines, captions, and opening statements present the news accurately?
6. Are editorials and commentaries clearly designated?
7. Which groups of people usually read the publication?[74]

Guidelines for Using Journals, General Magazines, and Newspapers

---

The following guidelines should assist teachers and students:

1. Be sure that journal, magazine, and newspaper articles are within the students' reading and comprehension range.

---

73 Donald C. Olrich et al., *Teaching Strategies: A Guide to Better Instruction*, 3rd ed. (Lexington, Mass.: Heath, 1990); Olrich, *Staff Development: Enhancing Human Potential* (Needham Heights, Mass.: Allyn & Bacon, 1989).

74 Association of Teachers of Social Studies in the City of New York, *A Handbook for the Teaching of Social Studies*, 4th ed. (Boston: Allyn & Bacon, 1977), p. 127.

2. Select materials that are readily available and affordable.
3. The journal, magazine, or newspaper articles should be compatible with your teaching goals, given the fact that these materials often express a particular view.
4. Train students in reading and evaluating these materials. Children and adolescents tend to believe that whatever is printed must be true. A useful project is a comparative analysis of articles that take different views on a controversial subject.
5. Train students in the use of card and periodical catalogs and the classification and retrieval systems of journals and magazines so they can use these materials in independent study and research.
6. Many students, especially at the secondary school and college level, clip excerpts from journals and magazines (also books) or cut out entire articles found in the library. As a teacher you must make the work of the librarian easier by discouraging this habit before students go to the library.
7. Journal, magazine, and newspaper articles are excellent primary sources for student reports. Encourage students to take notes, summarize main ideas, and interpret ideas.
8. These instructional materials are also excellent sources for thinking about ideas, selecting and using information for assignments, and identifying and solving problems independently or in a group. High-achieving students can work independently; low-achieving students will more likely need the security of the group and the assistance of the teacher.
9. Assist students in doing research reports by providing a list of journals and magazines that are relevant to the topic and can be understood by the student.
10. Keep a file of pertinent articles to supplement the text and incorporate into the unit or lesson plan. Update the file frequently.

Trade Books and Specialized Magazines

Whereas general magazines and newspapers are appropriate for a wide range of secondary students, trade books and specialized magazines are more appropriate as a reading source for average and high-achieving students. Particularly in social studies, "trade books provide abundant resources for helping (young) adolescents appreciate other cultures . . . and gain global awareness." They help students understand economic, political, and social diversities both "within our own country and among our neighbors." They help cultivate in our middle school and high school students "a sense of tolerance and understanding of those with whom we share the world," the nation, as well as our neighborhood, school, and classroom.[75]

---

75 Miriam B. Hansen and Kenneth C. Schmidt, "Promoting Global Awareness Through Trade Books," *Middle School Journal* (September 1989), pp. 34-35.

Trade books are also excellent instructional materials for English and science courses, to supplement or integrate the text. The number and type are limitless; indeed, they may be good literature—from Shakespeare to Steinbeck—or they may examine common or controversial scientific problems—from nuclear warfare to environmental pollution. Because these reading materials for English are usually written well, with strong characters and interesting plots, they can offer adventure-filled and highly motivating reading. Although science trade books often provide basic information, they, too, can be compelling reading; some are autobiographical and others deal with real-life problems that affect the reader.

Whereas research shows that the majority of secondary teachers primarily or exclusively use the textbook,[76] especially in math, science, and social studies, teachers are becoming more aware of the richness of trade books. Textbooks do have limitations (as previously discussed), which are compounded by constant reliance on them and often perpetuated since virtually every new textbook is closely modeled on profitable predecessors.

Teachers need to understand that trade books provide excellent opportunities for motivating readers in the various subject areas and developing critical thinking skills. They also offer possibilities for interdisciplinary discussions (e.g., Tolstoy's *War and Peace* or Hemingway's *A Farewell to Arms* can be used to teach both history and English), creative writing, dramatizations, role-playing, independent work, research, and problem-solving activities.[77]

Specialized magazines are appropriate for the academic subjects, including minor subject areas such as health, art, music, fitness and exercise, and computers. Although these magazines are usually incorporated into the curriculum as supplements to textbooks, especially for high-achieving students, other uses—based on a recent survey of 176 elementary teachers, 160 junior high teachers, and 139 high school teachers in San Antonio—are shown in Table 8.5. The five most popular uses of specialized magazines in the classroom were for (1) extension activities, (2) recreational reading, (3) motivation to read, (4) change of pace, and (5) current information.[78] In the junior high school, 76 percent of the language arts teachers, 43 percent of the social studies teachers, and 23 percent of the science teachers used this type of magazine in their classrooms. In the high school, 57 percent of the science teachers, 31 percent of the English teachers, and 24 percent of the social studies teachers used them. Frequency of use and type of student (student's ability or achievement) were not reported.

Considering that textbooks are adopted for a period of five years or more in some states, it is not surprising that teachers across the curriculum look to

76 Jean Craven, "A View from the Classroom," *Social Education* (April 1985), pp. 340–344; Bernstein, "The Academy's Contribution to the Impoverishment of America's Textbooks."

77 Hansen and Schmidt, "Promoting Global Awareness Through Trade Books."

78 Thomas C. Gee, Mary W. Olson, and Nora J. Forester, "Classroom Use of Specialized Magazines," *Clearing House* (October 1989), pp. 53-55.

current magazines for updated information in their respective subject areas. These magazines are excellent instructional tools to promote student research skills and for independent projects. They are catalysts for creative writing, providing students with ideas for their own stories or essays. Finally, a variety of specialized magazine articles can offer multiple viewpoints and thus encourage critical reading and controversial discussions, as well as in-depth understanding and learning of subject matter.

Guidelines for using trade books and specialized magazines and newspapers are basically the same as for general magazines and newspapers. Perhaps one difference is that trade books and specialized magazines may entail more homework and out-of-class reading time—and thus are more suitable for independent learners and high achievers.

SIMULATIONS AND GAMES

Play is pleasurable and natural for children and adolescents, and simulations and games are formalized expressions of play. They provide a wide range of social and cognitive experience. **Simulations** are abstractions of the real world, involving objects, processes, or situations. **Games** are activities with goals, rules, and rewards. *Simulated games* involve situations with goals, rules, and rewards.

Simulations and games in education are designed to (1) develop changes in attitudes or behaviors, (2) prepare participants to assume new roles, (3) help students understand current roles, (4) increase the learner's ability to apply concepts and principles, (5) reduce complex ideas or situations to manageable concepts, (6) illustrate how people live, (7) illustrate how roles may affect one's life that one may never assume, (8) motivate students, (9) develop or analyze ideas, and (10) sensitize individuals to another person's life situation.[79] All of these general purposes cannot be obtained from any one simulation or game. The teacher must select simulations or games appropriate for the objectives of the lesson.

Simulations have become increasingly popular among educators, after much success in military, business, medical, and public administration arenas. Many simulations are now produced commercially for teachers, especially for use in conjunction with computers and VCRs. However, teacher-made simulations (not for computer and VCR use) are more often used in the classroom, since they can be geared for specific students, subjects, or grade levels. Several "how-to-do-it" publications have been produced by teacher associations for would-be developers of simulations and games.

79 Theodore J. Kowalski, Roy A. Weaver, and Kenneth T. Henson, *Case Studies on Teaching* (New York: Longman, 1991); Olrich, *Teaching Strategies: A Guide to Better Instruction.*

Table 8.5 REASONS WHY TEACHERS USE SPECIALIZED MAGAZINES

	Percentage[a]	Rank order
Provide extension activities	84	1
Provide recreational reading material	74	2
Provide motivation to read	71	3
Change of pace of instruction	69	4
Provide current information	62	5
Develop awareness of real-life situations	59	6
Provide high interest materials	57	7
Provide research tools	48	8
Provide range of topics	48	8
Provide learning incentives	42	10
Provide visually attractive material	42	10
Provide catalyst for writing	36	12
Provide career information	36	12
Encourage critical reading	34	14
Provide models for expository reading	25	15
Provide models for expository writing	22	16
Provide problem-solving activities	20	17
Other	5	18

[a]Percentages total more than 100% because participants could check multiple responses.

Source: Thomas C. Gee, Mary W. Olson, and Nora J. Forester, "Classroom Use of Specialized Magazines," *Clearing House* (October 1989), p. 54.

A simulation of a school board meeting for students permits them to explore local community issues. A simulation in health science may permit students to gain insights into the need for diagnosing medical problems or the need for empathy and care of loved ones who are ill. The dynamics of business, politics, and warfare can also be simulated. For example, in a simulation of a political situation, playing the role of president, a congressman, or a Supreme Court justice is an excellent way for students to learn about the nature of government and how the branches of government work. (If students have little or no experience in role-playing, they should be briefed on the nature of role playing before the simulation starts.)

One educator reports four advantages of simulations.

1. A simulation is [an excellent motivating device].
2. A successful simulation demands the use of many study skills and techniques . . . A practical relationship is forged between study and fun.

3. A full-dress simulation is a powerful way to make many . . . topics. . . come alive.

4. A successful simulation is very rewarding to the teacher. [He or she] takes a back seat to let things develop [and watches] students live, talk, and enter into [active learning].[80]

In short, simulations permit students to experience the nearest thing to reality.

Games are more informal and cover a wide range of situations, while simulations reflect a real-life situation and are more structured. Games have been an important instructional tool dating back to early nineteenth-century educational pioneers such as Froebel and Pestalozzi and, later, to the play wing of the Progressive movement.

Almost any teacher guide, for almost all grade levels and subjects, will list several games for enriching learning. Educational games have social and cognitive purposes and are not designed solely to amuse, but any game may contribute to learning. For example, Monopoly is a game played for amusement, yet it has some value for young children in learning to count and deal with monetary value. Checkers and chess, besides being amusing, challenge the mind; they involve math, logic, and sequencing of moves.

For younger students the value of the game may lie in the game itself, in the experience it gives them in learning to discriminate sounds or objects, to manipulate and gain facility in motor skills, or to play together and socialize. For older students, the value may lie more in the postgame discussion, or what some educators call the "debriefing session." (Simulations can also incorporate post-activity discussions or debriefing sessions.) By proper questioning, the teacher brings out instances of questionable behavior, when the rules were ignored, and the reasons for such behavior. Life situations can be perceived as a series of games, where there are winners and losers, where there is cooperation and competition, and where rules are broken and enforced. In this connection, games are an excellent means for teaching morality and ethics, and value clarification.

Guidelines for Using Simulations and Games

Numerous simulations and games are commercially produced, but teachers must judge whether they are suitable for their students or if they

---

80 Edmund Sutro, "Full-Dress Simulations: A Total Learning Experience," *Social Education* (October 1985), p. 634.

need to be modified, or whether the teachers need to develop their own materials. Here are some guidelines to follow when incorporating simulations and games.

1. Every simulation and game must have an educational objective. Distinguish between amusement games and educational games, between game objectives and instructional objectives.
2. The purpose of using simulations is to enable students to understand the nature of a problem and how to solve the problem.
3. Games should be used for teaching thinking and socialization to children in the lower grades.
4. Simulations and games should be viewed as an experience for learning content. Students learn by organizing and familiarizing themselves with the content—by experiencing as much as possible the object, process, or situation.
5. Simulations and games must be related to the content (skills, concepts, values) you wish to teach; this content should correspond with reality, and the relationship between the real world and the simulation or game should be clarified to the participants.
6. Only variables, instances, or problems that are significant should be introduced as part of the simulation. Insignificant elements confuse and obscure.
7. In simulations and games, roles played by students must be clearly defined (for example, "If you had been president in 1990, how would you have responded to the Iraqi invasion of Kuiwait?").
8. When hindsight is being used to solve a simulated problem or to make a decision, the variables or background existing in the real-life situation should be introduced.
9. Have some students act out the simulation and other students observe. Have the students discuss the simulation.
10. Simulation and game rules must be concise and clear. Teachers must be able to answer questions from the class about hypothetical situations before a game begins.
11. Simulation and game rules should be understood with relative ease by the students (players) involved.
12. The postgame (or post-simulation) discussion is crucial for older students to clarify skills, concepts, and values to be learned.
13. The postgame (or post-simulation) discussion should incorporate case studies, draw on student experiences, apply what was observed to real-life situations, and lead to suggestions for further study.
14. The postgame (or post-simulation) discussion should not be terminated because of lack of time (rather continue the next day).
15. A class or homework writing exercise can be incorporated into the postgame (or post-simulation) discussion.

16. Employ a series of questions that requires students to discuss their thoughts during the activity: What thoughts governed their behavior? What experiences resulted in certain behavior? What strategies did they use to make decisions to achieve their goals? Which strategies were most effective? Could they predict the behavior of others?

17. In most simulations and games students will interact. Participants and observers should discuss the interaction, if they are old enough, in terms of cooperation and competition, rational and emotional behavior.

18. To determine whether your objectives have been achieved by the simulations or games, use some form of evaluation, feedback, or discussion.

SUMMARY

1. Good teachers become better teachers when they use appropriate materials in their lessons. Learning what materials to use, and how to use them, comes with experience.

2. Instructional materials may be printed (available from professional, governmental, and commercial sources) or duplicated (teacher-made or copied from printed material).

3. Materials should be selected in accordance with well-defined and agreed-upon criteria, such as whether they coincide with the teacher's objectives, are well organized and designed, and are suited to the reading level of the students.

4. In presenting materials, teachers need to consider student understanding, structure, sequence, balance, explanation, pace, elaboration, and transfer strategies.

5. Types of instructional materials include textbooks and workbooks; journals, magazines, and newspapers; and simulations and games. Textbooks and workbooks tend to dominate as the major instructional tools in most classrooms.

6. Important aspects of selecting textbooks deal with stereotyping, readability, comprehendability, textbook and pedagogical aids, and aids to student comprehension.

7. The differences between textbook aids, designed to facilitate student comprehension, and pedagogical aids, designed to facilitate the teacher's instruction, were noted. A host of examples of each type of aid was discussed.

8. Several strategies for incorporating journals, magazines, and newspapers, as well as simulations and games, into the daily lesson were examined.

CASE STUDY

Problem

An experienced eighth-grade social studies teacher decided to do something about the instructional limitations of using a single text. Another teacher felt the same way so together they developed a plan to collect instructional materials from magazines to be used (1) independently of the text, (2) in conjunction with the text, and (3) to assist colleagues.

Suggestions

1. *Collecting Instructional Materials*

   They gathered copies of:

   a. Professional magazines such as *Phi Delta Kappan, Middle Grade Journal*, and methods magazines from their field and others.

   b. Specialty magazines such as *American History Illustrated, Horizon, Military History,* and *Smithsonian.*

   c. Free magazines such as those from the National Wildlife Federation, history and geography societies, the state departments of conservation and education.

2. *Using Professional Magazines*

   They:

   a. Collected appropriate sample units suggested by the magazines or submitted by teachers.

   b. Used the units as suggested in the magazine or changed them to better fit their needs.

   c. Adapted the units, or parts of the units, to the requirements of the chapters in their text.

   d. Collected units and teaching hints from all subject areas and grade levels and filed these separately. They used these to assist colleagues having difficulty planning or teaching certain subjects.

3. *Using Specialty Magazines*

   They:

   a. Rewrote articles to fit various grade levels.

   b. Took interesting and exciting parts to use in their text units as well as use in the chapters.

   c. Used the information and visuals to construct grade level units based on the articles.

   d. Used the articles in conjunction with the text either as enrichment, as interest centers with manila folder covers, or as catalysts for extra credit research.

Discussion Suggestion

A twelfth-grade teacher wanted to use instructional materials to supplement her history text. She held antiwar, pacifist beliefs. She ordered materials from a variety of organizations that taught peace studies and used them for group lessons on reflective thinking and inquiry on ways war can be prevented. Neither she nor the materials presented any wars as possibly serving a "just" purpose or having a long-term positive result (e.g., in the field of ethics, the "just" war concept). This did not bother her since she thought *no* war was just.

Her position did bother a colleague in her department. He felt she was using her position to present materials reflecting her bias in a partisan fashion and cheating her students out of a true experience of reflective thinking, as well as over-simplifying the question of how to maintain a democracy when faced with totalitarian aggression. He provided materials on the Greeks, who defeated the Persians thus preserving the idea of freedom and of democracy; on World War II which liberated Europe and Asia and saved thousands from certain death in concentration camps. (His materials also argued that anti-war teachers helped Hitler—since no one stopped him in the beginning.)

The teacher ignored the materials he offered. The outcome: he went to the principal with his argument. The principal insisted she broaden her presentation. She accused them of censorship and stopping academic freedom. Some parents, reflecting both views, became upset, one side claiming overt censorship of materials and the other claiming covert censorship by the narrow use of biased and partisan materials. The newspaper was informed of the controversy and the battle was joined.

Discussion Questions

1. How might a beginning teacher use the ideas from magazine materials as units? Are there possible problems? Should a beginning teacher stay with the text to be safe?
2. What is your feeling regarding anti-war and pro-war materials? Is age or grade level a factor? Why? Why not?
3. Do you think the teacher in the second example, who used the peace studies material, was indeed a victim of censorship? What is your reaction to her colleague's and the parents' charges of censorship by selective use of materials?
4. Is it the teacher's job to use the materials to develop opinions and attitudes toward social issues? What is the alternative to this, if you think there is one?
5. What might be your conscious or unconscious biases regarding social or historical issues? How might you examine them? Do you consider it part of your job to present many sides or one that is considered "right"?

QUESTIONS TO CONSIDER

1. What is the main purpose of using instructional materials?
2. How would you determine if a textbook presents a stereotypical picture of an ethnic or religious group, sex, labor group, or any other minority?

3. Which textbook aids are most important? Why?
4. What are important factors to consider when supplementing the textbook with a workbook?
5. Is there a danger in using too many materials in a class? Explain.

THINGS TO DO

1. Discuss in class ten questions to consider in evaluating instructional materials. Which questions or concepts are the most important? Why?
2. List five steps in developing your own materials.
3. In class prepare a checklist for evaluating textbooks.
4. Discuss which textbook aids you like in a textbook. Why?
5. Give five suggestions for using the following materials: (a) workbooks, (b) journals and magazines, and (c) simulations and games.

RECOMMENDED READINGS

Anderson, Richard C., Jean Osborn, and Robert J. Tierney, eds. *Learning to Read in American Schools*. Hillsdale, N.J.: Erlbaum, 1984. An important discussion about using textbooks and workbooks, as well as how to improve the reading and learning skills of students.

Apple, Michael. *Teachers and Texts*. New York: Routledge & Kegan Paul, 1986. Analysis of the politics of textbook selection and the social and cultural implications of the content regarding class, race, and gender.

Greenblat, Cathy S. *Designing Games and Simulations: An Illustrated Handbook*. Newbury Park, Calif.: Sage, 1987. A systematic guide for teachers who wish to design games and simulations.

Heller, Mary F. *Reading-Writing Connections*. New York: Longman, 1991. Effective teaching of reading through an integrated reading-writing approach; also proposing that every teacher is a reading teacher.

Morlan, John E. and Leonard J. Espinoza. *Preparation of Inexpensive Teaching Materials*, 3rd ed. Belmont, Calif.: Fearon, 1988. Several ways of planning, preparing, using, and evaluating materials.

Russell, David, Etta Karp, and Anne M. Mueser. *Reading Aids Through the Grades*, rev. ed. New York: Teachers College Press, Columbia University, 1981. A classic text describing hundreds of activities and situations for teaching reading, divided into reading readiness, beginning reading, and advanced reading.

Standal, Timothy and Ruth E. Betza. *Content Area Reading: Teachers, Texts, and Students*, Englewood Cliffs, N.J.: Prentice-Hall, 1990. Guidelines and methods for teaching reading across content areas; integrates reading and writing skills.

KEY TERMS

Instructional aids

Verbal symbolism

Printed materials

Duplicated materials

Copyright law

Vertical relationships

Horizontal relationships

Reading formulas

Comprehendability

Textbook aids

Pedagogical aids

Default strategies

Narrative structure

Expository structure

Advance organizers

Text structures

Simulations

Games

Chapter 9

Instructional Technology

FOCUSING QUESTIONS

1. What technological advance do you consider most valuable in improving your instruction?

2. What problems are beginning teachers likely to have in using instructional technology?

3. For what purposes might films, filmstrips, and filmslides be used?

4. When is it best to use an overhead projector?

5. Why is television an important source of information? How can teachers best use television for improving instruction?

6. How do you expect to incorporate computers in the classroom?

7. What telecommunication systems might be useful in your teaching field?

8. What educational value, if any, do video games have?

*T*his chapter is an extension of the previous one and deals mainly with audiovisual aids and electronic media. Technology is conceived as instructional when, through specialized materials and equipment, it supplements the conventional process of instruction. The special materials and equipment make it possible for learners to experience stimuli that might otherwise be impossible or impractical to bring to the classroom or school. Places, objects, and events can be seen and heard in the classroom.

Just what technology you use will depend on your knowledge, the teaching assignment, the capability of the equipment, and its availability. Effective use does require some basic guidelines. Turning on a movie projector or computer is not quite as simple as opening a book, but important steps in their use are not unlike the steps recommended for all other instructional materials.

In using instructional technology, six steps are recommended:

1. *Prepare* the students for what they are going to see, hear, or do. This may entail a brief explanation.
2. *Arrange* conditions to show special materials under the best possible conditions so they do not interrupt the momentum of the lesson. This includes making necessary adjustments, such as changing a seat for a student in the rear who has trouble seeing the screen.
3. *Operate* the equipment efficiently. Either you or an assistant will probably be responsible for this task; in some cases, students will be responsible for operating equipment.
4. *Guide learners.* One of the "musts" in using media effectively is to focus learners' attention on specific things to attend to while viewing, listening, or reacting to assigned materials.
5. *Summarize* the experience or follow it up with a discussion.
6. *Evaluate the results.* To know whether the material and equipment have been used effectively, some kind of evaluation is necessary. Did the particular lesson accomplish your objectives? If not, why not? And what can be done to remedy the situation?[1]

Kemp and Smellie list eight slightly different steps for using instructional technology in the classroom, which are particularly useful for interactive media.

1. *Specify objectives.* Enumerate what is to be learned or performed.
2. *Structure content.* Divide the content or tasks into naturally grouped or sequenced segments.

---

1 Allan C. Ornstein, Harriet Talmage, and Ann Juhaus, *The Paraprofessional's Handbook* (Belmont, Calif.: Fearon, 1975); Charles F. Schuller, "Using Instructional Resources and Technology," in D. E. Orlosky, ed., *Introduction to Education* (Columbus, Ohio: Merrill, 1982), pp. 400–429.

3. *Provide for learner control*. Permit students to control the pace at which they wish to move through the instructional program.

4. *Provide feedback*. Immediately inform the learner, through words or pictures, the results of answering questions, making decisions, solving problems.

5. *Provide for higher levels of learning*. Plan to have the learner analyze and manipulate information, observe results, extrapolate, and derive generalizations.

6. *Develop a pretest*. Allow learners to find out how they are progressing; match objectives with related content.

7. *Provide directions*. Provide instructions to students on how to use equipment or obtain resources to be used for study.

8. *Evaluate*. Measure the extent to which students have learned objectives.[2]

A wide variety of technological instructional aids are available in most schools. We will discuss the materials you are most likely to encounter and some promising new ones. You may need to seek on-the-job instruction for use of the specific equipment at your school.

CHALKBOARDS AND DISPLAY BOARDS

Chalkboards and display boards certainly do not represent any advanced technology, but they are definitely visual aids. The **chalkboard** is probably the oldest and most traditional piece of equipment found in the classroom. Next to the textbook, it is the most widely used instructional aid. According to two educators, the chalkboard "is so omnipresent that many of us fail to think of it as an audiovisual aid at all; yet most teachers would be hard put if they had no chalkboards available."[3]

There is usually one chalkboard at the front of the classroom and sometimes others at the sides or back. In older schools most of the chalkboards are black (hence the name blackboard), but because black tends to absorb light and make the room gloomy, it is being replaced. Light green and yellow reduce glare and eyestrain, absorb less light, are cheerful, and provide a good contrast with white and colored chalk.

The chalkboard is popular because it allows for spontaneity, speed, and change. The chalkboard can fit the tempo of any lesson in any subject. It can be used for displaying pictures and important clippings; drawing sketches and

---

2 Jerrold E. Kemp and Don C. Smellie, *Planning, Producing, and Using Instructional Media*, 6th ed. (New York: Harper & Row, 1989).

3 Leonard H. Clark and Irving S. Starr, *Secondary and Middle School Teaching Methods*, 5th ed. (New York: Macmillan, 1986), p. 403.

The use of the chalkboard is still considered a viable method and instructional tool for conveying important concepts and skills.

diagrams to help illustrate points of a lesson; projecting films and other materials; listing suggestions as they are offered; writing outlines, summaries, and assignments; and examining problems and evaluating procedures and answers. The chalkboard is particularly valuable for emphasizing the major points of a lesson and working out problems for the whole class to see.

Because of the its flexibility and familiarity, the chalkboard is sometimes overused. Many secondary school teachers rely too heavily on it to the exclusion of other audiovisual aids. Instead of making elaborate drawings on the chalkboard, teachers can show them with an overhead projector. Or instead of writing long lists of problems or notes on the board for the students, the teacher can duplicate them and hand them out to the students. The time saved by these procedures can be devoted to other aspects of the lesson. The daily homework assignments can be duplicated on a weekly basis and handed out to the students, thus eliminating the need for the teacher to write them on the chalkboard and the need for the students to copy them down. This method also allows absent students to keep up with their assignments at home. This does not mean that the chalkboard should not be used, but that it should not be used when other procedures that are available might work more efficiently.

Display boards are used for displaying student projects and progress; displaying current items of interest related to a lesson or unit; posting announcements, memos, and routine assignments; and decorating the room. There are many types: bulletin board, pegboard, flannel board, magnetic board. The boards stimulate student creativity and interest, promote student participation in the learning activity, and make the room more cheerful and student-oriented. If there are no display boards in a room, a portion of the chalkboard can be reserved for this purpose. Especially in the middle grades, the display board is important enough that this would be a good use of some chalkboard space.

Guidelines for Using the Chalkboard

1. Write legibly and large enough for all to see. If your handwriting is cursive and you have trouble making it legible on the board, then print. Another way for compensating for a poor handwriting is to write with large letters.

2. Use the chalkboard as if you were writing on paper. Proceed from left to right. If crevices divide the chalkboard, treat them as margins—that is, end lines on the right side and start new lines on the left side. Try not to go beyond the margin for the sake of inserting one or two words.

3. While writing, stand to one side of the board as much as possible so you can maintain eye contact with the students.

4. When referring to work already on the chalkboard, stand to the side so you don't block the students' view. Use a pointer (a ruler or yardstick will do).

5. Don't talk toward the chalkboard while writing on it.

6. If the chalkboard space is limited, draw a line down the middle of the board, thus creating a margin and two smaller boards. This will allow you to use the space more efficiently.

7. Organize your chalkboard work ahead of time. When possible, outline items with a letter or numbering system. There are many possible systems, but use one form for purposes of consistency.

8. Don't clutter the board. Limit your writing or drawing to major ideas of the lesson.

9. If you must abbreviate, use standard forms. Don't use unusual or personal abbreviations. Check the dictionary if you are unsure.

10. Utilize colored chalk, rulers, string, stencils, and other materials to make your illustrations more effective.

11. Don't get embarrassed or show resentment if you make a mistake and a student corrects you. Instead, thank the student for the help.

12. If you are working with young or low-achieving students, write in complete sentences. They need practice in seeing and writing correct grammar.

13. Establish routine uses for the chalkboard. Have specific spaces for homework assignments, drill problems, or the instructional objective.

14. Erase the chalkboards completely after you finish, and keep them clean. If you are busy, ask a student to erase them while you continue with another part of the lesson.

15. Don't overuse the chalkboard. You can ditto or mimeograph lengthy or complicated materials.

FILMS, FILMSTRIPS, AND FILMSLIDES

According to one educator, **film** is the most influential and seductive educational medium for transmitting ideas and persuading an audience to a point of view.[4] Because of the vivid, often larger-than-life images it presents, the motion picture has a dramatic impact on its audience. Films both interest and motivate students. Thousands of good films have been made expressly for educational purposes. They can be divided into the following categories: (1) historical, (2) dramatic, (3) special topic, (4) "slice of life," and (5) animated.[5] The movie is particularly useful for showing processes in which motion is involved or in which slow motion can be used.

The **filmstrip** is a series of pictures in a fixed sequence on a strip of 35 millimeter film for still projection. Filmstrips are compact, easy to store, relatively inexpensive to buy, easy to project, and somewhat flexible in use because pictures thought to be unnecessary can be skipped over. Explanatory symbols or captions are often incorporated, and filmstrips with recorded sound narrations, called *sound filmstrips*, are being produced.

Filmslides are individual pieces of film for projection, mounted on thin cardboard or plastic frames, usually 2-inch squares. They are more flexible to use than filmstrips, since unnecessary slides can be omitted. Slide sets are sometimes accompanied by audiotape narrations. Slides may be changed manually or automatically with a device that advances the slides at preset time intervals.

The speed of showing both filmstrips and filmslides is adjustable. Each frame or slide can be discussed and the time allowed for discussion can vary; thus the teacher can set and change the pace of instruction. A film, on the other hand, is presented in a fixed, continuous sequence and the speed is also fixed (unless the images are such that the projector or video equipment can be slowed down or the projection can be stopped). Because students are forced to think at the speed and in the sequence determined by the film, it tends to create a passive rather than an active mind set. Since filmstrips and slides can be viewed on either a small or a large screen, they are suited to individual and small-group instruction as well as whole-class instruction.[6]

Several hundred commercial companies produce films, filmstrips, and filmslides for educational purposes. Catalogs listing producers, titles, rental or purchase rates, and ordering instructions are often circulated by school districts to local schools. Most films are rented on a daily or weekly basis, and most filmstrips and slides are bought. Some school systems maintain a film library. Films are also available on free loan or for a nominal fee from university and

---

4 Hart Wagner, *Teaching with Film* (Bloomington, Ind.: Phi Delta Kappa Foundation, 1977).

5 David F. Naylor and Richard Diem, *Elementary and Middle School Social Studies* (New York: Random House, 1987); William Louden, *Understanding Teaching* (Rutherford, N.J.: Cassell, 1991).

6 Schuller, "Using Instructional Resources and Technology."

public libraries and various political, social, and cultural groups. Enterprising students can take their own 8 millimeter films and 35 millimeter photographs for slides on field trips, in the classroom, or after school.

Guidelines for Using Films, Filmstrips, and Filmslides

1. Keep the film lists up to date.
2. When ordering from sources outside the school, be sure to order well in advance of the screening date.
3. Preview the film to make sure it is appropriate to the students' interests and maturity level and to familiarize yourself with the content.
4. Arrange to have the projector and screen or video equipment in the classroom and set up on the day scheduled for showing the film. Be sure to arrange for someone to run the projector if you do not know how. Check to see that the projector is operating properly before class starts.
5. Be sure all students can see the screen. The room should be dark enough to produce a quality picture. Good acoustics are also important. Sometimes a special room or the auditorium can be scheduled for showing a movie.
6. Prepare the students for the presentation. A list of major points or questions to answer, or a guide to the lesson is often helpful. Hand it out to the class before the showing.
7. Note-taking is difficult in a darkened room and should not be expected or encouraged while the projector is running.
8. Use the equipment properly. Turn off the projector when it is not in use. Handle film with care. Touch it only along the margins so you don't smudge it with fingerprints.
9. View a film without interruption, if possible. Save questions and comments for a summary discussion. Show filmstrips and filmslides frame by frame at a reasonable pace. Skip over or omit unnecessary ones.
10. If commentary is needed during the movie, either stop the projector or reduce the volume, but do this as little as possible. Allow time for discussion after the movie.
11. When showing filmstrips with written captions, call on volunteers to read them or summarize detailed captions. (Do not call on nonvolunteers, because it may be embarrassing for them if the captions are difficult to read.)
12. Allow time for discussion after the film.
13. Be sure to put the film back properly into its container.
14. Disconnect all wires. Store equipment in its appropriate place at the end of the lesson or day.

Overhead Projector

The **overhead projector** projects images of transparencies on a screen, wall, or chalkboard. The transparency is placed on the glass on top of the projector. Light from the lamp located in the projector produces an image that is reflected onto a viewing surface in back of the operator. The teacher can face the class while using it. Since the room does not need to be dark, students can take notes. The machine is lightweight and portable. Because the overhead projector is so convenient to use, it has become standard equipment in many classrooms and has replaced the chalkboard in many of their functions.[7]

Commercially prepared transparencies for the overhead projector are available for several subject areas. These materials can also be prepared by the teacher. The transparencies can be prepared before the class (which is best if materials are long or complex), or they can be made during a discussion and also changed as necessary to elaborate on a point. The teacher can point out various details on the projected image with a grease pencil while still facing the class.

Handmade transparencies are usually made of plastic and drawn with a felt-tip pen or grease pencil. To prevent smudging, start coloring in the center of the transparency and work toward the edges. Typed materials can be added with the use of a thermofax machine.

New overhead projectors have an extra feature or attachment to add motion and speed to special transparencies so that various moving elements can be shown.

Guidelines for Using Overhead Projectors

1. Keep the materials up to date.
2. Arrange ahead of time to have the projector and other necessary materials available when you need them. Arrange to have someone in the room who knows how to operate the projector if you do not know how.
3. Preview the materials or prepare them before class begins.
4. Handle overhead transparencies with care; don't smudge them, get fingerprints on them, or let the colors from the grease pens run together before drying.
5. Label materials properly for filing and reshowing.

---

7 Len Masterman, *Teaching the Media* (New York: Routledge, 1988); Marvin Pasch et al., *Teaching as Decision Making* (New York: Longman, 1991).

6. Be sure the materials are appropriate for the students' interests and maturity level and that they fulfill your instructional objectives.
7. Be sure all students can see the surface on which the material is projected. Focus the materials properly.
8. Arrange the materials in sequence with the lesson.
9. Explain and discuss each of the projected materials.
10. Shut off the machine when it is not in use during discussions.

TELEVISION

Recent evidence makes it clear that television has become "a second school system." Children under 5 years old watch television an average of 24 hours a week, or about one-fifth of their waking hours. By the time a child graduates from high school, he or she will have spent 15,000 to 20,000 hours in front of the screen as compared to 11,000 to 12,000 hours in school.[8] Before children reach 18, they will have seen 350,000 commercials "urging them to want, want, want."[9]

Rather than viewing television as a second school system, Neil Postman views it and other mass media (radio, comic books, movies) as the "first curriculum" because they appear to be affecting the way children develop learning skills and acquire knowledge and understanding.[10] According to Neil Postman, television's curriculum is designed largely to maintain interest; the school's curriculum is supposed to have other purposes, such as mastery of thinking skills. In addition, watching television requires little effort and few skills; children do not have to think about or solve problems.[11] Rather, they become accustomed to rapidly changing stimuli, quick answers, and "escapist" fantasies, not to mention overdoses of violent and sexual behaviors on the screen. See Tips for Teachers 9.1. In this connection, the Parent Teacher Association (PTA), consisting of more than 6.2 million members, has lobbied for years (and with some success) to curtail violent and sexual scenes on television, especially during prime time (7 to 10 P.M.).[12]

---

8 Aimee Dorr, *Television and Children* (Newbury Park, Calif.: Sage, 1986); John I. Goodlad, *A Place Called School* (New York: McGraw-Hill, 1984); and Kathy A. Kreudl, Kathryn Lasky, and Robert Dawson, "How Television Affects Adolescents," *Educational Horizons* (Spring 1989), pp. 88–91.

9 Evelyn Kaye, *The Family Guide to Children's Television* (New York: Pantheon, 1974), p. 7. Also see Stuart Oskamp, *Television as a Social Issue* (Newbury Park, Calif.: Sage, 1987).

10 Neil Postman, *Teaching as a Conserving Activity* (New York: Delacorte, 1979).

11 Neal J. Gordon, "Television and Learning," in H. J. Walberg, ed., *Educational Environment and Effects* (Berkeley, Calif.: McCutchan, 1979), pp. 57–65; Robert Hornik, "Out of School Television and Schooling: Hypotheses and Methods," *Review of Educational Research* (Summer 1981), pp. 193–214.

12 Nancy L. Cecil, "Help Children Become More Critical TV Watchers," *PTA Today* (April 1988), pp. 12–14; Joan M. Bergstran, "Help Your Child Find Great Alternatives to Television," *PTA Today* (April 1988), pp. 15–17.

Tips for Teachers 9.1

Tips for Parents for Guiding TV Watching

Teachers need to remind parents that too much time in front of the TV is harmful for their children. Research suggests that too much TV viewing interferes with reading, studying, and academic performance in general. Here are some tips in communicating with parents about their children's TV viewing.

1. Decide if children can watch television on school days and, if so, for how long.
2. Determine how much television can be watched on weekends.
3. Be clear about the time a child can watch television. Don't let children feel TV time can be saved up.
4. Establish rules about finishing homework, practicing, reading or doing chores before watching
5. Remind children that they have control over the television. When a show is too unbelievable or scary, they can turn it off.
6. Recognize that when a program is over, it is best not to just walk away. It is important to find out your child's feelings and impressions about the show.
7. Keep in mind that specials may arise that your child will want to see. Such an additional show may have to be worked into the weekly allotment.
8. Watch for children being captivated by habit-forming soap operas or serialized shows. There is little value in children keeping a daily appointment with such shows.
9. Be aware that when children are alone, they get bored. Sometimes they turn on the TV because they're frightened. Parents need to offer constructive alternatives.
10. Remember that just because a sensitive issue is mentioned on a TV show, it doesn't mean the show should be prohibited. If the program has merit, it may open discussion.
11. Observe whether children watch television even when they have friends over. Offer them something to do instead.
12. Ask yourself if television watching could be taking the place of activities that the family might do together. If the television is on during breakfast and dinner, this suggests that it is more important than conversation.
13. Consider reading aloud to children for 15 minutes each day. Some studies have shown that time spent each day reading aloud to children inspires them to turn off the TV.

Source: Joan Bergstrom, "Tips for Guiding TV Viewing," *PTA Today* (April 1988), p. 16.

The research suggests that selected programs for preschool and primary grade children such as "Sesame Street" and "Electric Company" are associated with improved cooperative behavior and cognitive skills. However, most of the data suggest that for upper elementary and secondary school students, watching television more than 4 hours a day is associated with lowered achievement in reading and mathematics.[13] Because of television's impact on the acculturation and socialization of children and youth and its influence on all of society, educators cannot ignore this medium. They must find ways to reverse the trend toward lower achievement resulting from too much time spent watching badly produced commercial television, and they must find ways to incorporate the medium into the school curriculum.

Two types of television programming can be employed in schools. **Educational television** refers to programs produced for broadcast on commercial or public television stations that are intended to inform and develop understanding. Students watch these programs at home. **Instructional television** refers to programs produced by schools to teach specific skills and subject matter and for viewing in school. Many commercial and public television stations produce programs that fit educational goals and objectives. In particular, public television, which is broadcast in many large cities, has real educational worth that has not been fully utilized by teachers. Many school systems rely on local television stations to provide most of the programming. Some large or innovative school systems and universities produce their own programs and have their own stations. Master teachers teach large numbers of classes simultaneously by means of television.

In order to guide students in selecting TV programs, some schools and districts form a committee consisting of teachers and administrators to obtain listing information in advance and to recommend programs. If there is no such committee, individual teachers can do the same job. The weekly schedule is published in local newspapers and magazines, and the three major networks (ABC, CBS, NBC), will supply outlines, suggestions, and schedules for several weeks in advance.

Recent developments in program recording and replaying suggest imaginative uses for television. For example, programs can be recorded on videotape so that they may be played back to the class immediately for further discussion, played back later at a more convenient time, or saved to show to another group the following year. Transcripts of programs are kept in stock in network libraries for loan or rental, making it possible to view a program at any suitable time so long as the school has playback capabilities.

Television has the potential for adding to students' knowledge. Students can learn about current events and scientific advances, be exposed to dramatic

---

13 Royal Van Horn, "Education Power Tools," *Phi Delta Kappan* (March 1991), pp. 527–533; Hersholt C. Waxman and Herbert J. Walberg, "Teaching and Productivity," *Education and Urban Society* (February 1986), pp. 211–220.

and musical performances, become better acquainted with leading figures in the worlds of the arts, science, politics, and business. When used properly, this instructional aid can stimulate discussion and further study of the topic. It can bring the specialist and the expert teacher to class in front of hundreds of students at once, or thousands of students over time if taped and played again. Schools that cannot offer specialized subject matter can use television as a means of providing instruction through prerecorded programs.

Guidelines for Using Television

1. Select programs to coincide with the learners' level of interest and maturity and with instructional objectives. Consider the educational significance, quality, content, writing, and production.
2. Make sure the classroom or media center is suitable for viewing the program. Check the lights and shades, acoustic arrangements, seating facilities, and placement of the television.
3. The classroom television set should have at least a 21-inch screen. It should be placed so that all students can see it well. It should not be less than 5 feet or more than 30 feet away from any student. It should be placed slightly above the height of the heads of seated students, or about 5 to 7 feet from the floor.
4. Lights should be left on if students are to take notes. If they are not expected to take notes, the lights may be dimmed somewhat for improved viewing.
5. There should be no glare or reflected light on the screen. Keep the television away from windows and mirrors and change the location of light fixtures as necessary. If the source of reflected light cannot be changed, either tilt the set downward or tape cardboard blinders to the set.
6. Before a program is viewed, give students any necessary background data and tell them what to expect. You may want to hand out question sheets that focus on major points. These are especially helpful if students are assigned to watch a program at home.
7. Avoid using the program as a lecturing device or a substitute for instruction. Integrate it into the lesson and discussion.
8. Keep questions and comments during the program to a minimum, or ask students to save them until the end of the program.
9. After the program, hold a discussion to analyze the main points.
10. The ideal program lasts no longer than two-thirds of the subject period so there is time for introduction and summary.
11. By using videotapes, programs can be fit into the daily class schedule. If a school system operates a network, it can play programs to fit class schedules.

12. When assigning programs for homework, make sure all students have access to a television set. Arrangements (such as a buddy system) should be made for those who do not.[14]

COMPUTERS

Computer technology for school purposes has been available since the 1950s, but it is in the last few years that computers have begun to have a major impact on classrooms and schools. Teachers are waking up to the fact that computers are here to stay and can be effective tools of instruction. In 1980 some 50,000 microcomputers were used in 15 percent of the nation's schools; by 1985 the numbers reached 500,000 in 92 percent of all public schools.[15] In 1990 there were some two million computers in use in nearly 99 percent of the schools. It is envisioned that most high schools will soon be offering students an average of 30 minutes per day at a computer terminal. Many elementary schools and most middle grade and junior high schools already have students learning on computers once or twice a week. Some 50,000 or more teachers are expected to be teaching computer technology as their main subject between 1990 and 1995.[16] What actually happens will depend to a large extent on the money available for the purchase of computers, the software available for student use, and the way computers are adopted into the curriculum.

In integrating computers into instructional methods, teachers should consider the following questions.

1. What are the objectives of using computers in schools?
2. Should they be restricted to students who have particular abilities? To particular grade levels? To particular subjects?
3. Should they be used to teach about computing and programming or to teach other subjects?
4. Should students be charged user fees for computers?
5. Who will train teachers in computer use?
6. Should the classroom be reorganized to have computers at every desk or should a computer center or laboratory be set up?[17]

---

14 Ornstein et al., *The Paraprofessional's Handbook.*

15 Arthur S. Melmed, "Information Technology for U.S. Schools," *Phi Delta Kappan* (January 1982), pp. 308–311; and *The Condition of Education 1987* (Washington, D.C.: U.S. Government Printing Office, 1987), Tables 258–259, p. 314.

16 Gary L. Donhardt, "Microcomputers in Education," *Educational Technology* (April 1984), pp. 30–32; Peter Smith and Samuel Dunn, "Human and Quality Considerations in High Tech Education," *Educational Technology* (February 1987), pp. 35–39.

17 Stephen M. Alessi and Stanley R. Trollip, *Computer-Based Instruction*, 2nd ed. (Needham Heights, Mass.: Allyn & Bacon, 1991); Robert L. Blomeyer and C. Dianne Martin, *Case Studies of Computer-Aided Learning* (New York: Falmer Press, 1990).

Most card catalogs in school libraries have been computerized.

The Role of Computers

Decker Walker maintains that few people really know how to use computers well for educational purposes.[18] Seymour Papert, the inventor of Logo and author of *Mindstorm*, argues that the computer is a medium of expression and should be used to build a sense of inquiry, to "mess about," to explore, and to improve thinking skills.[19] He also argues that the main impact of computers on learning will not come about through teaching students practical applications such as data processing and filing; the real impact will only come when students are taught how to program, because programming requires that they think logically and solve problems. When they learn how to program, "the world is open for very wonderful things to happen."[20]

---

18 Decker F. Walker, "Reflections on the Educational Potential and Limitations of Microcomputers," *Phi Delta Kappan* (October 1983), pp. 103–107.

19 Seymour Papert, "Computer Criticism vs. Technocentric Thinking," *Educational Researcher* (January/February 1987), pp. 22–30.

20 Charlotte Cox, "An Interview with Seymour Papert," *Curriculum Review* (January–February 1987), pp. 14–18.

We are in the midst of an "information explosion," the availability of an ever-increasing quantity of information through the use of the computer. People can participate in this explosion at three or four levels of **computer knowledge**: (1) *computer literacy*, general knowledge of what computers are used for and some general experience in using them; (2) *computer competency*, ability to use the computer as a tool for particular purposes; and (3) *computer expertise*, knowledge of how computers work and how to program them.[21] A fourth level is *computer hacking*, the activity of people who are more than experts—they spend days and even nights working on games or problems, transmitting messages across the country or across oceans, devising ingenious games and software to sell, and/or swapping new software among fellow hackers. In general, the hacker is freewheeling and addicted to the computer craze.

As educators, we should aim at making our students computer-literate at an early age and view computer literacy as "a fourth R" or a fundamental skill. Several questions arise, however. How computer-competent are teachers? Should every teacher be computer-competent? Should every teacher be at least computer-literate? Should we expect only a few teachers in each school to have the skills to teach students how to use the computer? Should we expect most teachers to have the skills to use the computer as an instructional aid?

A teacher can become computer-literature in a workshop that meets for a few practice sessions. The time spent in training is not critical to the teacher's ability to use the computer as an integral part of the teaching day; the key factor is the attitude of the teacher. If the teacher is hesitant about using the computer, many children will pick up on this attitude. If the teacher is enthusiastic, children will learn more eagerly and more easily. According to one educator, a 15–hour workshop laboratory experience reduces teaching anxiety (fear of helplessness in dealing with computers) from above average to below average anxiety (3.04 to 1.75 out of 5) and increases interest in computers from 1.96 to 4.08.[22]

Computer Programming

Because so much software with programs in so many subject areas and grade levels is now available, it is not essential for teachers to know how to program. Furthermore, a mass of educational software is now available from many companies to allow teachers to construct their own lessons without knowing a computer language. But the ability to program is still a valuable skill to acquire. It gives teachers facility in using computers and makes it easier for them to plan lessons and individualize instruction.

Programming is an active mental endeavor, and it fosters critical thinking, rational thinking, and problem-solving skills. Programmers must break down

---

21 Allan C. Ornstein, "Emerging Curriculum Trends: An Agenda for the Future," *NASSP Bulletin* (February 1989), pp. 37–48; Judith A. Turner, "Ohio State Eyes Computer Literacy," *Chronicle of Higher Education* (January 11, 1984), pp. 1, 14.

22 Ann D. Thompson, "Helping Preservice Teachers Learn Computers," *Journal of Teacher Education* (May–June 1985), pp. 52–54.

complex problems into subproblems and then develop procedural instruc-tors.[23] One research study found that programming is the only subject in the whole curriculum that succeeds in teaching students about things as a process, that writing and debugging a program forces the programmer to think logically and carefully about the subject.[24] An analysis of the program can also tell the user about the quality of the thinking that went into the solution. According to these results, students and teachers should be encouraged to learn how to program.

On the other hand, there is also research that suggests that there is no "convincing relationship between learning to program and learning to think."[25] Some studies suggest that computer programming "promises more than it has delivered" and that there are "no intellectual benefits" or measurable thinking skills produced by teaching how to program.[26]

Advocates counter these criticisms by arguing that the amount and quality of computer instruction varies from study to study, that different students respond differently to different learning environments, and that student groups are often not controlled properly. They further argue that when students master programming, it becomes possible for teachers to teach in different ways, ways that indirectly foster achievement in children. The point is also made that it is what students do with programming that counts, and it is not important to test its direct effects.[27] An analogy to learning how to read is made; what is learned as a result of learning how to read is more important than just learning how to read. Table 9.1 illustrates the potential relationship or chain of cognition and learning how to program. It should be repeated, however, that the data are mixed concerning the cognitive consequences of programming.

According to researchers, Logo is the programming language commonly used for elementary school children because of its simplicity and engaging stimuli. BASIC tends to be used most by middle grade and high school students because the educational market is dominated by Apple, which uses

23 Willis J. Horak and Edward B. Brown, "Using Computers to Develop Mathematical and Scientific Thinking Strategies," in Fifth Annual Microcomputers in Education Conference, *Tomorrow's Technology* (New York: Computer Science Press, 1984), pp. 163–167; Marcia C. Linn, "The Cognitive Consequences of Programming Instruction in Classrooms," *Educational Researcher* (May 1985), pp. 14–16, 25; and David Moursund, "Problem Solving: A Computer Educator's Perspective," *Computing Teacher* (February 1985), pp. 3–5.

24 Arthur Leuhrmann, "Adopting Microcomputers in Ways That Will and Won't Work," *Peabody Journal of Education* (Winter 1985), pp. 42–56; Leuhrmann, "Why Teach Programming? Two Good Reasons," *Electronic Learning* (May–June 1985), pp. 14–18.

25 Richard E. Mayer, "*Automaticity and Its Implications for Instructional Design*," paper presented at the annual meeting of the American Educational Research Association, San Francisco, April 1986.

26 David L. Lillie, Gary B. Stuck, and Wallace H. Hannum, *Computers and Effective Instruction* (New York: Longman, 1989); Richard E. Mayer, ed., *Teaching and Learning: Computer Programming* (Hillsdale, N.J.: Erlbaum, 1988).

27 Jodi Bonner, "Computer Courseware: Frame-Based on Intelligence," *Educational Technology* (March 1987), pp. 30–33; Cox, "An Interview with Seymour Papert"; and James E. Eisele, "Instructional Computing: What's New in Computing?" *Educational Technology* (August 1985), pp. 24–26.

Table 9.1 POTENTIAL RELATIONSHIP OF LEARNING TO PROGRAM AND COGNITIVE CONSEQUENCES

1. Language factors

   a. Students demonstrate knowledge of language commands (i.e., "Print," "If . . . then") by understanding how to use already coded features. For example, they might change a printed message or an arithmetic expression.

   b. Introductory programming courses usually emphasize learning the commands rather than how to use them in problem solving.

2. Design skills: templates

   a. Students learn a repertoire of *templates* that is, patterns of code using more than a single command.

   b. Templates are used to perform common tasks and complex activities such as sorting words or numbers in different situations.

   c. Templates enable the programmer to solve many problems without creating new codes; well-chosen templates facilitate good programming and in turn retrieval of information.

   d. Templates can be likened to what we call cognitive structure or cognitive schema among learners—methods for processing information.

3. Procedural skills

   a. Procedural skills are used to combine templates or language commands to solve problems. This includes *planning* a solution using available templates, *testing* the plan to see if it accomplishes the objectives, and *reformulating* the plan until it succeeds.

   b. Expert programmers spend a great deal of time planning, testing, and reformulating. In doing so they learn to test their thinking, to decompose a problem into subproblems, and to simplify complex tasks into less complex tasks.

   c. By developing a repertoire of generalized templates suitable for adaptation to new situations, programmers become better able to solve programming problems; they learn to plan, test, and reformulate problems in a variety of situations.

Source: Adapted from Marcia C. Linn, "The Cognitive Consequences of Programming Instruction in Classrooms," *Educational Researcher* (May 1985), pp. 14–16, 25.

Note: Advocates claim the above skills generalize or carry over to academic subjects; critics claim learning is much more content-oriented and when students learn to solve programming problems they do not automatically learn to solve subject-related problems.

BASIC as a standard feature with most of its computer models.[28] James Muller, the president of Young People's Logo Association, asserts that "youngsters are far more at home with computer technology than are the adults attempting to teach them computer literacy." Most teachers teach Logo and BASIC programming the same way they teach French, Spanish, English, and other subjects. They teach students "to memorize the commands, to practice them, to test their knowledge, . . . and then move on to more advanced procedures."[29] Many students have never learned Logo or BASIC per se, but rather use them "as merely another learning tool to accomplish their goal." In an age of computer technology, programming isn't something you just learn; it is something you learn with. You don't teach programming by rote procedures; rather you teach the children to think, observe, analyze, plan, hypothesize, and test strategies.

Computer Software

Instructional software offerings have gradually improved in quality and variety and are available for all subject areas and grade levels. No longer do they cover only isolated topics or provide practice in one or two skills; current software presents whole units and courses of instruction.[30]

However, there is still a good deal of criticism about the quality of the software. Recent studies reported that only 5 percent of software was rated "exemplary," and less than 25 percent met minimum state standards in California.[31] A Canadian research team was able to recommend only one out of ten software products previewed for use in the province of Alberta.[32] Another group concluded that only 5 percent of the software it studied was exemplary in terms of content, 5 percent in instructional presentation, 12 percent in documentation, and 9 percent in technical adequacy. Although fewer programs were classified as "deficient" in these four areas compared to earlier studies, the percentages still ranged from 9 to 29 percent. About a third of the programs were classified as "acceptable" or " desirable" in terms of content, instruction, documentation, and technical adequacy.[33] The most common explanation for

28 Douglas Clements, "Logo Programming: Can It Change How Children Think?" *Electronic Learning* (January 1985), pp. 28, 74–75; Richard Venezky and Luis Osin, *The Intelligent Design of Computer-Assisted Instruction* (New York: Longman, 1991).

29 James H. Muller, "Learning Must Be More Than Computer Literacy," *NASSP Bulletin* (April 1986), p. 37.

30 Pamela McCorduck and Avery Russell, "Computers in Schools," *Principal* (November 1986), pp. 16–21; Sherry Trimble, "Is Second Generation Software Any Better?" *NASSP Bulletin* (April 1986), pp. 32–35.

31 "Software for Schools," *Technological Horizons in Education Journal* (February 1989), pp. 15–16; "What's in the Educational Software Pool?" *Microgram* (March 1985), pp. 1–4.

32 *Computer Courseware Evaluations* (Edmonton, Alberta: Alberta Education Province, 1985).

33 Curt Dudley-Marling and Ronald D. Owston, "The State of Educational Software: A Criterion Based Evaluation," *Educational Technology* (March 1987), pp. 25–29.

the poor ratings in these studies has been that most software is written either by persons with expertise in computers but not in education or by persons with expertise in educational theory but not in computers.

Probably the most frequent criticism of software is the predominance of drill and tutorial programs. This is changing now, as more simulations and **interactive systems** are being introduced. Whereas the early software consisted of sequenced questions with specific answers, the new software permits a variety of student responses with branching to appropriate levels of instruction based on the student's response. If students fail to master a task or concept, the new drill and tutorial software breaks down the concept using analogies, examples, and suggestions rather than presenting a sequenced repetition of the subject matter.[34] Not only do graphics and sound enhance the overall appeal of the software, but the new simulations also permit students to experience something close to real-life situations. Students can conduct experiments; experience past events, current happenings, or future possibilities; and consider "what if" problems through simulations. Through interactive participation the new programs can promote logical thinking, hypothesizing, and problem-solving strategies, since the learner gets immediate feedback and the opportunity to analyze and pursue responses. Computerized simulations should soon interact in several ways with the learner, including tutoring systems, cognitive diagnosis, problem-solving tasks, experimental tasks, and predictive reasoning.

There is a small but growing number of technically sound programs that integrate high-level thinking skills through pattern-recognition, problem-solving, decision-making, and game-playing skills. Some educators refer to this software as "mindware." Examples are *Ace Detective* by Mindplay, *Balance of Power* by Mindscape, *Design Your Own Train* by Abracadata, *Pipeline* by Learning Technologies, and *Science Toolkit* by Broderbund.[35]

In selecting or purchasing software, teachers need to consider how well the program sustains student interest and, most important, how well students receive and process information. More specifically, teachers need to focus on (1) how well the software appeals to both the eyes and the mind and how well visual and textual data are integrated; (2) how well the software helps students selected and organize concepts and analyze and evaluate relationships; and (3) how well the software promotes subjective, divergent, and creative thinking.[36] Of almost equal importance is whether the software makes the best use of hardware capabilities, how free the system is of errors, and to what extent the

---

34 Alan D. Corré, *Icon Programming for Humanists* (Englewood Cliffs, N.J.: Prentice-Hall, 1990); Stellan Ohlsson, "Computer Simulation and Its Impact on Educational Practice," *Educational Research* (no. 1, 1988), pp. 5–34.

35 David Harte, "Purchasing Mindware," *Media and Methods* (March–April 1988), p. 22; Howard N. Sloane et al., *Evaluating Educational Software: A Guide for Teachers* (Englewood Cliffs, N.J.: Prentice-Hall, 1989).

36 Harte, "Purchasing Mindware."

program content coincides with the teacher's instructional objectives. See Tips for Teachers 9.2.

Computer Simulations

The idea of computer simulations as a method of teaching is rooted in Newell and Simon's classic text on problem solving, whereby it was theorized that if human cognition operates on internal representations, and if computers can manipulate arbitrary symbol-structures, then computer simulations have the potential to foster learning of knowledge, concepts, inferences, insights, and skills.[37]

Advocates or simulationists in secondary schools tend to focus on problem solving, especially in math, science, and geography. One approach used in the research is to simulate an expert problem solver and a novice, and then characterize the differences between their solutions. One major conclusion of this research is that errors are due not only to gaps in knowledge but to incorrect problem-solving strategies as well.[38] Because computer simulations contain explicit and implicit statements and tasks related to different capabilities, as well as requiring information-processing activities, they are considered ideal starting points for observing problem solving. The simulation can be made increasingly more difficult to trace the performance of the learner. However, some researchers contend that computer simulation contributes little to understanding human problem solving, because the simulations are based on over-simplified assumptions to facilitate implementation, the programs are written to work for a restricted set of examples, and performing the tasks does not necessarily coincide with the actual mental processes.[39]

Simulations can also be used for training that involves reaction-time tasks or real-life tasks in specified subject matter. The complexity and challenge of the simulation can be changed to coincide with the skills of the learner. Many choices can be built into the program such that as the learner advances he or she is presented with different representative cases to deal with. An interesting modification permits different learners to jointly participate in the simulation at the same time, dividing up the tasks so that each has specific responsibilities.

Even more interesting, simulations can be displayed on a telecommunications model so that participants can react over distance and take advantage of special training without traveling. Indeed, computer-based simulations, games, and microworlds can be integrated into a network of many different

37 Allen Newell and Herbert A. Simon, *Human Problem Solving* (Englewood Cliffs, N.J.: Prentice-Hall, 1972).

38 Ohlsson, "Computer Simulation and Its Impact on Educational Research and Practice"; Stephen T. Peverly, "Problems with the Knowledge-Based Explanation of Memory and Development," *Review of Educational Research* (Spring 1991), pp. 71–93.

39 Robert Neches, "Simulation Systems for Cognitive Psychology," *Behavioral Research Methods* (no. 14, 1982), pp. 77–79; Mitchell Rabinowitz et al., "Computer Simulation as Research Tools," *Educational Research* (no. 1, 1988), pp. 35–69.

Tips for Teachers 9.2

Evaluating Computer Software

Future teachers will be expected to know not only something about how to use computers in the classroom but also how to evaluate software. Several characteristics contribute to quality and usability. In many ways, the evaluation of computer software is like the evaluation of any other instructional material, whether it is a textbook, film, or television program.

1. *Content.* The program should be current and accurate. There should be no spelling or grammatical errors. Terminology and subject matter should be compatible with student achievement level, students' learning experiences, and course objectives.
2. *Educational quality.* The software material should be compatible with what we know about learning. The material should be well sequenced, built on prior learning, provide prompt feedback and provide time for review.
3. *Directions.* Clear, concise, and well-organized directions about use should be given within the program itself or as a supplement. The directions must match the skills and developmental levels of the students.
4. *Data flexibility.* The computer's ability to handle data quickly and easily makes it possible for software to include *branching*. In branching the answer to one question determines what material will come next. It is valuable for promoting individualized learning.
5. *Graphics and sound.* Graphics and sound should be designed to highlight data, elaborate on explanations, and emphasize causal relationships. It should be possible for the user to turn off the sound.
6. *Tracking and monitoring* The program should record scores and indicate problems or types of answers the students handle well or poorly. Access to this data should have security provisions, such as a secret password, to protect confidential information.
7. *Evaluation.* Does the program fit the curriculum? Is it compatible with available computer equipment in the school? Is it mistake-free? Is it easy to use? How does it deal with incorrect student responses? Does it promote student interaction? Is it too short or too long? What is the cost? How does it compare to other software packages?

Source: Adapted from Carol A. Doll, "Software Purchasing Strategies," *Media and Methods* (March–April 1988), pp. 19–23.

students from parts of the local community, nation, or world. Students can interchange data via electronic message systems and thus modify the simulations to fit local conditions and local problems.[40]

Finally, simulations can assist in learner self-evaluation by (1) providing feedback on progress, (2) recording and reviewing learning outcomes, and (3) serving as a database for students to learn from each other by providing on-screen retrieval of actions taken. By observing others attempting to solve a problem,[41] the student avoids making the same mistakes. The same retrieval of actions capability can be used to show proper moves or behaviors, which the learner or other learners can examine later. Because of this retrieval system, students can reflect on their own learning and that of others, and through this reflection learn a subject and improve their learning strategies.

Guidelines for Using Computers and Computer Software

1. A company that produces, distributes, or sells computers or computer materials should be willing to provide a number of services: (a) installation assistance as part of the purchase, not as an add-on cost; (b) user training as part of the computer purchase (the more complicated the computer hardware or software, the more important the user training); (c) a toll-free or local number to call for answers to questions and solutions to problems; and (d) updates to the software for little or no extra charge.

2. The use of the computer in the classroom should correspond with the school's goals.

3. If only one computer is available for class use, you will have to devise large-group instruction or divide the class into smaller groups to take turns at the computer. You will need several computers to permit several students to work on the program at the same time.

4. A group of teachers or curriculum specialists should preview software before it is purchased by the school. Individual teachers should preview material before using it in class.

5. Decide on what you want to do with the computer. Do you want to use it for practice and drill, problem solving, tutorial activities, simulations, or games?

6. Establish criteria for use based on your course objectives and the abilities and needs of your students.

---

40 James A. Levin et al., "Education on the Electronic Frontier," *Contemporary Educational Psychology* (March 1991), pp. 46–51

41 James A. Levin and Michael Waugh, "Educational Simulations, Tools, Games and Microworlds: Computer-Based Environments for Learning," *Educational Research* (no. 1, 1988), pp. 71–79.

7. The software should be suitable for your instructional grouping (individual, small group, or large group).

8. The software should be easy to use. The screen format should be clear. Instructions should be easy to follow. The software should have a complete menu (index or contents) for quick reference, a help section, and illustrations of input screen and output formats.

9. The software should be sound in terms of instructional and learning theory. It should motivate students more than conventional methods, because of its cost. It should be designed to foster students' critical thinking, problem-solving strategies, and creativity. It should be accurate, up to date, and clearly organized.

10. The software should be capable of being integrated with other software and with traditional materials into a comprehensive curriculum and instructional package.

11. You should know what supporting materials are available that can interface with your computer hardware and software.

12. You should know how to use both floppy and hard disks. Hard disks hold more data and access it more rapidly; however, floppy disks cost less and usually have adequate storage capacity for your purposes.

13. Software should provide user feedback on the display about what part of the process is taking place and whether it is proceeding normally. The user should be able to correct simple problems.

14. Periodically, review and evaluate the software for quality and variety on a team basis. Be prepared to recommend supplementary course materials.[42]

TELECOMMUNICATION SYSTEMS

Telecommunication refers to information exchange between two or more locations connected by electronic media, including television, radio, and telephone. Several hundred educational organizations (mostly large universities and state agencies and a few school systems) lease or own their own telecommunication system. About 50 percent own their system, 45 percent lease, and 5 percent operate a combined leased-owned system. Owned systems operate through television or radio broadcast systems; leased or leased-owned systems operate through telephone wires.[43] The systems permit traditionally underserved schools and areas with scarce resources, as well as innovative and large school districts, the opportunity to engage in long-distance learning.

---

42 Allan C. Ornstein, "Curriculum Computer Technology," *NASSP Bulletin* (in press 1992).

43 Allan C. Ornstein, "Video Technology and the Urban Curriculum," *Education and Urban Society Curriculum* (May 1991), pp. 335–341.

Satellite Dishes

Schools now can select television programs specifically developed for educational purposes and have the programs beamed into the classroom by satellite. Schools can subscribe to various program series, for example, 24 one-hour, commercial-free programs on how to improve writing or reading. The major producer of television programs for classroom use via satellite is the Agency for Instructional Television, a nonprofit American-Canadian organization. Regularly scheduled commercial satellite service can include educational programs for the home, but this will happen only if educators call for it and use it when available.

Electronic Mail

Electronic mail systems permit a message written with a word processor to be sent over telephone lines or network cables to a central facility often comprising a mainframe computer. Messages can be addressed to students or teachers (or professors) and can be stored in an electronic "mailbox" until the person receiving the message inputs the system at his or her convenience.[44]

The messages can be displayed on a computer screen, printed, and saved on a floppy disk. Messages can be sent across continents, across oceans. In this way, a class in New York City can communicate with a class in Chicago or in Tokyo.

Cable Transmission

In areas wired for cable television, teachers have the opportunity to deliver instruction to students who might not otherwise receive it. One school (or station) can serve as the transmitter to several schools within a school district or even within the state—an excellent vehicle for rural schools (hampered by size and location) to expand course offerings in math, science, and foreign language. Two-way audio and video capability can be added to the transmission so that students can interact with the teacher. Cable also offers an inexpensive communication opportunity for students to transmit and receive instruction at home from the school, library, or community facility (so long as the instructional delivery system is in place).[45]

Teleconferences

It is possible for people in different locations, even across state and national boundaries, to communicate and interact through television connections. Such conferences are widely used in business, government, and, to a lesser extent, universities. Teleconferencing is just appearing in a few school systems, as an experiment, on the secondary level. Groups of students can meet with teachers and other resource people through the television screen. The participants can

---

44 Glen Bull et al., "The Electronic Academic Village," *Journal of Teacher Education* (July–August 1989), pp. 27–31; Peter Grunwald, "The New Generation of Information Systems," *Phi Delta Kappan* (October 1990), pp. 113–114.

45 John K. Gilbert, Annette Temple, and Craig Underwood, eds., *Satellite Technology in Education* (New York: Routledge, 1991).

watch, listen, interrupt, ask questions, make decisions, as if they were across the table. It is a wonderful way for students to speak to an expert or communicate with their peers almost anywhere in the world. It is also an excellent way for small schools to have students meet with other teachers, especially if the schools lack specialized personnel (for example, a physics teacher).

Teletext Systems

Teletext systems are one-way systems in which information is sent to receivers through television broadcast. Receivers view what is sent, but there is no interaction and no sound transmission. Teletext information systems permit the viewer to receive news headlines, government reports, and various kinds of written data. Such systems are currently used in business, medicine, research, and government.

Educators will need to design teletext systems that can be used to advantage by students. For example, large information-based industries, such as publishing and newspaper companies or libraries and universities, might compile current information from various sources (books, reports, journals, newspapers) in electronic "bins."[46] By pressing the appropriate button, a user of the data bin from anywhere around the country could have selected information delivered electronically.

Telewriting

Telewriting operates through telephone lines. The visual is sent over a telephone line, and the audio is sent in conjunction through another telephone line. The telewriting device is sometimes called an electronic chalkboard, although an overhead projector can be used to enlarge the visual images for viewers. The fact that an oral presentation can accompany and explain the visual presentation makes the system more appealing for teachers. As with teletext, however, there is no two-way communication between sender and receiver; the device is useful for older students to receive information, but it does have limitations as an instructional tool since it does not permit two-way communication.

Telepicturephones

The telepicturephone is an offshoot of the telewriting system. It allows a person to send images from one monitor to another over telephone lines. By focusing a camera on a person or document and pressing a button, the sender can transmit a picture to another unit in 8 to 30 seconds. An ordinary phone is plugged into a machine similar to a television set with an attached camera; two-way voice

---

46 Marjorie Ferguson, *New Communication Technologies and the Public Interest* (Newbury Park, Calif.: Sage, 1986); Allan C. Ornstein, "Bringing Telecommunications and Videos into the Classroom," *High School Journal* (April-May 1990), pp. 252–257.

communication through that phone is temporarily interrupted when the picture is sent. Pictures can be stored for recall later, but prints of the pictures cannot be made.[47] For purposes of learning, older students (at least at the middle or junior high school level) can use this two-way audio and one-way video phone as a supplement to the typical classroom instruction both in school and at home.

As an offshoot of this picturephone system, it is possible for two distant schools (or colleges) to install a microwave transmission system that links the two points within a 200–mile range. The audio hookup is made with the telephone line and the visual is delivered through the television. This long-distance learning is achieved without being charged long-distance rates.

Telecourses

A few large universities are beginning to produce telecourse materials for local and national use. For an investment of $75,000 to $150,000, an institution can put into operation a studio with sufficient equipment, content experts, and telecommunication personnel to produce and market materials that can be used in the home as long as the user has a VCR and a television set. To recover costs, the university must produce several telecourses, use them for several years, and/or market them to other institutions.[48]

Local school districts have the opportunity to work with a local or regional university to develop telecourse materials. At the secondary level the materials can be used at home by students, since older students can work independently. At the elementary level they are better used in whole-group instruction in the school so teachers can provide necessary monitoring and feedback.

Charges for the telecourses vary, depending on whether the material has already been produced (and only needs to be modified) or has to be produced from the start. Charges might be as low as $500 to $2,500 to a school district for a set of tapes and the right to use them for a given period. Another method of payment might be on a per-student basis, almost like a user fee. See Tips for Teachers 9.3.

Guidelines for Using Telecommunications

1. Decide just what you want the system to do. Decide on objectives and the instructional use of the system (practice, tutoring, demonstrations, explanations, problem solving).

---

47 "Compact, Affordable Picture Phones May Revive Once-Heralded Technology," *Wall Street Journal* (November 16, 1985), p. 23.

48 John W. McCutcheon and James Swartz, "Planning for Cablecast Telecourses," *Technological Horizons in Education* (September 1987), pp. 98–100; Ornstein, "Video Technology and the Urban Curriculum."

2. Consider use of the system in relation to the abilities, needs, and interests of your students.
3. Find out what systems are available and how they work.
4. If programs are already available, preview them. Find out what supporting materials and equipment are necessary, suitable, and available.
5. Be sure that the system is easy to use and that the instructions are easy to follow for students and for you.
6. Be sure the system is manageable—that is, that not only will you know how to use it but also that you will be able to use it and supervise students at the same time they use it.
7. Find out what services and support the supplier will provide.
8. Consider both the cost and the reputation of the company who will install and repair the equipment.

VIDEOSYSTEMS

Video technology has made available another valuable tool for instruction. There are several different **videosystems** that make it possible for various audiovisual experiences to be produced, stored, and retrieved as needed. They permit the teacher and students to produce and create their own materials and to use audiovisual systems in numerous ways.

Teachers must plan how to integrate the new video technology into the curriculum. They also need to "train children to become critical video consumers who are literate in reading images."[49] On their own or through in-service training, teachers should investigate new methods to heighten awareness of how visual images affect us as individuals and as a society and how students can enhance their esthetic and thinking skills related to our television and video-dominated culture. In 1985 the number of videos rented from video stores surpassed the total number of books checked out of libraries.[50] The hope is that students will start checking out video documentaries—not only video movies and games—with gentle encouragement from teachers. One estimate is that by the year 2000 as much as 25 percent of all teaching tools will be based on computers and videos.[51]

---

49 Dennis M. Adams and Mary Hamm, "Teaching Students Critical Viewing Skills," *Curriculum Review* (January–February 1987), pp. 29–30.

50 Dennis M. Adams and Mary Hamm, "Changing Gateways to Knowledge: New Media Symbol Systems," *Tech Trends* (January 1988), pp. 2–23; Ornstein, "Curriculum Computer Technology."

51 "Preparing Students for the Year 2000," report prepared by the Society for Visual Education, Washington, D.C., 1987.

Tips for Teachers 9.3

Evaluating Telecourses

There may be telecourses available that suit your lesson, unit, or course objectives. Some telecourses require a great deal of teacher feedback and others very little. Start compiling a list of telematerials that coincide with your subject and grade level. Evaluation criteria should include the following:

1. Is the telecourse designed for a lesson, unit, or course?
2. Is the telecourse available for review?
3. Is the content presented in a varied and interesting format that takes full advantage of television's visual potential?
4. Does the telecourse include support materials such as transparencies, handouts, or test banks?
5. Can the telecourse be used in conjunction with the text being used or with existing classroom materials?
6. Is the content accurate and current?
7. What is the cost to purchase or use the material?
8. Will the producer permit making multiple copies of the telematerials?
9. What do other adopters say about the effectiveness of the telematerials?
10. Have the materials been pretested?

Source: Adapted from Allan C. Ornstein, "Bringing Telecommunications and Videos into the Classroom," *High School Journal* (April–May 1990), p. 254.

Videotapes

Videotapes have many applications for instruction. They can demonstrate, explain, record, and replay data. They can be used in classrooms, libraries, resource centers, and homes.

Recent advances have made video recording and playback equipment lightweight, portable, and relatively inexpensive. The teacher and students can record various events and play back the recording in class through a VCR system attached to a television. Interviews, community meetings, special events, and students' projects can be recorded. Students can produce videos based on their own stories or research.

Some large school districts now produce their own videos in recording departments and also distribute them to surrounding school systems. Students never have to miss a lesson, since the video can be stored and played back at a convenient time.

Videocassettes

Videocassettes are even easier than tapes to collect, store, and reuse as needed because they are extremely lightweight and small. Considering the low cost of equipment needed to record and play back the cassette, its potential is enormous.

There are also now many catalogs that list hundreds of commercially produced videos on educational subjects. There are even video "magalogs" (hybrids of magazines and catalogs) that are available at newsstands and libraries. Public libraries now rent or lend videocassettes, and school libraries are beginning to develop a sizeable collection of titles.

In theory, one might argue that there is little reason for students to come to class to listen to a teacher. All they have to do is ask the school or college to send them a videocassette, or check the library shelves, or go to the media store. These products should not be marketed as teacher substitutes, however, but as electronic tools to empower teachers to facilitate teaching and to empower students to facilitate learning.

Videodiscs

Most videos are recorded on tapes or cassettes. Recordings are also made on videodiscs, which resemble long-playing records, but have a larger storage capacity and are not subject to damage while in use. Videodiscs, usually made of metal, contain digitized information that is read by laser beams. The picture resolution and tuning is finer than that of magnetic tape, and the quality doesn't deteriorate with time. The disadvantages of videodiscs are that they are more expensive, they can be made only by professionals, and they cannot be erased or edited.

Videodiscs are coming to the classroom, despite the cost. Among the most interesting ones are (1) the *Knowledge Disc*, a disc-based encyclopedia with 32,000 entries and 9 million words (the equivalent of a 20–volume encyclopedia on a single disc; (2) *Bioscience*, with 6,000 still images of animals and plants that can be used with daily biology and general science lesson plans; (3) *History Disquiz*, containing 45 important newsreel film clips and several thousand "trivia" questions about them; and (4) the *Louvre* disc with 1,500 art images and the *National Gallery of Art* disc with 1,650 images.[52]

---

52 Royal Van Horn, "Isn't It About Time for Videodiscs to Come to School?" *PTA Today* (April 1988), pp. 22–25.

Interactive videodisks, to be used in conjunction with a computer, are being made. Realistic situations, simulations, and action-reaction situations can be presented as part of a training or learning program. Interactive videos have enormous teaching-learning potential—permitting students to receive and respond to a video program, to react accordingly, and to obtain information about the probable outcomes of their behavior (as if the situation had been real). The program can tell the viewer he or she is wrong or right, present the viewer with options, and show the outcome of these options. The program can be used for individual or small-group instruction. See Tips for Teachers 9.4.

Videoprinters

The videoprinter attaches to the television and produces a postcard-size color print of nearly anything you can see on the screen almost instantly. This includes not only regular broadcast television, but also teletext, videotape, videodisc, or anything transmitted through television. Pictures can be made at the rate of one a minute of such things as maps, weather forecast data for detailed study, or snapshots from student-made videotapes. Whatever material needs to be further explained can be printed and stored for future use.

Video Games

Video games are interactive; a microcomputer is programmed to respond to a player's move with a move of its own. All serious video game players play for mastery, but most video games are sufficiently difficult that novice players (including most students) are lucky if they can play more than two or three minutes on the first few tries.[53] Although this billion-dollar-a-year game industry has been criticized, mainly because the games tend to be escapist, some observers believe the effects can be positive. (Although not games, music videos are another problem, due to the proliferation of sex and violence found in them, and very few educators support their use.)[54] Practice in eye- and hand coordination and manual dexterity are obvious benefits. Also, educational material in video game format can be a pedagogical device—livening up practice and drill; teaching reading, writing, and other learning skills; and solving math and science problems.

---

53 Nancy R. Needham, "Thirty Billion Quarters Can't Be Wrong—Or Can They?" *Today's Education* (Annual 1982–1983), pp. 53–55.

54 Jennifer Norwood, "Music Videos—Have They Gone Too Far?" *PTA Today* (April 1988), pp. 26–28.

Tips for Teachers 9.4

Technology for Future Schools

Middle schools and high schools have had many successes over the decades. Careful planning must be undertaken by the schools to continue this tradition. American officials need to be sensitive to change, particularly how technology will impact schools of the future. Below are eight trends or tips to consider as we approach the year 2000.

1. There will be an ever-growing use of technology in the schools, especially computer simulations and interactive videos.
2. Educational software is becoming increasingly important and will supplement and in some schools may even replace traditional texts.
3. Films will be increasingly replaced by videos, and basic training in computers will be increased in lower grades to become the fourth R.
4. Emphasis on math, science, and English will continue, but computers will play a greater role in these courses in drills, simulations, and word processing.
5. Emphasis on creativity, flexibility, information evaluation and synthesis, as well as holistic thinking, will become increasingly important as the tools of technology become more complex and the thinking skills required to maximize their use become more sophisticated.
6. Computer, telecommunication, and video systems will eventually be designed for use in groups; students in classrooms will increasingly learn cooperatively, working in small groups.
7. Teachers will need to pay close attention to changes in society and the goals of the school to decide on the appropriate uses of technology. Such planning should include
   a. How technology can facilitate, not replace, the teacher.
   b. Time, expense, and effort in training teachers for using technology in schools.
   c. A balance between drill and practice versus open-ended and creative uses of computers, as well as between factual data bases versus complex data systems.
   d. The issue of access—sensitivity to the fact that low-income and minority students have limited access to computers and other technological tools.

(continues)

8. Teacher training programs must include an appropriate balance among teaching methods for subject areas such as English, social studies, math, and science; high-order processes such as problem solving, critical thinking, and creativity; and technology (including computer, telecommunication, and video capabilities).

Guidelines for Using Videosystems

1. The videoprogram will most likely be interesting, sometimes entertaining, but it should also have *educational value*.
2. The use of videosystems should lead to the attainment of the course *objectives*.
3. There are a host of videosystems and videoprograms already available. *Preview* the most promising systems and programs.
4. You need to *analyze* the video content, just as you analyze textbook content. Is the video worthwhile? Accurate? Interesting? Presented clearly? Technically sound? Free from bias? Content appropriate? Age appropriate?
5. *Excerpt* parts that are most useful. The equipment features on the VCR permit easy and effective use of limited sections of the program.
6. *Plan* how the video selected will be used in the teaching-learning process. Determine what supporting equipment is needed and what supporting software is available.
7. *Prepare* students for the video experience. Tell the students what to expect in the segment and what they are expected to get out of the experience. Provide questions or comments that will assist them in assessing the major points of the video.
8. Videosystems can be used in a variety of settings. Be clear on the *instructional place* for learning—classroom, library, resource center, home.
9. Videosystems can be used in conjunction with a variety of methods. Be clear on your *instructional method*—practice and drill, tutoring, simulations, problem solving.
10. Videosystems can be used in a variety of *instructional groups*: individualized instruction, small group instruction, and large-group instruction. Is the videoprogram usable for the type of instruction you are targeting?

11. The teacher needs to *monitor* student understanding. Some videos are interactive and provide immediate feedback so learners know the results of their activity immediately. Some videos provide learners with a sense of control and even excitement, allowing for active learning, and still others make learners into decision makers.

12. *Follow up* the video experience. Summarize the video lesson or remind students of what you had expected them to get from the program. Use questions or comments to encourage discussion or debate. Provide a number of review questions at the end of the lesson or for homework.

13. *Evaluate* the video experience. Did the program fit the objectives or needs of the curriculum? Were the students receptive? Did the subsequent learning experiences (and outcomes) justify the video use? Were the money and time well spent? Was a comparison or control group used to evaluate the video program?

SUMMARY

1. Basic guidelines for using instructional technology include (a) selecting equipment suitable to objectives, (b) learning how to operate the equipment, and (c) previewing the materials.

2. Visual images increase the effectiveness of the presentation of materials. Visual images can be incorporated into a presentation through the use of chalkboards and display boards; films, filmstrips, and filmslides; and overhead projectors.

3. Two types of television programming for use in schools are educational television (informative programs produced by commercial and public television stations) and instructional television (programs produced by educators for specific teaching purposes).

4. Teachers and students can participate in these levels of computer use: computer literacy, computer competency, and computer expertise. All students should be at least computer-literate.

5. The quality and variety of computer software has improved in recent years. The most challenging and interesting computer-based instructions is in the area of simulations and interactive systems.

6. Various telecommunication systems include satellite dishes, electronic mail, cable transmission, teleconferences, teletext systems, telewriting, telepicturephones, and telecourses.

7. Videosystems include videotapes, videocassettes, videodiscs, and video printers. The use of video games for educational purposes is controversial, but they can be used to liven up instruction.

CASE STUDY

Problem

A committee of experienced teachers was asked by the principal to design a plan for the introduction and use of computers into a middle school. They first took a survey of other schools to see what problems those faculties had experienced in their use of computers. Five major problems were identified: (1) too few computers for full implementation, (2) not enough time to learn the equipment, (3) difficulty in choosing software, (4) software using sounds as reinforcement distracted the students from other classwork, (5) purchasing software that was inappropriate for the intended grade levels.

Suggestion

Teachers from the other schools suggested the following ways to avoid these problems.

Problem 1: Use mobile carts; put all computers into one room and allot time by classes or individuals; ask PTA for funds to purchase more computers or write for grant monies; make the hard choice of giving some grade levels priority.

Problem 2: Send a volunteer teacher to take a "crash" course and then train others; select a company that supplies training; offer teachers incentives to take courses.

Problem 3: Select a company that will assist in software selection; insist that the school district allow adequate time to select software after it allocates the money; let resource people in the school become familiar with a computer magazine that reviews software, such as *Computing Teacher*.

Problem 4: Select software with silent reinforcers; use sound reinforcement software only for teachers not bothered by background noises.

Problem 5: Choose software only from companies offering an adequate review period (10 to 30 days).

Discussion Suggestion

This school also experienced problems in teachers' expectations regarding the students' initial knowledge of computers. Teachers found they needed to teach computer operation since many of the children were from low-income homes and did not have personal computers at home.

Another problem surfaced once the students began working with the software. The teachers assumed that when the computer signaled a correct response that the student had "learned" whatever was being worked on. They discovered that the students learned only how to get a correct response but were not retaining the answers or the process as part of their learning. The principal suggested that they use the computers only as a reinforcing tool rather than for initial teaching. The initial teaching would be performed in the usual manner or would be mixed with computer reinforcement. He insisted that the computer should *never* take the place of the teacher in the presentation of new learning or in the review of old subject matter.

Discussion Questions

1. How might you guard against your students using and learning only the computer operation and not the subject matter?
2. Choose two of the problems identified in the "problem" paragraph and provide some of your own suggestions. If you were teaching, to whom or where might you go for assistance?
3. How might you deal with the problem of some students having experience in computer operation while other students, and possibly the teacher, having limited experience?
4. How would you integrate computer instruction into a classroom schedule that concentrates on the basic skills such as reading, math, or English?
5. Which companies, in your view, offer the best educational software for secondary students? (Don't know? Think your supervisor will know?)

QUESTIONS TO CONSIDER

1. Do you agree that the chalkboard is still a valuable instructional aid? Explain.
2. What are five suggestions for using overhead projectors?
3. Some educators feel computers will revolutionize education. Do you agree? Explain.
4. What are three important factors to consider in choosing appropriate videosystems?
5. How can teachers encourage students to change their television and video viewing habits from movies to documentaries, from entertainment to education?

THINGS TO DO

1. Select one of the instructional aids discussed in this chapter. Do an oral report on its advantages and disadvantages.
2. Project a filmstrip or filmslide on a screen or light-colored curtain. Determine the minimum size of projection that all students in the room can see.
3. Write on a transparency with a variety of appropriate pencils and in a variety of sizes. Project the transparency to determine the best size, color, and type of markers for good visibility.
4. Invite an expert on computers to discuss with the class how to use them in instruction and how to teach computer literacy.
5. Check nearby colleges or local cable operators to find out what telecourses are available in your local community.

RECOMMENDED READINGS

Cuban, Larry. *Teachers and Teaching: The Classroom Use of Technology Since 1920.* New York: Teachers College Press, Columbia University, 1986. A compact book on the history of education technology—and why for many years teachers have not accepted machines in the classroom.

Gilbert, John K., Annette Temple, and Craig Underwood, eds. *Satellite Technology in Education.* New York: Routledge, 1991. Ideas and issues concerning the potential of satellite technology in education.

Mayer, Richard E., ed. *Teaching and Learning: Computer Programming.* Hillsdale, N.J.: Erlbaum, 1988. A collection of works describing how to teach students to use computers productively and what effect computer programming has on students.

Nickerson, Raymond S. and Philip P. Zodhiates, eds. *Technology and Education in the Year 2020.* Hillsdale, N.J.: Erlbaum, 1988. An analysis of how technology may influence secondary education in the future.

Oskamp, Stuart. *Television as a Social Issue.* Newbury Park, Calif.: Sage, 1987. Social issues relating to television viewing—violence, stereotyping of women and minorities, sex, and the potential of quality or prosocial programs.

Roberts, Nancy. *Integrating Telecommunications into Education.* Englewood Cliffs, N.J.: Prentice-Hall, 1990. A how-to-do text for establishing telecommunications in the school or home.

Sloane, Howard N. et al. *Evaluating Educational Software: A Guide for Teachers.* Englewood Cliffs, N.J.: Prentice-Hall, 1989. How to find and evaluate well-designed, instructionally sound, and technically reliable software for classroom use.

KEY TERMS

Chalkboards
Display board
Film
Filmstrip
Filmslide
Overhead projector
Educational television

Instructional television
Computer knowledge
Computer programming
Interactive systems
Telecommunications systems
Videosystems

Chapter 10

Instructional Grouping

FOCUSING QUESTIONS

1. When is it appropriate to use whole-group, small-group, and individual instruction?

2. What are the advantages and disadvantages of large-group instruction?

3. On what basis may students be organized into small groups?

4. What procedures should teachers follow in organizing small groups for instruction?

5. What methods can be used to provide individualized instruction?

6. What methods are recommended for using adaptive instruction? Mastery instruction?

7. How can computers be used for individualized instruction?

*T*he most common means of organizing students for instruction is to group 25 to 30 students according to age and grade level, and sometimes ability, and assign them to a specific classroom and teacher. When most instruction occurs in this setting, it is called a **self-contained classroom**. At the elementary school level a teacher is assigned to the class for the whole day. Students may travel as a class to another class one or two periods a day to receive special instruction (for example, in remedial reading, music, or physical education), or other teachers may visit the class to provide special instruction.

At the secondary level the self-contained classroom is modified by what is commonly called **departmentalization**. Students are assigned to a different teacher for each subject and may have six or seven different teachers each day. Departmentalization usually begins at the sixth, seventh, or eighth grade— depending on the school district.

There are three basic ways of grouping for instruction: (1) *whole-group instruction*, sometimes called large-group instruction, in which the entire class is taught as a group, (2) *small-group instruction*, in which the large group is broken up into subgroups according to ability, interest, project, or other criterion, and (3) *individualized instruction*, in which the individual student works alone or with another person on an individualized task or assignment. Different groupings require different physical settings, so we will take a look at some designs for seating arrangement, and then look at characteristics of instruction for each grouping.

CLASSROOM SEATING ARRANGEMENTS

In a classic study on teaching, Adams and Biddle found that, for the most part, what takes place in the classroom requires the attention of all the students. Teachers tend to stay in front of the classroom more than 85 percent of the time when teaching the whole class, but they change their location on the average once every 30 seconds. Elementary teachers tend to move around through the aisles more than secondary teachers.[1]

Adams and Biddle further found that student participation is restricted by the environment or physical setting itself in ways that neither the teacher nor the students seem to be aware of. It appeared to them that students who sit in the center of the room are the most active learners, or what they called "responders." The verbal interaction is so concentrated in this area of the classroom and in a line directly up the center of the room (which the teacher is

---

1 Raymond S. Adams and Bruce J. Biddle, *Realities of Teaching* (New York: Holt, Rinehart & Winston, 1970).

The "zone of action" for most teachers tends to be in the front and middle of the classroom.

in front of most of the time) that they coined the term "action zone" to refer to this area.

Teachers who are student-centered, indirect, and warm or friendly, as opposed to being subject-centered, direct, and businesslike, tend to reject the traditional **formal seating pattern** of rows of students directly facing the teacher at the front of the classroom. Formal seating patterns tend to reduce student-to-student eye contact and student interaction and to increase teacher control and student passivity. Student-centered teachers tend to favor **informal seating patterns**, such as rectangular (seminar), circular, and horseshoe (U-shaped) patterns, in which students face each other as well as the teacher (Figure 10.1).

What usually results when middle school students face each other is less time on tasks and more disruptive behavior by students who lack inner control.[2] At higher levels, or when being on task requires greater student interaction, the informal patterns are likely to be more effective. However, at all levels there is greater potential for discipline problems with nontraditional seating, and insecure teachers and those who are not good managers should keep to more traditional seating until they gain more experience.

2 Saul Axelrod et al., "Comparison of Two Common Classroom Seating Arrangements," *Academic Therapy* (September 1979), pp. 29–36; Valerie Caproni et al., "Seating Position, Instructor's Eye Contact Availability, and Student Participation," *Journal of Social Psychology* (December 1977), pp. 315–316. Also see Carolyn M. Evertson et al., *Classroom Management for Elementary Teachers*, 2nd ed. (Englewood Cliffs, N.J.: Prentice-Hall, 1989).

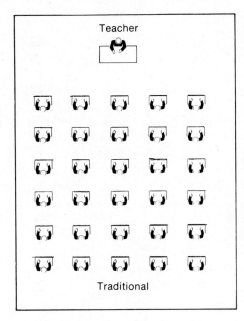

Traditional

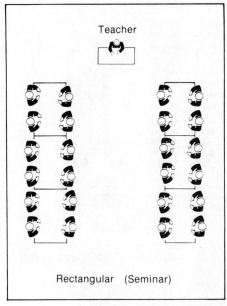

Rectangular   (Seminar)

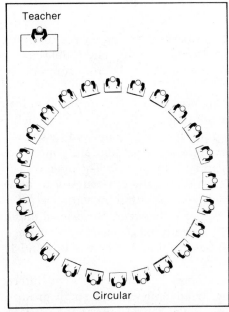

Circular

Horseshoe (U)

The teacher's desk is at the corner to avoid neck strain among students in the front of the classroom.

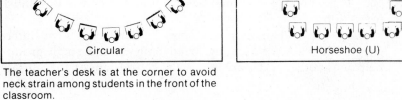

Figure 10.1   Four seating patterns.

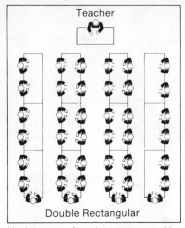

Teacher

Double Rectangular

Having rows of students separated by tables prevents students' from sitting too close to each other and reduces potential discipline problems.

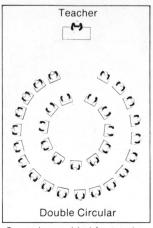

Teacher

Double Circular

Space is provided for teacher to move around and into smaller circle.

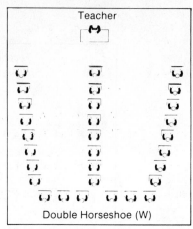

Teacher

Double Horseshoe (W)

If space permits seating may be arranged to form a double U instead of a W.

Figure 10.2 Three modified seating patterns.

Special Classroom Designs

The rectangular, circular, and horseshoe arrangements in Figure 10.1 assume no more than 20 to 25 students. Double rectangular, double circular, and double horseshoe (W-shaped) arrangements are needed to accommodate more than 25 students (Figure 10.2).

An **open classroom** seating arrangement is appropriate for middle grade and junior high school students (Figure 10.3). The many shelves, tables, and work areas allow for small-group and individualized instruction. The formal rows of fixed desks of the traditional classroom are gone. The desks are arranged in groups or clusters and can be moved. The open classroom increases student interaction and gives students the opportunity to move around and engage in different learning activities in different settings.

George Musgrave distinguishes between *home-based seating* and *special formations* designed for particular activities.[3] The classroom designs in Figures 10.1, 10.2, and 10.3 are home-based; those in Figures 10.4 and 10.5 are special formations.

These special seating arrangements enhance student interaction in large groups, cooperative learning arrangements, and small groups, for students help one another and share materials. The designs on the left side of Figure 10.4

3 George R. Musgrave, *Individualized Instruction: Teaching Strategies Focus on the Learner* (Boston: Allyn & Bacon, 1975).

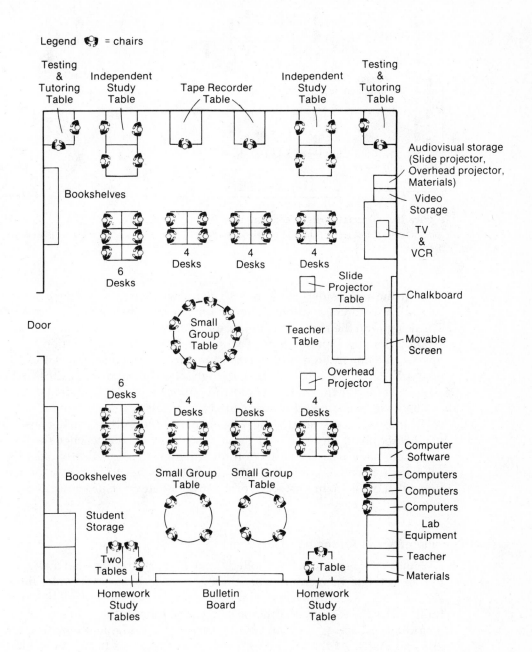

Figure 10.3 An open classroom seating pattern.

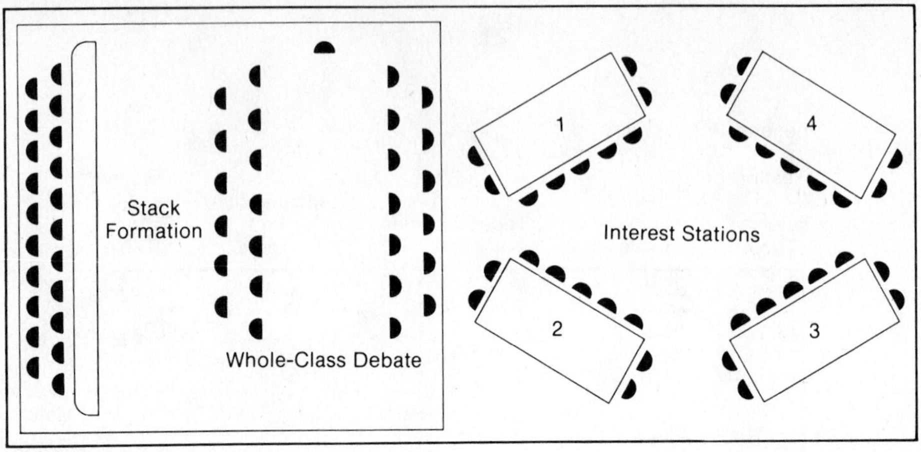

Figure 10.4 Special formation arrangements.

Source: George R. Musgrave, *Individualized Instruction: Teaching Strategies Focus on the Learner* (Boston: Allyn & Bacon, 1975), 48,63,65

and on the right side of Figure 10.5 work well for presenting instructional content, and enhance student interaction during debates, forums, or exhibits. The designs on the right side of Figure 10.4 and on the left side of 10.5 facilitate buzz sessions and special interest activities. These special formations are not as open as the one in Figure 10.3. The arrangements in Figures 10.4 and 10.5 are well suited to upper junior and senior high school groups, while those in Figure 10.3 are better for the middle grade and junior high school students.

Because of increased student interaction, discipline problems may arise with these special seating arrangements, unless the teacher has good managerial skill. However, all these designs allow the teacher flexibility in classroom activities. They function for small groups, create feelings of group cohesion and cooperation, and also allow the teacher to present a demonstration, ask the class to brainstorm a problem or debate an issue, or use audiovisual materials.

Physical Considerations in Arranging Classrooms

As long as the furniture is not bolted to the floor, the teacher can make changes in room design. Elementary teachers will need to be more flexible, since they are teaching several subjects; moreover, they can be more flexible, since they rarely share the room with other teachers. The room is theirs to set up learning areas, interest areas, work and study areas for reading, mathematics, science, arts and crafts. At the secondary level, where teachers teach one subject and other teachers share the room, the possibilities are reduced, but the room can still be divided into areas for small groups, audiovisual activities, projects, and independent study. Cooperation among teachers who share the room is needed.

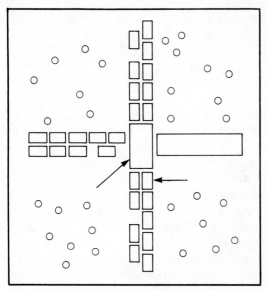

This "cross plan" creates more floor space. The open areas can be used for different activities.

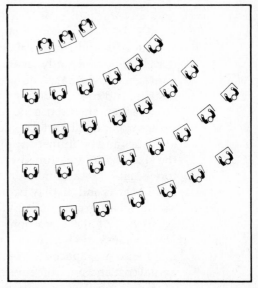

The class directs its attention to two or three people in front of the group. This arrangement can be used to prepare for a lesson or to summarize and evaluate a recently completed activity.

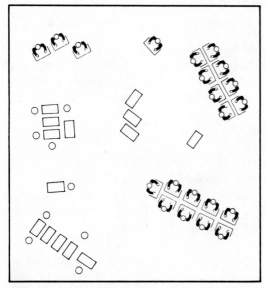

This arrangement allows pupils to work in small groups and move freely from one work area to another.

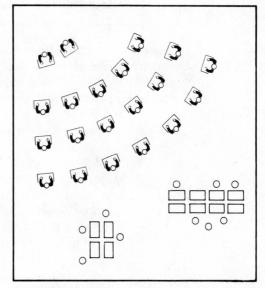

This plan provides for a large-group activity, while two smaller groups work on projects elsewhere in the room. To minimize distractions, children in the large group face away from the small-group areas.

Figure 10.5 Additional special formation arrangements.

Source: Robert E. Reys and Thomas R. Post, *The Mathematics Laboratory: Theory into Practice* (Boston: Prindle, Weber and Schmidt, 1973), p. 59.

Only through experience and time will teachers learn if a given arrangement suits their teaching style and the needs of their students. It may take several tries and continual revision to have a classroom design in which students work efficiently, materials and equipment are used to their best advantage, unnecessary equipment is removed, and the teacher finds it easy to instruct and to supervise the students.

Teachers should use four criteria in assessing classrooms: (1) *adequacy* refers to environmental factors such as sufficient light and heat; it also includes acoustics and equipment appropriate to the physical space; (2) *suitability* means the size, shape, and dimensions of the classroom, whether it is large enough (or too small) to accommodate the students, whether there are sufficient chalkboards and display boards, and whether the space is conducive to whole-group, small-group, or individualized learning; (3) *efficiency* involves the characteristics of the classroom space that are likely to improve instructional effectiveness, such as whether there are sufficient electrical outlets, shades to block out sun, space for computers, and so on; and (4) *economy* relates to the actual cost and possible savings that are achieved by the design or modification of an existing classroom for a particular group of students or a specific subject.[4]

Guidelines to Consider in Classroom Designs

Classroom design will be determined by the size of the room, the number of students in the class, the size and shape of tables and chairs, the amount of movable furniture, the location of fixed features such as doors, windows, closets, and chalkboard, the audiovisual equipment to be used, the school's practice, and the teacher's approach and experience. Seven factors should be considered in arranging the classroom.

1. *Fixed features*. The teacher cannot change the "givens" of a room and must take into account the location of doors, windows, closets, electric outlets, and so forth. For example, seats should not be too close to doors or closets. Electrical equipment needs to be near an outlet, and wires should not run across the center of the room. (If they must, they should be taped to the floor.)
2. *Traffic areas*. High traffic areas—such as supply areas, closets, and space near the pencil sharpener and wastebasket—need to be open and easily accessible. The teacher's desk should be located in a low traffic area.

---

4 Allan C. Ornstein, "Components of Curriculum Development," *Education and Urban Society* (Spring 1990), pp. 204–212.

3. *Work areas.* Work areas and study areas should be private and quiet, preferably placed in the corner or rear of the room, away from traffic lanes and noisy areas.

4. *Furniture and equipment.* The room, furniture, and equipment should be kept clean and in repair so that they can be used. Desks and chairs may be old, but they should be clean and smooth (make the appropriate requisition to the janitorial department or supervisor), and graphics and doodling should be discouraged immediately. The equipment should be stored in a designated space.

5. *Instructional materials.* All materials and equipment should be easily accessible so activities can begin and end promptly and cleanup time can be minimized. Props and equipment that are not stored in closets should be kept in dead spaces away from traffic.

6. *Visibility.* The teacher should be able to see all students from any part of the room to reduce managerial problems and enhance instructional supervision. Students should be able to see the teacher, chalkboard, projected images, and demonstrations without having to move their desks and without straining their necks.

7. *Flexibility.* The classroom design should be flexible enough so that it can be modified to meet the requirements of different activities and different groupings for instruction.[5]

WHOLE-GROUP INSTRUCTION

Whole-group instruction is the most traditional and common form of classroom organization. Teachers generally gear their teaching to the mythical "average" student on the assumption that this level of presentation will meet the needs of the greatest number of students. A common block of content (in any subject) is taught on the assumption that large-group instruction is the most effective and convenient format for teaching it.

In the large group the teacher lectures, explains, and demonstrates, asks and answers questions in front of the entire class, provides the same practice and drill exercises to the entire class, works on the same problems, and employs the same materials. Instruction is directed toward the whole group, but the teacher may ask specific students to answer questions, monitor specific students as they carry out the assigned activities, and work with students on an individual basis.

Whole groups can be an economical and efficient way of teaching. The method is especially convenient for teaching the same skills or subject to the

5 Edmund T. Emmer et al., *Classroom Management for Secondary Teachers*, 2nd ed. (Englewood Cliffs, N.J.: Prentice-Hall, 1989); Milbrey M. McLaughlin, Joan E. Talbert, and Nina Bascia, *The Contexts of Teaching in Secondary Schools* (New York: Teachers College Press, Columbia University, 1990).

entire class, making assignments, administering tests, setting group expectations, and making announcements. Bringing members of a class together for certain activities strengthens the feeling of belonging to a large group and can help establish a sense of community and class spirit. The whole group learns to cooperate by working with and sharing available resources, setting up rules and regulations for the learning environment, and exchanging ideas.[6] Finally, this method of grouping students is most effective for directing and managing large numbers of students.

The critics of whole-group instruction contend that it fails to meet the needs and interests of individual students. Teachers who use this method tend to look upon students as a homogeneous group with common abilities, interests, styles of learning, and motivation. Since instruction is geared to a hypothetical average student, all students are expected to learn and perform within narrow limits. Students are evaluated, instructional methods and materials are selected, and learning is paced on the basis of the group average.[7] High-achieving students eventually become bored, and low-achieving students eventually become frustrated. The uniqueness of each student is often lost in the large group. Extroverted students tend to monopolize the teacher's time, and passive students usually are not heard from or do not receive necessary attention. Finally, students sometimes act out their behavioral problems in the safety of numbers.

Although a good teacher can compensate for these problems, it is best not to use the whole group as the only grouping for instruction. Different grouping is essential for variety, motivation, and flexibility in teaching and learning.

Class Size and Achievement

Does class size affect whole-group learning? When it comes to improving student performance, common sense would expect a clear relationship to exist. Surprisingly, class size does not automatically lead to better student performance. In one review of 152 studies that analyzed smaller classes and student achievement, 82 percent found no significant impact, 9.2 percent saw positive results, and 8.6 percent found negative results.[8]

---

6 David W. Johnson and Frank P. Johnson, *Joining Together*, 4th ed. (Englewood Cliffs, N.J.: Prenctice-Hall, 1991); George J. Posner and Alan N. Rudnitsky, *Course Design: A Guide to Curriculum Development for Teachers*, 3rd ed. (White Plains, N.Y.: Longman, 1986).

7 Jeannie Oakes, "Tracking, Inequality, and the Rhetoric of Reform," *Journal of Education* (Summer 1986), pp. 60–80; Kimberly Trimble and Robert L. Sinclair, "*Ability Grouping and Differing Conditions for Learners*," paper presented at the annual meeting of the American Educational Research Association, San Francisco, April 1986.

8 Eric A. Hanushek, "The Impact of Differential Expenditures on School Performance," *Educational Researcher* (May 1989), pp. 45–51, 62.

In still another review of eight studies of low-achieving students, Robert Slavin found that differences in achievement levels of students in larger classes (22 to 37 students) compared to small classes (15 to 20 students) were insignificant. Across the eight studies the effect was only +.13—very disappointing given that the average class size in the large groups was 27 students compared to 16 in the small groups (40 percent difference).[9] In another review, Madden and Slavin found that only when class size is reduced to one-to-one teacher/student ratios, as in tutoring, does size make a difference.[10] Although Glass and his colleagues received considerable attention when they concluded that class size below 15 students had a substantial effect on student achievement, somewhat unknown, this was only significant in 10 out of 77 studies—and learning benefits did not really appear until class size was reduced to three students. The effects of class size and achievement were more positive in elementary grades than in middle grades and high school.[11]

These data correspond with the more recent "Prime Time" program in Indiana which showed that (in 300 observed classrooms) reduction in the average class size in the primary grades correlated with slight increases in student achievement.[12] One reason why the effects of class size in secondary schools seem indistinguishable is that size may have different effects on different subjects (English, social studies, etc.) and different tracks (academic, vocational, etc.). Both subjects and tracking are strongly correlated with social class, ability, motivation, etc., and these confounding variables may blur the effects of class size.

Similarly, in a review of Title I programs in 12 school districts, Harris Cooper pointed out that class size and additional academic time do not necessarily have an impact on reading achievement among low-achieving and at-risk students. Title I students spend about 13 minutes more instructional time per day in language arts and reading instruction than non-Title I students, and more than 50 percent of instruction for Title I students was at the individual level or in groups of 2 to 5 students.[13] What seems to be more important, based on a review of different class sizes, is the quality of instruction and degree of opportunity to learn the material on tests. Individualized learning is more beneficial than whole group instruction, but the teacher must know how to take

9 Robert E. Slavin, "Class Size and Student Achievement: Small Effects of Small Classes," *Educational Psychologist* (Winter 1989), pp. 99–110.

10 Nancy A. Madden and Robert E. Slavin, "Effective Pull-Out Programs for Students at Risk," in R. E. Slavin, N. L. Karweit, and N. A. Madden, eds., *Effective Programs for Students at Risk* (Needham Heights, Mass.: Allyn & Bacon, 1989), pp. 16–32.

11 Gene M. Glass and Mary L. Smith, *Meta-Analysis of Research on the Relationship of Class Size and Achievement* (San Francisco: Far West Laboratory for Educational Research and Development, 1978); Glass et al., *School Class Size* (Beverly Hills, Calif.: Sage, 1982).

12 Daniel J. Mueller, Clinton I. Chase, and James D. Walden, "Effects of Reduced Class Size in Primary Classes," *Educational Leadership* (February 1988), pp. 48–50.

13 Harris M. Cooper, "Does Reducing Student-to-Instructor Ratios Affect Achievement?" *Educational Psychologist* (Winter 1989), pp. 79–98.

advantage of the opportunity for greater individualization. Researchers maintain that efficient class size is a product of many factors, including subject area, students' prior achievement, and the instructional skills of the teacher.[14]

Guidelines for Teaching Whole Groups

When teaching whole groups or regular classes of 20 or more students, it is important to start well and on time. The teacher needs to set the tone for good classroom management and make good use of allocated time. Here are some practical suggestions to get the instructional ball rolling on the right path.

1. *Get your room ready.* If possible be in the room before the class arrives. Your appearance helps to start on time.
2. *Be sure the room conditions are appropriate.* Check the lighting, heat, ventilation, etc. Be sure the desks and chairs are in proper order. If there are closets in the room, be sure they are not gaping wide open. Check to see if the chalkboard is clear of "leftovers" from a previous period. (However, honor a colleague's request to save material so long as it is on the side.)
3. *Have your materials ready.* Attendance book, lesson plans, instructional materials, extra pencils or pens for students who may need them, chalkboard eraser, and other materials (charts, pictures, maps) that you may need should be readily available.
4. *When students arrive.* Be near the door (do not block it) to help direct middle grade or junior high school students to their seats; they need more controls or structure than high school students. Be sure students go to their assigned seats. If necessary, remind students that there is a homework assignment or review question to copy.
5. *Close the door when the late bell rings.* It is time to start. Don't wait for stragglers. If students arrive late, admit them but mark them late if they do not have a late pass. Take up the matter after class, if necessary, but not during class time.
6. *Give an assignment.* Obtain full attention. Start the students on a review exercise, warm-up drill, or set of problems. Explain instructions clearly. And be sure they begin the assignment.
7. *Check attendance; attend to clerical routines.* Now is the time to deal with clerical paperwork, attendance and late forms, and special notes or forms. These chores should take no more than five minutes.

---

14 Cooper, "Does Reducing Student-to-Instructor Ratios Affect Achievement?"; *Allan C. Ornstein, "In Pursuit of Cost-Effective Schools," Principal* (September 1990), pp. 28–30.

8. *Attend to special student needs.* While the students are completing the assignment, attend to special student requests or problems. Attend to one student at a time; otherwise, you may lose control.

9. *Circulate among students.* This bolsters classroom management and ensures students are prepared with books, pens, assignments, and the like.

10. *Check notebooks, homework, or other written work.* If time permits, check to see that students have their notebooks, homework, texts covered. Remind them that notebooks (homework assignments) will be frequently checked.

11. *Review assignment.* When most students seem finished with the assignment, start reviewing it. Make sure students understand the assignment. If needed, take extra time to discuss or reteach specific aspects of the assignment.

12. *Enforce written standards.* If the school, department, or you personally, has a specified method or procedure for students to write in notebooks, to submit homework or to do warm-up assignments, enforce it to the class.

13. *Attend to academic tasks.* Teach! This includes discussions, questions, explanations, demonstrations, projects, reports, and exams.

14. *Summarize the lesson.* Learn to pace your lesson. As the period ends, check your watch. Remind students classwork is to continue until you give the word that the class has ended.

15. *Dismiss the class.* Some schools provide a warning bell. Don't permit students to dismiss themselves, but don't keep them too long after the end-of-the-period bell (since they must report to another class on time).

SMALL-GROUP INSTRUCTION

Despite the data that suggest small-group instruction does not always improve achievement, dividing students into small groups seems to provide an opportunity for students to become more actively engaged in learning and for teachers to monitor student progress better. Between five and eight students seems to be an optimal number to ensure successful small-group activity. When there are fewer than five, especially in a group discussion, students tend to pair off rather than interact as a group.[15]

---

15 Robert E. Slavin, "Student Teams and Comparison among Equals: Effects on Academic Performance and Student Attitudes," *Journal of Educational Psychology* (August 1978), pp. 532–538; Noreen M. Webb, "Verbal Interaction and Learning in Peer-Directed Groups," *Theory into Teaching* (Winter 1985), pp. 32–39.

Student interaction is usually increased in small discussion groups or informal seating arrangements.

Small-group instruction works best in rooms with movable furniture, but it can also be used in classrooms with fixed furniture. Small groupings can enhance student cooperation and social skills. Appropriate group experiences foster the development of democratic values, cultural pluralism, and appreciation for differences among people. Small-group instruction can provide interesting challenges, permit students to progress at their own pace, provide a psychologically safe situation in which to master the material, and encourage them to contribute to class activities.

Dividing the class into small groups helps the teacher monitor work and assess progress through questioning, discussions, and checking workbook exercises and quizzes geared for the particular group. Small groups also give the teacher a chance to introduce new skills at a level suited to a particular group. Because the number of students assigned to each group is often determined by their progress, the group size will vary. Students may move from group to group if their progress exceeds or falls below that of their assigned group. In effect, the teacher is using grouping to restructure a heterogeneously grouped class into several homogeneous subgroups.

Small groups are typically used in reading and mathematics. The teacher divides the class into two or three groups, depending on the total number of students, their range of ability, and the number of groups the teacher is able to handle. The teacher usually works with one group at a time, while the other students do seatwork or independent work.

The use of small groups can be extended beyond the typical groupings in reading and mathematics to all grade levels and subjects. There are seven logical criteria on which grouping can be based.

1. *Ability*. Grouping by ability reduces the problems of heterogeneity in the classroom.
2. *Interest*. Students have some choice in group membership based on special interests in a particular subject matter or activity.
3. *Skill*. The teacher forms groups in order to develop different skills in students or to have them learn to work with different types of materials.
4. *Viewpoint*. Students have some choice in forming groups based on feelings about a controversial issue.
5. *Activity or project*. The teacher forms groups to perform a specific assignment.
6. *Integration*. The teacher forms groups considering race, ethnicity, religion, or sex to enhance human relations.
7. *Arbitrary*. Groupings are made at random or on the basis of alphabetical order, location in the room, or some other method not related to student or work characteristics.[16]

David Berliner contends that teachers who engage in small-group instruction seem to attend to five strategies of teaching: (1) *compensation*, favoring the shy, quiet, or low-achieving students, (2) *strategic leniency*, ignoring some inappropriate behaviors of students, (3) *proper sharing*, enlisting some students to aid in sharing homework or tutoring responsibility, (4) *progressive sharing*, compensating for the problems of low-ability students, and (5) *suppressing emotions*, limiting their emotions or feelings because they feel they are inappropriate or may lead to management problems.[17] Thus, the apparently simple task of organizing small groups involves numerous complex decisions and strategies.

Regardless of the basis of the grouping, assignments should be specific enough and within the range of the students' abilities and interests so the group can work on its own without teacher support. This permits the teacher to single out one group for attention or to help individuals by explaining, questioning, redirecting, and encouraging.

Small-group learning opportunities tend to be more effective in motivating black and female students to achieve than white and male students. In separate

---

16 Association of Teachers of Social Studies in the City of New York, *A Handbook for the Teaching of Social Studies*, 4th ed. (Boston: Allyn & Bacon, 1975); Allan C. Ornstein, Harriet Talmage, and Anne W. Juhasz, *The Paraprofessional's Handbook* (Belmont, Calif.: Fearon, 1975).

17 David C. Berliner, "Laboratory Setting and the Study of Teacher Education," *Journal of Teacher Education* (November–December 1985), pp. 2–8.

studies of young adolescent students, black students experience greater need for peer approval, group recognition, and group motivation regarding their achievement in school. White students tend to score higher on measures of achievement motivation that emphasize traits such as delayed gratification, sense of control, and self-esteem—so that the need for peer recognition for achievement is not as important. Moreover, the latter group score higher on measures of individualism and independence.[18] Female students also possess greater need for achievement in groups than males. This is perhaps due to the fact that boys are socialized to be individualistic, self-reliant, and competitive earlier and in different ways from girls and the idea of winning and succeeding on their own may be more important than sharing in group experiences.

Small-group instruction has been favorably compared to individualized instruction by many authorities in terms of practical advantages regarding teacher attention, more efficient use of teacher time, more efficient management of students, frequent student praise, good pacing, review and reinforcement of instruction, and increased peer-peer interaction.[19] Although these arguments appear convincing, the term "individualized instruction" can be misleading; that is, it often describes individualization for only a few moments within a regular class setting or a whole group of 20 to 30 students. Indeed, a one-to-one format has always showed superior achievement to students taught in groups.

In terms of precise benefits, a study of fifth-grade students with learning difficulties taught in small groups (of three) with direct instruction and one-to-one groups was compared for mastery (90 percent or more) in spelling and in math fractions. The mean time for spelling mastery in the small group was 570 minutes, and the one-to-one condition was 325 minutes, a mean percentage difference of 175 percent. For fractions, the small group was 253 minutes and for the one-to-one condition, 202 minutes. This was a mean difference of 116 percent. But the total instructional time for teachers to teach the small group of three students was 248 minutes for fractions and 598 minutes for spelling. The total time to teach the same content to the same number of students in the one-to-one setting or individually was 606 minutes for fractions and 974 minutes for spelling. The one-to-one setting in fractions required 245 percent of the time needed for the small group, and 163 percent for spelling.[20]

---

18 Louis A. Castenell, "Achievement Motivation: An Investigation of Adolescents' Achievement Patterns," *American Educational Research Journal* (Winter 1983), pp. 503–510; Edgar Epps, "Correlates of Academic Achievement among Northern and Southern Urban Negro Students," *Journal of Social Issues* (Summer 1969), pp. 55–70.

19 Allan C. Ornstein, "Practice and Drill: Implications for Instruction," *NASSP Bulletin* (February 1990), pp. 112–116; Barak V. Rosenshine, "Synthesis of Research on Explicit Teaching," *Educational Leadership* (April 1986), pp. 60–69; and Robert E. Slavin and Nancy L. Karweit, "Effects of Whole-Class, Ability Grouped, and Individualized Instruction on Mathematics Achievement," *American Educational Research Journal* (Fall 1985), pp. 351–367.

20 Jeremy Baker, Margaret Young, and Meredith Martin, "The Effectiveness of Small-Group versus One-to-One Remedial Instruction," *Elementary School Journal* (September 1990), pp. 65–76.

The implications seem clear: small-group instruction is efficient in terms of total instructional minutes a teacher needs to teach all the members of a group certain content, but student time is wasted. It can be argued that such a waste of student time is not justified when the major goal is remedial instruction, but in a regular instructional setting the increased use of teacher time (and the related economics) is a powerful factor to consider. However, there are ways in which one-to-one instruction may be built into whole-group instruction. The most obvious way is to withdraw a student in need of remedial instruction to a separate setting for brief periods of individual instruction. Peer tutors, adult volunteers, or parents can also serve as instructors on a one-to-one basis. But a teacher charged with teaching a number of students will always be more efficient (not necessarily more effective) with a larger group in terms of use of time.

Ability Grouping

The most common means of dealing with heterogeneity is to assign students to classes and programs according to ability. In high schools students may be tracked into college preparatory, vocational or technical, or general programs. In many middle and junior high schools, students are sometimes assigned to a class by ability and stay with that class as it moves from teacher to teacher. In a few cases, and more often in elementary schools, students are assigned to a class on the basis of a special characteristic, such as being gifted, handicapped, or bilingual. Elementary schools may use several types of **ability grouping**. In addition to the types used in the secondary schools, they may assign students to a heterogeneous class and then regroup them homogeneously by ability in selected areas, such as reading and mathematics.

Despite widespread criticism of **between-class ability grouping** (separate classes for students of different abilities), teachers overwhelmingly support the idea because of the ease in teaching a homogeneous group; it continues to be a common grouping pattern at the secondary level where students are tracked on several academic levels of achievement and aptitude.[21] Whereas high school students are often assigned to academic, vocational, and general programs, middle and junior high school students are often assigned to advanced, basic, and remedial classes. (In both cases, we are dealing with tracking and homogeneous grouping.) The major advantages of such grouping are that it permits adaptation of instructional methods to the needs of students; it helps maintain student interest, because high achievers are not bored or slowed down by the participation of low achievers; it makes pacing, instructional smoothness, probing, reinforcement, classroom management, and general teaching

---

21 Jeannie Oakes, "The Reproduction of Inequality: The Content of Secondary School Tracking," *Urban Review* (Summer 1982), pp. 107–120; Aretha B. Pigford, "Instructional Grouping: Purposes and Consequences," *Clearing House* (February 1990), pp. 261–263.

easier; and it makes possible greater teacher attention and individualized instruction to low achievers.[22]

The major criticisms is that separating students into high- and low-achieving groups fosters corresponding expectations among teachers and students (self-fulfilling prophecies), and perpetuates the same students in the same tracked classes.[23] Ability grouping is perceived to perpetuate social class and racial inequalities because lower-class and minority students are disproportionately represented in lower tracks and that such tracks have negative impact on achievement.[24]

Some researchers have found that high-ability students benefit from such grouping, but this does not compensate for the losses for students in low-ability groups. Not only do slow or remedial classes reinforce low achievement among low achievers, but also discipline problems, lack of participation, slower paced instruction, and lack of interest in the subject are greatest in these classes—causing the gap between ability groups to widen compared to its size when low achievers are placed in mixed classes.[25] (Discipline problems are minor as long as low achievers are in a minority in mixed classes.) In short, the argument is that students in low homogeneous groups receive lower quality of instruction than do students in higher tracks.

When Slavin reviewed some 30 studies and weighed the outcomes of all students (high and low) in ability-grouped classes, he found the effects to be close to zero in both elementary and secondary schools. (Most of the studies involved grades 7 to 9, and the one exception was in social studies which showed relatively strong effects favoring homogeneous grouping for average and high achievers.)[26]

However, instruction in mixed ability, untracked classes more closely resembles instruction in high-achieving and middle-track classes than instruc-

---

22 Robert E. Slavin, "Achievement Effects of Ability Grouping in Secondary Schools: A Best-Evidence Synthesis," *Review of Educational Research* (Fall 1990), pp. 471–499; Aage B. Sorensen and Maureen T. Hallinan, "Effects of Ability Grouping on Growth in Academic Achievement," *American Educational Research Journal* (Winter 1986), pp. 519–542.

23 Susan D. Allan, "Ability Grouping Research Reviews," *Educational Leadership* (March 1991), pp. 60–65; Adam Gamoran and Robert D. Mare, "Secondary School Tracking and Educational Inequality," *American Journal of Sociology* (March 1989), pp. 1146–1183; and Thomas L. Good, "Two Decades of Research on Teacher Expectations," *Journal of Teacher Education* (July–August 1987), pp. 32–47.

24 Jomilla H. Braddock, *Tracking: Implications for Student Race-Ethnic Subgroups* (Baltimore: Center for Research on Effective Schooling for Disadvantaged Students, 1990); Adam Gamoran, "Measuring Curriculum Differentiation," *American Journal of Education* (February 1989), pp. 129–143.

25 James A. Kulik, "Findings on Grouping Are Often Distorted," *Educational Leadership* (March 1991), p. 67; James A. Kulik and Chen-Lin C. Kulik, "Effects of Ability Grouping on Student Achievement," *Equity and Excellence* (Spring 1987), pp. 22–30; and John M. Peterson, "Remediation Is No Remedy," *Educational Leadership* (March 1989), pp. 24–25.

26 Robert E. Slavin, "Achievement Effects of Substantial Reductions in Class Size," in R. E. Slavin, ed., *School and Classroom Organization* (Hillsdale, N.J.: Erlbaum, 1989), pp. 247–257; Slavin, "Achievement Effects of Ability Grouping in Secondary Schools: A Best-Evidence Synthesis," *Review of Educational Research* (Fall 1990), pp. 471–499.

tion in low-track classes; so the mixed-ability grouping tends to benefit low-ability students. Thus, two large school districts (Denver and San Diego) have begun to eliminate remedial classes at the middle schools and high schools, on the basis that elimination of such classes will raise expectations for students who would otherwise remain stuck in low-level courses for most of their academic lives.[27]

Within-class ability grouping is commonly found at the elementary school level, as well as in a small number of middle schools, whereby students are grouped heterogeneously at the class level, but usually divided into smaller groups for reading and math, as well as possibly for particular topics. This grouping pattern is assessed as effective; students in heterogeneous classes who are regrouped homogeneously learn more than students in classes that do not use such grouping. This is especially true in reading and math, for which within-class grouping is common, as well as for low-achieving students.[28]

The research data suggest that a small number of within-class groups (two or three) is better than a large number, permitting more monitoring by and feedback from the teacher and less seatwork time and transition time.[29] For example, in a class of three ability groups students spend approximately two-thirds of the time doing seatwork without direct supervision, but with four groups they spend three-quarters of the class time doing seatwork. See Tips for Teachers 10.1.

When within-class ability groups are formed, students proceed at different paces on different materials. The tasks and assignments tend to be more flexible than those in between-class groups. Teachers also tend to try to increase the tempo of instruction and the amount of time for instruction in low-achieving within-class groups to bring students closer to the class mean.[30] There is less stigma for low-ability groups in within-class grouping

27 Daniel Gursky et al., "A New Approach for Low Achievers," *Teacher* (December 1989), p. 22; Peterson, "Remediation Is No Remedy."

28 James M. McPartland et a.l., *School Structures and Classroom Practices in Elementary, Middle and Secondary Schools* (Baltimore: Johns Hopkins University Press, 1987); Jeannie Oakes, "Tracking in Secondary Schools: A Contextual Perspective," *Educational Psychologist* (Spring 1987), pp. 129–153; and Slavin and Karweit, "Effects of Whole-Class, Ability Grouped and Individualized Instruction on Mathematics Achievement."

29 Hilda Borko and Jerome Niles, "Teaching Strategies for Forming Reading Groups," paper presented at the annual meeting of the American Educational Research Association, New Orleans, April 1984; Elfrieda Heibert, "An Examination of Ability Grouping in Reading Instruction," *Reading Research Quarterly* (Winter 1983), p. 231–255; and Peter Winograd and Scott G. Paris, "A Cognitive and Motivational Agenda for Reading Instruction," *Educational Leadership* (December–January 1989), pp. 30–35.

30 Benjamin S. Bloom, "The 2 Sigma Problem: The Search for Methods of Instruction as Effective as One-to-One Tutoring," *Educational Researcher* (June 1984), pp. 4–16; Brian Rowan and Andrew W. Miracle, "Systems of Ability Grouping and the Stratification of Achievement in Elementary Schools," *Sociology of Education* (July 1983), pp. 133–144; and Joseph S. Yarworth, Timothy L. Schwambach, and Robert F. Nicely, "Organizing for Results in Elementary and Middle School Mathematics," *Educational Leadership* (October 1988), pp. 61–67.

Tips for Teachers 10.1

Components of Direct Instruction

Most teachers rely on whole-group instruction, and evidence suggests that for teaching low-achieving and at-risk students in this type of setting, a high-structured approach is the most effective method. This approach, today, is often called "direct" instruction or "explicit" instruction. The major aspects of direct instruction are listed below. (Note, however, this approach is not suitable for high-achieving or independent learners who prefer a low-structured and flexible situation so they can utilize their initiative.)

1. Begin a lesson with a short statement of goals.
2. Begin with a short review of previous, prerequisite learning.
3. Present new material in small steps, with student practice after each step.
4. Give clear and detailed instructions and explanations.
5. Provide a high level of active practice for all students.
6. Guide students during initial practice.
7. Ask a large number of questions, check for student understanding, and obtain responses from all students.
8. Provide systematic feedback and corrections.
9. Obtain a student success rate of 80 percent or higher during initial practice.
10. Provide explicit instruction for seatwork exercises, and, where possible, monitor and help students during seatwork.
11. Provide for spaced review and testing.

Source: Barak Rosenshine, "Explicit Teaching and Teacher Training," *Journal of Teacher Education* (May–June 1987), p. 34.

than in between-class grouping, since grouping is only for part of the day and the class is integrated the rest of the time. In addition, regrouping plans tend to be more flexible than in between-class groups, because moving students from group to group is less disruptive within a class than between classes.

In the final analysis, many teachers use many forms of ability grouping. The important point is that the teacher ask appropriate questions before grouping students such as:

1. *What is the purpose of grouping?* Is it to group for instructional efficacy? If so, grouping by ability enables you to increase the effectiveness of teaching and learning. Is it to promote race relations, cooperative learning, or self-esteem among low achievers?

2. *What tasks are to be completed?* Mechanical or rote tasks tend to be independent tasks, and offer the greater possibility that each student can work on his own at his seat. Interdependent tasks, or team assignments, are more conducive for grouping students.

3. *What are the management skills of the teacher?* Grouping by itself does not result in increased student achievement. You must be able to manage students so as to create an effective classroom environment. Multiple groups tend to create problems for teachers who are poor classroom managers.

4. *What are the results of grouping?* The more groups that are formed, the more time teachers must spend in small-group instruction. During this time, the remaining students (those not in the group receiving instruction) usually engage in other instructional tasks—some of which are often of questionable value. Students in classrooms with many within groups have fewer direct contacts with their teachers than those in nongrouped classrooms.[31]

Guidelines for Ability Grouping Instruction

Slavin and Karweit have developed a step-by-step procedure for teaching mathematics in middle grade and junior high classes which can also be utilized for reading groups.[32] The program, called Ability-Grouped Active Teaching (AGAT), uses two ability groups rather than the typical three to increase the amount of time the teacher can spend with each group. Studies have found that students gained approximately one grade equivalent more with the AGAT program than with large-group instruction. The procedures are as follows.

1. *Assign* students to one of two groups—the top 60 percent to the high-middle teaching group and the remaining 40 percent to the low teaching group.

---

31 Maureen T. Hallinan, "The Effects of Ability Grouping in Secondary Schools," *Review of Educational Research* (Fall 1990), pp. 501–504; Aretha B. Pigford, "Instructional Grouping: Purposes and Consequences," *Clearing House* (February 1990), pp. 261–263.

32 Robert E. Slavin and Nancy L. Karweit, *Ability-Grouped Active Teaching (AGAT): Teacher's Manual* (Baltimore: Center for Social Organization of Schools, Johns Hopkins University, 1982); Slavin and Karweit, "Effects of Whole Class, Ability Grouped, and Individualized Instruction on Mathematics Achievement."

2. *Pace* the lesson and teach at a level according to the abilities of each group. The low ability group, for example, may require twice as much time to cover the same material.

3. *Quiz* students frequently. Give a pretest to determine their initial ability and then quizzes about once a week to determine if they are learning the material and if the pace of the lesson should be adjusted.

4. *Prepare* separate lessons for each group. The lessons should include (a) starter problems every day, which should last about 3 minutes (or up to 5 to 8 minutes); (b) instructional materials such as pictures, graphs, and illustrations; (c) practice problems or seatwork activities for about half the class period; (d) homework every day except perhaps Friday, and (e) quizzes at least once a week.

5. *Arrange seating* so that groups are separate during group work but students are in a mixed arrangement for the rest of the day.

6. *Schedule activities* to make the best use of teacher and student time (or time on task), and be sure activities are clear to students and consistent each class period.[33]

Peer Tutoring

Peer tutoring, also called *pairing students*, is the assignment of students to help one another on a one-to-one basis or in small groups in a variety of situations. According to Ornstein, there are three types of pairing students: (1) Students may tutor others *within* the same class; (2) older students may tutor students in lower grades outside of class; (3) two students may work together and help each other as equals with learning activities.[34] The purpose of the first two types is to pair a student who needs assistance with a tutor on a one-to-one basis, although small groups of two or three tutees and one tutor can also be formed. The third type of pairing students, also called *peer-pairing*, is nontutorial. More than two students working together as equals is sometimes called *cooperative learning*.

Of all three pairing arrangements, peer tutoring within the same class is the most common. A student who has completed a lesson and has shown understanding of the material is paired with a student who needs help. The research suggests that because students are less threatened by peers, they are more willing to ask fellow students questions that they fear the teacher might consider "silly." In addition, they are less afraid that fellow students might criticize them for being unable to understand an idea or problem after a second or third explanation.[35] It has also been found that a student can usually explain a concept in language that another student can grasp; unfamiliar vocabulary is

---

33 Robert E. Slavin, *Using Student Team Learning*, 3rd ed. (Baltimore: Center for Research on Elementary and Middle Schools, Johns Hopkins University, 1986); Slavin, *Cooperative Learning: Theory, Research and Practice* (Englewood Cliffs, N.J.: Prentice-Hall, 1990).

34 Ornstein, Talmage, and Juhasz, *The Paraprofessional's Handbook*.

35 Slavin, *Cooperative Learning*.

cut to a minimum, and sometimes a few choice slang terms can make a difficult concept comprehensible. Also, because the faster student has just learned the concept, he may be more aware than the teacher of what is giving the slower student difficulty. Peer tutors benefit from the relationship; their own understanding is reinforced by explaining the idea or problem, and their social skills are enhanced.[36] The teacher benefits by having additional time to work with students who have more severe learning problems.

David and Roger Johnson find these advantages of peer tutoring.

1. Peer tutors are often effective in teaching students who do not respond well to adults.
2. Peer tutoring can develop a bond of friendship between the tutor and tutee, which is important for integrating slow learners into the group.
3. Peer tutoring allows the teacher to teach a large group of students, but still gives slow learners the individual attention they need.
4. Tutors benefit by learning to teach, a general skill that can be useful in adult society.[37]

The help that one student gives another can be *explanatory* or *terminal*. Explanatory help consists of step-by-step accounts of how to do something. Terminal help consists of correcting an error or giving the correct answer without explaining how to obtain the answer or solve the problem. Most studies of explanatory and terminal help conclude that giving explanations aids the tutor in learning the material, whereas giving terminal help does not.[38] In giving explanations the tutor clarifies the material in her own mind, may see new relationships, and builds a better grasp of the material. Giving terminal help involves little restructuring of concepts.[39]

Not surprisingly, receiving explanations is correlated with achievement. Students who receive terminal help or receive no help tend to learn less than students who receive explanatory help.[40] The benefit of receiving explanations

---

36 Russel Ames and Carole Ames, *Research on Motivation in Education* (Orlando, Fla.: Academic Press, 1984); Penelope L. Peterson et al., "Ability X Treatment and Children's Learning in Large-Group and Small-Group Approaches," *American Educational Research Journal* (Winter 1981), pp. 453–473.

37 David W. Johnson and Roger T. Johnson, *Learning Together and Alone*, 3rd ed. (Englewood Cliffs, N.J.: Prentice-Hall, 1990).

38 Susan R. Swing and Penelope L. Peterson, "The Relationship of Student Ability and Small-Group Interaction to Student Achievement," *American Educational Research Journal* (Summer 1982), pp. 259–274; Noreen M. Webb, "Predicting Learning from Student Interaction: Defining the Interaction Variables," *Educational Psychologist* (Spring 1983), pp. 33–41.

39 John A. Bargh and Yaacov Schul, "On the Cognitive Benefits of Teaching," *Journal of Educational Psychology* (October 1980), pp. 593–604; Webb, "Verbal Interaction and Learning in Peer-Directed Groups."

40 Swing and Peterson, "The Relationship of Student Ability and Small-Group Interaction to Student Achievement"; Penelope L. Peterson et al., "Merging the Process-Product and the Sociolinguistic Paradigms: Research on Small Group Processes," in P. L. Peterson, L. C. Wilkerson, and M. Hallinan, eds., *The Social Context of Instruction* (New York: Academic Press), pp. 126–152.

seems to be that it fills in incomplete understanding of the material and corrects misunderstandings; it also increases effort and motivation to learn. Receiving terminal help or receiving no help is frustrating and causes students to lose interest in learning.

Peer tutors trained in direct instructional methods (using frequent repetition, drill, and monitoring of a tutee's performance) are more effective (at least in teaching reading comprehension to their peers) than their tutor counterparts who use inquiry methods or receive no training. As few as three short training sessions are required. Although direct instructional methods are better than inquiry methods or no training at delivering information, tutees in general who receive peer instruction in any form perform significantly higher on post–reading tests than nontutees who receive no such instruction.[41]

Benjamin Bloom argues that tutoring (with preferably a 1:1 student-student ratio, but no more than 3:1) is the most effective method of grouping for instruction compared to conventional methods (30:1 student-teacher ratio) and even mastery learning methods (which he helped develop) when the mastery methods are used in a class of about 30 students. Bloom found that as many as 90 percent of the tutored students and 70 percent of the mastery learning students attained a level of increased achievement reached by only 20 percent of the students with conventional instruction over a three-week period.[42] Figure 10.6 compares achievement with conventional, mastery, and tutor instruction.

Nancy Madden agrees with one-to-one tutoring, especially for elementary school students, and adds three more dimensions: it is most effective when (1) tutors are teachers, (2) tutees spend most of the day in heterogeneous classes, and (3) tutors work with the same students for a minimum of eight weeks to ensure continuity.[43] Madden adds, during whole-group reading instruction, the tutors should serve as additional reading teachers to reduce student-teacher ratios to no more than 15 to 1. (Where all the money will come from to implement this program on a large scale is another issue.) Whether the program can be implemented at the secondary level is still another issue, but the idea has merit for prevention and intervention.

Tutoring programs that seem most effective, both for tutors and tutees, have the following characteristics: (1) formal organization with procedural rules established by the teacher, (2) instruction in basic skills and content, (3)

---

41 Judith E. Judy et al., "Effects of Two Instructional Approaches and Peer Tutoring on Gifted and Nongifted Sixth-Grade Students' Analogy Performance," *Reading Research Quarterly* (Spring 1988), pp. 236–255.

42 Benjamon S. Bloom, "Helping All Children Learn in Elementary School—and Beyond," *Principal* (March 1988), p. 12–17; Bloom, "The 2 Sigma Problem: The Search for Methods of Group Instruction as Effective as One-to-One Tutoring."

43 Nancy A. Madden et al., "Restructuring the Urban Elementary School," *Educational Leadership* (February 1989), pp. 14–18.

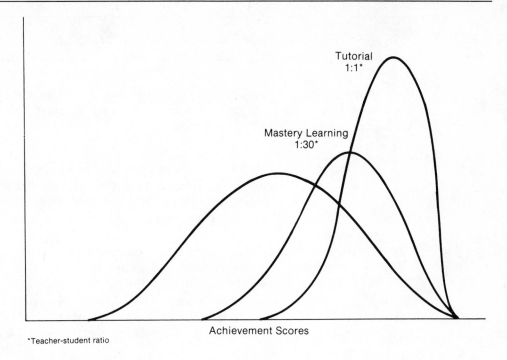

*Teacher-student ratio

Figure 10.6 Achievement distribution for students with conventional, mastery learning, and tutor insturction.

Source: Benjamin S. Bloom, "The 2 Sigma Problem: The Search for Methods of Group Instruction as Effective as One-to-One Tutoring," *Educational Researcher* (June–July 1989), p.5.

explanatory rather than terminal help given, (4) no more than three tutees per tutor and ideally one tutee per tutor, and (5) short duration, about four weeks.[44] (This last point contradicts Madden's eight-week recommendation.) When a tutorial program with these features is combined with regular classroom instruction, "the students being tutored not only learned more than they did without tutoring, they also developed a more positive attitude about what they were studying." In addition, the "tutors learned more than students who did not tutor."[45]

44 Peter A. Cohen, James A. Kulik, and Chen-Lin C. Kulik, "Educational Outcomes of Tutoring: A Meta-Analysis of Findings," *American Educational Research Journal* (Summer 1982), pp. 237–248; Linda Devin-Sheehan, Robert S. Feldman, and Vernon I. Allen, "Research on Children Tutoring Children: A Critical Review," *Review of Educational Research* (Summer 1976), pp. 355–385.

45 *What Works: Research about Teaching and Learning* (Washington, D.C.: U.S. Government Printing Office, 1986), p. 36.

Guidelines for Peer Tutoring

Peer tutoring, like ability grouping, can be effective if implemented properly, but it takes substantial time and effort to get off to a good start. Following are some suggestions for effective peer tutoring.

1. The teacher assesses students' needs. Needs may be mainly academic (for example, specific students may need remedial instruction in specific subjects). Needs may be social (another goal of tutoring is to enhance peer group relations or cross-cultural relations).

2. The teacher creates the expectation that everyone can learn from one another through verbalization and modeling.

3. Specific class time is set aside for tutoring.

4. The teacher provides directions for each tutor about time schedules and exactly what to do (for example, "Read the sentence to the group and get at least two students to identify the adjectives and nouns").

5. No tutor should work with the same students for more than a month at a time. This will prevent the tutor's assuming the role of substitute teacher, limit extended mismatching, and prevent boredom.

6. Tutors should not administer tests to tutees. One reason for peer tutoring is to develop a nonthreatening relationship, and testing may defeat this purpose.

7. Shy students should be assigned to work with cooperative, friendly tutors.

8. The teacher must be sure students understand their respective roles. He or she should select a student and demonstrate tutoring to the class. The teacher should model appropriate tutor behavior, provide examples of what is to be achieved, and show how it is to be achieved.

9. Pairing of good friends is unwise because they tend to drift from cognitive tasks into social interaction.

10. It is the teacher's job to plan tutoring arrangements well so that tutors understand and use a mix of materials, media, and activities (for example, one week doing review and drill in the workbooks, the next week doing library research, the next week writing and discussing stories).

11. Parents should be informed about the organization, purpose, and procedures of the tutoring program.

12. Parents can help in developing the classroom and schoolwide tutoring programs, collecting resources, gaining community support, assess-

ing student needs, matching and assigning students, and helping tutors and tutees.[46]

Cooperative Learning

Grouping students to work together instead of competing is becoming a more and more accepted practice by teachers. In the traditional classroom structure, students compete for teacher recognition and grades. The same students tend to be "winners" and "losers" over the years. High-achieving students continually receive rewards and are motivated to learn, and low-achieving students continually experience failure (or near-failure) and frustration. Reducing competition and increasing cooperation among students may diminish hostility, prejudice, and patterns of failure among students.

This does not mean that competition has no place in the classroom or school. Even the advocates of cooperation feel that competition under the right conditions and with evenly matched individuals or groups can be a source of motivation, excitement, fun, and improve performance—for example, in simple drill activities, speed tasks, low-anxiety games and psychomotor activities, and athletics.[47]

According to a review of the research, cooperation among participants helps build (1) positive and coherent personal identity, (2) self-actualization and mental health, (3) knowledge and trust of others, (4) communication, (5) acceptance and support of others, (6) wholesome relationships, and (7) reduction of conflicts. The data also suggest that cooperation and group learning are considerably more effective in fostering these social and interpersonal skills than competitive or individualistic efforts.[48]

In **cooperative learning**, students are divided into heterogeneous groups of two to six to work together on tasks assigned by the teacher. They engage in a variety of learning activities that require collaboration, teamwork, and/or mutual support. They help one another (especially the slow members), praise and criticize one another's efforts and contributions, and receive a group performance score.

Although several cooperative learning models exist, and school districts tend to adapt or modify existing models to suit their own needs, Johnson and Johnson's five basic components usually appear in the models: (1) *positive interdependence*—students understand they are responsible for their own learn-

---

46 Thomas L. Good and Jere E. Brophy, *Looking into Classrooms*, 5th ed. (New York: HarperCollins, 1991); Michael Webb and Wendy Schwartz, "Children Helping Children: A Good Way to Learn," *PTA Today* (October 1988), pp. 16–17.

47 Johnson and Johnson, *Joining Together*; Robert E. Slavin, *Student Team Learning* (Washington, D.C.: National Education Association, 1983).

48 David W. Johnson and Roger T. Johnson, *Learning Together and Alone* (Englewood Cliffs, N.J.: Prentice-Hall, 1991); D. Johnson, *Reaching Out: Interpersonal Effectiveness and Self-Actualization*, 4th ed. (Englewood Cliffs, N.J.: Prentice-Hall, 1990).

ing and the learning of members in their group; (2) *individual accountability*— each student must contribute effort and demonstrate mastery in their group; (3) *face-to-face interaction*—students have the opportunity to work together on assignments and to help and learn from each other; (4) *social skills*—students are expected to communicate with each other, assume leadership roles, and resolve conflicts within the group; and (5) *group processes*—students must periodically assess how they are working together and how their group behavior may be improved.[49] These five components can be applied to several different cooperative learning situations, and nearly any other group situation that seeks to break from the teacher-dominated instructional setting.

Based on several reviews of studies, remarkable claims have been made about cooperative learning: that achievement effects have been relatively and equally high for high, average, and low achievers, boys and girls, students of various ethnic backgrounds, handicapped students, and in elementary and secondary schools alike. A close scrutiny of the data suggests, however, the most effective methods should include (1) group goals and group recognition, (2) group success dependent on individual learning of all group members, and (3) individual accountability toward the group.[50]

Added to these three methods is a fourth—individual recognition. The latter point is often overlooked: group goals and group processes may be necessary to motivate students to work as a team and help one another, but if individuals are not recognized for their own performance then it becomes counterproductive for high achievers (even average students) to provide help at the expense of their own efforts, much less to give extra effort or time. If they are not given bonuses or higher grades for individual performance a regression to the group mean will become the norm—and the mean will continue to drop over an extended period as high achievers learn to devote less time on subjects organized around cooperative learning. Common sense reminds us that group goals and group success must be balanced with individual recognition and success; group scores alone will have less achievement effect in the long run. (The Soviets have learned that the hard way.)

Of all the cooperative learning arrangements, the two developed by Slavin are most popular: student team achievement divisions (STAD) and team-assisted instruction (TAI). Both arrangements have been found to increase student achievement, given the proper implementation. In *STAD*, teams of four or five members are balanced by ability, gender, and ethnicity. Students are ranked by previous test scores or grades and divided into threes or quarters.

---

49 David W. Johnson and Roger T. Johnson, *Cooperation and Competition: Theory and Research* (Edina, Minn.: Interaction Publishers, 1987); Johnson and Johnson, "Toward A Cooperative Effort," *Educational Leadership* (April 1989), pp. 80–81.

50 Robert E. Slavin, "Cooperative Revolution Catches on Fire," *School Administrator* (January 1988), pp. 9–13; Slavin, "Cooperative Learning and Student Achievement," *Educational Leadership* (October 1988), pp. 31–33; and Slavin, "Group Rewards Make Groupwork Work," *Educational Leadership* (February 1991), pp. 89–92.

Each team consists of one student from each of the thirds or quarters of the class ranking, with extra middle-ranked students becoming the fourth or fifth members. STAD involves five basic steps.

1. The teacher presents the *lesson to the whole group* in one or two class periods.

2. *Team study* follows for one or two class periods. Students who have already mastered the material help slower teammates with it. Drill is stressed, although students can engage in discussion and questioning. In a group of four students only two copies of the work sheets and answer sheets are given to each team to encourage team interaction and support. Students can work alone, if they prefer, or in pairs or threes. The team is not finished with the assignment until all members can score 100 percent on a practice quiz. (This figure may be a little impractical and need to be lowered.) Students are supposed to give one another explanations, not just check answer sheets and supply answers. The teacher moves around the room to monitor the teams' activities, and provides additional assistance.

3. *Class quizzes* are given frequently to see if students have learned the material while in the group. Students return to their assigned seats or move their desks apart for quizzes. The student scores are averaged into a team score, so that group members are more likely to help each other. Quizzes are scored in terms of progress so that slow-performing groups have the opportunity to gain recognition. The teacher grades the quizzes promptly, or students may exchange test papers for faster feedback.

4. *Recognition* is given teams for high average scores or improvement scores. Recognition can be given through bulletin boards, certificates, class newsletters, and letters to parents. Individuals are also recognized for good performance to maintain motivation, but a balance between individual reward and team accomplishment must be found. Giving too many individual rewards heightens competition and reduces cooperation.

5. *Teams are changed* every five or six weeks to give students an opportunity to work with other students and to give members of low-scoring teams a new chance.[51]

The steps involved in *team-assisted instruction (TAI)* are similar to those in STAD, but there is more emphasis on diagnosing through pre- and posttesting and on mastery of skills through practice. Instead of first studying the material together and then checking understanding through practice quizzes in teams,

51 Robert E. Slavin, *School and Classroom Organization* (Hillsdale, N.J.: Erlbaum, 1988); Slavin, *Using Student Team Learning*.

students first work on their own skill sheets and then have their team members check their answers and provide assistance. Not until a student gets 80 percent or higher on the practice quiz is he or she certified by the team to take the final test. Teams are given achievement and improvement scores and recognized as in STAD, but in addition they are labeled "super teams" (high performing), "great teams" (moderate performing), or "good teams" (minimum passing grade). Each day the teacher works for about 5 to 15 minutes (based on a 45–minute lesson) with two or three groups who are at about the same point in the curriculum. The other teams work on their own during this time.[52]

The emphasis of TAI is on teaching basic skills more through a type of mastery learning than through direct instruction. The approach is designed for the elementary, middle and junior high school, not the senior high school, and has been successfully implemented in teaching reading and mathematics. In some comparisons to students in traditional classes in mathematics, for example, TAI students have tended to show nearly twice as much progress in learning over the same period of time.[53]

A cooperative learning approach designed for middle school and senior high school students is called the **jigsaw classroom**. It is an old idea with a new name. Students work together in a small group on a specific academic task, assignment, or project.[54] They depend on each other for resources, information, and study assignments. It is an excellent method not only for reducing class-room competition and increasing cooperation, but also for reducing classroom or student prejudices, if any exist, and improving human relations.

While the teacher instructs the rest of the class, one group works in a study area on a special task. Students share materials, help one another, and evaluate each other's ideas and assignments. Each group meets once a week for a half or or whole period. Groups can also meet outside of class, say in the library, before school, or at someone's home after school. The group is required to finish its task in a specified period of time, and, depending on the task, they may report their results to the whole class or turn in the finished product to the teacher. Students are evaluated on an individual and group basis. New groups are formed when new assignments are given by the teacher. Groups are formed according to interests, but are mixed according to ability, gender, and ethnicity, thus promoting concepts of democracy and integration.

---

52 Robert E. Slavin, "Student Teams and Comparison among Equals," *Journal of Educational Psychology* (August 1978), pp. 532–538; Slavin, "Student Teams and Achievement Division," *Journal of Research and Development in Education* (Fall 1978), pp. 38–49; and Slavin, "Synthesis of Research on Cooperative Learning," *Educational Leadership* (February 1991), pp. 71–82.

53 Thomas L. Good, Douglas A. Grouws, and Howard Ebmeier, *Active Math Teaching* (New York: Longman, 1983); Robert E. Slavin, "Team Assisted Individualization: Combining Cooperative Learning and Individualized Instruction in Mathematics," in R. E. Slavin, ed., *Learning to Cooperate, Cooperating to Learn* (New York: Plenum, 1985), pp. 177–209.

54 Elliot Aronson et al., *The Jigsaw Classroom* (Beverly Hills, Calif.: Sage, 1978).

Another cooperative learning approach is *structured academic controversy,* also geared for secondary school students. The academic controversy centers on a controversial issue (ideal for science, social studies, or language arts). Students pair off in two-member teams and learn to (1) advocate a position in debate form, (2) share knowledge with team members and later with opposing teams, (3) analyze and critically evaluate positions, (4) rebut information, and (5) synthesize and integrate information into factual and judgmental conclusions (that can be summarized into a joint position to which all sides can agree).[55]

After each team presents its own position, it must reverse positions and debate just as forcefully based on new information learned. Then both opposing teams must synthesize the best arguments of both points of view, reach a consensus supported by the facts, and write a report which may include (if the teacher wants to add it) a rationale for the synthesis that all members of both groups can agree on. Students, in this cooperative model, learn group management and social skills, debating skills, and how opposing groups come together; they learn to compromise, cooperate, and keep an open mind for changing personal viewpoints when facts indicate they should.

Guidelines for Cooperative Learning

In addition to the general steps for STAD and TAI already mentioned, some specific strategies for cooperative approaches have been developed by David and Roger Johnson in several texts. A number of these strategies are presented below.

1. *Arrange the classroom to promote cooperative goals.* Students will need to work in clusters, and seating arrangements should reflect this need. Provide sufficient space and study areas for students to share; position media equipment in a way that students have easy access as a group.
2. *Present the objectives as group objectives.* The group and not the individual is the focus. Gear the reward structure to achieving group objectives.
3. *Communicate intentions and expectations.* Students need to understand what is being attempted. They should know what to expect from the teacher and from each student in the group and what the teacher expects them to accomplish.

---

55 David W. Johnson and Roger T. Johnson, "Critical Thinking Through Structured Controversy," *Educational Leadership* (May 1988), pp. 58–64.

4. *Encourage a division of labor where appropriate.* Students should understand their roles and responsibilities. This will take time and practice.

5. *Encourage students to share ideas, materials, and resources.* Students should look to each other and not the teacher. The teacher may act as a catalyst in making suggestions, but not be the major source of ideas.

6. *Supply a variety of materials.* Since the sharing of materials is essential to the group, sufficient quantities and variety are needed. If materials are insufficient, the group may bog down and perhaps become disruptive.

7. *Encourage students to communicate their ideas clearly.* Verbal messages should be clear and concise. Verbal and nonverbal messages should be congruent with each other.

8. *Encourage supportive behavior and point out rejecting or hostile behavior.* Behaviors such as silence, ridicule, personal criticism, one-upmanship, and superficial acceptance of an idea should be discussed and stopped since they hinder cooperation and productive group behavior.

9. *Provide appropriate cues and signals.* Point out when the noise level is too high ("Things are getting a little too boisterous"). Direct the group's attention to individual problems and encourage students to use the group ("Check with the group"; "Would you please add this problem to the group's agenda?").

10. *Monitor the group.* Check progress of individuals in a group and of the group as a whole. Explain and discuss problems, assist, and give praise as appropriate.

11. *Evaluate the individual and group.* In evaluation focus on the group and its progress. Evaluate the individual in the context of the group's effort and achievement. Provide prompt feedback.

12. *Reward the group for successful completion of its task.* After evaluation, recognition and rewards should be given on a group basis so that individuals come to realize that they benefit from each other's work and will help each other succeed.[56]

In a supplementary review of cooperative learning, the Johnsons point out that each lesson in cooperative learning should include five basic elements: (1) *positive interdependence*—students must feel they are responsible for their own learning and the learning of the other members of the group; (2) *face-to-face interaction*—students must have the opportunity to explain what they are learning to each other; (3) *individual accountability*—each student must be held accountable for mastery of the assigned work; (4) *social skills*—each student must communicate effectively, maintain respect among group members, and

---

[56] Johnson and Johnson, *Learning Together and Alone.*

work together to resolve conflicts; and (5) *group processing*—groups must be assessed to see how well they are working together and how they can improve.[57]

Group Activities

In various kinds of group activities the teacher's role moves from engineer or director to facilitator or resource person, and many leadership functions transfer from the teacher to the students. Although there is no clear research showing that the group techniques below correlate with student achievement, it is assumed that under appropriate circumstances, operating in these groups can be as effective as or more effective than relying on the teacher as the major source of learning. It is also assumed that many kinds of group activities (1) help teachers deal with differences among learners, (2) provide opportunity for students to plan and develop special projects on which groups can work together, and (3) increase student interaction and socialization. In short, they achieve social and emotional as well as cognitive purposes.

There are many ways for teachers to arrange activity in groups. Different group arrangements, also called group projects, result in different roles and responsibilities for the students and teacher. Listed below are 15 possible group projects.

1. *A committee* is a small group working together in a common venture for a given period of time. Committees succeed to the extent that members grow socially in the group process and are able to accomplish cognitive tasks without close teacher direction. Committee representatives may be chosen to report to the entire class.

2. *Brainstorming* is a technique to elicit large numbers of imaginative ideas or solutions to open-ended problems. Group members are encouraged to expand their thinking beyond the routine sorts of suggestions. Everyone's suggestions are accepted without judgment, and only after all the ideas are put before the group do the members begin to focus on a possible solution.

3. *A buzz session* provides an open environment in which group members can discuss their opinions without fear of being "wrong" or being ridiculed for holding an unpopular position. Buzz sessions can also serve to clarify a position or bring new information before the group to correct misconceptions.

4. *The debate and panel* are more structured in format than some of the other small-group activities. In a debate, two positions on a controversial issue are presented formally; each debater is given a certain amount of time to state a position, to respond to questions from others

---

57 Johnson and Johnson, "Toward a Cooperative Effort," pp. 80–81.

in the group, and to pose questions. The panel is used to present information on an issue and, if possible, to arrive at group consensus. Several students (three to eight) may sit on a panel. Each panel member may make an opening statement, but there are no debates among panel members.

5. *A symposium* is not as structured as a debate and not as relaxed as the give-and-take exchange of a panel. The symposium is appropriate for airing topics that divide into clear-cut categories or viewpoints. Participants are expected to represent a particular position and try to convince others, but the method of interaction is more spontaneous and no one is timed as in a debate.

6. *Role playing and improvisation* are techniques for stepping outside of one's own role and feelings and placing oneself in another's situation. Role playing also serves for exploring intergroup attitudes and values.

7. *Fish bowl* is a technique in which members give their full attention to what one individual wants to express. The whole group sits in a circle. Two chairs are placed in the center of the circle. A member who wants to express a point of view does so while sitting in one of the chairs. Any other member who wants to discuss his or her view takes the other chair, and the two converse while the others listen. To get into the discussion, students must wait for one chair to be vacated.

8. *A critiquing session* is the examination of members' work by the group. The group offers constructive comments and suggestions about ways to improve the work.

9. *Round table* is a quiet, informal group, usually four or five students, who sit around a table conversing either among themselves (similar to a buzz session) or with an audience (similar to a forum).

10. *A forum* is a panel approach in which members interact with an audience.

11. *Jury trial* is a technique in which the class simulates a court room. It is excellent for evaluating issues.

12. *Majority-rule decision making* is a technique for arriving at an agreement or selecting an individual for a task when members of the group hold different opinions. It involves discussion, working out compromises, and making decisions based on the wishes of the majority.

13. *Consensus decision making* requires group members to agree. Consensus requires the views of all members of the group be considered, since the group must arrive at a conclusion or agree on a plan of action.

14. *A composite report* synthesizes and summarizes the views or information of all members of a group. Rather than a series of reports by individual members, one report is presented in written or oral form to the class or teacher.

15. *An agenda* is a formal method for organizing a group task. Students or the teacher can plan the agenda, and members of the group must keep to it.

Using group techniques in flexible and imaginative ways can have important instructional advantages. They give students some control over their own personal adjustment as well as over their cognitive learning. They allow the teacher to plan different lessons to meet the needs and interests of different groups. They permit the teacher to vary instructional methods, to plan interesting and active (as opposed to passive) activities, and to supplement the lecture, questioning, practice and drill methods.

The key to the success of group projects is the way the teacher organizes them. Flexible space and furniture undoubtedly make them easier, but furniture is not the critical factor. All of the group techniques, if planned and implemented properly, tend to promote five group-oriented characteristics in the classroom: (1) task structures that lend themselves to cooperation among group members, 2) a chance for students to work at their own pace but think in terms of group goals, (3) the development of social and interpersonal skills among participants—students learn to communicate with and trust one another, (4) a reward structure based on the performance of the group (which encourages helping behaviors), and (5) a variety of team-building strategies—students learn to work together, appreciate individual diversities, and capitalize on individual strengths (see Tips for Teachers 10.2).

Based on a five-year longitudinal study, Daniel Solomon and his colleagues list five major behaviors that should evolve with an effective group project.

1. *Cooperative activities* in which students work on learning tasks or play together.
2. *Regular participation in helping and sharing activities.*
3. Experiencing the *positive expectations* of others (that is, the group expects members to be considerate, cooperate, take responsibility, help, and share).
4. Role playing and other activities designed to enhance children's *understanding of other people's needs, intentions, and perspectives.*
5. *Positive discipline,* which includes the development and clear communication of rules and norms that emphasize the individual's rights and responsibilities with respect to others.[58]

David Johnson points out that when students work on group projects, they must learn to disclose their attitudes and behaviors in an honest way

---

58 Daniel Solomon et al., "A Program to Promote Interpersonal Consideration and Cooperation in Children," in Slavin, ed., *Learning to Cooperate, Cooperating to Learn,* pp. 7–8; Solomon et al., "Promoting Prosocial Behaviors in Schools: An Intervention Report of a Five-year Longitudinal Intervention Program," paper presented at the annual meeting of the American Educational Research Association, San Francisco, April 1986.

Tips for Teachers 10.2

Basic Rules of Group Participation

In order for students to benefit from a group exercise, they must learn to participate in a way that adds to other students' ideas while confirming their feelings of competence. Students can learn to value differing views as opportunities for learning, not to fear or reject them as personal attacks, so long as every group member learns some basic rules of group participation.

1. I am critical of ideas, not people.
2. I focus on making the best decision possible, not on "winning."
3. I encourage everyone to participate and master all of the relevant information.
4. I listen to everyone's ideas, even if I do not agree.
5. I restate what someone has said if it is not clear.
6. I first bring out all the ideas and facts supporting both sides and then try to put them together in a way that makes sense.
7. I try to understand both sides of the issue.
8. I change my mind when the evidence clearly indicates that I should do so.

Source: David W. Johnson and Roger T. Johnson, "Critical Thinking Through Structured Controversy," *Educational Leadership* (May 1988), p. 63.

(1) giving and receiving supporting feedback, (2) focusing on specific problems, not personalities, (3) providing feedback that the receiver can understand, and (4) providing feedback on actions that the receiver can change.[59] In this way, mutual trust and communication are improved. Basically, the giving and receiving of feedback in this way requires courage, understanding, and respect for others and oneself. The teacher should stress that honesty and support are important and can be used to improve or hinder people's attitudes and actions, and therefore they should not be taken lightly.

---

59 Johnson, *Reaching Out*.

Guidelines for Group Activities

Students can be assigned to group projects by interest, ability, friendship, or personality. The teacher must know the students and the objectives for using small groups before establishing the groups. If the objective is to get the job done expeditiously, the teacher should assign a strong leader to each group, rely on high-achieving students to lead the activities, avoid known personality conflicts, and limit the group size to five. If the objective is more interpersonal than cognitive, the students may be grouped according to their diversities rather than similarities and the group might be larger.

In order to organize such group activities, the following recommendations should be considered. They are basically sequential, although each recommendation should be used only if it coincides with your circumstances and teaching style.

1. Select the group project to enhance objectives and outcomes.
2. Consider social and cognitive purposes (intermixing students by ability, matching students and topics, blending personalities, promoting social or racial integration) and potential managerial problems when assigning members to groups.
3. Solicit volunteers for membership in group projects, reserving the right to decide final membership.
4. Go over directions for carrying out each phase of the group activity in writing or orally to the point of redundancy.
5. Explain the role of participants, the way they are to interact, and whatever problems might occur. Define roles, interactions, and problems through examples and preliminary simulations.
6. Be sure that individuals can function socially, emotionally, and intellectually in their roles as members of a particular group.
7. Allot class time for groups to organize, plan, and develop some of their projects or assignments, with supervision as needed.
8. Be sure a group is able to function effectively and do a good job before asking it to perform for the class.
9. Allow group members to decide on the nature of the class presentation, within general rules that have been established.
10. Do not allow any individual to dominate the activities or responsibilities of the group. All members of the group should participate, within the limits of their abilities, and assume responsibility for the success of the project.
11. Evaluate the completed group project with the students. Discuss problems and decisions participants had to face and the strategies chosen by each participant. Note recommendations and revisions that should be implemented with the next group project.

12. Do not direct a class into a group project unless you are willing to work harder than you would in large-group instruction. The process of organizing and supervising group projects from behind the scenes of the classroom is almost always more taxing than the process of direct teaching in the foreground of the classroom.[60]

INDIVIDUALIZED INSTRUCTION

In the past three decades several systematic programs for **individualized instruction** have been advanced. Although the approaches vary somewhat, all the programs seem to attempt to maximize individual learning by (1) diagnosing the student's entry achievement levels or learning deficiencies; (2) providing a one-to-one teacher-to-student or machine-to-student relationship; (3) introducing sequenced and structured instructional materials, frequently accompanied by practice and drill; and (4) permitting students to proceed at their own rate. Most of the approaches combine behavioral and cognitive psychology, although the behaviorist component seems more in evidence because of the stress on instructional objectives and drill exercises, small instructional units and sequenced materials, evaluation of instruction in terms of changes in learning or progress, and reinstruction based on posttest evaluations.

Early Individualized Programs

One of the early programs for individualized instruction was the Project on Individually Prescribed Instruction (IPI), developed at the University of Pittsburgh in the late 1950s and early 1960s. For every student an individual plan was prepared for each skill or subject based on a diagnosis of the student's proficiency levels. Learning tasks were individualized, and the student's progress was continually evaluated.[61]

The Program for Learning in Accordance with Needs (PLAN), developed in the 1960s and 1970s, relies on instructional objectives and two-week modules arranged according to the student's level of achievement. Instructional materials are ungraded, and alternative sets of materials are available for each unit of instruction.[62]

---

60 Gail M. Inlow, *Maturity in High School Teaching*, 2nd ed. (Englewood Cliffs, N.J.: Prentice-Hall, 1970); George W. Maxim, *Social Studies and the Elementary School Child*, 2nd ed. (Columbus, Ohio: Merrill, 1983); and Ornstein, Talmage, and Juhasz, *The Paraprofessional's Handbook*.

61 Robert Glaser and Lauren B. Resnik, "Instructional Psychology," *Annual Review of Psychology* (no. 23, 1973), pp. 207–276. Also see Robert Glaser, ed., *Advances in Instructional Psychology* (Hillsdale, N.J.: Erlbaum, 1978).

62 John C. Flanagan, "Program for Learning in Accordance with Needs," paper presented at the annual meeting of the American Educational Research Association, Chicago, February 1968.

Research indicates that probably the most effective method for increasing student achievement is individualized instruction.

Individually Guided Education (IGE) is a total educational system developed at the University of Wisconsin and introduced in several thousand schools. Planned variations are made in what and how each student learns. The program includes individual objectives, one-to-one relationships with teachers or tutors, diagnostic testing, independent study, small-group instruction, and large-group instruction.[63]

A more behaviorist and teacher-directed approach is the Personalized System of Instruction (PSI), sometimes called the Keller plan after its originator. It was developed initially for high school and college students. PSI makes use of study guides (which break the course down into small units with specific objectives); individuals progress through the units as fast or slow as they wish, master units (80 percent or better) before proceeding to the next unit, and act as proctors (high-achieving students assisting others).[64]

Field testing of these individualized instruction programs has generally been positive. Some reports on IPI, PLAN, IGE, and PSI have shown significant gains in student achievement, especially with low-achieving students, since

---

63 Herbert J. Klausmeier and Richard E. Ripple, *Learning and Human Abilities*, 3rd ed. (New York: Harper & Row, 1971).

64 Fred S. Keller, "Good-bye Teacher," *Journal of Applied Behavioral Analysis* (April 1968), pp. 79–84.

they seem to prefer a structured approach to learning.[65] Of the four programs, IPI and IGE were the most widely used and seemed to report the most consistent rise in student test scores.[66] Nevertheless, individualized plans are expensive to implement, and most schools today continue to employ group methods of instruction, partly out of habit and because it is easier for teachers.

Independent Study

Although the idea dates back to the 1920s and 1930s, independent study is still practiced today because of its application in a variety of instructional settings (including outside the classroom). **Independent study** involves work conducted by the student on a topic using school or nonschool resources under the direction of the teacher. It was introduced in the 1960s as part of **flexible module scheduling**—dividing the class day or schedule into small time units to enhance flexibility—and **nongraded education**—advancement of students in each skill area or subject at their own rate so they may be at one level of learning in mathematics and another in reading.[67]

Independent study has been used by curriculum and instructional experts particularly in connection with the "self-directed learner," the student who has developed the desire to learn and the study skills needed for pursuing independent study. Although independent study is most applicable at the high school level, because students have mastered certain basic skills, middle school students can be moved from dependence on the teacher toward self-directed learning according to their abilities. In general, independence in performing academic tasks or projects is an extension of having learned how to learn; it requires curiosity, interest, and independent reading and study skills. See Tips for Teachers 10.3.

According to two educators who have provided in-service workshops on independent study for 20 years, teachers need to include the following elements in planning independent instructional activities: (1) *preparation*, getting students ready and explaining the activity; (2) *guidance*, showing students how to apply appropriate study skills; (3) *independence*, encouraging students to learn from their own reading or study; and (4) *instruction*, sharing and applying what they have learned to what others have learned.[68]

---

65 Margaret C. Wang and Herbert J. Walberg, eds., *Adapting Instruction to Individual Differences* (Berkeley, Calif.: McCutchan, 1985). Also see N. L. Gage and David C. Berliner, *Educational Psychology*, 5th ed. (Boston: Houghton Mifflin, 1992).

66 Herbert Klausmeier, *Learning and Teaching Concepts* (New York: Academic Press, 1980); Deborah B. Strother, "Adapting Instruction to Individual Needs," *Phi Delta Kappan* (December 1985), pp. 308–311.

67 B. Frank Brown, *The Non-Graded High School* (Englewood Cliffs, N.J.: Prentice-Hall, 1963); J. Lloyd Trump and Dorsey Baynham, *Focus on Change* (Chicago: Rand McNally, 1961).

68 Harold L. Herber and Joan Nelson-Herber, "Helping Students Become Independent Learners," *Journal of Reading* (April 1987), pp. 584–588.

Tips for Teachers 10.3

Providing for Individual Differences in Whole Grouped Classes

Some schools group students homogeneously, others heterogeneously, and still others rely on a compromise or mixed classroom setting (predominantly homogeneous or heterogeneous). In all cases, there is need to individualize instruction—such as course content, methods, and learning tasks. Below are suggestions that should help the teacher in this instructional agenda, especially with high-achieving and low-achieving students.

For Rapid Learners, High Achievers

1. Provide for student participation in planning content and instructional activities

2. Plan instructional activities that have minimal detail and routine and greater originality and inquiry

3. Emphasize abstract ideas and problem-solving experiences

4. Provide many individualized, self-paced, and independent activities

5. Provide a wide range of materials; use in-depth materials and original sources

6. Encourage students to tutor classmates and to assume leadership roles in group activities

7. Encourage independent study, research, and reports in subject area

For Slow Learners, Low Achievers

1. Provide guidance and clear directions in performing tasks

2. Plan practice and drill activities, along with continuous feedback and monitoring of students' work

3. Emphasize concrete learning experiences and fewer abstractions

4. Provide structured activities. Keep tasks and instructional activities short and clear but not infantile

5. Vary instructional methods and activities during the same class period; use interesting materials and lively approaches

6. Encourage students to assume tutee role and to participate in group activities

7. Emphasize study skills and reading practice in subject area

continues

For Rapid Learners, High Achievers	For Slow Learners, Low Achievers
8. Use lecture, discussion, inquiry, and discovery approaches; apply new learning to high-level analysis and critical thinking	8. Minimize lecture, inquiry, and discovery approaches; apply new learning to practical situations or life experiences
9. Vary homework assignments, avoid routine and drill exercises; ask for analysis of facts and opinions	9. Be clear on homework directions; use routine and drill exercises to reinforce main ideas of lesson; provide extra practice in thinking logically
10. Use homework the next day as springboard for new learning; don't repeat what students already know	10. Review homework the following day; be detailed and sure students understand homework before introducing new learning
11. Give fewer summaries and reviews; provide greater depth and breadth of content	11. Present numerous opportunities for summaries and reviews; teach the same content in different ways
12. Provide in-depth reading assignments. Encourage students to read at home for pleasure; assign supplementary books and magazine articles related to subject	12. Occasionally give students free time in class to read for pleasure; be prepared to rewrite materials or provide supplementary materials for students who may not be able to read the text
13. Teach students how to read faster and better, skim, and read for inferences	13. Teach students how to read; help students read for comprehension of content
14. Rely on verbal and numerical symbolism; stress ideas, not facts	14. Incorporate audiovisual stimuli; allow students to work with things rather than words
15. Present instruction at a faster place; cover several topics, ideas in depth; let students analyze and synthesize data; show cause-effect relations	15. Present learning in small steps; give students adequate time to respond and think; discuss same topics as you would with high achievers but focus on basic information

continues

For Rapid Learners, High Achievers	For Slow Learners, Low Achievers
16. Use academic work to motivate students; adjust content to intrinsic motivating experiences	16. Use motivating methods and materials to help students learn; adjust content to extrinsic motivating experiences
17. Have high standards, but do not push them too far or too hard; encourage students to use their abilities	17. Maintain realistic standards; be patient and understanding; avoid labeling; begin at student's level and then introduce new information
18. Get to know students as individuals; provide interesting and challenging work that gives students the opportunity to use their special abilities; hold students accountable	18. Get to know students as individuals; give individual attention; make it evident you expect students to learn; hold students accountable
19. Let students learn on their own; emphasize individual goals and individual recognition; avoid overly competitive situations.	19. Let students learn from each other; emphasize group goals and group approval; build students' confidence and self-concept
20. Allow students to evaluate their own progress; encourage students to select rigorous subjects	20. Provide opportunities to succeed; give students additional help or recommend remedial assistance before or after class

Although many schools say they make independent study available, it often means different things to different educators. It might mean working in various work areas or resource centers, such as in libraries, in labs, or on computers for portions of the day, or it might mean being assigned to a cafeteria or auditorium when other students are not using the facility and working on homework. Despite this confusion, a review of the research shows that students in traditional classes in English and history do just as well as students engaged in independent study the first year. It is not until the second or third year, as students and teachers become better acquainted with the approach, that students in independent study show significant differences in achievement.[69] As

---

69 Don H. Richardson, "Independent Study: What Difference Does It Make?" *NASSP Bulletin* (September 1967), pp. 53–62.

students gain more experience in independent study programs, they tend to show higher creative scores, more satisfaction with school, better study habits and library skills, more individual resourcefulness, and less group dependence in school compared to students not involved in independent study.[70]

Guidelines for Independent Study

Basic requirements for an independent study program include (1) a clear set of objectives for students to follow, (2) a variety of materials and resources for students to use, (3) outlining of methods or steps for students to follow to carry out tasks and assignments, (4) checks by the teacher at intervals to assess progress and problems, (5) discussion of problems that a student has encountered or is likely to encounter on the basis of other students' experience, (6) schedules to allow for individual research or study, and (7) interest-area arrangements in class and outside of class (library, computer lab). Some educators also advocate a "contract" between the teacher and each student on what is to be learned or demonstrated during independent study.

Trump and Miller make the following recommendations for a successful program.

1. Independent study may be an individual activity or involve a small group of students with similar needs or interests.
2. Independent study can take several different forms and be used in several different skill areas or subjects.
3. At the high school level students should spend as much as 12 hours of the usual 30 hours per school week in independent study. (No corresponding provision is discussed at the middle school level.)
4. The cooperation of teachers, supervisors, counselors, and resource personnel is needed for a full program.
5. The use of five school locations or interest areas is recommended: (a) libraries, (b) resource centers, (c) small-group conferences, (d) relaxation rooms, and (e) restriction zones (usually called study halls).
6. Out-of-school study is recommended, such as work involving industrial sites, social and community agencies, government agencies, museums, and local businesses.[71]

---

70 William M. Alexander and William I. Burke, "Independent Study in Secondary Schools," *Interchange* (no. 3, 1972), pp. 101–113; Herber and Herber, "Helping Students Become Independent Learners;" and Selma Wasserman, "Reflections on Measuring Thinking, While Listening to Mozart's *Jupiter Symphony*," *Phi Delta Kappan* (January 1989), pp. 365–370.

71 J. Lloyd Trump and Delmas F. Miller, *Secondary School Curriculum Improvement*, 3rd ed. (Boston: Allyn & Bacon, 1979).

Adaptive Instruction

Two individualized instructional programs, adaptive instruction and mastery learning, have stood the test of time and are still used in many schools today. Developed and refined during the past three decades, both programs recognize that students differ at any given point not only in learning capacity but also in the degree to which they are able to understand the instruction and move to the next task or topic. Both programs attempt to adapt instruction to the individual, not to the group or to some hypothetical average.

Adaptive instruction, sometimes called adaptive education, grew out of the University of Pittsburgh's IPI. Under this program adaptations occur on two levels: (1) developing the learning skills of the student and (2) altering the instructional environment to correspond to the individual's learning skills.[72]

The first level is achieved by determining in what way and to what extent the students' basic cognitive structure needs to be developed. This includes techniques they use for processing information, their skills for learning how to learn, their interests, attitudes, and behavior in class—all of which affect learning. Adaptations are made on the basis of an initial and then periodic diagnosis of the students' competence and also on the assumptions that academic performance can be influenced by what the school does, particularly by the quality and quantity of instruction, and that in no way are students fixed in one track.

The second level is achieved by flexibility in instruction to meet the needs and abilities of each child in the classroom. Instruction is individualized in several ways—for example, varying the amount of time allowed for different students to learn each skill, topic, or subject; establishing different goals for different students rather than uniform goals; grouping students according to abilities, needs, tasks; adjusting tasks and assignments to coincide with patterns of learning, problems, talents, aptitudes, interests; and providing different curriculum content and choices for students.

The research in general indicates that students who are taught by teachers who adapt instruction to their needs, especially low-achieving or mildly handicapped students, learn more than students in traditional classes or in large-group instruction. High-achieving students are capable of learning more than less able students in the same class without this approach; however, both groups are capable of learning more when instructional methods, materials, and assignments mesh with their abilities.[73]   A quantitative synthesis of 38

---

72 Robert Glaser, *Adaptive Education: Individual Diversity and Learning* (New York: Holt, Rinehart & Winston, 1977); Lauren B. Resnick and Robert Glaser, *The Nature of Intelligence* (Hillsdale, N.J.: Erlbaum, 1976); and Margaret C. Wang, *The Rationale and Design of the Self-Schedule System* (Pittsburgh: University of Pittsburgh, Learning Research and Development Center, 1974).

73 Sandra Cohen and Laurie Debettencourt, "Teaching Children To Be Independent Learners: A Step by Step Strategy," *Focus on Exceptional Children* (no. 3, 1983), pp. 1–12; Margaret C. Wang and Herbert J. Walberg, "Adaptive Instruction and Classroom Time," *American Educational Research Journal* (Winter 1983), pp. 601–626.

studies of 7,200 students over a 10–year period indicates that adaptive instruction in various grade levels and content areas (21 of these studies involved math or reading) has a strong influence (.45 or nearly half a standard deviation) on student achievement. Students in adaptive programs score on average at the 67th percentile, while students not in such programs (the control group) scored at the 50th percentile.[74]

Guidelines for Adaptive Instruction

Patterns of adaptation are numerous, but the overall emphasis should be on matching the student's abilities and needs with various instructional paths. Robert Glaser outlines seven basic characteristics of adaptive instruction.

1. *Time, materials, and resources are flexible.* Time in school is made flexible to accommodate different styles and rates of learning. Materials and resources are varied and used in context with the students' needs and abilities. Module materials, with various entry points and options for students to choose, skip, or go back to certain items, are made available.

2. *The curriculum provides sequence, structure, and multiple options for learning.* The subject matter is sequenced and structured so that skills or concepts build upon one another; prerequisite content is defined and mastered before moving to a more advanced level of learning. The curriculum permits movement in several directions to facilitate instruction that best suits the individual. Students can slow down and review or move more rapidly through a defined sequence of the curriculum, depending on their abilities and needs.

3. *There is open display of and access to instructional materials and media equipment.* Various learning environments are created by organizing and modifying the arrangement of the classroom. There is a place for browsing through books and materials, for reading, for studying or doing quiet work, for reviewing or tutoring, and for engaging in independent work. Seats and desks are changed, depending on the materials and activities that are being stressed.

4. *Tests provide information for teachers to make decisions.* Performance is measured at several points, including before instruction. The function of tests is not so much to compare students (norm reference) as to assess initial abilities and progress (criterion reference). Tests are used primarily for diagnostic reasons, not for grading.

---

74 Hersholt C. Waxman et al., "Synthesis of Research on the Effects of Adaptive Instruction," *Educational Leadership* (September 1985), pp. 26–29.

5. *Teaching students how to learn is emphasized.* Students are taught "management" skills that allow them to assess instructional materials and media for their own purposes and use them wisely, and to search out information that will help them learn. They learn to assess their own performance and behavior, to learn from past experiences, and to plan future activities. They learn to take greater responsibility in their own learning and thus come to understand their own learning and cognitive strategies. Students learn study skills, homework skills, concentration skills, test-taking skills, and problem-solving skills.

6. *The role of the student is expanded.* Students who work at their own pace have a chance to choose their materials and activities. Students help one another to achieve individual and group goals. Students are able to move about, talk quietly with one another, and make decisions about what they will learn by themselves and in conjunction with the classmates and teacher. The learner takes on added responsibilities about his or her own education.

7. *The role of the teacher as instructor is expanded.* Teachers learn to use their particular strengths in different ways to help students learn. Teachers direct, guide, and encourage students on a one-to-one basis. They learn pedagogical, monitoring, and tutoring skills for organizing and running a classroom in which instruction is individualized. They move about the classroom providing appropriate assistance, attention, correction, direction, and praise for specific students. They learn to identify students who need support and feedback to accomplish a task and those who can work on their own with little assistance.[75]

Mastery Instruction

Mastery instruction is a desired educational goal for all grade levels and subjects. The approach being used most widely in the public schools is Learning for Mastery (LFM), often referred to as **mastery learning**. It was associated originally with John Carroll and later with James Block and Benjamin Bloom. Their mastery learning ideas have gained supporters particularly in urban school districts, where there is an obvious need to improve academic performance among inner-city students.

Carroll maintained that if students are normally distributed by ability or aptitude for some academic subject and are provided with appropriate instruction tailored to their individual characteristics, the majority should achieve mastery of the subject and learning should be dramatically improved. He also held that if a student does not spend sufficient time to learn a task, he or she will not master it. However, students vary in the amount of time they need to complete a task. Nearly all students (assuming no major learning disability) can achieve at grade level if given sufficient time.[76]

---

75 Glaser, *Adaptive Education.*

76 John B. Carroll, "A Model of School Learning," *Teacher's College Record* (May 1963), pp. 723–733.

Table 10.1 highlights Carroll's model of learning; it deals with conditions and time for learning, as well as instructional factors. Two assumptions (not by Carroll) are worth noting: (1) Quality of instruction is difficult to measure and thus it is difficult to predict learning. Most researchers of mastery learning, therefore, focus on various aspects of academic time and avoid instructional variables. (2) When quality of instruction is high, many students should become similar in terms of time needed for learning and rate of learning.

Carroll and, later, Robert Slavin distinguish between time needed to learn (based on student characteristics such as aptitude) and time available for learning (under the teacher's control). High-achieving students need less time than low-achieving students to learn the same material. Group instruction, large or small, rarely accommodates varying learner characteristics or considers the time needed to learn. The teacher has the ability to vary instructional time for different individuals or groups of students with mastery instruction, especially for low-achieving students who usually need additional time.[77]

Block and Bloom argue that 90 percent of public school students can learn much of the curriculum at the same level of mastery, with the slower 20 percent of students in this 90 percent needing 10 to 20 percent more time than the faster 20 percent.[78] Although slower students require a longer period of time to learn the same materials, they can succeed if their initial level of knowledge is correctly diagnosed, and if they are taught with appropriate methods and materials in a sequential manner beginning at their initial competency level.

To accomplish this goal, criterion-reference tests must be used to determine whether a student possesses skills required for success in each step in the learning sequence. Also, small units of instruction must be used. An entire course such as eighth-grade mathematics or ninth-grade social studies is too complex to be studied in large units. Instead it should be broken down into smaller pieces following some of the principles of programmed instruction. Students must also be given precise diagnostic information, or feedback, on their learning progress. Together with feedback, they must be given specific guidance or correctives to remedy their learning problems. Finally, students who demonstrate that they have learned the material must be provided with worthwhile enrichment activities to extend their learning while others continue to master the initial tasks.

A substantial body of data indicates that mastery learning can result in large learning gains for students. One observer, for example, has reviewed more than a hundred studies on mastery learning and concludes that the results "indicate

77 John B. Carroll, "The Carroll Model: A 25-Year Retrospective and Prospective View," *Educational Researcher* (January–February 1989), pp. 26–31; Robert E. Slavin, "Mastery Learning Reconsidered," *Review of Educational Research* (Summer 1987), pp. 175–214.

78 James H. Block, *Mastery Learning: Theory and Practice* (New York: Holt, Rinehart & Winston, 1971); Benjamin S. Bloom, *Human Characteristics and School Learning* (New York: McGraw-Hill, 1976); and Bloom, *All Our Children Learning* (New York: McGraw-Hill, 1981).

Table 10.1   MODEL OF SCHOOL LEARNING; FIVE VARIABLES

1. *Aptitude*. The name given to the variable(s) that determines the amount of time a student needs to learn a given task or unit of instruction under *optimal* learning conditions.

2. *Opportunity to learn*. The amount of time allowed for learning by the school schedule; frequently the time is less than that required in view of the student's aptitude.

3. *Perseverance*. The amount of time a student is willing to spend on learning a task or unit of instruction; it is related to and helps define motivation.

4. *Instructional quality*. Time needed for learning is increased when instructional quality is low.

5. *Understanding instruction*. To the extent the student lacks ability to understand instruction, the amount of time needed to learn is increased.

Source: Adapted from John B. Carroll, "The Carroll Model: A 25-Year Retrospective and Prospective View," *Educational Researcher* (January–February 1989), pp. 26–31.

that mastery strategies do indeed have moderate to strong effects on student learning when compared to conventional methods of instruction."[79] Similarly, in a review of more than 25 studies, Block and Burns found that 61 percent of the mastery-taught students scored significantly higher on achievement tests than nonmastery-taught students.[80] In studies of entire school districts the results show that mastery approaches are successful in teaching basic skills, such as reading and mathematics, that form the basis for later learning; moreover, inner-city students profit more from this approach than from traditional groupings for instruction.[81]

A review of 108 experimental-controlled studies by the Kuliks showed that mastery learning has positive effects on student achievement in secondary schools and colleges. The effects were stronger for the lower-achieving students (who seem to prefer and make better use of direct or explicit instructional approaches). In two-thirds of the cases, the learning outcomes in the mastery group were large enough to be significant; on the average, the final exam scores increased by .5 standard

79 Robert B. Burns, "Mastery Learning: Does it Work?" *Educational Leadership* (November 1979), p. 112.

80 James H. Block and Robert B. Burns, "Mastery Learning," in L. S. Shulman, ed., *Review of Research in Education*, vol. 4 (Itasca, Ill.: Peacock, 1976), pp. 118–146. Also see James H. Block, Helen E. Efthim, and Robert B. Burns, *Building Effective Mastery Learning Schools* (White Plains, N.Y.: Longman, 1989).

81 Daniel U. Levine, "Achievement Gains in Self-Contained Chapter I Classes in Kansas City," *Educational Leadership* (March 1987), pp. 22–23; Levine, "Creating Effective Schools," *Phi Delta Kappan* (January 1991), pp. 389–393; and Daniel U. Levine and Allan C. Ornstein, "Research on Classroom and School Effectiveness and its Implications for Improving Big City Schools," *Urban Review* (June 1989), pp. 81–94.

deviation, or from the 50th to the 70th percentile. The largest achievement gains were in classes (i.e., social studies) in which the pace of the materials was controlled by the teacher, not at individual student rates (i.e., mathematics).[82]

Another major review of mastery programs was reported by Guskey and Gates concerning elementary and secondary students. They reported an average improvement on examination scores of .78 standard deviation, or even stronger positive effects.[83] Their review was limited to only one mastery program model, that is, LFM (or the one developed by Carroll, Block, and Bloom).

The favorable findings do not mean that all the important questions have been answered or that mastery strategies do not have critics. Educators do not know, for example, how well differing mastery approaches can work for high-order learning and affective learning or for different types of students (high-achieving, middle-class students, and ethnic groups other than black and Hispanic). Moreover, we are unsure to what extent teachers are teaching the tests to their students in order to avoid blame, since the assumption is that students can master the material.[84] And since most teachers rely on criterion-reference or teacher-made tests to provide evidence of mastery, there is a question of the reliability and validity of the criteria used in determining mastery; different teachers may reach different conclusions about what students know by using a different criterion for testing.[85]

Other critics claims that basic skills—reading, writing, and mathematics—are being broken down into discrete tasks that students master, but the students still do not acquire the actual skill—they cannot read, write, or compute any better. Students may show gains in small skill items, but this does not necessarily prove learning.[86] "It is quite possible," adds Walter Doyle, "for a teacher to achieve high work involvement and study productivity by simplifying task demands to the point that students learn very little."[87] What happened to the notions of wholeness and the importance of concepts and problem-solving skills? More important, Robert Slavin has questioned much of the findings as

---

82 Chen-Lin C. Kulik, James A. Kulik, and Robert L. Bangert-Drowns, "Effectiveness of Mastery Learning Programs: A Meta-Analysis," *Review of Educational Research* (Summer 1990), pp. 265–299.

83 Thomas R. Guskey and Sally L. Gates, "A Synthesis of Research on Group-Based Mastery Learning Programs," paper presented at the annual meeting of the American Educational Research Association, Chicago, April 1985.

84 Allan C. Ornstein, "Emphasis on Student Outcomes Focuses Attention on Quality of Instruction," *NASSP Bulletin* (January 1987), pp. 88–95; Grant Wiggins, "Teaching to the (Authentic) Test," *Educational Leadership* (April 1989), pp. 41–47; and Blaine R. Worthen and Vicki Spandel, "Putting the Standardized Test Debate in Perspective," *Educational Leadership* (February 1991), pp. 65–70.

85 Lorin W. Anderson, "Values, Evidence, and Mastery Learning," *Review of Educational Research* (Summer 1987), pp. 215–223; Thomas R. Guskey, "Rethinking Mastery Learning Reconsidered," *Review of Educational Research* (Summer 1987), pp. 225–229.

86 Linda Darling-Hammond, "Mad-Hatter Tests of Good Teaching," *New York Times* (January 8, 1984), sec. 12, p. 57; Ornstein, "Emphasis on Student Outcomes."

87 Walter Doyle, "Effective Teaching and the Concept of the Master Teacher," *Elementary School Journal* (September 1985), p. 31.

artificial and fuzzy and has argued that (1) there are different mastery-learning programs, (2) not all are of equal value, and (3) the whole-class ones (which provide only a period or two of corrective instruction) are not effective (at least in Baltimore and Philadelphia where he has conducted studies).[88]

Traditionally, teachers have held time constant so that individual differences were reflected in achievement differences. A mastery learning situation, which varies time among students, will narrow achievement differences among students in favor of those who need extra time at the expense of other students.[89] Also, in a situation in which high-achieving students must wait for slow students to catch up, and high achievers must wait for the teacher's attention because the teacher spends an inordinate amount of time with low achievers so they can gain mastery, the high achievers are being discriminated against, they will become bored, and their learning outcomes will probably suffer.

These criticisms do not nullify the importance of mastery learning or other direct instructional approaches. However, questions arise whether any instructional approach that breaks learning into tiny, sequenced items has desirable end results with all students, especially high-achieving, talented, or creative students; whether all students need so much practice to master fundamental skills and tasks; and whether it should be considered acceptable to vary instructional time to the disadvantage of higher achievers.

Guidelines for Implementing Mastery Instruction

Mastery instruction is not easy to implement. The teacher must adapt the instruction to the student, rather than the student adapting to the instruction. The teacher must continually monitor each student's work, provide a variety of instructional materials and activities, determine which skills and tasks each student has mastered, and provide immediate feedback—not an easy task in a class of 25 or more students. As more studies on mastery learning are conducted in various settings, educators will discover whether these problems and issues can be resolved.

Table 10.2 lists suggestions for using mastery instruction by Hyman and Cohen, who have summarized the mastery approaches adopted in more than

---

88 Robert E. Slavin, "Mastery Learning Reconsidered," *Review of Educational Research* (Summer 1987), pp. 175–213; Slavin, "On Mastery Learning and Mastery Teaching," *Educational Leadership* (April 1989), pp. 77–79; and Robert E. Slavin and Nancy A. Madden, "Synthesis of Research on What Works for Students at Risk," *Educational Leadership* (February 1989), pp. 4–13.

89 Marshal Arlin, "Time, Equality, and Mastery Learning," *Review of Educational Research* (Spring 1984), pp. 65–86; Arlin, "Time Variability in Mastery Learning," *American Educational Research Journal* (Spring 1984), pp. 103–120.

3,000 schools, and by Carroll and then Block and Anderson, who promoted and developed mastery learning. In all three approaches it is clear that mastery learning requires careful teacher planning and organization. It requires extensive diagnostic criterion-reference testing. It is necessary to determine different standards for mastery for each class depending on the students' abilities. Teachers have to devise alternative assignments (remedial, corrective, or enrichment) for different students at different stages and at least two forms of tests to measure changes in learning. Teachers must cope with individual rates of learning and vary content coverage and time. You can be sure that it takes a master teacher who is willing to work hard to implement mastery instruction successfully.

Strategic Instruction

Strategic instruction is a method by which the teacher helps students become independent learners, to learn on their own without the assistance of an adult, by explaining and demonstrating useful learning strategies. For example, Weinstein and Mayer suggest four major groupings of strategies.

1. *Strategies for basic learning*, such as enumerating, sequencing, classifying, comparing/contrasting, and generalizing content. The student learns to collect and describe information.
2. *Strategies for complex learning*, such as paraphrasing, skimming, summarizing, note taking, and creating analogies. These techniques include integration of prior information with new information and transferring learning from one situation (long-term memory) to a new situation (short-term memory).
3. *Strategies for comprehension monitoring*, which refer to the students' knowledge of their own cognitive processes (what they are doing) and their ability to control and modify these processes when learning. These strategies require the student to assess learning goals, the degree to which the goals are being met, and, if necessary, to modify the strategies to meet the goals.
4. *Affective strategies*, such as the student's ability to focus attention, maintain concentration, manage performance anxiety, avoid frustration, establish and maintain motivation, and manage time effectively. These affective strategies interact with and influence the first three.[90]

Winograd and Paris suggest five strategies for fostering reading comprehension and independent readers; the strategies can apply as well to any subject.

1. *Recruitment.* The teacher must engage the student's interest.

---

90 Claire F. Weinstein and Richard F. Mayer, "The Teaching of Learning Strategies," in M. C. Wittrock, ed., *Handbook of Research on Teaching*, 3rd ed. (New York: Macmillan, 1986), pp. 315–327.

Table 10.2 SUGGESTIONS FOR MASTERY LEARNING

Hyman and Cohen

1. Define instructional objectives behaviorally so the teacher and learner know exactly where they are and what they must accomplish.

2. Teach the behavior (or skill) sought in the objective directly rather than "building" to or around it.

3. Provide immediate feedback to all learner responses.

4. Set the level of instruction so that students are maximally successful (80–90 percent correct).

5. Divide instruction into small, self-contained and sequenced modules.

6. Control the stimulus (materials, media, activities) so the teacher knows exactly what the learner is responding to.

7. Provide positive feedback to reinforce the learner's "critical response" (the response that corresponds to the instructional stimulus precisely defined by the instructional objective).

Carroll

1. Specify what is to be learned.

2. Motivate pupils to learn it.

3. Provide instructional materials.

4. Present materials at a rate appropriate for different pupils.

5. Monitor students' progress.

6. Diagnose difficulties and provide remediation.

7. Give praise and encouragement for good performance.

8. Maintain a high rate of learning over a period of time.

Block and Anderson

1. Inform students about the features of the model, including what they are expected to learn, how they will be graded, and that extra time will be allowed if needed.

2. Teach the lesson relying on large-group or whole-group instruction.

3. Give a "formative" quiz on a no-fault basis to assess student progress: Students can check their own papers or switch papers.

4. Based on the results, divide the class into a "mastery" group and "nonmastery" group; 90 percent is considered mastery.

5. Give "enrichment" to mastery group—group projects, independent study, etc.

6. Give "corrective" instruction to nonmastery group—small study groups consisting of two or three students, individual tutoring, alternative instructional materials, rereading materials, practice and drill, etc.

7. Give time and support to each group depending on its size; however, the teacher should spend more time with the students of the "nonmastery" group.

8. Give a "summative" or final quiz on the unit or topic; students who achieved mastery on the "formative" quiz do not need to take this quiz; at least 75 percent of the students should have achieved mastery by the summative test.

9. If not, repeat procedures 6 through 8, from "corrective" instruction to "summative" test.

Source: Adapted from Joan S. Hyman and S. Alan Cohen, "Learning for Mastery: Ten Conclusions After 15 Years and 3,000 Schools," *Educational Leadership* (November 1979), pp. 104–109; John B. Carroll, "On Learning from Being Told," *Educational Psychologist* (Winter 1968), pp. 5–10; and James H. Block and Lorin W. Anderson, *Mastery Learning in Classroom Instruction* (New York: Macmillan, 1975).

2. *Reduction in freedom*. The teacher must reduce the scope or size of the task (problem) to the abilities of the learner so the person can cope with requirements of the task (problem).

3. *Emphasizing critical features*. The teacher must accentuate specific features of the task or problem so the student can proceed and use correct procedures on his or her own.

4. *Frustration control*. The teacher must help reduce the learner's stress, through monitoring and tutoring.

5. *Demonstration*. The teacher must demonstrate ideal strategies that the learner can initiate.[91]

The overarching goal of strategic instruction is to have students learn on their own by teaching them to process information about the strategies they use. The cognitive agenda is to make students more thoughtful and selective about learning: to know what strategies to use, how to use them, and when and where to use them. Most schools focus on knowledge, or at best knowledge of a skill, without requiring students to demonstrate how and when to use the skill, why it works, and when it does not work. For example, students often learn to blindly use math formulas or science methods without demonstrating that they can discriminate when the formula or method is appropriate, and how and when to modify its use in certain situations. Strategic instruction provides such opportunities for students—at least in theory it does.

The goal is to introduce this type of instruction early in the student's school career; hence, to reduce the number (in the millions) who are crippled learners by the time they enter middle or junior high school—and to continue this instruction in the upper grades as a reinforcement procedure.

Scaffolding is another form of strategic instruction; it permits the student to solve a task or problem by carrying it out, achieving a learning outcome which would be beyond his unassisted efforts. In class, the teacher focuses on a number of learning strategies (one at a time) and leads students in refining and reformulating their knowledge of the strategies they use. According to Beau Jones, the teacher scaffolds instruction by (1) *supporting* the student's attempt to use the strategy, providing additional examples and modeling as required; (2) *adjusting* the task and related materials to suit the learner's abilities or level; and (3) *removing support* structures gradually as the student shows increased competence.[92]

The teacher must be able to assess the students' cognitive abilities to explain and apply the appropriate strategy (or strategies). Teachers need to ask themselves the following questions: (1) Are my students in control of their own

91 Peter Winograd and Scott G. Paris, "A Cognitive and Motivational Agenda for Reading Instruction," *Educational Leadership* (December–January 1989), pp. 30–36.

92 Beau Fly Jones, *Strategic Teaching and Learning: Cognitive Instruction in the Content Areas* (Elmhurst, Ill.: North Central Regional Educational Laboratory, 1987).

learning as a result of my instruction? (2) Can students use the knowledge and strategies with increasingly difficult tasks (or problems)? (3) Can students transfer the learning to new situations?[93] (4) Are students aware of their own thinking as they undertake the task(s) or problem(s)? (5) Does my instruction promote independent learning, that is, learning on one's own without an adult present?

Guidelines for Teaching Strategic Instruction

Strategic instruction has the dual function of teaching subject *content* and teaching *strategies* for learning that can be applied to new learning contexts, thus making the student independent of the teacher. Some of these strategies help students link prior and new knowledge, whereas other strategies help students consolidate, integrate, and extend information.

Guidelines for strategic instruction should be aligned with the objectives of the lesson, the students' abilities or capabilities, and the level of learning expected. Focus on the guidelines that coincide with your own teaching style (and omit the others). Ask what can be done to help students learn and transfer what they have learned to new learning situations. With this in mind, a series of instructional strategies are recommended; they are divided into three main processes: preparation, presentation, and application of what is to be taught and learned.

I. Preparation for Learning
  1. *Discuss objective/task*
     Discuss/define nature of task
     Discuss audience/learning goals
     Model/elicit criteria for success
  2. *Preview/select materials*
     Model/guide previewing of materials
     Elicit content focus/organizational pattern
  3. *Activate/provide background knowledge*
     Elicit/provide content and vocabulary
     Confront misconceptions, discuss strategies
     Elicit/provide categories and structural pattern
  4. *Focus interest/set purpose*
     Brainstorm, model/guide hypotheses and predictions
     Model/guide formulating questions

---

93 Beau Fly Jones and Lawrence B. Friedman, "Active Instruction for Students at Risk," *Educational Psychologist* (Summer 1988), pp. 299–308; Jones, *Strategic Teaching and Learning*.

II. Presentation of Content
1. *Pause and reflect/discuss (after segments)*
   Model/guide checking predictions
   Model/guide comparing to prior knowledge
   Model/guide asking clarification questions
   Elicit/discuss faulty logic/contradictions/gaps
   Model/guide raising issues/formulating questions
2. *Integrate ideas (after segments)*
   Brainstorm, model/guide reasoning for selection
   Model/guide summarizing text segments
3. *Assimilate new ideas (after segments)*
   Brainstorm, model/guide articulation
   Provide conferences/feedback, correctives
   Discuss reasons for withholding judgment
III. Application and Integration
1. *Integrate/organize meaning for whole*
   Brainstorm key ideas, find categories/patterns
   Discuss organizational patterns/standards, model
   Guide return to standards/evaluation process
2. *Assess achievement of purpose*
   Discuss "old" misconceptions/new learnings
   Guide identification, diagnose/prescribe, coach
   Provide opportunities for questions and follow-up
3. *Extend learning*
   Increase complexity/diversity of content and task
   Discuss/guide mnemonics and in-depth study skills[94]

Computerized Instruction

Patrick Suppes, an innovator in computer use in schools, coined the term **computer-assisted instruction** (CAI). Suppes defined three levels of CAI: practice and drill, tutoring, and dialogue.[95] At the simplest level, students work through drills in spelling, reading, foreign languages, simple computations, and so forth. At the second level, the computer acts as a tutor, taking over the function of presenting new concepts. As soon as the student manifests a clear understanding, he or she moves to the next exercise. The third and highest level, dialogue, involves a sophisticated interaction between the student and the computer. The student can not only give responses but also ask new questions, and the computer will react appropriately. Computers that can conduct a true

---

94 *Thinking Skills Instruction in English/Language Arts* (Washington, D.C.: National Education Association, 1987).

95 Patrick Suppes, "Computer Technology and the Future of Education," *Phi Delta Kappan* (April 1968), pp. 420–423.

dialogue with students are still in the developmental stage, but many educators expect them to reach the mass market in the late 1990s.

Other educators tend to envision the role of the computer in terms of three types of application: tool application, computer-assisted instruction, and computer-managed instruction.

Computer application is the use of the computer by the student to accomplish some task, for example, word processing to write a report or solving mathematical problems. The use of the computer is a personal decision on the part of the student and not requested by the teacher.

Computer-assisted instruction is the use of the computer by the student to facilitate learning. This type of application involves tutoring and practice and drill programs and is appropriate when subject matter needs to be mastered or for practice of critical skills before advancing to higher levels of learning. It coincides with Suppes's first and second levels of computerized instruction.

Computer-managed instruction is the use of the computer by the teacher and school for the systematic control and organization of aspects of instruction including testing, diagnostics data, learning prescriptions, and record keeping. If programmed properly, and if the computer has sufficient memory and storage capacity, the computer can monitor, test, prescribe programs for, and keep the records for more than 100,000 students throughout a school district.[96]

Most instructional use of computers is one of the first two types of application. Increasingly, however, teachers of students with handicaps or learning disabilities are using the third type to monitor, test, prescribe instruction for, and store information on each student they teach. In fact, the procedure is often part of the individualized education program (IEP) developed by the special educators. For slow students and students with disabilities, computer-managed instruction can help the teacher diagnose the students' difficulties, analyze instructional techniques, and replace ineffective techniques with alternative strategies. For average and rapid learners, it offers increased capacities for self-teaching, problem-solving, and independent instruction.

Summaries of the research on computer-assisted instruction suggest that it is effective as a *supplement* to regular instruction. At higher grade levels, particularly college, it can be used effectively as a *replacement* for regular instruction.[97] CAI has been shown to be effective for short-term achievement gain (quizzes and examinations), but not for long-term gains

96 John C. Cook, "Creating a Statewide Computer Education Network," *Education Digest* (October 1985), pp. 36–39; Alan M. Hofmeister, "The Special Educator in the Information Age," *Peabody Journal of Education* (Fall 1984), pp. 5–21; and Allan C. Ornstein, "Curriculum Computer Technology," *NASSP Bulletin* (in press 1992).

97 James A. Kulik, Chen-Lin C. Kulik, and Peter A. Cohen, "Effectiveness of Computer-Based College Teaching," *Review of Educational Research* (Winter 1980), pp. 525–544; David M. Miller, "The Great American History Machine," *Academic Computing* (October 1988), pp. 28, 43–47, 50–55.

(retention).[98] Some studies show that low-achieving students make significant gains in reading and math skills with 10 to 20 minutes daily of CAI that emphasizes practice and drill.[99] However, others show no significant differences in achievement between CAI and non-CAI students, suggesting that CAI is not uniformly effective, and the teacher or instructor may be a crucial variable.

Given the computer craze, an additional word of caution is needed. In computerized instruction students interact with machines and materials that have no emotional and affective components. Critics contend that substituting a machine for a human teacher leaves students with no true guidance and with too little personal interaction. Ralph Tyler concludes that the use of computers in education is based on two faulty assumptions: "that teaching is mostly, if not solely, presenting materials to students [and] that teaching is primarily a technical activity, whereas, in fact, it is a human service."[100] Actually, the computer is only as good as the person (teacher or student) who is using it and the person who wrote the software that accompanies it; the key to successful computer use is still the human factor. See Tips for Teachers 10.4.

Guidelines for Using Computers in Classrooms

Unquestionably, computers are here to stay. Questions arise, however. How computer-competent are teachers? Are the research findings on computerized instruction mixed because teacher competency is mixed? Should every teacher have facility in computer application and for what type of application? Is there an appropriate grade level to introduce computerized instruction? Should computers be taught as a separate subject, as part of mathematics, or as part of several subjects? Should computers be used only in a computer laboratory or should they be installed in classrooms as part of the daily teaching-learning process? It is hard for educators to agree on the answers to these questions. Below are specific procedures on which educators can usually find agreement.

---

98 Judith Edwards et al., "How Effective is CAI? A Review of the Research," *Educational Leadership* (November 1975), pp. 147–153; James A. Kulik, Robert L. Bangert, and George Williams, "Effects of Computer-Based Teaching on Secondary School Students," *Journal of Educational Psychology* (February 1983), pp. 19–26; and Peter Smith and Samuel Dunn, "Human Quality Considerations in High Tech Education," *Educational Technology* (February 1987), pp. 35–39.

99 Richard E. Clark, "Reconsidering Research on Learning from Media," *Review of Educational Research* (Winter 1983), pp. 445–459; Paul A. McDermott and Marley W. Watkins, "Computerized vs. Conventional Remedial Instruction for Learning Disabled Pupils," *Journal of Special Education* (Spring 1983), pp. 81–88; and "CAD Software: Packages Flex New Muscles," *Technological Horizons in Education Journal* (February 1989), pp. 18–20.

100 Ralph W. Tyler, "Utilization of Technological Media, Devices, and Systems in School," *Educational Technology* (January 1980), pp. 13–14.

Tips for Teachers 10.4

Different Group Designs for Different Classroom Conditions

Just as it is important to use different instructional methods and materials, it is important to mix instructional groupings to meet classroom conditions and student characteristics and to provide variety. No one grouping approach is appropriate for every circumstance. A mixture of large-group, small-group, and individualized instruction should be used. Here we provide a few commonsense methods, a wrap-up or review, for large-group, small-group, and individualized instruction.

For Whole-Group Instruction

1. Make the classroom attractive and safe. Consider flexible spacing and furnishings.
2. Consider the physical conditions of the classroom when arranging desks and tables.
3. Allow for the physical and psychological needs of the students. Some students will have to sit close to the chalkboard for vision reasons; some students will have to be separated because they are too friendly or disruptive.
4. Involve all students in the instructional activities. Avoid emphasizing teacher-student interaction on one side or in the middle of the room.
5. Encourage dialogues among students. Avoid monologues by the teacher or extended dialogues between the teacher and one student.
6. Arrange instructional materials and media equipment so that all students can readily see and participate in the activities.
7. Direct and monitor classroom activities.
8. Make smooth transitions from large-group activities to either small-group or individualized instruction. Maintain a brisk pace when making transitions.

For Small-Group Instruction

1. Make sure students know what to do and how to proceed. Be sure they understand the objectives or tasks and when they have achieved them.
2. Make sure students are aware of their responsibilities while working in small groups.

continues

3. Enhance communication and minimize conflicts by discussing appropriate behavior for individuals within groups.

4. When organizing groups, consider the abilities and needs of the students. Mix groups by ethnicity, social class, and sex for purposes of integration; mix groups by ability so they are relatively equal on a cognitive basis.

5. Take into account special learning and behavior problems. Separate students who do not work well together.

6. Encourage small groups to direct their own learning experiences. The teacher is no longer the director of activities and the source of knowledge, but a facilitator and resource person.

7. Permit students to work at their own pace within their respective groups. Permit the entire group to work at its own pace.

8. For high-achieving students and those who can work by themselves, give them latitude and encourage a sense of independence and resourcefulness. For low-achieving students and those who need extra encouragement or assistance, provide the necessary support and feedback. Try to improve their sense of self-esteem and achievement.

9. Monitor the work of each group. Make comments, ask questions, and assist the group as necessary.

10. Conduct periodic probes. Stop the lesson and bring everyone to attention to discuss common problems or errors experienced by two or more groups.

11. Provide knowledge of group results to the class. Emphasize the positive. Provide immediate feedback and group rewards for achievement.

12. Provide smooth transitions from small-group activities to either large-group or individualized instruction. Maintain the momentum of the lesson when making transitions.

For Individualized Instruction

1. Make sure students know what to do and how to proceed. Objectives, tasks, and achievement levels should be stated.

2. Make sure students understand their responsibilities when working on individual assignments or independent study.

3. Select diverse materials and media based on individual needs and abilities. Explain the various materials and media available and where they may be found. Permit students latitude in selecting instructional tools.

4. Arrange instructional materials in small, sequenced units to enhance correct responses from students, especially low-achieving students.

continues

5. Permit students to work at their own pace.
6. Monitor and check for understanding. Permit independent work after students indicate understanding of the main skills or concepts of the lesson.
7. Provide enrichment activities for high-achieving students; give them more latitude in selecting materials and activities. Provide corrective activities for low-achieving students; give them more assistance and encouragement.
8. Evaluate student work and provide immediate feedback, if possible.
9. Assess for the purpose of guiding, modifying instruction, and measuring progress; do not compare or rank students.
10. Provide smooth transitions from individualized instruction to either large-group or small-group instruction. Maintain the pace of the lesson when making transitions. Avoid abrupt transitions.

I. *Integrate computer use with underlying instruction.*
   1. Match computer application with objectives of the course.
   2. Match computer application with specific lesson plans.
   3. Include a computer-based testing system that measures students, abilities, including test-retest (pre- and posttests).
   4. Use a program that can manage large amounts of student data, including daily attendance, student grades on homework and quizzes, and standardized test data.
II. Keep apprised of the software available to meet your students' needs.
   1. If possible, obtain a preview copy from the company.
   2. Examine advertisements in computer magazines; read software reviews published in computer magazines.
   3. Solicit recommendations from teachers who are using computers.
   4. Be sure the word processing software can run on the school's computer.
   5. Look for software that has several different ways of teaching the same concept while offering different levels of difficulty. (This gives the student the opportunity to learn at his or her own pace.)

6. Ensure that the software can identify individual learning problems and automatically provide a tutorial set of exercises.
7. The software should be able to distinguish between a user's typing mistakes and basic errors in understanding the material.
8. The software should have a branching function, so that if the student is having difficulty with a specific task or problem, the program can offer remedial exercises or alternative ways for learning the material.

III. What schools can do to enhance computer use among students.
1. Schools should make sure students have adequate access to computers. Students who have computers at home are more likely to be interested in school computers and have extra time at home to practice their computer skills. Students who do not have computers at home are at a disadvantage in school and need extra computer time in school.
2. Schools need to provide students with opportunities for extracurricular computer experiences before and after school.
3. Schools should establish computer clubs and closely monitor them to ensure they do not become monopolized by students who are computer-proficient.
4. Schools should restructure courses in computers (or in specific subjects) so all students become computer-literate.
5. Since many classrooms do not have computers, or have only one or two, the schools should provide computer labs or classrooms that can house 15 to 30 students at one time.

SUMMARY

1. Classroom seating arrangements include traditional, rectangular, circular, horseshoe, and various special formations designed to meet special activities.
2. Instruction may take place in large-group, small-group, and individual settings. The teacher is responsible for varying these three groupings according to the needs of the students and the objectives of the lesson.
3. Large-group or whole-group instruction is the most common form of classroom organization, suitable for the teacher when lecturing and explaining, questioning, and providing practice and drill.
4. Whole-group instruction tends to be geared to the average learner, and the students are expected to perform within a narrow range.
5. Small groups give the teacher flexibility in instruction and an opportunity to introduce skills and tasks at the level suited to a particular group of students.

6. There are several methods for organizing students in small groups, including grouping by ability, peer tutoring, cooperative learning, and group activities. Small-group activities are best achieved when group size is limited to from five to eight students per group.

7. Individualized instruction permits the student to work alone at his or her own pace and level over short or long periods of time. Individualized instruction permits the teacher to adapt instruction to the abilities, needs, and interests of the learner.

8. Programs for individualized study developed in the past include Individually Prescribed Instruction, Program for Learning in Accordance with Needs, Individually Guided Education, and Personalized System of Instruction. Current types of individualized instruction include independent study, adaptive instruction, mastery instruction, and computer-assisted instruction.

CASE STUDY

Problem

A beginning teacher was assigned an eighth-grade class in a middle school, having gotten a bachelor's degree after four years of military service. The class lacked cohesion and a sense of identity and had a poor reputation in the school. A large number of the students were unsuccessful or marginally successful, with very low self-esteem. The teacher tried two ways of building self-esteem and class identity. Both used tutoring as the vehicle, and grouping the students was a major part of one approach.

Suggestion

Before implementing the tutoring or change in grouping, the teacher systematically let her students know she considered them the "leaders" of the school by virtue of their being eighth graders, and informed them that she would be demanding of them, but fair. She told them that when they left her room, they were the "elite." She reinforced this by encouraging her students to join the safety patrol or be recess assistants. She encouraged her colleagues to use her students for errands, with the request that they, too, mention the leadership role.

She met with the sixth-grade teachers and they planned a program of cross-age tutoring. Carefully chosen students began the tutoring although the full class received special training in the "needs of young children" and for their roles as "personnel and teaching mentors." Those not initially selected as tutors were assigned room tasks or put on standby or used as runners for other rooms while awaiting rotation to tutoring assignments.

The tutors, at the end of their tour, were invited to the principal's office, complimented on their work, and given certificates. The tutoring process eventually became the hallmark of the room, with an article planted by the teacher in the neighborhood newspaper. There was no indication that the tutoring assisted the sixth graders, except to excite their interest in becoming big sixth graders, but the effect on the eighth-grade classroom was astounding. Students developed a responsible attitude toward their own academic work and pride in being in the class.

Discussion Suggestion

This same teacher changed the grouping in the room. Rather than having the desks face each other in groups of four, they were placed in straight rows. She felt that the intensity and the time spent in face-to-face small-group interaction by the groups of four had developed subgroupings whose identification was more with the group than with the room as a whole.

She had the first student in each row became a row leader, the last student an assistant row leader. The row leader's task was to take attendance, provide books to new students, inform them of the room procedures, and put assignments collected by the assistant into an "In" box. The assistants were to act as room leaders when needed. The room leaders were changed throughout the semester, with only those who were up to date with homework and other assignments eligible for leadership.

In-class tutoring of both an academic and a nonacademic nature accompanied the new grouping. Academic tutoring was distributed among students proficient in different subject areas, the pattern of tutoring based on the instruction used for the cross-age tutoring.

But everyone tutored in some topic. A student proficient in sports assisted others in the physical education classes. A student accordion player gave a class recital and lesson in accordion playing. A student good in art gave students lessons, etc. These proficiencies were identified by the teacher when she developed a Class Roster of Talents, a segment of a bulletin board which featured monthly student Polaroid pictures and *any* accomplishment or skills they had. The bulletin board was placed next to the principal's office.

The change to straight rows worked to unify the room by breaking up the subgrouping identifications. It also facilitated the tutoring since the room tutor was not seen as one subgroup member intruding on another subgroup, but one classmate assisting other classmates. The row leader idea helped to develop responsibility among all the students.

The class developed an *espirt de corps* and became a positive force in the school; an academic climate emerged in the classroom.

Discussion Questions

1. Should a beginning teacher, just out of college, attempt the same kinds of tutoring and room arrangements cited here? What would be realistic and what would not?

2. What tutoring generalities cited here could be used in the classroom or school you expect to teach? How might these similarities be implemented?
3. Did the rather manipulative use of tutoring bother you? What of the structured arrangement of the desks and the quasimilitary use of students? To discuss, use findings from this chapter and others, as well as your own personal opinions.
4. Using the discussion on tutoring and room arrangements in your text, develop a scenario of how the teacher might have prepared the students for tutoring and apply these methods to a situation of your own description.
5. Compare and contrast the suggestions in the case study in Chapter 3, Classroom Management and Discipline, to those in this chapter. Could they be used simultaneously? Would you be able to use some or all of them or are these suggestions tied to a specific kind of personality?

QUESTIONS TO CONSIDER

1. What type of seating arrangements do you prefer during large-group instruction? What does this say about your teaching approach?
2. Which small-group instructional methods do you prefer? Why?
3. Which individualized instructional methods do you prefer? Why?
4. What are three advantages and three disadvantages of mastery learning?
5. In what ways can teachers of various grade levels or subjects work together to develop strategic instruction?

THINGS TO DO

1. Discuss the advantages and disadvantages of three seating arrangements for the subject level and grade level you wish to teach.
2. Defend or criticize the nature of competitive and cooperative classrooms. Be sure to describe the advantages of each, whatever your overall preference. How would you change the reward structures in school?
3. Observe a tutoring program for students in a local school. Report back to the class on the merits of the program.
4. Observe a teacher applying adaptive instruction and another one using scaffolding instruction. Enumerate the similar and dissimilar instructional strategies.
5. Discuss your views about computerized instruction. Describe how you expect to use computers for instructional purposes.

RECOMMENDED READINGS

Block, James H., Helen E. Efthim, and Robert B. Burns. *Building Effective Mastery Learning Schools*. White Plains, N.Y.: Longman, 1989. The major features of mastery instruction and how it can be adopted in various school settings.

Bloom, Benjamin S. *Human Characteristics and School Learning*. New York: McGraw-Hill, 1976. Emphasis on individual instruction and school learning, with methods of changing the level and rate of learning through mastery approaches.

Fenstermacher, Gary D. and John I. Goodlad. *Individual Differences and the Common Curriculum*, Eighty-second Yearbook of the National Society for the Study of Education, Part I. Chicago: University of Chicago Press, 1983. Several chapters written by well-known authorities on individualized instruction and learning; easy to read and yet grounded in research.

Glaser, Robert. *Adaptive Education: Individual Diversity and Learning*. New York: Holt, Rinehart & Winston, 1988. Compact description of various conditions and characteristics of instruction that can be adapted to the individual student.

Johnson, David W. and Roger T. Johnson, et al., *Circles of Learning: Learning Together and Alone*. Englewood Cliffs, N.J.: Prentice-Hall, 1991. How to improve the teaching-learning process through small group and individual methods.

Jones, Beau Fly. *Strategic Teaching and Learning: Cognitive Instruction in the Content Areas*. Elmhurst, Ill.: North Central Regional Educational Laboratory, 1987. Application of strategic instruction in the major content areas—science, social studies, math, and English.

Louden, William. *Understanding Teachers*. New York: Teachers College Press, Columbia University, 1991. An analysis of how teachers think and teach, with emphasis on instructional methods and groups.

KEY TERMS

Self-contained classroom

Departmentalization

Formal seating pattern

Informal seating pattern

Open classroom

Whole-group instruction

Small-group instruction

Ability grouping

Between-class ability grouping

Within-class ability grouping

Peer tutoring

Cooperative learning

Jigsaw classroom

Individualized instruction

Independent study

Flexible module scheduling

Nongraded education

Adaptive instruction

Mastery learning

Strategic instruction

Computer-assisted instruction

Chapter
11

Instructional Planning

FOCUSING QUESTIONS

1. How do teachers plan for instruction? At what levels do they plan?

2. How do teachers map a course of study?

3. What are the main components of a unit plan?

4. What are the main components of a lesson plan?

5. What components would be stressed in a mastery lesson plan? Creativity lesson plan?

6. How do unit and lesson plans facilitate teaching and instruction?

*E*ffective planning is based on knowledge of (1) the general goals of the school, (2) the objectives of the course and subject, (3) students' abilities, aptitudes, needs, and interests, (4) content to be included and appropriate units into which the subject can be divided, and (5) techniques of short-range instruction or lesson planning.

Although planning is the shared responsibility of administrators, supervisors, and teachers, the individual teacher must organize content, methods, and materials and originate his or her own plans for daily instruction in the classroom.

HOW TEACHERS PLAN

Teacher planning is a form of decision making. Planning a course, unit, or lesson involves decisions in two areas: (1) *subject matter knowledge*, concerning organization and presentation of content, knowledge of student understanding of content, and knowledge of how to teach the content, and (2) *action system knowledge*, concerning teaching activities such as diagnosing, grouping, managing, and evaluating students and implementing instructional activities and learning experiences.[1]

Both kinds of knowledge are needed for effective planning. Most teachers have knowledge of subject matter, but lack expertise in various aspects of action system knowledge. Shavelson and Stern found that while various planning models are included in teacher training (mostly based on subject matter knowledge), the models are not always used by teachers once they begin planning in schools. "Obviously, there is a mismatch between the demands of classroom instruction and the prescriptive planning model."[2] According to Good and Brophy, this mismatch occurs because teachers are easily "overwhelmed by the rapid pace" of the classroom "and become simply *reactive* to classroom events."[3]

According to John Zahorik, who sampled some 200 teachers, most teachers do not engage in rational planning or make use of objectives. They tend to emphasize content, materials, resources, and learning activities.[4]

In a study of experienced teachers, Penelope Peterson also found that teachers emphasize subject matter content and instructional activities when planning a daily lesson. Of five planning categories, they spend the least time on planning objectives.[5]

---

1 Pamela L. Grossman and Anna E. Richert, "Unacknowledged Knowledge Growth," *Teaching and Teacher Education* (no. 4, 1988), pp. 53–62; Gaea Leinhardt and David Smith, "Expertise in Mathematics Instruction: Subject Matter Knowledge," paper presented at the annual meeting of the American Educational Research Association, New Orleans, April 1984.

2 Richard Shavelson and Paula Stern, "Research on Teachers' Pedagogical Thoughts, Judgments, Decisions, and Behavior," *Review of Educational Research* (Winter 1984), p. 477.

3 Thomas L. Good and Jere E. Brophy, *Educational Psychology: A Realistic Approach*, 4th ed. (White Plains, N.Y.: Longman, 1988), p. 25.

4 John A. Zahorik, "Teachers' Planning Models," *Educational Leadership* (November 1975), pp. 134–139.

5 Penelope L. Peterson, Christopher W. Marx, and Ronald M. Clark, "Teacher Planning, Teacher Behavior, and Student Achievement," *American Educational Research Journal* (Summer 1978), pp. 417–432.

According to Gail McCutcheon, when plans are required by supervisors, teachers tend to turn in "a shorthand description" of what they plan to do in class. They "[list] objectives for a lesson in their plan books only if requested to do so by the principal." In the teachers' view, objectives are implicit in the content and activities of the lesson and need not be shown. For many teachers, "planning serves as a memory jogger, a list of things to be sure to accomplish."[6] Because of this view, most teachers do not value the use of objectives or of detailed or elaborate plans. Although researchers tend to see logic in planned lessons, Elliot Eisner points out that most of what happens in the classroom cannot be observed, measured, or preplanned, and much of teaching is based on impulse and imagination.[7]

The views expressed by McCutcheon and Eisner are contrary to Lee Shulman's observations. The decisions teachers make during planning strongly influence their classroom instruction; plans serve as scripts to which teachers adhere in classrooms.[8] In addition, collaborative planning has an important influence on the behavior of beginning teachers whereby they tend to consider content and activities, as well as pedagogy, in groups by themselves or with mentors. What teachers plan together is associated with classroom instruction and student performance on tests.[9]

Of all the subtasks or exploratory considerations analyzed in collaborative planning, what occupies the most time or discussion are lesson plan activities (i.e., pacing and timing of instructional materials, various instructional methods) and teacher-centered approaches (what the teacher will be doing during the lesson).[10] Surprisingly, however, beginning teachers frequently ignore a central element of planning—the students—as well as how their lesson plans coincide with long-range curriculum goals.

Planning by Level of Instruction

Teachers engage in five levels of planning: yearly, term, unit, weekly, and daily. Planning at each level involves a set of goals, sources of information, forms or outlines, and criteria for judging the effectiveness of planning (Table 11.1).

---

6 Gail McCutcheon, "How Do Elementary School Teachers Plan?" *Elementary School Journal* (September 1980), pp. 4–23.

7 Elliot W. Eisner, *The Educational Imagination*, 2nd ed. (New York: Macmillan, 1985).

8 Lee S. Shulman, "Knowledge and Teaching: Foundations of the New Reform," *Harvard Educational Review* (February 1987), pp. 1–22.

9 Rosary V. Lalik and Jerome A. Niles, "Collaborative Planning by Two Groups of Student Teachers," *Elementary School Journal* (January 1990), pp. 319–336; Terry M. Wildman et al., *Teachers Learning From Teachers* (Blacksburg, Va.: Virginia Polytechnic Institute, College of Education, 1987).

10 Lalik and Niles, "Collaborative Planning by Two Groups of Student Teachers"; Patricia H. Phelps, "Expanding Beginning Teachers' Perspectives on Planning," *Clearing House* (February 1990), pp. 251–252.

One researcher points out that, in their year and term planning, middle grade teachers rely most heavily on (1) previous successes and failures, (2) district curriculum guides, (3) textbook content, (4) student interest, (5) classroom management factors, (6) school calendar, and (7) district proposals and workshops. At the unit, weekly, and daily levels, they are mostly influenced by (1) availability of materials, (2) student interest, (3) schedule interruptions, (4) school calendar, (5) district curriculum guides, (6) textbook content, (7) classroom management, (8) classroom activity flow, and (9) prior experience.[11] Such factors as other teachers' suggestions, professional journals, in-service training, or undergraduate training were ranked lowest. This suggests professional training and associates have little influence on teacher planning—which does not speak highly for the profession.

According to Robert Yinger, planning is perceived as rational, logical, and structured, and as being reinforced by a number of instructional and managerial routines. By the middle of the school year about 85 percent of the instructional activities are routine.[12]   In planning teachers use instructional routines for questioning, monitoring, and managing students, as well as for coordinating classroom activities.

But the teacher needs to consider variety and flexibility in planning, as well as structure and routine, to take into account the students' differing developmental needs and interests. Some students, especially high achievers, divergent thinkers, and independent learners, learn more in nonstructured and independent situations, whereas many low achievers, convergent thinkers, and dependent learners prefer highly structured and directed environments.[13]

Mental versus Formal Planning

McCutcheon maintains that the most valuable form of teacher planning at the classroom level is "the reflective thinking that many teachers engage in before writing a unit or lesson plan, or while teaching a lesson."[14] Often the exact weekly or daily lesson plan is sketchily outlined. Much of what happens is a reflection of what happened in other years when a similar lesson was taught. It develops as the teaching-learning process unfolds and as teachers and students interact in the classroom. Many actions related to planning cannot be

---

11 Deborah S. Brown, "Twelve Middle School Teachers' Planning," *Elementary School Journal* (September 1988), pp. 69–87.

12 Robert J. Yinger, "A Study of Teacher Planning," *Elementary School Journal* (January 1980), pp. 107–127.

13 Stephen F. Foster, "Ten Principles of Learning Revised in Accordance with Cognitive Psychology," *Educational Psychologist* (Summer 1986), pp. 235–243; N. L. Gage and Margaret C. Needels, "Process-Product Research on Teaching: A Review of the Criticisms," *Elementary School Journal* (January 1989), pp. 253–300; and Richard E. Snow, "Individual Differences and the Design of Educational Programs," *American Psychologist* (October 1986), pp. 1029–1039.

14 McCutcheon, "How Do Elementary School Teachers Plan?" p. 7.

Table 11.1   LEVELS OF TEACHER PLANNING

Level	Goals of planning	Sources of information	Form of plan	Criteria for judging effectiveness of planning
Yearly planning	1. Establishing general content (fairly general and framed by district curriculum objectives) 2. Establishing basic curriculum sequence 3. Ordering and reserving materials	1. Students (general information about numbers and returning students) 2. Resources available 3. Curriculum guidelines (district objectives) 4. Experience with specific curricula and materials	1. General outlines listing basic content and possible ideas in each subject area (spiral notebook used for each subject)	1. Comprehensiveness of plans 2. Fit with own goals and district objectives
Term planning	1. Detailing of content to be covered in next three months 2. Establishing a weekly schedule for term that conforms to goals and emphases for the term	1. Direct contact with students 2. Time constraints set by school schedule 3. Resources available	1. Elaboration of outlines constructed for yearly planning 2. A weekly schedule outline specifying activities and times	1. Outlines— comprehensiveness, completeness, and specificity of elaborations
Unit planning	1. Developing a sequence of well-organized learning experiences 2. Presenting comprehensive, integrated and meaningful content at an appropriate level	1. Students' abilities, interests, etc. 2. Materials, length of lessons, setup time, demand, format 3 District objectives 4. Facilities available for activities	1. Lists or outlines of activities and content 2. Lists of sequenced activities 3. Notes in plan book	1. Organization, sequence, balance, and flow of outlines 2. Fit with yearly and term goals 3. Fit with anticipated student interest and involvement
Weekly planning	1. Laying out the week's activities within the framework of the weekly schedule 2. Adjusting schedule for interruptions and special needs 3. Maintaining continuity and regularity of activities	1. Students' performance in preceding days and weeks 2. Scheduled school interruptions (for example, assemblies, holidays) 3. Materials, aides, and other resources	1. Names and times of activities in plan book 2. Day divided into instructional blocks punctuated by a.m., lunch, and p.m.	1. Completeness of plans 2. Degree to which weekly schedule has been followed 3. Flexibility of plans to allow for special time constraints or interruptions 4. Fit with goals

Table 11.1   (Continued)

Level	Goals of planning	Sources of information	Form of plan	Criteria for judging effectiveness of planning
Daily planning	1. Setting up and arranging class-room for next day 2. Specifying activity components not yet decided upon 3. Fitting daily schedule to last-minute intrusions 4. Preparing students for day's activities	1. Instruction in materials to be used 2. Set-up time re-quired for activities 3. Assessment of class "disposition" at start of day 4. Continued interest, involvement, and enthusiasm	1. Schedule for day written on the chalkboard and discussed with students 2. Preparation and arrangement of materials and facilities in the room	1. Completion of last-minute preparations and decisions about content, materials, etc. 2. Involvement, enthusiasm, and interest communi-cated by students

Source: Robert J. Yinger, "A Study of Teacher Planning," *Elementary School Journal* (January 1980), pp. 114–115.

predetermined in a classroom of 30 students or more who are rapidly interact-ing with their teacher.

Mental planning is the teacher's spontaneous response to events in the classroom; the teacher considers situations and responds intuitively. (Of course, that intuition must be well grounded in subject matter and action system knowledge.) Mental planning is a part of teaching that is crucial for effectiveness, but it cannot be easily observed, recorded, or detailed. Therefore, it often goes unnoticed and unmentioned as part of the planning process. Mental planning suggests that instruction (or teaching) is an art that cannot be planned in advance—that a theory of principles (or methods) of teaching cannot easily be determined or agreed upon. But mental planning is a practical, common, and effective method of instructional planning. **Formal planning** is what most educators and researchers recognize as a legitimate and necessary instructional activity. Perhaps it is examined so often simply because it can be prescribed, categorized, and classified. Formal planning is structured and task-oriented; it suggests that teaching and instruction can be taught as part of teacher training and staff development.

In connection with formal planning, teachers need opportunity for (1) planning in groups or pairs without the presence of supervisors, (2) seeing visual or video demonstrations of master teachers, followed by reflection and discussion, (3) helping teachers learn more about their students' academic needs and behaviors, such as making use of their cumulative records, test scores, and portfolios, (4) discussing innovative methods or ideas on a regular basis at faculty, departmental, curriculum, or in-service meetings, and (5) avoiding pitfalls in planning, such as rigidly following a lesson plan regardless of intervening variables.[15]

In addition, with the current emphasis on mandated curriculum, standardized testing, and required state or district competencies, beginning teachers are vulnerable to becoming merely *implementers* rather than *developers* of curriculum. Even experienced teachers tend to forfeit their role as curriculum developers, partially because professional time during the school day is not provided and some teachers feel the extra time needed to fulfill this role is an imposition that extends beyond the school day.

Course Plans: Mapping

A long-range teacher guide is usually called a *map* or *course of study*. In large school districts the map is often prepared by a committee of experts. In small school districts the teachers of a subject, working as a group or as individuals, may develop their own map, within limits defined by state guidelines. As a teacher plans a map, he or she must consider: (1) goals of the school (or school district); (2) needs assessment data, if available, by the school or district; (3) preassessment or placement evaluation data of the students, such as reading tests, aptitude tests, self-report inventories, observational reports; and (4) instructional objectives of the course according to district or state guidelines and grade level or departmental publications.[16]

Mapping details the content, concepts, skills, and, sometimes, values to be taught for the entire course. Performing this task places the teacher in a better position to do unit and lesson planning. The mapping process also helps connect the goals and objectives of the course. It helps teachers to view the course as a whole and to see the relationship of content, concepts, and skills being stressed.[17] Mapping requires that the teacher know, before the term or school years begins, what the important content areas, concepts, and skills of the course are. See Tips for Teachers 11.1.

In general, the map or course of study provides a total view of the entire term's or year's work without specifying sequences or relationships of tasks. As an example, the map in Table 11.2 identifies the major content, concepts, skills, and values for any subject or grade level.

---

15 Phelps, "Expanding Beginning Teachers' Perspectives on Planning."

16 Walter Dick and Robert A. Reiser, *Planning Effective Instruction* (Englewood Cliffs, N.J.: Prentice-Hall, 1989); Bruce W. Tuckman, *Evaluating Instructional Programs*, 2nd ed. (Boston: Allyn & Bacon, 1985).

17 George J. Posner and Alan N. Rudnitsky, *Course Design: A Guide to Curriculum Development for Teachers*, 2nd ed. (White Plains, N.Y.: Longman, 1986); John Wiles and Joseph C. Bondi, *Curriculum Development: A Guide to Practice*, 3rd ed. (Columbus, Ohio: Merrill, 1989).

Tips for Teachers 11.1

Planning a Course

Here are a few recommendations for the map or course level of planning.

1. Be sure you understand the rationale for the course in the context of the goals of the school or district.
2. Be sure you understand the objectives of the course, according to state or district guidelines.
3. Clarify the focus of the course. Should it be designed to stress subject matter, learner needs, or societal needs?
4. Determine if there is a special need (special audience, special instructional program) for the course.
5. Identify the important components: content, concepts, skills, values.
6. Examine the components to see if they (a) meet the important objectives of the course; (b) foster critical or high-order thinking; (c) match student abilities, according to data obtained from preplanning evaluation; (d) stimulate student interest; (e) are realistic in terms of school time allotted to the course and school resources; and (f) are balanced in terms of sequence (vertically related) and scope (horizontally related).
7. Decide on important components so that they can be used as a framework for your unit planning.
8. Show the map to an experienced colleague or supervisor. Revise it in light of the feedback received.
9. As you use the map, evaluate, modify, and improve it. Note components that should be (a) added to cover gaps; (b) eliminated to avoid redundancy, trivia, and unnecessary complications; or (c) changed to avoid unanticipated negative effects and to provide better guidance for you and the students.

Interdisciplinary Planning: Science-Technology-Society (STS)

Regardless of the level of planning, instruction should be related to the students' lives and to current as well as future problems. Students should be able to make connections between subject matter and real problems and issues. They should understand the value of studying their subjects, and what they study should be relevant to their needs and useful to their lives.

Table 11.2   MAPPING: IDENTIFYING MAJOR CONTENT, CONCEPTS, SKILLS, AND VALUES

Content areas*	Concepts (major ideas of the course)
1. According to headings (such as chapters or topics in the text)	1. Classifying information with a focus
2. According to similarities and differences (such as communities, cities, states, nations, and continents)	2. Grouping information with a focus
	3. Categorizing information with implicit relationships
3. According to "what" or "who" relationships (such as Matisse, Picasso, and Miro)	4. Categorizing information with explicit relationships
4. According to a system of classification (such as animals, foods, chemicals, governments)	5. Comparing information with a focus
	6. Comparing information with qualifications
5. According to "why" or explanation of phenomena (such as "what" if questions, possibilities, probabilities, and projections)	7. Explaining (interpreting) information by logical relationships
	8. Explaining (interpreting) information by separating relevant from irrelevant information
6. According to "how" (such as working out problems of weight, volume, density, motion)	9. Organizing information based on principles, formulas, or cause-effect relationships
	10. Assimilating new information with old information based on principles, formulas, or cause-effect relationships
	11. Applying principles, formulas, or cause-effect relationships to explain new information
	12. Applying principles, formulas, or cause-effect relationships to predict trends, events, or measurements

Basic academic skills	Learning skills

1. Speaking
   Listening
   Debating
   Rethinking
   Concluding
	1. Note taking
	   Outlining main ideas only
	   Outlining main and subordinate ideas
	   Classifying information
	   Grouping information
	   Outlining from chalkboard
	   Outlining from text

2. Reading
   Vocabulary
   Skimming
   Comprehension
   Interpreting pictures and graphs
	2. Homework
	   Routine homework
	   Problem-solving homework
	   Independent work
	   Reporting
	   Special projects (library, laboratory, etc.)

3. Writing
   Essay
   Reporting
   Creative
	Group assignments

Table 11.2 (Continued)

Basic academic skills	Learning skills
4. Computer Skills	3. Studying
Practice and drill	Copying from text
Using or transferring information	Underlining text
Writing ideas or stories	Notes in text margins
Reporting	Studying alone
Problem solving	Studying in groups
Simulations	Reviewing while reading assignments
Programming	Reviewing for quizzes or tests

Higher-cognitive functioning	Values
Using facts	Affirming one's identity
Analyzing	Affirming one's group
Synthesizing	Listening to others
Inferring	Appreciating others
Drawing conclusions	Working with others
Evaluating	Choosing friends
Problem solving	Making choices
Predicting	Being responsible for one's actions
	Understanding legal issues
	Understanding moral and ethical issues

*Content areas can be based on the units of the course. Units should be organized around one of the items listed.

The six content areas and twelve concepts suggest a hierarchy based on difficulty and sophistication in thinking. There seems to be a correlation with content 1 and concept 1; content 2 and concepts 2–4; content 3 with concepts 5–6; content 4 with concepts 7–8; content 5 with concepts 9–10; and content 6 with concepts 11–12. No proof of the correlation has been established.

In this connection, a major interdisciplinary effort in United States schools, called **Science-Technology-Society** (STS), was developed by Penick and Yager. The thrust is to combine subject matter in science and social studies, then subsequently with technological issues and vocational education. Several professional organizations, such as the National Science Foundation and National Council for the Social Studies, have endorsed the STS courses.[18]

18 John E. Penick, Robert E. Yager, and Ronald Bonnstetter, "Teachers Make Exemplary Programs," *Educational Leadership* (October 1986), pp. 14–20; John E. Penick and Robert E. Yager, "A Model School-Based Program for Science Education Majors," *Action in Teacher Education* (October 1989), pp. 4–6; and Robert E. Yager, "Problem Solving: The STS Advantage," *Curriculum Review* (January–February 1987), pp. 19–21.

Basic to the goals of STS is the education of an informed citizenry capable of understanding and functioning in a technological society, one that is changing rapidly, in which critical social issues must be resolved. Teachers who wish to plan instruction on an interdisciplinary basis, combining scientific, technological, and societal issues, would do well to examine the characteristics and processes of STS compared to a standard program, as highlighted by Table 11.3. STS attempts to move teaching and learning from the classroom to the community, from knowledge derived from texts to active problem solving, and from a passive student role to an active one.

Guidelines for Developing Instructional Plans

How can teachers plan and organize instruction and improve the curriculum? In many cases, teachers work in small groups at the subject or grade level or at the schoolwide level. Here are some steps for improving instructional planning.

1. Work collaboratively with colleagues, and possibly include representatives from the administration, parents, and students to consider school (and school district) goals.
2. Identify plans needed to achieve school (and school district) goals.
3. Collect data from students, parents, staff, and administration regarding existing plans.
4. Develop a plan with time lines.
5. Review the literature in the specific subject area.[19]
6. Consult with subject specialists and psychologists of learning.
7. Develop a philosophy and learning theory that coincides with the goals of the school and the knowledge derived from subject specialists and learning theorists.
8. Outline the content and learning skills (e.g., critical thinking) to be covered.[20]
9. Develop criteria for selecting instructional materials that cover recommended content and learning skills.
10. Develop guidelines for instructional methods that implement recommended content and learning skills.
11. Monitor the plans at the classroom level; seek feedback from other teachers working with the plan.

---

19 Tom Maglaras and Deborah Lynch, "Monitoring the Curriculum: From Plan to Action," *Educational Leadership* (October 1988), pp. 58–60.

20 Allan C. Ornstein, "Components of Curriculum Development," *Illinois School Research and Development Journal* (Spring 1990), pp. 204–211.

Table 11.3 STANDARD INSTRUCTION COMPARED TO SCIENCE-TECHNOLOGY-SOCIETY (STS) INSTRUCTION

Standard	STS
1. Major content/concepts found in texts	1. Identification of real-life problems
2. Use of activities suggested by or supplementary to text	2. Use of local resources (human and material) to assist in problem resolution
3. Passive involvement of students in assimilating text data	3. Active involvement of students in seeking information
4. Learning primarily contained in classroom	4. Learning in several settings
5. Limited attention to social issues or career awareness; occasional reference to a famous person (often dead)	5. Focus on social issues and career awareness that related to research and technology
6. Students concentrating on problems or issues provided by teachers	6. Students performing citizenship roles as they attempt to resolve problems or issues in local community
7. Learning focused on current explanations and understanding	7. Learning focused on the future
8. Learning is test driven	8. Learning occurs through activity
9. Students see process skills separate from content	9. Content and process skills are integrated
10. Teacher's concerns for process are not clear to students	10. Students readily see the relationship of process to their own actions
11. Student curiosity and creativity decline across grade levels	11. Student curiosity and creativity increase from grade to grade
12. Students see teacher as purveyor of information	12. Students see teacher as resource and facilitator
13. Students rarely initiate questions; they react to teacher's questions	13. Students ask more questions of other students and the teacher
14. Students have few novel or original ideas	14. Students seem to have many novel or original ideas
15. Students see little practical value to their study	15. Students can relate their study to their daily living

Source: Adapted from Robert E. Yager, "New Goals for Students," *Education and Urban Society* (November 1989), pp. 16–18.

12. Establish an in-service or staff development program to provide peer training with regard to the plan(s).

13. Require trainers to develop training packets, as well as informal and formal training sessions.

14. Evaluate the plans; provide for modification and recycling.

UNIT PLANS

A **unit plan** is a blueprint to clarify what content will be taught by what learning experiences during a specific period of time. It is a segment of the map or course of study. One reason for developing unit plans is the theory that learning by wholes is more effective than piece-by-piece learning. Another is the need for teachers to plan experiences in advance to meet the different objectives. Advance planning at the unit plan level enables teachers to survey the entire subject and be more effective in designing and structuring the instructional process. The overall view helps them anticipate problems that may arise, especially in terms of prerequisite content, concepts, and skills.

Components of the Unit Plan

The unit plan consists of six basic components: objectives, content, skills, activities, resources and materials, and evaluation (Table 11.4). All should be considered in planning a unit, although your school (or immediate supervisor) may not require that you specify them all.

Objectives

Objectives can be behavioral or nonbehavioral (topics, problems, questions). Most teachers today rely on behavioral objectives partly because of recent emphasis on them in the professional literature. The method you use as the core of your plan will depend on your approach and the schools' approach to planning units.

Content

The scope of the content should be outlined. The content often includes three major categories: knowledge, skills, and values.[21] The development of skills is usually more important at the elementary school level and with teachers who emphasize behaviorist or mastery learning. Knowledge is more important at the secondary school level and with teachers who emphasize cognitive or inductive learning. Valuing is more a reflection of the individual teacher and school then the specific grade level.

---

21 Ronald C. Doll, *Curriculum Improvement: Decision Making and Process*, 8th ed. (Needham Heights, Mass.: Allyn & Bacon, 1992); Ralph W. Tyler, *Basic Principles of Curriculum and Instruction* (Chicago: University of Chicago Press, 1949).

Table 11.4   UNIT PLAN COMPONENTS

1. Objectives
   General objectives and specific objectives
   Behavioral objectives or nonbehavioral objectives (topics, problems, questions)

2. Content
   Knowledge (concepts, problem solving, critical thinking)
   Skills (cognitive, affective, psychomotor)
   Values (personal, social, moral)

3. Skills
   Work habits
   Discussion and specific communication skills
   Reading skills
   Writing skills
   Note-taking skills
   Dictionary skills
   Reference skills (table of contents, glossary, index)
   Library skills
   Reporting and research skills
   Computer skills
   Interpreting skills (maps, charts, tables, graphs, legends)
   Inquiry skills (problem solving, experimenting, hypothesizing)
   Social skills (respecting rules, accepting criticism, poise and maturity, peer acceptance)
   Cooperative and competitive skills (leadership, self-concept, participation in group)

4. Learning activities
   Lectures and explanations
   Practice and drill
   Grouping activities (buzz sessions, panels, debates, forums)
   Role playing, simulations, dramatizations
   Research, writing projects (stories, biographies, logs)
   Experiments
   Field trips
   Reviews

5. Resources and materials
   Written materials (books, pamphlets, magazines, newspapers)
   Audiovisual materials (films, records, slides, television, videotapes)
   Programmed or computer materials
   Models, replicas, charts, graphs, specimens

6. Evaluation procedures
   Demonstrations, exhibits, debates
   Reviews, summaries
   Quizzes, examinations
   Reteaching
   Remediation
   Special training

Teachers can enrich students' learning experiences by inviting resource people from the community into class to talk about specific content.

Skills

A list of cognitive and social skills to be developed is sometimes optional. The skills should be based on the content to be taught and are sometimes listed as part of the content. Important basic skills to develop include critical reading, skimming and scanning, reading graphic materials (maps, diagrams, charts, tables) library skills, composition and reporting skills, note-taking, homework skills, study skills, social and interpersonal skills, discussion and speaking skills, cooperative and competitive skills, and leadership skills.

Learning Activities

Learning activities, sometimes called *student activities*, should be based on implementing objectives and students' needs and interests. Only special activities, such as guest speakers, field trips, debates and buzz sessions, special reports, projects, experiments, and summative examinations, need be listed. The recurring or common activities can be shown as part of the daily lesson plan.

Resources and Materials

The purpose of including resources and materials in the plan is to guide the teacher in assembling the reading material, library and research materials, and audiovisual equipment needed to carry out instruction. This list at the unit plan level should include only essential resources and materials. A list of resources is sometimes included as part of learning activities and so is sometimes considered an optional element in a unit plan.

Evaluation Procedures

The major evaluation procedures and culminating activities should be included. These include formative and summative evaluations: student exhibits and demonstrations, summary debates and discussions, quizzes and examinations, reteaching, remedial work, and special tutoring or training. Evaluation can be conducted by students or the teacher or both. The intent is to appraise whether the objectives have been achieved and to obtain information for improving the unit plan. See Tips for Teachers 11.2.

Approaches to Unit Planning

The teacher might check with his or her supervisor before planning a unit. Some school districts have a preferred approach for developing units, and others permit their teachers more latitude. Some supervisors require teachers to submit units for final approval, while others give teachers more professional authority. Below are three basic approaches to unit planning that teachers may wish to consider.

Behavioral Approach

In this approach (see Table 11.5), the teacher designates the topic, instructional objectives, concepts, materials, and time (number of lessons needed to teach the topic). The topics are broken down into lesson plans. Emphasis is on objectives, written on a cognitive level, closely corresponding to the taxonomy and Mager approaches (see Chapter 6). The concepts, what we call content and skills, are mainly categorized according to the six levels of the cognitive domain of learning, except the concepts in topic 5. Most of the objectives have a proficiency level (and some have a condition), suggesting the Mager style of writing objectives. The concepts and materials indicated parallel the objectives, and the time is shown as a guide for the teacher who expects to complete this unit in eleven days. Note that each of the topics dealing with length, mass, and volume are really each three separate subtopics combined into one; a separate lesson (one day) is schedule for each subtopic.

Topic Approach

Table 11.6 illustrates the topic approach. The unit plan is organized by topics and objectives. Objectives introduce the lesson, but the topics serve as the major basis for outlining the unit. The objectives coincide with the recommendation that content focus on concepts, skills, and values. Note that the objectives (related to knowledge, skills, and values) do not build upon one another (they are somewhat independent) nor are they divided into general and specific. The topics are arranged in the order in which they will be treated, suggesting that they correspond to the table of contents of a textbook. Indeed, it is appropriate

Tips for Teachers 11.2

Organizing and Implementing Unit Plans

As you prepare your unit and lesson plans, you should be aware of common mistakes. The idea is to minimize them by following guidelines that have proved to be practical, by discussing plans with your colleagues or supervisor, and by practicing.

Below is a list of suggestions that apply to all levels of unit planning and can be adapted to accommodate your school's requirements and your teaching style and instructional approach.

1. Ask your principal or supervisor for curriculum plans pertaining to your subject and grade level to guide your planning.
2. Ask your colleagues or supervisor for a file of unit plans to guide your planning.
3. Check the instructor's manual of the textbook or workbook, if you are using one; many have excellent examples of unit plans.
4. Consider vertical (different grades, same subject) and horizontal (same grade, different subjects) relationships of subject matter in formulating your unit plans. Be sure you understand the relationship between new information and prior knowledge.
5. Consider students' abilities, needs, and interests as you plan your unit.
6. Decide on objectives and related content for the various units of the subject.
7. After objectives and content have been established, sequence the units.
8. Determine the order of the content by considering cognitive processes (skills, concepts, problems) and affective processes (attitudes, feelings, values) involved. Developmental theories, mastery learning, or task analysis can be used to determine the order of the units as well as the content.
9. Consider appropriate time allocation for each unit. Most units will take one to three weeks to complete.
10. Investigate resource materials and media available in your district and school; incorporate appropriate materials and media.
11. Provide opportunities for student practice and review.
12. Provide opportunities for evaluation (not necessarily testing or grades).
13. Ask your colleagues or supervisor for feedback after you implement your unit plan; discuss questions, problems, and proposed modifications.

continues

> **14.** Rewrite or at least modify your unit plan whenever you teach the same subject and grade level; the world changes, classes change, and students differ.
> **15.** Be patient. Do not expect immediate results. Practice will not make you perfect, but it will make you a better teacher.

to follow a text, as long as it is well planned and the teacher knows when to modify or supplement the text with related activities and materials.

The topics here represent daily lesson plans. The activities listed are non-recurring, special activities; repeated activities can be listed at the lesson plan level. The activities are listed in the order in which they will occur, but there is not one particular activity listed for each topic (as in Table 11.5). The evaluation component is separate and includes formative and summative tests, discussion, and feedback.

Activities Approach

Table 11.7 illustrates a unit approach that deemphasizes topics and objectives (which most units are based on) and emphasizes various activities. The activities are sequenced, correspond with the first two (cognitive) objectives, and determine the lesson plan schedule. The third objective overlaps with the first two objectives—almost as a by-product. The unit consists of a minimum of six lessons, listed under activities (sometimes called "class sessions"), and a possible seventh lesson (review) depending on the results of the unit examination. The evaluation component consists of a pretest and a posttest, with follow-up for review and reteaching if necessary. In general, the approach is not detailed and assumes a certain amount of flexibility and fill-in on the unit as it is taught by the teacher.

Diagnostic Profile Chart

The unit plan described in Table 11.5 places heavy emphasis on the linear and metric system as well as on problem solving and experimenting. Table 11.8 is an extension of that unit plan; the teacher develops a diagnostic profile of each student to identify quickly those who need supplementary work to assist them in mastering the content and skills of the unit plan. The diagnostic profile provides an overview of the members of the class and of any specific areas that many students have had difficulty learning. If only a few problems exist for a few students, then this would suggest supplementary work on an individual or small-group basis. If a specific problem exists for many students in the class, then this would suggest reteaching the whole group.

Table 11.5   UNIT PLAN: BEHAVIORAL APPROACH IN SCIENCE

Theme: Problem Solving in the Laboratory

1. *Topic*: Knowledge of laboratory safety procedures
   a. *Objective*: Each learner will identify appropriate laboratory safety procedures by correctly answering 12 out of 15 items on a short-answer item quiz
   b. *Concepts*: Comprehension and application of safety equipment, safety procedures
   c. *Materials*: Safety goggles, fire extinguisher, fire blanket, sand, and laboratory workbook
   d. *Time*: 1 day

2. *Topic*: Properties of length, mass, and volume
   a. *Objective*: Each student will differentiate among symbols used to identify length, mass, and volume by answering 16 out of 20 matching questions in the laboratory workbook
   Objective: Each student will work out 8 of the 10 problems dealing with length, mass, and volume in the laboratory
   b. *Concepts*: Comprehending length, mass, and volume
   c. *Materials*: Yardstick, ounce scale, quart cylinders, chocolate bars, cookies, and water
   d. *Time*: 3 days

3. *Topic*: Conversion of units of length, mass, and volume to metric system
   a. *Objective*: Each student will convert 16 out of 20 laboratory problems regarding length, mass, and volume into metric answers
   b. *Concepts*: Translating linear answers to metric answers
   c. *Materials*: Yardstick and meter stick, ounce scale and kilogram scale, quart and liter cylinders
   d. *Time*: 3 days

4. *Topic*: Classification of variables
   a. *Objective*: Each learner will classify and distinguish among control, treatment, and responding variables by answering 4 out of 5 questions in a laboratory experiment
   b. *Concepts*: Analyzing scientific variables
   c. *Materials*: Buscocopters, scissors, glycerin, alcohol, water, crayfish, tadpoles
   d. *Time*: 1 day

5. *Topic*: Steps in problem solving
   a. *Objective*: Each learner will sequence and provide a rationale for the steps of the scientific method
   b. *Concepts*: Hypothesizing, verifying, and concluding
   c. *Materials*: Tray of ice, water, beakers, graduated cylinders
   d. *Time*: 1 day

6. *Topic*: Implementing your own experiment
   a. *Objective*: Each student will explain to the class the control, treatment, and responding variables in their own experiment
   Objective: Each student will explain to the class the procedures used in their experiment
   b. *Concepts*: Analyzing and evaluating scientific experiments
   c. *Materials*: Glycerin, alcohol, water, eyedroppers, beakers, graduated cylinders
   d. *Time*: 2 days

Source: Adapted from David G. Armstrong, *Developing and Documenting the Curriculum* (Needham Heights, Mass.: Allyn & Bacon, 1989), pp. 190–191, 194–195.

Table 11.6   UNIT PLAN: TOPIC APPROACH FOR AMERICAN HISTORY

Objectives

I. Knowledge
1. To recognize that the U.S. Constitution is rooted in English law
2. To identify the causes and events leading to the forming of the U.S. Constitution
3. To argue the advantages and limitations of the U.S. Constitution
4. To illustrate how amendments are enacted

II. Skills
1. To expand vocabulary proficiency
2. To improve research skills
3. To improve oral reporting skills
4. To expand reading habits to include historical events and people
5. To develop debating techniques

III. Values
1. To develop an understanding that freedom is based on laws
2. To recognize the obligations of freedom (among free people)
3. To appreciate how rights are protected
4. To develop a more positive attitude toward minorities
5. To develop a more positive attitude toward classmates

Topics

I. Historical Background of the Constitution
1. English common law
2. Magna Carta
3. Mayflower Compact
4. Colonial freedom
5. Taxation without representation
6. Boston Tea Party
7. First and second Constitutional Congress
8. Declaration of Independence
9. Age of Enlightenment and America

II. Bill of Rights and the Constitution
1. Constitutional Convention
2. Framing of the Constitution
3. Bill of Rights
   a. Reasons
   b. Specific freedoms
4. Powers reserved to the states
5. Important amendments
   a. Thirteenth, Fourteenth, Fifteenth (slavery, due process, voting rights)
   b. Nineteenth (women's suffrage)
   c. Twentieth (progressive tax)
   d. Twenty-second (two-term limit to presidency)
   e. Others

Table 11.6   (Continued)

Activities

1. Filmstrip introducing part I
2. List of major points to be discussed in part I
3. Homework—reading list for each lesson (I.1–9; II.1–5)
4. Television program on "American Freedom" and discussion after I.9
5. Field trip to historical museum as culminating activity for I and introduction to II
6. Topics and reports for outside reading, with two-day discussion of reports after II.3
7. Two-day debate (with four teams): "What's wrong with our Constitution?" "What's right with our Constitution?" after II.5

Evaluation

1. Short quiz for I.1–9
2. Graded reports with specific feedback for each student; half a lesson
3. Discussion of students' role as citizens in a free society; compare rights and responsibilities of American citizens with rights and responsibilities of students; a full lesson or one day
4. Unit test; review I.1–9; II.1–5

Source: Adapted from Gail M. Inlow, *Maturity in High School Teaching*, 2nd ed. (Englewood Cliffs, N.J.: Prentice-Hall, 1970), pp. 110–112.

In the diagnostic chart shown in Table 11.8, the X's identify weakness in the category where they appear. The chart allows easy identification of students who need assistance, such as Cox (four areas) and Miller and Doyle (five areas). In general, the students seem to have difficulty with skill areas dealing with metrics and problem solving; this suggests some extended instruction on these two topics.

Regardless of the diagnostic method used (the table represents only one method), the teacher should organize information about each student's ability, as well as the performance of the whole class, by specific areas of study. Such diagnosis shows each student's progress, as well as how he or she performs in relation to classmates.

Guidelines for Developing Unit Plans

The number of units and the time allotted and emphasis for each unit are matters of judgment, although experts tend to recommend about 10 to 30 units for a year's course and about 5 to 15 lessons per unit. Consideration is usually

Table 11.7   UNIT PLAN: ACTIVITIES APPROACH FOR ENGLISH

Topic: Correctly punctuating with commas

Objectives: Upon completion of this unit the students will

1. Correctly use comma rules found in the grammar text
2. Correctly punctuate with commas in writing compositions
3. Recognize the value of correct commas in comprehensible writing

Content (concepts)

1. Comma use in a series of three or more items, persons, or places—one class session
2. Comma use to separate appositives—one class session
3. Comma use in prepositional phrases—one class session
4. Comma use in compound sentences—two class sessions

Activities (class sessions)

1. Pretest (see evaluation): short-answer questions and descriptive paragraphs
2. Discussion and explanations of comma rules based on test and text
3. Practice writing sentences and paragraphs orally and in writing
4. Pair off students to edit each other's personal letters and compositions
5. Follow-up discussion related to letters and compositions
6. Posttest (see evaluation)
7. Review (if necessary)

Materials (media)

1. Text: Jones and Jones, *Language Use for Students*
2. Students' sentences, paragraphs, letters, and compositions
3. Overhead projector

Evaluation

1. Pretest: ten sentences, two student paragraphs
2. Posttest
   a. Twenty sentences with at least 80 percent correct
   b. Students' composition with at least 80 percent correct

Review

1. Review: based on posttest scores

Table 11.8　DIAGNOSTIC UNIT CHART

Students' names	Linear Measurement			Metric Measurement			Controlling Variables	Problem-solving steps	Experimenting
	Inches, feet	Ounces, pounds	Pints, quarts	Centimeters, meters	Grams, kilograms	Liters, kiloliters			
Anderson								X	
Arnold		X			X				
Bailey		X							
Baker					X			X	X
Bantz			X						X
Belmont				X					
Carroll	X			X				X	
Cox					X	X	X		X
Dahl									
Doyle				X		X	X	X	X
Evans									
Fien			X			X			
Franks				X					X
Grant		X							
Heniz								X	
Hoffman					X				X
Jordan				X					
Katz			X				X		
Marks									
Miller			X		X	X		X	X
Roberts							X		X
Thompson						X		X	

given to the organization of the textbook, the emphasis suggested by state and school district curriculum guides, and the special abilities, needs, and interests of the students. Also, according to test specialists, there is an increasing tendency for teachers to plan units around national, state, and school district testing programs, what is sometimes called "focused" instruction or "high-stakes" evaluation.[22]

---

22 W. James Popham, "Can High-Stakes Tests Be Developed at the Local Level?" *NASSP Bulletin* (February 1987), pp. 77–84; Herbert C. Rudman, "Classroom Instruction and Tests," *NASSP Bulletin* (February 1987), pp. 3–22.

Having already outlined the basic components of the unit plan, we now provide suggestions that deal with some of the details. These suggestions are applicable for all subjects and grade levels.

1. Develop the unit plan with a particular class or group of students in mind.
2. Indicate the subject, grade level, and length of time to teach the unit.
3. Outline the unit around a general theme or idea (the unit title).
4. Identify the general objectives, problems, or topics of the unit. Each objective, problem, or topic should correspond to a lesson plan (to be discussed below).
5. Include one or more of the following: (a) content and activities, (b) cognitive processes and skills, (c) psychomotor skills, (d) attitudes and values.
6. Match objectives (problems or topics) with content and activities (processes and skills).
7. Identify methods for evaluating the outcomes of the unit. Possibly include a pretest and posttest to determine learning outcomes or improvement in learning.
8. Include resources (materials and media) needed to supplement the text.
9. Plan an effective way of introducing the unit, possibly an overview exercise, problem, or recent event.
10. Classify the unit, if possible, according to different levels of problem solving, creative work, or achievement.
11. Design parts of the unit for low-achieving, average-achieving, and high-achieving students.
12. Plan the unit so it is vertically related to other parts of the course or subject and, if possible, horizontally related to other subjects.
13. Develop the unit to include the life experiences of the students or out-of-school activities, such as field trips or work in the library or community.
14. Duplicate the unit plan for the students so they can follow it.
15. Periodically modify and update the unit plan for subsequent use.

LESSON PLANS

A **lesson plan** sets forth the proposed program, or instructional activities, for each day; it is sometimes referred to as a *daily plan*. In general, the lesson plan should be planned around the fixed periods (usually 35 to 50 minutes) of the typical school schedule, allowing adequate time for teachers or students to arrive (if they are changing classrooms) and to leave at the end of the period. Shorter blocks of time may be allowed for younger students or for those whose

Schools provide different opportunities for students to learn their lessons.

attention span is limited. Good planning or scheduling is an aid to good instruction and good classroom management.

Although special school activities may require shortened or lengthened periods, most lessons should be planned for full periods. Sometimes students need more or less time to finish an activity or assignment, and teachers need to learn how to be flexible in adjusting timing. As teachers develop their planning and pacing skills, they learn to plan better schedules in advance and to plan supplementary activities and materials for use or elimination as the need arises, to maintain a good pace. Additional activities might include performing a committee function, completing a research assignment, finishing a workbook assignment, illustrating a composition or report, working on a study activity, performing an honor or extra credit assignment, or tutoring another student. Additional materials might include pictures, charts, and models to further demonstrate a major point in the lesson, practice and drill for review purposes, and a list of summary questions to review major points of the lesson.

To avoid omissions, underemphasis, or overemphasis, the teacher needs to consider his or her style of teaching and the students' abilities and interests. The teacher should review the progress of each day's lesson and periodically take notes on important student responses to different methods, media, and activities—to reuse with another class or at another time. Inexperienced teachers need to plan the lessons in detail, follow the plan, and refer to it frequently. As they grow in experience and confidence, they become able to plan with less detail and rely more on their spontaneous responses to what happens in the classroom as the teaching-learning process unfolds.

Lesson Plans by Authorities

Many current authorities who write about what a lesson plan should contain write from the point of view of direct instructional methods, that is, a view of the classroom in which teaching is teacher-directed, methods and materials are sequenced, content is extensive and focused, students are provided with practice as the teacher checks or monitors the work, and the teacher provides evaluation of performance. The objectives are clearly stated in the beginning of the lesson, and a review either proceeds or follows the statement of objectives. Learning takes place in an academic, subject-centered environment. There is little mention or concern about student needs or interests; emphasis is on student abilities and achievement.

The authors listed in Table 11.9 all exhibit this direct, step-by-step approach to learning. The categories or components are lined up within the table to show similarities among approaches. All lesson plan components and classroom events are controlled by the teacher; no provision is made for student choice or planning, and the classroom is highly structured and businesslike. Most important, the emphasis is on knowledge, skills, and tasks, as well as practice, review, and testing; very few, if any, of their prescriptions seem directed to problem solving, critical thinking, or creativity, much less personal, social, or moral development.

Although the authorities listed in the table might not admit it or agree, their approaches apply mainly to the teaching of basic skills and basic subjects such as reading, mathematics, and foreign language, where practice and drill are often recommended. They are not as effective, if they can be used at all, in teaching inquiry or discovery learning or creative thinking. Nevertheless, since the approaches do receive much attention in the professional literature and since they are applicable in more than one teaching area, they should be read. Later, we will present a less direct approach, along with sample lesson plans, that provides teachers with greater flexibility in teaching.

Teaching Techniques

The authorities listed in Table 11.9, as well as other advocates of direct instruction, emphasize structured and sequenced strategies for enhancing student understanding while teaching from the lesson plan. Barak Rosenshine, for example, refers to **teaching functions**—that is, *checking* procedures to ensure full student comprehension. Throughout the lesson the teacher engages in a series of functions to check student understanding, outlined below.

Table 11.9   LESSON PLAN COMPONENTS BY AUTHORITIES

Mastery learning (Hunter)	Instructional design (Gagné)	Lesson planning (Slavin)	Instructional behaviors (Good and Grouws, Good and Brophy)
1. *Review.* Focus on previous lesson; ask students to review questions orally or in writing; ask students to summarize main points.		1. *State learning objectives.* Explain what students are expected to learn; provide background information.	1. *Review.* Review concepts and skills related to homework; provide review exercises.
2. *Anticipatory set.* Focus students' attention on lesson to be presented; stimulate interest in new material.	1. *Gain attention.* Alert students to what to expect; get students started on a routine or warm-up drill.	2. *Review prerequisites.* Have students recall major points of previous lesson.	
3. *Objective.* State explicitly what will be learned; state rationale or how it will be useful.	2. *Inform learners of objective.* Activate the learners' motivation by informing them of the objective to be achieved.		
4. *Input.* Identify needed knowledge and skills for learning new lesson; present material in logical and sequenced steps.	3. *Recall prior knowledge.* Remind students of previously learned knowledge or concepts germane to new material; recall relevant prerequisites.	3. *Present new material.* Teach the lesson; present new information; provide examples; illustrate concepts.	2. *Development.* Promote student understanding of new material; provide examples, explanations, demonstrations.
	4. *Present the stimulus material.* Present new knowledge or skills; indicate distinctive properties of the concepts to be learned.		
5. *Modeling.* Provide several examples or demonstrations throughout the lesson.			
6. *Check for understanding.* Monitor students' work before they become involved in lesson activities; check to see they understand the directions or tasks.	5. *Provide learning guidance.* Elaborate on directions, provide assistance; integrate new information with previous (long-term memory) information.	4. *Conduct learning probes.* Pose questions to assess student understanding; provide "corrective instruction" or assistance when necessary.	3. *Assess student comprehension.* Ask questions; provide controlled practice.

Table11.9   (Continued)

Mastery learning (Hunter)	Instructional design (Gagné)	Lesson planning (Slavin)	Instructional behaviors (Good and Grouws, Good and Brophy)
7. *Guided practice.* Periodically ask students questions or problems and check their answers. The same type of monitoring and response formats are involved in checking for understanding as in guided practice.	6. *Elicit performance.* Suggest, do not specify, methods for performing tasks or problems; provide cues or directions, not answers; students are to provide answers.		
	7. *Provide feedback.* Reinforce learning by checking students' work and providing frequent feedback, especially during the acquisition stage of the new material; use feedback to adapt instruction to individual students.		
8. *Independent practice.* Assign independent work or practice when it is reasonably sure that students can work on their own with minimal effort.		5. *Provide independent practice.* Give students practice exercises or problems; permit students to apply new information on their own.	4. *Seatwork.* Provide uninterrupted seatwork; get everyone involved; sustain momentum.
	8. *Assess performance.* Inform students of their performance in terms of outcomes; establish an "expectancy" level.	6. *Assess performance and provide feedback.* Review independent practice; provide feedback; reteach whatever is necessary.	5. *Accountability.* Check the students' work.

Table 11.9   (Continued)

Mastery learning (Hunter)	Instructional design (Gagné)	Lesson planning (Slavin)	Instructional behaviors (Good and Grouws, Good and Brophy)
	9. *Ensure retention and transfer.* Utilize various instructional techiques to ensure retention (outline, classify information, use tables, charts, and diagrams). Enhance transfer of learning by providing a variety of cues, practice situations, and interlinking concepts.	7. *Provide practice and review.* Assign homework; review material in next lesson; integrate material in later lessons.	6. *Homework.* Assign homework regularly; provide review problems.
			7. *Special reviews.* Provide weekly reviews (exercises, quizzes) each Monday to enhance and maintain learning; provide monthly reviews every fourth Monday to further enhance and maintain learning.

I. To check previous work
   1. Asking questions or problems about concepts or skills.
   2. Administering a short quiz on previous lessons or homework.
   3. Having students correct their own quizzes or homework.
   4. Organizing small student groups to review previous lessons or homework.
   5. Encouraging students to prepare questions about previous lessons or homework to ask each other or the teacher.
   6. Having students prepare a written summary of previous lessons.
   7. Reteaching and providing additional practice.

II. To check current work
   1. Asking students several questions concerning the main points of the new material.
   2. Calling on nonvolunteers.

3. Asking students to summarize main points on paper or at the chalkboard.
4. Having students write answers on paper and then check answers with a neighbor.
5. Discussing main points of the lesson in small groups and preparing a summary for presentation to the class.
6. Providing sufficient practice exercises, monitoring for understanding, and providing feedback.
7. Reteaching when necessary.
8. Providing additional successful repetitions.[23]

Emmer and Evertson present five categories of *clarifying* techniques. Their suggestions pertain to both elementary and secondary school in all subjects.

I. Communicate lesson objectives
   1. State the objectives at the beginning of the lesson.
   2. Explain to students what they will be accountable for knowing or doing.
   3. Emphasize major ideas as they are presented.
   4. Review the objectives or major points at the end of the lesson.
II. Present information systematically
   1. Outline the lesson in an easy-to-follow sequence.
   2. Stick to the topic.
   3. Summarize previous points; make transitions between major ideas or concepts.
   4. Provide step-by-step directions when necessary.
   5. Check for understanding at intervals before proceeding to the next major idea or concept.
   6. Maintain an appropriate pace.
III. Avoid vagueness
   1. Provide concrete examples to explain and reinforce information.
   2. Use appropriate vocabulary.
   3. Be specific and precise; refer to concrete objects, events.
IV. Check for understanding
   1. Ask questions or obtain work samples before proceeding.
   2. Have students summarize main points to show understanding.
   3. Call on slower students and nonvolunteers.
   4. Reteach necessary parts.
V. Provide practice and feedback
   1. Provide adequate practice of objectives to be mastered.

---

23 Barak V. Rosenshine, "Teaching Functions in Instructional Programs," *Elementary School Journal* (March 1983), pp. 335–351; Barak V. Rosenshine and Robert Stevens, "Teaching Functions," in M. C. Wittrock, ed., *Handbook of Research on Teaching*, 3rd ed. (New York: Macmillan, 1986), pp. 376–391.

2. Reinforce learning with review assignments.
3. Check work on a regular basis.
4. Reexplain and reteach when appropriate.[24]

The assumption here is that the step-by-step components listed in Table 11.9, as well as the teaching functions and clarifying techniques of Rosenshine and Evertson, result in highly structured lesson plans. Beginning teachers welcome this type of structure in their quest for "how-to" approaches, but carried to an extreme the learning process for students becomes task-based, convergent-oriented, and lower-level thinking.

Concern for broad-based, divergent-oriented, and higher-level thinking is what teaching and learning should be about; it can be best illustrated in a study of 60 high school teachers who were divided into two groups: those who emphasized and those who deemphasized critical thinking as an instructional goal with their students. Teachers were observed on ten dimensions. Significant differences were found on eight out of ten dimensions. Teachers who emphasized critical thinking exhibited the following lesson plan practices:

1. *Fewer lesson plan topics were discussed.* Topics and ideas were elaborated.
2. *Lesson plan content was coherent.* Arguments or positions for issues were clearly stated; hypothetical situations were analyzed.
3. *Teachers provided students with challenging tasks.* Students had to identify, describe, analyze, and assess aspects of the lesson; students were encouraged to discuss information without their notes or texts.
4. *Teachers modeled thoughtfulness.* They complimented students on their thinking during the lesson, especially when good questions were raised; they recognized student ownership of ideas; and shared with the class their position on issues.
5. *Students were encouraged to give reasons and explanations for statements.* Yes-no responses had to be defended with supporting evidence or with "because . . . ".
6. *Teachers encouraged student discussion.* Data were carefully analyzed by the teacher and students; student viewpoints were elaborated.
7. *Teachers engaged individual students in Socratic dialogue.* Students had to clarify, analyze, and evaluate their opinions or answers.
8. *Teachers revealed disagreement exists among authorities within the field.* Different assumptions and methods were noted; competing views were introduced and discussed.[25]

---

24 Edmund T. Emmer et al., *Classroom Management for Secondary Teachers*, 2nd ed. (Englewood Cliffs, N.J.: Prentice-Hall, 1989); Carolyn M. Evertson et al., *Classrooom Management for Elementary Teachers*, 2nd ed. (Englewood Cliffs, N.J.: Prentice-Hall, 1989).

25 Joseph J. Onosko, "Comparing Teachers' Instruction to Promote Students' Thinking," *Journal of Curriculum Studies* (September–October 1990), pp. 443–461.

These teachers were not content driven but thought (or process) driven; they were not concerned with precise tasks, but rather challenging tasks; they were not concerned with sequenced or structured procedures, but rather thoughtful discussions; and they were not concerned with correct responses by students, but rather the logic or analysis associated with the responses. It should be noted, however, that these teachers were experienced and considered as master teachers by their supervisors. Hence they were not ordinary teachers; they were the best the schools had to offer. Furthermore, one gets the sense that the students were above average—thus it is possible the direct, structured instruction reflected in Table 11.9 is still appropriate for lower-achieving students.

We know that many teachers challenge their students, but challenge is easier and more often exhibited in classrooms comprising high achievers. We need greater understanding of the instructional practices of teachers who succeed in promoting higher-level thinking with low-achieving students. Many beginning teachers lack this knowledge base because the research on this aspect of teaching and learning is still at its infancy stage. Despite more than 25 years of research and thousands of studies concerning inner-city, low-income, and disadvantaged students, we can agree on very little about teaching high-level thinking skills to low-achieving students; instruction for low achievers continues to emphasize mechanical, rote learning and structured, sequenced tasks—as, according to this author, in explicit instruction, direct instruction, and mastery learning.

Components of the Lesson Plan

There is no one ideal format to follow for a lesson plan. Teachers should modify the suggestions of methods experts and learning theorists to coincide with their teaching style and the suggestions of their school or district. For example, the New York City school system recommends that beginning teachers include the following seven components in a lesson plan.

1. Specific *objectives* of the lesson
2. Appropriate *motivation* to capture the students' interest and maintain it throughout the lesson
3. *Development* or *outline* of a lesson (sometimes referred to as content or activities)
4. Varied *methods*, including drill, questions, and demonstrations, designed to keep the lesson on track
5. Varied *materials and media* to supplement and clarify content
6. Medial and final *summaries*
7. Provision for an *assignment* or *homework*.[26]

This list of components can serve as a logical framework for constructing a lesson plan. The teacher can vary how much time he or she spends on each component,

---

26 *Getting Started in the Secondary School: A Manual for New Teachers*, rev. ed. (New York: Board of Education of the City of New York, 1986).

how much detail is included in each, and which components are included. With experience the teacher discovers the most useful components to include and the amount of detail needed in the plan as a whole. See Tips for Teachers 11.3.

Objectives

The first questions a teacher considers when sorting out the content he or she plans to teach are: What do I plan to teach? What do I want the students to learn from the lesson that will be worthwhile? The answers to these questions are the objectives; they form the backbone of the lesson. Motivation, methods, and materials are organized to achieve the objectives. Establishing objectives ensures against aimlessness.

Objectives may be phrased as statements or questions. (Most people think they can only be written as statements.) The question form may encourage students to think. Regardless of how they are phrased, they should be written on the chalkboard or on a printed handout for students to see. Here are some examples of objectives for a lesson plan, written first as a statement and then as a question.

1a. To compare the prices of agricultural goods and industrial goods during the depression.

1b. Why did the prices of agricultural goods decline more than the prices of industrial goods during the depression?

2a. To recognize that the production of oil in the Middle East affects economic conditions in the United States.

2b. How does the production of oil in the Middle East affect economic conditions in the United States?

3a. To recognize that the skin protects people from diseases.

3b. How does our skin protect us from diseases?

The major objective of a lesson may have ancillary (secondary) objectives. Ancillary objectives divide the lesson into segments and highlight or supplement important ideas. Below is an example of a lesson objective with two ancillary objectives (expressed as statements and then questions).

1a. *Lesson objective*: To explain the causes of World War I. *Ancillary objectives*: To compare nationalism, colonialism, and militarism; to distinguish between propaganda and facts.

1b. *Lesson objective*: What were the causes of World War I? *Ancillary objectives*: How are nationalism, colonialism, and militarism related? How can we distinguish between propaganda and facts?

Motivation

Motivational devices or activities arouse and maintain interest in the content to be taught. Fewer motivational devices are needed for students who are intrinsically motivated, that is, are motivated to learn to satisfy some inner need or interest, than for students who are extrinsically motivated, that is, require incentives or reinforcers for learning. Lesson planning and instruction must seek to enhance both forms of motivation.

Tips for Teacher 11.3

Monitoring the Lesson Plan

One school district in Aurora, Colorado, has devised a procedure for monitoring the lesson plan, that is, seeing if the curriculum is being implemented at the classroom level. Events in the classroom are identified as green or red flags, with green signifying effective strategies and red signifying ineffective strategies. The teacher can use this list for self-evaluation; or, students, colleagues, or supervisors can use it to provide feedback to the teacher.

GREEN FLAGS

1. Heretogeneous classes with groups within
2. Student interest and teacher enthusiasm
3. Recognizing that students may change in skills
4. Integration of problem solving
5. Students applying [content] to real-life situations
6. Use of manipulatives
7. Enrichment activities available to students

RED FLAGS

1. All students in the class doing the same assignments
2. No or excessive homework
3. Students grouped homogeneously
4. Excessive or no purpose for chalkboard work
5. Teacher grading papers while students do homework or students doing homework on own; homework consisting of an excessive number of similar problems
6. Students repeating operations they have mastered
7. Class bogged down on "mastery" of specific operations
8. No diagnostic testing
9. Lack of variety of strategies and class activities
10. Too much or too little [explanation and] demonstration
11. Students not understanding purposes of their homework
12. Rigidity of [student] groupings—no fluidity of movement to allow for weaknesses, strengths, or ability
13. [Lack of] checking for understanding
14. Overemphasis on drill and practice
15. Never any use of [supplementary materials or media]

Source: Tom Maglaras and Deborah Lynch, "Monitoring the Curriculum: From Plan to Action," *Educational Leadership* (October 1988), p. 59.

1. *Intrinsic motivation*. **Intrinsic motivation** involves sustaining or increasing the interest students already have in a topic or task. The teacher selects and organizes the lesson so that it will (a) whet students' appetite at the beginning of the lesson; (b) maintain student curiosity and involvement in the work by using surprise, doubt, and perplexity; novel as well as familiar materials; interesting and varied methods; (c) provide active and manipulative opportunities; (d) permit students autonomy in organizing their time and effort; and (e) provide choices or alternatives to meet requirements of the lesson. Some activities and materials that can be used to enhance intrinsic motivation are:

1. *Challenging statements.* Nuclear power plants are unnecessary and potentially dangerous.
2. *Pictures and cartoons.* How does this picture illustrate the American public's feelings toward Japanese-made automobiles?
3. *Personal experiences.* What type of clothing is best to wear during freezing weather?
4. *Problems.* What metals conduct heat well? Why?
5. *Exploratory and creative activities.* I need three volunteers to come to the chalkboard to fill in the blanks of the puzzle, while the rest of you do it in your seats.
6. *Charts, tables, graphs, maps.* From a study of the chart, what characteristics do all these animals have in common?
7. *Anecdotes and stories.* How does the paragraph I have just read convey the author's feelings about the South?
8. *Contests and games.* Let's see how well you remember yesterday's homework. We will organize five teams by rows. In your notebooks, list eight different string instruments. You will have two minutes. We will average the scores. The winning row, with the highest average score, will receive extra credit.

2. *Extrinsic motivation*. **Extrinsic motivation** focuses on cognitive strategies. Activities that enhance success and reduce failure increase motivation. High-achieving students will persist longer than low-achieving students, even when experiencing failure, so incentives for learning are more important for average- and low-achieving students.[27] They are important for all students when the subject matter or content is uninteresting or difficult.[28]

Nine basic principles can be used by teachers for enhancing extrinsic motivation.

---

27 Franz E. Weinert and Rainer H. Kluwe, *Metacognition, Motivation and Understanding* (Hillsdale, N.J.: Erlbaum, 1986); Raymond J. Wlodkowski and Judith H. James, *Eager to Learn* (San Francisco: Jossey-Bass, 1990).

28 Ellis D. Evans, "The Effects of Achievement Motivation and Ability upon Discovery Learning and Accompanying Incidental Learning under Two Conditions of Incentive Set," *Journal of Educational Research* (January 1967), pp. 195–200; Eva Sivan, "Motivation in Social Constructionist Theory," *Educational Psychologist* (Summer 1986), pp. 209–233.

1. *Clear directions and expectations.* Students must know exactly what they are expected to do and how they will be evaluated.
2. *Time on task.* Keep students on task. The amount of time allocated to a particular topic or task varies considerably from school to school and from teacher to teacher. Time on task, student motivation, and student achievement are related.
3. *Cognitive match.* Student motivation is highest when students work on tasks or problems appropriate to their achievement levels. When they are confused or when the work is above their abilities, they resist or give up. When it is below their abilities, they seek other interests or move through the lesson as fast as possible.
4. *Prompt feedback.* Feedback on student performance should be constructive and prompt. A long delay between behavior (or performance) and results diminishes the relationship between them.
5. *Relate past learning with present learning.* Use reinforcers to strengthen previous learned content.
6. *Frequent rewards.* No matter how powerful a reward, it may have little impact if it is provided infrequently. Small, frequent rewards are more effective than large, infrequent ones.
7. *Praise.* Verbal praise ("Good," "Great," "Fine work") is a powerful motivating device.
8. *High expectations.* Students who are expected to learn will learn more and be motivated to learn more than students who are not expected to learn.
9. *Value of rewards.* Motivation is partially based on the value an individual places on success, as well as the individual's estimate of the possibility of success. Thus, incentives used for students should have value for them.[29]

Development

Lesson development, sometimes called the *outline,* can be expressed as topics and subtopics, a series of broad or pivotal questions, or a list of activities (methods and materials). Most secondary teachers rely on topics or questions, and most elementary teachers refer to activities.

Emphasis on topics, concepts, or skills indicates a content orientation in teaching approach. Emphasis on activities has a more sociopsychological orientation; there is more stress on student needs and interests. For example, outlining the problems of the ozone layer on the chalkboard is content-oriented. Interviewing someone about the ozone layer is an activity that encompasses a wide range of social stimuli.

---

29 N. L. Gage and David C. Berliner, *Educational Psychology,* 4th ed. (Boston: Houghton Mifflin, 1988); Robert E. Slavin, *Educational Psychology: Theory into Practice,* 3rd ed. (Englewood Cliffs, N.J.: Prentice-Hall, 1991); and Merlin C. Wittrock and Eva L. Baker, *Testing and Cognition* (Needham Heights, Mass.: Allyn & Bacon, 1991).

1. *Content.* Several criteria have been proposed for selecting and organizing appropriate content and experiences in the development section. The following are criteria for *content* developed by Ornstein and Hunkins.

1. *Validity.* The content selected should be verifiable, not misleading or false.
2. *Significance.* The content needs to be constantly reviewed so that worthwhile content—basic ideas, information, principles of the subject—is taught, and lessons do not become cluttered by masses of more trivial content now available through the "information explosion."
3. *Balance.* The content should promote macro- and microknowledge; students should experience the broad sweep of content, and they should have the opportunity to dig deep.
4. *Self-sufficiency.* The content should help students learn how to learn; it should help them gain maximum sufficiency in the most economic manner.
5. *Interest.* Content is best learned when it is interesting to the student. Some progressive educators urge that the child should be the focus of the teaching and learning process.
6. *Utility.* The content should be useful or practical in some situation outside the lesson, either to further other learning or in everyday experiences. How usefulness is defined depends on whether a teacher is subject-centered or student-centered, but most teachers would agree that useful content enhances the human potential of the learner.
7. *Learnability.* It should be within the capacity of the students to learn the content. There should be a cognitive match between the students' attitudes and the subject (and between their abilities and academic tasks).
8. *Feasibility.* The teacher needs to consider the time needed, resources and materials available, curriculum guides, state and national tests, existing legislation, and the political climate of the community. There are limitations on what can be planned and taught.[30]

2. *Experiences.* Ronald Doll has raised several questions useful in developing appropriate learning activities, which he refers to as *experiences.* This term connotes a larger concept, including classroom and school activities, as well as out-of-school and community activities.

1. Can the experiences profit the [pupils] we teach?
2. Do the experiences help to meet the needs of our pupils?
3. Are our pupils likely to be interested in the experiences?

---

30 Allan C. Ornstein and Francis P. Hunkins, *Curriculum: Foundations, Principles, and Issues* (Englewood Cliffs, N.J.: Prentice-Hall, 1988).

4. Do the experiences encourage pupils to inquire further?
5. Do the experiences seem real?
6. How do the experiences accord with the life patterns of our pupils?
7. How contemporary are some of the major experiences?
8. How fundamental to mastery of total learning content are they?
9. Do the experiences provide for attainment of a range of objectives?
10. Do the experiences provide opportunities for both broad study and deep study?[31]

Methods

Relying on the same methods day after day would be boring, even for adults. Different procedures sustain motivation throughout the lesson. Although many different procedures can be employed in a lesson, four basic methods are (1) practice and drill, (2) questioning, (3) explanations and lectures, and (4) demonstrations and experiments. Depending on the type of lesson—as well as the students, subject, and grade level—these instructional methods should be used in varying degrees. We have already discussed these methods at length (Chapter 6), but we will review them here in a different mode.

1. *Practice/Drill.* There is general agreement that students need *practice exercises* to help them transfer new information into long-term memory and integrate new and old learning. Practice problems may come from workbooks, textbooks, and teacher-made materials. Practice, in the form of seatwork, can be helpful for students if it is given for limited time periods (no more than ten minutes per class session), the instructions for it are clear, and it is integrated into the lesson (not assigned to fill time or to maintain order). *Drill* can be helpful for basic skills, such as reading, mathematics, and foreign language, and in lower grades and with low-achieving students who need more practice to learn new skills or integrate information.

Robert Slavin is a strong advocate of incorporating practice and drill as a major component of the lesson plan. He recommends six steps for enhancing what he calls *"independent practice."*

1. *Be sure students can do the work.* Do not assign the work until you are sure students understand or can do almost all items on the practice sheet or worksheet. A high success rate on practice items is important for student learning.
2. *Assign short independent practice.* Implement short practice sessions at one sitting; otherwise, the result becomes neutral or negative. (The trouble is that many teachers assign long practice sessions.)
3. *Give clear instructions.* It instructions are unclear, the practice session will be confusing or wasteful. In lower grades, it is sometimes necessary to elaborate on instructions and give examples.

---

31 Doll, *Curriculum Improvement: Decision Making and Process.*

4. *Get students started*. Once students start, it is best to avoid interrupting them. See to it that the students are working before attending to problems of individual students.

5. *Monitor the work*. Circulate around the room to help students or to resolve questions.

6. *Collect and assess work*. A problem with seatwork is that many students see little need to do it since it has no bearing on grades. Students should know that the practice work will be collected and graded; moreover, immediate feedback should be provided.[32]

A short drill provides a quick and efficient way for teachers to check on the effectiveness of instruction before moving to the next stage or level in the lesson. It is well suited for mastery and direct methods of lesson planning, and especially for low-achieving students.[33] Following are some drill techniques that can be used in your lesson planning.

1. Ask pupils to repeat answers.
2. List facts or concepts to be remembered.
3. Identify characteristics or attributes of the content.
4. Review answers to questions.
5. State answers in different ways.
6. Have volunteers answer a number of questions and discuss answers.
7. Give a short quiz and have students grade papers.
8. Assign exercises from the workbook or text.
9. Monitor seatwork and provide immediate feedback.
10. Discuss or review common problems, as revealed by a short quiz or monitoring of the seatwork.

2. *Questioning*. Teachers should include four to six broad *questions* that serve the dual purpose of stimulating discussion among students and outlining the major topics or parts of the lesson. Teachers who emphasize critical thinking or problem solving tend to rely on questions to stimulate the lesson. Such questions should:

1. Be simple and direct.
2. Encourage critical thought.
3. Be aimed at eliciting broad answers, not memory or factual information.

---

32 Slavin, *Educational Psychology: Theory into Teaching*.

33 John V. Hamby, "How to Get an 'A' on Your Dropout Prevention Report Card," *Educational Leadership* (February 1989), pp. 21–28; Gavriel Salomon and David N. Perkins, "Rocky Road to Transfer: Rethinking Mechanisms of a Neglected Phenomenon," *Educational Psychologist* (Spring 1989), pp. 113–142.

4. Be asked in an order that corresponds to the content of the lesson.
5. Build on each other, that is, be sequential.
6. Challenge students, yet not be above the level of the class.
7. Be framed to meet the needs and interests of the students.
8. Vary in difficulty and abstractness to encourage participation by different students.[34]

Good questioning, according to Jerome Bruner, leads to higher modes of learning. In answering a thought-provoking question, a high-achieving student limits it, analyzes parts of it, reformulates it, and decides on the best methods to use for answering.[35] Thought-provoking questions usually ask how and why, not when, where, who, or what, unless introduced by a provocative comment. Questions that call for a yes-or-no answer do not promote discussion or stimulate critical thinking or problem-solving strategies. Examples of thought questions are:

1. The temperature was identical on Thursday and today, yet today we feel warmer. What accounts for this difference?
2. How can we determine whether the author is serious or poking fun?
3. How did the concept of Manifest Destiny lead to our Latin American colonial policy during the nineteenth century?
4. Why are Japan and Korea outproducing Americans in manufacturing goods?

3. *Lectures/Explanations.* Teachers are often required to give *lectures* and *explanations* to emphasize an important point, to fill in content gaps in the workbook or textbook, or to elaborate on a specific content area. Short explanations may be embedded in the lesson plan without writing or noting it.

In planning an explanation or short lecture, the teacher should keep in mind the following characteristics.

I. Continuity
1. *Sequence of discourse.* The lesson should follow a planned sequence, with few diversions or tangential discussions. Explanations should be included at proper places to maintain the sequence of the lesson.
2. *Fluency.* The teacher should speak in clear, concise, complete grammatical sentences.

---

34 J. T. Dillon, *Questioning and Teaching: A Manual of Practice* (New York: Teachers College Press, Columbia University, 1988); Francis P. Hunkins, *Teaching Thinking Through Questioning* (Needham Heights, Mass.: Gordon Publishers, 1989).

35 Jerome S. Bruner, *Toward a Theory of Instruction* (Cambridge, Mass.: Harvard University Press, 1966).

II. Simplicity
1. *Visual aids.* Pictures, tables, charts, models, and computer graphics or videos can be used to enhance verbal explanations.
2. *Vocabulary.* The teacher should use the students' normal vocabulary for effective explanations. Technical or new terms pertaining to the content should be introduced and clearly defined during the explanation.
III. Explicitness
1. *Inclusion of elements.* The major ideas of the lesson should be elaborated with specific descriptions or examples.
2. *Explicit explanations.* Causal and logical relationships should be made explicit.[36]

4. *Demonstrations/Experiments.* Demonstrations and experiments play an important role in *inductive inquiry.* They are ideal for creative and discovery methods of lesson planning, whereby the teacher and students integrate the subject matter by collecting data, observing, measuring, identifying, and examining causal relationships.

Young students and low-achieving students will need more instruction and feedback from the teacher. Older and high-achieving students work more independently and participate more in demonstrations and experiments because they are more able to handle quantities of information, reorganize it into new forms, and transfer it to new learning situations.[37] In either case the recommendations below ensure the effectiveness of the demonstration and experiment.

1. Plan and prepare for the demonstration (or experiment). Make certain that all materials needed are available when you begin. Practice the demonstration (if conducted for the first time) before the lesson to see what problems may arise.
2. Present the demonstration in context with what students have already learned or as a stimulus for searching for new knowledge.
3. Make provisions for full participation of the students.
4. Maintain control over the materials or equipment to the extent the students are unable to work on their own.
5. Pose both close-ended and open-ended questions according to students' capacity for deductive and inductive responses. ("What is

---

36 Elizabeth Perrott, *Effective Teaching: A Practical Guide to Improving Your Teaching* (New York: Longman, 1982).

37 Ruth Gardner and Patricia A. Alexander, "Metacognition: Answered and Unanswered Questions," *Educational Psychologist* (Spring 1989), pp. 143–158; Robert Glaser, "The Reemergence of Learning Theory within Instructional Research," *American Psychologist* (January 1990), pp. 29–39.

happening to the object?" is a close-ended question; "What can you generalize from . . . ?" is open-ended.)

6. Encourage students to ask questions as they arise.
7. Encourage students to make observations first and then to make inferences and generalizations. Encourage them to look for and express new information and insights.
8. Allocate sufficient time so that (a) the demonstration can be completed, (b) students can discuss what they have observed, (c) students can reach conclusions and apply principles they have learned, (d) students can take notes or write up the demonstration, and (e) materials can be collected and stored away.

Materials and Media

Media and materials, sometimes referred to as resources or instructional aids, facilitate understanding and foster learning by clarifying verbal abstractions and arousing interest in the lesson. Many materials and media are available (Table 11.10). The teacher's selection should depend on the objectives and content of the lesson plan; the age, abilities, and interests of the students; the teacher's ability to use the resources; the availability of the materials and equipment; and the classroom time available. The materials and media should be:

1. Accurate and up to date.
2. Large enough to be seen by all the students.
3. Ready for use (check in advance of the lesson).
4. Interesting and varied.
5. Suited for developing the objectives of the lesson.
6. Properly displayed and used throughout the lesson.

Many lessons fail because materials or media that were needed were inadequate, unavailable, or inappropriate for the level of the students. If students need to bring special materials for a task or project, they should be told far in advance so that they may obtain them. The teacher should be sure that necessary equipment is available, scheduled in advance, set up on the appropriate day, and in working order.

Summaries

Teachers cannot assume that learning is taking place in the class as a whole (or even with the majority) just because some students give correct answers to their questions or because they have presented well-organized explanations and demonstrations. Some students may have been daydreaming or even confused while other students answered questions and while the demonstrations took place. To ensure understanding of the lesson and to determine whether the objectives of the lesson have been achieved, teachers should include one or more summaries.

Table 11.10   MATERIALS AND MEDIA FOR LESSON PLAN USE

Input suggestions			Output suggestions		
View/ Observe	Read	Listen	Make/ Construct	Verbalize	Write
Visuals	*Materials*	*Media*	*Materials*	*Verbalizations*	*Written*
Bulletin boards	Books	Radio	Dioramas	Oral reports	*Performance*
Banners	Comic books	Records	Collages	Panels	Themes
Posters	Pamphlets	TV	Scrolls	Debates	Research
Transparencies	Posters		Sand -	Discussions	papers
Slides	Newspapers	*Verbalizations*	paintings	Brainstorming	Reports
Films/filmstrips	Bulletin boards	Speeches	Diaries	Oral ques-	Workbook
Flashcards	Flashcards	Lectures	Pictographs	tions and	answers
TV	Reports	Debates	Maps	answers	Blackboard
Graphs	Wall graffiti	Discussions	Models		problems
	Letters	Dramatic/	Timelines	*Solve*	Poems,
Community		interpretive	Paintings	Puzzles	essays, etc.
Events	*Smell/Taste/Touch*	readings	Food	Mazes	
Field trips	Objects	Interviews	Clothing	Problems	*Perform*
Dramatic	Textures		Bulletin boards	Equations	Simulations
presentations	Food	*Try/Do/Use*	Banners	Games	Role plays
	Temperatures	Games	Graphs	Riddles	Sociodramas
	Chemicals	Experiments	Word wall		Concerts
		Exercises	Drawings		Pantomimes
		Manipulative			Interpretive
		materials	*Presentations*		readings
			Films		Dramas
			Filmstrips		
			Tapes		

Source: Carol Barber, *Mastery Learning Training Manual* (Price, Utah: Southeastern Education Service Center, 1985), p. 1.

There should be a short *review* of each lesson in which the lesson as a whole and important or confusing parts are summarized. A short review can take the There should be a short *review* of each lesson in which the lesson as a whole and important or confusing parts are summarized. A short review can take the following forms:

1. Pose several thought-provoking questions that summarize previous learning (or previous day's homework).
2. Ask for a comparison of what has already been learned with what is being learned.
3. Ask a student to summarize the main ideas of the lesson. Have other students make modifications and additions.
4. Assign review questions (on the chalkboard or in the workbook or textbook).
5. Administer a short quiz.

During the lesson at some point when a major concept or idea has been examined, it is advisable to present a **medial summary**—a series of pivotal questions or a problem that will bring together the information that has been discussed. Medial summaries slow down the lesson; however, they are important for low-achieving and young students who need more time to comprehend new information and more links with prior knowledge. A **final summary** is needed to clinch the basic ideas or concepts of the lesson. If you realize that it is impossible to teach all you planned, then end the lesson at some logical point and provide a summary of the content you have covered. Each lesson should be concluded by a summary activity, not by the bell.

Following are *chalkboard activities* that can be used as summaries.

1. Refer to the outline on the chalkboard that has been developed during the lesson. Erase all but the headings. Have students supply the details.
2. Ask two or three students to go to the chalkboard and have them list or identify people, places, or outcomes.
3. Ask two or three students to go to the chalkboard and have them each solve a problem that reviews what has been learned. Discuss steps of the problem.

Following are types of *thought questions* that can be used as summaries.

1. Who can review the four steps in . . . ?
2. Who can solve the following problem: . . . ?
3. In light of what we have learned, who can describe the best method for . . . ?
4. Based on what we have learned, who can discuss the causes for . . . ?
5. Would you recommend this story to others? Why? Why not?
6. What would happen if . . . ?

The following *activities* are suited for summaries.

1. Ask students to interpret a cartoon, map, or model related to the lesson.
2. Ask students to draw a diagram or chart labeling the major parts or areas that have been discussed.
3. Have one or two students give a short oral report.
4. Have a few students debate the issues or conclusions.
5. Have students make predictions based on the data or problems that have been discussed.

Assignments

The work that students are requested to do at home should furnish them with the content (knowledge, skills, and tasks) needed to participate in the next day's lesson. Following are some characteristics of effective assignments.

1. The homework should be interesting.
2. Attention should be directed to definite concepts or problems.

3. Questions should be framed so as to provide background information necessary to answer the teacher's questions on the following day.

4. Homework should periodically incorporate previously taught content to reinforce learning.

5. The assignment should provide opportunities for students to grow in written (or symbolic) expression, reading, or important skills related to the subject.

6. Provision should be made for individual differences. There should be minimum assignments for all students with enrichment levels for high-achieving students.

7. The new assignment can be copied or given at the beginning or end of the period, but any discussion should be at the end and grow out of the lesson in a logical manner.

8. Homework should be explained, and practice or examples given if necessary. Problems that may arise when doing the homework should be briefly examined in class at the end of the period.

9. Assignments should not be dictated, because of the time dictation takes and the errors students make in recording oral assignments. Either the homework should be written on and copied from the chalkboard at the beginning of the period while the teacher engages in administrative or clerical tasks, or it should be duplicated and handed out on a weekly basis (for middle-grade students) or monthly basis (for high school students).

10. The length of the assignment will vary by grade level and subject. It is generally thought that homework in grades 1 to 3 should not exceed 15 to 30 minutes per day; grades 4 to 6, 45 minutes, grades 7 to 9, 20 to 30 minutes per subject, and grades 10 to 12, 30 to 45 minutes per subject. Lengthy assignments discourage students, especially slow students, and create anxiety and stress.

11. For variety, assignments might include: (a) notebook and textbook assignments, (b) working on projects, (c) writing letters, articles, or reports, (d) analyzing television programs, (e) reading related books and articles, (f) interviewing people and visiting places in the community, and (g) conducting or summarizing an experiment or being involved in a hands-on activity.

12. Homework should be monitored for completion and accuracy, and students should receive timely, specific, and constructive feedback. Where performance is poor, teachers should provide not only feedback and additional time for review, but also additional assignments designed to ensure mastery of content.

13. It is important for the school to have a coordinated homework/tutoring program for students who need assistance—and the assistance should be provided on a daily basis, if necessary. Provisions must be made for students who do not understand the daily assignment;

otherwise frustration and lack of interest take over and interfere with learning.

SAMPLE LESSON PLANS

Five sample lesson plans are included to illustrate how the various components of the lesson can be used. Explanations accompanying each plan give some sense of what the teacher is trying to achieve. The lesson plans are written for different grade levels and subjects, but the lesson types can be used for all students regardless of age, ability, or subject matter.

The first three samples are lesson plans for structured approaches. The remaining two are plans for more divergent and flexible approaches. The words in italics coincide with the previously discussed components of a lesson plan.

Flexible Grouping Lesson Plan (Table 11.11)

1. *The lesson topic* is derived from the unit plan on vocabulary.
2. The *primary objective* is to teach the meaning of 10 new words. The two *secondary objectives* accomplish the primary objective and enhance dictionary and writing skills.
3. The teacher immediately starts the lesson with a *review* of the previous homework. The class as a whole discusses the homework.
4. Only *materials* specific to the lesson are noted in the lesson plan.
5. The teacher uses the term *activities* to organize the development or outline, since the focus of attention is on classroom activities.
6. The class is divided into *two groups* for the activities. Group I is slower or lower achieving than Group II.
7. Both groups do similar *seatwork*. Group I is given the extra step of alphabetizing for extra practice in the process. Group II understands the need for alphabetical order in searching through the dictionary, so this step is omitted. Group II is given another, more difficult task of dividing words into syllables to make up for the one task that was omitted. The teacher monitors the seatwork of the students and helps anyone with individual problems.
8. After seatwork, the two groups engage in different activities. The teacher works with one group while the other is involved in independent work. For Group I the teacher provides a *medial summary* for feedback, review, and assessment. (Prompt and varied feedback and review are needed for the slower group.) Group II engages in *independent work*, having selected their own books to read for enjoyment. The teacher then works with Group II in a *summary* activity, connecting the original objective with the students' independent work, while Group I does its independent assignment. Group I has 5 minutes less independent work and 5 minutes more teacher-directed summary work because these students need more teacher time, are less able to

Table 11.11   FLEXIBLE GROUPING LESSON PLAN

Grade: 6–8

Lesson Topic: Vocabulary

Objective: To define 10 new words

1. To deduce the meaning of the words using a dictionary

2. To write the meaning of the new words in a sentence

Review: Both groups (10 minutes)

1. Correct homework, workbook, pp. 36–39

2. Focus on questions, p. 39

Materials: Dictionaries, logs, supplementary books

Development:

Group I: Activities	Group II: Activities
Seatwork (15 minutes)	Seatwork (15 minutes)
1. Alphabetize the following 10 words: explicit, implicit, appropriate, inappropriate, potential, encounter, diminish, enhance, master, alligator. 2. Find each new word in the dictionary. 3. Write a definition for each new word.	1. Find each of the following 10 words in the dictionary: explicit, implicit, appropriate, inappropriate, potential, encounter, diminish, enhance, master, alligator (same words for both groups). 2. Write a definition for each new word. 3. Divide each new word into syllables.
Medial summary (15 minutes) 1. Teach new words; students give examples and discuss meaning of new words.	Independent work (15 minutes) 1. Continue reading supplementary books. 2. Underline at least five new words in the pages you read. 3. Find their meaning in the dictionary.
Independent work: (10 minutes) 1. Get up to date with logs. 2. Include at least 5 new words in logs.	Final summary (10 minutes) 1. Discuss the 10 assigned words and the words students have chosen in their independent reading.

Homework: Both groups
1. Continue with logs.
2. Write each new word in an original sentence.

---

work independently of the teacher, and are likely to have more problems that need to be discussed.

9. The whole class receives the same *homework* assignment. Group I is permitted to start the homework in class so the assignment at home does not overwhelm them. The lesson for the day is integrated into the homework in both the logs and the writing assignment.

Thinking Skills Lesson Plan (Table 11.12)

1. The *lesson topic* can be part of a separate unit on critical thinking skills, or it can serve as an introductory lesson for a unit in almost any subject.

Table 11.12   THINKING SKILLS LESSON PLAN

Grade: 6–12
Lesson Topic: Classifying information
Objective: To arrange information into groups on the basis of similar or common attributes
Motivation:
1. Why should we learn to classify information into categories or groups?
2. Into what groups would you classify the following information: Kennedy, table, elephant, Lincoln, Roosevelt, Chicago, Nixon, Boston, Bush, donkey and San Francisco?

Development:	Pivotal Questions
1. Procedures. Discuss at least three reasons for classifying information.	1a. When do you classify information? Why? 1b. What happens to information that is not organized? Why?
2. Skim text (pp. 48–55) to get an idea of important items or ideas that might be classified.	
3. Agree on categories (groups or labels) to be used in classifying information in text.	3a. What advantages are there to the categories? 3b. What are their unifying attributes? 3c. What other categories could we have used? Explain.
4. Focus on three practice items in the text and agree on related categories for purpose of ensuring understanding.	
5. Read carefully the same pages and place selected items into appropriate categories.	5. Why raise your hand if you are stuck on a particular item?
6. Discuss similar or common attributes.	6a. Why did you identify these items with those categories? 6b. Why did you choose these common attributes as a category to classify the items? 6c. What other common attributes might you have chosen?
7. Modify (change, subtract, or add) categories, if necessary.	7a. Why did you change these categories? 7b. What can we do with the items that fit into more than one category? Which items fit into more than one category?
8. Repeat procedures using other important items; read pp. 56–63.	8. What categories did you select? Why?
9. Combine categories or subdivide into smaller categories.	9a. Why did you reclassify (add or subdivide) these categories? 9b. What should we do with the leftover items? Which ones are left over?

Summary:
1. What important things have you learned about classifying information?
2. What are different ways of classifying information?
3. When is it appropriate to subdivide categories?
4. Look at the chalkboard (text). Who wishes to categorize these five new items into one of the categories we have already established?

Homework:
1. Read Chapter 7.

2. There is only one *objective*. It pertains to classifying—a critical thinking skill.

3. The *motivation* assumes a certain amount of abstract thinking on the part of the students. It is verbal as opposed to visual or auditory. The first question is divergent and provocative. The second question is more convergent and focused. The short exercise provides students with a challenge, introduces them to the main part of the lesson, and shows how they handle certain information before the lesson. Some words (*elephant, donkey, Lincoln*, etc.) can be categorized into various groups, and *table* does not belong in any category. (It serves as irrelevant information to see how students handle it.)

4. The *development* is a set of *procedures* or operations to teach students how to classify information. The *pivotal questions* are to be introduced at different stages of the lesson. They stimulate discussion, clarify points, and check understanding. They are divergent in nature and provide students with latitude in the way they can answer; the teacher must listen carefully to the responses, since the answers are not necessarily right or wrong, but involve, in part, viewpoints and subjectivity.

5. The *summary* is a series of important or key questions that lead to a discussion and elaboration of what has been taught. The length of the summary discussion is based on the time permitted. Question 1 is vague, and students may not respond, or may respond in a way that the teacher does not expect. Questions 2 and 3 are more focused. Question 4 leads to a good overview and reinforcement exercise. (The teacher may or may not have time to use it.)

6. The homework is based on the lesson and leads to the next step or slightly more advanced aspect of classifying.

Mastery Learning Lesson Plan (Table 11.13)

1. Fractions as a *lesson topic* are introduced in the seventh grade in most school districts and continued in the eighth grade.

2. The *objective* is written in terms of a performance level.

3. Mastery learning lessons entail a good deal of *review*.

4. The *motivation* is in the form of two separate problems that involve real-life experiences in another subject—art.

5. Only unusual *materials* are listed. Empty tubes are used to avoid potential clean-up problems. Other items easy to count can be used in lieu of paint tubes.

6. The *development* is in the form of problems and related activities. The problems, like fractions and mixed numbers, coincide with the worksheet the students are up to. The teacher explains each problem and then introduces the related activities. While students work on the activities, the teacher moves around the room and monitors their work. The problems get progressively more difficult. Each item that

Table 11.13 MASTERY LEARNING PLAN

Grade: 7–8

Lesson Topic: Fractions

Objective: Students will perform the worksheet items on fractions (worksheet 12), with at least 80 percent accuracy after the lesson

Review: Review yesterday's homework on fractions

Motivation:

1. Joel used several tubes of paint to illustrate a landscape: $\frac{1}{3}$ tube of white paint, $\frac{1}{3}$ tube of yellow paint, and $\frac{2}{3}$ tube of blue paint. How many tubes of paint did he use in all?

2. Stacey painted a more detailed landscape. She used $1\frac{1}{4}$ tubes of green paint, $1\frac{3}{4}$ yellow tubes, and $2\frac{1}{4}$ blue tubes. How many tubes did she use in all?

Materials: Overhead projector, empty tubes of paint

Development:

Problems	Activities
1a. With overhead projector explain how to solve first problem: $\frac{1}{3} + \frac{1}{3} + \frac{2}{3} = n$	1a. At their desks students solve 5 problems (adding and subtracting *like fractions*) in workbook.
1b. Have all students together solve a similar problem: $\frac{1}{6} + \frac{3}{6} + \frac{4}{6} = n$	1b. Students are to write sum in lowest terms.
	1c. Students record work (and answers) in their notebook.
	1d. Discuss all items missed by more than 10 percent of the students.
2a. With overhead project explain how to solve second problem: $1\frac{1}{4} + 1\frac{3}{4} + 2\frac{1}{4} = n$	2a. At their desks students solve 5 problems (adding and subtracting *mixed numbers)* in workbook.
2b. Have all students together solve a similar problem: $3\frac{1}{3} + 4\frac{2}{3} + 1\frac{1}{3} = n$	2b. Repeat 1b.
	2c. Repeat 1c.
	2d. Repeat 1d.

Practice:

1. Hand out worksheet 12.

2. Call on volunteer to do first sample item in worksheet.

3. Call on second and third volunteers to do next two sample items.

4. Have students complete remaining worksheet on their own at their own pace.

Summary (Evaluation):

1. With overhead projector show correct answers for all the items.

2. Ask students how many got each item right.

3. Discuss all the items, but emphasize items that 20 percent or more missed.

4. Have students score their own papers and turn them in.

Homework:

1. Distribute homework or explain new worksheet that is to be answered (*unlike fractions*).

2. Review assignment next day.

3. Reteach problem items (items that 20 percent or more missed during previous lesson).

is missed by even a small percentage of students must be further explained, since the work builds on previous learning.

7. The teacher provides additional *practice* before asking students to complete the worksheet on their own. Only volunteers are called on because the work is new. Three items are explained. The teacher moves around the room monitoring the students' work and providing additional help when necessary.

8. As a *summary* all items are discussed. All items missed by students, especially those that are missed by 20 percent or more, are discussed in greater detail. Individuals' scores on the worksheet determine how much practice is needed the next day in the form of review.

9. The *homework* is related to the lesson; it is assigned and explained. The next day it will be reviewed.

Inquiry-Discovery Lesson Plan (Table 11.14)

1. The *lesson topic* is derived from the unit on energy and environment.
2. The two *objectives* are written as questions to stimulate curiosity and indicate problems students are to solve.
3. The *materials* needed are supplementary readings that examine efficiency and cost of various forms of insulation.
4. The *development* of the lesson consists of two sections corresponding to the two objectives. Each section contains a problem and related problems. The problems serve as motivating devices, since students are challenged to investigate answers and make decisions about ranking. Thus the component on motivation is unnecessary.
5. Each problem includes a *medial summary*; a student works out a problem at the chalkboard while the other students do the same at their seats. The whole class discusses the problems during the *medial summaries*, which replace the usual final summary. The *related problems* are written as statements, but could be rewritten as *questions* ("What is the cost for each insulating item?"). The time devoted to the related problems will depend on the time required for students to work out the two major problems and discuss them in the medial summaries.
6. The *homework* is a series of investigative activities. These activities set the stage for another set of related problems to be worked out in class the next day.

Creativity Lesson Plan (Table 11.15)

1. The *lesson topic* provides an opportunity for students to create or develop their own project, based on key geographical terms they have learned.
2. The *objectives* focus on understanding terms that describe and distinguish special features considered essential to geographic education.

Table 11.14   INQUIRY-DISCOVERY LESSON PLAN

Grades: 9–12

Lesson Topic: Energy conservation

1. How can (heating) energy be conserved at home?

2. How can (gasoline) energy be saved in driving?

Materials: Supplementary readings on insulation

Development:

Conserving Energy in Home Heating

1. Problem: Investigate the best ways to save energy in the house, and rank them. Assume a 1,200–foot house, no insulation in ceiling or walls, no storm windows (15 windows), and poor weatherstripping around windows and doors (2 doors).

Rank	Item	Gallons of oil saved (average temperature 30°F over 8 months)
2	Add storm windows	290
1	Add 2 inches of fiberglass insulation to ceiling	1,044
4	Close drapes	58
3	Renew weatherstripping	203

2. Medial summary: Discuss reasons for ranking and best insulators.

3. Related problems (questions): (a) Discuss costs for each insulating item. (b) Compare the cost and energy saved. (c) Determine payback period.

Conserving Gasoline in Driving

1. Problem: Investigate the best ways to save energy while driving and assume a car that gets 10 miles per gallon (mpg) and is driven 15,000 miles per year.

Rank	Item	Gallons of gas saved
4	Drive only 12,000 miles	300
2	Buy a compact car (30 mpg) and drive 15,000 miles	1,000
1	Buy a compact car (30 mpg) and drive 12,000 miles	1,100
3	Buy a standard car (20 mpg) and drive 15,000 miles	750

2. Medial summary: Investigate actual savings for each item by assuming the cost of gasoline at $1.25 per gallon.

3. Related problems (questions): (a) Discuss factors influencing energy used—amount of driving, driving speed (wind resistance), efficiency of car. (b) Discuss need to travel less than 55 mph. (c) Discuss ways to improve efficiency of car.

Homework:

1. Select 10 electrical appliances at home.

2. Determine wattage for each appliance.

3. Determine annual usage of each appliance (consult with parents).

4. Be prepared to discuss the wattage and kilowatt use of your appliances.

Source: The two tables on oil and gas are adapted from Alfred E. Friedl, *Teaching Science to Children: An Integrated Approach* (New York: Random House, 1986), pp. 298–299; the other components are the author's ideas.

Table 11.15   CREATIVITY LESSON PLAN

Grade: 6–12

Lesson Topic: Creating an island

Objectives:

1. To understand that all places on earth have special features that distinguish them from other places
2. To become familiar with terms that identify landforms and bodies of water
3. To apply terms for geographical landforms and bodies of water to an original student project

Review/Introductory Activity (10 minutes):

1. Students use atlases and maps to review land and water terms.
2. Students create a glossary of important geographical land and water terms in the form of a three-column chart giving terms (basin, bay, canyon, cape, cove, delta, gulf, hill, inlet, island, lake, mountain, peninsula, plateau, river, sea, valley), definitions, and examples (Florida is a peninsula).

Materials: Atlases, wall maps, textbooks, glossary, large pieces of drawing paper or poster board, felt tip pens or markers

Development (Activities):

1. The class is divided into groups of four (or five). Group members are to work cooperatively to plan and draw an imaginary island.
2. Each island should feature at least 10 (or 15 depending on grade level and previous related lessons) of the following geographical forms: basin, bay, canyon, cape, cove, etc.
3. Students are to give all features on the island names of their choice. The names are to be related to one theme, for example, Computer Island, Bytes Bay, and Microchip Mountain.
4. Students who finish early are to include map features (depending on the grade level) such as latitude, longitude, elevation key, scale.

Summary (10–15 minutes):

1. Each group shows its completed map to the class. Students discuss each group's portrayal of the geographical terms.
2. If time permits, students are to place five cities on each island and discuss the locations of cities, reasons for their choice, best locations.

Homework:

1. Determine the island's climate and natural resources based on latitude and longitude coordinates given by the teacher.
2. Discuss where most of the island's population would most likely live, given the island's configuration and natural resources.
3. Discuss possible environmental problems that might develop as a result of using the available resources (only for upper grade levels).
4. Discuss possible trade problems that might develop as a result of using available resources (only for upper grade levels).

Source: Adapted from "Geography Lesson Plan," *National Geographical Society Update* (Fall 1987), pp. 9–10. The basic ideas have been restructured to coincide with the author's lesson plan components.

Students move from understanding geographical concepts to applying them in class.

3. The *review* component of the lesson may also be considered an introductory activity. The activity provides background information for the main part or development of the lesson.

4. Different *materials* are displayed, available for research, and distributed to students for use.

5. The *development* employs cooperative learning. Rules in working together need to be briefly discussed. The number of land and water terms should depend on the students' grade level. The naming of features on the island can be optional, based on time considerations, but it provides a way of relating the content of the lesson to the experiences of the students.

6. The *summary* component is achieved in part through cooperative learning as students discuss the groups' projects. Provision is made for supplementary discussion and review of hypothetical cities if the lesson is finished with time remaining. This activity can also be assigned as part of the homework.

7. The *homework* is an extension of the class activity. It tests further understanding of the subject and critical thinking. The last two homework problems are geared for advanced students.

Guidelines for Implementing Lesson Plans

You will need to consider several factors as you begin to move from planning to performance. Even after you have had some experience, it is wise to review the following factors to ensure your success in the execution of the lesson plan: student differences, length of period, flexibility, student participation, student understanding, and evaluation.

1. *Student Differences.* Individual and group differences must be considered as you plan your lesson and then teach it. Teachers need to make provisions for student differences in ability, age, background, and reading level.

2. *Length of Period.* One of the major problems beginning teachers have is planning a lesson that will coincide with time allotted (the 30, 40, or 50 minutes of each period). New teachers must learn to pace themselves, not to plan too much (and have to end abruptly) or too little (and have nothing planned for the last 5 to 10 minutes of the period).

If during a lesson a teacher realizes too little has been planned, he or she can:

1. Pose additional questions to explore various facets of the content.
2. Drill the students on the major points of the lesson.

3. Set up a short panel in which students take a position on the issues or topics discussed.
4. Spend additional time on the new assignment, discussing problems that may arise and going over sample questions.

If during a lesson the teacher realizes too much has been planned, he or she should:

1. Select a major subheading or breakpoint in the development to end the lesson.
2. End the lesson with a brief summary.
3. Conclude the lesson the next day by including in the new lesson the content that was not covered the previous period.

3. *Flexibility.* The teacher must be flexible, that is, prepared to develop a lesson along a path different from the one set down in the plan. Student reactions may make it necessary or desirable to elaborate on something included in the plan, or to pursue something that arises as the lesson proceeds. Although effective teachers tend to encourage on-task behavior and discourage off-task behavior, they are willing to make corrections and take advantage of unforeseen developments. The basis for the change is more intuitive than objective, more unplanned than preplanned.

4. *Student Participation.* Teachers must encourage the participation of the greatest number of students in each lesson. They should not permit a few students to dominate the lesson and should draw nonvolunteers into the lesson. They should not talk too much or dominate the lesson with teacher-directed activities. The need is to encourage student participation, student-to-student interaction, and increased performance among shy students, low-achieving students, and students on the sides and in the rear rows (as opposed to students in the middle or front of the room).

5. *Student Understanding.* There is often a gap between what students understand and what teachers think they understand. Part of the reason for this gap has to do with the rapidity of the teaching process—so much happens at once that the teacher is unaware of everything that goes on in the classroom. Following are suggestions to increase student understanding as you teach the lesson.

1. Insist that students respond to the questions put to them. Students who do not know answers or have trouble in understanding the lesson tend to mumble or speak too quietly to be heard clearly, try to change the subject, or ask another question instead of responding to the original question. These are some of the strategies students adopt to outwit teachers.

2. If a student answer lacks detail, does not cover the major aspects of the problem, or is partially or totally incorrect, (a) probe the student by rephrasing or simplifying the question, using another question to lead the student toward the desired answer, or providing additional information, or (b) call on another student to help the first student.

3. If, after calling on a few students, you are unable to obtain the desired response, you may have to reteach parts of the lesson. Although this is not planned, you cannot ignore that several students are having problems understanding the lesson.

4. Prepare students for demonstrations and experiments, ask questions during these activities, and follow up with written exercises in which students analyze or synthesize what they observed or performed.

5. Include practice, review, or applications in every lesson. The amount of time you spend on these activities will depend on the students' abilities. Low-achieving and younger students need more practice, review, and concrete application.

6. Be sure to include medial and final summaries. Low-achieving and younger students need more medial summaries than high-achieving students.

6. *Evaluation.* The lesson plan must be evaluated so that it can be modified and improved. At the end of a lesson, the teacher should have a clear idea about how the students reacted and whether they understood and enjoyed the lesson. To appraise your lesson plan, ask yourself the following questions.

1. Was the instruction congruent with the objectives?
2. Were the students motivated throughout the lesson?
3. What parts of the lesson were boring, confusing, or inappropriate? How can these parts be improved?
4. Do I need to spend more time reviewing parts of the lesson?
5. Were the questions appropriate? Which ones came up that were not planned and can be used in the future?
6. What problems arose? How can I correct them?
7. What other activities can be used to improve the planning?
8. Was there sufficient time to complete the lesson?
9. What did I fail to accomplish in the lesson?
10. Should certain parts of the lesson be omitted, condensed, or elaborated on?

A good teacher, no matter how experienced, is a critic of his or her lesson plan and seeks new ways for improving the teaching-learning situation. The teacher is aware of what is happening during the lesson and intuitively judges what is worthwhile and what needs to be modified for the next time the lesson plan is used. See Tips for Teachers 11.4.

Tips for Teachers 11.4

Organizing and Implementing Lesson Plans: A Checklist

The teacher should always look for ways to improve the lesson plan. Below are 25 research-based tips that correlate with student achievement; as many as possible (not necessarily all in one lesson) should be incorporated into portions of the lesson plan. Although most of the statements seem to be based on a mastery approach, the checklist can be used for most types of teaching.

1. Plan lesson toward stated objectives or topics of the unit plan.
2. Require academic focus of students.
3. Follow the plan. Keep to a schedule, start the lesson on time, and be aware of the time.
4. Provide a review of previous lesson or integrate previous lesson with new lesson.
5. Indicate to students the objectives of the lesson; explain what is to be accomplished.
6. Utilize whole groups and small groups and independent study.
7. Present lesson with enthusiasm; motivate students.
8. Present lesson at appropriate pace, not too slow or too fast.
9. Explain things clearly. Be sure students understand what to do and how to do it.
10. Give students a chance to think about what is being taught.
11. Try to find out when students don't understand.
12. Provide sufficient time for practice.
13. Ask frequent questions; be sure they are challenging and relevant.
14. Answer student questions or have other students answer them.
15. Provide explanations, demonstrations, or experiments.
16. Elaborate on difficult points of the lesson; give details, provide examples.
17. Show how students are to do classwork.
18. Choose activities that are interesting and promote success.
19. Make smooth transitions between activities.
20. Incorporate supplementary materials and media.
21. Summarize the lesson.
22. Schedule seatwork; monitor and assess student work.
23. Give homework, provide examples of how to do homework, and collect and check homework.
24. Evaluate lesson plan after teaching.

continues

25. Be open to feedback and modification; listen to students, colleagues, supervisors, and other observers.

Source: Adapted from James H. Block, Helene E. Efthim, and Robert B. Burns, *Building Effective Mastery Learning Schools* (White Plains, N.Y.: Longman, 1989); Carolyn M. Evertson et al., *Classroom Management for Elementary Teachers*, 2nd ed. (Englewood Cliffs, N.J.: Prentice-Hall, 1989).

SUMMARY

1. Teachers plan at five different levels: yearly, term, unit, weekly, and daily.
2. Mapping takes place at different subject and grade levels; it helps clarify what content, skills, and values you wish to teach.
3. Science-Technology-Society planning emphasizes problems with local interest and actively involves students beyond traditional textbook and classroom learning experiences.
4. The basic components of a unit plan are objectives, content, skills, activities, resources, and evaluation.
5. Three types of unit plans are the behavioral approach, topic approach, and activities approach.
6. The basic components of a lesson plan are objectives, motivation, development, methods, materials and media, summaries, and homework.
7. Five lesson plans were discussed: flexible grouping, thinking skills, mastery learning, inquiry-discovery, and creativity.

CASE STUDY

Problem

A ninth-year teacher had difficulty constructing units and lesson plans. She felt obligated to deal with every skill, concept, and learning activity in the district's manual and in the list of objectives from the text. In an attempt to cover everything, little opportunity was provided for review or questions. Students learned superficially, forgot easily, and were generally confused. A colleague who had been in the Air Force's Academic Instructors' School showed her how he was taught to deal with information overload.

Suggestion

He told her everything cannot be equally important. Some things are more critical to the students than others. Topics can be divided into three categories: *Must Knows* (MK), *Should Knows* (SK), and *Nice to Knows* (NTK). "Must knows" are what the teacher decides are (1) necessary for *basic success* in the subject and (2) must be *mastered before progressing* to succeeding steps or concepts. "Should knows" are not as critical as MKs, and are covered as *examples*, levels of *enrichment*, or *addendums* to the MKs. "Nice to knows" are all *enrichment* or *extensions* of the SKs, such as interest centers, reports, guests. The *teacher* determines which objectives go into which category.

The MKs are taught to the full class in whole-group instruction. When the teacher is satisfied that the class has mastered the MKs, the students can extend the concepts or skills to the SKs. In other words, the SKs become MKs for students. NTKs can remain as is since they are not critical at this stage in the students' schooling and *will probably be covered as MKs as they progress through school.*

Using these categories, and this progression, relieves the teacher from the pressure of feeling students must have complete mastery of every topic or skill, and it also allows realistic planning for individual differences.

Discussion Suggestion

A principal found almost every new teacher had difficulty developing scope and sequence in planning, getting ideas for lesson materials, deciding which part of the subject matter was most important and how to make it interesting once it was decided. They had methods skills, but they had difficulty providing a structure within which to implement these skills.

A major part of the problem was their use of the university model for teaching. They first turned to their university texts for information, along with the students' texts, as well as getting topical books from the libraries. Surrounded by this plethora of information, they spent hours trying to prepare a cohesive, sustained, and patterned series of lessons with internal consistency.

The principal suggested they not start with the adult books, with their disparate organization, but start with students' books (*not texts*) from the students' section of the library. These authors have already ordered the topic in sequence and scope, logically and clearly. Professional illustrators have planned the illustrations placed at critical points for maximum impact. The books offer suggestions for developing teaching bulletin boards. Frequently, the teacher can find a whole unit already developed, with individual chapters, or portions of chapters, suggesting daily lessons.

The principal suggested the following sequence: (1) first use a good encyclopedia to get a firm background, (2) use the students' books to develop sequence and scope, (3) use the text to shape specifics, (4) use the college texts last to choose interesting "filler" information.

Discussion Questions

1. Choose a topic from a text used in your school or a methods class. See if you can establish the Must Knows for your teaching. How would you plan to cover the Should Knows and Nice to Knows both while you are concentrating on the Must Knows and after most of the class has succeeded in them?
2. What might the evaluation problems be when using the MK, NTK, and SK system? Those who have used the system claim evaluation is actually simple and more fair than evaluating across the whole spectrum of learning. Why might that be?
3. Is the use of students' material in instructional planning a lazy way of planning and possibly cheating the students? Why? Why not?
4. Ask the opinions of different methods instructors at your college, cooperating and supporting teacher, and experienced teachers about their ideas of using students' materials. Then go to the students' section and check out some of the materials to see how you might use them. Then see if you agree or disagree with those with whom you've spoken.
5. How would you define and sequent in planning?

QUESTIONS TO CONSIDER

1. Why do educators advise planning in cooperation with students? Why do many teachers ignore student input when planning?
2. What are the criteria for a good unit plan?
3. According to what approach do you think a unit for your subject or grade could best be planned? Why?
4. Which are the most essential components to consider when planning a lesson? Why?
5. Which instructional methods do you plan to stress in your lesson plans? Why?

THINGS TO DO

1. Prepare a map or course of study for your subject and grade level.
2. Speak to an experienced teacher. Ask the teacher to provide you with a series of unit plans for the subject or grade level you plan to teach. Examine the major components in class.
3. Select one of the above units and list the activities and resources that could be incorporated into it.
4. Plan a lesson in your subject and grade level; then teach it according to the specifications listed. What were the good parts of the lesson? What were the unsatisfactory parts?

5. List some common mistakes in lesson planning. Ask experienced teachers: What are ways to prevent some of these mistakes?

RECOMMENDED READINGS

Beyer, Barry K. *Teaching Thinking Skills*. Needham Heights, Mass.: Allyn & Bacon, 1991. How thinking skills can be planned and taught in most secondary classrooms, including sample exercises and lesson plans.

Block, James H., Helene E. Efthim, and Robert B. Burns. *Building Effective Mastery Learning Schools*. White Plains, N.Y.: Longman, 1989. A mastery approach to teaching and learning, including how to plan unit plans and lesson plans for mastery.

Gagné, Robert M., Leslie J. Briggs, and Walter W. Wager. *Principles of Instructional Design*, 3rd ed. New York: Holt, Rinehart & Winston, 1988. Methods and steps in planning for instruction, starting with performance objectives and ending with student performance.

Good, Thomas L. and Jere E. Brophy. *Looking in Classrooms*, 5th ed. New York: Harper-Collins, 1991. A research-oriented book on several aspects of teaching including lesson planning.

Grambs, Jean D. and John C. Carr. *Modern Methods in Secondary Education*, 5th ed. New York: Holt, Rinehart & Winston, 1991. Varied teaching methods with emphasis on unit and lesson planning.

Kindsvatter, Richard, William Wilen, and Margaret Ishler. *Dynamics of Effective Teaching*. White Plains, N.Y.: Longman, 1988. An up-to-date introduction to the principles of classroom instruction and planning, with numerous instruments for evaluating instruction and planning.

Posner, George J. and Alan N. Rudnitsky. *Course Design: A Guide to Curriculum Development for Teachers*, 3rd ed. White Plains, N.Y.: Longman, 1986. Numerous examples of course planning, unit planning, and lesson planning.

KEY TERMS

Mental planning	Teaching functions
Formal planning	Intrinsic motivation
Mapping	Extrinsic motivation
Science-Technology-Society	Lesson Development
Unit plan	Medial summary
Lesson plan	Final summary

Teacher Professionalism

The Effective Teacher

FOCUSING QUESTIONS

1. Do teachers have an effect on student outcomes?

2. What is the difference between teacher processes and teacher products?

3. Are different teacher strategies effective with different types of students?

4. How can the interaction between the teacher and the students in the classroom be measured?

5. What are the characteristics of a good teacher?

6. What is the difference between teacher characteristics and teacher competencies?

7. Can we determine teacher effectiveness?

*T*o help you appreciate the research findings in this chapter, you might try this exercise. Make a list of teachers you have had about whom you have pleasant memories. List those teachers in whose classes you were not happy. What do you remember about the attitudes and behaviors of both types of teachers? As you read this chapter, think about how the attitudes and behaviors of the teachers on the two lists correspond to research findings and information about effective and ineffective teachers.

We will present first an overview of the research on effective teaching and then five basic aspects of teachers: teacher style, teacher interactions, teacher characteristics, teacher competencies, and teacher effects. In the early stages of research, up to the mid-1970s, theorists were concerned with **teacher processes**, that is, teacher behaviors, or what teaching was going on in the classroom. The attempt to define and explain good teaching focused on teacher styles, teacher interactions, and teacher characteristics. More recently, researchers have become concerned with **teacher products**, that is, student outcomes. The assessment of products focuses on teacher competencies and teacher effects.

REVIEW OF THE RESEARCH ON TEACHING

Over the years thousands of studies have been conducted to identify the behaviors of successful and unsuccessful teachers. However, teaching is a complex act; what works in some situations with some students may not work in different school settings with different subjects, students, and goals. There will always be teachers who break many of the rules of procedures and methods and yet are profoundly successful. There will always be teachers who follow the rules and are unsuccessful.

Some educational researchers maintain that we cannot distinguish between "good" and "poor," or "effective" and "ineffective" teachers, that no one knows for sure what the competent teacher is, that few authorities can "define, prepare for, or measure teacher competence."[1] They point out that disagreement over terms, problems in measurement, and the complexity of the teaching act are major reasons for the negligible results in judging teacher behavior. The result is that "much of the data have been confusing, contradictory, or confirmations of common sense (i.e., a friendly teacher is a good teacher), and that so-called acceptable findings have often been repudiated."[2] The more one views teaching as being complex or unpre-

1 Bruce J. Biddle and William J. Ellena, "The Integration of Teacher Effectiveness," in B. J. Biddle and W. J. Ellena, eds., *Contemporary Research on Teacher Effectiveness* (New York: Holt, Rinehart & Winston, 1964), p. 3.

2 Allan C. Ornstein, "Teacher Effectiveness Research: Some Ideas and Issues," *Education and Urban Society* (February 1986), p. 168.

dictable, the more one is compelled to conclude that it is difficult to agree upon generalizations about successful teaching.[3]

Other researchers assert that appropriate teaching behaviors can be defined (and learned by teachers), that good or effective teachers can be distinguished from poor or ineffective teachers, and that the magnitude of the effect of these differences on students can be determined.[4] They conclude that the kinds of questions teachers ask, the ways they respond to students, their expectations of and attitudes toward students, their classroom management techniques, their teaching methods, and their general teaching behaviors (sometimes referred to as "classroom climate") all make a difference. However, in some cases the positive effects of teachers upon student performance may be masked or washed out by the relative negative effects of other teachers in the same school.[5] The teacher may not be the only variable, or even the major one, in the teaching-learning equation, but teachers do make a difference, either a positive one or a negative one, as a group and as individuals.

If teachers do not make a difference, then the profession has problems. If teachers do not make a difference, the notions of teacher evaluation, teacher accountability, and teacher performance are nonworkable—and sound educational policy cannot be formulated, there is little hope for many students, and there is little value in trying to learn how to teach. However, even if we are convinced that teachers have an effect, it is true that we were unable to assess with confidence the influence a teacher has on student performance or behavior because the learning variables are numerous and the teaching interactions and relationships are complex.

Empirical findings are needed if we are to establish realistic expectations concerning teacher effects. In the meantime, we must find strength and confidence in the belief that we can, and often do, make a difference with our students. You may not be successful with all of your students all of the time, but as long as you give your best, you will have served well your students, yourself, your colleagues, and your profession. Most of you will succeed—

3 Homer Coker, Donald M. Medley, and Robert S. Soar, "How Valid Are Expert Opinions about Effective Teachers?" *Phi Delta Kappan* (October 1980), pp. 131–134; Lee S. Schulman, "A Union of Insufficiencies: Strategies for Teacher Assessment," *Educational Leadership* (November 1988), pp. 35–41; and Robert S. Soar, Donald M. Medley, and Homer Coker, "Teacher Evaluation: A Critique of Currently Used Methods," *Phi Delta Kappan* (December 1983), pp. 239–246.

4 Jere E. Brophy, "Classroom Management Techniques," *Education and Urban Society* (February 1986), pp. 182–194; Carolyn M. Evertson et al., "Making a Difference in Education Quality Through Teacher Education," *Journal of Teacher Education* (May–June 1985), pp. 2–12; N. L. Gage, "What Do We Know about Teaching Effectiveness?" *Phi Delta Kappan* (October 1984), pp. 87–90; and Nancy L. Zimpher, "A Design for the Professional Development of Teacher Leaders," *Journal of Teacher Education* (January–February 1988), pp. 53–61.

5 Thomas L. Good, Bruce J. Biddle, and Jere E. Brophy, *Teachers Make a Difference* (New York: Holt, Rinehart & Winston, 1975); Allan C. Ornstein, "Theoretical Issues Related to Teaching," *Education and Urban Society* (November 1989), pp. 96–105.

through experience, self-reflection, and productive supervision. See Tips for Teachers 12.1.

TEACHER STYLES

Teaching style is viewed as a broad dimension or personality type that encompasses a teacher's stance, pattern of behavior, mode of performance, and attitude toward self and others. Penelope Peterson defines teacher style in terms of how teachers utilize space in the classroom, their choice of instructional activities and materials, and their choices of grouping students.[6] Donald Medley refers to teacher style as a dimension of classroom climate.[7] Still others describe teacher style as an *expressive* aspect of teaching (characterizing the emotional relationship between students and teachers, such as warm or businesslike) and as an *instrumental* aspect (how teachers carry out the task of instruction, organize learning, and set classroom standards).[8]

Regardless of which definition of teacher style you prefer, the notion of stability or pattern is central. Certain behaviors and methods are stable over time, even with different students and different classroom situations. There is a purpose, rationale—a predictable teacher pattern even in different classroom contexts. Aspects of teaching style dictated by personality can be modified by early experiences and perceptions and by appropriate training as a beginning teacher. As years pass, a teacher's style becomes more ingrained and it takes a more powerful set of stimuli and more intense feedback to make changes. If you watch different teachers at work, including your college professors, you can sense that each one has a style of his own for teaching, for structuring the classroom and delivering the lesson.

Descriptive Models of Teaching Styles

Many educators have delineated various teaching styles in descriptive and colorful terms. Herbert Thelen attempts to compare teaching styles with characteristics of societal positions or with what appear to be roles associated with other occupations. Frank Riessman's eight teaching styles describe personality types; they were originally based on observations of effective teachers of inner-city students, but they can be used for all teachers. Louis Rubin, more

---

6 Penelope L. Peterson, "Direct Instruction Reconsidered," in P. L. Peterson and H. J. Walberg, eds., *Research on Teaching: Concepts, Findings, and Implications* (Berkeley, Calif.: McCutchan, 1979), pp. 57–69.

7 Donald M. Medley, "The Effectiveness of Teachers," in Peterson and Walberg, eds., *Research on Teaching: Concepts, Findings and Implications*, pp. 11–27.

8 Allan C. Ornstein and Harry L. Miller, *Looking into Teaching* (Chicago: Rand McNally, 1980). Also see Bruce R. Joyce and Marsha Weil, *Models of Teaching*, 3rd ed. (Englewood Cliffs, N.J.: Prentice-Hall, 1986).

Tips for Teachers 12.1

Observing Other Teachers to Improve Teaching Practices

The statement "Teachers are born, not made" fails to take into account the wealth of knowledge we have about good teaching and how children learn. Teachers can supplement their pedagogical knowledge and practices by observing other good teachers. Assuming that your school has a policy of observations or your supervisor can make arrangements with experienced teachers, you will be able to see how other teachers organize their classrooms. The next step is to ask yourself which of their practices are compatible with your approach to teaching and which you might be able to use. The questions below indicate some of the things to look for when you are observing.

STUDENT-TEACHER INTERACTION

1. What evidence was there that the teacher truly understood the needs of the students?
2. What techniques were used to encourage students' respect for each others' turn to talk?
3. How did the teacher react to students who interrupted the class routine?
4. What student behaviors in class were acceptable and unacceptable?
5. How did the teacher motivate students?
6. How did the teacher encourage student discussion?
7. In what way did the teacher see things from the students' point of view?
8. In what way did the teacher provoke and use students' curiosity?
9. What evidence was there that the teacher responded to students' individual differences?
10. What evidence was there that the teacher responded to students' affective development?

TEACHING-LEARNING PROCESSES

1. Which instructional methods interested the students?
2. How did the teacher provide for transitions between instructional activities?
3. Which instructional materials (or media) interested students?
4. What practical life experiences (or activities) were used by the teacher to integrate concepts being learned?

continues

5. How did the teacher minimize student frustration or confusion concerning the skills or concepts being taught?
6. How did the teacher promote a positive learning environment?
7. In what way did the teacher encourage creative, imaginative work from students?
8. What instructional methods were used to make students think about ideas, opinions, or answers?
9. How did the teacher arrange the groups? What social factors were evident within the groups?
10. How did the teacher encourage independent (or individualized) student learning?
11. What methods reflected sound knowledge of subject matter?
12. How did the teacher integrate the subject matter with other subjects?

CLASSROOM ENVIRONMENT

1. How did the teacher utilize classroom space effectively?
2. How were the desks and chairs arranged? Why?
3. In what ways was the classroom aesthetically pleasant?
4. How did the teacher utilize classroom equipment effectively?
5. What did you like and dislike about the physical environment of the classroom?

recently, defines six kinds of teaching styles related to the act of teaching. These descriptions of teaching styles are summarized in Table 12.1.

The models by Thelen, Riessman, and Rubin are not research-based, but you may find these educators quite insightful about the qualities of an effective teacher and how these qualities relate to classroom teaching. Each style results in different teaching techniques and methods. As long as positive results are obtained, and as long as the teacher feels at ease with a particular style, it is important to follow personal preferences.

There are many other teacher styles. Teachers must develop their own style and teaching techniques based on their own physical and mental characteristics. Teachers must feel at ease in the classroom; if they are not genuinely themselves, students see through them and label them as "phony." The social, psychological, and educational climate in the classroom and school also has something to do with determining teaching style. Nonetheless, no one should be locked into a recommended style, regardless of conventional wisdom, con-

Table 12.1   DESCRIPTIONS OF TEACHING STYLES

Thelen (1954)

1. *Socratic*. The image is a wise, somewhat crusty teacher who purposely gets into arguments with students over the subject matter through artful questioning.

2. *Town-Meeting*. Teachers who adapt this style use a great deal of discussion and play a moderator role that enables students to work out answers to problems by themselves.

3. *Apprenticeship*. This person serves as a role model toward learning, as well as toward occupational outlook, perhaps even toward general life.

4. *Boss-Employee*. This teacher asserts his or her own authority and provides rewards and punishments to see that the work is done.

5. *Good-Old Team Person*. The image is a group of players listening to the coach and working as a team.

Riessman (1967)

1. *Compulsive Type*. This teacher is fussy, teaching things over and over, and is concerned with functional order and structure.

2. *Boomer*. This teacher shouts out in a loud, strong voice: "You're going to learn"; there is no nonsense in the classroom.

3. *Maverick*. Everybody loves this teacher, except perhaps the principal. She raises difficult questions and presents ideas that disturb.

4. *Coach*. This teacher is informal, earthy, and maybe an athlete; he is physically expressive in conducting the class.

5. *Quiet One*. Sincere, clam, but definite, this teacher commands both respect and attention.

6. *Entertainer*. This teacher is free enough to joke and laugh with the students.

7. *Secular*. This person is relaxed and informal with children; she will have lunch with them, or play ball with them.

8. *Academic*. The teacher is interested in knowledge and in the substance of ideas.

Rubin (1985)

1. *Explanatory*. The teacher is in command of the subject matter and explains particular aspects of the lesson.

2. *Inspiratory*. The teacher is stimulating and exhibits emotional involvement in teaching.

3. *Informative*. The teacher presents information through verbal statements. The student is expected to listen and follow the instructions of the teacher.

4. *Corrective*. The teacher provides feedback to the student—analyzing the work, diagnosing for errors, and presenting corrective advice.

5. *Interactive*. Through dialogue and questioning, the teacher facilitates the development of students' ideas.

6. *Programmatic*. The teacher guides the students' activities and facilitates self-instruction and independent learning.

Source: Adapted from Frank Riessman, "Teachers of the Poor: A Five Point Plan," *Journal of Teacher Education* (Fall 1967), pp. 326–336; Louis Rubin, *Artistry in Teaching* (New York: Random House, 1985); and Herbert A. Thelen, *Dynamics of Groups at Work* (Chicago: University of Chicago Press, 1954).

temporary history, or popular opinion. Teacher style is a matter of choice and comfort, and what works with one teacher may not work with another teacher. Similarly, operational definitions of good teachers and good teaching styles vary among and within school districts. There is no ideal teacher type or teacher style—and no educational institution (school or college) should impose one on its staff or faculty.

Research on Teacher Styles

Lippitt and White laid the groundwork for a more formal classification of what a teacher does in the classroom. Initially, they developed an instrument for describing the "social atmosphere" of children's clubs and for quantifying the effects of group and individual behavior. The results have been generalized in numerous research studies and textbooks on teaching. The classic study used classifications of *authoritarian, democratic,* and *laissez-faire* styles.[9]

The *authoritarian* teacher directs all the activities of the program. This style shares some characteristics with what is now called the *direct teacher.* The *democratic* teacher encourages group participation and is willing to let students share in the decision-making process. This behavior is typical of what is now called the *indirect teacher.* The *laissez-faire* teacher (now often considered to be an unorganized or ineffective teacher) provides no (or few) goals and directions for group or individual behavior.

Investigations based on Lippitt and White found that children taught by the authoritarian teacher failed to initiate activity and became dependent upon the teacher; some of the authoritarian groups exhibited aggressive and rebellious behavior toward the leader. The democratic teacher generated a friendly and cooperative group atmosphere; students' output was the highest in this group and the students carried through work assignments without the aid of the teacher for periods of time. The laissez-faire style of leadership generated confusion and minimal student productivity.

The authoritarian-democratic-laissez-faire constructs led to hundreds of empirical studies that concentrated on the same or similar teacher categories, such as (1) direct versus indirect teaching; (2) dominative-integrative teaching; (3) teacher-centered, student-centered, and problem-centered teaching; and (4) inclusive-conjunctive-preclusive teaching.[10]

One of the most ambitious research studies on teacher styles was conducted by Ned Flanders and his associates between 1954 and 1970. Flanders focused

---

9 Ronald Lippitt and Ralph K. White, "The Social Climate of Children's Groups," in R. G. Barker, J. S. Kounin, and H. F. Wright, eds., *Child Behavior and Development* (New York: McGraw-Hill, 1943), pp. 485–508. Also see Kurt Lewin, Ronald Lippitt, and Ralph K. White, "Patterns of Aggressive Behavior in Experimentally Created Social Climates," *Journal of Social Psychology* (May 1939), pp. 271–299.

10 Allan C. Ornstein, "Research on Teaching: Trends and Policies," *High School Journal* (December–January 1986), pp. 160–170.

on developing an instrument for quantifying verbal communication in the classroom.[11] Every three seconds observers sorted teacher talk into one of four categories of *indirect* behavior or one of three categories of *direct* behavior. *Student talk* was categorized as response or initiation and there was a final category representing *silence* or when the observer could not determine who was talking. The ten categories are shown in Table 12.2.

Flanders' indirect teacher tended to overlap with Lippitt and White's democratic teaching style, and the direct teacher tended to exhibit behaviors similar to their authoritarian teacher. Flanders found that students in the indirect classrooms learned more and exhibited more constructive and independent attitudes than students in the direct classrooms. All types of students in all types of subject classes learned more working with the indirect (more flexible) teachers. In an interesting side note, Flanders found that as much as 80 percent of classroom time is generally consumed in teacher talk. We will return to this point later.

The following questions, developed by Amidon and Flanders, represent a possible direction for organizing and analyzing observations.

1. What is the relationship of teacher talk to student talk? This can be answered by comparing the total number of observations in categories 1 to 7 with categories 8 and 9.
2. Is the teacher more direct or indirect? This can be answered by comparing categories 1 to 4 (indirect) with categories 5 to 7 (direct).
3. How much class time does the teacher spend lecturing? This can be answered by comparing category 5 with the total number of observations in categories 1 to 4 and 6 and 7.
4. Does the teacher ask divergent or convergent questions? This can be answered by comparing category 4 to categories 8 and 9.[12]

The data obtained from this system do not show when, why, or in what context teacher-student talk occurs, only how often particular types of interaction occur. Nonetheless it is considered a useful device for making teachers aware of their interaction behaviors in the classroom.

The Flanders system can be used to examine teacher-student verbal behaviors in any classroom, regardless of grade level or subject. Someone can observe the verbal behavior of a prospective, beginning, or even experienced teacher and show how direct or indirect the teacher is. (Most prospective and beginning teachers tend to exhibit direct behavior, since they talk too much. Professors, also, usually lecture and thus exhibit many direct behaviors while teaching.)

---

11 Ned A. Flanders, *Teacher Influence, Pupil Attitudes, and Achievement* (Washington, D.C.: U.S. Government Printing Office, 1965); Flanders, *Analyzing Teaching Behavior* (Reading, Mass.: Addison-Wesley, 1970).

12 Edmund J. Amidon and Ned A. Flanders, *The Role of the Teacher in the Classroom* (St. Paul, Minn.: Amidon & Associates, 1971). Also see Robert F. McNergney and Carol A. Carrier, *Teacher Development* (New York: Macmillan, 1981).

Table 12.2   FLANDERS CLASSROOM INTERACTION ANALYSIS SCALE

| Teacher talk | | Student talk | Silence |
Indirect behavior	Direct behavior		
1. *Accepts feeling*: Accepts and clarifies the tone of feeling of the students in an unthreatening manner. Feelings may be positive or negative. Predicting or recalling feelings is included. 2. *Praises or encourages*: Praises or encourages student action or behavior. Jokes that release tension, but not at the expense of another individual; nodding head or saying "Um hm?" or "Go on" are included. 3. *Accepts and uses ideas of student*: Clarifying, building ideas suggested by a student. As teacher brings more of his own ideas into play, shift to category 5. 4. *Asks questions*: Asking a question about content or procedure with the intent that a student answer.	5. *Lectures*: Gives facts or opinions about content or procedure; expresses his own ideas, asking rhetorical questions. 6. *Gives directions*: Gives directions, commands, or orders with which students are expected to comply. 7. *Criticizes or justifies authority*: Statements are intended to change student behavior from unacceptable to acceptable pattern; bawling someone out; stating why the teacher is doing what he is doing; extreme self-reference.	8. *Response*: Talk by students in response to teacher. Teacher initiates the contact or solicits student statement. 9. *Initiation*: Talk initiated by students. If "calling on" student is only to indicate who may talk next; observer must decide whether student wanted to talk.	10. Silence or confusion: Pauses, short periods of silence, and periods of confusion in which communication cannot be understood by the observer.

Source: Ned A. Flanders, *Teacher Influence, Pupil Attitudes, and Achievement* (Washington, D.C.: U.S. Government Printing Office, 1965), p. 20.

Current research on teacher style tends to reflect a diverse group of *qualitative* and *interpretive* studies that refer to: (1) classroom ecology, (2) detailed and descriptive accounts of classroom events, and (3) extensive interviews with teachers and students that shed light on what teachers do and how they do it. Some of these studies are conducted in schools cooperatively with classroom teachers and university-based researchers, some take place in laboratory settings or assessment centers, and still others are part of the new, alternative

Some people looking at this teacher might characterize her as Rubin's "explanatory" teacher or Flanders' "direct" teacher.

"portfolio" system, that includes such items as videotapes of teachers at work and teachers' and students' samples of work.

In most cases, the new research on teacher style emphasizes the popular process-product research, where teacher behaviors and student outcomes are viewed in a linear relationship: teacher behaviors or methods produce observable or measurable student outcomes. According to some educators, *qualitative* research presumes that teaching is a highly complex and context-specific act in which differences across classrooms and schools are critical; and that process-product (or *quantitative*) research, and its assumptions about direct teacher-student relationships, is misleading for many teachers.[13] Professional judgments of teachers, along with hunches and intuitive actions, are as important as recommended research-based behaviors or methods. Such personality charac-

---

13 Marilyn Cochran-Smith and Susan L. Lytle, "Research on Teaching and Teacher Research: The Issues That Divide," *Educational Researcher* (March 1990), pp. 2–11; Elliot W. Eisner, "What Really Counts in School," *Educational Leadership* (February 1991), pp. 10–17; and Lee Schulman, "Knowledge and Teaching: Foundations of the New Reform," *Harvard Educational Review* (February 1987), pp. 1–22.

teristics as empathy, enthusiasm, friendliness, nurturing, etc., are very important for good teaching, perhaps more important than learning or teaching content. Such characteristics are part of personality or teacher style and have very little to do with technical know-how, teacher training, or generalizable prescriptions.

Teachable Groups

The analysis of teaching styles eventually leads to two questions: is student learning affected by the teachers' use of different approaches or styles? Are different teaching strategies effective for different students? Assuming the answer is "yes" in both cases, the aim is to match the appropriate teacher style and strategies with the appropriate group of students in order to achieve the best teaching-learning situation.

Herbert Thelen calls this the proper "fit." He states that teachers recognize four kinds of students: good, bad, indifferent, and maladjusted. Each teacher places different students in these categories, and teachable students for one teacher may be quite different for another. The proper fit between teacher and students results in the best kind of classroom or best group—what is defined as the **teachable group**. He contends that homogeneous grouping is essential for a group to become more "teachable."[14] A teacher in such a group accomplishes more with students than in groups in which the range of ability and behavior is wide; moreover, it is easier to fit students and teachers together to achieve the best combinations. Any grouping that does not attempt to match students and teachers can have only "accidental success."

Of special interest to the concept of teaching style is the classic work of Heil and Washburne. On the basis of observing fifth- and sixth-grade classrooms in New York City, students were divided into four categories: (1) *conformers*, characterized by high academic standards, high social orientation, and control over impulses; (2) *opposers*, characterized by conflict with authority, hostile or pessimistic tone, intolerance toward disappointment, easy frustration; (3) *waverers*, characterized by anxiety, ambivalence, fear and indecision; and (4) *strivers*, characterized by marked drive for recognition, especially in school achievement and exhibitionistic activities. The teachers were divided into three personality types: *turbulent* (sloppy, inconsistent, impatient), *controlling* (orderly, businesslike, organized, yet sensitive to students' feelings), and *fearful* (anxious, dependent on approval from students and supervisors, unable to bring structure and order to their teaching task).[15]

---

14 Herbert A. Thelen, *Classroom Grouping for Teachability* (New York: Wiley, 1967).

15 Louis M. Heil and Carlton Washburne, "Brooklyn College Research on Teacher Effectiveness," *Journal of Educational Research* (May 1962), pp. 347–351.

Neither the striving nor the conforming students were affected by the teacher type, but teaching type made a difference in achievement for the opposers and waverers (behaviors exhibited by many problem and at-risk children). For opposers and waverers, the controlling teachers were the most effective. The turbulent teachers were less successful in teaching opposers, who evidenced the highest intolerance toward ambiguity. The fearful teachers were the least effective with all kinds of students, but especially with the opposers and waverers. Heil's findings, though apparently inconclusive, are consistent with the idea of grouping students according to cognitive and sociopsychological characteristics and "matching" them with teaching styles (and the belief that teachable students for one teacher may be quite different for another). This would lead to the formation of teachable groups.

Other researchers have addressed the problem of teachable groups and point out that effective teachers vary for students with different learning characteristics and socioeconomic backgrounds, as well as for different grade levels and subjects. For example, Donald Medley presents one of the most comprehensive reviews of 289 teacher process and product studies.[16] He concludes that effective teachers behave differently with different types of students. As shown in Table 12.3, the most effective teachers of low socioeconomic status school students (1) spend less time discussing matters unrelated to lesson content, (2) present structured and sequential learning activities, (3) permit little time on independent and small-group work, (4) initiate low-level and narrowly defined questions and are less likely to amplify or discuss student answers, (5) spend little time on and discourage student-initiated questions and comments, (6) provide less feedback on student-initiated questions, (7) engage in fewer teacher rebukes, and (8) spend less time on discipline matters. The type of instruction, type of questions, and management techniques tend to be opposite for middle-class students.

Three things are important to note from Medley's review. First, his notion of changing teaching strategies for different students is similar to Heil's "match" between teacher and student types and Thelen's "fit" between teachers and students to establish teachable groups. Teachable students for one teacher may be quite different for another, not all students are easy to teach or even teachable under normal conditions, some good teachers cannot successfully teach some types of problem students, and different students need different teaching techniques.

Second, his description of effective teaching behaviors for low socioeconomic students does not resemble the current progressive model of instruction. The least effective teachers are those who ask the most high-level

16 Donald M. Medley, *Teacher Competence and Teacher Effectiveness: A Review of Process-Product Research* (Washington, D.C.: American Association of Colleges for Teacher Education, 1977); Medley, "The Effectiveness of Teachers," in Peterson and Walberg, eds., *Research on Teaching: Concepts, Findings, and Implications*, pp. 11–27.

Table 12.3   EFFECTIVE AND INEFFECTIVE BEHAVIORS IN TEACHING LOW SOCIOECONOMIC
STUDENTS IN THE ELEMENTARY GRADES

Teaching function	Effective behaviors	Ineffective behaviors
Maintenance of learning environment	Less deviant, disruptive pupil behavior	More deviant, disruptive pupil behavior
	Fewer teacher rebukes	More teacher rebukes
	Less criticism	More criticism
	Less time spent on classroom management	More time spent on classroom management
	More praise, positive motivation	Less praise, positive interaction
Use of pupil time	More class time spent in task-related "academic" activities	Less class time spent in task-related "academic" activities
	More time spent working with large groups or whole class	Less time spent working with large groups or whole class
	Less time spent working with small groups	More time spent working with small groups
	Small groups of pupils work independently less of the time	Small groups of pupils work independently more of the time
	Less independent seatwork	More dependent seatwork
Method of instruction	More "low-level" questions	Fewer "low-level" questions
	Fewer "high-level" questions	More "high-level" questions
	Less likely to amplify, discuss, or use pupil answers	More likely to amplify, discuss, or use pupil answers
	Fewer pupil-initiated questions and comments	More pupil-initiated questions and comments
	Less feedback on pupil questions	More feedback on pupil questions
	More attention to pupils when they are working independently	Less attention to pupils when they are working independently

Source: Adapted from Donald M. Medley, *Teacher Competence and Teacher Effectiveness* (Washington, D.C.: American Association of Colleges for Teacher Education, 1977), pp. 11–24, 65.

and fewest low-level questions, whose students ask more questions and get more feedback, and who amplify or discuss student-initiated comments. Teachers who use more low-level questions and fewer high-level ones, whose students initiate fewer questions and who tend not to discuss what students say are the most effective. Unquestionably, Medley's ideas are threatening and open to criticism, since they can lead to tracking students by ability and restricting low socioeconomic status students to limited cognitive experiences.[17]

17 Allan C. Ornstein, "How Good Are Teachers in Affecting Student Outcomes?" *NAASP Bulletin* (December 1982), pp. 61–70; Ornstein, "A Difference Teachers Make," *Educational Forum* (Fall 1984), pp. 109–118.

Third, Medley's ideas appear to be very much in line with teaching approaches and methods that have been identified by current researchers as highly successful with low-achieving students, both at the elementary and secondary grade levels: basic skills, drill, time on task, feedback, competency and mastery learning approaches; they coincide with instruction labeled direct and explicit. Such teacher styles tend to be in line with the Brophy, Doyle, Evertson, Good and Rosenshine models (discussed below in this chapter), but in opposition to a good deal of traditional and conventional wisdom that favors a warmer, more humanistic teacher (especially at the elementary school level).

Beyond Medley, on a generic basis, teaching style influences how we use teacher behavior research. The "theories" and "practices" described in the professional literature must be matched to fit the teacher's style. An experienced teacher learns to select only those recommended behaviors that he or she feels comfortable with in the classroom. Teachers must learn a body of knowledge (theory) essential for teaching, and how to apply it (practice). They need to learn to be analytical and reflective as they develop and grow as a teacher. This connotes that teachers learn to choose among alternatives, including various theories and practices of teaching which can be adapted either on an "as is" basis or modified to fit their particular style of teaching.[18] This calls for a mature and reflective teacher, one who engages in a cycle of thought based on previous experience and who is willing to ask himself: What did I do? Why? How ought I do things differently (to improve)?[19]

TEACHER INTERACTION

An approach to the study of teacher behavior is based on systematic observation of **teacher-student interaction** in the classroom, as, for example, in the work of Flanders, which we have already described. The analysis of interaction often deals with a specific teacher behavior and a series of these behaviors constituting a larger behavior, described and recorded by an abstract unit of measurement that may vary in size and time (for example, every three seconds a recording is made).

Verbal Communication

In a classic study of teacher-student interaction, Arno Bellack analyzed the linguistic behavior of teachers and students in the classroom.[20]   Classroom

18 Allan C. Ornstein, "A Look at Teacher Effectiveness: Research, Theory, and Practice," *NASSP Bulletin* (October 1990), pp. 78–88.

19 Christine Canning, "What Teachers Say About Reflection," *Educational Leadership* (March 1991), pp. 18–21; Gaea Leinhardt, "Capturing Craft Knowledge of Teaching," *Educational Researcher* (March 1990), pp. 18–25.

20 Arno A. Bellack et al., *The Language of the Classroom* (New York: Teachers College Press, Columbia University, 1966).

activities are carried out in large part by verbal interaction between students and teachers; few classroom activities can be carried out without the use of language. The research, therefore, focused on language as the main instrument of communication in teaching. Four basic verbal behaviors or "moves" were labeled.

1. Structuring moves serve the function of focusing attention on subject matter or classroom procedures and beginning interaction between students and teachers. They set the context for subsequent behavior. For example, beginning a class by announcing the topic to be discussed is a structuring move.
2. Soliciting moves are designed to elicit a verbal or physical response. For example, the teacher asks a question about the topic with the hope of encouraging a response from the students.
3. Responding moves occur in relation to and after the soliciting behaviors. Their ideal function is to fulfill the expectations of the soliciting behaviors.
4. *Reacting moves* are sometimes occasioned by one or more of the above behaviors, but are not directly elicited by them. Reacting behaviors serve to modify, clarify, or judge the structuring, soliciting, or responding behavior.[21]

According to Bellack, these pedagogical moves occur in combinations he called "teaching cycles." A cycle usually begins with a structuring or soliciting move by the teacher, both of which are initiative behaviors, continues with a responding move from a student, and ends with some kind of reacting move by the teacher. In most cases the cycle begins and ends with the teacher. The investigators' analysis of the classroom also produced several insights.

1. Teachers dominate verbal activities. The teacher-student ratio in words spoken is 3:1. (This evidence corresponds with Flanders' finding that teacher talk is 80 percent of classroom activity.)
2. Teacher and student moves are clearly defined. The teacher engages in structuring, soliciting, and reacting behaviors, while the student is usually limited to responding. (This also corresponds with Flanders' finding that most teachers dominate classrooms in such a way as to make students dependent.)
3. Teachers initiate about 85 percent of the cycles. The basic unit of verbal interaction is the soliciting-responding pattern. Verbal interchanges occur at a rate of slightly less than 2 cycles per minute.

---

21 Ibid.

4. In approximately two-thirds of the behaviors and three-fourths of the verbal interplay, talk is content-oriented.

5. About 60 percent of the total discourse is fact-oriented.

In summary, the data suggest that the classroom is teacher-dominated, subject-centered, and fact-oriented. The students' primary responsibility seems to be to respond to the teacher's soliciting behaviors. (As a teacher, you should want to break this cycle of teaching.)

In another study Smith and Meux focused on the linguistic behavior of the teacher.[22] It was divided into "episodes" and "monologues." The **teacher episode** is defined as one or more verbal exchanges between two or more speakers. Questions by the teacher and answers by the students constitute the most common episode. The **teacher monologue** consists of a solo performance by a speaker addressing the group; the teacher who gives directions or a command is engaged in a monologue. Effective teachers tend to engage in episodes. The ideal episode seems to be an exchange in which several speakers respond to an original question or statement. Thus the most effective linguistic behavior is not teacher to student or student to teacher, but teacher to several students.

A series of episodes or monologues form a cycle that includes one or more of several verbal entries (that is, questions or statements that initiate the exchange):

1. *Defining* entries are concerned with how words are used to refer to objects: "What does the word . . . mean?"

2. *Describing* entries ask for an explanation or description about something: "What did John find out?"

3. *Designating* entries identify something by name: "What mountain range did we see in the film?"

4. *Stating* entries involve statements of issues, proofs, rules, theories, conclusions, beliefs, and so on: "What is the plot of the story?"

5. *Reporting* entries ask for a summary or a report on a book or document: "Can you summarize the major points of the book?"

6. *Substituting* entries require the performance of a symbolic operation, usually of mathematic or scientific value: "Who can write the equation on the chalkboard?"

7. *Evaluating* entries ask for judgment or estimate of worth of something: "Would you like to assess the validity of the argument?"

8. *Opinioning* entries ask for a conclusion, affirmation, or denial based upon evidence: "How do you feel President Bush will be judged by historians?"[23]

---

22 B. Othaniel Smith and Milton Meux, *A Study of the Logic of Teaching*, 2nd ed. (Urbana, Ill.: University of Illinois Press, 1970).

23 Ibid.

Language, Thought, and Teaching

Joan Tough's longitudinal study of students in classrooms has resulted in a functional description of seven categories of spontaneous language in learning.

1. *Self-Maintaining*. Students' use of language to protect or assert their needs or interests, to justify behavior or answers, or to criticize others.
2. *Directing*. Use of language to monitor their own actions, to give directions, to give answers, or to plan collaborative actions; this coincides with knowledge and comprehension levels of thinking.
3. *Reporting*. Use of language to illustrate what they have read, heard, seen, experienced, or performed; this refers to sequencing, making comparisons, recognizing related aspects, and analyzing features.
4. *Reasoning*. Use of language to explain how or why, or to deduce the particular from the general or induce the general from the particular; this includes recognizing causal relationships, relating solutions to problems, justifying opinions, and formulating principles.
5. *Predicting*. Use of language to anticipate or predict the unknown; this includes forecasting, recognizing sequence of events, and recognizing alternative actions.
6. *Projecting*. Use of language to explain what they themselves or others feel or think; refers to experiences and feelings of others, projecting the reactions of others, as situations never experienced.
7. *Imagining*. Use of language to express fantasy or imagination; this sometimes connotes a creative mind and hard-to-agree-upon reference points or features.[24]

While thought and speech are not the same, the development of language overlaps with intellectual development, and verbal intercourse with adults is important in influencing cognition. Teachers who ask questions that require students to use proper language for a variety of tasks stimulate students to use a variety of cognitive processes.[25] To this end, a questioning strategy that considers the seven functional categories of students—i.e., matching questions to the students' stage of language development and level of comprehension—correlates with academic achievement.[26]

By the time students have reached sixth grade, most of them should be able to use (with varying degrees of facility) all seven functions of language. Low achievers, however, mainly operate at the self-maintaining and directing func-

24 Joan Tough, *Listening to Children Talk* (London: Ward Lock, 1976); Tough, *The Development of Meaning* (New York: Wiley, 1977).

25 Jean Piaget and Barbel Inhelder, *The Early Growth of Logic in the Child* (London: Routledge & Kegan Paul, 1964); Lev S. Vigotsky, *Thought and Language* (Cambridge, Mass.: MIT Press, 1962).

26 Thema Harms, Roberta Woolever, and Richard Brice, "A Questioning Strategies Training Sequence," *Journal of Teacher Education* (September–October 1989), pp. 40–45.

tions, and not all high achievers use all the functions as a basis for learning. Furthermore, most students are used to operating in the classroom at the lower language functions, simply because the common method of teaching permits and even encourages simple responses to questions and other low-level academic tasks (such as practice, drill, review). Teachers are keyed to right answers, not complex thought. In their defense, however, they are victimized by the need to make use of time, teach the required content, and test students. Only confident and mature teachers are comfortable enough to slow down—and not be time-driven, curriculum-driven, or test-driven—given pressured administrators and a demanding public concerned with results.

The teacher needs to listen to the students' responses to questions to determine whether they are ready to answer with logical reasoning, predicting, projecting, and so on. To facilitate students' strategies in using more complex functions of language (functions 4–7), the teacher needs to ask questions at the appropriate level; allow adequate wait-time; talk less and listen more; use probes at the appropriate time; ensure that all students, especially low achievers, are called on; not be so ready to answer questions or provide answers; and provide feedback and encourage elaboration and interaction among students. See Tips for Teachers 12.2.

Nonverbal Communication

According to Miles Patterson, nonverbal behavior in the classroom serves five teacher functions: (1) *providing information,* or elaborating upon a verbal statement; (2) *regulating interactions,* such as pointing to someone; (3) *expressing intimacy or liking,* such as smiling or touching a student on the shoulder; (4) *exercising social control,* reinforcing a classroom rule, say, by proximity or distance, and (5) *facilitating goals,* as when demonstrating a skill that requires motor activity or gesturing.[27] These categories are not mutually exclusive; there is some overlap, and nonverbal cues may serve more than one function depending on how they are used.

Although the teaching-learning process is ordinarily associated with verbal interaction, **nonverbal communication** operates as a silent language that influences the process. What makes the study of nonverbal communication so important and perhaps fascinating is that some researchers contend that it comprises about 65 percent of the social meaning of the classroom communication system.[28] As the old saying goes, "Actions speak louder than words."

In a recent study of 225 teachers (and other educators with authority) in 45 schools, Stephens and Valentine observed 10 specific nonverbal behaviors: (1) smiles or frowns, (2) eye contact, (3) head nods, (4) gestures, (5) dress,

---

27 Miles L. Patterson, *Nonverbal Behavior: A Functional Perspective* (New York: Springer, 1983).

28 Aron W. Siegman and Stanley Feldstein, eds., *Nonverbal Behavior and Communication* (Hillsdale, N.J.: Erlbaum, 1978).

Tips for Teachers 12.2

Relating Students' Use of Language to Teaching Strategies

Teachers can be trained to understand the students' use of functional language, then to stimulate students to use language for a variety of purposes and to elicit more complex responses by modifying their lesson plans and questioning approach. Below are directions for lesson planning and a self-evaluation or guide for questioning; they are precise and more suitable for a beginning teacher than an experienced one.

Directions for Lesson Planning

Before beginning to write your plan:

1. Select and preview the material (book, story, film, article, etc.) you are going to present.
2. Decide on the *unit of intake* (that is, the amount of material the pupils will read/listen to before you ask your first questions): one paragraph, one page, several pages, the whole story or film, etc.
3. Decide on the level of the initial question for each unit intake. Select an opening question on the highest level the group can handle. Children who need to be made aware of the central meaning or basic idea may need a *reporting* question such as, "What is happening here?" More mature or able students may respond better to an initial *logical reasoning* question such as, "Why do you think . . . ?"
4. Decide on a target proportion of *reporting, logical reasoning, predicting*, and *projecting* questions that seems appropriate for the particular group of students. For example, you might decide to aim for 35% *reporting* questions, 30% *logical reasoning*, 20% *predicting*, and 15% *projecting*.

Steps in writing your plan:

1. *Add* the following objective to your lesson plan: "The pupils will successfully respond to a total of _____ questions distributed as follows: _____% *reporting,* _____% *logical reasoning,* _____ % *predicting,* _____% *projecting.*
2. Write your plan out in detail, with the questions (verbatim) you intend to ask, including possible probes. Code each question to indicate the categories of language function the question is intended to elicit—(R), (LR), (PRE), or (PRO). For example: "What happened to the cat next?(R)."

continues

Questions for Self-Evaluation (Record and analyze on tape if possible)

1. Was there more student talk than teacher talk?
2. Did I allow sufficient wait-time between asking a question and calling on a student to respond?
3. Did I call on all students equally?
4. Did I *actively* listen to students as they gave their responses (maintain eye contact, nod head, etc.)?
5. Did I provide feedback on correctness of responses?
6. Was the unit of intake appropriate for the group?
7. Were my initial questions on an appropriate level?
8. Did I use "backtracking" (i.e., *reporting*) probes if the student was not able to answer the initial question correctly?
9. Did I use "follow-up" probes after a correct response to a reporting question to elicit *logical reasoning*, *predicting*, and/or *projecting*?
10. Were my target proportions (%) of questions in each of the four categories appropriate for this group?

Source: Thema Harms, Roberta Woolever, and Richard Brice, "A Questioning Strategies Training Sequence," *Journal of Teacher Education* (September-October 1989), p. 45.

(6) interaction distance, (7) touch, (8) body movement, (9) posture, and (10) seating arrangements.[29] In general, the first four behaviors are easily interpreted by the observer; some smiles, eye contact, head nods, and gestures are expected, but too many make students suspicious or uneasy. Dress is a matter of professional code and expectation. Distance, touch, body movement, posture, and seating are open to more interpretation, are likely to have personal meaning between communicators, and are based on personalities and social relationships.[30] Different types of these five behaviors, especially distance, touch, and body movement, can be taken as indications of the degree of formality in the relationship between the communicators, from intimate to personal to social to public. Teachers should maintain a social or public relationship—that is, a formal relationship—with their students. Behaviors that

29 Pat Stephens and Jerry Valentine, "Assessing Principal Nonverbal Communication," *Educational Research Quarterly* (Winter 1986), pp. 60–68.

30 Ibid.

coincide with or could be interpreted as indicating intimate and personal relations should be avoided.

When the teacher's verbal and nonverbal cues contradict one another, according to Charles Galloway, the students tend to read the nonverbal cues as a true reflection of the teacher's real feelings. Galloway developed global guidelines for observing nonverbal communication of teachers, which he referred to as the "silent behavior of space, time, and body."[31]

1. *Space.* A teacher's use of space conveys meaning to students. For example, teachers who spend most of their time by the chalkboard or at their desk may convey insecurity, a reluctance to venture into student territory.
2. *Time.* How teachers utilize classroom time is an indication of how they value certain instructional activities. The elementary teacher who devotes a great deal of time to reading but little to mathematics is conveying a message to the students.
3. *Body maneuvers.* Nonverbal cues are used by teachers to control students. The raised eyebrow, the pointed finger, the silent stare all communicate meaning.

As shown in Table 12.4, Galloway suggests that various nonverbal behaviors of the teacher can be viewed as encouraging or restricting. By their facial expressions, gestures, and body movements, teachers affect student participation and performance in the classroom. The concept of encouraging versus restricting behavior can help in analyzing interactions. In referring to the table, we might ask the following questions:

1. How much time does the teacher spend on encouraging versus restricting behavior?
2. When (and why) does the teacher use encouraging and restricting cues?
3. Does the teacher's nonverbal behavior reveal his or her true feelings?
4. Is the teacher's verbal behavior (questions, directions, responses) accompanied by nonverbal cues?
5. Does the teacher's verbal behavior coincide with his or her nonverbal behavior?
6. To what extent do indirect and direct teachers, as defined by Flanders and Rosenshine, exhibit encouraging and restricting nonverbal behavior, as defined by Galloway?

---

31 Charles M. Galloway, "Nonverbal Communication," *Theory into Practice* (December 1968), pp. 172–175; Galloway, "Nonverbal Behavior and Teacher Student Relationships: An Intercultural Perspective," in A. Wolfgang, ed., *Nonverbal Behavior: Perspectives, Applications, Intercultural Insights* (Toronto: Hogrefe, 1984), pp. 411–430.

Table 12.4   ENCOURAGING AND RESTRICTING TEACHER NONVERBAL BEHAVIORS

Encouraging behaviors	Restricting behaviors
Facial expression connotes enjoyment or satisfaction.	Teacher avoids eye contact, communicating inattention, disinterest, or unwillingness to listen.
Facial expression implies understanding or acceptance of student's need or problem.	Facial expression implies that he or she is unenthusiastic, condescending, impatient, or unsympathetic.
Teacher maintains eye contact, indicating patience, attention, and willingness to listen.	
Teacher moves toward students.	Teacher scowls, frowns, sneers.
Teacher pats student on back.	Teacher slouches or stands in a way that suggests disinterest or absorption in own work or thought.
Teacher uses gesture that indicates student is on the right track.	
Teacher stands or sits in a way that suggests alertness or readiness to respond to student.	Teacher uses gestures or facial expressions to indicate that students stop, e.g., hand up, waving, angry look.
Voice intonation or inflection suggests approval or support.	Teacher pokes, slaps, grabs student.
Teacher utters approval or suggests that student go on, e.g., "um-hm."	Teacher uses vocal utterance to indicate that students are to stop talking or one that interrupts, e.g., "shhh," "ugh."
Teachers displays understanding, compassion, supportiveness by laughing.	Voice intonation or inflection suggests antagonism, irritability, depreciation, or discouragement.

Source: Adapted from Charles M. Galloway, *Silent Language in the Classroom* (Bloomington, Ind.: Phi Delta Kappa Foundation, 1976); Galloway, "Nonverbal Behavior and Teacher Student Relationships: An Intercultural Perspective," in A. Wolfgang, ed., *Nonverbal Behavior: Perspectives, Applications, Intercultural Insights* (Toronto: Hogrefe, 1984), pp. 411–430. Also based on conversations with Galloway, September 18, 1987.

The related concept of attentive and inattentive nonverbal behavior by students is also important in analyzing teacher-student interactions. See Tips for Teachers 12.3.

Students exhibit nonverbal behavior that influences teachers' impressions, attitudes, reciprocal behavior, expectations, and existing and future student-teacher interactions. Nonverbal communication of students has been organized by researchers into four different categories.

1. *Location/proximity*. Where a student chooses to sit at the beginning of the year, assuming choice is available, influences the teacher's impression of how likable, initiating, and responsive the student is.
2. *Attentiveness*. Nonverbal behaviors such as erect posture, eye contact, and smiling communicate attention and are related to positive evaluations of the student's competence, learning, and attitude.
3. *Disruptive behaviors*. The absence of eye contact and verbal responsiveness is associated with negative teacher impressions. Rejecting help

Tips for Teachers 12.3

Inattentive and Attentive Nonverbal Behaviors

The teacher should look for nonverbal student behavior to determine whether the student is attentive (or engaged in an appropriate activity) or inattentive (not engaged). This awareness on the part of the teacher should take place regardless of the classroom activity. Below are cues that are useful in recognizing attentiveness and inattentiveness.

INATTENTIVE BEHAVIORS

1. Moving around the room without permission or at an inappropriate time
2. Reading a book or doing homework during class discussion
3. Doodling with a pencil; drawing instead of doing the assigned activity
4. Laying head on desk
5. Gazing out the window or at someone in the hallway
6. Staring fixedly at an object not related to a class activity
7. Sitting with elbows on desk or hands underneath thighs
8. Poking or annoying a classmate
9. Being unprepared (no pencil, pen, notebook)
10. Tipping the chair back and forth

ATTENTIVE BEHAVIORS

1. Raising a hand to volunteer a response
2. Maintaining eye contact with the teacher
3. Working on the assigned activity; academically engaged
4. Turning around to listen to a student who is speaking
5. Engaging in some task during a free activity or independent study period
6. Being prepared (with pencil, pen, notebook)
7. Alert, energetic, positive facial expressions
8. Nonjerky movement in seat, quiet sitting in front of classroom

Source: Adapted from Thomas L. Good and Jere E. Brophy, *Looking in Classrooms*, 5th ed. (New York: HarperCollins, 1991). Six of the inattentive behaviors and five of the attentive behaviors are based on Good and Brophy; the remaining items are the author's.

from the teacher and responding to teacher initiatives with negative nonverbal behaviors indicate disinterest or dislike to many teachers, and teachers often respond in kind with negative nonverbal behavior.

4. *Timing.* Students who make requests at inappropriate times are perceived negatively by teachers. Students who respond quickly to teacher requests appear to be perceived more positively by their teacher. "Successful interrupters" pick the best time to engage in mischief or deviant behavior, that is, when the teacher is engaged in an activity; "unsuccessful interrupters" get caught because their timing is wrong.[32]

Speaking and Listening

By the same token, the teacher's nonverbal behavior influences students (as well as other colleagues). According to one study on listening, only 7 percent of a speaker's message comes from verbal communication (the words that are used). As much as 38 percent comes from the *tone* (not what one says but how one says it), and 55 percent comes from body language (face, arms, clothing, territory, etc.).[33] The notion that words have so little meaning compared to nonverbal behavior is hard to believe—given a society in which precision in words (*who* that modifies a person and *which* that modifies a group or corporation, liable versus nonrecourse, can mean the difference between winning or losing a $10 million lawsuit) is so important.

The way one stands, moves, or walks can express confidence or weakness, friendliness or hostility. It is important that a speaker's verbal messages, tone, and body language are congruent, otherwise, the listener is confused or misled; it is particularly important for a teacher to be precise in communicating to students, since they can easily become confused in a teacher-student relationship that starts off power-oriented and unequal.

Two of the most common irritating listening habits are interrupting and lack of eye contact. Other poor listening habits include looking at one's watch, attending to other tasks, completing the sentence or phrase for the speaker, and correcting the speaker in the middle of a thought. Other irritants' include doing something else while listening, such as reading, writing, or listening to other people at the same time, and nervousness (tapping, scratching, biting nails).[34] Teachers must avoid disagreeable listening habits and model good ones to develop student rapport and trust, maintain discipline, and communicate effectively.

---

32 Walter Doyle, "Classroom Organization and Management," in M. C. Wittrock, ed., *Handbook of Research on Teaching*, 3rd ed. (New York: Macmillan, 1986), pp. 392–431; Thomas L. Good and Jere E. Brophy, *Educational Psychology: A Realistic Approach*, 3rd ed. (White Plains, N.Y.: Longman, 1986).

33 Alex Mehrabian, *Silent Messages* (Belmont, Calif.: Wadsworth, 1971).

34 Donald Klopf and Ronald E. Cambra, *Speaking Skills for Prospective Teachers* (Englewood, Colo.: Norton Publishers, 1983); William J. Serler, L. David Schuelke, and Barbara Lieb-Brilhart, *Communication for the Contemporary Classroom* (New York: Holt, Rinehart & Winston, 1984).

Different people have different listening styles; one educator lists six:

1. *Leisure listener's* mind tends to wander and pick up pleasant or positive messages. The person is relaxed and tunes into only portions of what is being communicated. Teachers who fall into this category are usually positive persons; nonetheless, they should be more focused as listeners.
2. *Inclusive listener* is a comprehensive listener and reacts to the literal meaning of what is being communicated. However, this person usually gets impatient with ramblers. A teacher who falls into this category needs to be a little more patient and listen to tone and other nonverbal messages.
3. *Stylistic listener* focuses on the mannerisms and nonverbal cues of the speaker and categorizes the speaker favorably or unfavorably. A teacher who is stylistic needs to avoid quick judgments.
4. *Technical listener* gathers data while listening; he or she focuses on the content and avoids nonverbal cues. The teacher in this category would profit from paying more attention to the speaker's mannerisms and nonverbal cues.
5. *Emphatic listener* is a sensitive listener and is aware of the speaker's feelings. As a teacher, this person is usually warm and friendly; however, he or she can become more effective by focusing more on content while continuing to focus on the emotions of the speaker.
6. *Nonconforming listener* usually agrees or disagrees quickly; this person usually challenges the speaker, asks questions, or listens for supporting information in agreeing or disagreeing with the speaker. He or she is good at probing. A teacher in this category should listen more and avoid hasty judgments; too much probing is also annoying.[35]

You might ask yourself what style of listener are you? What type of listening behaviors or body language do you exhibit as a teacher—with your students, colleagues, and supervisors? How can you improve your listening style? In terms of how people react to you, why is it important to understand your own speaking and listening characteristics?

Teacher Expectations

Teachers communicate their expectations of students through verbal and nonverbal cues. It is well established that these expectations affect the interaction between teachers and students and, eventually, the performance of students. In many cases teacher expectations become **self-fulfilling prophecies**; that is,

35 Frank W. Freshour, "Listening Power: Key to Effective Leadership," *Illinois School Research and Development Journal* (Fall 1989), p. 17–23. The accompanying suggestions are the author's.

if the teacher expects students to be slow or exhibit deviant behavior, he or she treats them accordingly, and in response they adopt such behaviors.

The research on teacher expectations is rooted in the legal briefs and arguments of Kenneth Clark prepared during his fight for desegregated schools in the 1950s and in his subsequent description of the problems in New York City's Harlem schools.[36] He pointed out that prophesying low achievement for black students not only provides teachers with an excuse for their students' failure but also communicates a sense of inevitable failure to the students.

Clark's thesis was given empirical support a few years later by Rosenthal and Jacobsen's *Pygmalion in the Classroom*, a study of students in the San Francisco schools.[37] After controlling for the ability of students, teachers were told that there was reason to expect that certain students would perform better, and the expectancy was fulfilled. However, confidence in *Pygmalion* diminished when Robert Thorndike, one of the most respected measurement experts, pointed out that there were several flaws in the methodology and that the tests were unreliable.[38]

Interest in teacher expectations and the self-fulfilling prophecy reappeared in the 1970s and 1980s. Cooper and then Good and Brophy outlined how teachers communicate expectations to students and thus influence student behavior.

1. The teacher expects specific achievement and behavior from particular students.
2. Because of these different expectations, the teacher behaves differently toward various students.
3. This treatment suggests to students what achievement and behavior the teacher expects from them, which affects their self-concepts, motivation, and performance.
4. If the teacher's treatment is consistent over time, it will shape the students' achievement and behavior. High expectations for students will influence achievement at high levels, and low expectations will produce lower achievement.
5. With time, student achievement and behavior will conform more and more to the original expectations of the teacher.[39]

---

36 Kenneth B. Clark, *Dark Ghetto* (New York: Harper & Row, 1965).

37 Robert Rosenthal and Lenore Jacobson, *Pygmalion in the Classroom* (New York: Holt, Rinehart & Winston, 1968).

38 Robert Thorndike, "Review of Pygmalion in the Classroom," *American Educational Research Journal* (November 1968), pp. 708–711.

39 Jere E. Brophy and Thomas L. Good, *Teacher-Student Relationships* (New York: Holt, Rinehart & Winston, 1974); Harris M. Cooper, "Pygmalion Grows Up: A Model for Teacher Expectation Communication and Performance Influence," *Review of Educational Research* (Summer 1979), pp. 389–410; Cooper and Good, *Pygmalion Grows Up* (New York: Longman, 1983); and Thomas L. Good and Rhona G. Weinstein, "Teacher Expectations: A Framework for Exploring Classrooms," in K. Kepler-Zumwalt, ed., *Improving Teaching* (Alexandria, Va.: Association for Supervision and Curriculum Development, 1986), pp. 63–85.

Cooper and Good and Brophy represent conventional wisdom: teachers not only tend to convey lower expectations for low achievers and higher expectations for high achievers, but also exhibit worse academic treatment for low achievers and better academic treatment for high achievers—all which affect the students' cognitive abilities in class (see Table 12.5). But the issue concerning expectations deals with realism; there are relative differences in academic performance among students, and there should be no stigma attached to the teachers' awareness of these differences. It is a problem only if the teachers' perceptions result in differential treatment that is harmful for any group of students, including the possibility of harming high achievers.

The consistency between teachers' perceptions and their interactions with students is mixed and uncertain—and not as clear-cut as the conventional wisdom would have us believe. For example, other research suggests that high achievers are more likely than low achievers to be called on by the teacher in class discussion, but when students are doing seatwork activities teachers are likely to spend more time with and talk to low achievers. In addition, low achievers are more likely to receive praise after a correct answer in large groups and receive sustained feedback after an incorrect answer.[40]

The problem of expectations is further compounded by the fact that high achievers seem more prone to view themselves in more favorable terms whereas researchers see no differences in teacher-student interactions between high and low achievers. Even when observers see interaction differences favoring low achievers, the low achievers are not prone to see themselves favorably. For example, low achievers more often than high achievers perceive teachers as calling on another student after calling on them, and spending less wait-time with them, but observers have reported that teachers more often turned to other students after incorrect answers were made by high achievers, and spent less time waiting for the high achievers to respond.[41] How these perceived student differences interact with researchers who continuously criticize teachers and their different perceptions and behaviors regarding high and low achievers is unclear.

In short, the most effective teacher is realistic about the differences between high and low achievers. The teacher who develops a rigid or stereotyped perception of students is likely to have a harmful effect on them. The teacher who understands that uniqueness and differences exist and adapts realistic methods and content accordingly will have the most positive effect on students. The need is not to get "hung up" or defensive when teachers treat students in a different way, say in terms of a homework or reading assignment, or in the

---

40 Alexis L. Mitman and Andrea A. Lash, "Students' Perceptions of their Academic Standing and Classroom Behavior," *Elementary School Journal* (September 1988), pp. 55–68.

41 Dona Kagan, "Ways of Evaluating Teacher Cognition," *Review of Educational Research* (Fall 1990), pp. 419–469; Mitman and Lash, "Students' Perceptions of their Academic Standing and Classroom Behavior."

Table 12.5 TEACHER BEHAVIOR WITH LOW ACHIEVERS AND HIGH ACHIEVERS

1. *Waiting less time for low achievers to answer questions*. Teachers often given high-achieving students more time to respond than low-achieving students.

2. *Interrupting low achievers more often*. Teachers interrupt low achievers more often than high achievers when they make reading mistakes and/or are unable to sustain a discussion about the content or lesson.

3. *Giving answers to low achievers*. Teachers more frequently respond to incorrect responses of low achievers by giving them the answer or calling on another student to answer the question than they do with high achievers.

4. *Rewarding inappropriate behavior*. Teachers at times praise inappropriate responses of low achievers, which serves to dramatize the weakness of such students.

5. *Criticizing low achievers more often and praising them less often*. Some teachers criticize low achievers more than high achievers, a practice that is likely to reduce initiative and risk-taking behavior. Moreover, low achievers seem less likely to be praised, even when they get the correct answer.

6. *Not confirming responses of low achievers*. Teachers sometimes respond to answers from low achievers with indifference. Even if the answers are correct, they call on other students to respond without confirming answers, a practice that is likely to sow seeds of doubt concerning the adequacy of their response.

7. *Paying less attention to low achievers*. Teachers simply pay less attention to low achievers. For example, they smile more frequently and maintain more eye contact with high achievers, give briefer and less informative feedback to low achievers' questions, and are less likely to follow through on time-consuming instructional methods with low achievers.

8. *Calling on low achievers less often*. Teachers seem inclined to call on high achievers more often than low achievers.

9. *Using different interaction patterns*. Contact patterns between teachers and students are different for high and low achievers. Public response patterns dominate in interaction with high achievers, but low achievers have more private contacts with teachers. For low achievers, private conferences may be a sign of inadequacy.

10. *Seating low achievers further from the teacher*. Teachers often place low achievers in locations that are more distant from them.

11. *Demanding less from low achievers*. Teachers are more likely to demand little from and give up on low achievers and let them know it. Teachers demand more work from high achievers and ask more high-level questions.

12. *Administering different tests and grades*. Teachers often give low achievers less demanding tests and assignments. They are more likely to give high achievers the benefit of the doubt in borderline cases involving grades.

Source: Adapted from Thomas L. Good, "Two Decades of Research on Teacher Expectations: Findings and Future Directions," *Journal of Teacher Education* (July–August 1987), pp. 32–47; Thomas L. Good and Jere E. Brophy, *Educational Psychology: A Realistic Approach*, 3rd ed. (White Plains, N.Y.: Longman, 1986).

types of questions they ask, without first giving the benefit of doubt to the teacher. Sometimes it is necessary to give students different tasks, according to abilities, needs, and/or interests—as long as they are pushed to their potential.

TEACHER CHARACTERISTICS

In the reams of research published on teacher behavior, the greatest amount concerns **teacher characteristics**. The problem is that researchers disagree on which teacher characteristics constitute successful teaching, on how to categorize characteristics, and on how to define them. In addition researchers use a variety of terms to name what they are trying to describe, such as "teacher traits," "teacher personality," "teacher performance," and "teacher outcomes."[42] Descriptors or characteristics have different meanings to different people, and even when similar descriptors are used, categories have dissimilar meanings. Warm behavior for one investigator often means something different for another; effects of such behavior may be seen differently. Further, it can be assumed that a warm teacher would have a different effect on students according to age, sex, achievement level, socioeconomic class, ethnic group, subject, and classroom context.[43]

These differences tend to operate for every teacher characteristic and to affect every study on teacher behavior. Although a list of teacher characteristics may be suitable for a particular study, the characteristics (as well as the results) cannot always be compared with another study. The fact is, they often are compared, integrated, and built upon each other to form a theory or viewpoint about which teacher characteristics are most effective.

Nonetheless, many researchers feel that certain teacher characteristics can be defined, validated, and generalized from one study to another, that recommendations can be made from the generalizations, and that the recommendations can be used in a practical way.

Classic Research on Teacher Characteristics

Although researchers have named literally thousands of teacher characteristics over the years, A. S. Barr organized recommended behaviors into a manageable list.[44] Reviewing some 50 years of research, he listed and defined 12 successful characteristics (Table 12.6). Other authorities have made other summaries of teacher characteristics, but Barr's work is considered most comprehensive.

---

42 Biddle, "The Integration of Teacher Effectiveness Research"; Gary D. Borich, ed., *The Appraisal of Teaching* (Reading, Mass.: Addison-Wesley, 1979).

43 Allan C. Ornstein, "Do Teachers Make a Difference?" *Childhood Education* (May–June 1983), pp. 342–351; Ornstein, "Teacher Effectiveness Research"; and Soar, Medley, and Coker, "Teacher Evaluation: A Critique of Currently Used Methods."

44 A. S. Barr, "Characteristics of Successful Teachers," *Phi Delta Kappan* (March 1958), pp. 282–284.

Table 12.6   BARR'S CHARACTERISTICS IMPORTANT FOR SUCCESSFUL TEACHING

1. *Resourcefulness*. Originality, creativeness, initiative, imagination, adventurousness, progressiveness.

2. *Intelligence*. Foresight, intellectual acuity, understanding, mental ability, intellectual capacity, common sense.

3. *Emotional stability*. Poise, self-control, steadfastness, sobriety, dignity, nonneuroticism, emotional maturity, adjustment, constancy, loyalty, easygoing realism in facing life, not excitable, stable, integrated character.

4. *Considerateness*. Appreciativeness, kindliness, friendliness, courteousness, sympathy, tact, good-naturedness, helpfulness, patience, politeness, thoughtfulness, tolerance.

5. *Buoyancy*. Optimism, enthusiasm, cheerfulness, gregariousness, fluency, talkativeness, sense of humor, pleasantness, carefreeness, vivaciousness, alertness, animation, idealism, articulativeness, expressiveness, wit.

6. *Objectivity*. Fairness, impartiality, open-mindedness, freedom from prejudice, sense of evidence.

7. *Drive*. Physical vigor, energy, perseverance, ambition, industry, endurance, motivation, purposefulness, speediness, zealousness, quickness.

8. *Dominance*. Self-confidence, forcefulness, decisiveness, courageousness, independence, insensitiveness to social approval, self-sufficiency, determination, thick-skinnedness, self-reliance, self-assertiveness.

9. *Attractiveness*. Dress, physique . . . personal magnetism, neatness, cleanliness, posture, personal charm, appearance.

10. *Refinement*. Good taste, modesty, morality, conventionality, culture, polish, well-readness.

11. *Cooperativeness*. Friendliness, easygoingness, geniality, generosity, adaptability, flexibility, responsiveness, trustfulness, warm-heartedness, unselfishness, charitableness.

12. *Reliability*. Accuracy, dependability, honesty, punctuality, responsibility, conscientiousness, painstakingness, trustworthiness, consistency, sincerity.

Source: A. S. Barr, "Characteristics of Successful Teachers," *Phi Delta Kappan* (March 1958), pp. 282–283.

While Barr presents an overview of hundreds of studies of teacher characteristics, the single most comprehensive study was conducted by David Ryans.[45] More than 6,000 teachers in 1,700 schools were involved in the study over a six-year period. The objective was to identify through observations and self-ratings the most desirable teacher characteristics. Respondents were asked to identify and describe a teaching act that they felt made a difference between success or failure. These critical behaviors were reduced to the list of 25 effective

45 David G. Ryans, *Characteristics of Teachers* (Washington, D.C.: American Council on Education, 1960).

Effective teachers exhibit various styles and behaviors. Viewed broadly, this teacher seems to portray Ryans' "understanding, friendly teacher" and Barr's "buoyant, cheerful" teacher.

behaviors and 25 ineffective behaviors (Table 12.7). The lists, combined with Barr's recommendations, serve as good guidelines for beginning and even experienced teachers. The teacher should examine them in terms of his or her own personality and perceptions of good teaching.

Ryans went on to develop a bipolar list of 18 teacher characteristics (for example, original versus conventional, patient versus impatient, hostile versus warm). Respondents were asked to identify the approximate position of teachers for each pair of characteristics on a seven-point scale. (A seven-point scale makes it easier for raters to avoid midpoint responses and nonpositions).

The 18 teacher characteristics were defined in detail and further grouped into three "patterns" of successful versus unsuccessful teachers:

1. *Pattern X*: understanding, friendly, responsive, versus aloof, egocentric
2. *Pattern Y*: responsible, businesslike, systematic, versus evading, unplanned, slipshod
3. *Pattern Z*: stimulating, imaginative, original, versus dull, routine

These three primary teacher patterns were the major qualities singled out for further attention. Elementary teachers scored higher than secondary teachers on the scales of understanding and friendly classroom behavior (Pattern X). Differences between women and men teachers were insignificant in the elementary schools, but in the secondary schools women consistently scored

Table 12.7   RYANS' CRITICAL TEACHER BEHAVIORS

Effective behaviors	Ineffective behaviors
1. Alert, appears enthusiastic.	1. Is apathetic, dull, appears bored.
2. Appears interested in pupils and classroom activities.	2. Appears uninterested in pupils and classroom activities.
3. Cheerful, optimistic.	3. Is depressed, pessimistic; appears unhappy.
4. Self-controlled, not easily upset.	4. Loses temper, is easily upset.
5. Likes fun, has sense of humor.	5. Is overly serious, too occupied for humor.
6. Recognizes and admits own mistakes.	6. Is unaware of, or fails to admit, own mistakes.
7. Is fair, impartial, and objective in treatment of pupils.	7. Is unfair or partial in dealing with pupils.
8. Is patient.	8. Is impatient.
9. Shows understanding and sympathy in working with pupils.	9. Is short with pupils, uses sarcastic remarks, or in other ways shows lack of sympathy with pupils.
10. Is friendly and courteous in relations with pupils.	10. Is aloof and removed in relations with pupils.
11. Helps pupils with personal as well as educational problems.	11. Seems unaware of pupils' personal needs and problems.
12. Commends effort and gives praise for work well done.	12. Does not commend pupils, is disapproving, hypercritical.
13. Accepts pupils' efforts as sincere.	13. Is suspicious of pupils' motives.
14. Anticipates reactions of others in social situations.	14. Does not anticipate reactions of others in social situations.
15. Encourages pupils to try to do their best.	15. Makes no effort to encourage pupils to try to do their best.
16. Classroom procedure is planned and well organized.	16. Classroom procedure is without plan, disorganized.
17. Classroom procedure is flexible within overall plan.	17. Shows extreme rigidity of procedure, inability to depart from plan.
18. Anticipates individual needs.	18. Fails to provide for individual differences and needs of pupils.
19. Stimulates pupils through interesting and original materials and techniques.	19. Uninteresting materials and teaching techniques used.
20. Conducts clear, practical demonstrations and explanations.	20. Demonstrations and explanations are not clear and are poorly conducted.
21. Is clear and thorough in giving directions.	21. Directions are incomplete, vague.
22. Encourages pupils to work through their own problems and evaluate their accomplishments.	22. Fails to give pupils opportunity to work out own problems or evaluate their own work.
23. Disciplines in quiet, dignified, and positive manner.	23. Reprimands at length, ridicules, resorts to cruel or meaningless form of correction.
24. Gives help willingly.	24. Fails to give help or gives it grudgingly.
25. Foresees and attempts to resolve potential difficulties.	25. Is unable to foresee and resolve potential difficulties.

Source: David G. Ryans, *Characteristics of Teachers* (Washington, D.C.: American Council on Education, 1960), p. 82.

higher in Pattern X and in stimulating and imaginative classroom behavior (Pattern Z), and men tended to exhibit businesslike and systematic behaviors (Pattern Y). Younger teachers (under 45 years) scored higher than older teachers in patterns X and Z; older teachers scored higher in pattern Y.

A similar but more recent list of teacher characteristics was compiled by Bruce Tuckman, who has developed a feedback system for stimulating change in teacher behavior.[46]   His instrument contains 28 bipolar items on which teachers are also rated on a seven-point scale (Table 12.8).

The characteristics cluster into four teacher "dimensions," similar to Ryans patterns:

1. *Creative.* The creative teacher is imaginative, experimenting, and original; the noncreative teacher is routine, exacting, and cautious.
2. *Dynamic.* The dynamic teacher is outgoing, energetic, and extroverted; the nondynamic teacher is passive, withdrawn, and submissive.
3. *Organized.* The organized teacher is purposeful, resourceful, and in control; the disorganized teacher is capricious, erratic, and flighty.
4. *Warm.* The warm teacher is sociable, amiable, and patient; the cold teacher is unfriendly, hostile, and impatient.[47]

TEACHER COMPETENCIES

Because of the problem with lack of agreement in defining teacher characteristics, Medley and others recommend more precise terms, what they call **teacher competencies.**[48] These competencies may or may not stem from broad teacher characteristics, but they are "specific items of behavior" that can be defined with the care necessary for inclusion in a manual of instruction or in a teacher-appraisal system.

The University of Toledo and the Salt Lake City school district have developed reliable lists of competencies. The 49 Toledo competencies were designed to measure five broad areas of behaviors (called topics) that student teachers should be expected to exhibit (Table 12.9). They reflect some 2,000 behavioral objectives on which the instrument was developed; they can apply to all preservice teachers K–12, and they can be used to assist beginning teachers as well. The Salt Lake City list contains 24 competencies in four broad categories (Table 12.10). The instrument was developed by administrators and teachers of

---

46 Bruce W. Tuckman, "Feedback and the Change Process," *Phi Delta Kappan* (January 1986), pp. 341–344; Tuckman, *Evaluating Instructional Programs*, 2nd ed. (Boston: Allyn & Bacon, 1985).

47 By 1990 Tuckman added two more bipolar adjectives (a total of 30) and one more dimension (flexibility); he termed the dimensions "interpersonal styles." See Bruce W. Tuckman, "An Interpersonal Construct Model of Teaching," paper presented at the annual meeting of the American Educational Research Association, Chicago, April 1991.

48 Donald M. Medley, Homer Coker, and Robert S. Soar, *Management-Based Evaluation of Teacher Performance* (New York: Longman, 1984), p. 58.

Table 12.8   TUCKMAN'S TEACHER CHARACTERISTICS

1.	Original	___	___	___	___	___	___	___	Conventional
2.	Patient	___	___	___	___	___	___	___	Impatient
3.	Cold	___	___	___	___	___	___	___	Warm
4.	Hostile	___	___	___	___	___	___	___	Amiable
5.	Creative	___	___	___	___	___	___	___	Routinized
6.	Inhibited	___	___	___	___	___	___	___	Uninhibited
7.	Iconoclastic	___	___	___	___	___	___	___	Ritualistic
8.	Gentle	___	___	___	___	___	___	___	Harsh
9.	Unfair	___	___	___	___	___	___	___	Fair
10.	Capricious	___	___	___	___	___	___	___	Certain
11.	Cautious	___	___	___	___	___	___	___	Outspoken
12.	Disorganized	___	___	___	___	___	___	___	Organized
13.	Unfriendly	___	___	___	___	___	___	___	Friendly
14.	Resourceful	___	___	___	___	___	___	___	Unresourceful
15.	Reserved	___	___	___	___	___	___	___	Sociable
16.	Imaginative	___	___	___	___	___	___	___	Exacting
17.	Erratic	___	___	___	___	___	___	___	Systematic
18.	Aggressive	___	___	___	___	___	___	___	Passive
19.	Accepting	___	___	___	___	___	___	___	Critical
20.	Quiet	___	___	___	___	___	___	___	Bubbly
21.	Outgoing	___	___	___	___	___	___	___	Withdrawn
22.	In control	___	___	___	___	___	___	___	On the run
23.	Flighty	___	___	___	___	___	___	___	Conscientious
24.	Dominant	___	___	___	___	___	___	___	Submissive
25.	Observant	___	___	___	___	___	___	___	Preoccupied
26.	Introverted	___	___	___	___	___	___	___	Extroverted
27.	Assertive	___	___	___	___	___	___	___	Soft-spoken
28.	Timid	___	___	___	___	___	___	___	Adventurous

Source: Bruce W. Tuckman, "Feedback and the Change Process," *Phi Delta Kappan* (January 1976), p. 342. Also see Tuckman, *Evaluating Instructional Programs*, 2nd ed. (Boston: Allyn & Bacon, 1985), p. 95.

Table 12.9   UNIVERSITY OF TOLEDO COMPETENCY INDICATORS

Topic: Planning, teaching materials/equipment and evaluation

1. Plans units of instruction.
2. Plans instruction at a variety of cognitive levels.
3. Can state pupil outcomes and/or student course objectives in behavioral terms (behavioral objectives).
4. Has realistic expectations for the learning process and student readiness for learning.
5. Gathers, organizes, and evaluates pertinent information about students for effective instruction.
6. Identifies and evaluates learning problems of students in content area being taught.
7. Keeps informed of current professional/subject area literature and curricular learning materials/resources available.
8. Knows how to select (or construct), organize and use appropriate instructional materials and equipment to facilitate learning activities.
9. Uses criteria and effective procedures for determining pupil achievement of learning objectives.
10. Selects/develops appropriate assessment techniques and instruments for instructional activities.
11. Collects, quantifies, and interprets data from appropriate assessment instruments.
12. Maintains evaluation records.
13. Engages in professional development by obtaining and analyzing evaluative information concerning the effectiveness of instruction.
14. Uses information about the effectiveness of instruction to revise it, with possible curriculum modifications.
15. Relates to accountability issues concerning responsibilities to students, parents, and the instructional process.

Topic: Instructional strategies, techniques, and/or methods

16. Uses a variety of instructional strategies.
17. Uses convergent and divergent inquiry strategies.
18. Develops and demonstrates problem-solving skills.
19. Establishes transitions and sequences in instruction which are varied.
20. Modifies instructional activities to accommodate identified learner needs.
21. Demonstrates ability to work with individuals, small groups and large groups.
22. Structures the use of time to facilitate student learning.
23. Uses a variety of resources and materials.
24. Provides learning experiences which enable students to transfer principles and generalizations to situations outside of school.
25. Provides assignments/learning opportunities interesting and appropriate to different ability levels of pupils.
26. Demonstrates knowledge in the subject areas.

Table 12.9 (Continued)

27. Demonstrates self-direction and conveys the impression of knowing what to do and how to do it.

28. Works effectively as a member of an instructional team.

29. Uses acceptable written and oral expression with learners.

30. Adjusts components of the physical/learning environment over which the teacher has control to facilitate learning.

Topic: Communication with learners

31. Provides group communication (cooperation, interaction, learning from others).

32. Uses a variety of functional verbal and nonverbal communication skills with students.

33. Gives clear directions and explanations.

34. Motivates students to ask questions.

35. Uses questions that lead students to analyze, synthesize and think critically.

36. Accepts varied student viewpoints and/or asks students to extend or elaborate answers or ideas.

37. Demonstrates proper listening skills.

38. Provides feedback to learners on their cognitive performance.

39. Expresses a positive personal attitude toward the teaching profession.

Topic: Learner reinforcement-involvement

40. Maintains an environment in which students are actively involved, working on-task.

41. Implements an effective classroom management system for positive student behavior (discipline).

42. Uses positive reinforcement patterns with students.

43. Assists students in discovering and correcting errors and inaccuracies.

44. Develops student feedback, evaluation skills and student self-evaluation.

Topic: Professional standards

45. Accepts responsibility, is dependable.

46. Evidences cooperation with others (teachers, administrators, support staff, parents, etc.) in planning and teaching.

47. Acts as an appropriate model in terms of ethics, attitudes and values.

48. Attends teacher and other professional meetings.

49. Understands and follows school law, policies, and procedures and their effects on teachers and teaching, including professional conduct standards.

Source: Thomas Gibney and William Wiersma, "Using Profile Analysis for Student Teacher Evaluation," *Journal of Teacher Education* (May–June 1986), p. 43.

the school district and therefore is valid for that particular school setting. It is used chiefly for purposes of remediation and improvement and is applicable to teachers of all grades and subjects.

Both sets of competencies deal mainly with what the teacher is doing while teaching. Both sets deal with specific behaviors as opposed to broad characteristics or teaching patterns. Because the competencies are more specific, long lists are needed to get an idea of the teacher's performance. The longer the list, however, the greater the chance that the competencies will overlap and cluster in other broad categories, which brings us back to the problem of many teacher characteristic inventories.

Because such long lists of competencies can be generated, it is important to determine which competencies school principals believe to be significant, since they invariably play a role in developing teacher evaluation plans, in observing and judging teachers (usually at the elementary and junior high level), and in assigning supervisors to evaluate teachers' performance (usually at the high school level). In a nationwide study of 202 secondary schools selected for special recognition for effectiveness in educating their students (conducted under the aegis of the U.S. Department of Education), principals were asked to identify and rank the competencies they emphasized with teachers.[49] The top 11 competencies are presented in Table 12.11.

The five competencies most important for principals—task orientation, enthusiasm and interest, direct instruction, pacing, and feedback—emphasize the "active" dimension of teaching and businesslike behaviors. Principals of effective schools expect their teachers to teach and in a way that can be observed and measured. One might assume, however, that elementary principals might have emphasized fewer task-oriented explicit behaviors and more socially oriented and humanistic behaviors.

In general, most measurements of teacher competence focus on minimal competencies. According to Arthur Wise, school districts and administrators that evaluate competencies of teachers spend "little time evaluating teachers who appear to be competent"; therefore, competent teachers often are not threatened by the process nor do they consider it useful. "Rather they criticize evaluations for providing too few observations and evaluators for making [too few] comments . . . [that] relate specifically to . . . their particular teaching assignment." This does not mean that teacher competency instruments are invalid or unreliable measures; rather, their present utility is linked to identifying teacher incompetence. In some school districts, for example, "the absence of minimal teaching competence, especially the inability to manage the classroom triggers remediation, probation, or intervention."[50]

---

49 John W. Arnn and John N. Mangieri, "Effective Leadership for Effective Schools: A Survey of Principal Attitudes," *NASSP Bulletin* (February 1988), pp. 1–7.

50 Arthur E. Wise et al., "Teacher Evaluation: A Study of Effective Practices," *Elementary School Journal* (September 1985), p. 94.

Table 12.10   SALT LAKE CITY SCHOOL DISTRICT COMPETENCY INDICATORS

1. Determines standards of expected student performance

   a. Preassessment (diagnosis)

   b. Competencies expected at a given level

   c. Determines individual needs

   d. Expected goals for student achievement

   e. Evaluation of goals

2. Provides learning environment

   a. Availability of resource personnel

   b. Availability of variety of resource materials

   c. Physical organization and learning process

   d. Positive attitude toward students

   e. Exhibits an attitude that all students can learn

   f. Teacher shows enthusiasm and commitment for the subject taught

   g. Student behavior demonstrates acceptance of learning experience

3. Demonstrates appropriate student control

   a. Evidence that student knows what to do

   b. Evidence that student is working at task

   c. Demonstrates fairness, acceptance, and flexibility

   d. Appropriate control in difficult situations

   e. Anticipates and avoids crisis situations

4. Demonstrates appropriate strategies for teaching

   a. Demonstrates techniques that are appropriate to different levels of learning

   b. Adjusts techniques to different learning styles

   c. Uses variety of techniques to teach specific skill or concept

   d. Gives directions that are clear, concise, and appropriate to the student learning level

   e. Establishes two-way communication with students and utilizes feedback to determine teaching strategies

   f. Demonstrates that a purpose has been determined for the instruction

   g. Exhibits evidence of effective planning

Source: A Continuing Written Agreement . . . Between the Board of Education of Salt Lake City . . . and Salt Lake Teachers Association, 1988–89. (Salt Lake City, Utah: Salt Lake Teachers Association, 1988), Article 11, pp. 36–37.

Table 12.11   PRINCIPALS' RANKING OF EFFECTIVE TEACHER COMPETENCIES

Rank of importance	Competency	Definition
1	Task orientation	The extent to which the classroom is businesslike, the students spend their time on academic subjects, and the teacher presents clear goals to the students
2	Enthusiasm and interest	The amount of the teacher's vigor, power, and involvement
3	Direct instruction	The extent to which the teacher sets and articulates the learning goals, actively assesses student progress, and frequently makes class presentations illustrating how to do assigned work
4	Pacing	The extent to which the level of difficulty and the pace of the lesson is appropriate for the students' ability and interest
5	Feedback	The extent to which the teacher provides the students with positive and negative feedback
6	Management	The extent to which the teacher is able to conduct the class without instruction being interrupted
7	Questioning	The extent to which the teacher asks questions at different levels and adjusts them appropriately in the classroom
8	Instructional time	The allocation of a period of time for a lesson adequate to cover the material yet flexible enough to allow for the unexpected
9	Variability	The amount of flexibility or adaptability of teaching methods; the amount of extra material in the classroom
10	Structuring	The extent to which the teacher directs instruction
11	Opportunity to learn criterion material	The extent to which criterion material is covered in class

Source: John W. Arnn and John N. Mangieri, "Effective Leadership for Effective Schools: A Survey of Principal Attitudes," NAASP Bulletin (February 1988), p. 4.

A further word of caution is needed. Many school districts (even entire states such as Florida and North Carolina) have developed a specific list of teacher competencies as a basis for appraisal and merit pay plans. Teachers who do not exhibit explicit behaviors are often penalized, labeled as "marginal" or "below standard," and in some cases they may lose their jobs. According to critics, these lists of competencies tend to reflect a narrow and behaviorist view of a "good" teacher and to ignore humanistic or affective behaviors that also contribute to good teaching.[51] Brophy takes a middle position: describing uses and misuses. He maintains that schools should develop guidelines for teaching "based on process-outcome research linking teaching behavior to student outcomes," but also warns that there are "limitations of scientific data in general and of teacher effects data in particular."[52] He asserts that the new research on teacher effectiveness allows schools "to attain given sets of prioritized objectives," as well as teaching "norms and guidelines ... within a range of variance," but it can also "subject [teachers] to overly rigid or otherwise inappropriate prescriptions."[53]

Nevertheless, the national movement for reform in education, coupled with the influence of the behaviorist movement in psychology, has pushed for an appraisal system based on specific teacher competencies. When used for such purposes, multiple observations are required. If inferences or decisions about teaching competencies are to be the grounds for personnel decisions, then adequate sampling of teacher performance is necessary (especially in an era of litigation).

Wise maintains that successful appraisal of competencies requires four factors: (1) *commitment*—top level leadership must approve of the evaluation process and allocate institutional resources for it; (2) *evaluator competence*—the evaluator (or user) must have the expertise to perform the task of observation (or analysis); (3) *collaboration*—administrators, supervisors, and teachers must develop a common understanding of the goals and processes involved; and (4) *compatibility*—there must be joint decision making, agreed-upon support systems, and agreement between evaluation goals and processes and school or district goals and processes.[54]

Successful appraisal also requires a degree of willingness to give the teacher being appraised the benefit of doubt and a chance to remediate before being terminated. It also calls for an open mind so that other competencies not listed

51 David Holdzkom, "Appraising Teacher Performance in North Carolina," *Educational Leadership* (April 1987), pp. 40–44; Allan C. Ornstein, "The Changing Status of the Teaching Profession," *Urban Education* (October 1988), pp. 261–279; and Ornstein, "Theoretical Issues Related to Teaching."

52 Jere E. Brophy, "Research on Teacher Effects: Uses and Abuses," *Elementary School Journal* (September 1988), pp. 5–6.

53 Ibid., pp. 6, 14.

54 Wise et al., "Teacher Evaluation: A Study of Effective Practices"; Arthur E. Wise, Linda Darling-Hammond, and Barnett Berry, *Effective Teacher Selection: From Recruitment to Retention* (Santa Monica, Calif.: The Rand Corporation, 1987).

can be incorporated into the appraisal system. It also calls for common sense—that there is more than one preferred model that connotes teacher competency.

Guidelines for Evaluating Teacher Characteristics and Competencies

Having to be evaluated in terms of characteristics or competencies can generate marked anxiety in beginning teachers. They need extra counseling and support to reduce their fears and to make them aware that a teacher's probationary period involves evaluation as a guide to improvement. One researcher suggests seven means of support that should be made available to beginning teachers who must be evaluated for minimal teacher competencies.

1. *System information*, providing information related to procedures, guidelines, and expectations of the school district.
2. *Resources and materials*, disseminating materials that explain the rationale of the process.
3. *Instructional information*, giving information about recommended teaching and instructional methods.
4. *Emotional support*, offering support by colleagues and supervisors through conferences and by sharing experiences.
5. *Classroom management suggestions*, providing ideas and guidance on effective management.
6. *Classroom environment suggestions*, providing ideas and guidance on arranging and organizing the physical setting of the classroom.
7. *Demonstration teaching*, permitting new teachers to observe experienced teachers and to discuss competencies in a follow-up conference.[55]

The model developed by Ben Harris provides a method for improving teaching by analyzing classroom behavior. It requires teachers and supervisors to agree upon behaviors that will be observed and analyzed, and upon the importance of those behaviors.

1. Establish criteria that indicate positive teacher characteristics or competencies.
2. Observe the teacher three separate times by three different "sources," or professionals (colleague, supervisor, principal).

---

55 Sandra J. Odell, "Induction Support of New Teachers: A Functional Approach," *Journal of Teacher Education* (January–February 1986), pp. 26–29.

3. Rate the teacher on the agreed-upon criteria.
4. Compare the perceptions or analyses of the three observers.
   a. All agree behaviors are clearly demonstrated.
   b. All agree behaviors are not demonstrated.
   c. Two out of three agree behaviors are demonstrated.
   d. Two out of three agree behaviors are not demonstrated.
5. Generate four types of diagnoses.
   a. *Accomplishments*—areas where all three sources (observers) agree that characteristics or competencies are clearly demonstrated.
   b. *Need for improvement*—areas where all three sources agree that characteristics or competencies are not demonstrated.
   c. *Uncertainty* (need attention)—areas where sources disagree or question.
   d. *Refine/upgrade*—areas where sources agree that refinement or upgrading is required.[56]

TEACHER EFFECTS

Teacher behavior research has shown that teacher behaviors, as well as specific teaching principles and methods, make a difference with regard to student outcomes. Rosenshine and Furst analyzed some 42 correlational studies in their often quoted review of **process-product research**. They concluded that there were 11 teacher processes (behaviors or variables) strongly and consistently related to products (outcomes or student achievement). The first five teacher processes showed the strongest correlation to positive outcomes.

1. *Clarity* of teacher's presentation and ability to organize classroom activities
2. *Variability* of media, materials, and activities used by the teacher
3. *Enthusiasm*, defined in terms of the teacher's movement, voice inflection, and the like
4. *Task orientation* or businesslike teacher behaviors, structured routines, and an academic focus
5. *Student opportunity to learn*, that is, the teacher's coverage of the material or content in class on which students are later tested.[57]

---

56 Ben M. Harris, *Developmental Teacher Evaluation* (Boston: Allyn & Bacon, 1986); Harris, *In-Service Education for Staff Development* (Needham Heights, Mass.: Allyn & Bacon, 1989).

57 Barak V. Rosenshine and Norma F. Furst, "Research in Teacher Performance Criteria," in B. O. Smith, ed., *Research on Teacher Education* (Englewood Cliffs, N.J.: Prentice-Hall, 1971), pp. 337–372; Rosenshine and Furst, "The Use of Direct Observation to Study Teaching," in R. M. Travers, ed., *Second Handbook of Research on Teaching* (Chicago: Rand McNally, 1973), pp. 122–183. Note that the first five processes also appear in Arnn and Mangieri's list of competencies (Table 12.11), but in different order of importance.

The six remaining processes were classified as promising: use of student ideas, justified criticism, use of structuring comments, appropriate questions in terms of lower and higher cognitive level, probing or encouraging student elaboration, and challenging instructional materials.

With the Rosenshine and Furst review, it appeared that research on **teacher effectiveness** had begun to provide objective information about what teachers do, how it relates or contributes to student learning, and how it can be measured. As critics pointed out, however, the studies cited in their review and even their own analysis were marked by serious technical problems and made prescriptions based on such evidence hazardous.[58]

Rosenshine himself later revised his conclusions; subsequent analysis showed that only two behaviors or processes consistently correlated with student achievement: (1) task orientation (later referred to as *direct instruction*) and (2) opportunity to learn (later referred to as *academic time, academic engaged time,* and *content covered*). On a third behavior, clarity, he wavered, pointing out that it seemed to be a correlate of student achievement for students above the fifth grade. The other eight processes appeared to be less important and varied in importance not only according to grade level, but also according to subject matter, instructional groups and activities, and students' social class and abilities.[59] Nevertheless, the original review remains a valuable study on how teacher processes related to student products.

The Gage Model

Nate Gage recently analyzed 49 process-product studies. He identified four clusters of behaviors that show a strong relationship to student outcomes: (1) *teacher indirectness,* the willingness to accept student ideas and feelings and the ability to provide a healthy emotional climate; (2) *teacher praise,* support and encouragement, use of humor to release tensions (but not at the expense of others), and attention to students' needs; (3) *teacher acceptance,* clarifying, building, and developing students' ideas; and (4) *teacher criticism,* reprimanding students and justifying authority. The relationship between the last cluster and outcome was negative; where criticism occurred, student achievement was low.[60] In effect, the four clusters suggest the traditional notion of a democratic or warm teacher (nothing more than what has been emphasized for several decades).

---

58 Robert W. Heath and Mark A. Nielson, "The Research Bias for Performance Based Teacher Education," *Review of Educational Research* (Fall 1974), pp. 463–484; Ornstein, "How Good Are Teachers in Affecting Student Outcomes?"

59 Barak V. Rosenshine, "Content, Time and Direct Instruction," in Peterson and Walberg, eds., *Research on Teaching: Concepts, Findings, and Implications,* pp. 28–56.

60 N. L. Gage, *The Scientific Basis of the Art of Teaching* (New York: Teachers College Press, Columbia University, 1978).

From a review and synthesis of teaching and achievement in reading and mathematics, Gage presents successful teaching principles and methods that seem relevant to most subjects and grades. These strategies are summarized below. Bear in mind that they are commonsense strategies; they apply to many grade levels, and most experienced teachers are familiar with them. Nonetheless, they provide guidelines for education students or beginning teachers who say, "Just tell me how to teach."

1. Teachers should have a system of rules that allows students to attend to their personal and procedural needs without having to check with the teacher.
2. A teacher should move around the room, monitoring students' seatwork and communicating an awareness of their behavior while also attending to their academic needs.
3. To ensure productive independent work by students, teachers should be sure that the assignments are interesting and worthwhile, yet still easy enough to be completed by each student without teacher direction.
4. Teachers should keep to a minimum such activities as giving directions and organizing the class for instruction. Teachers can do this by writing the daily schedule on the board and establishing general procedures so students know where to go and what to do.
5. In selecting students to respond to questions, teachers should call on volunteers and nonvolunteers by name before asking questions to give all students a chance to answer and to alert the student to be called upon.
6. Teachers should always aim at getting less academically oriented students to give some kind of response to a question. Rephrasing, giving clues, or asking leading questions can be useful techniques for bringing forth some answer from a silent student, one who says "I don't know," or one who answers incorrectly.
7. During reading group instruction, teachers should give a maximum amount of brief feedback and provide fast-paced activities of the "drill" type.[61]

The Good and Brophy Model

Good and Brophy have identified several factors related to effective teaching and student learning. They are basically principles of teaching, but not teacher behaviors or characteristics. In this connection, the researchers contend that teachers today are looking more for principles of teaching than for prescriptions.

---

61 Ibid. The author disagrees with item 5; see Chapter 7 on questioning; also, some reading experts recommend less drill and more reading for enjoyment.

1. *Clarity* about instructional goals (objectives).
2. Knowledge about *content* and ways for teaching it.
3. *Variety* in the use of teaching methods and media.
4. *"With-it-ness,"* awareness of what is going on, alertness in monitoring classroom activities.
5. *"Overlapping,"* sustaining an activity while doing something else at the same time.
6. *"Smoothness,"* sustaining proper lesson pacing and group momentum, not dwelling on minor points or wasting time dealing with individuals, and focusing on all the students.
7. *Seatwork* instructions and management that initiate and focus on productive task engagement.
8. Holding students *accountable* for learning; accepting responsibility for student learning.
9. *Realistic expectations* in line with student abilities and behaviors.
10. *Realistic praise*, not praise for its own sake.
11. *Flexibility* in planning and adapting classroom activities.
12. *Task orientation* and businesslike behavior in the teacher.
13. *Monitoring* of students' understanding; providing appropriate feedback, giving praise, asking questions.
14. *Providing students the opportunity to learn* what is to be tested.
15. Making comments that help *structure learning* of knowledge and concepts for students; helping students learn how to learn.[62]

The fact that many of these behaviors are classroom management techniques and structured learning strategies, rooted in Kounin's model of classroom management and discipline, suggests that good discipline is a prerequisite for good teaching.

The Evertson and Emmer Model

The Evertson and Emmer model is similar to the Good and Brophy model (in fact, Evertson has written several texts and articles with Brophy). The models are similar in three ways: (1) teacher effectiveness is associated with specific teaching principles and methods; (2) organization and management of instructional activities are stressed, and (3) the conclusions of the educators are based primarily on process-product studies. A good deal of the work is stems from the time when Evertson, Emmer, and Brophy were colleagues at the University

---

62 Thomas L. Good and Jere E. Brophy, *Looking in Classrooms*, 5th ed. (New York: HarperCollins, 1991); Good and Brophy, "Teacher Behavior and Student Achievement," in M. C. Wittrock, ed., *Handbook of Research on Teaching*, 3rd ed. (New York: Macmillan, 1986), pp. 328–375. Also see Andrew C. Porter and Jere Brophy, "Synthesis of Research on Good Teaching," *Educational Leadership* (May 1988), pp. 74–85.

of Texas at Austin (they all went their separate ways by the mid-1980s). Their work is also based on nearly 15 years of collaborative research.

Nine basic teaching principles represent the core of Evertson's work with Emmer and, to a lesser extent, with Brophy. Effectiveness is identified as raising student achievement scores.

1. *Rules and procedures.* Rules and procedures are established and enforced and students are monitored for compliance.
2. *Consistency.* Similar expectations are maintained for activities and behavior at all times for all students. Inconsistency causes confusion in students about what is acceptable.
3. *Prompt management of inappropriate behavior.* Inappropriate behavior is quickly stopped to prevent its spread.
4. *Checking student work.* All student work, including seatwork, homework, and papers, is corrected; errors are discussed; and feedback is provided promptly.
5. *Interactive teaching.* This takes several forms and includes presenting and explaining new materials, question sessions, discussions, checking for student understanding, actively moving among students to correct work, providing feedback, and, if necessary, reteaching materials.
6. *Academic instruction,* sometimes referred to as "academic learning time" or "academic engaged time." Attention is focused on the management of student work.
7. *Pacing.* Information is presented at a rate appropriate to the students' ability to comprehend it, not too rapidly or too slowly.
8. *Transitions.* Transitions from one activity to another are made rapidly, with minimum confusion about what to do next.
9. *Clarity.* Lessons are presented logically and sequentially. Clarity is enhanced by the use of instructional objectives and adequate illustrations and by keeping in touch with students.[63]

Principles of Instruction

From the integration of research on how young children learn, Linda Anderson and her colleagues (Evertson and Brophy) have developed an instructional model consisting of 22 specific principles. The model was based on process-

---

63 Edmund T. Emmer, Carolyn M. Evertson, and Jere E. Brophy, "Stability of Teacher Effects in Junior High Classrooms," *American Educational Research Journal* (Winter 1979), pp. 71–75; Emmer et al., *Classroom Management for Secondary Schools,* 2nd ed. (Englewood Cliffs, N.J.: Prentice-Hall, 1989); Evertson, "Do Teachers Make a Difference?" *Education and Urban Society* (February 1986), pp. 195–210; Evertson and Emmer, "Effective Management at the Beginning of the School Year in Junior High Classes," *Journal of Educational Psychology* (August 1982), pp. 485–498; and Evertson et al., *Classroom Management for Elementary Teachers,* 2nd ed. (Englewood Cliffs, N.J.: Prentice-Hall, 1989).

product studies on teaching reading to primary grade students in whole-group instruction. However, the researchers contend that the principles are curriculum-neutral and apply across subject matter and grade levels. The principles, listed in Table 12.12, correlate with student achievement and provide guidelines for organizing, managing, and instructing classroom groups as a whole. They make it possible for the teacher to provide as much individual attention as possible in a group setting. By and large, the 22 principles coincide with direction instruction and mastery learning.

The Master Teacher

The national interest in education reform and excellence in teaching has focused considerable attention on the notion of the "master teacher." The instructional principles suggested by Anderson, the direct behaviors suggested by Medley, and the Good, Brophy, and Evertson models correspond with Walter Doyle's task-oriented and businesslike description of a master teacher. Such teachers "focus on academic goals, are careful and explicit in structuring activities . . . , promote high levels of student academic involvement and content coverage, furnish opportunities for controlled practice with feedback, hold students accountable for work, . . . have expectations that they will be successful in helping students learn, [and are] active in explaining concepts and procedures, promoting meaning and purpose for academic work, and monitoring comprehension."[64]

When 641 elementary and secondary teachers were asked to "rate criteria for recognition of a master teacher," they listed in rank order: (1) knows the subject matter, (2) encourages student achievement through positive reinforcement, (3) uses a variety of strategies and materials to meet the needs of all students, (4) maintains an organized and disciplined classroom, (5) stimulates students' active participation in classroom activities, (6) maximizes student instruction time, (7) has high expectations of student performance, and (8) frequently monitors student progress and provides feedback regarding performance.[65]

Although the sample of teachers was predominately female (71 percent), so that it can be argued that the recommended behaviors reflect female norms, it must be noted that the teaching profession is predominately female (67 percent, according to NEA survey data). Most important, the teachers were experienced (77 percent had been teaching for at least 11 years) and their rank order list of criteria corresponds closely to the principals' rank order list (see Table 12.11) and to Doyle's notion of a master teacher. The teachers emphasize academic

---

64 Walter Doyle, "Effective Teaching and the Concept of Master Teacher," *Elementary School Journal* (September 1985), p. 30.

65 Jann E. Azumi and James L. Lerman, "Selecting and Rewarding Master Teachers," *Elementary School Journal* (November 1987), p. 197.

Table 12.12   PRINCIPLES OF INSTRUCTION AND THE EFFECTIVE TEACHER

I. Obtaining group attention

1. *Getting started*. The lesson should start quickly; use standard and predictable signals to get the attention of the class.

2. *Seating*. Seat the class so you can work with the whole group and individuals at the same time.

II. *Introducing the lesson*

3. *Overview*. Provide an overview of the lesson to prepare students for the remaining presentation.

4. *New learning*. Present new words, skills, and tasks in the beginning of the lesson so they can be used and integrated into the instructional activities.

5. *Practice*. Provide practice in new skills and tasks until they are understood. Phase in new learning gradually while old learning is being mastered.

6. *Work assignments*. Be sure students know what to do and how to do it. Before asking them to work independently, have them explain or demonstrate how the activities will be accomplished.

III. *Ensuring everyone's attention*

7. *Monitoring*. Move around the room and check everyone's work during the lesson; provide feedback.

8. *Ordered turns*. Adopt a pattern or style of selecting students to read or answer questions; students should know when to expect their turn, thus reducing their anxiety about being called to recite.

9. *Alertness*. Keep students alert between turns by occasionally questioning a student about a previous response from another student.

10. *Minimizing call outs*. Don't allow call outs; emphasize that everyone must wait his or her turn.

IV. *Meeting individual needs within the group*

11. *Differences in learning*. Be aware of different rates of learning; consider when the group as a whole can or cannot move on to the next part of the lesson.

12. *Needed assistance*. Provide extra help when necessary, after class or the next day before class begins.

13. *Models*. Use students who have mastered the content as models for others.

14. *Tutorial assistance*. If one or more students still have difficulty mastering the content, provide tutorial assistance.

V. *Teacher questioning and students responding*

15. *Academic focus*. Concentrate questions on academic content; minimize questions that deal with personal experiences.

16. *Wait for answers*. After asking a question, wait for the students to answer. Some students need extra time to think. Do not continue to wait if the student seems confused or embarrassed.

17. *Providing the answer if necessary*. When a student is unable to respond to a question, call on another student or give the answer, especially if the question deals with factual knowledge.

Table 12.12   (Continued)

18. *Explaining and elaborating if necessary.* If a question requires thinking, explain the steps involved in answering the question. If the student is unable to respond to a question or is incorrect, rephrase the question or provide clues.

19. *Acknowledging correct answers.* Acknowledge correct responses; make sure everyone hears and understands the answer.

20. *Follow-up questions.* Occasionally use follow-up questions to the same student (or to another student) to help integrate information or extend ideas to a logical conclusion.

VI. *Praising and criticizing*

21. *Praising in moderation.* Provide moderate praise for specific achievements and behaviors. Recognize effort and creative thinking, even if the answer is wrong.

22. *Avoiding criticism.* Use correction, not criticism; specify correct or desirable alternatives.

Source: Adapted from Linda M. Anderson, Carolyn M. Evertson, and Jere E. Brophy, "An Experimental Study of Effective Teaching in First-Grade Reading Groups," *Elementary School Journal* (March 1979), pp. 193–223; Anderson, Evertson and Brophy, *Principles of Small Group Instruction in Elementary Reading*, paper no. 58 (East Lansing, Mich.: Institute for Research on Teaching, Michigan State University, 1982). Also see Jere E. Brophy and Thomas L. Good, "Teaching Behavior and Student Achievement," in M. C. Wittrock, ed., *Handbook of Research on Teaching*, 3rd ed. (New York: Macmillan, 1986), p. 346.

focus, high expectations, organized classrooms, and variety in strategies and methods. They stress task orientation (although not as much as the principals do), enthusiasm and interest, direct instruction, and feedback. Finally, both teachers and principals consider working with and responding to students to be important.

Cautions and Criticisms

Although the notions of teacher competencies and teacher effectiveness are often identified as something new in research efforts to identify good teaching, they are nothing more than a combination of teaching principles and methods that good teachers have been using for many years prior to this recent wave of research. What these product-oriented researchers have accomplished is to summarize what we have known for a long time but often passed on in the form of "tips for teachers" or practical suggestions (which were once criticized by researchers as being recipe-oriented). These researchers confirm the basic principles and methods of experienced teachers; however, they give credibility to the teachers' practices by correlating their behaviors (processes) to student achievement (products). The researchers do dispel the notion that teachers have little or no measurable effect on student achievement.

More important, the new research on teaching helps provide a professional knowledge base for teacher educators and teacher training institutions. If this knowledge base continues to develop and is appropriately used, it can help provide information to use when making decisions about appropriate teaching techniques—even who should teach. Jere Brophy goes so far as maintaining that this new knowledge base empowers teachers because it allows them to act confidently on the basis of well-established principles rather than on trial and error. He compares the potential power of this new knowledge base with the medical profession—and how scientific knowledge influences and upgrades the practice of medicine.[66]

But knowing the past limitations of so-called scientific research on teaching, coupled with what we know about the art of teaching, it might be an overstatement to maintain there is an agreed-upon knowledge base undergirding the profession of teaching. Instead of an agreed-upon knowledge base, what we have in the literature is a host of theories, models, and ideas that are floating around—to be analyzed and reanalyzed—and very little of this "new" knowledge differs from the "old" knowledge: what teachers have been calling "common sense."

Indeed, there is some danger in the new research. The conclusions overwhelmingly portray the effective teacher as task-oriented, organized, and structured (nothing more than Ryans' Pattern Y teacher). But the teacher competency and teacher effectiveness models tend to overlook the friendly, warm, and democratic teacher; the creative teacher who is stimulating and imaginative; the dramatic teacher who bubbles with energy and enthusiasm; the philosophical teacher who encourages students to play with ideas and concepts; and the problem-solving teacher who requires that students think out the answers. In the new researchers' desire to identify and prescribe behaviors that are measurable and quantifiable, they overlook the emotional, qualitative, and interpretive descriptions of classrooms, and the joys of teaching. One would expect more social and psychological factors to be observed, recorded, and recommended as effective. A good portion of their work also deals with low achievers and at-risk students—perhaps the reason why many of their generalizations or principles coincide with classroom management and structured and controlling techniques, as well as explicit teaching.

Maxine Greene asserts that a good deal of teaching is not subject to empirical inquiry or correlates of student achievement. For Greene, good teaching and learning involve values, experiences, insights, imagination, and appreciation—the "stuff" that cannot be easily observed or measured. For her, teaching and learning are an existential encounter, a general philosophical process involving ideas and creative inquiries, which cannot be easily quantified.[67]

---

66 Brophy, "Research on Teacher Effects: Uses and Abuses"

67 Maxine Greene, "Philosophy and Teaching," in Wittrock, ed., *Handbook of Research on Teaching*, pp. 479–500; Greene, *The Dialectic of Teaching* (New York: Teachers College Press, Columbia University, 1988).

Elliot Eisner is concerned that what is not measurable goes unnoticed in a product-oriented teaching model. By breaking down the teaching act into dimensions and competencies and criteria that can be defined operationally and quantified, educators overlook the hard-to-measure aspects of teaching, the personal, humanistic, and playful aspects of teaching.[68] To say that excellence in teaching requires measurable behaviors and outcomes is to miss a substantial part of teaching—what some educators refer to as artistry, drama, tone, and flavor.[69]

Gerald Unks is also concerned that the teacher effectiveness models are too behaviorist and product-oriented. Teacher behaviors that correlate with measurable outcomes often lead to rote learning, "learning bits" and not wholes, memorization, drill, and automatic responses. This current teaching-learning set treats the "mind as a jug" to be filled up with facts that will later be funneled out in a test.[70] The new models also seem to miss moral and ethical outcomes, as well as social, personal, and self-actualizing facets related to learning and life—in effect, the affective domain of learning and the psychology of being human. In their attempt to observe and measure what teachers do, and detail whether students improve their performance on reading or math tests, these models ignore the learner's imagination, fantasy, and artistic thinking—their dreams, hopes, and aspirations, and the impact teachers have on these hard to define but very important aspects of the students' life. The chief variable of this current research is cognitive performance; if there is a secondary variable, it is student control. Learning experiences that deal with character, spiritual outlook, and philosophy are absent.[71] The whole person and human dimension of teaching is usually ignored—a sad commentary for a helping profession.

The new and popular teacher competency and teacher effectiveness models lock us into a narrow mold that misses many nuances of teaching. Many of these prescriptions (which the researchers call principles) themselves are old ideas bottled under new labels such as "with-it-ness," "smoothness," and "clarity." They seem to confirm what effective teachers have been doing for many years but never knew what to call it. The new research helps us label and confirm what is needed so that beginning teachers have a better yardstick or starting point.

Finally, the new models of research on teaching are paying closer attention to the content component of teaching and learning. In the past there has been

---

68 Elliot W. Eisner, *The Educational Imagination*, 2nd ed. (New York: Macmillan, 1985).

69 Ornstein, "Theoretical Issues Related to Teaching."

70 Gerald Unks, "Product-Oriented Teaching: A Reappraisal," *Educational and Urban Society* (February 1986), pp. 242–254.

71 Allan C. Ornstein, "A Look at Teacher Effectiveness Research: Theoretical Considerations," in H. C. Waxman and H. J. Walberg, eds., *Effective Teaching* (Berkeley, Calif.: McCutchan, 1991), pp. 63–80; Ornstein, "A Look at Teacher Effectiveness Research."

little mention by these researchers of the subject knowledge of the teacher, how it relates to student understanding, how it is taught, and how it can be integrated with the principles and methods they recommend. But they still pay little attention to the thought processes of learning, especially critical thinking, problem solving, creativity, and other forms of high-level cognition. By increasing the teacher's ability to teach students how to learn and by increasing the students' repertoire of tactics for learning, we can increase student achievement and learning beyond the classroom.

Thus the research on teacher effectiveness in the 1990s should be expanded to include more humanistic and affective principles, more emphasis on content or subject matter, and more emphasis on learning how to learn, or learning strategies. See Tips for Teachers 12.4.

The Human Factor

Good teachers know, although they may not be able to prove it, that good teaching is really about caring and sharing; the capacity to accept, understand, and appreciate students on their terms and through their world; making students feel good about themselves; having positive attitudes, and setting achievement goals; and getting all fired up with enthusiasm and a cheerful presence.[72]

These are basically fuzzy qualities that the scientific theories and paradigms of teaching tend to overlook. Indeed, teachers who place high priority on humanistic and affective practices, and on the personal and social development of their students, are not really interested in devoting much time to the empirical or behavioral literature, or in teaching small pieces of information that can be measured and correlated with their own teaching behaviors.

Researchers have found a direct relationship between student learning and teacher esteem. The higher the teacher's esteem, the more the students learned.[73] No one taught these teachers how to build their own self-esteem, or the esteem of their students. Yet, teachers who are confident about themselves are not overly concerned about their evaluation ratings, or even what the research has to say about their teacher behaviors. How does the profession reconcile the fact that so many competent teachers consider teacher research as "irrelevant and counterintuitive" to their own practice of teaching? Why do we often hear the complaint: "That's all good theory, but it does not work in practice."

---

72 Ron Abrell, "If Only I Had Known the ABCs," *Kappa Delta Pi Record* (Fall 1989), pp. 31–32; Margaret Mooney, "What Do You Do when You Teach?" *Teaching K-8* (August–September 1990), pp. 52–54.

73 Alan Hofmeister and Margaret Lubke, *Research into Practice: Implementing Effective Teaching Strategies* (Needham Heights, Mass.: Allyn & Bacon, 1991).

Tips for Teachers 12.4

Reaching and Teaching At-Risk Students

Most of the research on teacher competencies and teacher effectiveness stresses direct and explicit instructional techniques and overlooks attitudinal and motivational factors related to learning. The current principles of teaching tend to emphasize structure, sequence, seatwork, practice, monitoring, and feedback. Below are some methods that deal with the human side of teaching at-risk children. They have proven to be successful and complement and fill a void in the recent research on teaching.

ACHIEVEMENT

1. Focus on teaching basic skills as well as higher cognitive functioning levels based on knowledge of the skills.
2. Develop individualization and self-pacing, as well as mastery approaches to learning.
3. Recognize absolute achievement as well as improvement by expanding achievement awards, sending letters to parents, and notifying school officials.
4. Involve parents in their children's learning, especially in early grades.
5. Develop a peer tutoring program using classmates or upper-grade students.

ATTITUDE

1. Provide support, encouragement, and realistic praise.
2. Recognize good work, and provide confirmation of success.
3. Develop a class philosophy that each student is worthwhile and can learn.
4. Help students build self-esteem, a sense of responsibility, and self-respect.
5. Help students clarify values, deal with personal choices, and realize responsibility for themselves and for learning.
6. Hold "rap" sessions with students; listen to what they have to say, permit them to get to know one another, and express individual perspectives.
7. Involve students in school services and extracurricular activities to build self-confidence and group identification.
8. Invite people who dropped out to talk to students in class.

continues

9. Enforce classroom rules; instill a sense of pride in the students and the classroom.
10. Involve students in real-life situations; encourage them to deal with personal issues.
11. Use community resources by bringing people into the schools and by taking students on field trips.
12. Supply career education and information about jobs starting at an early grade level; provide work-related experiences in higher grades.

Source: Adapted from John V. Hamby, "How to Get an 'A' on Your Dropout Prevention Report Card," *Educational Leadership* (February 1989), pp. 21–28; Bettie B. Youngs, "The Phoenix Curriculum," *Educational Leadership* (February 1989), p. 24.

Teaching is a people industry, and people (especially young people) perform best in places where they feel wanted and respected. To be sure, it is possible for a teacher to "disengage" or "disinvite" students by belittling them, ignoring them, undercutting them, comparing them to other siblings or students, or even yessing them (failing to hold them accountable for the right answer), and still perform high on other discrete competencies or behaviors associated with the teacher as a technician: "The teacher came to class on time." "The teacher checked homework on a regular basis." "The teacher was clear about objectives of the course." "The teacher graded quizzes on a timely basis," etc. Such a competency-based model, checklist, or behaviorist approach is very common, as we search for a research-based model of what is a "good" teacher. But it ignores being part of a helping or caring profession, being a kind and generous teacher, or working with students so they develop their own uniqueness.

The focus of teacher research should be on the learner, not on content; on the feelings and attitudes of the student, not on knowledge and skills (since feelings and attitudes will eventually determine what knowledge and skills are sought after and acquired); and on long-term development and growth of the students, not on short-term objectives or specific tasks. But if teachers spend more time on the learner, on his or her feelings and attitudes, and on the social or personal growth and development of their students, they may be penalized when cognitive outcomes (little pieces of information) are correlated with their teaching behaviors.

Students need to be encouraged and nurtured by their teachers, especially when they are young (certainly up to the end of middle school and junior high school). They are too dependent on approval from significant adults—first their parents, then their teachers. The research suggests that parents and teachers need to help young children and adolescents establish a source for self-esteem by focusing on their strengths, supporting them, discouraging negative self-talk, and helping them take control of their lives and living by their own values.[74]

People (including young people) with high esteem achieve at high levels; and the more one achieves, the better one feels about oneself. The opposite is also true: students who fail to master the subject matter, get down on themselves—and eventually give up. Students with low self-esteem give up quickly. In short, student esteem and achievement are related, as are student esteem and self-reliance.[75] Put in different words, if we can nurture the students' self-esteem, almost everything else will fall into place, including achievement scores and academic outcomes.

This builds a strong argument for creating success experiences for students to help them feel good about themselves. The long-term benefits are obvious: the more students learn to like themselves, the more they will achieve; and, the more they achieve, the more they will like themselves. But that's down the road; that takes time, that's nurturing for future benefits; that does not show up on a classroom or standardized test within a semester or school year; it doesn't help the teacher who is being evaluated by a content-driven or test-driven school administrator. It certainly does not benefit the teacher who is being evaluated for how many times he or she attended departmental meetings or whether the shades in the classroom were even.

The research on teaching is primarily concerned with the present—with processes and products that are measured in one term (or year) and by a standardized test of cognitive outcomes (not affective outcomes). Thus, one might conclude that the new teacher effectiveness research misses the main mark. Students need to engage in growth-enhancing experiences; and we need to recognize that the most effective teachers endow their students with a "you can do it" attitude, with good feelings about themselves, which are indirectly and eventually related to cognitive achievement. While every teacher needs to demand high academic standards, and teach the content, there needs to be understanding that the content interacts with the process; if the process can be cultivated in a humanistic way, then the outcomes of the content will be improved.

The current research on teacher effectiveness needs to be revised to fit the context of varied teaching styles. Teachers must be permitted to incorporate

---

74 Judy Arin Krupp, "How Do You Feel About Yourself?" *Teaching K–8* (January 1991), pp. 63–68; T. R. Ellis, "Touch Therapy: When Hugging Helps," *Principal* (September 1990), pp. 34–36.

75 David W. Barnett and Karl B. Zucker, *The Personal and Social Assessment of Children* (Needham Heights, Mass.: Allyn & Bacon, 1990); Alan S. Kaufman, *Assessing Adolescent and Adult Intelligence* (Needham Heights, Mass.: Allyn & Bacon, 1991).

specific teacher behaviors and methods according to their personality, philosophy, and goals—to pick and choose from a wide range of research and theory and to discard other teacher behaviors that conflict with their style, without being considered ineffective.

It is obvious that certain behaviors contribute to good teaching. The trouble is, there is little agreement on exactly what behaviors or methods are most important. There will be some teachers who learn most of the rules about "good" teaching, yet they will be unsuccessful. There will be other teachers who break many of the rules of "good" teaching, yet be profoundly successful. There will be some teachers who gain theoretical knowledge of "what works," but will be unable to put the ideas into practice. Some teachers will act effortlessly in the classroom and others will consider teaching a chore. All this suggests that teaching cannot be described in terms of a checklist or a precise model. It also suggests that teaching is a holistic activity that deals with whole people (not tiny behaviors or competencies) and how people (teachers and students) develop and behave in a variety of classroom and school settings.

While the research on teacher behavior, teacher competencies, and teacher effectiveness provides a vocabulary and system for improving our insight into good teaching, there is a danger that it may lead to some of us becoming too rigid in our view of teaching. Following only the research on teaching can lead to too much emphasis on specific behaviors that can be easily measured or prescribed in advance.

Most teacher evaluation instruments tend to deemphasize the human side of teaching, because it is difficult to measure. In an attempt to be scientific, to predict and control behavior, and to assess group patterns, we sometimes lose sight of affective behaviors and individual differences. Although some educators have moved to a search for humanistic factors that influence teaching, we continue to define most teacher behaviors in terms of behaviorist and cognitive factors.

Similarly, most teacher evaluation processes do not address the question of how to change teacher behavior. The developers of evaluation instruments assume that once they have discovered what ought to be done, teachers will naturally do what is expected. If our purpose is to change or improve the practices of teachers, then it is necessary to come to grips with teachers' beliefs and attitudes and with their concepts of "good" or "effective."

In providing feedback and evaluation of teachers many factors need to be considered so the advice or information does not fall on deaf ears. Teachers appreciate feedback processes whereby they can improve their teaching, so long as the processes are honest and fair and are professionally planned and administered; so long as teachers are permitted to make mistakes; and so long as more than one model of effectiveness is considered so that teachers can adopt recommended behaviors and methods that fit their personality and philosophy of teaching.[76]

---

76 Ornstein, "Teacher Effectiveness Research: Theoretical Considerations."

SUMMARY

1. Research on teacher behavior has looked at teacher styles, teacher-student interactions, teacher characteristics, teacher competencies, and teacher effects.
2. Although much remains to be learned about successful teaching, research has identified some teacher behaviors that seem to be effective and influence student performance.
3. Recent research on effective teaching has shifted from the process of teaching to the products of teaching.
4. The classic, important research on teaching, prior to the 1970s, was the work of A. S. Barr, Arno Bellack, Ned Flanders, and David Ryans. These researchers focused on teacher styles, teacher-student interaction, and teacher characteristics—that is, the process, what was happening in the classroom, and the behavior of the teacher.
5. Recent research on teaching tends to emphasize classroom management and explicit, organized, and businesslike teaching.
6. The more recent research on teaching effectiveness is based on the work of Jere Brophy, Walter Doyle, Carolyn Evertson, N. L. Gage, Thomas Good, Donald Medley, Barak Rosenshine, and Arthur Wise. Their research tends to focus on the products or outcomes of teaching.

CASE STUDY

Problem

A newly graduated ninth-grade teacher signed a contract in a progressive and affluent school district. She was shocked to hear teachers speaking to other teachers of students' academic skills and personal characteristics that they had retrieved from personnel files and cumulative records. Having heard in her curriculum and methods classes of the self-fulfilling prophecy and the "Pygmalion effect," derived from the book, *Pygmalion in the Classroom*, she was certain these teachers were eventually going to prejudge these students. She vowed she would never look at a child's prior records, but would judge them only on their work and behavior in *her* classroom.

After she was there for a while, she began having behavioral problems with a few students and she found it difficult to assist others who were slow in some subjects.

Suggestion

When discussing her problem with the principal, she received specific teaching assistance but was also told to consult the curriculum specialist/teacher in the building, talk to the students' former teachers, and review their personnel files and cumulative records. She did all but the review. The curriculum specialist also suggested she review the records; she did not review them, convinced that the principal and specialist were unaware of the prophecy idea and the Pygmalion research. Problems continued and the principal, during a hurried lunchroom session, suggested she once again review the records. She did not.

Later a boy in her class had a grand mal seizure. She was unprepared for this and froze. Two children, after a while, ran to get the previous year's teacher who cleared the tongue which was beginning to choke the boy. Afterward, the former teacher asked the teacher why she wasn't prepared for this since it was in bold type in the child's records. The principal became incensed when the teacher said she knew nothing of not only the potential medical problems of the students but also of those students diagnosed as having learning disabilities, and those who needed special behavioral assistance and what curriculum methods had been tried by their teachers.

The teacher was near tears when the principal had her review, in his office, in his presence, all 23 students' records. In this review the teacher discovered children with specific learning disabilities, suggestions from other teachers for types of remedial work, and those with medical problems including one student who was a diabetic. After hearing her defense the principal replied, "The hell with the university. This is reality and the reality is that you, we, and the district might face a lawsuit because of *your* negligence in taking advice."

Discussion Suggestion

School staff worked out a procedure for discreet use of documentary information. On "records day," each teacher would, along with a listing of new students, pass to the receiving teacher an abbreviated list of students with specific needs such as health or academic problems and behavioral irregularities. Teachers could then make an initial seating to disperse troublemakers, identify those needing review and assistance so as not to "lose" them, and be prepared for health emergencies or to recognize health problems before they got serious. No information was provided on I.Q.s and no information of a diagnostic psychological nature, since these could lead to a lawsuit and the teachers were not psychologists. The teachers thought this procedure was very helpful for monitoring special students and becoming aware of academic or behavioral problems.

Discussion Questions

1. How might the beginning teacher have followed the principal's specific advice and still not have prejudged her studies?
2. If you decide to become familiar with your students' histories, what information might you ask for from parents? When would you ask?
3. How important to your effectiveness are other kinds of behavior besides knowing aspects of student backgrounds and needs? Are there factors that you consider more important?
4. Using your text, identify at least four teaching instructions and four student characteristics that you consider will contribute to your effec-

tiveness. Why? Identify at least three of those that you consider detrimental or even harmful. Why?

5. To what extent do you expect to use student records as a source for influencing your teaching?

QUESTIONS TO CONSIDER

1. Do teachers make a difference in student outcomes? If you say yes, to what extent? If your answer is no, why?
2. How would you describe your teaching style in the terms used by Riessman, Rubin, Anderson, and Lippitt?
3. How would you use the Flanders interaction analysis scale to provide feedback for a beginning teacher?
4. What teacher competencies listed in the tables of this chapter seem most important to you? Why?
5. What behaviors listed by Brophy and Good and Evertson and Emmer coincide with your own teacher style? What behaviors seem to conflict with your teacher style?

THINGS TO DO

1. Evaluate the behaviors Medley labels as "effective" for low socioeconomic students. Discuss in class whether these behaviors make sense for low socioeconomic students of different sex, age, and achievement scores.
2. Volunteer to teach a lesson in class for about ten minutes. Use a simplified version of the Flanders interaction analysis scale (direct versus indirect) or Bellack's verbal behaviors (structuring, soliciting, responding, reacting). Note whether there is agreement among class members in categorizing your teacher behavior.
3. Observe two or three professors while they teach and take note of the amount of time they talk compared to student talk. Use every 3 seconds as a time interval to calculate the ratio of teacher to student talk. Report to the class.
4. Recall three or four of your favorite teachers. Compare their teacher characteristics, as you remember, with the list of successful characteristics compiled by Barr. Which characteristics on Barr's list do you think they possess?
5. Interview several experienced teachers concerning the recommended teacher principles and methods of Rosenshine, Gage, Good and Brophy, and Evertson and Emmer. Do the teachers support or reject the recommendations? What reservations do teachers bring up? What do they like about the recommendations?

RECOMMENDED READINGS

Flanders, Ned A. *Analyzing Teaching Behavior*. Reading, Mass.: Addison-Wesley, 1970. Description of the chain of classroom events, interaction of teacher and students, and activities for helping the teacher organize his or her behavior in the classroom.

Gage, Nathaniel L. *The Scientific Basis of the Art of Teaching*. New York: Teachers College Press, Columbia University, 1978. A discussion of teacher effectiveness studies, successful teaching strategies, and the notion of teaching as a "practical" art with a scientific basis.

Good, Thomas L. and Jere E. Brophy. *Looking in Classrooms*, 5th ed. New York: Harper-Collins, 1991. An important book that helped move the field from the study of teacher processes to teacher products, and a convincing argument that teachers do make a difference.

Joyce, Bruce and Marsha Weil. *Models of Teaching*, 2nd ed. Englewood Cliffs, N.J.: Prentice-Hall, 1986. A book that combines theory with practice and examines various cognitive and behavioral teaching models.

Medley, Donald M., Homer Coker, and Robert S. Soar. *Measurement-Based Evaluation of Teacher Performance*. New York: Longman, 1984. A theoretical book on evaluating teachers, with emphasis on measurement problems and methods.

Rosenholtz, Susan J. *Teachers' Workplace*.. White Plains, N.Y.: Longman, 1989. Quantitative and qualitative data on differences in teacher effectiveness.

Waxman, Hersholt C. and Herbert J. Walberg, eds. *Effective Teaching*. Berkeley, Calif.: McCutchan, 1991. A book of readings that blends current research and practice.

KEY TERMS

Teacher processes	Nonverbal communication
Teacher products	Self-fulfilling prophecy
Teaching style	Teacher characteristics
Teachable groups	Teacher competencies
Teacher-student interaction	Process-product research
Teacher episode	Teacher effectiveness
Teacher monologue	

Professional Growth

FOCUSING QUESTIONS

1. How would you improve the support system for student teachers?

2. What are some methods for improving the support and learning opportunities for teachers during the first few years of their teaching career?

3. How can students evaluate their teachers?

4. How does self-evaluation improve a person's capabilities as a teacher? What methods of self-evaluation might a teacher use?

5. How do peer evaluation and supervisory evaluation contribute to evaluating teachers?

6. What sources and products can supply information to be used for teacher evaluation and growth?

7. How do professional organizations serve teachers?

You can always improve your teaching. The extent of improvement is related to how much improvement you think you need and how hard you work at it. Beginning teachers in particular should expect to encounter some problems and frustrations, but they should also learn from their experiences and improve their technical skills over time.

If you hope to be an effective teacher who enjoys his or her work, not only will you need to be well prepared for each day's lessons but also you will need to possess a variety of skills in working with people—with students, colleagues, supervisors, and parents. You will need to have a general education, knowledge of the subject you teach, and training in teaching your grade level and type of student. The preceding chapters in this book dealt with methods of teaching. This final chapter is intended to help you grow as a teacher.

PROGRAM REQUIREMENTS AND COMPONENTS

The most prevalent teacher education programs offered to entering teachers are elementary and secondary education. About 75 percent of teacher education institutions offer both of these programs. Although there is great diversity in admission requirements into teacher education programs, most colleges and universities have raised the grade point average (GPA) from 2 to 2.3 on a 4–point scale. Nationwide approximately 20 percent of all students applying for admission into teacher education are rejected.[1] This represents a significant increase in rejection rate, largely reflecting the national reform trend to upgrade the profession, especially admission requirements, and the recent increases in teacher education enrollments (expected to continue into the mid-1990s).

Typically, the average elementary education student takes 58 credits in arts and science, 30 credits in academic concentrations and minors, 42 credits for professional preparation, including 9 credits for methods and 12 credits for student teaching. The secondary education student averages 54 hours in arts and science, 39 hours in an academic major and minor, and 30 hours in professional preparation, including 7 hours in methods and 9 hours in student teaching.

Field Experiences

Most teacher education programs provide early **field experiences** for education students to visit schools, observe teachers in classrooms, work with teachers, and in some cases teach. Field experiences are increasingly becoming a required

---

1 Gary R. Galluzzo and Richard I. Arends, "The Rate Project: A Profile of Teacher Education Institutions," *Journal of Teacher Education* (July-August 1989), pp. 56–58.

component of the preservice education program. Nationwide, about 140 hours of fieldwork is required in elementary education programs and 90 hours are required in secondary programs.[2]

Field experience visits help education students understand the reality of schooling, and the classroom observations give insights into the work of teachers and various types of teaching strategies. They also provide opportunities for prospective teachers to familiarize themselves with the workings of the classroom from a teacher's perspective and to integrate teaching methods learned in textbooks by studying the teaching of others. Without these observations, preservice teachers have greater difficulty linking theoretical knowledge (gained by textbook readings and discussions in methods courses) with events and situations in the classroom. In fact, until preservice teachers can integrate what they read with the reality of teaching, almost everything they read as principles or methods of teaching remains theoretical.

Some teacher educators propose that "simulated field" experiences, through written teacher logs, case studies, autobiographies, and videotaped classes, are more appropriate in the initial stages of teacher preparation. These experiences provide shared experiences in college settings, can be reread or replayed for further discussion and analysis, and can illustrate many concrete examples in short periods of time.[3] Nonetheless, most teacher educators do agree that on-site field experiences in classrooms and schools should be provided to prospective teachers.[4] Indeed, the more schools you visit and the more teachers you observe or better yet work with, the more you will understand the reality of school life and teaching; in fact, the more you should be able to conceptualize and integrate principles and methods of teaching and learning.

Most education students will be given a guided tour of the building, visiting such places as the teachers' lounge, teachers' cafeteria, school auditorium, library, and resource center, and they may be introduced to the principal or assistant principal and one of the guidance counselors or deans.

If given an opportunity to visit a class in session, it might be profitable to note the following things which you can discuss the next day in your education class:

1. The general teaching style of the teacher.
2. Classroom routines and rules.

---

2 Galluzzo and Arends, "The Rate Project"; Virginia Richardson, "Significant and Worthwhile Change in Teaching Practice," *Educational Researcher* (October 1990), pp. 10–18.

3 Carol Livingston and Hilda Borko, "Expert-Novice Differences in Teaching," *Journal of Teacher Education* (July-August 1989), pp. 36–42; G. Williamson McDiarmid, "Challenging Prospective Teachers' Beliefs During Early Field Experience," *Journal of Teacher Education* (May–June 1990), pp. 12–20.

4 *Tomorrow's Teachers: A Report of the Holmes Group* (East Lansing, Mich.: The Holmes Group, 1986); *Toward High and Rigorous Standards for the Teaching Profession* (Washington, D.C.: National Board for Professional Teaching Standards, 1989).

3. How the lesson was started, developed and ended.
4. Instructional materials and equipment used during the lesson.
5. Interaction among students and with the teacher.
6. Range of abilities and interests of the students and how the teacher handled these differences.
7. Teaching strategies and methods that motivated the students or bored them.
8. The general classroom climate.

In some cases, field experiences will include an assignment to a school in which you do not actually teach. Instead, you get to know the students and teachers through various activities such as tutoring, working with small groups of students, conducting a portion of the lesson, assisting the teacher in clerical work (e.g., taking attendance or filling out forms), grading quizzes or tests, or acting as a member of a small teaching team. These activities provide insight into various teaching roles and help you get to know students and acquire skills in dealing with school routines and paperwork.

According to researchers, both elementary and secondary education students often have several field experiences that can be categorized as "noninteractive routines," such as grading papers, putting up bulletin boards, and correcting homework. However, elementary education students more frequently observe cooperating teachers than do their secondary counterparts; the former group engages more in small-group and large-group teaching (as an assistant), whereas secondary education students are more likely to tutor individual students. As students move further along into their field experiences (considered a second term in the research study), they take on more varied roles and responsibilities, including planning lessons and assisting the teacher with activities that require increasing interaction with students.[5]

Students assigned to junior high school and senior high school have similar experiences in five out of eight recorded activities: (1) observing cooperating teachers, (2) assisting with noninteractive routines, (3) assisting with interactive routines, (4) individual tutoring, and (5) small-group teaching. Students assigned to junior high schools observe other teachers, prepare lesson plans, and assist in teaching large groups more often than students placed in senior high schools.[6]

In order to promote thoughtful reflection of field experiences that extend beyond observation and discussion guidelines, a number of teacher preparation institutions are experimenting with different activities. Among the most popular strategies is the use of (1) *critical incident summaries*, a short writing exercise or diary in which education students are asked to report about an

---

5 Joyce E. Killian and D. John McIntyre, "Grade Level as a Factor in Participation During Early Field Experiences," *Journal of Teacher Education* (March–April 1988), pp. 36–46.

6 Ibid.

important teacher-related event they observed during the previous week and to discuss the event at the university setting; (2) *case reports or studies*, expanding an incident into a more complete account incorporating contextual variables, teaching principles and methods, and the students' analysis and evaluation of the incident;[7] (3) *using exemplars or models*, organizing teaching behaviors into categories or patterns, observing or videotaping as teachers conduct lessons, and then recalling or analyzing what happened in relation to the categories;[8] and (4) *reflective discussions* that go beyond generic techniques into the realm of personalized techniques and that focus on attitudes and attributes that can be developed during the preservice and early years of teaching.[9]

Four points are worth noting. (1) Research suggests that about 60 percent of these four practices focus on problems and 40 percent on successes that occur while observing (or teaching).[10] (2) While there is great variety in critical incidents, case reports, models, and reflective discussions, they can be used for beginning teachers in colleges and school district sites alike. (3) The first two activities can be summed as part of journal writing, which requires some reflection (the fourth activity) on practice. (4) The third and fourth activities emphasize the analysis of teaching and teacher self-awareness; they help the beginning teacher develop more philosophical and mature ways of teacher thinking.

According to Francis Bolin, these types of activities help student teachers (and beginning teachers) think about (1) what they know, (2) what they feel, (3) what they do, and (4) why they do it.[11] Research also suggests that these four field experiences help future teachers exhibit more mature judgment and behavior in their first year of teaching and in their relationship with colleagues and administrators.[12] A certain amount of "nontext wisdom," or larger "doses of reality," is gained through these field experiences, as well as through traditional field activities such as observing, assisting, and teaching in classrooms.

Student Teaching

The newly assigned student teacher has many questions: What clothes should I wear? Will I be assigned to a "good" school? Will it be close to home (or work)?

---

7 Diane S. Murphy, Carolyn Colvin, and Ann I. Morey, "Helping New Teachers Become Thoughtful Practitioners," *Educational Horizons* (Summer 1990), pp. 183–186.

8 Dona M. Kagan, "The Cost of Avoiding Research," *Phi Delta Kappan* (November 1989), pp. 220–224.

9 Sheila W. Moran, "Schools and the Beginning Teacher," *Phi Delta Kappan* (November 1990), pp. 210–213; Terry M. Wildman and Jerry A. Niles, "Reflective Teachers: Tensions Between Abstractions and Realities," *Journal of Teacher Education* (May 1989), pp. 46–50.

10 Murphy, Colvin, and Morey, "Helping New Teachers Become Thoughtful Practitioners."

11 Francis S. Bolin, "Helping Student Teachers Think About Teaching," *Journal of Teacher Education* (January–February 1990), pp. 38–42. Also see Richard Yinger and Christopher M. Clark, *Reflective Journal Writing: Theory and Practice* (East Lansing, Mich.: Michigan State University Institute for Research on Teaching, 1991).

12 Karen Kilgore, Dorene Ross, and John Zbikowski, "Understanding the Teaching Perspectives of First-Year Teachers," *Journal of Teacher Education* (January–February 1990), pp. 28–38; McDiarmid, "Challenging Prospective Teachers' Beliefs During Early Field Experience."

Will the students like me? Will I get along with my cooperating teacher? When will I get to teach? Will my cooperating teacher be in the back of the room or leave me on my own? Will I be provided with feedback from my cooperating teacher? College professor? Will my cooperating teacher and college professor get along? Who will be responsible for grading my work?

Most student teachers feel stress. Frequently used words to describe how they feel are "pressured," "anxious," "tense," and "overwhelmed." When asked to identify factors within their student teaching experience that contribute to creating stress, 44 secondary student teachers cite four main factors: (1) time pressure (38% of the responses), not having sufficient time to do all the things that are required such as planning lessons, constructing tests, and marking papers; (2) classroom situation (19%), maintaining classroom control, teaching slow or unmotivated students; (3) lack of direction to the student teacher by the cooperating teacher (19%), demands upon the student teacher, different expectations of the student teacher and cooperating teacher; and (4) being in a new situation (12%), that is, being unfamiliar with school or classroom rules, the other teachers, and students.[13]

Obviously, students need more time to devote to the many roles and tasks associated with student teaching; their course loads should be light during the semester they student teach. College advisers need to inform students that student teaching is almost like a full-time job, and they should not have to work while student teaching. Student teachers, ideally, should observe and participate in the same school prior to student teaching; and their roles, and the roles of the cooperating teacher and supervising professor, need to be clarified before they are assigned to their respective schools.

The relationship among the student teacher, cooperating teacher, and supervising professor is crucial to the student teaching experience. Although student teaching is a time for trial and error, for making mistakes and learning from them, how well you develop as a "teacher to be" during this period will have a lot to do with the help you receive from the cooperating teacher and the supervising professor.

Student teaching programs are increasingly addressing the three-way relationship of student-teacher-supervisor. In California, for example, a pilot program, the Clinical Supervision Initiative (CSI), was launched to improve the relationship; cooperating teachers and supervising professors take workshops together to agree on common language and common teaching strategies for training and supervising student teachers. The program also emphasizes a three-stage supervision process: (1) *pre-observation* conferences where the supervising professor and student teacher review lesson plans and agree on a focus for observation; (2) *observation*, aided by detailed note taking; and (3) *post-observation*, using the notes to promote self-reflection and self-assessment

---

13 Jerry B. Davis, "Stress Among Secondary School Student Teachers," *High School Journal* (April–May 1990), pp. 240–244.

by the student teacher, followed by constructive feedback from the supervisor.[14]

In Florida a similar model has been developed, involving the same three players but with slightly different labels: student intern, directing teacher, and university supervisor. Called the Supervision Throughput Model (STM), a primary component of the model is a series of conferences involving the triad in which the teacher and professor orient the student intern and identify and later diagnose methods for improving the intern's performance. The initial conferences define observable behaviors to be exhibited, give specific assignments to the intern, decide how responsibility will be transferred from the directing teacher to the intern, and establish the schedule for subsequent conferences and observations.[15]

With both programs the teacher and professor hold post-observation conferences in which specified behaviors are identified and constructively critiqued. One of several recording or observation systems is used: category, frequency count, sequential record, or event system. The triad is supposed to agree on the behaviors and recording method together, incorporating the principles of participatory decision making.[16]

During the post-observation conference, the teacher or professor relies on open-ended questions—for example, "If you were doing it again, what would you do differently?" "What can you improve on?"—rather than on telling students or giving "right" answers. The teacher or professor listens carefully, uses the student's response, and suggests alternative or modified strategies.

HELPING THE BEGINNING TEACHER

What are the general needs of the beginning teacher? Most schools plan for teacher orientation, but in spite of efforts to help teachers succeed, many still encounter adjustment problems. A review of the research on problems of beginning teachers shows that feelings of isolation; poor understanding of what is expected of them; work load and extra assignments that they were unprepared to handle; lack of supplies, materials, or equipment; poor physical facilities; and lack of support or help from experienced teachers or supervisors contribute to their feelings of frustration and failure.[17]

14 Susan Mata and Beth Ann Berliner, "A Boost for Those Who Supervise Student Teachers," *Far West Laboratory: Research and Practice* (Winter 1989), pp. 1–3; telephone conversation with Beth Ann Berliner, December 20, 1989.

15 Lawrence J. O'Shea, Nora L. Hoover, and Robert G. Carroll, "Effective Intern Conferencing," *Journal of Teacher Education* (March–April 1988), pp. 17–21.

16 Nora L. Hoover, Lawrence J. O'Shea, and Robert G. Carroll, "The Supervisor-Intern Relationship and Effective Interpersonal Communication Skills Used in Conducting Intern Conferences," *Journal of Teacher Education* (March–April 1988), pp. 22–27.

17 Jerry A. Ligon, "Four Ways to Reduce Worry for New Teachers," *American School Board Journal* (March 1988), p. 50; Simon Veenman, "Perceived Problems of Beginning Teachers," *Review of Educational Research* (Summer 1984), pp. 143–178.

Problems of Education Students and Beginning Teachers

Frances Fuller suggests a progression in the types of concerns teachers have. Education students are characterized by "nonconcern;" student teachers are characterized by "increased concern;" beginning teachers are preoccupied with "survival concerns;" and experienced teachers have gotten past initial survival and are more involved with "self" concerns.[18]

A number of factors contribute to the concerns of student teachers about the difficulty of teaching, including the fact that most people do fear the unknown when they are about to embark on a new job (especially their first job). However, the content of introductory teacher education courses does not seem to prepare teachers for the realities of the job. Another factor may be that age and optimism may be inversely related. It takes a few years of seasoning to face reality, and college students at the prestudent teaching level tend to have confidence in their own abilities and to believe they are better equipped than others (older people) to be teachers. What young student cannot, after all, reasonably criticize many former teachers and say, "I can do a better job"?

In a recent study, beginning teachers and education students were asked to rank problems they expected.[19] The problems perceived by the teachers as the ten most important are listed in Table 13.1. Although there is some agreement between the groups in the ranking of important problems, there is significant disagreement on the perceived difficulty of the problems. First-year teachers consistently rank the items as more difficult than education students, and that difference is noted in Column 4 by the minus sign. For problems teachers considered less important (not shown on the table), there seems to be strong agreement in the ranking. The less important items dealt with getting along with colleagues, following school policies, being accepted by students, dealing with administrative constraints, and knowledge of subject matter. However, the mean scores in perceived difficulty show that beginning teachers also view the less important problems more seriously.

Numerous reports over the last several years document the shock for the new teacher that accompanies the realities of the school and classroom.[20] Organized programs and internal support systems for beginning teachers are scarce. Mentor relations between experienced and beginning teachers and

---

18 Frances F. Fuller, "Concerns for Teachers: A Developmental Conceptualization," *American Educational Research Journal* (March 1969), pp. 207–226.

19 Carol S. Weinstein, "Preservice Teachers' Expectations about the First Year of Teaching," *Teaching and Teacher Education* (no. 1, 1988), pp. 31–40.

20 Judith E. Lanier and Judith W. Little, "Research on Teacher Education," in M. C. Wittrock, ed., *Handbook of Research on Teaching*, 3rd ed. (New York: Macmillan, 1986), pp. 527–569; Ronald N. Marso and Fred L. Pigge, "Differences Between Self-Perceived Job Expectations and Job Realities of Beginning Teachers," *Journal of Teacher Education* (November–December, 1987) pp. 53–56; and Terry M. Wildman and Jerry A. Niles, "Essentials of Professional Growth," *Educational Leadership* (February 1987), pp. 4–10.

Table 13.1   PERCEIVED PROBLEMS OF BEGINNING TEACHERS AND EDUCATION
STUDENTS

Ranking of first-year teachers	Questionnaire item	Ranking of education students	Mean score difference in perceived difficulty[*]
1	Dealing with work load	1	−.49
2	Improving academic performance of low-achieving students	3	−.62
3	Adapting curriculum and instruction to needs of slow learners	5	−.68
4	Teaching students from different cultures and backgrounds	21	−1.17
5	Figuring out why students are having difficulties with assignments	6	−.61
6	Responding effectively to student misbehavior	11	−.61
7	Maintaining discipline	11	−.87
8	Dealing with insufficient materials and supplies	2	−.43
9	Dealing with a lack of supplementary and enriching materials	4	−.47
10	Planning lessons and units	14	−.81

[*]All differences in the degree of difficulty are significant at the .0001 level; they reflect differences in difficulty between beginning teachers (always ranked more difficult) and education students.

Source: Adapted from Carol S. Weinstein, "Preservice Teachers' Expectations about the First Year of Teaching," *Teaching and Teacher Education* (no. 1, 1988), p. 35.

support from colleagues for continued learning and professional development are still exceptions, not the rule.[21]

Without question, there is recognition that the **induction period**, the first two or three years of teaching, is critical in developing teachers' capabilities, and that beginning teachers should not be left alone to sink or swim. Several state education agencies have recently developed internship programs for new teachers, while other states have increased staff development activities.[22] However, it is the internal support systems and strategies that the schools adopt,

21 Ann Liebermann and Lynne Miller, eds., *Staff Development for the '90s* (New York: Teachers College Press, Columbia University, 1991); Gene I. Maeroff, *The Empowerment of Teachers* (New York: Teachers College Press, Columbia University, 1988).

22 Carolyn M. Evertson, "Do Teachers Make a Difference?" *Education and Urban Society* (February 1986), pp. 195–210; Joseph R. Jenkins and Linda M. Jenkins, "Making Peer Tutoring Work," *Educational Leadership* (March 1987), pp. 64–68; and Deborah S. Saltrick et al., "Establishing Organization Development Strategies in Secondary Schools," *Journal of Staff Development* (Winter 1991), pp. 52–55.

that is, the daily support activities and continual teaching opportunities, that are most important for the professional development of new teachers.

Common causes of failure of new teachers need to be identified and addressed. One school administrator has identified six general causes of failure that the schools should rectify.

1. *Assignment to difficult classes.* "Good" courses and "good" students are assigned to teachers on the basis of seniority; beginning teachers are given the "dregs" or "leftovers" to teach. A better balance is required (actually the opposite assignments) to permit beginning teachers to survive and learn from their mistakes in the classroom.

2. *Isolation of classrooms from colleagues and supervisors.* The classrooms furthest from the central office are usually assigned to beginning teachers. Isolating the new teacher from experienced teachers contributes to failure. Beginning teachers need to be assigned to rooms near the main office and near experienced teachers to encourage daily communication.

3. *Poor physical facilities.* Classrooms, room fixtures, and equipment are usually assigned on the basis of seniority. Providing the leftovers to new teachers is damaging to morale. A more equitable assignment of facilities is needed.

4. *Burdensome extra class assignments.* Extra class duties are cited as a source of ill feelings more than any other item. New teachers are often assigned burdensome or tough assignments that they were unprepared for and did not expect as teachers, such as yard patrol, hall patrol, cafeteria patrol, or study hall duties. Furthermore, the afternoon and evening assignments for which teachers are paid extra usually go to senior teachers. Assignments given to beginning teachers should not be so burdensome that they affect the quality of their teaching; also, the assignments with pay should be awarded on a merit basis.

5. *Lack of understanding of the school's expectations.* School officials should clarify the school's goals and priorities and the responsibilities of teachers early in the first term. Administrators do provide orientation and written guides about roles and responsibilities, but the problem seems to be the dearth of continuing communication and reinforcement as the teacher progresses through various stages of role acquisition.

6. *Inadequate supervision.* Most problems of beginning teachers could be either prevented or curtailed with proper supervision. Supervision often consists of only two or three formal visits a year to the classroom and possibly a few informal contacts and one or two meetings. The need is for increased supervisory contact, both formal and informal,

so that assistance is provided regularly in the early stages of the teacher's career.[23]

Perhaps the best way of assisting new teachers, and making their transition easier and more profitable, is to introduce them early (before the school term starts) to school policy (attendance, record keeping, lesson assignments, homework policy, grading policy, etc.); provide a "buddy" teacher, friend, or mentor to provide ongoing assistance for the entire first year; assign one less class (recognize the extra professional time needed to adjust to a new job, especially the demands of teaching), ensure they do not teach the "leftover" or "difficult" classes during the first year, and provide ongoing training (say on a weekly basis) to help them with problems and meet the demands of the new job. Each school district should have a comprehensive induction program to help new teachers adjust more quickly to the realities of teaching. The reason is clear: the move from a safe college campus, where theory is expounded, to the classroom/school setting, where practice is required, often involves a change in lifestyle and a period of adjustment.

Problems of Teaching in Inner-City Schools

In general, beginning teachers experience a great deal of anxiety the first year on the job as they make the transition from student teacher to beginning teacher and adjust to their new professional roles and responsibilities.[24]

Teachers assigned to inner-city schools tend to feel significantly greater anxiety, even symptoms of exhaustion and battle fatigue; they deal with classroom management and discipline problems as well as with the inability of most of their students to grasp the basic fundamentals, the nonavailability or nonresponsiveness of parents, and the lack of assistance from supervisors and administrators.[25] Whereas teachers assigned to middle-class and suburban schools can learn on the job and profit from their mistakes with proper supervision or feedback from colleagues, teachers assigned to lower-class and inner-city schools often fail on the job and lack support mechanisms.

In this connection, Ornstein and Levine summarize forty years of research aimed at understanding and overcoming the problems of teaching low-achieving and inner-city students. The problems are categorized into ten

---

23 William H. Kurtz, "How the Principal Can Help Beginning Teachers," *NASSP Bulletin* (January 1983), pp. 42–45.

24 David W. Grissmer and Sheila N. Kirby, *Teacher Attrition: The Uphill Climb to Staff the Nation's Schools* (Santa Monica, Calif.: The Rand Corporation, 1987); Frederick J. McDonald and Patricia Elias, *The Transition into Teaching: The Problems of Beginning Teachers and Programs to Solve Them* (Princeton, N.J.: Educational Testing Service, 1983).

25 Joseph J. Blase, "A Qualitative Analysis of Sources of Teacher Stress," *American Educational Research Journal* (Spring 1986), pp. 13–40; Thomas J. Sergiovanni, "The Dark Side of Professionalism in Educational Administration," *Phi Delta Kappan* (March 1991), pp. 521–526.

realities, illustrated in Table 13.2. The first five are teacher related and the remaining five are student or school related. The inference is that the finger of responsibility should not be pointed at only one group or one person. The researchers provide six teacher-education solutions for the five teacher-related problems: (1) Increase the number of minority education students, (2) teach effective instruction for low achievers, (3) improve practice teaching by permitting student teachers more opportunity to develop their skills under the influence of an effective cooperating teacher, (4) provide greater assistance to teachers during the first three years (intern period) of teaching, (5) put greater emphasis on classroom management techniques during the preservice and intern period, and (6) consider several teacher effectiveness models in preservice and in-service education.[26]

Support from Colleagues for Beginning Teachers

In general, having to learn by trial and error without much support and supervision has been the most common problem faced by new teachers. Expecting teachers to function without support is based on the false assumptions that (1) teachers are well prepared for their initial classroom and school experiences, (2) teachers can develop professional expertise on their own, and (3) teaching can be mastered in a relatively short period of time. Researchers find that there is little attempt to lighten the class load and limit extra class assignments to make the beginning teacher's job easier. In the few schools that do limit these activities, teachers have reported that they have had the opportunity to "learn to teach."[27]

Studies of secondary schools have shown that teachers expect to learn from one another when the school provides opportunities for teachers (1) to talk routinely to one another about teaching, (2) to be observed regularly in the classroom, and (3) to participate in planning and preparation.[28] Teachers who are given opportunity to (1) develop and implement curriculum ideas, (2) join study groups about implementing classroom practices, or (3) experiment in new skills and training feel more confident in their individual and collective ability to perform their work.[29]

---

26 Allan C. Ornstein and Daniel U. Levine, "Social Class, Race, and School Achievement: Problems and Prospects," *Journal of Teacher Education* (September–October 1989), pp. 17–23.

27 Judith E. Lanier and Joseph Featherstone, "A New Commitment to Teacher Education," *Educational Leadership* (November 1988), pp. 18–22; Phillip C. Schlechty, "A School District Revises the Functions and Rewards of Teaching," paper presented at the annual meeting of the American Educational Research Association, 1984; and Deborah B. Strother, "Peer Coaching for Teachers: Opening Classroom Doors," *Phi Delta Kappan* (June 1989), pp. 824–827.

28 Judith W. Little, *School Success and Staff Development* (Boulder, Colo.: Center for Action Research, 1981); Little, "District Policy Choices and Teacher Professional Development Opportunities," paper presented at the annual conference of the American Educational Research Association, New Orleans, April 1988.

29 Thomas D. Bird, "Early Implementation of the California Mentor Teacher Program," paper presented at the annual meeting of the American Educational Research Association, San Francisco, April 1986; Aurora Chase and Pat Wolfe, "Off to a Good Start in Peer Coaching," *Educational Leadership* (May 1989), pp. 37–38.

Table 13.2   REALITIES OF TEACHING INNER-CITY, LOW-ACHIEVING STUDENTS, WITH
POTENTIAL SOLUTIONS

Realities

1. *Differences in teacher-student backgrounds.* Teachers with middle-class backgrounds may have difficulty understanding and motivating inner-city students; this may be particularly salient with white teachers working with minority students.

2. *Teacher perceptions of student inadequacy.* Many teachers working with inner-city students conclude from achievement test scores that large numbers are incapable of learning; hence the teachers may work less hard to improve student performance.

3. *Low standards of performance.* By the time many inner-city students reach middle or senior high school, low performance has become the norm, expected and accepted by both students and teachers.

4. *Ineffective instructional grouping.* Low achievers are frequently grouped into slow classes (or subgrouped in regular classes) where instruction proceeds at a slow rate.

5. *Poor teaching conditions.* As inner-city students fall further behind academically, and as both they and their teachers experience frustration and disappointment, classroom behavior problems increase and teachers find working conditions more difficult; the words "battle fatigue," "battle pay," and "blackboard jungle" have been used in the literature to describe teaching conditions in inner-city schools.

6. *Differences between parental and school norms.* Differences between the way the inner-city home (physical punishment) and the school (internalization of norms) punish, shame, or control youngsters make it difficult for many students to follow school rules or for teachers to enforce them.

7. *Lack of previous success in school.* Lack of academic success in earlier grades hinders learning more difficult material and damages a student's perception of what he or she is capable of learning.

8. *Negative peer pressure.* High-achieving inner-city students are frequently ridiculed and rejected by peers for accepting the middle-class school norms.

9. *Inappropriate instruction.* As inner-city students proceed through school, academic tasks and concepts become increasingly more abstract, and many of these students fall further behind because their level of mastery is too rudimentary to allow for fluent learning.

10. *Delivery of services.* The tasks of delivering effective instruction and related services to students are increasingly more difficult in a classroom or school comprised mainly of lower-achieving, inner-city students (because their learning problems are more serious) than in a middle-class classroom or school that has a small percentage of lower-achieving, inner-city students.

Source: Adapted from Allan C. Ornstein and Daniel U. Levine, "Social Class, Race, and School Achievement: Problems and Prospects," *Journal of Teacher Education* (September–October 1989), pp. 17–23.

According to Joyce and Showers, an experienced teacher who acts as a **peer coach** or **resource teacher** for an inexperienced teacher performs five functions: (1) *companionship*, discussing ideas, problems, and successes; (2) *technical feedback*, especially related to lesson planning and classroom observations; (3) *analysis of application*, integrating what happens or what works as part of the beginning teacher's repertoire; (4) *adaptation*, helping the beginning teacher adapt to particular situations; and (5) *personal facilitation*, helping the teacher feel good about himself or herself after trying new strategies.[30] See Tips for Teachers 13.1

Similar data have been reported by Neubert and Bratton, involving visiting resource teachers in Maryland school districts who, rather than observe classroom teachers, teach alongside them. Five characteristics of the resource teachers that promote an effective coaching relationship are (1) *knowledge*—more knowledge about teaching methods than the classroom teacher; (2) *credibility*—demonstrated success in the classroom; (3) *support*—a mix of honest praise and constructive criticism; (4) *facilitation*—recommending and encouraging rather than dictating, assisting rather than dominating in the classroom; and (5) *availability*—accessible to the classroom teacher for planning, team teaching, and conferences.[31]

In the Sonoma County, California, school district, experienced teachers are called "colleague coaches" and "peer coaches"; they help train new and probationary teachers. The coaches attend seven training sessions to learn how to observe, conference, and communicate. Table 13.3 briefly illustrates the seven sessions. The pre-observation conference is used to make explicit for the new/probationary teacher the purpose of the lesson, expected teacher behaviors and student outcomes, and strategies to enhance the lesson. During the observation, the coach collects information. The post-observation conferences discuss what actually happened during the lesson, as opposed to what was planned.[32]

The coach asks questions that encourage the teacher to reflect, not react or defend. An integral part of the post-conference is to discuss what facilitated or hindered the teaching-learning process. The training is ongoing; the coaches continue to meet as a group to learn from each other and to discuss how they can continuously provide support for the teachers. The spirit of the program is exemplified by the term sometimes used—"peer sharing and caring"—to describe the new openness and learning among colleagues.

---

30 Bruce Joyce and Beverly Showers, *Power in Staff Development Through Research in Training* (Alexandria, Va.: Association for Supervision and Curriculum Development, 1983); Joyce and Showers, *Student Achievement Through Staff Development* (White Plains, N.Y.: Longman, 1988).

31 Gloria A. Neubert and Elizabeth C. Bratton, "Team Coaching: Staff Development Side by Side," *Educational Leadership* (February 1987), pp. 29–32.

32 Patricia Raney and Pam Robbins, "Professional Growth and Support Through Peer Coaching," *Educational Leadership* (May 1989), pp. 35–38.

Tips for Teachers 13.1

Improving Your Teaching

Beginning teachers need help from mentors in lesson planning and in the preparation and organization of instruction; they also need to know what to do as classroom problems arise. Problems cannot be predicted with exact accuracy, but one group of educators has suggested possible solutions of some common problems that may take shape as teaching unfolds.

I. *Problem*: The teacher wastes the first five minutes of class time.
   Possible Solutions:

   *1. Introduce learning activities as soon as students enter the room.
   2. Briefly review information covered in previous lesson.
   *3. Direct students to copy homework assignment on chalkboard.
   *4. Provide a warm-up activity or exercise for students to complete.
   5. Write or state the objectives of the day so students know what to expect.
   6. Catch the immediate attention of the students—with an interesting story, startling fact, set of questions, or hypothetical situation.
   *7. Be sure all students are in their seats before starting the lesson; a student out of his seat when the late bell rings is marked late.

II. *Problem*: Students do not take good notes.
   Possible Solutions:

   1. Preview the main types or headings to be covered.
   2. Use advance organizers to introduce what students will be learning.
   3. Use slides or opaque projector to distinguish main ideas.
   *4. Walk around the room and check notes.
   *5. At the end of the lesson review main ideas.

III. *Problem*: Students become confused or frustrated.
   Possible Solutions:

   1. Check the students' records, and preview students' abilities and needs.
   2. Monitor students' seatwork.

continues

3. Be aware of nonverbal cues (facial expressions, eye contact) to help determine if students understand the lesson.

*4. Slow down, probe, repeat if necessary.

5. Modify materials to fit students' abilities and needs.

*6. Relate content to students' life experiences.

*7. Provide medial summaries for each main topic or idea.

*8. Review first, then reteach, if necessary.

IV. *Problem*: Students are bored and uninterested.
   Possible Solutions:

1. Move around the room; don't stay glued to one spot.

2. Change inflection and volume of voice to separate one idea from another or to create interest; move your hands.

3. Look directly at students—use nonverbal behavior (smile, wink, hand signal).

4. Show enthusiasm—use animation, surprise, humor, and stories.

5. Reduce one-way (student-teacher), traditional communication pattern.

*6. Encourage two-way or three-way communication (among students).

*7. Reduce teacher talk; encourage students to ask and answer questions.

*8. Ask for students' viewpoints, opinions, insights, and personal examples.

9. Supply variety—statistics, definitions, quotes, testimony, analogies.

*10. Challenge students to defend their answers, to go beyond the information, to hypothesize, to predict.

*11. Evenly distribute questions to whole class, don't only call on volunteers or exploit one or two students who usually have the answers.

12. Ask questions of whole class, then call on a student.

*13. Vary methods—questions, discussions, demonstrations, dramatizations, role playing, etc.

14. Vary visual aids—maps, graphs, pictures, charts, models, slides, tapes, videos, etc.

continues

V. *Problem*: Students do poorly on quizzes or tests.
   Possible Solutions:

1. Help students to determine what is important to study.
2. Use simplified objectives; explain to students what is expected of them.
*3. Review homework on a daily basis.
4. Hand out sample test questions (not test questions) so students know what is expected.
*5. Give several small quizzes or tests to reduce test anxiety.
*6. Discuss how to review for a test, and how to take a test.
*7. After tests, provide immediate feedback; discuss common problems.

VI. *Problem*: Teachers waste the last five minutes of the lesson.
   Possible Solutions:

*1. Be aware of the clock; pace the lesson.
2. Refocus on main points; summarize the lesson.
3. If extra time permits, ask students to summarize important points.
4. Have students provide examples, personal impressions.
5. Distribute short summary quiz.
6. If time is limited, provide a closure or wrap-up statement.
*7. Have a final or summary slide or transparency on hand and introduce it if needed.
*8. Review homework for tomorrow.
9. Discuss the next lesson or objective for tomorrow.
*10. Don't permit students to close their books and/or pack up a few minutes prior to the bell; the teacher dismisses the students.

Note: The possible solutions with the asterisks are the author's—based on his experience.

Source: Peter E. Weiss, Richard L. Weaver, and Howard W. Cotrell, "Using Public Speaking Skills to Improve Classroom Instruction," *Educational Horizons* (Spring 1990), pp. 117–120.

Table 13.3   TRAINING SESSIONS FOR PEER COACHES

Session 1:

Overview of the research on peer coaching

A context for peer coaching

 collaborative goal structures in schools

 peer coaching, school norms, and culture

 social and technical principles of coaching

 organizing for peer coaching

Exemplary peer coaching models

Sessions 2, 3:

Overview of observation instruments for coaching: from mirroring to coaching

 interaction analysis

 time-off-task

 drop-in observation

 cognitive coaching

 script-taping

 checklists

Session 4:

Factors influencing peer coaching relationships: how we look, what we value

A model of factors influencing teacher thinking and behavior

 modality preferences

 educational beliefs

 cognitive style

Session 5:

Advanced conferencing skills

 pre-conferencing

 observing

 post-conferencing

Session 6:

Fine-tuning communication skills

 mediational questions

 probing for specificity

 identifying and staying aware of presuppositions

Session 7:

Change theory and effective staff development practices

 what the research says

 implications for peer coaching

 planning for maintenance

Source: Patricia Raney and Pam Robbins, "Professional Growth and Support Through Peer Coaching," *Educational Leadership* (May 1989), p. 36.

Guidelines for Improving Support for Beginning Teachers

Whatever the existing provisions for the induction period for entry teachers, there is the need to improve provisions for their continued professional development, to make their job easier, to make them feel more confident in the classroom and school, to reduce the isolation of their work settings, and to enhance interaction with colleagues. Below are some recommendations for achieving these goals.

1. Schedule beginning teacher orientation in addition to regular teacher orientation. Beginning teachers need to attend both sessions.
2. Appoint someone to help beginning teachers set up their rooms.
3. Provide beginning teachers with a proper mix of courses, students, and facilities (not all leftovers). If possible, lighten their load for the first year.
4. Assign extra class duties of moderate difficulty and requiring moderate amounts of time, duties that will not become too demanding for the beginning teacher.
5. Pair beginning teachers with master teachers to meet regularly to identify general problems before they become serious.
6. Provide for coaching groups, tutor groups, or collaborative problem-solving groups for all beginning teachers to attend. Encourage beginning teachers to teach each other.
7. Provide for joint planning, team teaching, committee assignments, and other cooperative arrangements between new and experienced teachers.
8. Issue newsletters that report on accomplishments of all teachers, especially beginning teachers.
9. Schedule reinforcing events, involving beginning and experienced teachers, such as tutor-tutee luncheons, parties, and awards.
10. Provide regular (say, twice monthly) meetings between the beginning teacher and supervisor to identify problems as soon as possible and to make recommendations for improvement.
11. Plan special and continuous in-service activities with topics directly related to the needs and interests of beginning teachers. Eventually, integrate beginning staff development activities with regular staff development activities.
12. Carry on regular evaluation of beginning teachers; evaluate strengths and weaknesses, present new information, demonstrate new skills, and provide opportunities for practice and feedback.[33]

---

33 Bruce Joyce and Renee T. Clift, "The Phoenix Agenda: Essential Reform in Teacher Education," *Educational Researcher* (April 1984), pp. 5–18; Joyce L. Epstein, Brian L. Lockard, and Susan L. Dauber, "Staff Development for Middle-School Education," *Journal of Staff Development* (Winter 1991), pp. 36–41; and Kurtz, "How the Principal Can Help Beginning Teachers."

STUDENT EVALUATION

Teachers can learn a lot from student evaluations. In trying to analyze their own effectiveness and ways to improve, it may be difficult for teachers to recognize mistakes. Colleagues and supervisors are usually present in the classroom only briefly and infrequently, but students observe the teacher all day every day. Teachers receive student feedback continually as soon as they enter the classroom, regardless of how and what they teach and how and what the students learn. Student feedback is both overt and covert, ranging from facial expressions and gestures to focused attention or disruptive behavior. Moreover, the students' feelings and attitudes affect the quality of the teaching and the teacher's products.

Honest evaluation and feedback can be obtained from students through questionnaires and rating forms that are filled out anonymously. Some teachers develop their own forms, which are probably not the most reliable and valid instruments, but can serve if the teacher is uncomfortable or dissatisfied with prepared forms. In constructing a form, researchers tend to agree that the teacher should focus on eight areas: (1) objectives, (2) content, (3) methods, (4) materials, (5) homework, (6) classroom management, (7) tests and evaluation, and (8) behavior or interaction with students.[34] The easiest rating method is a five-point rating scale from "strongly agree" to "strongly disagree" or from "very good" to "very poor." It is not so much the content of the instrument or the point scale as the acceptance of student evaluation by the teacher that is important for professional growth and development.

For the teacher who wishes to use an evaluation instrument with more reliability and validity, there are many sources. A supervisor or principal will probably recommend an instrument used by the school or school district. One instrument designed by the state of Florida (and now used in parts of Colorado and Washington) has been tested for reliability in grades K–12; the coefficients from many pilot tests range from .79 to .98. The instrument comprises a formative scale (designed to identify problems) and a summative scale (which shows positive relationships between instrument scores and student achievements).[35] A section of the Florida performance measurement instrument is shown in Table 13.4. Although originally designed for supervisors to rate teachers, it can also be used by many different groups of raters, including secondary school students, to rate teachers. The instrument focuses on 4 out of 6 teacher domains or clusters and 21 bipolar items of teacher behavior identified

---

34 Milbrey W. McLaughlin and R. Scott Pfeifer, *Teacher Evaluation: Improvement, Accountability, and Effective Learning* (New York: Teachers College Press, Columbia University, 1988); Donald M. Medley, Homer Coker, and Robert S. Soar, *Measurement-Based Evaluation of Teacher Performance* (New York: Longman, 1984).

35 B. O. Smith, Donovan Peterson, and Theodore Micceri, "Evaluation and Professional Improvement Aspects of the Florida Performance Measurement System," *Educational Leadership* (April 1987), pp. 16–19.

Table 13.4 Florida Performance Measurement System

	Total freq.	Frequency	Frequency	Total freq.	
					Domain: Instructional organization and development
1. Begins instruction promptly					1. Delays
2. Handles materials in an orderly manner					2. Does not organize or handle materials systematically
3. Orients students to classwork/maintains academic focus					3. Allows talk/activity unrelated to subject
4. Conducts beginning/ending review					4.[a]
5. Questions: academic comprehension/lesson development					5a. Allows unison response
a. single factual (domain 5.0)					b. Poses multiple questions asked as one
b. requires analysis/reasons					c. Poses nonacademic questions/nonacademic procedural questions
6. Recognizes response/amplifies/gives correct feedback					6. Ignores student or response/expresses sarcasm, disgust, harshness
7. Gives specific academic praise					7. Uses general, nonspecific praise
8. Provides for practice					8. Extends discourse, changes topic with no practice
9. Gives directions/assigns/checks comprehension of homework, seatwork assignments/gives feedback					9. Gives inadequate directions on homework/no feedback
10. Circulates and assists students					10. Remains at desk/circulates inadequately

Domain: Presentation of subject matter

11. Treats concepts—definition/attributes/examples/nonexamples		11. Gives definition or examples only
12. Discusses cause-effect/uses linking words/applies law or principle		12. Discusses either cause or effect only/uses no linking word(s)
13. States and applies academic rule		13. Does not state or does not apply academic rule
14. Develops criteria and evidence for value judgment		14. States value judgment with no criteria or evidence

Domain: Communication: verbal and nonverbal

15. Emphasizes important points		15.[a]
16. Expresses enthusiasm verbally/challenges students		16.[a]
17.[a]		17. Uses vague/scrambled discourse
18.[a]		18. Uses loud-grating, high pitched, monotone, inaudible talk
19. Uses body behavior that shows interest—smiles, gestures		19. Frowns, deadpan or lethargic

Domain: Management of student conduct

20. Stops misconduct		20. Delays desist/doesn't stop misconduct/desists punitively
21. Maintains instructional momentum		21. Loses momentum—fragments nonacademic directions, overdwells

Note: [a] No item listed.
Source: "Florida Performance Measurement System," rev. ed. (Tampa, Fla.: University of South Florida, Teacher Evaluation Assessment Center, 1987).

over 50 years of teacher behavior research.[36] The measurement procedure is based on recording the actual frequency of each behavior. However, when used by raters such as students at the end of a school term, the measurement procedure should involve estimating behavior on a seven-point scale (to prevent mid-range scores), with a high effectiveness rating equivalent to "very often" and a low rating equivalent to "rarely."

Many teachers will use more than one type of evaluation, both informal and formal, throughout the year. The formal evaluation is one of the best instruments to use because of its consistency in format and ease of interpretation. The most important thing to keep in mind is that all raters and ratings are imperfect, but the data suggest that students actually make the best raters in terms of reliability and validity. Since they see the teachers in different situations over an extended period of time, they cannot be fooled or misled by a single day's performance as a formal observer might be.[37]

Student ratings will probably never become institutionalized as long as teachers have some say in the evaluation process. To the extent that teachers feel insecure about their own teaching, they are likely to oppose such ratings. But this is not an instrument that teachers should be required to use. Rather, it is an instrument that can and should be used by teachers who wish to improve their teaching through realistic evaluation, and whose personal and professional self-concepts are positive enough to risk feedback from their students.

Guidelines for Implementing Student Evaluations

In using student evaluations it is important to clarify (1) the policy for their use—for example, whether the results will be seen by supervisors, whether teachers will discuss the results with the students, whether the results will be used officially for evaluating teachers, and (2) standards to ensure reliability and validity—for example, appropriate conditions, clear directions, suitable questions.

Lawrence Kult recommends the following procedures for having the students do the evaluations.

---

36 Donovan Peterson et al., "Evaluation of a Teacher's Classroom Performance: Using the Florida Performance Measurement System," *Teaching and Teacher Education* (no. 4, 1986), pp. 309–314. The other two teacher domains deal with planning and testing. Since they are difficult to observe they are not part of this instrument but can be used for rating purposes.

37 N. L. Gage, "What Do We Know about Teaching Effectiveness?" *Phi Delta Kappan* (October 1984), pp. 87–90; Allan C. Ornstein, "Can We Define a Good Teacher?" *Peabody Journal of Education* (April 1976), pp. 201–207; and Ornstein, "Teacher Effectiveness Research: Some Ideas and Issues," *Education and Urban Society* (February 1986), pp. 168–175.

1. An informative discussion in class should precede the actual evaluation, preferably just before it. The reasons for the evaluation and the kinds of questions to expect should be discussed. The positive effect that the evaluation can have for both students and teacher should be stressed. All questions by the students should be answered by the teacher.
2. All evaluations should be anonymous, and students must be assured that in no way will their grades be affected by the evaluations.
3. Sufficient time should be given to students to complete the evaluation.
4. The completed evaluations should be collected in such a way that a particular evaluation form cannot be identified with a student.
5. Any problems that surfaced during the evaluation should be discussed after the completion of the evaluation to improve the next one.
6. To alleviate some of the pressure concerning the evaluation, the students may be permitted to converse among themselves for a few minutes following the completion of the evaluation.
7. Positive acknowledgment of the students' participation should be made by the teacher after the completion of the evaluation.[38]

The assumption is that most teachers, if they are candid with themselves, will find that student evaluations parallel most of their own beliefs concerning their strong and weak teaching points. In some cases, they will gain knowledge about their teaching and instruction. The interpretation of the results should be performed with the idea of gaining personal insight. Negative comments should be read as guides for making corrections in the future, not as personal attacks that must be repudiated. The results will have more meaning if they are reviewed more than once, and they should be saved to compare with results on the next evaluation to see if changes have been made. The whole process will probably have a more beneficial effect on the professional growth of the teacher if the evaluations are optional and not required to be turned over to a supervisor.

SELF-EVALUATION

Teaching presents ample opportunities for self-evaluation. The teacher who does a good job, and knows it, has the satisfaction of seeing students grow, feeling their respect and affection and obtaining the recognition of colleagues, parents, and the community.

---

38 Lawrence E. Kult, "Using Teacher Evaluation by Students," *Clearing House* (September 1975), pp. 11–13.

Self-evaluation by the teacher can contribute to professional growth. This idea is a logical outgrowth of modern belief in the value of teacher-supervisor cooperation. If teacher evaluations are accepted as an integral part of an effective supervisory situation for professional development, then teachers should be involved in the clarification and continual appraisal of their goals and effectiveness.

According to Good and Brophy, teachers "seek opportunities to evaluate and improve their teaching, if acceptable and useful methods are available." The trouble is, these researchers continue, teachers have not been encouraged or taught to engage in self-criticism, to recognize weaknesses, and to "link criticisms with constructive plans designed to improve . . . skills."[39] Bruce Tuckman concludes that teachers are willing to engage in and even welcome self-evaluation as long as it is conducted in an appropriate manner, they participate in the planning stages, and they have some assurance of how the results will be used.[40]

Recent data also indicate the teachers favor self-evaluation over evaluation by students, peers, and supervisors. Teachers rated as "good" by supervisors picked self-evaluation as their first choice among instruments to use in judging their own effectiveness (selected by 37 percent of more than 2,700 teachers surveyed). Objective evaluations by students and reactions of other teachers familiar with their work were second (19 percent) and third (16 percent) choices for assessing their own performance. Furthermore, as many as 52 percent of teachers assert that it is *relatively easy* to know when one is teaching effectively.[41]

Another reason for self-evaluation is that nearly three-fourths (72%) of all school teachers in a recent Rand Corporation survey of 32 school districts and 192 schools indicate that they have "strong" or "complete" control over what goes on in the classroom, and 92 percent indicate "strong" or "complete" control over teaching strategies and methods. While 46 percent of the sampled teachers report that their principal, chair, or supervisor was "moderately helpful" or "extremely helpful," more than one-third (36%) report little or no help from these people.[42] Teachers have learned to fend for themselves and to evaluate themselves and what goes on in the classroom intuitively—without procedures that are tested for reliability and validity and without the assistance of staff or administration.

In this connection, a U.S. government survey of 10,000 secondary teachers and 400 schools revealed that one-fourth (26%) of the respondents indicated

---

39 Thomas L. Good and Jere E. Brophy, *Looking in Classrooms*, 5th ed. (New York: HarperCollins, 1991), pp. 526–527.

40 Bruce W. Tuckman, *Evaluating Instructional Programs*, 2nd ed. (Boston: Allyn & Bacon, 1985).

41 Robert B. Kottkamp, Eugene F. Provenzo, and Marilyn M. Cohn, "Stability and Change in a Profession: Two Decades of Teacher Attitudes, 1964–1984," *Phi Delta Kappan* (April 1986), pp. 559–566.

42 Arthur Wise et al., *Case Studies for Teacher Evaluation: A Study of Effective Practices* (Santa Monica, Calif.: The Rand Corporation, 1984).

they were "never" evaluated by their building principal or supervisor the previous year and another 27 percent indicated only one visit. When teachers were asked how many times they visited other teachers to observe or discuss teaching techniques, 70 percent said "never."[43] In other words, teacher evaluation and feedback from administrators, supervisors, or colleagues is infrequent and, in many cases, nonexistent.

Indeed, teacher acceptance of an evaluation/feedback process is affected by the frequency of observations. Since most teachers operate with virtual autonomy in the classroom and receive minimal assistance from supervisors or colleagues, it follows that self-evaluation may be more useful than an evaluation based on one or two visits, at best, by an outsider.

There are basically two forms of self-evaluation. First, teachers can rate themselves on their *teaching methods* at the classroom level. This type of evaluation can be developed by the teacher, a group of teachers, the school district, or by researchers. The eight areas of behavior, previously discussed under student evaluation or the instrument used in Florida, or any other instrument the teacher is comfortable with, can be modified for the purpose of self-evaluation.

Second, teachers can rate themselves on their *professional responsibilities* at the school and community level. According to two administrators, this form might include (1) classroom techniques, (2) contractual responsibilities, (3) service to school, and (4) professional development.[44] To this list might be added (5) relations with students, (6) relations with colleagues, (7) relations with parents, and (8) service to the community.

The evaluation instrument used by the Chicago public school system combines both teaching and professional elements of evaluation (Table 13.5). It assumes that teachers are responsible not only for good instruction, school environment, and personal standards (Parts I, II, and III of the evaluation form), but also for good community relations and professional and personal growth (Parts IV and V). The school principal is required to use the form in evaluating teachers, and the Chicago handbook for teachers suggests that teachers themselves use it as a guide for self-improvement.

Guidelines for Self-evaluation

Self-evaluation can serve as the initial step in continuing attempt to improve teaching and instructional procedures. A *forced-choice instrument* (with three or five choices per item) or an open-ended technique with minimal boundaries or

---

43 *High School and Beyond: Teacher and Administrator Survey* (Washington, D.C.: National Institute for Education, 1985).

44 Eileen Pembroke and Edmund R. Goedert, "What Is the Key to Developing an Effective Teacher Evaluation System," *NASSP Bulletin* (December 1982), pp. 29–37.

Table 13.5   CRITERIA FROM THE CHICAGO PUBLIC SCHOOLS FOR EVALUATING
                TEACHERS

I. *Instruction*
  a. Provides written lesson plans and preparation in accordance with the objectives of the
     instructional program.
  b. Establishes positive learning expectation standards for all students.
  c. Periodically evaluates pupils' progress and keeps up-to-date records of pupils'
     achievements.
  d. Applies contemporary principles of learning theory and teaching methodology.
  e. Draws from the range of instruction materials available in the school.
  f. Exhibits willingness to participate in the development and implementation of new ideas
     and teaching techniques.
  g. Provides bulletin board and interest areas reflective of current student work.
  h. Exhibits and applies knowledge of the curriculum content related to subject area and
     instructional level.
  i. Shows evidence of student performance and progress.
II. *School Environment*
  a. Establishes and maintains reasonable rules of conduct within the classroom consistent
     with the provisions of the school district discipline code.
  b. Maintains attendance book(s), lesson plans, seating chart(s), and grade book
     accurately.
  c. Uses recommendations and suggestions from conferences and special education
     staffings.
  d. Encourages student growth in self-discipline and positive self-concept.
  e. Makes students aware of the teacher's objectives and expectations.
  f. Practices fairness in teacher-pupil relationships.
  g. Exhibits an understanding and respect for students as individuals.
III. *Personal Standards*
  a. Presents an appearance that does not adversely affect the students' ability to learn.
  b. Demonstrates proper diction and grammatical usage when addressing students.
  c. Uses sound judgment.
IV. *Community Relationships*
  a. Uses appropriate resources available in the community.
  b. Initiates appropriate conferences with parents, administrators, and/or ancillary
     personnel, in accordance with school procedures.
  c. Performs professional responsibilities in an atmosphere of mutual respect with parents
     and other community members.
  d. Communicates the academic progress, attendance and conduct of students to their
     parents.
  e. Endeavors to understand the lifestyles and values of the school community.
V. *Professional Responsibilities*
  a. Is punctual and regular in attendance to school and duty assignments.
  b. Participants in in-service meetings and uses information and materials provided.
  c. Exhibits cooperative attitude toward students, parents, community, and school
     personnel.
  d. Adheres to the Rules of the Board of Education and policies and procedures of the
     school district and the local school unit.
  e. Makes proper use of professional preparation periods.

Note: Provision is made for school principals to add "local school criteria" as long as teachers are informed
about them prior to the evaluation.
Source: *Teacher Evaluation Plan and Handbook of Procedures* (Chicago: Office of the Superintendent, 1990),
pp. 11–12.

guides to choose from might be used. A written self-evaluation can be used to describe almost any aspect of teaching and instruction, with freedom to focus on any item perceived as important. Regardless of which method is used, the following suggestions are worth noting.

1. The value of self-evaluations is dependent upon how they are used.
2. The teacher's ability to assess his or her weaknesses and strengths is important for self-improvement. This ability can be enhanced through good relations and communication between the teacher and supervisor.
3. Self-evaluation of overall teaching competence used for personnel (or salary) decisions entails many problems, most notably credibility.
4. Self-evaluation for self-improvement is more acceptable than judgments of worth for supervisory decisions.
5. If performance contracts are used in a school, self-evaluations may be used as part of the contract or formal evaluation process.
6. Self-ratings should be compared with student ratings if the same items are included in the forms. Discrepancies between the ratings should be interpreted or analyzed.
7. Self-evaluations can be better utilized by discussing them with colleagues or staff members in charge of staff development.
8. Self-evaluations can be used as a starting point for the formal evaluation of the teacher by the supervisor.
9. Teachers wishing to focus on specific behaviors or instructional activities should videotape a particular lesson in conjunction with the self-evaluation of that lesson.

PEER EVALUATION AND ASSISTANCE

No matter how successful individuals are as student teachers and how good their preservice training is, they can benefit from the advice and assistance of experienced colleagues. Talking to other teachers gives people the chance to sound out ideas and pick up information. "Self-confidence is often developed through the reactions of fellow teachers. Thus, to create a healthy and productive teaching environment, there must be opportunities and a willingness to share information and ideas."[45]

Unquestionably, new teachers need the feedback and encouragement experienced teachers can provide. The exchange of ideas can take place in school and out, such as sharing a ride to a local meeting. Most important, experienced

---

45 Shirley F. Heck and C. Ray Williams, *The Complex Roles of the Teacher* (New York: Teachers College Press, Columbia University, 1984), p. 17.

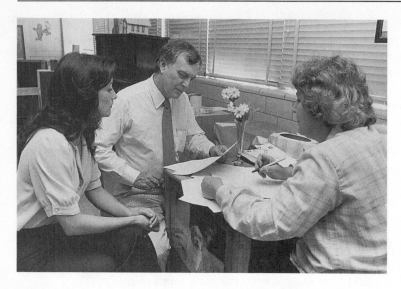

Working together and maintaining good collegial relations are important ingredients for staff development.

teachers must be willing to open their classrooms to new teachers. Because of the desire for autonomy in their classrooms that most teachers develop, there is "seldom as much communication or visitation between classrooms as there should be."[46] In some studies as many as 45 percent of the teachers report no contact with other teachers during the school day, and another 32 percent report having infrequent contact with other teachers.[47]

Whether observing other teachers is done on an informal or formal basis, permission should be granted by the teacher to be observed and by the supervisor or administrator in charge of the new teacher's professional development. The new teachers should look for techniques of teaching and lesson planning that they were not aware of, that coincide with their teaching style, and that are an improvement over what they are doing. A short follow-up conference to go over specific points should be scheduled either the same day or the next day while the observation is fresh.

It is perhaps more beneficial for new teachers to ask one or more experienced teachers to observe them teach. The observers should have teaching assignments (by subject or grade level) similar to those of the new teachers and some experience as observers. Untrained observers, for example, often focus on the teacher and not on the students, so they miss clues and behaviors that indicate degree of student interest and involvement and aspects of student-

---

46 Ibid., p. 19.

47 *What Works: Research about Teaching and Learning* (Washington, D.C.: U.S. Department of Education, 1986). Also see Sylvia Me-ling Yee, *Careers in the Classroom* (New York: Teachers College Press, Columbia University, 1990).

teacher interaction. New teachers need to have self-confidence to be willing to be observed, but they do have a lot to gain from informed comments about their teaching and lesson planning.

Schools often schedule **staff development** or in-service time for teachers to work in small groups with other teachers. In elementary schools teachers are often divided into groups by grade level. In secondary schools they may be divided by subject. In these small in-service groups teachers may discuss specific or general aspects of teaching and instruction, focus on students who have learning or behavioral problems, or work on curriculum development. The members of the group may observe each other regularly.

Joyce and Showers, who have studied staff-development programs, describe **mentor programs**, which should involve the following activities: (1) discussion of the theory and practice of teaching strategies and methods, (2) modeling or demonstration of teaching strategies, (3) practice in simulated and real classrooms, (4) feedback about performance, and (5) coaching on problems and transferring new skills to the classroom.[48]

Such structured in-service programs encourage professional exchanges and mentor relations that can help teachers develop teaching and instructional skills. These small groups should emphasize self-improvement, be voluntary, and be conducted without the presence of a supervisor. As Good and Brophy assert, "sharing information and the search for new alternatives" mean more when people want to participate than when they have to do so.[49] Similarly, discussion is more open without the presence of a supervisor; the members of the group are more likely to say what they want and help each other in the way they want, not to say and do what they think the supervisor wants. See Tips for Teachers 13.2

Based on studies of New York City teachers who assumed diverse staff development roles, Ellen Saxl and her colleagues developed 18 key skills for teachers who assist other teachers in school-site activities; they are listed in Table 13.6. Their data suggest that teachers can make a significant contribution as either part-time or full-time mentors or staff developers, and that ongoing training and support for the mentors are a vital part of the process.[50]

The mentor program of the Toledo schools has gained national recognition as a model of peer evaluation of and assistance to beginning teachers during an induction period, and of peer assistance to experienced teachers. The model is different from others because it is a full peer review system. Experienced teachers determine whether a beginning teacher (or intern) becomes a full-

---

48 Joyce and Showers, *Student Achievement Through Staff Development.*

49 Good and Brophy, *Looking into Teaching,* p. 557.

50 Ellen R. Saxl, Ann Liebermann, and Matthew B. Miles, "Help Is at Hand: New Leadership for Teachers as Staff Developers," *Journal of Staff Development* (Spring 1987), pp. 7–11; Saxl, Miles, and Liebermann, *Professional Assister Training* (Alexandria, Va.: Association for Supervision and Curriculum Development, 1988).

Tips for Teachers 13.2

Enhancing Professional Interaction in Staff Development Programs

In various staff development programs, exchanging ideas and asking teachers to examine what they observed or did in the classroom makes them feel less isolated and more confident about their teaching. Questions designed to promote professional dialogue and reflective thinking in such programs include:

1. What do you remember about the classroom situation?
2. What do you recall were your thoughts at the time?
3. What seemed to be the most important issue in the situation?
4. What alternatives did you consider?
5. Why did you select the action you did?
6. Did it turn out to be the right choice? How did you know it was the right choice?
7. What was inappropriate about the other alternatives in this situation?
8. What might have happened if you had chosen another alternative? Take one alternative and describe specifically what you anticipate might have happened.
9. How did you know this might happen?
10. What knowledge did you use in making this decision?
11. What is another situation that this one was like?
12. What percentage of this decision was based on intuition and what percentage on knowledge?
13. How would you act in a similar situation in the future?
14. What might you change?
15. What did you learn from this situation that you can transfer from intuition to knowledge for the future?

Source: Adapted from Joellen P. Killion and Cynthia R. Harrison, "Evaluating Training Programs: Three Critical Elements for Success," *Journal of Staff Development* (Winter 1988), p. 36.

Table 13.6   KEY SKILLS FOR STAFF DEVELOPERS

Skill	Examples
1. *Interpersonal ease*. Relating to and directing others.	Very open person; nice manner; has always been able to deal with staff; knows when to stroke, when to hold back, when to assert; knows "which buttons to push"; gives individuals time to vent feelings, lets them know her interest in them; can talk to anyone.
2. *Group functioning*. Understanding group dynamics, able to facilitate teamwork.	Has ability to get a group moving; started with nothing and then made us come together as a united body; good group facilitator; lets the discussion flow.
3. *Training/doing workshops*. Directing instruction, teaching adults in systematic way.	Gave workshops on how to develop plans; taught us consensus method with 5-finger game playing; prepares a great deal and enjoys it; has the right chemistry and can impart knowledge at the peer level.
4. *Educational general (master teacher)*. Wide educational experience, able to impart skills to others.	Excellent teaching skills; taught most grades, grade leader work, resource teacher; has done staff development with teachers; was always assisting, supporting, being resource person to teachers; a real master teacher; much teacher training work.
5. *Educational content*. Knowledge of school subject matter.	Demonstrates expertise in a subject area; showed parents the value of learning the subject; knows a great deal about teaching; what she doesn't know she finds out.
6. *Administrative/organizational*. Defining and structuring work, activities, time.	Highly organized, has everything prepared in advance; could take an idea and turn it into a program; good at prioritizing, scheduling; knows how to set things up.
7. *Initiative-taking*. Starting or pushing activities, moving directly toward action.	Assertive, clear sense of what he wanted to do; ability to poke and prod where needed to get things done; had to assert myself so he didn't step on me.
8. *Trust/rapport-building*. Developing a sense of safety, openness, reduced threat on part of clients; good relationship-building.	In 2 weeks he had gained confidence of staff; had to become one of the gang, eat lunch with them; a skilled seducer (knows how to get people to ask for help); "I have not repeated what they said so trust was built"; did not threaten staff; was so open and understanding that I stopped feeling uneasy.
9. *Support*. Providing nurturant relationship, positive affective relationship.	Able to accept harsh things teachers say, "It's OK, everyone has these feelings"; a certain compassion for others; always patient, never critical, very enthusiastic.
10. *Confrontation*. Direction expression of negative information, without generating negative effect.	Can challenge in a positive way; will lay it on the line about what works and what won't; is talkative and factual; can point out things and get away with being blunt; able to tell people they were wrong, and they accept it.

Table 13.6   (Continued)

Skill	Examples
11. *Conflict mediation*. Resolving or improving situations where multiple incompatible interests are at play.	Effected a compromise between upper and lower grade teachers on use of a checklist; spoke to the chair about his autocratic behavior and things have been considerably better; able to mediate with the principal to soften her attitude; can handle people who are terribly angry, unreasonable; keeps cool.
12. *Collaboration*. Creating relationships where influence is mutually shared.	Deals on same level we do, puts in his ideas; leads and directs us, but as peers; doesn't judge us or put us down; has ideas of her own, but flexible enough to maintain the teachers' way of doing things too.
13. *Confidence-building*. Strengthening client's sense of efficacy, belief in self.	She makes all feel confident and competent; doesn't patronize; "You can do it"; has a way of drawing out teachers' ideas; injects a great deal, but you feel powerful; makes people feel great about themselves; like a shot of adrenaline boosting your ego, talents, and professional expertise.
14. *Diagnosing individuals*. Forming a valid picture of the needs/problems of an individual teacher or administrator as a basis for action.	Realizes that when a teacher says she has the worst class, that means "I need help"; has an ability to focus in on problems; picks up the real message; sensitive, looks at teacher priorities first; knows when an offhand joke is a signal for help.
15. *Diagnosing organizations*. Forming a valid picture of the needs/problems of the school organization as a basis for action.	Analyzes situation, recognizes problems, jumps ahead of where you are to where you want to go; anticipates problems schools face when they enter the program; helped us know where we should be going; helped team look at the data in the assessment package.
16. *Managing/controlling*. Orchestrating the improvement process; coordinating activities, time, and people; direct influence on others.	Prepared materials and coordinated our contact with administration and district; is a task master and keeps the process going; makes people do things rather than doing them himself.
17. *Resource-bringing*. Locating and providing information, materials, practices, equipment useful to clients.	He uses his network to get us supplies; brings ideas that she has seen work elsewhere; had the newest research methods, articles, and ideas and synthesizes them for our needs.
18. *Demonstrating*. Modeling new behavior in classrooms or meetings.	Willing to go into classrooms and take risks; modeling; showed the chair by his own behavior how to be more open.

Source: Ellen R. Saxl, Ann Liebermann, and Matthew B. Miles, "Help Is at Hand: New Knowledge for Teachers as Staff Developers," *Journal of Staff Development* (Spring 1987), p. 9.

fledged teacher.[51]   The assumption is that new teachers lack practical experience and that experienced teachers have a legitimate professional role in screening and assisting new entrants. The experienced teachers tend to emphasize the same skills that were previously emphasized by supervisors and principals in their evaluation of new teachers, but too often the supervisory group lacked time to provide ongoing assistance. Teachers who are not new entrants but who never mastered basic teaching techniques or have trouble managing students are also assigned to the program.

Under the Toledo mentor program, a new teacher and an experienced teacher are matched on the basis of subject or grade level. The evaluation of the beginning teacher is a continuing process involving detailed observations and analysis of the novice's teaching behaviors and instructional methods. The experienced teacher may point out a deficiency, suggest a new teaching method, or demonstrate a sample lesson. The program has the blessing of the local teachers' union and school administrators and is bound to spread as the idea of peer evaluation and mentor assistance programs becomes incorporated as part of the reform of teacher education.

Most teachers, in the past, have relied heavily on school district manuals, administrative mandates, supervisory advice, as well as directives from community and state agencies. They accepted the status quo and doubted whether challenging it would have much effect. Most teachers consider themselves conservative and believe it best to keep their noses clean and not rock the boat. Teachers, in large numbers, have accepted (without questioning or challenging) the reform measures of the past—accountability, competency testing, master teachers, merit pay, behavioral objectives, and so on. Although these reform ideas have had an impact on the teaching profession, teachers themselves have had a minimal input; these measures have been imposed from the outside. Consequently, teacher reform has often ignored the concerns of teachers and realities of teaching.

Mentor/staff development programs bring teachers together and increase teacher influence over the teaching profession. Not only do these programs help teachers become more collegial and helpful with each other but also they encourage teachers to share ideas, test and try out new materials and media, and contribute to the knowledge base of teaching. They help sustain interest in teachers and rekindle commitments with teachers who are in midcareer. In general, the mentor/staff development programs create a new sense of personal accomplishment and professionalism among teachers. Moreover, they recognize teachers—and stress the need for improved morale, motivation, and participation.[52] See Tips for Teachers 13.3.

---

51 Personal letter to author from Albert Shanker, president of the American Federation of Teachers, June 21, 1988.

52 Robert Evans, "The Faculty in Midcareer," *Educational Leadership* (May 1989), pp. 10–14; Lanier and Featherstone, "A New Commitment for Teacher Education."

Tips for Teachers 13.3

Professional Development for Teachers

Teachers must continue to learn and acquire professional skills in order to be current and informed. Professional development for teachers must be ongoing and systematic and supported by the school district. The best payoff comes when teachers participate and plan with colleagues for their own growth. Following are 18 recommendations for getting teachers involved in professional development plans.

The professional development plan should:

1. Match individual expectations and interests with institutional (school) roles and needs.
2. Provide for individual differences.
3. Be based on a positive model for improvement, not coercion or punishment.
4. Reassure teachers, not threaten them.
5. Include rewards, recognition, and reinforcement for achievement.
6. Build on the desire for personal approval and need for personal success.
7. Be developed collaboratively.
8. Provide leadership roles for teachers.
9. Be directed at changing teacher behavior, not student behavior.
10. Introduce new strategies and methods slowly.
11. Accept the influence of the past, not personal differences.
12. Expect some resistance or discontent.
13. Link on-the-job performance and training.
14. Provide opportunity to refine skills.
15. Develop low-cost support strategies.
16. Include short-term (one year) and long-term (about three years) goals.
17. Include strategies for achieving the goals, with target dates and assessment strategies.
18. Rely on formative and summative evaluation.

Guidelines for Peer Evaluation and Assistance

In all the methods of peer evaluation, there is opportunity for feedback. In order to effect change, feedback must be handled properly. Bruce Tuckman offers 12 rules for implementing effective feedback for purposes of improving teaching.

1. Feedback must be specific and involve concrete behaviors and activities.
2. Feedback must be clear and describe how one appears to behave.
3. The feedback source must be reputable and believable.
4. Feedback must be in terms that the teacher understands and relates to.
5. The feedback recipient must have an understanding of an acceptable standard so the discrepancy between what is and what should be is clear.
6. The feedback recipient must know the expectations of others so he or she can meet them.
7. The feedback recipient must be personally committed to change.
8. The feedback recipient's commitment to change must be public.
9. The feedback process must create some tension.
10. The feedback recipient needs support from others; the receptivity to change must involve low risk.
11. Models for change and self-improvement must be provided.
12. Both the feedback recipient and the giver must use feedback in a constructive way that contributes to each other's professional growth.[53]

SUPERVISORY EVALUATION AND ASSISTANCE

Beginning teachers should welcome supervision as a means to develop professionally. In most schools the purpose of supervisory observation and conferences is to increase morale and effective teaching.

Teacher-supervisor interaction, often referred to as **clinical supervision**, follows a similar pattern in many schools. Members of the supervisory and administrative staff meet with new teachers at the beginning of the school year to acquaint them with school policies and programs. As the school year gets under way, a grade-level or subject-related supervisor helps the novice plan lessons, suggests appropriate materials and media, and provides curriculum

---

53 Bruce W. Tuckman, "Feedback and the Change Process," *Phi Delta Kappan* (January 1976), p. 341–344; Tuckman, *Evaluating Instructional Programs*.

suggestions. Ideally, he or she informally visits the class for short periods of time to learn about the new teacher's style, abilities, and needs. Later, at the teacher's invitation or by mutual agreement, the supervisor observes a complete lesson. Such a visit is often formally planned in conjunction with a **pre-observation conference** to talk over the plans for the lesson and a **post-observation conference** to discuss the observation and evaluation of the lesson.

This three-step process (pre-observation conference, observation, and post-observation conference) has been enlarged to eight "phases" by Morris Cogan, a major theorist in the area of supervision of teachers: (1) establishing the teacher-supervisor relationship, (2) planning the lesson with the teacher, (3) planning the strategy of observation, (4) observing instruction, (5) analyzing the teaching-learning process, (6) planning the strategy of the conference, (7) the conference, and (8) renewed planning.[54]

Robert Goldhammer, a student of Cogan, developed a similar model consisting of five "stages": (1) pre-observation conference, (2) observation, (3) analysis and strategy, (4) supervision conference, and (5) post-conference analysis. In both of these models the teacher's behavior and techniques are observed, analyzed, and interpreted, and decisions are made in order to improve the teacher's effectiveness.[55]

According to Ben Harris, the teacher can assume increasing responsibilities for each step in the process. As the teacher learns to analyze and interpret observational data and confronts his or her own needs, he or she should become less dependent on the supervisor and more capable of self-analysis.[56]

Supervisory evaluation involves judgments about the teacher and can put teachers on the defensive. Albert Shanker questions the value of "having a supervisor sit in the back of the classroom, watch a lesson, write an evaluation, and then meet with [the teacher] to discuss the evaluation." He believes the practice is "ineffective" but that supervisors stick to the practice "because everybody else does it."[57] Experienced teachers are often uncomfortable with the idea that the supervisor is seeing only a fragment of a lesson or only one or two lessons and that their techniques and methods may be misinterpreted.

Obviously, several observations and conferences are needed before any formal judgment is made about a teacher's performance. However, even one or two observations by a skilled supervisor can be helpful to the teacher, especially for the new teacher who lacks practical experience in the classroom. There is also evidence, according to both Brookover and Wise, that beginning (and experienced) teachers value supervisory feedback and appreciate supervisors'

---

54 Morris Cogan, *Clinical Supervision* (Boston: Houghton Mifflin, 1973).

55 Robert Goldhammer et al., *Clinical Supervision: Special Methods for the Supervision of Teachers*, 2nd ed. (New York: Holt, Rinehart & Winston, 1980).

56 Ben M. Harris, *Supervisory Behavior in Education*, 4th ed. (Englewood Cliffs, N.J.: Prentice-Hall, 1990); Harris, *In-Service Education for Staff Development* (Needham Heights, Mass.: Allyn & Bacon, 1989).

57 Albert Shanker, "The Revolution That's Overdue," *Phi Delta Kappan* (January 1985), p. 314.

and principals' input in diagnosing, prescribing, and recommending teaching strategies and skills. The input helps teachers learn to teach and to understand the expectations of the school district. The latter is considered important in view of the fact that the turnover among new teachers (those with less than three years of experience) may be as high as 40 percent.[58]

Some researchers distinguish between *peer coaching* (already discussed) and **technical coaching,** or supervisor-teacher evaluation. Technical coaching includes supervisory evaluations; it assists teachers in developing new teaching strategies and skills and helps them attain new knowledge about the strategies for longer periods than peer coaching. But it has a price: it tends to inhibit professional dialogue and peer exchange, and teachers often focus on the presence or absence of a particular behavior or item on an evaluation form that may have little value for an individual teacher or for students.

The supervisor-teacher system, however, assumes that objective feedback and evaluation, given in a nonthreatening and constructive climate, can improve teaching. According to some supervisors, the key to developing an effective supervisor-teacher evaluation system is that it must:

1. Be accepted as fair and objective by teachers.
2. Be related to the requirements of the job and needs of the school.
3. Specify the factors and behaviors on which the teacher will be judged.
4. Reliably measure teacher performance and indicate how the measurement will be performed.
5. Clearly communicate the expectations for performance to the teacher.
6. Provide for teacher development as part of the system.[59]

Table 13.7 summarizes the major characteristics of a supervisory evaluation system that achieves maximum teacher growth and accountability. Both teachers and supervisors understand the mechanics of the system, accept its purpose and utility, and recognize it as only one method for evaluation.

Guidelines for Supervisory Evaluation and Assistance

Procedures for the pre-observation, observation, and post-observation of supervisory evaluation are interrelated. During the pre-observation conference,

---

58 Wilbur B. Brookover et al., *Creating Effective Schools: An Inservice Program for Enhancing School Learning Climate and Achievement* (Holmes Beach, Fla.: Learning Publications, 1982); Arthur E. Wise et al., *Effective Teacher Selection: From Recruitment to Retention* (Santa Monica, Calif.: The Rand Corporation, 1987).

59 Robert J. Garmston, "How Administrators Support Peer Coaching," *Educational Leadership* (February 1987), pp. 34–36; Pembroke and Coedert, "What Is the Key to Developing an Effective Teacher Evaluation System."

Table 13.7   CHARACTERISTICS OF AN EFFECTIVE SUPERVISORY EVALUATION SYSTEM

1. *All participants accept the validity of the system.* The supervisor and teachers must believe that the evaluation methods and procedures employed will accurately reflect the teachers' performance.

2. *All participants thoroughly understand the mechanics of the system.* This includes frequency of evaluation, forms, methods of data collection, timeliness, purpose of conferences, relation of process to personnel decisions, and rebuttal and appeal procedures.

3. *Teachers know that the performance criteria have a clear, consistent rationale.* They understand where the criteria came from, why they are important, and what standards or outcomes are being compared.

4. *Supervisors are properly trained in using the system.* The supervisor needs technical skills (data collection, methods of observation, data analysis) and personal skills (communicating, conferencing, changing teacher behavior).

5. *Evaluation results in distinctions of level of performance.* Effective methods distinguish among above standard, standard, and below standard performance, telling teachers how they rate.

6. *There is a distinction between formative evaluation during the growth period and summative evaluation for final determinations.* The distinction is valuable, especially for teachers in a remedial track, to reduce anxiety about formative evaluation and allow teachers in the development period to make better use of it.

7. *A variety of sources of evaluation are used.* Although supervisory evaluation is an accepted practice, other methods of assessing performance are also included.

8. *Evaluation is a district priority.* The system must be formal and tie into district goals. It should be emphasized that the system is designed to meet the needs of professional growth and accountability.

Source: Adapted from David T. Conley, "Critical Attributes of Effective Evaluation Systems," *Educational Leadership* (April 1987), pp. 60–64.

the teacher and supervisor get to know each other and build mutual trust and respect. According to Harris, pre-observation preparations should include:

1. Identifying and accepting the purpose of observation.
2. Setting the time of the observation.
3. Selecting and agreeing on an instrument or method for observation.
4. Reviewing observation procedures.
5. Reassuring the teacher.
6. Deciding on follow-up activities.[60]

60 Harris, *Supervisory Behavior in Education.*

During the observation the supervisor should pay attention to specific behaviors and teacher-student interactions. The observation should be objective and free of any prejudgments about the teacher. Eight suggestions for the overall observation process are made by John Robinson.

1. Analysis of the classroom observation should be written in a report by the supervisor and include comments on actual events, an overall evaluation of the lesson, and recommendations for improving instruction.

2. Supervisors should make an effort to observe classes more than they do at the present (on the average teachers are only observed twice during a school year).

3. Supervisors should announce in advance when they intend to visit the teacher. (Many teachers claim their observations are unannounced.)

4. The pre-observation conference should be emphasized as an integral and necessary part of the observation report.

5. Observations should be planned with the goal of effecting long-range improvement of instruction in a few basic but important areas.

6. The observation report should concentrate on major points, both favorable and unfavorable. Minor recommendations should be made in the post-observation conference and should not be part of the report.

7. The report should be sent to the teacher before the post-observation conference.

8. School districts should offer an in-service course in observation and feedback methods. (Supervisors report they receive little help from their district in these supervisory functions.)[61]

The post-observation conference is essential for analyzing the lesson and the teacher's behavior in general. Agreements reached during the pre-observation conference about what is to be observed should be helpful in focusing the post-observation discussion. The observer should also bring up any specific problem or recurring behavior that came to his or her attention (for example, the teacher repeatedly calls the name of the student before asking a question; the teacher repeatedly turns his or her back to the class when writing on the chalkboard). According to Lovell and Wiles, analysis of behavior should include the following:

1. Compare anticipated (ideal) teacher and student behavior with actual behavior.

61 John J. Robinson, "The Observation Report—A Help or a Nuisance?" *NASSP Bulletin* (March 1978), pp. 22–26.

2. Identify consequences of discrepancies between anticipated and actual behavior.

3. Decide on what should be done about the discrepancies between anticipated and actual behavior.

4. Compare projected (ideal) use of materials, media, equipment, physical space, and social environment with actual use; identify consequences of discrepancies and make recommendations for future use.

5. Compare desired learning outcomes with actual learning outcomes (as observed during the lesson) and make recommendations to improve learning outcomes in the future.[62]

As the teacher receives feedback on his or her behavior, tensions and anxiety are likely. A solid base of mutual trust and respect must exist for maximum benefit to be derived from these supervisor-teacher functions.

ALTERNATIVE FORMS OF EVALUATION

Some school districts have been experimenting with other forms of evaluation or with eliminating evaluation entirely. Some of these suggestions follow.

Artifacts of Teaching

Samples or **artifacts of teaching** are sources of data for teacher evaluation and growth. Rarely considered as a source of feedback or information, teachers should recognize that these products offer prime examples of their workmanship and are representative of their performance. They can serve as excellent alternative sources for evaluating teachers.

1. *Lesson plans and unit plans.* Examination of lesson and unit plans should indicate whether the curriculum or course syllabus is being taught, whether the teacher's pace and focus are correct, how individual student differences are provided for, whether the instructional objectives are clear and activities are appropriate, and whether study and homework exercises are adequate.

2. *Tests.* Do quizzes and examinations reflect the important objectives and learning outcomes? Are the directions clear? Are the test questions appropriately written? Is there a good mix of different types of questions?

3. *Laboratory and special projects.* These handouts should be examined for clarity, spelling, punctuation, and appropriateness. They should coin-

---

62 John T. Lovell and Kimball Wiles, *Supervision for Better Schools*, 5th ed. (Englewood Cliffs, N.J.: Prentice-Hall, 1983).

cide with the important objectives and content of the course and motivate students and enrich their learning experiences.

4. *Materials and media.* The quality and appropriateness of materials and media and the way they are incorporated into the instructional process partially reveal the teacher's knowledge, skills, and effort.

5. *Reading lists and bibliographies.* These lists should accommodate varied student abilities, needs, and interests.

6. *Student outcomes.* Samples of student work and test results indicate students' mastery of skills and subject matter. They provide feedback for teachers and a basis on which to judge whether the teacher has achieved his or her own objectives as well as the standards set by the school.[63]

These artifacts (when several, not just one or two, are considered) are sources of valid and valuable data that can be used by the teacher for self-examination. They can also be used by supervisors as a supplement to the formal evaluation process. One advantage of these artifacts is that they can be collected quickly and examined with a colleague or supervisor to provide objective feedback and recommendations for improvement. Another is that they enable the teacher to look at his or her teaching and instructional skills over an extended period of time, even the entire school year (or longer), as opposed to a one-time rating or classroom observation. Also, since the teacher selects the artifacts, he or she may feel more at ease and be more willing to examine the data than when evaluation is based on formal rating scales or observations where the teacher has less input and control. Finally most colleagues and supervisors do not have enough time for thorough classroom observations and pre- and post-observation conferences, and examining the artifacts is much less time-consuming.

New Development Programs

Some school districts are experimenting with eliminating formal teacher evaluations on the assumption that staff development programs can be sufficient to improve teaching and instruction. It can also be tried in places where the majority of teachers are tenured and expect little supervisory or administrative assistance and in school districts that have a strong sense of collegiality and professionalism and feel that less supervision and good in-service programs would best serve teacher growth.

For example, the Valley Stream, New York, suburban school district has designed a five-year staff development program that eliminates supervisory

---

63 John G. Savage, "Teacher Evaluation Without Classroom Observation," *NASSP Bulletin* (December 1982), pp. 41–45. Also see Peter Oliva, *Supervision for Today's Schools*, 3rd ed. (White Plains, N.Y.: Longman, 1989).

observations of teachers. The following resources are used: (1) consultants; (2) professional materials, including videotapes, journals, and books; (3) experts within the system, such as experienced teachers, principals, district directors, and department heads; (4) professional networks, such as educational associations, research agencies, and teaching laboratories; (5) staff development programs from commercial or professional groups; (6) statewide and regional education agencies; and (7) colleges and universities. The format includes (1) summer workshops, (2) summer projects, (3) conference attendance (local, state, and national), (4) teacher centers, (5) faculty meetings (school and district), (6) in-service days and administrative days, (7) inter-visitations, (8) after-school seminars and workshops, and (9) university courses.[64] Demonstrations, coaching, and feedback are provided, and the sessions are spaced over the entire school year. Most of the in-service activities take place on school grounds or school district grounds. There is an attempt to integrate new research and theories about teaching and learning with practical application in the classroom.

In New Jersey, one high school has organized departments without chairs in which teachers collectively make all instructional, staff development, and managerial decisions. They select their courses and texts; schedule classes; allocate budget items, books, and materials; and participate in hiring new staff and administrators. The teachers observe their peers, but the principal still evaluates the teachers. Nearly every teacher acknowledges the principal as a leader, but the principal describes himself as a facilitator who shares governance with the teachers.[65] At times the teachers want the principal to make decisions for them, because they are forced to spend extra time at meetings, although he encourages them to reach their own solutions and provide their own help for each other. In this school, the supervisors are in the background, to the extent that the teachers have recently recommended adding a new supervisory position.

The National Education Association's (NEA) response to staff development has led to the Mastery in Learning Project, a five-year program involving 26 schools across the country. The program emphasizes school-site (sometimes called school-based) initiated improvement activities as opposed to school-district initiated activities. The staff development program emphasizes teacher collaboration and teacher leadership. In these schools, teachers and administrators share governance and mutually decide on goals and curriculum/instructional programs to achieve the goals. Each faculty of these 26 schools must collaborate together and embark on their own activities to improve teaching and learning. The staffs tend to move through nine stages of

64 Glen Grube, Henry G. Crain, and Timothy M. Melchior, "Taking Risks to Improve Instruction," *Educational Leadership* (October 1988), pp. 17–21.

65 Vicki I. Karant, "Supervision in the Age of Teacher Empowerment," *Educational Leadership* (May 1989), pp. 27–29.

collegiality, as illustrated in Table 13.8. Most schools involved in the project, after two years, have reached steps 8 or 9 in the table (according to the NEA).

The National Board

In 1990, the **National Board of Professional Teaching Standards** (NBPTS) launched its $50 million research and development program to improve teacher certification and teacher assessment. Its mission is to develop a voluntary certification system that establishes high standards of what teachers should *know* and be able to *do*, and identifies a governing board (comprised mainly of teachers) to enforce these standards.

The new certification system will consist of 30 different teaching certificates that consider two dimensions: developmental level of students (how they should be taught) and subject matter (what should be taught). Four developmental levels have been identified: early childhood, middle childhood, early adolescence, and adolescence/young adulthood.[66] This new focus differs from traditional practices of state licensing by school level; the new process focuses on developmental levels of learners and yields teaching certificates for generalists (e.g., Early and Middle Childhood Generalists [K–6] and subject specialists (i.e., Early Adolescence English, Adolescence Math). The Board will also develop certificates for special education, bilingual education, and vocational education.[67]

Most of the guidelines of the National Board deal with new assessment procedures for teachers. Among the ten recommended procedures is that assessment should (1) correlate with student learning; (2) consist of a variety of methods (including some that may involve assessment centers); (3) detect and eliminate external and internal biases with respect to age, gender, and ethnicity among teachers; (4) provide constructive feedback; and (5) involve professional teacher associations, academic institutions, and state agencies.[68]

These five procedures are probably most important. It is essential that the criteria for assessment be reliable, valid, and cost-effective; that multiple criteria for good teaching be accepted; and that the evaluation system be constructive and bolster excellence in teaching (and provide concurrent rewards) and not minimum competency or political pork barrel and favoritism. To be sure, the evaluation system should place what we know about good teaching in appropriate classroom and school contexts and should coincide with sound evaluation methodologies.

---

66 Joan Baratz-Snowden, "The NBPTS Begins its Research and Development Program," *Educational Researcher* (August-September 1990), pp. 19–24; *Toward High and Rigorous Standards for the Teaching Profession.*

67 Baratz-Snowden, "The NBPTS Begins its Research and Development Program"; Arthur E. Wise, "Policies for Reforming Teacher Education," *Phi Delta Kappan* (November 1990), pp. 200–202.

68 Ibid.

Table 13.8   STEPS TOWARD COLLEGIALITY

1. *Testing*. The teachers examine the nature of the program or activity and vote whether to participate; 75 percent or more of the staff must agree.

2. *Exhilaration*. The faculty feel elated to discover they are being treated as professionals and given increased power to improve teaching and learning.

3. *Commitment*. In this stage, teachers commit their energies to solving schoolwide problems they have identified.

4. *Dispirit*. When they realize that no one from outside the school is going to provide solutions to existing problems, many become dispirited; some staff members drop out of the project, and others confront it.

5. *Regeneration*. The remaining participants become committed and assess how many other teachers can be recruited into active work.

6. *Small successes*. The staff acts on a few small, simple ideas such as improving school discipline or increasing parental involvement in the school.

7. *Research*. Teachers, at this stage, begin to examine the research related to the problems they wish to act on; they seek out resource specialists, central district personnel, and university professors.

8. *Experimentation*. Teachers select and introduce pilot programs and assess their outcomes. If they adopt a program, they continue to monitor and assess it in relation to their own school (as opposed to relying on broad-based findings).

9. *Comprehensiveness*. At this stage, teachers move from fragmented approaches to comprehensive reform; professional activities become mutually supporting.

Source: Robert M. McClure, "The Evolution of Shared Leadership," *Educational Leadership* (November 1988), pp. 60–62.

PROFESSIONAL ASSOCIATIONS AND ACTIVITIES

Membership in professional organizations and participation in meetings, research, and advanced study can contribute to professional growth and help improve conditions for teachers.

Teacher Associations

There are two major teacher associations, the American Federation of Teachers (AFT) and the National Education Association (NEA). In most school districts teachers vote on which of the two associations all of them will join. In some school districts, the choice of joining or not joining a local chapter of the AFT or a state affiliate of the NEA is left to the individual. If you have a choice, you should not be rushed into making a decision. Keep in mind, however, that both organizations have helped improve salaries, benefits, and working conditions for teachers and that you should join one of them. At present nearly 85 percent of public school teachers belong to either the AFT or the NEA.[69]

The AFT has approximately 750,000 members, organized in 2,200 locals mainly in cities. Included in the membership are some 550,000 teachers, 100,000 municipal workers and nurses who are not teachers, 75,000 college teachers and 25,000 auxiliary staff (secretaries, paraprofessionals, cafeteria workers, etc.).[70] By 1995 the AFT membership is expected to reach 950,000. (See Table 13.9.) The AFT publishes a monthly newspaper, *American Teacher*; a professional magazine, *Changing Education*; and a yearly policy statement, *Consortium Yearbook*. It requires members to join the local, state, and national organizations simultaneously. The AFT has not been involved in publishing research. It focuses on issues of conditions of employment and professional status.

The NEA has a membership of more than 2 million, including 50,000 students, 100,000 retired members, 90,000 auxiliary staff, 75,000 college professors, 200,000 professional support staff (guidance counselors, librarians, administrators), and nearly 1.6 million classroom teachers, more than half the nation's 2.4 million public school teachers.[71] This figure is expected to grow to 2.2 million by 1995, as shown in Table 13.9.

Disproportionately suburban and rural, the membership is served by a large network of affiliates in every state, Puerto Rico, and the District of Columbia. There are more than 12,000 local affiliate groups, but unlike the AFT (where the local affiliate is powerful), most of the power is derived from the state affiliates. In terms of numbers the NEA represents the second largest lobby force in the country, trailing only behind the Teamsters.

The NEA publishes the *NEA Research Bulletin* and several research reports and opinion surveys about teachers each year. Its major publication is *Today's Education*, now an annual publication, with a supplementary monthly newspaper.

Although the two organizations occasionally take different positions on educational matters and battle over membership, "no raid" efforts have been discussed at the state level. Most important, both organizations seek to improve the status of the teaching profession, agree on many issues concerning teachers and schools, and sometimes join forces on policy matters. Merger talks have begun to sound serious in more than 15 states in recent years, and there would be immense political and economic advantages to be gained from the formation of a united "super" teacher organization.[72]

---

69 Allan C. Ornstein and Daniel U. Levine, *Foundations of Education*, 4th ed. (Boston: Houghton Mifflin, 1989).

70 Telephone conversation with Robert Porter, Secretary-Treasurer of the American Federation of Teachers, March 7, 1989; March 12, 1991.

71 *NEA Handbook, 1989–1990* (Washington, D.C.: National Education Association, 1990); telephone conversation with Margaret Jones, Director of Research, National Education Association, February 17, 1989; March 11, 1991.

72 Allan C. Ornstein, "The Changing Status of the Teaching Profession," *Urban Education* (October 1988), pp. 261–279.

Table 13.9   MEMBERSHIP IN AFT AND NEA

Year	AFT	NEA
1857*		43
1870		170
1880		354
1890		5,474
1900		2,322
1910		6,909
1916*	1,500	
1920	10,000	22,850
1930	7,000	216,188
1940	30,000	203,429
1950	41,000	453,797
1960	59,000	713,994
1970	205,000	1,100,000
1980	550,000	1,650,000
1985	600,000	1,700,000
1990**	750,000	2,000,000
1995**	950,000	2,200,000

*Year organization was founded.
**Estimated membership.
Source: Allan C. Ornstein and Daniel U. Levine, Foundations of Education, 4th ed. (Boston: Houghton Mifflin, 1989), p. 61.

Professional Organizations

At the working level of the classroom, the professional organization of greatest benefit to a teacher (and education student) is usually one that focuses on his or her major field. Each professional association provides a meeting ground for teachers of similar interests. The activities of these professional organizations usually consist of regional and national meetings and publication of a monthly or quarterly journal that describes accepted curriculum and teaching practices.

Some organizations are *subject-centered*. Others focus on the needs and rights of *special students* and are organized to ensure that these children and youth are served by well-prepared school personnel and to improve specialized teaching techniques. Table 13.10 lists 15 major teaching organizations that focus on specific subject matter and specific types of students.

Still another type of professional organization cuts across subjects and student types. These organizations tend to highlight innovative teaching and

Table 13.10   PROFESSIONAL TEACHING ORGANIZATIONS

Specialization by subject

1. American Alliance for Health, Physical Education, Recreation and Dance
2. American Council on the Teaching of Foreign Languages
3. American Industrial Arts Association
4. American School Health Association
5. American Vocational Association
6. Association for Education in Journalism
7. International Reading Association
8. Modern Language Association
9. Music Teachers National Association
10. National Art Education Association
11. National Business Education Association
12. National Council for the Social Studies
13. National Council of Teachers of English
14. National Council of Teachers of Mathematics
15. National Science Teachers Association

Specialization by type of student

1. American Association for Gifted Children
2. American Association of Workers for the Blind
3. American Association for Asian Studies
4. American Montessori Society
5. American Speech-Language-Hearing Association
6. Association for Gifted Children
7. Association for Children with Learning Disabilities
8. Convention of American Instructors of the Deaf
9. Council for Exceptional Children
10. Middle School Association
11. National Association for Bilingual Children
12. National Association for Creative Children and Adults
13. National Rehabilitation Association
14. National Scholarship Service and Fund for Negro Students
15. Rural Education Association

Source: Allan C. Ornstein and Daniel U. Levine, *Foundations of Education*, 4th ed. (Boston: Houghton Mifflin, 1989), pp. 71–72.

instructional practices in general. They describe, in their journals, new trends and policies that affect the entire field of education, have a wide range of membership including teachers, administrators, and professors, and work for the advancement of the teaching profession in general.

Perhaps the best known organization of this type is Phi Delta Kappa, which includes 585 local and 7 regional chapters in the United States and Canada and 8 international chapters. As of 1992, it had approximately 165,000 members, with no distinctions made among graduate students, administrators, and grade school and college-level teachers. Originally open only to men, it opened its membership to women in 1974. The purpose of the organization is to promote quality and equality of education, with particular emphasis on public education. Members receive *Phi Delta Kappan*, a highly respected journal published 10 times a year, and the fraternity newsletter. Paperback publications of interest are available at reduced rates for members.

Professional Activities

If you are to continue to do a good job teaching, you must keep up with your subject and the latest teaching and instructional trends in your specialization. Without continued updating, one's teaching becomes dated and dry. To keep abreast of developments in your field you will need to do three things: (1) read professional books and journals; (2) attend professional conferences, at least one or two a year; and (3) enroll in advanced courses in conjunction with a university-sponsored program or a school district in-service program. All three activities will help you keep up on changes in methods and materials, teaching and learning theories, and current experimentation.

Readings

Almost any professional organization you join should have a monthly or quarterly journal. The journal that will have the most immediate value for you focuses on your subject and grade level. For example, reading teachers might subscribe to the *Journal of Reading, Reading Teacher*, or *Reading Today*. Math teachers might subscribe to the *Arithmetic Teacher* or *Mathematics Teacher*, and social studies teachers would do well to read *Social Education* and *Social Science Quarterly*. Middle school teachers might subscribe to *Middle School Journal*, while high school teachers might want *Clearing House* or *High School Journal*.

There are many professional journals in education (more than 200 are available), and the need is to pick and choose wisely because of time and the cost of subscriptions. The answers to two questions can help determine your reading and subscription focus: Do I want practical advice and easy-to-read articles or theoretical and in-depth reading? Do I want to focus on subject or grade level issues or do I want a broad discussion of education issues?

Meetings

The two major teacher organizations—American Federation of Teachers and National Education Association—meet annually in different cities. If you become a member of one of these organizations, it would be beneficial to be an active participant and attend the annual meeting. The various subject-related associations and specialized student associations also have conferences. Keep an eye on your local colleges and universities; their departments or schools of education often sponsor professional meetings and short seminars that are excellent for updating your knowledge about teaching and for meeting other professionals in the local area. State departments of education and local school districts frequently organize in-service workshops and one- or two-day conferences on timely educational topics and teaching techniques.

The idea is to choose wisely which meetings and conferences best serve your professional needs and interests and to organize your schedule so you can attend them. Become acquainted with the scheduling and travel policy of your school district. If the meetings take place during the school calendar, you will need special permission to attend. Some school districts allow travel reimbursement for certain meetings. Local meetings sponsored by colleges or universities, state departments, regional education agencies, or local school districts often convene after school hours or on weekends. These sessions are easier to attend in terms of scheduling, time, and cost.

Course Work

You should take advantage of university course work and programs that lead to a graduate degree and state certification in a field of study. You may also attend summer sessions, workshops, special institutes, and in-service courses conducted by a local college or the school district.

Check to see whether special stipends, scholarships, or grants are available. Several states offer monetary incentives for enrolling in programs in special fields, especially in science, math, and special education. Many school districts offer partial or full reimbursement for graduate work.

Many of the recent reports on excellence in education recommend reducing the role of teacher training institutions in the preparation and certification of teachers by limiting the number of professional educational courses. Others, such as the Carnegie Report and the National Commission on Excellence in Education, call for increased professional education and field experiences. Reports by the Education Commission of the States, the National Governors' Association, and the Holmes Group call for a fifth-year (not a five-year) program, where education courses are offered after the student receives a bachelor's degree.[73] Perhaps the most consistent recommendation is for closer cooperation between schools and universities in offering preservice and in-service education of teachers.

---

73 *Report Card on School Reform* (Princeton, N.J.: Carnegie Foundation for the Advancement of Teaching, 1988); *Tomorrow's Teachers: A Report of the Holmes Group* (East Lansing, Mich.: The Holmes Group, 1986). Also see Mary H. Futrell, "Standards for the Teaching Profession: A Call for Collaborative Action," *Peabody Journal of Education* (Spring 1988), pp. 4–71.

Researcher-Teacher Collaboration

Increasingly, university researchers are joining with schools in an effort to deal with a range of educational problems. The action research model of the 1950s encouraged cooperative study of problems by practitioners and researchers. In the 1980s Gary Griffin and Ann Liebermann developed three models for collaborative research centers, which they termed Interactive Research and Development in Schooling (IR&DS), involving (1) single school districts, (2) state regional agencies, and (3) teacher centers sponsored by the AFT.[74]

The **collaborative research model** has spread because of the belief that through cooperative problem solving researchers can get a better grasp of practitioners' problems and develop strategies that improve teaching and benefit teachers and schools. In fact, a large portion of the new research on teacher effectiveness is derived from such cooperative efforts. The new collaborative centers (sometimes called R&D education centers or laboratory research centers) tend to focus less on theory and what researchers want to study and more on practical and enduring problems of teachers.

Decisions regarding research questions, data collection, and reporting are jointly determined by the university and the school. Collaboration between teachers and researchers is stressed, and both groups work together to improve the theory and practice of education. Researchers are learning to respect teachers and to conduct research of practical value, and teachers are learning to appreciate the work of researchers and to do research.[75]

A most interesting development in collaborative relationships is that many teachers no longer want anonymity in studies conducted by researchers. With the old relationship, the need was to protect the rights and anonymity of "informants" or "respondents" in qualitative research. The participants of the new research on teaching, in which teachers or schools participate, seek recognition—especially if the results are positive or methods and recommendations are being reported by professors in journals or books. According to one researcher, "If research and practice are truly interdependent, then researchers must provide opportunities for teachers to be recognized for their own accomplishments."[76] This is an ethical issue that has not been pressed in the past and may very well become an issue as experienced teachers develop relation-

---

74 Gary A. Griffin, Ann Liebermann, and Joann Jacullo-Noto, *Interactive Research and Development in Schooling* (Austin: University of Texas at Austin, Research and Development Center for Teacher Education, 1983). Also see Gary A. Griffin, ed., *Staff Development*, Eighty-second Yearbook of the National Society for the Study of Education (Chicago: University of Chicago Press, 1983); and Ann Liebermann, ed., *Rethinking School Improvement* (New York: Teachers College Press, Columbia University, 1986).

75 Christopher M. Clark, "Teacher Preparation: Contributions of Research on Teacher Thinking," *Educational Researcher* (March 1988), pp. 5–12; Ornstein, "The Changing Status of the Teaching Profession."

76 Judith H. Shulman, "Now You See Them, Now You Don't," *Educational Researcher* (August-September 1990), p. 11.

ships with researchers—and perceive only the researchers' benefit when the materials are published. This also deals with the teachers' sense of ownership and empowerment, as well as how we can improve teacher-researcher relations so that theory and practice are blended better in the future.

To be sure, a large part of today's teacher effectiveness research is based on the contributions of teachers who have been interviewed, observed, and studied; they were never credited or even recognized for their time and input, yet others (mainly researchers on teacher behavior) benefited by publications and name recognition, promotions, salaries, and even book royalties.

EMPLOYMENT OPPORTUNITIES

Procedures and criteria for hiring new teachers are not standardized. Thus, new graduates and teachers wishing to change school districts do not have a clear picture of how to present themselves and what qualities to stress.

According to school administrators, the credential file and interview are most important. The credential file often determines whether a candidate will make it to the interview, and the interview often determines whether the candidate will get the job.[77]

Key items in a credential file are letters of reference and the résumé. General letters rarely convey fitness for a specific position; they send a vague message, and the employer perceives that the candidate is applying to many school districts. Targeting is important; letters should communicate qualifications in ways that relate directly to the needs of a particular school.[78] The résumé should detail education, employment, and skills related to the position.

More than 85 percent of the principals responding to a survey saw the interview as a very important factor in teacher selection.[79] Questions in an interview can be divided into four types:

1. *Questions designed to help relax candidates*, for example, asking applicants how they liked their student teaching experience or previous teaching experience.
2. *Questions designed to assist candidates to express themselves openly*, for example, asking applicants about their philosophy of classroom management or special interests or talents.

---

77 Robert J. Olney, "How Employers View Résumés," *Journal of College Placement* (Spring 1982), pp. 64–67; Jo Roberts, "How to Make the Most of Teacher Interviews," *NASSP Bulletin* (December 1987), pp. 103–108.

78 Herman Holtz, *Beyond the Résumé* (New York: McGraw-Hill, 1984); Dick Viering, "How to Survive the Paper Screening in a Job Search," *NASSP Bulletin* (December 1987), pp. 109–114.

79 James A. Vornberg and Kelsey Liles, "Taking Inventory of Your Interviewing Techniques," *NASSP Bulletin* (January 1983), pp. 88–91.

3. *Questions designed to evaluate candidates' competence*, for example, asking questions related to specific problems or actions rather than philosophy, such as how they would handle the gifted learner, the slow learner.

4. *Questions designed to evaluate candidates' enthusiasm about teaching*, for example, asking about specific activities to make the classroom an exciting place for students, and asking why candidates became teachers.[80]

In most cases the principal and three to five school people participate in the interview. Although some interviewers ask superficial questions and are influenced by the physical characteristics and personality of the applicant, most interviewers structure the interview around certain questions and emphasize the responses of the candidate. See Tips for Teachers 13.4.

In a survey of 271 elementary and secondary principals, it was found that the five most important variables in reviewing a candidate's *application* were: (1) correct spelling and punctuation in the candidate's application letter, (2) letters of recommendation(s) from those who were familiar with the candidate's work with children, (3) letters of recommendation(s) from administrators, (4) neatness of materials, and (5) evaluation of student teaching from the cooperating teacher.[81] This data is shown in Table 13.11. The variables considered most important about the candidate *interview* were, in rank order, (1) honesty of responses, (2) interpersonal skills, (3) use of oral English, (4) personal appearance, (5) anticipated ability to adjust to the community, and (6) sophistication of responses.[82]

Regardless of what you think about interviews, it still remains the most direct and important screening tool available to the vast majority of school districts (with the exception of very large ones that still rely on bureaucratic forms and pen-and-paper tests). You need to know what to expect from interviewers. According to one school administrator, veteran interviewers:

1. Focus not on questions of competency (that should be investigated before they meet with candidates), but rather on those of philosophy and the roles of how you might fit into the system.

2. Are impressed not by verbal glibness, but rather by physical attractiveness and personal charm.

3. Are not rigid about time, but rather are willing to allow you to ask questions and clarify points.

---

80 Ibid.

81 Joseph A. Braun et al., "A Survey of Hiring Practices in Selected School Districts," *Journal of Teacher Education* (March–April 1987), pp. 45–49.

82 Ibid.

Tips for Teachers 13.4

Questions Interviewers Ask Teacher Candidates

Applying for a teacher's job? Here are some questions written by an administrator for administrators to ask young teachers being interviewed for a job. Although not all these questions will be asked or will be asked in this exact form during your interview, anticipating these types of questions should help you to prepare. Good luck.

1. *Philosophy of education.* In your opinion, what are the purposes of public education?
2. *Age/grade level suitability.* What do you see as the main differences between the needs of middle grade students and high school students?
3. *Subject matter competence.* What would you say are the comparative strengths and weaknesses of the ____ book series?
4. *Discipline and class management.* Have you found that any one form of disciplinary action is more effective than any other?
5. *Lesson planning skills.* What variety of teaching techniques would you plan to use in the classroom and in what situations?
6. *Flexibility within ability levels.* What special talents or abilities are needed to help a slow learner?
7. *Adaptability to administrative decisions.* What would be your attitude and reaction to an administrative decision with which you do not wholeheartedly agree?
8. *Expected relationship with peers.* How do you feel you will go about fitting into an established teaching staff that has had little turnover?
9. *Extracurricular interests.* Which activities would you be willing and able to direct if the opportunity should arise?
10. *Plans for professional improvement.* Where do you hope to be as an educator in approximately 10 years?

Source: Thomas P. Kopetskie, "An Administrator's Guide to Hiring the Right Person," *NASSP Bulletin* (January 1983), p. 14.

Table 13.11 RANK ORDER OF VARIABLES IN CONSIDERING A CANDIDATE'S APPLICATION

Variable	Mean*
Correct spelling, punctuation, and English usage	5.52
Letters of recommendation from those who have seen candidate work with children	5.33
Letters of recommendation from administrators	5.26
Neatness of materials, e.g., quality of reproduction	5.13
Evaluation from cooperating teacher of student teaching	5.03
Previous employment experience	4.99
Typed vs. untyped materials	4.80
Closed or confidential letters of recommendation	4.54
Candidates' narrative statement	4.28
Substitute teaching experience	4.27
Evaluation from university supervisor of student teaching experience	4.15
Extracurricular activities	4.13
Grade point average	4.01
Honors, awards, scholarships	3.86
Work as aide	3.80
Letters of reference from personal contact	3.11
Institution certifying candidate	3.09
Age	2.76
Military experience	2.15

*Mean based on ratings of 271 principals on a scale from 6 for most important to 1 for least important.
Source: Joseph A. Braun et al., "A Survey of Hiring Practices in Selected School Districts," *Journal of Teacher Education* (March–April 1987), p. 46.

4. Sometimes have you meet individually with key members of the staff or screening committee, say before or after the formal interview.
5. Make notes after the interview to recall impressions and characteristics to distinguish between you and other candidates.
6. Send candidates material about the school system, which is important to read (to show you care) and ask related questions. The material should help prepare you with basic demographics, problems, and challenges that you will face in the school (or school district).[83]

---

83 Clarence Ham, "Interview How-To," *American School Board Journal* (September 1990), pp. 25, 36.

The Teacher's Extra Duties

The teacher's job includes many nonteaching activities outside the classroom. This fact often comes as a surprise to beginning teachers who were not introduced to the varied responsibilities of teachers, since their field and student teaching experiences focused on classroom activities and pedagogical skills. The courts generally place three legal duties on the shoulders of teachers: instruction, supervision, and provision for a safe environment for students. In addition, the courts have defined and upheld the school district's assignment of extra teaching duties, and the professional teaching organizations have recognized them as within the scope of the teacher's job, so long as they are reasonable adjuncts to the normal school day, not discriminatory, demeaning, or unusually time consuming.[84]

In using the criteria cited by the courts, one administrative observer elaborates on ten extra assignments or duties teachers can expect to perform: (1) take over study hall, (2) supervise student organizations or clubs, (3) supervise field trips, (4) attend parent-teacher meetings, (5) provide bus supervision, (6) supervise the school's breakfast or lunch program, (7) supervise the school's detention program, (8) supervise teacher aides, (9) supervise at athletic games, music performances, school parties or pep rallies, and other school-related programs, and (10) serve on schoolwide or districtwide committees.[85]

There are other duties, not specifically listed here or not always specified in the school manual or rules, also within the scope of the teacher's job. Although they are not always spelled out in the contract, or specifically listed in conjunction with the position, teachers can be expected to perform duties outside the classroom, especially if they are associated to student health or safety, academic or social growth. The best a new teacher can hope is for the school district to spell out these extra duties at the interview stage, or certainly at the acceptance stage.

THE JOB AHEAD

Ralph Tyler points out that we are now learning that most professionals reach their peak performance by their seventh year of practice, and then performance begins declining.[86] If the number who express fatigue, show stress symptoms, or drop out is any indication, the peak may be earlier. In order to prevent this decline, teachers need challenging and practical in-service programs. Each school has to concentrate on a few of its most serious needs and then develop

---

84 William B. Valente, *Education and Law: Public and Private* (St. Paul, Minn.: West Publishers, 1987).

85 Nathan L. Essex, "What Extra Duties Should Teachers Be Expected to Perform," *NASSP Bulletin* (October 1989), pp. 96–102.

86 Ralph W. Tyler, "What We've Learned from Past Studies of Teacher Education," *Phi Delta Kappan* (June 1985), pp. 682–684; personal conversation by author with Ralph Tyler, July 6, 1989.

in-service programs to meet these needs. In-service programs can be vastly improved if the staffs of teacher education institutions and school districts work together to identify and focus on serious problems.

Your Mental Health

If you expect to be an effective teacher, you will need to be able to cope with frustrations and problems that arise on the job. Regardless of the amount of satisfaction you obtain from teaching, there will be dissatisfying aspects. What follows is a list of **mental health strategies**, a mix of common sense and psychology for self-understanding, developed to help you deal with problems or dissatisfactions that may arise.

1. *Develop self-awareness.* The better you understand yourself, the less likely you are to be overwhelmed by events or feel out of control.
2. *Evaluate dissatisfactions.* If you are dissatisfied with aspects of teaching, try to deal with parts of the problem that can be remedied. Don't give up.
3. *Expose yourself to new professional experiences.* Broaden your professional experiences. Volunteer for workshops and exchange teaching. Devote time to study and travel.
4. *Reevaluate total load.* Maintain a balance between work and social activities. Try to reduce work tension. Too much work leads to undue pressure and too little work leads to boredom.
5. *Study someone else with similar problems.* It helps to assess people with similar problems to see what they are doing wrong to avoid making the same mistakes.
6. *Evaluate personal problems.* Evaluate what problems affect your job performance. How serious are they? How widespread are they? What can be done to improve the situation? Try to confront, not avoid, the source of the problems. Try to deal with one problem at a time.
7. *Look for help on specific questions.* Often teacher dissatisfaction pertains to a specific problem, for example, the inability to maintain discipline. Consulting with an experienced colleague or supervisor sometimes helps.
8. *Talk to friends.* Talking to friends about a problem often clarifies the problem and sometimes, even what can be done to help alleviate it.
9. *Get professional help.* When friends or family cannot help with your problems, it is wise to seek professional help.
10. *Participate in group discussions.* Since many problems of teachers are similar, pool ideas and experiences. Even the "gripe" session in the teachers' lounge has benefits in expressing one's dissatisfactions and learning that others have similar problems.
11. *Develop supplementary areas of your life.* Participate in various community and social activities to broaden your experiences and to maintain a healthy outlook on life.

12. *Recognize new possibilities in teaching.* Many teachers have remedied dissatisfaction by discovering new teaching responsibilities, such as work on workshops, experimental programs, and staff development projects.

13. *Don't take out your frustrations in class.* Don't vent your dissatisfactions on your students. It solves nothing and adds to your teaching problems.

14. *Be willing to admit failure.* In extreme cases it is best to withdraw from the school or profession if you find that teaching in the present situation has too many problems or that you simply don't enjoy teaching.[87]

Facing Yourself

Your ability to learn from experience and to grow professionally and personally depends in large part on your capacity to face, analyze, and deal constructively with the realities of your life and work conditions. Ten strategies for understanding yourself in relation to the realities of your school situation are listed below.

1. *Strengths and weaknesses.* The ability to make realistic self-estimates is crucial, given the fact that your students and colleagues will observe and make judgments about your behavior, attitude, and abilities. Learn to see yourself as others see you and to compensate for or modify areas that need to be improved.

2. *Ability to make use of resources.* As a teacher you will come across many different texts, tests, materials, and people. You will need to make judgments about their value and how to best utilize these resources for your growth.

3. *Social and personal skills.* You will need to understand the attitudes and feelings of your students, colleagues, and supervisors, how to adapt to and interact with different persons, how to learn from them, and how to work cooperatively with them.

4. *Ability to function in a bureaucratic setting.* Schools are bureaucracies, and you must learn the rules and regulations, as well as the norms and behaviors of the school. As a teacher, you are an employee of an organization that has certain expectations of you and all employees.

5. *Forms, reports, and records.* Schools expect teachers to complete a host of forms, reports, and records accurately and on time. The quicker you

---

87 The first 12 items are derived from Fritz Redl and William W. Wattenberg, *Mental Hygiene in Teaching*, 2nd ed. (New York: Harcourt Brace, 1959). The last two are derived from Robert F. Biehler and Jack Snowman, *Psychology Applied to Teaching*, 6th ed. (Boston: Houghton Mifflin, 1990).

become familiar with this work, the smoother it will be for you. At first the various forms, reports, and records may seem burdensome, yet neither you, your supervisors, nor the school can function without them.

6. *Ability to make choices.* You will need to understand and apply the decision-making process purposefully and logically. Learn to be consistent and rational when making a choice. Think about the impact your decisions have on others in the school.

7. *Understanding your role as a teacher.* The teacher's role goes far beyond teaching a group of students in class. Teaching occurs in a particular social context, and much of what you do and are expected to do is influenced by this context. Different students, supervisors, administrators, parents, and community members expect different things from you. You must expect to perform varied roles depending on the realities, demands, and expectations of a school's culture.

8. *Know how to organize your time.* There are only so many hours in a day, and many demands and expectations are imposed on you as a person and professional. You will need to make good use of time, to set priorities, to plan, and to get your work done.

9. *Separate your job from your personal life.* Never let the teaching job (or any job) overwhelm you to the point that it interferes with your personal life. There are times when you may have to spend a few extra hours in school helping students or working with colleagues, and there are times when you will have to spend extra after-school hours grading papers and tests, preparing lessons, and performing clerical tasks, but for your own mental health be sure you have time left for your private, family, and social life.

10. *Develop a professional identity.* Professional identity involves an understanding of the relation between your professional training and professional roles; knowledge of yourself and how others perceive you, your teaching style and capabilities, the teaching styles and capabilities of your colleagues, your expectations as a teacher, and the expectations of your supervisor or administrators; and the ability to select and evaluate future career plans.

As we conclude this chapter, it is important to note that teaching can be difficult and rewarding. Few roles are more exciting and important than teaching. When competent teachers work with children and adolescents, there is rarely a dull moment. Through their students, teachers can contribute to the shaping and growth of the community and the nation; the teachers' impact is long term—and we are unable to determine where the influence ceases. Teaching is a proud profession, and professional growth and development are an important part of the life of a teacher. Take the job seriously, and work at improving your skills and abilities as a teacher.

SUMMARY

1. The student teaching experience is largely influenced by the expectations of the supervising professor and clinical teacher, as well as the relationships they develop between themselves and with the student.
2. Beginning teachers need support and assistance to ease into their position and improve their instructional skills.
3. To become a master of the trade, you will need to continually improve your teaching abilities. People closely associated with your teaching and instruction, including students, peers, and supervisors, are best able to provide feedback and evaluation. Several procedures for utilizing the ratings and observations of these three groups have been outlined.
4. Research suggests that student raters of teachers are more reliable and valid than other raters, since students see teachers over an extended period in various situations.
5. Teachers favor self-evaluation over all other forms of evaluation, including student, peer, and supervisory evaluation.
6. Supplementary sources for evaluating teachers include lesson and unit plans, special projects, instructional materials and media, reading lists, and student work and test outcomes.
7. There are hundreds of education associations for teachers to join; the two largest ones and the ones that have probably done the most to improve teacher salaries and working conditions are the American Federation of Teachers and the National Education Association.
8. Several other opportunities exist to help teachers grow as professionals, including reading the professional literature, attending conferences, taking courses, and collaborating with researchers.
9. When pursuing a job, it is important to realize that letters of reference and the résumé are the key items that school officials look at. These items help you get the interview for which interpersonal and communication skills are important factors for being hired.
10. The type of teacher you become, and the way you professionally grow, is related to the way you deal with the realities of the job and your life away from work.

CASE STUDY

Problem

A newly married eleventh-grade teacher, with two years experience, transferred from an academically oriented school to a low-academic, semi-problem-oriented school. Her intent was to "help children really needing help" and "make a significant difference." She continued to take courses for another degree, teach piano, and work as a pianist/entertainer in a private club. She intended to keep the same schedule in her new school.

She had been a successful teacher in her former school, but in her new school she soon had behavior problems along with academic failure in her class. She needed to prepare more careful and detailed lessons, modifying the curriculum, and do more individual and remedial work; she felt drained by an increase in truancy forms, parent conferences, record keeping to justify grades, overt and covert hostility, and playground and lunchroom monitoring duties. Her enjoyment of teaching lessened and problems began to develop in her marriage. She turned to the principal for help.

Suggestion

The principal knew that a beginning teacher's main problem is not being able to do all the activities he or she could do. These other activities must be kept to a minimum, especially in "difficult" schools. First the teacher gave up the piano and then her graduate classes; she devoted her time to teaching.

The principal then suggested she give her marriage role and her personal needs first priority, *before* teaching. If she did not do this, the principal suggested, she would not have the "inner support" to help others.

The principal then assigned her a mentor teacher to assist her with suggestions for day-to-day teaching planning and practices. They met a few times but the mentor was unable to meet regularly, having his own class and family.

As her students became more rebellious she began to react in a hostile manner, feeling betrayed by them for their not "appreciating" her efforts to help them, usually at the expense of her own personal life and sacrifice of time. The affective, "understanding" approach which had worked in her former school made things worse. And the end of the semester she left teaching to concentrate on a Master's in Business Administration.

Discussion Suggestion

Independent of the principal and mentor, a colleague urged the teacher not to see herself in the missionary role and to quit trying to "save" her students; just *teach* them. Defining a teaching role in highly personalized ways forced her into multiple roles of parent/social worker, "nurturant" mother/"loving" teacher; such roles are impossible to fulfill, and it is unfair to expect reciprocation from the students. The students, it was suggested, don't want her "love"; they want respect. Respect is earned through professional interaction with clients (in this case students) and not through making one personal sacrifice after another.

Discussion Questions

1. Identify the progression of disenchantment the teacher experienced and the reasons for this disenchantment. Was there a more basic problem with this teacher than one of trying too hard? Analyze your

own motivations for teaching and share them with someone to see if they are realistic.

2. Considering the emotional problems many students face today, do you consider the admonition to "respect" rather than "love" your students as coldhearted? What does either term mean in influencing behavior or expectations?

3. The phenomenon of the sexual and emotional abuse of children has made teachers a high risk group for accusations by students. How does this alter your ideas of teachers "loving," hugging, and becoming actively involved with a student?

4. Compare the information in this chapter to the expectations of parents, state legislatures, the platform of teacher unions, the public, and your own observations in order to answer the question: Is teaching a profession? What kinds of support will you need to feel successful or "professional?"

5. Did the teacher do the right thing by leaving teaching?

QUESTIONS TO CONSIDER

1. Why should you begin now to consider ways for improving your skills as a teacher?

2. What are some ways for coping with problems or concerns related to the job of teaching?

3. Which of your experiences as a preservice teacher do you think will help you as a beginning teacher?

4. Of the following evaluation alternatives—student, peer, self, and supervisory—which would you prefer as a beginning teacher? Why? As an experienced teacher? Why?

5. Name two or three professional organizations you expect to join as a teacher. How do you expect to benefit from membership in these organizations?

THINGS TO DO

1. Survey the class on the basic adjustment problems of new teachers. Rank order them. Discuss in class how problems considered important (top 5) can be remedied.

2. Study the important evaluation techniques of teaching. If your professor permits, select one instrument and evaluate his or her performance.

3. Have a class member teach a sample lesson in his or her subject or grade level. Evaluate the lesson in terms of instructional methods, use of media, and organization of subject matter.

4. Invite a representative of the AFT and NEA to your class to discuss the organizations.

5. The text lists several professional organizations and several professional journals. Identify the ones that offer potential for your professional development. Explain the reasons to the class.

RECOMMENDED READINGS

Chiarelott, Leigh, Leonard Davidman, and Kevin Ryan. *Lens on Teaching*. New York: Holt, Rinehart & Winston, 1991. A combination lab manual and text devised for field-based courses.

Jackson, Philip W. *The Practice of Teaching*. New York: Teachers College Press, Columbia University, 1986. The complexity of teaching and the uncertainties teachers face in classrooms and schools.

Kowalski, Theodore, Roy A. Weaver, and Kenneth T. Henson. *Case Studies of Teaching*. White Plains, N.Y.: Longman, 1989. Thirty-six case studies of first-year teachers, providing an analysis of common experiences faced by new teachers.

McNergney, Robert, ed. *Guide to Classroom Teaching*. Needham Heights, Mass.: Allyn & Bacon, 1989. An outline of the methods and skills of teaching and an understanding of the roles and responsibilities of teachers.

Ornstein, Allan C. *Strategies for Effective Teaching*. New York: HarperCollins, 1990. The book pulls together current research on effective teaching and how students learn.

Rubin, Louis J. *Artistry in Teaching*. New York: Random House, 1985. Aimed at trainers of teachers and teachers in training who believe that teaching is more art than science and that prescriptive practices cannot really be taught in advance.

Tom, Alan R. *How Should Teachers Be Educated?* Bloomington, Ind.: Phi Delta Kappa, 1987. An overview and analysis of several reports calling for major reforms and restructuring of teacher education.

KEY TERMS

Field experiences

Induction period

Peer coach

Resource teacher

Staff development

Mentor program

Clinical supervision

Pre-observation conference

Post-observation conference

Technical coaching

Artifacts of teaching

National Board of Professional Teaching Standards

Collaborative research model

Mental health strategies

Name Index

Subject Index

Ability grouping, 491–496
  Ability-Grouped Active Teaching program, 495–496
  between-class ability grouping, 491–493
  guidelines for, 495–496
  pre-grouping considerations, 494–495
  within-class ability grouping, 493–495
Absolute standards, grading, 250–251
Academic time, 29–41
  academic allocated time, 29, 32–35
  academic engaged time, 31, 38, 40
  academic instructional time, 29, 35–38
  academic mandated time, 29, 31–32
  tips for increasing instructional time, 39–40
Acceptance approach, classroom management, 120–122
Achievement. See Student achievement
Achievement tests, 170–172
  competency tests, 172
  diagnostic tests, 171
  subject exit tests, 172
  types of, 170–171
Activities approach, unit plans, 563
Adaptive instruction, 519–521
  guidelines for, 520–521

nature of, 519–520
Adolescents
  concerns of, 54–55
  and cults, 56–57
  latchkey children, 55, 57–58
  outcomes of adolescent problems, 53
  school support of, 58, 60–61
  and stress, 52–54
Advance organizers, 359–360, 414
Affective domain, taxonomy of educational objectives, 294, 295, 300
Affective strategies, 81, 526
Agenda, 508
Aims
  Cardinal Principles of Secondary Education, 276–277
  nature of, 275
Allocated time, academic, 29, 32–35
Allport Submission Reaction Study, 173
Allport-Vernon-Lindsey Study of Values, 173
Alterable environments, 28
American College Test (ACT), 172, 176–178
  coaching for, 176–178
American Federation of Teachers (AFT), 712, 713, 716
American Teacher, 713
Analogies, 373
Analysis, 80
Application of skills, 83

Aptitude tests, 172–173
  general aptitude tests, 172
  talent aptitude tests, 172
  types of, 172
Artifacts of teaching, 708–709
Assertive approach, classroom management, 104–106
Association for Supervision and Curriculum Development, goals of, 278, 279
At-risk children, teaching of, 659–660
Attitudinal scales, 173
Authoritarian teacher, 613

Back-to-basics approach, 322
Balancing, presentation of materials, 395
Behavioral approach
  practice and drill method, 322–323
  unit plans, 557, 560
Behavior modification, 110–112
  basic principles in, 110–111
  modeling, 112
Between-class ability grouping, 491–493
Block time schedule, 65
Brainstorming, 507
Business-academic approach, classroom management, 106–110
Busywork, 321–322
Buzz session, 507

Photo Credits